The U.S. Supreme Court

The U.S. Supreme Court
A Bibliography

Fenton S. Martin
Robert U. Goehlert
Indiana University

Congressional Quarterly
1414 22nd Street N.W.
Washington, D.C. 20037

Congressional Quar

Congressional Quarterly, an editorial research service and publishing company, serves clients in the fields of news, education, business, and government. It combines Congressional Quarterly's specific coverage of Congress, government, and politics with the more general subject range of an affiliated service, Editorial Research Reports.

Congressional Quarterly publishes the *Congressional Quarterly Weekly Report* and a variety of books, including college political science textbooks under the CQ Press imprint and public affairs paperbacks on developing issues and events. CQ also publishes information directories and reference books on the federal government, national elections, and politics, including the *Guide to the Presidency,* the *Guide to Congress,* the *Guide to the U.S. Supreme Court,* the *Guide to U.S. Elections, Politics in America,* and *Congress A to Z: CQ's Ready Reference Encyclopedia.* The *CQ Almanac,* a compendium of legislation for one session of Congress, is published each year. *Congress and the Nation,* a record of government for a presidential term, is published every four years.

CQ publishes the *Congressional Monitor,* a daily report on current and future activities of congressional committees, and several newsletters including *Congressional Insight,* a weekly analysis of congressional action, and *Campaign Practices Reports,* a semimonthly update on campaign laws.

An electronic online information system, Washington Alert, provides immediate access to CQ's databases of legislative action, votes, schedules, profiles, and analyses.

Library of Congress Cataloging-in-Publication Data

Martin, Fenton S.
   The U.S. Supreme Court: a bibliography / Fenton S. Martin, Robert U. Goehlert.
      p.   cm.
   ISBN 0-87187-554-3
   1. United States. Supreme Court--Bibliography.   2. Courts of last resort--United States--Bibliography.   I. Goehlert, Robert, 1948– .   II. Title.
   KF8741.A1M37 1990
   016.34773'26--dc20
   [016.34730735]   90-1842
                                                                              CIP

Table of Contents

Preface

In *The U.S. Supreme Court: A Bibliography* we offer a comprehensive listing of references to works about the Supreme Court. The volume contains citations about the Court, including its history, development, powers, and relations with the other branches of the federal government. This book also focuses on the accomplishments and activities of the individual justices, including their private lives and public careers.

This bibliography is designed to assist librarians, researchers, government personnel, and the general reader interested in the Supreme Court. The citations were drawn from a variety of fields, including business, economics, political science, law, history, public administration, and the general social sciences and humanities. The bibliography cites books, articles, dissertations, essays, and research reports. Because of the overwhelming array of U.S. government documents dealing with the Supreme Court, we have omitted them. Consequently, the bibliography does not include nomination hearings, memorials, or other government documents about the Court or individual justices. However, an annotated list of guides to government documents is included in the introduction to this volume. Since the bibliography is intended primarily for an English-speaking audience, the citations are to English-language works. In general, the time period covered is from 1850 to 1989, although the occasional citation to materials published earlier is included.

For the most part, works included in the bibliography fulfill three main criteria: writings are analytical, scholarly, and not merely descriptive. Consequently, the emphasis is on research monographs, articles from major journals, and dissertations. Because the amount of descriptive materials aimed at policy makers is enormous, we selectively chose to include such works in some categories, especially in areas where little scholarly work has been done. Thus, while the bibliography does contain a considerable amount of popular literature, it is by no means complete. Generally, we tended to list only materials that were commercially available and that could be found in academic libraries and large public libraries.

In addition to the bibliographic citations, this book also includes an introduction to research resources on the Supreme Court. The introduction is intended to acquaint the researcher with the different types of resources available when researching the Supreme Court. Some of these resources are specific guides to finding or interpreting statutes, whereas others are general guide books to government and legal publications. Also discussed are books, periodicals, indexes, and on-line databases that provide background information on the Supreme Court and current events. We were selective in the resources included in the introduction, and the annotations were kept as simple as possible.

The bibliographic citations are separated into two major sections. The first section of the bibliography focuses on the Supreme Court, and is divided into fourteen subject areas: The Development of the Court, The Court and the Federal Government, The Organization of the Court, The Work of the Court, The Court and Civil Liberties, The Court and Equal Rights, The Court and Due Process, The Court and Regulation, The Court and Economic Issues, The Court and Education, Liability, Public Opinion of the Court, The Impact and Implementation of Decisions, and The Members of the Court. The second section of the bibliography is arranged by individual justice in alphabetical order. We also have provided a detailed Subject Index, which identifies more specific subjects, and an Author Index. Because we have listed the bibliographic citations in a classified arrangement, the best way to look for materials is to use the Table of Contents and the Subject Index.

In compiling this bibliography, we checked a variety of sources. Primarily, we searched forty-six indexes, either in their paper form, on CD-ROM, or on-line:

ABC POLSCI
ABS Guide to Recent Publications in Social and Behavioral Sciences
Abstracts on Criminolgy and Penology
Air University Library Index to Military Periodicals
America: History and Life
American Political Science Research Guide
Annual Legal Bibliography
Art Index
Arts and Humanities Citation Index
British Humanities Index
Business Periodicals Index
Combined Retrospective Index to Journals in History
Combined Retrospective Index to Journals in Political Science
Criminal Justice Periodical Index
Current Contents: Social and Behavioral Sciences
Current Index to Journals in Education
Current Law Index
Education Index
Historical Abstracts
Human Resources Abstracts
Humanities Index
Index to Legal Periodicals
Index to Periodical Articles Related to Law
Index to U.S. Government Periodicals
International Bibliography of the Social Sciences: Political Science
International Political Science Abstracts
Journal of Economic Literature
Legal Resource Index
Library Literature
Monthly Digest of Legal Articles
Police Science Abstracts
Psychological Abstracts
Public Affairs Information Service Bulletin
Quarterly Strategic Bibliography
Reader's Guide to Periodical Literature

Religion Index One
Sage Public Administration Abstracts
Sage Urban Studies Abstracts
Selected Rand Abstracts
Social Sciences Citation Index
Social Sciences Index
Sociological Abstracts
United States Political Science Documents
Urban Affairs Abstracts
Women's Studies Abstracts
Writings on American History

For dissertations, we made an exhaustive key word search of *Comprehensive Dissertation Index* and *Dissertation Abstracts*. For books and research reports, we checked *Books in Print, Cumulative Book Index, American Book Publishing Record, Public Affairs Information Service Bulletin, National Union Catalog, Biographical Books 1876-1949*, and *Biographical Books 1950-1980* as well as the holdings of the Indiana University libraries.

In addition, we searched the following bibliographies dealing with the Supreme Court and the justices:

Andrews, Joseph L. *The Law in the United States of America: A Selective Bibliographical Guide.* New York: New York University Press, 1965.

Burke, Robert E., and Richard Lowitt. *The New Era and the New Deal, 1920-1940.* Arlington Heights, IL: Harlan Davidson, 1981.

Cassare, Ernest. *History of the United States: A Guide to Information Sources.* Detroit: Gale Research, 1977.

Chambliss, William J., and Robert B. Seidman. *Sociology of the Law: A Research Bibliography.* Berkeley, CA: Glendessary Press, 1970.

Cronon, E. David. *The Second World War and the Atomic Age, 1940-1973.* Northbrook, IL: AHM, 1975.

Dahl, Richard C., and C. E. Bolden. *The American Judge: A Bibliography.* Vienna, VA: Coiner Publications, 1968.

De Santis, Vincent P. *The Gilden Age, 1877-1896.* Northbrook, IL: AHM, 1973.

Donald, David. *The Nation in Crisis, 1861-1877.* New York: Appleton and Company, 1969.

Fehrenbacher, Don E. *Manifest Destiny and the Coming of the Civil War, 1840-1861.* New York: Appleton and Company, 1970.

Ferguson, E. James. *Confederation, Constitution, and Early National Period, 1781-1815.* Northbrook, IL: AHM, 1975.

Fremlin, Ronald H. *Modern Judicial Administration: A Selected and Annotated Bibliography.* Reno, NV: National College of the State Judiciary, 1973.

Hightower, James A. *A Bibliography of Books and Documents Written about the One Hundred Men Who Have Sat as Supreme Court Justices, 1789-1971.* Washington, DC: Library of Congress, 1972.

Johnsen, Julia E., comp. *Limitation of Power of Supreme Court to Declare Acts of Congress Unconstitutional*. New York: H. W. Wilson, 1935.

Klein, Fannie J. *The Administration of Justice in the Courts: A Selected Annotated Bibliography*. Dobbs Ferry, NY: Oceana Publications, 1976.

Leary, William M., and Arthur S. Link. *The Progressive Era and the Great War, 1896-1920*. Arlington Heights, IL: AHM, 1978.

McCarrick, Earlean M. *The U.S. Constitution: A Guide to Information Sources*. Detroit: Gale Research, 1978.

Mason, Alpheus T., and D. Grier Stephenson, Jr. *American Constitutional Development*. Arlington Heights, IL: AHM, 1977.

Mauer, David J. *United States Politics and Elections: Guide to Information Sources*. Detroit: Gale Research, 1978.

Mersky, Roy M. *Selected Bibliography on the History of the United States Supreme Court*. Austin, TX: n.p., 1969.

Millet, Stephen M. *A Selected Bibliography of American Constitutional History*. Santa Barbara, CA: ABC-Clio, 1975.

Remini, Robert V., and Edwin A. Miles. *The Era of Good Feeling and the Age of Jackson, 1816-1841*. Arlington Heights, IL: AHM, 1979.

Senior, Mildred R. *The Supreme Court: Its Power and Judicial Review*. Washington, DC: Division of Library Science, George Washington University, 1937.

Smith, Dwight L., and Lloyd W. Garrison, eds. *The American Political Process: Selected Abstracts of Periodical Literature (1954-1971)*. Santa Barbara, CA: ABC-Clio, 1972.

Stephenson, D. Grier, Jr. *The Supreme Court and the American Republic: An Annotated Bibliography*. New York: Garland, 1981.

Tingley, Donald F. *Social History of the United States: A Guide to Information Sources*. Detroit: Gale Research, 1979.

Tompkins, Dorothy. *Court Organization and Administration: A Bibliography*. Berkeley: Institute of Governmental Studies, University of California, 1973.

Tompkins, Dorothy. *The Supreme Court of the United States: A Bibliography*. Berkeley: Bureau of Public Administration, University of California, 1959.

U.S. Congress. *List of References on the Supreme Court of the United States with Particular Reference to the Doctrine of Judicial Review*. Washington, DC: U.S. Government Printing Office, 1935.

We hope that this bibliography will prove beneficial to researchers and students in the field of American politics and history. The book also is intended to generate more interest in research on the Supreme Court by surveying what has been done and pointing out areas that have been neglected.

We wish to thank the Political Science Department at Indiana University for its support of our research. Thanks go to Steve Flinn (Systems Manager) for his technical assistance and wizardry. Special thanks go to Richard L. Pacelle, Jr., for the many helpful suggestions he made about the bibliography and for the time he spent answering the seemingly endless questions we asked about the Supreme Court. For their invaluable assistance, our thanks go to Indiana University law librarians Keith Buckley, Marianne Mason, and Linda Farris. And we thank Nancy Kervin of Congressional Quarterly for her careful readings of the manuscript.

Fenton S. Martin
Robert U. Goehlert

Introduction

This introduction identifies a selected list of books, periodicals, indexes, on-line databases, and other publications and services that are useful in conducting research on the Supreme Court. The research resources are grouped by category, and short descriptions are provided for many of the resources.

General government research guides are described in the first part of this section. These guides present an overview of the type and variety of government publications available to the legal researcher. This is followed by a discussion of specific legal resources that are useful in finding and interpreting statutes, as well as resources that provide information on topics related to the Supreme Court, such as the Constitution, the role of the Supreme Court, and biographical data on the justices.

The second part of this introduction covers research resources not directly related to the Supreme Court, but still useful to the legal researcher. These resources—including almanacs, dictionaries, encyclopedias, general news publications, and general biographical sources—are important in that they provide background or historical information, which helps put the Supreme Court's actions in perspective. In addition, the news publications—including newspapers, newsmagazines, news services, and journals—provide current information on the Supreme Court.

Pertinent indexes, abstracting services, on-line databases, and CD-ROM services also are described in each section. These publications and services are key not only in pinpointing specific information, but in simplifying the research process.

Research Guides on Government Publications

The five annotated entries listed below are the best guides to government and legal resources, both for current and historical materials. These guides describe how to find and use government and legal research resources.

Sears, Jean L., and Marilyn K. Moody. *Using Government Publications.* 2 vols. Phoenix: Oryx Press, 1986.

The first volume of this set discusses searching publications by subjects and government agencies. Each of twenty-seven chapters covers a single subject or agency, such as foreign policy, occupations, elections, or the president. Each chapter includes a search strategy and describes indexes, on-line databases, and general sources. The second volume covers finding statistics and using special techniques, including historical searches, legislative histories, budget analyses, and treaties. This set is an excellent tool for the first-time use of government documents.

Bitner, Harry, Miles O. Price, and Shirley R. Bysiewicz. *Effective Legal Research*. 4th ed. Boston: Little, Brown, 1979.

This work provides descriptions of all resources related to legal research. It contains an in-depth examination and explanation of the reference works used in legal research. There also are chapters on finding federal statutes, treaties, and other international acts; federal administrative law; and the rules and decisions of federal courts and administrative and regulatory agencies. This volume is an excellent guide to government documents.

Morehead, Joe. *Introduction to United States Public Documents*. 3d ed. Littleton, CO: Libraries Unlimited, 1983.

Although this work is a textbook for library school students and professional librarians, it is a valuable guide for anyone interested in researching federal documents. The chapter on sources of legal information contains a wealth of information. There also are separate chapters on the executive branch, regulatory agencies, and advisory commissions. The book has especially useful information on how the depository library system works and on the work of the Government Printing Office (GPO) and GPO's superintendent of documents (SuDocs). This volume is especially useful for learning the technical aspects of documents, such as the SuDocs classification system.

Boyd, Anne Morris. *United States Government Publications*. 3d ed. Revised by Rae Elizabeth Rips. New York: H. W. Wilson, 1949.

Even though this work is somewhat outdated, its discussion of government publications is still useful for understanding the nature, types, and value of government publications. The work also is important when researching legal publications in the eighteenth and nineteenth centuries.

Schmeckebier, Laurence F., and Roy B. Eastin. *Government Publications and Their Use*. 2d rev. ed. Washington, DC: Brookings Institution, 1969.

This well-known and respected reference work contains extensive information on all forms of publications published by the government and, like the Boyd volume, has much information not found elsewhere. Although the volume does not include information about the numerous reference tools published in the last two decades, Schmeckebier does provide an excellent description and analysis of documents published prior to 1900.

There are many other research guides to political science and government publications that also contain sections or chapters on judicial research. Most of these guides are available in any college or university library. Several of them are listed below.

Andriot, John L. *Guide to U.S. Government Publications*. Rev. ed. McLean, VA: Documents Index, 1988.

Bailey, William G. *Guide to Popular U.S. Government Publications*. 2d ed. Englewood, CO: Libraries Unlimited, 1990.

Brock, Clifton. *The Literature of Political Science: A Guide for Students, Librarians, and Teachers*. New York: R. R. Bowker, 1969.

Freides, Thelma. "A Guide to Information Sources on Federal Government Agencies." *News for Teachers of Political Science* 18 (Summer 1978): 6-13.

Government Reference Books: A Biennial Guide to U.S. Government Publications. Littleton, CO: Libraries Unlimited, 1968/1969 —.

Holler, Frederick L. *Information Sources of Political Science.* 4th ed. Santa Barbara, CA: ABC-Clio, 1986.

Jacobstein, J. Myron, and Roy M. Mersky. *Fundamentals of Legal Research.* Rev. ed. Mineola, NY: Foundation Press, 1990.

Lu, Joseph K. *U.S. Government Publications Relating to the Social Sciences: A Selected Annotated Guide.* Beverly Hills, CA: Sage Publications, 1975.

Mason, John B. *Research Resources: Annotated Guide to the Social Sciences.* 2 vols. Santa Barbara, CA: ABC-Clio, 1968-1971.

Palic, Vladimir M. *Government Publications: A Guide to Bibliographic Tools . . . , Incorporating Government Organization Manuals: A Bibliography.* New York: Pergamon Press, 1977.

Robinson, Judith S. *Subject Guide to Government Reference Books.* Littleton, CO: Libraries Unlimited, 1985.

Robinson, Judith S. *Tapping the Government Grapevine: The User-Friendly Guide to U.S. Government Information Sources.* Phoenix: Oryx Press, 1988.

Van Zant, Nancy P. *Selected U.S. Government Series: A Guide for Public and Academic Libraries.* Chicago: American Library Association, 1978.

Vose, Clement E. *A Guide to Library Resources in Political Science: American Government.* Washington, DC: American Political Science Association, 1975.

Williams, Wiley J. *Subject Guide to Major United States Government Publications.* 2d ed. Chicago: American Library Association, 1987.

Wynar, Lubomyr R. *Guide to Reference Materials in Political Science.* Littleton, CO: Libraries Unlimited, 1967.

The following publications are indexes or catalogs of general government publications. The first five guides are especially useful for identifying documents of the eighteenth and nineteenth centuries. For more information regarding the use of these resources, consult the guides in the previous section, especially the works by Morehead, Boyd, and Schmeckebier.

Poore, Ben P. *Descriptive Catalog of the Government Publications of the United States, September 5, 1774-March 4, 1881.* Washington, DC: U.S. Government Printing Office, 1885.

This publication attempted to list all governmental publications, but many department publications were omitted. It is a chronological, annotated list of government publications dated from September 1774 to March 1881. This work is known as *Poore's Descriptive Catalog.*

Ames, John G. *Comprehensive Index to the Publications of the United States Government, 1881-1893.* 2 vols. Washington, DC: U.S. Government Printing Office, 1905.

This is known as *Ames' Comprehensive Index.* Entries are arranged alphabetically by subject. There is an index of personal names. Some departmental publications were omitted.

Checklist of United States Public Documents, 1789-1976. Arlington, VA: U.S. Historical Documents Institute, 1976.

This is the most comprehensive single bibliographical source for U.S. government documents. The entries provide full bibliographic citations for all of the entries in the *1789-1910 Checklist*; the *Document Catalog*; the *Monthly Catalog, 1895-1976*; and the shelf list of the Government Printing Office's Public Documents Library.

Lester, Daniel, and Sandra Faull, comps. *Cumulative Title Index to United States Public Documents, 1789-1976*. Arlington, VA: U.S. Historical Documents Institute, 1978.

This index lists all of the titles in the *Checklist of United States Public Documents, 1789-1976*.

Catalog of the Public Documents of the [53rd to 76th] Congress and All Departments of the Government of the United States [for the Period of March 4, 1893, through December 31, 1940]. Washington, DC: U.S. Government Printing Office, 1896-1945.

This publication, known as the *Document Catalog*, was the first truly systematic record of U.S. public documents. It is the only complete list of executive orders from 1893 to 1940. It also contains presidential proclamations. There are alphabetical entries for authors, subjects, and some titles. This catalog has been discontinued.

U.S. Superintendent of Documents. *Monthly Catalog of United States Government Publications*. Washington, DC: U.S. Government Printing Office, 1895 —.

The *Monthly Catalog* is the *Reader's Guide* of U.S. government publications. While this catalog is not inclusive of all publications, it does index by author, title, subject, and so on, the majority of the most important publications issued by the federal government. There also is a CD-ROM version of the *Monthly Catalog*. It is called Government Documents Catalog Subscription (GDCS) and includes materials from 1976 to the present. Access is by author, title, subject, Superintendent of Documents number, and report number. Features include browse and keyword searching.

The following four publications serve as indexes to the *Monthly Catalog* for the years it had no indexing or for later cumulative indexing.

Kanely, Edna A., comp. *Cumulative Subject Index to the Monthly Catalog of United States Government Publications, 1895-1899*. 2 vols. Arlington, VA: Carrollton Press, 1977.

Buchanon, William A., and Edna A. Kanely, comps. *Cumulative Subject Index to the Monthly Catalog of United States Government Publications, 1900-1971*. Arlington, VA: Carrollton Press, 1973.

Monthly Catalog of United States Government Publications Cumulative Index, Set 1: 1976-1980. 6 vols. Phoenix: Oryx Press, 1987.

Monthly Catalog of United States Government Publications Cumulative Index, Set 2: 1981-1985. 6 vols. Phoenix: Oryx Press, 1987.

Parish, David W. *Changes in American Society, 1960-1978: An Annotated Bibliography of Official Government Publications*. Metuchen, NJ: Scarecrow Press, 1980.

This book describes important government publications in the last twenty years. It is arranged under broad subject areas and lists publications from congressional committees.

Finding Statutes

If the president signs a bill or a bill becomes law without his signature, the enrolled billed is sent from the White House to the General Services Administration (GSA) for printing. If a bill is passed by both houses over the objections of the president, the chamber that last overrides the veto transmits it to the GSA. There it is assigned a public law number and paginated for the *United States Statutes at Large* volume covering that session of the Congress. The public laws are numbered in sequence starting with the beginning of each Congress. Since 1957, the laws have been prefixed for ready identification by the number of the Congress.

The first official publication of a statute is in the form of a slip law, which is a separately published unbound pamphlet. The heading indicates the public law number, the date of approval, and the bill number. Since 1976, the heading also has indicated the *United States Statutes at Large* citation. If the statute has been passed over the veto of the president or has become law without his approval, a statement is inserted in place of the usual notation of approval.

The Office of the Federal Register supplies annotations in the margins of slip laws giving the citations to statutes mentioned in the text and other explanatory notes. Since 1974, the notes have given the citations to the *United States Code*, enabling a reader to immediately determine the legislative history of the law, which consists of the committee report numbers, the names of the committees, the dates of consideration and passage in each chamber, and reference to the *Congressional Record*. Since 1971, a reference to presidential remarks has been included in the legislative history by citing the *Weekly Compilation of Presidential Documents*.

Using the *United States Statutes at Large*

Each year, the General Services Administration prepares the *United States Statutes at Large*, which is a permanent collection of the statutes of each session of Congress. Each volume contains a complete index and a table of contents. From 1956 through 1975, the volumes contained a table of earlier laws affected, and from 1963 through 1974, they contained a table showing the legislative history of each law. The latter table was discontinued in 1975, as the legislative histories now appear on the back of each slip law.

Using the *United States Code*

The *United States Code* is a codification of the statutes of the United States arranged according to subjects under fifty title headings. The purpose of the *Code* is to present the current status of laws in a concise and usable form without requiring one to use numerous volumes of the *Statutes at Large* containing every amendment. Revised editions of the *Code* are published every six years and cumulative supplements are printed at the end of each session of Congress.

Statutes Indexes

Since the *Statutes at Large* and the *Code* comprise the official record of statutory law, they are the primary sources and indexes for finding laws. But there are several commercial reference series that also can be used to locate statutes, either by number or popular name, and to determine the present legal status of a statute. These reference resources can be used by themselves, but it is always best to use them in conjunction with the *Statutes at Large* and the *Code*.

Shepard's Acts and Cases by Popular Names: Federal and State. Colorado Springs, CO: Shepard's Citations, 1968—.

This index cites the location in the *Statutes at Large* and the *Code* by the popular name of the statute. It similarly indexes state acts. Federal cases referred to by popular names can be accessed by using the section that contains references to the *United States Supreme Court Reports* and *National Reporter System.*

Shepard's United States Citations Statute Edition. Colorado Springs, CO: Shepard's Citations, 1955 —.

This citator, published irregularly, allows one to determine the validity of an act or judicial decision by providing citations to earlier and later statutes and cases, as well as to other legal sources. A student or researcher can determine the current status of a decision or act by identifying which amendments, other enactments, or legal decisions have affected a particular statute or decision.

United States Code Annotated. St. Paul, MN: West Publishing Company, 1927 —.

Although this annual set reprints the *United States Code*, the statutes are accompanied by extensive annotations, legal notes, and analytic comments on the specific statute and its legislative history. This supplemental material is invaluable for anyone interested in researching the original intent and later interpretation of the statute.

United States Code Service. Rochester, NY: Lawyers Co-Operative Publishing Company, 1972 —.

This service is very similar to the *United States Code Annotated.* Published irregularly, it reprints the *United States Code* and includes annotations, notes, and legislative histories. One of the volumes in the set, the *United States Code Guide*, is especially useful. It can be used to relate the *Code* to several other reference resources, including the *United States Supreme Court Reports: Lawyers' Edition* and *American Jurisprudence.*

Because these four reference sets are complex tools, one should consult some of the following guides to find more detailed descriptions of how they work and the various ways they can be used. Also, Harry Bitner's *Effective Legal Research* (Boston: Little, Brown, 1979) and J. Myron Jacobstein and Roy M. Mersky's *Fundamentals of Legal Research* (Mineola, NY: Foundation Press, 1990) have excellent chapters on how to use the four services.

Cohen, Morris L. *How to Find the Law.* 9th ed. St. Paul, MN: West Publishing Company, 1989.

Dickerson, Reed. *The Interpretation and Application of Statutes.* Boston: Little, Brown, 1975.

How to Use Shepard's Citations: A Presentation of the Scope and Functions of Shepard's Citation Books and Services with Methods and Techniques to Enhance Their Value in Legal Research. Colorado Springs, CO: Shepard's/McGraw-Hill, 1987.

Statsky, William P. *Legislative Analysis and Drafting.* 2d ed. St. Paul, MN: West Publishing Company, 1984.

Interpreting Statutes

Judicial decisions, both by the Supreme Court and lower courts, are important in determining whether a particular statute or presidential action is constitutional. Since decisions by the courts affect statutory law and administrative law, it is important to be able to identify decisions and know how to follow judicial interpretations.

Constitution

Any analysis of statutes and the rules, regulations, and orders that constitute administrative law must start with the Constitution. The powers of the president are specified in the Constitution. While there are gray areas of legality, executive orders and presidential proclamations are not to supersede statutes. Consequently, it is important to have an understanding of the Constitution to know what the powers of the president are, as well as how statutes are made.

U.S. Library of Congress. Congressional Research Service. *Constitution of the United States of America, Analysis and Interpretation: Annotations of Cases Decided by the Supreme Court of the United States to . . . .* Washington, DC: U.S. Government Printing Office, 1913 — .

This publication, which commonly is referred to as the *Constitution Annotated*, is updated irregularly, and supplements are issued every two years. Extensive case annotations and scholarly analysis and interpretations make this work the best compendium on the Constitution.

Mitchell, Ralph. *CQ's Guide to the U.S. Constitution: History, Text, Index, Glossary.* Washington, DC: Congressional Quarterly, 1986.

This "Constitution-in-a-nutshell" contains a detailed alphabetical index by topic that makes it easy to find the specific part of the Constitution and amendments for which one is looking. It also contains an excellent glossary of legal terms.

Constitutional Law Texts

The following texts can be used to find information about specific cases as well as essays about major turning points in the development of constitutional law.

Berns, Walter. *Constitutional Cases in American Government.* 7th ed. New York: Crowell, 1989.

Corsi, Jerome R., and Matthew Lippman. *Constitutional Law: A Political Science Casebook.* Englewood Cliffs, NJ: Prentice-Hall, 1985.

Cushman, Robert F. *Cases in Constitutional Law.* 7th ed. Englewood Cliffs, NJ: Prentice-Hall, 1989.

Ducat, Craig R., and Harold W. Chase. *Constitutional Interpretation.* 4th ed. St. Paul, MN: West Publishing Company, 1988.

Grossman, Joel B., and Richard S. Wells. *Constitutional Law and Judicial Policy Making.* 3d ed. New York: Longman, 1988.

Kauper, Paul G. *Constitutional Law: Cases and Materials.* 5th ed. Boston: Little, Brown, 1980.

Killeen, Denis. *United States Constitution: Supreme Court Cases.* West Hartford, CT: Hartfordshire Press, 1987.

Kutler, Stanley, I., ed. *The Supreme Court and the Constitution: Readings in American Constitutional History.* New York: W. W. Norton, 1984.

Lockhart, William B., Yale Kamisar, and Jesse H. Choper. *The American Constitution: Cases, Comments, and Questions.* 6th ed. St. Paul, MN: West Publishing Company, 1986.

Mason, Alpheus T., and D. Grier Stephenson, Jr. *American Constitutional Law: Introductory Essays and Selected Cases.* 9th ed. Englewood Cliffs, NJ: Prentice-Hall, 1990.

Mendelson, Wallace. *The Constitution and the Supreme Court.* 2d ed. New York: Dodd, Mead, 1970.

Shapiro, Martin M., and Rocco J. Tresolini. *American Constitutional Law.* 6th ed. New York: Macmillan, 1983.

Stephens, Otis H., Jr., and Gregory J. Rathjen, eds. *The Supreme Court and the Allocation of Constitutional Power: Introductory Essays and Selected Cases.* San Francisco: W. H. Freeman, 1980.

Swisher, Carl B. *American Constitutional Development.* Boston: Houghton Mifflin, 1978.

Tribe, Laurence H. *American Constitutional Law.* 2d ed. Mineola, NY: Foundation Press, 1988.

Legal Dictionaries

Dictionaries can be used in a variety of ways for studying the Supreme Court. Most of all, they are useful for finding the answers to ready reference questions, such as a date, a definition, the name of an individual, and the like. Some dictionaries are more scholarly and detailed than others, providing short essays rather than dictionary-style entries.

Anderson, William S., ed. *Ballentine's Law Dictionary, with Pronunciations.* 3d ed. Rochester, NY: Lawyers Co-Operative Publishing Company, 1969.

Black, Henry C. *Black's Law Dictionary.* 5th ed. St. Paul, MN: West Publishing Company, 1979.

Chandler, Ralph C., Richard A. Enslen, and Peter G. Renstrom. *The Constitutional Law Dictionary.* 2 vols. Santa Barbara, CA: ABC-Clio, 1985-1987.

Gifis, Steven H. *Law Dictionary.* 2d ed. Woodbury, NY: Barron's Educational Series, 1984.

Kling, Samuel G. *The Legal Encyclopedia and Dictionary.* New York: Pocket Books, 1970.

Radin, Max. *Radin Law Dictionary.* Rev. ed. Dobbs Ferry, NY: Oceana Publications, 1970.

Volkell, Randolph Z. *Quick Legal Terminology.* New York: John Wiley, 1979.

Legal Encyclopedias

Legal encyclopedias are excellent sources of information on the Supreme Court, yet most students and researchers tend to overlook them in their search for information. All of the encyclopedias cited below contain lengthy essays. The entries usually are written by experts in the field, providing concise overviews and histories. These encyclopedias should be the first place one looks before searching for documents, legal cases, and the like.

American Jurisprudence. 2d ed. San Francisco: Bancroft-Whitney, 1962 — .

This multivolume encyclopedia contains treatises covering federal and state laws. Each volume is indexed, and there is an index to the whole set as well as annual supplements.

Corpus Secundum Secundum. New York: American Law Book Company, 1937-1960, 1961 —.

Over 400 articles on U.S. law are arranged under topical headings in this work. Citations to law cases are given. The citations are indexed in each volume as well as in a separate index. There are annual supplements.

The Guide to American Law: Everyone's Legal Encyclopedia. 12 vols. St. Paul, MN: West Publishing Company, 1983.

This encyclopedia contains entries for over 5,000 topics, including articles on legal cases, statutes, terms and concepts, and notable persons. Each volume is individually indexed; the last volume indexes and cross-references the entire set. New information can be found in *The Guide to American Law Yearbook, 1987: Everyone's Legal Encyclopedia.* St. Paul, MN: West Publishing Company, 1987.

Hixson, Richard F. *Mass Media and the Constitution: An Encyclopedia of Supreme Court Decisions.* New York: Garland, 1989.

This volume covers over two hundred First Amendment decisions made by the Supreme Court during the nineteenth and early twentieth centuries. It includes the name and date of each decision, along with the ruling, precedents, and circumstances.

Levy, Leonard W., ed. *Encyclopedia of the American Constitution.* 4 vols. New York: Free Press, 1986.

This four-volume set is the only encyclopedia specifically about the Constitution. Articles were written by 262 contributors, including lawyers, political scientists, historians, and journalists. There are more than 2,200 articles about constitutional history, concepts and terms, Supreme Court cases, and public acts. The encyclopedia includes a guide to legal citations and a chronology of 100 significant dates in constitutional history as well as a subject index and index of cases.

Bibliographies

The researcher who is interested in the Supreme Court will have no difficulty finding materials. Perhaps the only problem the researcher will face is focusing in on a particular topic and weeding through citations and sources. The bibliographies mentioned in this section cover all kinds of materials, including books, periodical literature, and government documents. By consulting these bibliographies the researcher will have thousands of citations from which to choose. One also can consult the bibliographies listed in the preface; those volumes were searched in compiling this bibliography.

General

Bibliographic Index: A Cumulative Bibliography of Bibliographies. New York: H. W. Wilson, 1937 —.

This work lists bibliographies by subject. The bibliographies listed are separate books, parts of books, periodical articles, or pamphlets. There is a semiannual index and a cumulated index issued each December.

Constitution

Andrews, Joseph L. *The Law in the United States of America: A Selective Bibliographical Guide.* New York: New York University Press, 1966.

This bibliography selectively lists and annotates legal publications. There are two parts, the first listing primary materials and the second, secondary works. The entries are found under broad subject headings.

Chambliss, William J., and Robert B. Seidman. *Sociology of the Law: A Research Bibliography*. Berkeley, CA: Glendessary Press, 1970.

This bibliography contains some material on the Supreme Courts and constitutional law, but it is most useful for finding citations to jurisprudence, judicial review, and more theoretical aspects of judicial behavior.

Hall, Kermit L. *Bibliography of American Constitutional and Legal History, 1896-1979*. 5 vols. Millwood, NY: Kraus International Publications, 1984.

This five-volume work cites over 18,000 major writings on the history of U.S. legal culture from 1896 through 1979. It covers books, dissertations, and scholarly journal articles published in English in the United States. The bibliography is organized into seven parts: (1) general surveys and texts, (2) institutional, (3) constitutional doctrine, (4) legal doctrine, (5) biographical, (6) chronological, and (7) geographical.

McCarrick, Earlean M. *The U.S. Constitution: A Guide to Information Sources*. Detroit: Gale Research, 1980.

All aspects of constitutional law, including its development, amendments, and the role of the Supreme Court and individual justices, are covered in this guide. It is better for finding citations to books than to journals.

Mason, Alpheus T., and D. Grier Stephenson, Jr. *American Constitutional Development*. Arlington Heights, IL: AHM, 1977.

This is an excellent guide to the literature on constitutional law and statutory interpretation. The citations are taken mostly from the field of legal studies, but there are some citations from the social sciences and humanities.

Millet, Stephen M. *A Selected Bibliography of American Constitutional History*. Santa Barbara, CA: ABC-Clio, 1975.

This bibliography contains citations to the origins and development of the Constitution; the history of amendments; and the role of the Court, Congress, and the president in the judicial system.

Ontiveros, Suzanne R., ed. *The Dynamic Constitution: A Historical Bibliography*. Santa Barbara, CA: ABC-Clio, 1986.

More than 1,370 citations to books, articles, and dissertations are included in this bibliography. There are annotations for the articles but not for the books and dissertations. The bibliography is arranged in five chapters, each with an introductory survey. The first chapter provides citations to materials that are historiographies, and the following four chapters are by time period. The volume includes an author and a title index.

Reams, Bernard D., and Stuart D. Yoak. *The Constitution of the United States: A Guide and Bibliography to Current Scholarly Research*. Dobbs Ferry, NY: Oceana Publications, 1987.

This unannotated bibliography includes citations to essays, articles, books, and government documents about the Constitution and all the amendments. The citations are arranged by branches of government and by each amendment.

Supreme Court

Brenner, Saul. "Game Theory and Supreme Court Decision Making: A Bibliographic Overview." *Law Library Journal* 72 (Summer 1979): 470-475.

Browning, James R., and Bess Glenn. "The Supreme Court Collection at the National Archives." *American Journal of Legal History* 4 (July 1960): 241-256.

Coppa and Avery Consultants. *The Supreme Court: A Bibliographical Overview of an Institutional Decision Maker*. Monticello, IL: Vance Bibliographies, 1980.

Feinberg, Renee. *The Equal Rights Amendment: An Annotated Bibliography of the Issues, 1976-1985*. Westport, CT: Greenwood Press, 1986.

Garcia, Lana C. "Role and Experiences of Supreme Court Law Clerks: An Annotated Bibliography." *Law Library Journal* 70 (August 1977): 338-342.

Hallam, H. Charles, Jr., and Edward G. Hudon. "United States Supreme Court Records and Briefs: A Union List, with a Note on Their Distribution and Microfilming." *Law Library Journal* 40 (May 1947): 82-84.

Marshall, Geoffrey. "Some Recent Books about the Supreme Court." *Political Studies* 5 (June 1957): 186-188.

Mastrangelo, Paul J. "A Supreme Court Mediagraphy." *Law Library Journal* 78 (Spring 1986): 279-306.

Meyer, Hermann H. *List of Works Relating to the Supreme Court of the United States*. Washington, DC: U.S. Government Printing Office, 1909.

Miller, Arthur S. "The Supreme Court of the United States: A Bibliographical Essay." *American Studies International* 16 (Winter 1977): 5-14

Nunis, Doyce B., Jr. "Historical Studies in United States Legal History, 1950-1959: A Bibliography of Articles Published in Scholarly Non-Law Journals." *American Journal of Legal History* 7 (January 1963): 1-27.

Spector, Robert M. "Judicial Biography and the United States Supreme Court: A Bibliographical Appraisal." *American Journal of Legal History* 11 (January 1967): 1-24.

Stephenson, D. Grier, Jr. "The Judicial Bookshelf." *Supreme Court Historical Society Yearbook* 1985 (1985): 128-145.

Stephenson, D. Grier, Jr. *The Supreme Court and the American Republic: An Annotated Bibliography*. New York: Garland, 1981.

Surrency, Erwin C. "Documentary Sources for Study of United States Supreme Court Litigation: Parts I-II." *Law Library Journal* 69 (November 1976): 440-452.

Wigdor, Alexandra K. *The Personal Papers of Supreme Court Justices: A Descriptive Guide*. New York: Garland, 1986.

Guides to the Supreme Court

The following two guides are excellent starting places for anyone looking for either the answer to a specific question or an overview of some aspect of the Supreme Court.

Guide to the U.S. Supreme Court. 2d ed. Washington, DC: Congressional Quarterly, 1989.

This one-volume guide is more like an encyclopedia on the Supreme Court. It is a massive handbook divided into five chapters covering the origins and development of the

Court, the Court and the federal system, the Court and the individual, pressures on the Court, and the Court at work. It also includes a section on the justices, providing background information, and a section summarizing major decisions of the Court since 1789.

Elliott, Stephen P., ed. *A Reference Guide to the United States Supreme Court*. New York: Facts on File, 1986.

This volume includes four chapters on the Supreme Court, including the role of the Court, constitutional power of the branches, the division of power between the federal government and the states, and individual rights. There is an excellent section on landmark cases providing good summaries, and on biographies of the justices. There are numerous appendixes, including an alphabetical listing of chief justices, an alphabetical listing of associate justices, two chronological tables for the chief justices and associate justices providing basic information about their careers, a listing of sitting courts, and a chronological listing of landmark cases. The volume also includes a short bibliography and subject index.

Supreme Court Casebooks

Supreme Court decisions are first issued as "slip opinions." These are published within three days and are available in depository libraries. In addition to the slip opinions there are several casebooks a researcher can use for finding Supreme Court decisions.

U.S. Law Week. Washington, DC: Bureau of National Affairs, 1933 — .

This weekly periodical service includes important sections on the Supreme Court. It has four indexes: a topical index, a table of cases, a docket number table, and a proceedings section. In addition to containing the full text of all decisions, the periodical has a number of useful sections, including (1) cases filed last week, (2) summary of cases filed recently, (3) journal of proceedings, (4) summary of orders, (5) arguments before the Court, (6) argued cases awaiting decisions, (7) review of the Court's work, and (8) review of the Court's docket.

U.S. Supreme Court. *Supreme Court Reporter*. St. Paul, MN: West Publishing Company, 1983 — .

This weekly nongovernmental publication contains annotated reports and indexes of case names. It includes some material not covered in the *United States Reports*, such as opinions of justices in chambers.

U.S. Supreme Court. *United States Reports*. Washington, DC: U.S. Government Printing Office, 1790 — .

The *Reports*, an annual publication, contain the official text of all opinions of the Supreme Court. Also included are tables of cases reported, cases and statutes cited, miscellaneous materials, and a subject index. All written reports and most *per curiam* reports of decisions are printed.

U.S. Supreme Court. *United States Supreme Court Reports: Lawyers' Edition*. Rochester, NY: Lawyers Co-Operative Publishing Company, 1970 — .

All other casebooks contain the official reports, but this service contains numerous *per curiam* decisions not found elsewhere. The annual service also summarizes individually the majority and dissenting opinions and counsel briefs. The index to annotations leads one to the legal notes provided for each case.

West's Federal Case News. St. Paul, MN: West Publishing Company, 1978 — .

This weekly publication provides summaries of cases decided in the Supreme Court but also does so for a number of other courts, including the U.S. Court of Appeals, U.S. Court of Claims, U.S. district courts, and selected cases from state courts.

Decisions of lower courts (district courts and courts of appeals) are not reported officially by the government. However, decisions of these courts are printed unofficially. The *National Reporter System* is a privately published edition of law reports covering most of the lower federal courts. The *Federal Reporter* contains the decisions of federal intermediate appellate courts and some selected district courts, and the *Federal Supplement* contains mainly the decisions of the U.S. district courts.

Besides publishing the decisions of the Supreme Court, the government also publishes on a regular basis the decisions of the following courts: court of claims, court of customs and patent appeals, customs court, commerce court, tax court, and court of military appeals.

Digests of Supreme Court Decisions

There are several excellent reference resources that contain digests analyzing court decisions by subject and case name. *Shepard's United States Citations* also identifies every time a decision has been cited in a later case, whereby one can follow changes in legal interpretation.

Blandford, Linda A., and Patricia Russell Evans, eds. *Supreme Court of the United States, 1789-1980: An Index to Opinions Arranged by Justice.* 2 vols. Millwood, NY: Kraus International Publications, 1983.

Digest of United States Supreme Court Reports, Annotated with Case Annotations, Dissenting and Separate Decisions since 1900. Rochester, NY: Lawyers Co-Operative Publishing Company, 1948.

Guenther, Nancy A. *United States Supreme Court Decisions: An Index to Excerpts, Reprints, and Discussions.* 2d ed. Metuchen, NJ: Scarecrow Press, 1983.

Shepard's United States Citations: Case Edition. Colorado Springs, CO: Shepard's Citations, 1947 — .

Significant Decisions of the Supreme Court. Washington, DC: American Enterprise Institute for Public Policy Research, 1969 — .

United States Supreme Court Digest. St. Paul, MN: West Publishing Company, 1940 — .

Briefs and Records of the Supreme Court

Several resources can be used to locate the briefs and oral arguments used by counsel on both sides. The briefs and records are a valuable resource for understanding the eventual decision of a case and the interpretation of a statute or administrative rule.

Complete Oral Arguments of the Supreme Court of the United States. Frederick, MD: University Publications of America, 1980 — .

Kurland, Philip B., and Gerhard Casper. *Landmark Briefs and Arguments of the Supreme Court of the United States: Constitutional Law.* Frederick, MD: University Publications of America, 1975—.

U.S. National Archives and Records Service. *Tape Recordings of Oral Arguments before the U.S. Supreme Court.* Washington, DC: National Archives and Records Service, 1955—.

U.S. Supreme Court. *Records and Briefs.* Washington, DC: Government Printing Office, 1832—.

Legal Newspapers

We have listed legal newspapers in a separate category since they are a special kind of publication. Although these newspapers are written with the legal profession in mind, they contain a wealth of information for anyone studying the Supreme Court. They include stories about major issues, appointments, and controversies surrounding the Supreme Court. For anyone following national politics, these newspapers should be required reading.

Legal Times of Washington. Washington, DC: Legal Times of Washington, 1978—.

This weekly periodical contains accounts of current developments in the legal world.

National Law Journal. New York: New York Publishing Company, 1978—.

This is a legal newspaper geared for a general audience. It offers a weekly selective index to legal materials.

U.S. Law Week. Washington, DC: Bureau of National Affairs, 1933—.

This weekly newspaper has four major sections. Section one provides summaries and analyses of major court decisions. The second section deals with new court decisions and agency rulings. The third section contains information on Supreme Court decisions. The last section contains information on Supreme Court opinions.

Other publications regarding interpretations of the law and legal issues are issued by the Justice Department and General Accounting Office (GAO). *Official Opinions of the Attorneys General* and *Opinions of the Office of Legal Counsel* both are issued by the Department of Justice. In the GAO's *Decisions of the Comptroller General,* one can find legal decisions regarding the disbursement of appropriated monies. The last source, *Court Proceedings and Actions of Vital Interest to the Congress,* issued by the House Judiciary Committee, is rather specialized. Its focus is primarily on decisions affecting members of Congress, such as immunity, election disputes, and the scope of their powers.

Legal Journals

Legal journals are a primary source for articles relating to the study of the Supreme Court. They are indispensable for legal research, and also can be useful for other approaches to the Supreme Court since they contain an enormous number of articles on all aspects of the Court. It is impossible to cite all the journals that would be useful; only a few representative journals are listed here. Omitted are university journals (*Harvard Law Review, Georgetown Law Journal*), state journals (*Illinois Bar Journal, Maryland Law Review*), and some specialized journals (*Antitrust Law and Economic Review, Tax*

Law Review) that can be especially important when researching a topic related to specific areas. One should always take the time to see what specialized journals exist since they may contain primary sources of information.

Administrative Law Review. Chicago: American Bar Association, 1973 — . (Published quarterly.)

American Bar Association Journal. Chicago: American Bar Association, 1915 — . (Published monthly.)

American Journal of Legal History. Philadelphia: American Society for Legal History, 1957 — . (Published quarterly.)

Federal Bar Journal. Washington, DC: Federal Bar Association, 1931 — . (Published quarterly.)

Federal Rules Decisions. St. Paul, MN: West Publishing Company, 1941 — . (Published monthly.)

Supreme Court Historical Society Yearbook. Washington, DC: Supreme Court Historical Society, 1976 — . (Published annually.)

U.S. Law Week: A National Service of Current Law. Washington, DC: Bureau of National Affairs, 1933 — . (Published weekly.)

Legal Indexes

Indexes and abstracting services are crucial research tools for studying the Supreme Court; they are the key to finding journal literature. While almost every index will contain citations to articles on the Supreme Court, we have selected the indexes most likely to be used in the study of the Court. But students and researchers should always check to see if there are any other indexes that would prove useful to their research. For example, to research the role of women and the courts, *Women's Studies Abstracts* would be useful; to explore efforts in the area of law and order, the *Abstracts on Criminology and Penology* would be helpful, as well as several other indexes in the field of criminal justice, including *Police Science Abstracts* and the *Criminal Justice Periodical Index*.

In addition, since many indexes are now available on CD-ROM, one should check to see if these versions are in a library. CD-ROM products can save time and effort. One also can check the indexes listed later in this introduction in the section on general research resources.

Annual Legal Bibliography. Cambridge: Harvard University Law School Library, 1961 — .

This bibliography covers books and articles acquired by the Harvard University Law School Library. The entries are classified into the following groups: common law, civil law and other jurisdictions, private international law, and public international law. The entries are not annotated. This bibliography provides excellent coverage of administrative law and congressional relations with the president and the Supreme Court.

Contents of Current Legal Periodicals. Los Angeles: Law Publications, 1975 — .

The articles listed in the tables of contents of legal journals are indexed by subject in this monthly publication. The virtue of this service is the currency of its indexing.

Current Law Index. Menlo Park, CA: Information Access Corporation, 1980 — .

This monthly index covers legal periodicals and newspapers. Its microfilm counterpart, *Legal Resources Index*, cumulates the information found in the paper copy. *Legal Re-*

sources Index also is available on CD-ROM, where it is called LEGALTRAC. While most students and researchers only would use these tools when researching specific legal issues, these indexes should be consulted for any literature search on the Supreme Court.

The Federal Index. Cleveland: Predicasts, 1976 — .

This is a monthly index covering the congressional, executive, and judicial branches of government. It indexes the *Federal Register*, the *Congressional Record*, the *Weekly Compilation of Presidential Documents*, and *U.S. Law Week*. The index is cumulated annually. It is enormously useful for keeping up to date on federal policies, rules, and decisions. As a commercial index to documents and selected secondary sources, it can save time when searching for judicial documents.

Index to Legal Periodicals. New York: H. W. Wilson, 1908 — .

This monthly work indexes articles appearing in legal periodicals of the United States, Canada, Great Britain, Northern Ireland, Australia, and New Zealand. Indexes are provided for authors, subjects, book reviews, and cases. This is another legal index that should be used in almost every literature search on the Supreme Court. Since it is the oldest legal index, it can be used for historical research as well.

Index to Periodical Articles Related to Law. Dobbs Ferry, NY: Glanville Publications, 1958 — .

This quarterly index lists by author and subject articles found in journals published by law schools, lawyers associations, and law institutes. It contains some citations to the study of the Supreme Court, but it should be used only after consulting other legal indexes.

Monthly Digest of Legal Articles. Greenville, NY: Research and Documentation Corporation, 1969 — .

This is another service best used for finding recent journal literature on the Supreme Court.

Legal Databases

Bibliographic databases that cover all areas of the social sciences are extremely useful in that they retrieve information quickly and are available at most university and other research libraries. Many libraries subscribe to on-line bibliographic databases such as Knight-Ridder's DIALOG Information Retrieval Service, and Maxwell Systems' Bibliographic Retrieval Service (BRS) and ORBIT. The two legal database systems are LEXIS and WESTLAW. The Information Bank of the New York Times includes materials from the *New York Times* and selected materials from other newspapers and magazines. Librarians are trained to use these databases and can advise the researcher about the cost and effectiveness of the various systems.

Two journals, *Online* and *Database: The Magazine of Database Reference and Review*, report on new databases, new searching techniques, and possible future developments. For additional information, one also can consult the databases listed later in this introduction in the section on general research resources.

LEGAL RESOURCES INDEX. Menlo Park, CA: Information Access Corporation, 1980 — .

This database indexes over 660 journals and five legal newspapers as well as legal monographs and government publications from the Library of Congress. It provides the best overall look at legal materials and can be used when researching almost any topic related to the Supreme Court.

LEXIS. Dayton, OH: Mead Data Central, 1973 —.

This system searches through legal documents to retrieve needed information. With a LEXIS terminal and a telephone, text is retrieved from a computer in Dayton, Ohio. This system can be used for finding citations to several different perspectives on the Supreme Court, including legal analyses of decisions, administrative decision making, and regulatory politics.

WESTLAW. St. Paul, MN: West Publishing Company, 1978 —.

All recent U.S. state and federal court decisions are abstracted in this database. It covers judicial decision making and the court system, so it can be used most effectively for finding citations related to the interpretation of public laws.

Biographical Directories on the Justices

Listed below are several directories that can be used to find biographical information about Supreme Court justices. Some of the directories also contain information about judges at other levels of the judicial system.

Barnes, Catherine. *Men of the Supreme Court: Profiles of the Justices*. New York: Facts on File, 1978.

This volume includes biographical essays of the twenty-six men who served as Supreme Court justices between 1945 and 1976. Each essay includes information on the justices' education, legal training, and work as a justice.

Chase, Harold, Samuel Krislov, Keith O. Boyum, and Jerry N. Clark. *Biographical Dictionary of the Federal Judiciary*. Detroit: Gale Research, 1976.

Basic biographical data for federal judges from 1789 to 1974, including Supreme Court justices, are contained in this work.

Friedman, Leon, and Fred L. Israel. *The Justices of the United States Supreme Court*. New York: R. R. Bowker, 1969-1978.

This five-volume set contains detailed biographical essays on the 101 Supreme Court justices who served during the period from 1789 to 1976. It also includes representative opinions of each justice, plus an annotated bibliography for each justice.

United States Court Directory. Washington, DC: U.S. Government Printing Office, 1981 —.

This semiannual volume provides the names, addresses, and phone numbers of judges of the Supreme Court, court of appeals, court of claims, court of customs and patent appeals, and court of military appeals.

General Research Resources

Almanacs

Most almanacs can be used as ready reference sources. While every almanac uses a different format, they all contain essentially the same information.

Information Please Almanac. New York: Simon and Schuster, 1947 – .

Official Associated Press Almanac. Maplewood, NJ: Hammond Almanac, 1974 – .

World Almanac and Book of Facts. New York: Newspaper Enterprise Association, 1868 – .

World Almanac of U.S. Politics. New York: World Almanac, 1989 – .

Dictionaries

Dictionaries in the fields of political science and history contain a variety of information. In addition to definitions of terms and concepts, one can find entries for legal cases, court decisions, histories of government agencies, and biographical sketches. Most political science and history dictionaries contain hundreds of entries relevant to the study of the Supreme Court.

Political Science

Holt, Sol. *The Dictionary of American Government.* Rev. ed. New York: Woodhill Press, 1970.

Plano, Jack C., and Milton Greenberg. *The American Political Dictionary.* 8th ed. New York: Holt, Rinehart, and Winston, 1989.

Whisker, James B. *A Dictionary of Concepts in American Politics.* New York: John Wiley, 1980.

History

Adams, James T. *Dictionary of American History.* Rev. ed. New York: Charles Scribner's Sons, 1976.

Martin, Michael R., and Leonard Gelber. *Dictionary of American History: With the Complete Text of the Constitution of the United States.* Rev. ed. Totowa, NJ: Rowman and Allanheld, 1989.

Encyclopedias

Encyclopedias in the field of political science and history can be used to find information about important dates, biographies, and significant historical events. Encyclopedias are especially useful for finding basic information on unfamiliar events, names, or issues.

Political Science

Encyclopedia of the Social Sciences. 15 vols. New York: Macmillan, 1930-1935.

This encyclopedia contains scholarly articles on the concerns of the social sciences. The articles usually are lengthy, supply bibliographies, and are signed by the author. The entries are arranged alphabetically.

Sills, David L., ed. *International Encyclopedia of the Social Sciences.* 17 vols. New York: Macmillan, 1968.

Articles with a general subject matter are arranged alphabetically in the encyclopedia. There are cross-references and an index to aid the reader in finding materials. The articles are written by social scientists and include material on the Supreme Court relating to the disciplines of political science, law, history, economics, and sociology. This encyclopedia is not a revision of the earlier *Encyclopedia of the Social Sciences.*

History

Morris, Richard B., and Jeffrey B. Morris. *Encyclopedia of American History.* 6th ed. New York: Harper and Row, 1982.

This one-volume work covers chronologically the important events in American history. There is a section devoted to biographies of notable U.S. figures.

Newspapers and Indexes

All newspapers generally cover the Supreme Court, reporting on national implications of and local reactions to its activities. Newspapers are unrivaled for their ability to provide almost instantaneous reports on Supreme Court activities. The two best newspapers for following the Supreme Court are the *New York Times* (indexed in the *New York Times Index*) and the *Washington Post* (indexed in the *Washington Post Index*).

The New York Times Information Bank, which began in 1969, is a unique on-line database service. Articles published in the *New York Times,* as well as articles from more than seventy additional periodicals, are indexed and abstracted in the database. One can use the database to retrieve the bibliographic citations or the abstracts of the articles. The indexing and abstracting is selective; there is a strong emphasis on political issues and officials.

The *National Newspaper Index* indexes the *New York Times, Wall Street Journal, Christian Science Monitor, Los Angeles Times,* and *Washington Post.* This microfilm index is cumulative and updated regularly. Because it covers more than a single calendar year, it is easier to use than the separate annual indexes to these newspapers. For research on current issues, the *National Newspaper Index* is the first place one should look. The *National Newspaper Index* also is available on CD-ROM on INFOTRAC. The CD-ROM version dates back to 1985 and is updated monthly.

Another important on-line database service is the *NewsBank Electronic Index. NewsBank* indexes selected articles from more than 450 U.S. newspapers, beginning with January 1982. The full text of articles is available on microfiche. This index also is on CD-ROM, which makes searching for articles much easier.

In addititon to the newspaper indexes, both the *Public Affairs Information Service Bulletin* and the *Business Periodicals Index* selectively index stories from the *New York Times* and the *Wall Street Journal.*

Newsmagazines

Weekly and monthly newsmagazines are an excellent source of current information about the Supreme Court. They include not only news stories but also editorials and feature articles.

Newsweek and *Time* are especially useful for weekly reports on the Supreme Court. *Human Events* and *Washington Monthly* both focus specifically on politics in Washington, DC. *Human Events* contains sections entitled "Capitol Briefs" and "This Week's News in Washington." *Washington Monthly,* in addition to several feature articles, has information on new government appointments, news briefs on all activities of the government, and reviews of books on American politics. The other magazines listed below regularly carry articles on the Supreme Court written from a variety of philosophical viewpoints, from liberal to conservative.

The best indexes to use for finding articles from newsmagazines are the *Reader's Guide to Periodical Literature* and the *Magazine Index*. Another tool is the INFOTRAC CD-ROM index that includes the *Magazine Index* and *Business Index*. INFOTRAC is updated quarterly and indexes materials back to 1980. It also indexes the *Wall Street Journal* and has an option for full-text retrieval.

Although the following magazines do publish some scholarly articles on the Supreme Court, they usually are not thought of as research journals. They are most useful for keeping up on current events and as a record of public opinion, as evidenced in their editorials and opinion articles.

Atlantic Monthly. Boston: Atlantic Monthly Company, 1857 — .

Center Magazine. Santa Barbara, CA: Center for the Study of Democratic Institutions, 1967 — .

Commentary: Journal of Significant Thought and Opinion on Contemporary Issues. New York: American Jewish Committee, 1945 — .

Commonweal. New York: Commonweal Publishing Company, 1924 — .

Conservative Digest. Falls Church, VA: Viguerie Communications Corporation, 1975 — .

Current. Washington, DC: Heldref Publications, 1960 — .

Harper's Magazine. New York: Harper's Magazine Company, 1851 — .

Human Events: The National Conservative Weekly. Washington, DC: Human Events, 1944 — .

National Review: A Journal of Fact and Opinion. New York: National Review, 1955 — .

New Republic: A Journal of Opinion. Washington, DC: New Republic, 1914 — .

Newsweek. New York: Newsweek, 1933 — .

Progressive. Madison, WI: Progressive, 1909 — .

Society: Social Science and Modern Society. New Brunswick, NJ: Transactions Periodicals Consortium, Rutgers University, 1963 — .

Time: The Weekly Newsmagazine. New York: Time-Life, 1923 — .

U.S. News and World Report. Washington, DC: U.S. News and World Report, 1933 — .

Washington Monthly. Washington, DC: Washington Monthly Company, 1969 — .

News Services

While newspapers provide day-to-day coverage of political events, the time lag for published indexes is one of the most frustrating problems that researchers encounter. Indexes to newspapers generally are three or more months behind. Consequently, if one is interested in finding information about an event that took place a month ago, one may not be able to search newspapers through an index. It is in these situations that news services can be most useful since they are only about two weeks behind in their publication. *Facts on File* and *Keesing's Contemporary Archives* are often the only indexed sources available for information about very recent events.

Editorials on File: Semi-Monthly Compilation from 140 U.S. and Canadian Newspapers. New York: Facts on File, 1977 — .

Editorials are reproduced and indexed in this reference work. This resource can be used to study public opinions and attitudes about the Supreme Court.

Facts on File: Weekly News Digest and Index. New York: Facts on File, 1940—.

This is a weekly digest of world events, but the emphasis is on the United States. The entries are grouped under broad topics such as world affairs or national affairs. There is a cumulative index. *Facts on File News Digest* also is available on CD-ROM; it covers 1987-1988 and is updated annually. It can be searched by date, index topic, keyword, and with Boolean logic.

Keesing's Contemporary Archives: Weekly Diary of World Events. London: Keesing's
Publications, 1931—.

This publication summarizes news reports for the week. There is strong coverage of news events in the United Kingdom and Europe. It is indexed cumulatively every two weeks, three months, year, and two years.

Journals

Virtually every journal in political science and history at one time or another will contain an article on the Supreme Court. The journals listed below either publish articles on the Supreme Court on a regular basis or are useful for specialized areas of study, such as public opinion. Besides journals in political science and history, there are many journals in the fields of economics, sociology, psychology, and policy studies that publish articles related to the study of the Supreme Court. Again, the best method for finding articles from journals in those disciplines is to use a variety of indexes, abstracting services, and on-line databases.

Political Science

American Academy of Political and Social Sciences, The Annals. Philadelphia: American
Academy of Political and Social Science, 1890—. (Published bimonthly.)

American Journal of Political Science. Detroit: Midwest Political Science Association,
1957—. (Published quarterly.)

American Political Science Review. Washington, DC: American Political Science Association, 1907—. (Published quarterly.)

American Politics Quarterly. Beverly Hills, CA: Sage Publications, 1973—. (Published
quarterly.)

Journal of Law and Politics. Charlottesville: University of Virginia, 1983—. (Published
quarterly.)

Journal of Politics. Gainesville, FL: Southern Political Science Association, 1939—.
(Published quarterly.)

Law and Contemporary Problems. Durham, NC: Duke University, School of Law,
1933—. (Published quarterly.)

Policy Review. Washington, DC: Heritage Foundation, 1977—. (Published quarterly.)

Political Behavior. Albany, NY: Agathon Press, 1979—. (Published quarterly.)

Political Science Quarterly. New York: Academy of Political Science, 1886—. (Published
quarterly.)

Polity. Amherst, MA: Northeastern Political Science Association, 1968—. (Published
quarterly.)

Public Administration Review. Washington, DC: American Society for Public Administration, 1940 —. (Published quarterly.)

Public Interest. New York: National Affairs, 1965 —. (Published quarterly.)

Public Opinion. Washington, DC: American Enterprise Institute for Public Policy Research, 1978 —. (Published bimonthly.)

Public Opinion Quarterly. New York: American Association for Public Opinion Research, Columbia University, 1937 —. (Published quarterly.)

Review of Politics. Notre Dame, IN: University of Notre Dame, 1938 —. (Published quarterly.)

Social Science Quarterly. Austin, TX: Southwestern Social Science Association, 1920 —. (Published quarterly.)

Western Political Quarterly. Salt Lake City, UT: Western Political Science Association, 1948 —. (Published quarterly.)

Wilson Quarterly. Washington, DC: Woodrow Wilson Center for Scholars, 1976 —. (Published quarterly.)

History

American Heritage: The Magazine of History. New York: American Heritage Publishing Company, 1949 —. (Published bimonthly.)

American Historical Review. Washington, DC: American Historical Association, 1895 —. (Published five times a year.)

American Studies. Lawrence, KS: Midcontinent American Studies Association, 1960 —. (Published quarterly.)

Current History. Philadelphia: Current History, 1943 —. (Published monthly.)

Historian: A Journal of History. Allentown, PA: Alpha Theta International Honor Society in History, 1938 —. (Published quarterly.)

Journal of American History. Bloomington, IN: Organization of American Historians, 1914 —. (Published quarterly.)

Journal of Southern History. New Orleans: Southern Historical Association, 1935 —. (Published quarterly.)

Pacific Historical Review. Berkeley, CA: American Historical Association, Pacific Coast Branch, 1932 —. (Published quarterly.)

Prologue: The Journal of the National Archives. Washington, DC: U.S. National Archives and Records Administration, 1969 —. (Published quarterly.)

Indexes

In addition to the legal indexes discussed earlier, the following indexes are the most useful in finding journal articles that pertain to the Supreme Court.

General

British Humanities Index. London: Library Association, 1963 —.

This work indexes articles from over 275 periodicals in the humanities and social sciences, arranged by subject. In addition to indexing all of the major British journals in political science that would have articles on the Supreme Court, the work also indexes journals such as *New Society* and the *Guardian*, which can be used as sources for studying British views of the Supreme Court and American politics. This index is issued quarterly.

Business Periodicals Index. New York: H. W. Wilson, 1958 —.

This work, published monthly except August and cumulated annually, indexes articles appearing in English-language business periodicals published in the United States. It covers accounting, advertising, finance, labor, management, public administration, and general business. The index can be used two ways to study the Supreme Court: (1) finding articles describing what the business and industrial sectors think of the Supreme Court, and (2) following the views and actions of interest groups and associations, because the work indexes a considerable number of trade and professional magazines.

Magazine Index. Menlo Park, CA: Information Access Corporation, 1978 —.

Articles and reviews appearing in general U.S. magazines are listed in this monthly index. It is most useful for following current events relating to the Supreme Court and finding articles reflecting various opinions on issues. This index also is included in INFOTRAC, the CD-ROM service.

Public Affairs Information Service Bulletin (PAIS). New York: PAIS, 1915 —.

This weekly subject guide to American politics in general indexes government publications, books, and periodical literature. It includes citations to many congressional committee hearings. Additionally, it indexes the *National Journal, CQ Weekly Report, Congressional Digest*, and, selectively, the *Weekly Compilation of Presidential Documents*. A fifteen-volume *Cumulative Subject Index to the PAIS Annual Bulletins, 1915-1974* has been published by Carrollton Press. *PAIS* is cumulated quarterly and annually. This index also is available on CD-ROM.

Reader's Guide to Periodical Literature. New York: H. W. Wilson, 1905 —.

Articles in popular periodicals published in the United States are indexed in this semimonthly guide. Articles are indexed by author and subject. Each yearly cumulation of this index includes hundreds of citations about the Supreme Court. While one would not use this index for scholarly research, it is always worthwhile to see what it does have about the Supreme Court. It is a vital reference tool for researching events within the past year. This guide is now available on CD-ROM.

Social Sciences Citation Index (SSCI). Philadelphia: Institute for Science Information, 1973 —.

Items appearing in the *SSCI* have been cited in footnotes or bibliographies in the social sciences. The cited works are books, journal articles, dissertations, reports, proceedings, and the like. There are four separate indexes: a source (author) index, a citation index, a corporate index, and a key word subject index. Although this index is difficult to use, it does have several unique features that are helpful for studying the Supreme Court. By using the corporate index, one can identify publications issued by particular organizations, such as the Brookings Institution. The source and citation indexes can be used to identify the writings of a particular scholar who has written extensively on the Supreme Court, as well as to identify other researchers who have cited their writings. *SSCI* is published three times a year.

Social Sciences Index. New York: H. W. Wilson, 1975 —.

This quarterly work indexes articles found in about 150 social science journals. The index covers all of the major journals in political science as well as the other social sciences. Every literature search on the Supreme Court, regardless of the topic, should include this index. It also is available on CD-ROM.

Political Science

ABC POL SCI: A Bibliography of Contents: Political Science and Government. Santa Barbara, CA: ABC-Clio, 1969 —.

Tables of contents from about 300 journals, both U.S. and foreign, are published six times a year in this bibliography. Because it is published in advance of the journals' publication dates, it is especially useful for finding very recent articles on the Supreme Court.

Combined Retrospective Index to Journals in Political Science, 1886-1974. 8 vols. Arlington, VA: Carrollton Press, 1978.

This work indexes articles from approximately 180 English-language political science periodicals appearing since 1886 by subject and author. Since most indexes in the field of political science date back to only the past twenty years, this one is invaluable for anyone interested in articles published about the Supreme Court in the nineteenth and early twentieth centuries. It is the only resource for systematically searching for older articles about the Supreme Court.

International Bibliography of the Social Sciences: Political Science. Chicago: Aldine, 1962 —.

This annual bibliography lists books, articles, reports, and other research publications classified under these six sections: political science, political thought, government and public administration, governmental process, international relations, and area studies. Entries are selected from more than 2,000 journals. This is another source for foreign-language materials on the Supreme Court although it includes many English-language citations as well.

International Political Science Abstracts. Oxford, England: Basil Blackwell, 1952 —.

This bimonthly work abstracts articles published in 600 English-language and foreign-language political science journals. The abstracts for the English-language journals appear in English, while the foreign-language articles are abstracted in French. This abstracting service is the best source for finding foreign-language articles about the Supreme Court. Even if one is not interested in foreign-language material, one should check to see if this service has citations on the Supreme Court that have not appeared in other indexes.

Sage Public Administration Abstracts. Beverly Hills, CA: Sage Publications, 1974 —.

This quarterly publication abstracts articles selected from approximately 200 English-language journals, as well as books, pamphlets, and government publications dealing with public administration. Although this abstracting service does not have an enormous number of citations to the Supreme Court, it should be consulted when searching for information related to policy analysis, public management, bureaucratic studies, and federal programs.

United States Political Science Documents. 2 vols. Pittsburgh: University Center for International Studies, University of Pittsburgh, 1976 —.

About 120 U.S. political science journals are indexed and abstracted in this annual work. The first volume contains indexes by author, subject, geographic area, proper name, and journal title. The second volume abstracts the articles indexed in Volume 1. This is another index that should be used for studying any topic on the Supreme Court. It indexes many of the newer journals in political science that are not covered elsewhere.

History

America: History and Life. Santa Barbara, CA: ABC-Clio, 1964 —.

Articles, book and film reviews, and dissertations are covered in this serial bibliography. A streamlined format adopted in 1989 offers quarterly indexes containing abstracts and citations. There also is a cumulative annual index. This abstracting service provides excellent coverage of materials in the field of history. For historical research on the Supreme Court, one always should include this index.

Arts and Humanities Citation Index. Philadelphia: Institute for Scientific Information, 1978 —.

Published three times a year, this work indexes books, journal articles, theses, dissertations, reports, proceedings, congresses, and unpublished papers cited in footnotes or bibliographies in the humanities. There is an author index, citation index, subject index, and corporate index to the citations. This work can be used to find citations to the Supreme Court from history journals as well as to the arts. For anyone interested in judicial activities and actions related to the arts, culture, and humanties, this index is most helpful.

Combined Retrospective Index to Journals in History, 1838-1974. 11 vols. Arlington, VA: Carrollton Press, 1978.

This work indexes over 150,000 articles published in more than 200 English-language journals in history since 1838. Five of the eleven volumes cover U.S. history. There is an author index in addition to the subject index. Besides providing indexing of journals for the nineteenth century, this work is very good for biographical research on judicial figures.

Humanities Index. New York: H. W. Wilson, 1974 —.

This is a quarterly index to English-language journals in the humanities. The articles are indexed by author and subject. This work covers the major journals in history and is best utilized in searches for citations related to the history of the Supreme Court. This index also is available on CD-ROM.

Writings on American History: A Subject Bibliography of Articles. Millwood, NY: KTO Press, 1974 —.

This is an annual bibliography of journal articles on American history from about 500 periodicals. The entries are arranged chronologically, geographically, and by subject. Although this work only has an author index, not a subject index, it includes a wealth of citations on almost every topic related to the Supreme Court. Its scope goes beyond the field of history to include journals from political science, economics, and other social sciences.

Databases

In addition to indexes, on-line databases can be used to research the Supreme Court. Some databases are on-line versions of paper indexes, while some only exist in an on-line format.

Current Affairs

MAGAZINE INDEX. Menlo Park, CA: Information Access Corporation, 1976 — .

This database indexes articles from over 370 general magazines and provides good coverage of current affairs. While not as extensive in scope as the NATIONAL NEWSPAPER INDEX or NEWSEARCH, this resource can be useful to research major stories about the Supreme Court as well as current issues and controversies surrounding the Supreme Court.

NATIONAL NEWSPAPER INDEX. Menlo Park, CA: Information Access Corporation, 1979 — .

This database indexes the *Christian Science Monitor*, the *New York Times*, and the *Wall Street Journal*. It indexes all items except weather charts, stock market tables, crossword puzzles, and horoscopes. It provides good coverage of government relations. This database is especially useful for finding articles related to current judicial activities.

NEWSEARCH. Menlo Park, CA: Information Access Corporation, 1979 — .

Updated daily, this database indexes more than 2,000 news stories, information articles, and book reviews from over 1,400 newspapers, magazines, and periodicals. It indexes articles for the current month. At the end of the month, the magazine article data are transferred to the MAGAZINE INDEX and the newspaper data are transferred to the NATIONAL NEWSPAPER INDEX. This is another excellent source for keeping up-to-date on the Supreme Court.

Documents

FEDERAL INDEX. Washington, DC: Capitol Services, 1976 — .

This database indexes the *Washington Post, Congressional Record, Federal Register*, and other documents, including rules, regulations, bills, speeches, hearings, roll-call votes, reports, vetoes, court decisions, and executive orders. It is the best single source for finding information about the federal government.

FEDERAL REGISTER ABSTRACTS. Washington, DC: Capitol Services, 1977 — .

Materials in the *Federal Register* are abstracted in this database. It covers government regulations, proposed rules, and legal notices, such as presidential proclamations, executive orders, and presidential determinations.

GPO MONTHLY CATALOG. Washington, DC: U.S. Government Printing Office, 1976 — .

This database contains records of reports, studies, and the like, issued by all federal government agencies, including Senate and House committee hearings. It is useful for finding documents issued through the Office of the President and the Executive Office. While it is best suited for finding documents issued by departments of the executive branch, this database also can be used in searching for judicial documents. The GPO MONTHLY CATALOG database may be accessed through the DIALOG on-line service.

GPO SALES PUBLICATIONS REFERENCE FILE. Washington, DC: U.S. Government Printing Office, 1971 —.

This database essentially is an on-line version of the *GPO Publications Reference File*. It is best suited for finding citations to new publications, especially those that have not yet been cited in the *Monthly Catalog*, and for determining whether a particular document is still available for purchase. This database may be accessed through the DIALOG on-line service.

Social Sciences

AMERICA: HISTORY AND LIFE. Santa Barbara, CA: ABC-Clio, 1964 —.

This database provides comprehensive coverage of all areas of U.S. history, international relations, and politics and government. It is the best database for finding articles dealing with the history of the Supreme Court, and for biographical materials on the justices.

COMPREHENSIVE DISSERTATION INDEX. Ann Arbor, MI: Xerox University Microfilms, 1861 —.

This database indexes American dissertations written since 1861 by subject, title, and author. Since thousands of dissertations have been written about various aspects of the Supreme Court, this database has a wealth of information. In addition, the *Comprehensive Dissertation Index* is available in print and CD-ROM versions.

PSYCINFO. Washington, DC: American Psychological Association, 1967 —.

Each year, citations covering psychology and related areas are chosen from over 900 journals, 1,500 books, and numerous technical reports for this database. A search can produce numerous citations to psychological and behavioral studies of the Court. The database contains a considerable number of materials in the fields of political behavior and psychology, so it is quite useful for anyone studying the Supreme Court on a microlevel. The print version of this index, *Psychological Abstracts*, also is available on CD-ROM.

PUBLIC AFFAIRS INFORMATION SERVICE (PAIS) INTERNATIONAL. New York: PAIS, 1976 —.

Approximately 25,000 citations found in more than 1,200 journals and 800 books, pamphlets, government documents, and agency reports are added to this database each year. All fields of social sciences, including political science, public administration, international relations, law, and public policy, are covered. This database is useful not only for finding materials related to current events, but also for researching specific topics. Since there are indexes to books, documents, and articles from journals such as the *CQ Weekly Report* and the *National Journal*, this database can yield a wide variety of citations both to primary and secondary sources.

SOCIAL SCISEARCH. Philadelphia: Institute for Scientific Information, 1972 —.

All areas of the social and behavioral sciences are covered in this database. Entries are chosen from the 1,000 most important social science journals as well as from 2,200 others in the natural, physical, and biomedical sciences. As this is the largest in scope of any database, in terms of both the numbers of journals and the disciplines covered, one can find citations to almost any facet of judicial studies. Of all the databases, this one will most likely yield the greatest number of citations to any single topic related to the Supreme Court.

SOCIOLOGICAL ABSTRACTS. San Diego, CA: Sociological Abstracts, 1963 —.

Abstracts covering sociology and related areas in the social and behavioral sciences are included in this database. Entries are chosen from over 1,200 periodicals and other serial publications. In addition to citations to sociological and behavioral studies of the Supreme Court, this database also includes citations to public opinion and political communication as well as to the impact of judicial decisions and programs. The print version of this database, *Sociological Abstracts*, also is available on CD-ROM.

UNITED STATES POLITICAL SCIENCE DOCUMENTS. Pittsburgh: University Center for International Studies, University of Pittsburgh, 1975—.

Articles from approximately 120 major political science journals published in the United States are abstracted and indexed. This database can be best utilized for finding citations to the major journals in the field of political science. It is also the best database for identifying articles on the Supreme Court from the growing number of policy studies journals.

Biographical Directories and Indexes

Listed below are several directories that can be used to find information on politicians, at both the federal level and the state and local level. They also include party leaders and other important political leaders. Following the annotated entries is a list of other directories, some of which are more specialized or historical in nature. Depending on a researcher's need, they can be invaluable reference tools.

American Leaders 1789-1987. Washington, DC: Congressional Quarterly, 1987.

This biographical directory provides information for presidents, vice presidents, senators, representatives, Supreme Court justices, and state governors. It includes dates of birth and death, political affiliation, and dates and places of service.

Who's Who in American Politics: A Biographical Directory of United States Political Leaders. New York: R. R. Bowker, 1967—.

This directory presents biographical data for approximately 12,500 political figures, from presidents down to local leaders. Included are federal government employees, national party leaders, state legislators, local officials of large cities, county chairmen of parties, and minority party leaders. Also provided are address, party affiliation, education, family data, political and business background, and achievements. The directory is revised biennially.

Who's Who in Government. 3 vols. Indianapolis: Marquis Who's Who, 1972-1977.

Biographical information on political leaders on the federal and state level is provided in this directory. It presents basically the same information as the directory listed above. The value of this directory lies in the format of its indexes. One index arranges political figures according to office within the government structure; the other arranges politicians according to type of responsibilities.

Morris, Dan, and Inez Morris, eds. *Who Was Who in American Politics. A Bibliographical Dictionary of over 4,000 Men and Women Who Contributed to the United States Political Scene from the Colonial Days up to and Including the Immediate Past*. New York: Hawthorn Books, 1974.

Other biographical directories include the following:

Dearborn, L. E., ed. *A Supplement to Appleton's Cyclopaedia of American Biography*. 6 vols. New York: Press Association Compilers, 1918-1931.

Dictionary of American Biography. New York: Charles Scribner's Sons, 1928.

Garraty, John A., ed. *Encyclopedia of American Biography*. New York: Harper and Row, 1974.

Johnson, Rossiter, ed. *The Twentieth Century Biographical Dictionary of Notable Americans*. 10 vols. Boston: The Biographical Society, 1904.

The National Cyclopaedia of American Biography. New York: James T. White and Company, 1892.

Preston, Wheeler. *American Biographies*. New York: Harper and Brothers Publishers, 1940.

Van Doren, Charles, ed. *Webster's American Biographies*. Springfield, MA: G & C Merriam Company, 1984.

Who Was Who in America. Historical Volume, 1607-1896. A Companion Volume of Who's Who in American History. Rev. ed. Chicago: Marquis Who's Who, 1967.

Who Was Who in America. Volume One, 1897-1942. A Companion Volume of Who's Who in American History. Chicago: Marquis, 1943.

Who Was Who in America. Volume Two, 1943-1950. A Companion Biographical Reference Work to Who's Who in America. Chicago: Marquis, 1963.

Who Was Who in America. Volume Three, 1951-1960. A Companion Biographical Reference Work to Who's Who in America. Chicago: Marquis, 1963.

Who Was Who in America. Volume Four, 1961-1968. A Companion Biographical Reference Work to Who's Who in America. Chicago: Marquis, 1968.

Who Was Who in America. Volume Five, 1969-1973. A Companion Biographical Reference Work to Who's Who in America. Chicago: Marquis, 1973.

Who Was Who in America. Volume Six, 1974-1976. A Companion Biographical Reference Work to Who's Who in America. Chicago: Marquis, 1976.

Who Was Who in America. Volume Seven, 1977-1981. A Companion Biographical Reference Work to Who's Who in America. Chicago: Marquis, 1981.

Who Was Who in America. Volume Eight, 1982-1985. A Companion Biographical Reference Work to Who's Who in America. Chicago: Marquis, 1985.

Who Was Who in America. Volume Nine, 1985-1989. Chicago: Marquis, 1989.

Wilson, James Grant, and John Fiske. *Appleton's Cyclopaedia of American Biography*. 6 vols. New York: D. Appleton, 1888-1894.

Wilson, James Grant, ed. *Appleton's Cyclopaedia of American Biography*. 2 vols. New York: D. Appleton, 1901.

Biographical indexes provide references to more complete information in periodicals, books, or biographical encyclopedias. While it is possible to identify biographical information through newspapers and general indexes, it is time-consuming and haphazard. Biographical indexes can be especially useful in finding information about emerging politicians.

Bio-Base. 2d ed. Detroit: Gale Research, 1981 — .

This index is a microfiche reference service that provides citations to biographical sketches in more than 375 biographical indexes. In part, some of the citations come from the hardcover edition of the two Gale indexes listed below. But because it includes thousands of other citations, this is the most complete single index to biographical materials.

Biographical Dictionaries Master Index. Detroit: Gale Research, 1975.

This volume, along with its 1979 and 1980 supplements, is a guide to biographical listings in over fifty current biographical reference works. This is a valuable resource for finding information about recent political actors.

Biography and Genealogy Master Index. 8 vols. Detroit: Gale Research, 1980.

This guide provides citations to information in all of the major biographical dictionaries in political science and history. By using this guide to identify information about political figures, both living and dead, it is possible to find several—and sometimes dozens—of references to information about a single person. In 1982, a three-volume supplement to the *Index* was published.

Biography Index. New York: H. W. Wilson, 1946 —.

This quarterly index identifies biographical materials in books and magazines. It includes references to obituaries, diaries, collections of letters, and memoirs. The entries are arranged by the name of the biographee, and the profession/occupation index makes it possible to identify various kinds of political figures. There also is a *Current Biography Cumulated Index, 1940-1979*, which was published by H. W. Wilson in 1973.

There is essentially only one on-line biographical database, BIOGRAPHY MASTER INDEX, produced by Gale Research. Basically, it is an expanded on-line version of *Bio-Base*. It is an index to biographical information contained in more than 600 source publications, including the *Who's Who* series, dictionaries, handbooks, and encyclopedias. Records include the name of the individual, birth and death dates, and the names and dates of biographical sources.

In addition to BIOGRAPHY MASTER INDEX, it is possible to use a variety of other databases to identify information about political figures as well as materials written by them. Most databases can be searched by author and key words in the title, so it is possible to search a database to see what a particular justice has written. Likewise, the titles of entries can be searched to gather citations about individuals. This strategy can be advantageous if applied to a number of databases, including AMERICA: HISTORY AND LIFE, COMPREHENSIVE DISSERTATION INDEX, PAIS INTERNATIONAL, PSYCINFO, SOCIAL SCISEARCH, SOCIOLOGICAL ABSTRACTS, and U.S. POLITICAL SCIENCE DOCUMENTS. As political biographies long have been a traditional form of research for dissertations written in the fields of history and political science, a subject search for dissertations written about a justice can yield hundreds of citations.

I. The Development of the Court

General Studies

1. Abraham, Henry J. *The Judiciary: The Supreme Court in the Governmental Process.* 7th ed. Boston: Allyn and Bacon, 1987.

2. Acheson, Patricia C. *The Supreme Court: America's Judicial Heritage.* New York: Dodd, Mead, 1961.

3. Adams, Arlin M. "The Role of the Federal Judiciary." *Proceedings of the American Philosophical Society* 128 (September 1984): 231-237.

4. Alfange, Dean, Jr. *The Supreme Court and the National Will.* Port Washington, NY: Kennikat, 1967.

5. Angell, Ernest. *Supreme Court Primer.* New York: Reynal and Hitchcock, 1937.

6. Arnot, Raymond H. "The Supreme Court of the United States." *Modern Culture* 12 (January 1901): 453-457.

7. Auerbach, Carl A., Lloyd Garrison, Williard Hurst, and Samuel Mermin. *The Legal Process.* San Francisco: Chandler Publishing Company, 1961.

8. "Backstage at the Supreme Court." Illustrated by Betty Wells. *American Bar Association Journal* 65 (July 1979): 1058-1062.

9. Bains, Rae. *The Supreme Court.* Mahwah, NJ: Troll Associates, 1985.

10. Balch, Thomas W. *A World Court in the Light of the United States Supreme Court.* Philadelphia: Allen, Lane, and Scott, 1918.

11. Baldwin, Simeon E. *The American Judiciary.* New York: Century Company, 1905.

12. Baldwin, Simeon E. "The American System of Supreme Courts and What It Accomplishes." In *The Making of America,* Vol. 2, edited by Robert M. La Follette, 76-92. Chicago: Making of America Company, 1906.

13. Ball, Milner S. *The Promise of American Law.* Athens: University of Georgia Press, 1981.

14. Barnes, William H. *The Supreme Court of the United States.* New York: Nelson and Phillips, 1875.

15. Barth, Alan. *The Heritage of Liberty.* St. Louis: McGraw-Hill, 1965.

16. Bates, Earnest S. *The Story of the Supreme Court.* Indianapolis: Bobbs-Merrill, 1938.

17. Baum, Lawrence. *The Supreme Court.* 2d ed. Washington, DC: Congressional Quarterly Press, 1985.

18. Beale, Joseph H. "Social Justice and Business Costs: A Study in the Legal History of Today." *Harvard Law Review* 49 (February 1936): 593-609.

19. Beaney, William M. "The Federal Courts." *Current History* 60 (June 1971): 347-352, 369.

20. Beck, James M. "The Golden Age of

the Supreme Court." *American Law Review* 57 (July/August 1923): 599-618.

21. Beck, James M. "The Supreme Court of the United States." *West Virginia Law Quarterly* 31 (April 1925): 139-165.

22. Benham, George A. "The Supreme Court of the United States." *North American Review* 163 (October 1896): 505-509.

23. Benson, Lee. *Turner and Beard: American Writing Reconsidered*. Glencoe, IL: Free Press, 1960.

24. Berger, Raoul. "Role of the Supreme Court." *University of Arkansas at Little Rock Law Journal* 3 (1980): 4-12.

25. Berle, Adolf A. "Making Democracy Work." *Current* 96 (June 1968): 15-19.

26. Berman, Harold J., ed. *Talks on American Law*. Rev. ed. New York: Vintage Books, 1971.

27. Beth, Loren P. "The *Slaughter House Cases* Revisited." *Louisiana Law Review* 23 (April 1963): 487-505.

28. Beth, Loren P. "The Supreme Court as Scapegoat: A Comment on Mr. Hogan's View of History." *Journal of Politics* 33 (May 1971): 521-524.

29. Bickel, Alexander M. *The Least Dangerous Branch: The Supreme Court at the Bar of Politics*. New Haven, CT: Yale University Press, 1986.

30. Bickel, Alexander M. *The Supreme Court and the Idea of Progress*. New Haven, CT: Yale University Press, 1978.

31. Bizzell, William B. *Judicial Interpretation of Political Theory: A Study in the Relation of the Courts to the American Party System*. New York: Burt Franklin, 1974.

32. Black, Charles L. *The Occasions of Justice: Essays Mostly on Law*. New York: Macmillan, 1963.

33. Black, Charles L. "The Supreme Court and Democracy." *Yale Review* 50 (December 1960): 188-201.

34. Black, Forrest R. "The American Constitutional System: An Experiment in Limited Government." *Kentucky Law Journal* 24 (November 1935): 11-26.

35. Blodgett, Nancy. "Windows into the Legal Past." *American Bar Association Journal* 71 (January 1985): 44-48.

36. Bloomfield, Maxwell. "The Supreme Court in American Popular Culture." *Journal of American Culture* 4 (Winter 1981): 1-13.

37. Boudin, Louis B. *Government by Judiciary*. 2 vols. New York: Russell and Russell, 1968.

38. Bowman, Harold M. "The Supreme Court's Part in the Building of the Nation." *Boston University Law Review* 11 (November 1931): 445-484.

39. Bradley, Joseph P. "Office and Nature of Law as the Basis and Bond of Society." *Legal Intelligencer* 41 (1884): 396.

40. Brenner, Saul, ed. *American Judicial Behavior*. New York: MSS Information Corporation, 1973.

41. Brigham, John. *The Cult of the Court*. Philadelphia: Temple University Press, 1987.

42. Broderick, Albert. "Constitutional Politics: The Supreme Court's Second Fifty Years." *Oklahoma City University Law Review* 12 (Fall 1987): 657-708.

43. Broderick, Albert. "From Constitutional Politics to Constitutional Law: The Supreme Court's First Fifty Years." *North Carolina Law Review* 65 (June 1987): 945-956.

44. Brooks, Frank H. "United States Supreme Court." *Chicago Legal News* 21 (March 23, 1889): 257.

45. Brownell, Herbert, Jr. "The United States Supreme Court: Symbol of Orderly, Stable, and Just Government." *American*

Bar Association Journal 43 (July 1957): 595-599.

46. Bryce, James. *The American Commonwealth.* 3d ed. 2 vols. New York: Macmillan, 1893-1895.

47. Buchanan, G. Sidney, and Gaye Rothman. "Quest for Freedom: Legal History of the 13th Amendment, Chapter 6; Supreme Court and 13th Amendment in Modern Era." *Houston Law Review* 12 (May 1975): 844-870.

48. Butler, Charles H. *A Century at the Bar of the Supreme Court of the United States.* New York: Putnam's, 1942.

49. Cabanillas, Jose M. "A Nation without a Supreme Court." *University of Richmond Law Notes* 2 (Spring 1964): 94-99.

50. Cahill, Fred V., Jr. *Judicial Legislation: A Study in American Legal Theory.* New York: Ronald Press, 1952.

51. Cahn, Edmond N., ed. *Supreme Court and Supreme Law.* Bloomington: Indiana University Press, 1954.

52. Caldwell, Millard F. "The Third Legislative Chamber." *Florida Bar Journal* 38 (June 1964): 327-336.

53. Carr, Robert K. *Democracy and the Supreme Court.* Norman: University of Oklahoma Press, 1936.

54. Carson, Hampton L. *The History of the Supreme Court of the United States: With Biographies of All the Chief and Associate Justices.* 2 vols. Philadelphia: P. W. Ziegler, 1902.

55. Carson, Hampton L. "The Place Occupied by the Judiciary in Our American Constitutional System." *Pennsylvania Bar Association Report* 20 (1914): 39-67.

56. Carson, Hampton L. "The Place Occupied by the Judiciary in Our American Constitutional System." *Virginia State Bar Association Report* 26 (1913): 321-345.

57. Carson, Hampton L. *The Supreme Court of the United States: Its History.* 2d ed. Philadelphia: A. R. Keller, 1892.

58. Carter, Lief H. *Contemporary Constitutional Lawmaking: The Supreme Court and the Art of Politics.* Elmsford, NY: Pergamon Press, 1985.

59. Clark, A. Inglis. "The Supreme Court of the United States during the First Half Century of Its Existence." *Commonwealth Law Review* 1 (October/December 1903): 3-12, 69-78.

60. Clark, Charles E. *The Judicial Process: A Series of Cases Illustrating the Place of the United States Supreme Court in Our Legal System.* New Haven, CT: Yale University Press, 1933.

61. Clayton, James E. *The Making of Justice: The Supreme Court in Action.* New York: Dutton, 1964.

62. Cohen, Edward C. "The Early Supreme Court of the United States in Perspective." *Notre Dame Lawyer* 7 (March 1932): 320-324.

63. Collins, Ronald K., ed. *Constitutional Government in America.* Durham, NC: Cardiner Academy, 1980.

64. Collins, Ross A. "The Supreme Court of the United States." *Mississippi Law Journal* 29 (March 1958): 192-202.

65. Collyer, Rita. *In Defense of the Constitution: Excerpts from Addresses and Opinions of the Chief Justices of the United States and an Excerpt from the Recent Minority Opinion in the So Called "Gold Clause" Case by Associate Justice McReynolds of the Supreme Court.* Washington, DC: n.p., 1935.

66. Colt, James D. "The Supreme Court of the United States." *New England Magazine* 2 (March 1890): 21-38.

67. Commager, Henry S. "The American Legal Tradition." *Cambridge Journal* 1 (January 1921): 233-239.

68. Congressional Quarterly. *Congres-*

sional Quarterly's Guide to the U.S. Supreme Court. 2d ed. Washington, DC: Congressional Quarterly, 1989.

69. Congressional Quarterly. *The Supreme Court, Justice, and the Law.* 3d ed. Washington, DC: Congressional Quarterly, 1983.

70. Corwin, Edward S. *The Constitution and What It Means Today.* Princeton, NJ: Princeton University Press, 1958.

71. Corwin, Edward S. "The Constitution as Instrument and as Symbol." *American Political Science Review* 30 (December 1936): 1071-1085.

72. Corwin, Edward S. *Liberty against Government: The Rise, Flowering, and Decline of a Famous Judicial Concept.* Baton Rouge: Louisiana State University Press, 1948.

73. Corwin, Edward S. *Our Constitutional Revolution and How to Round It Out.* Philadelphia: Brandeis Lawyers Society, 1951.

74. Costigan, George P., Jr. "The Supreme Court." *Yale Law Journal* 16 (February 1907): 259-272.

75. Cover, Robert M. *Justice Accused: Antislavery and the Judicial Process.* New Haven, CT: Yale University Press, 1975.

76. Cox, Archibald. *The Role of the American Supreme Court in American Government.* New York: Oxford University Press, 1976.

77. Coy, Harold. *The First Book of the Supreme Court.* New York: Watts, 1958.

78. Coy, Harold. *The Supreme Court.* New York: Watts, 1981.

79. Craig, Walter. "The Supreme Court of the United States: A Look at Its Critics." *Trust Bulletin* 43 (March 1964): 36-42.

80. Cullen, Charles T. "Toward a History of American Law: A Review Essay." *New York History* 54 (April 1973): 191-199.

81. Currie, David P. *The Constitution in the Supreme Court: The First Hundred Years, 1789-1888.* Chicago: University of Chicago Press, 1986.

82. Curtis, Charles P. *Law as Large as Life: A Natural Law for Today and the Supreme Court as Its Prophet.* New York: Simon and Schuster, 1959.

83. Curtis, Charles P. *Lions under the Throne: A Study of the Supreme Court of the United States, Addressed Particularly to Those Laymen Who Know More Constitutional Law than They Think They Do, and to Those Lawyers Who Know Less.* Boston: Houghton Mifflin, 1947.

84. Curtis, George T. *Commentaries on the Jurisdiction, Practice, and Peculiar Jurisprudence of the Courts of the United States.* Vol. I of *Containing a View of the Judicial Power, and the Jurisdiction and Practice of the Supreme Court of the United States.* Philadelphia: T. and J. W. Johnson, 1854.

85. Cushman, Robert E. "The History of the Supreme Court in Résumé." *Minnesota Law Review* 7 (March 1923): 275-305.

86. Cushman, Robert E. *Role of the Supreme Court in a Democratic Nation.* Washington, DC: Public Affairs Committee, 1940.

87. Damon, Allan L. "A Look at the Record: The Supreme Court." *American Heritage* 26 (October 1975): 49-51, 80-84.

88. Danforth, Henry G. *A Digest of the United States Supreme Court Reports from the Organization of the Court to October 1885: Comprising Dallas, Cranch, Wheaton, Peters, Howard, Black, Wallace, and United States Reports (Otto and Davis) to Volume 115.* Albany, NY: Banks and Brothers, 1885.

89. Daniels, William J. "Public Perceptions of the United States Supreme Court." Ph.D. diss., University of Iowa, 1970.

90. Davenport, William H., ed. *Voices in Court: A Treasury of the Bench, the Bar, and the Courtroom.* New York: Macmillan, 1958.

91. David, Andrew. *Famous Supreme Court Cases.* Minneapolis: Lerner, 1980.

92. Davis, Warren. *Law of the Land.* New York: Carlton Press, 1962.

93. Dawson, Mitchell. "Birth of the Supreme Court." *Missouri Bar Journal* 11 (March 1940): 50-52.

94. Denenberg, R. V. "The U.S. Supreme Court: An Introductory Note." *Cambridge Law Journal* 29 (April 1971): 134-147.

95. Depew, Chauncey M. "The United States Supreme Court." *Munsey's Magazine* 17 (May 1897): 169-178.

96. Deutsch, Jan G. "Harvard's View of the Supreme Court: A Response." *Texas Law Review* 57 (November 1979): 1445-1454.

97. Didier, Eugene L. "The Supreme Court of the United States." *Chautauquan* 11 (September 1890): 718-721.

98. Dimond, Raul R. *Supreme Court and Judicial Choice: The Role of Provisional Review in a Democracy.* Ann Arbor: University of Michigan Press, 1989.

99. Dionisopoulos, P. Allan. "The Uniqueness of the Warren and Burger Courts in American Constitutional History." *Buffalo Law Review* 22 (Spring 1973): 737-767.

100. Dolbeare, Kenneth M., and Phillip E. Hammond. "The Political Party Basis of Attitudes toward the Supreme Court." *Public Opinion Quarterly* 32 (Spring 1968): 16-30.

101. Dorfman, Joseph. *Early American Policy.* New York: Columbia University Press, 1960.

102. Dorsen, Norman. "Trends and Prospects in the United States Supreme Court."

Public Law 1986 (Spring 1986): 83-98.

103. Doyle, William F. "From *Swift vs. Tyson* to *Erie R. R. vs. Tompkins*: Ninety-six Years of Supreme Court History." *Dicta* 15 (December 1938): 307-315.

104. Duke, R. T., Jr. "Future of the Supreme Court." *Virginia Law Register* 13 (March 1908): 898-899.

105. Early, Stephen T. *Constitutional Courts of the United States: The Formal and Informal Relationships between the District Courts, the Courts of Appeals, and the Supreme Court of the United States.* Totowa, NJ: Littlefield, Adams, 1977.

106. Edwards, Percy L. "The Federal Judiciary and Its Attitudes towards the People." *Michigan Law Journal* 5 (June 1896): 183-194.

107. Ernst, Morris L. *The Law of the Land.* New York: Weybright and Talley, 1969.

108. Esterline, Blackburn. "The Supreme Law of the Land." *American Law Review* 40 (July/August 1906): 566-579.

109. Farnum, George R. "The Constitution and the Embattled Court since 1801." *Boston University Law Review* 17 (April 1937): 281-292.

110. Farrand, Max, ed. *The Records of the Federal Convention of 1787.* 4 vols. New Haven, CT: Yale University Press, 1937.

111. Feinstein, Isidor. *The Court Disposes.* New York: Covici, Friede, 1937.

112. Finkin, Matthew W. "Does Karl Klare Protest Too Much?" *Maryland Law Review* 44 (Fall 1985): 1100-1110.

113. Finley, S. W. "Daniel Webster Packed 'Em In." *Supreme Court Historical Society Yearbook* 1979 (1979): 70-78, 83.

114. Forte, David F. *The Supreme Court.* New York: F. Watts, 1979.

115. Foster, Joseph. "William Whipple, Signer of the Declaration of Independence." *Granite Monthly* 43 (July 1911): 205-219.

116. Fraenkel, Osmond K. "Still the Best of Judicial Worlds." *Progressive* 21 (February 1957): 18-21.

117. Frank, Jerome. *Courts on Trial: Myth and Reality in American Justice.* Princeton, NJ: Princeton University Press, 1949.

118. Frank, Jerome. "What Courts Do in Fact." *Illinois Law Review* 26 (February 1932): 645-666.

119. Frank, John P. "Court and Constitution: The Passive Period (1846-1950)." *Vanderbilt Law Review* 4 (April 1951): 400-426.

120. Frank, John P. "The Historic Role of the Supreme Court." *Kentucky Law Journal* 48 (Fall 1959): 26-47.

121. Frank, John P. "Historical Bases of the Federal Judicial System." *Indiana Law Journal* 23 (April 1948): 236-270.

122. Frank, John P. *Marble Palace: The Supreme Court in American Life.* New York: Knopf, 1958.

123. Freedman, Max, William M. Beaney, and Eugene V. Rostow. *Perspectives on the Court.* Evanston, IL: Northwestern University Press, 1967.

124. Freund, Paul A. *On Law and Justice.* Cambridge: Harvard University Press, 1968.

125. Freund, Paul A. *On Understanding the Supreme Court.* Boston: Little, Brown, 1951.

126. Freund, Paul A. "A Supreme Court in a Federation: Some Lessons from Legal History." *Columbia Law Review* 53 (May 1953): 597-619.

127. Freund, Paul A. *The Supreme Court in Contemporary Life.* Dallas: Southern Methodist University School of Law, 1965.

128. Freund, Paul A. "Supreme Court of the United States." *Canadian Bar Review* 29 (December 1951): 1080-1094.

129. Freund, Paul A. *The Supreme Court of the United States: Its Business, Purposes, and Performance.* Cleveland, OH: World Publishing Company, 1961.

130. Fribourg, Marjorie G. *The Supreme Court in American History: Ten Great Decisions: The People, the Times, the Issues.* Philadelphia: Macrae Smith, 1965.

131. Fried, Charles. "Two Concepts of Interests: Some Reflections on the Supreme Court's Balancing Test." *Harvard Law Review* 76 (February 1963): 755-778.

132. Friedlander, Robert A. "Social Utility, and the American Transformation of the English Common Law." *Chitty's Law Journal* 26 (October 1978): 279-282.

133. Friedman, Lawrence M. *A History of American Law.* New York: Simon and Schuster, 1973.

134. Fritz, Mechthild. "Religion in a Federal System: Diversity versus Uniformity." *University of Kansas Law Review* 38 (Fall 1989): 37-79.

135. Frodin, Reuben. "The Supreme Court in American Government and Politics, 1900-1950." *Journal of General Education* 6 (October 1951): 46-58.

136. Funston, Richard Y. *Judicial Crisis: The Supreme Court in a Changing America.* New York: Wiley, 1974.

137. Funston, Richard Y. *A Vital National Seminar: The Supreme Court in American Political Life.* Palo Alto, CA: Mayfield, 1978.

138. Gabriel, Ralph H. *The Course of American Democratic Thought.* 2d ed. New York: Ronald Press, 1956.

139. Galloway, Russell W., Jr. *The Rich and the Poor in Supreme Court History, 1790-1982.* Greenbrae, CA: Paradigm Press, 1982.

140. Galloway, Russell W., Jr. "The Supreme Court since 1937." *Santa Clara Law Review* 24 (Summer 1984): 565-648.

141. Garland, Augustus H. "The Court a Century Ago." *Supreme Court Historical Society Yearbook* 1976 (1976): 37-44.

142. Garvey, Gerald. *Constitutional Bricolage*. Princeton, NJ: Princeton University Press, 1971.

143. Gilmore, Grant. *The Ages of American Law*. New Haven, CT: Yale University Press, 1977.

144. Goldman, Sheldon, and Austin Sarat, eds. *American Court Systems: Readings in Judicial Process and Behavior*. San Francisco: W. H. Freeman, 1978.

145. Goode, Stephen. *The Controversial Court: Supreme Court Influences on American Life*. New York: Messner, 1982.

146. Goodell, Thomas D. "An Athenian Parallel to a Function of Our Supreme Court." *Yale Review* 2 (May 1893): 64-73.

147. Goodnow, Frank J. *Social Reform and the Constitution*. New York: Macmillan, 1911.

148. Grossman, Joel B., and Joseph Tanenhaus, eds. *Frontiers of Judicial Research*. New York: Wiley, 1969.

149. Guitteau, William B. "Fictions about the Supreme Court." *Social Studies* 30 (March 1939): 103-109.

150. Haar, Charles M., ed. *The Golden Age of Law*. New York: George Braziller, 1965.

151. Habenstreit, Barbara. *Changing America and the Supreme Court*. New York: J. Messner, 1970.

152. Haines, Charles G. "Histories of the Supreme Court of the United States Written from the Federal Point of View." *Southwestern Political and Social Science Quarterly* 4 (June 1923): 1-35.

153. Hamilton, Jack A. *The Supreme Court, Guardian or Ruler?* New York: Scholastic Book Services, 1968.

154. Harrell, Mary Ann, and Stuart E. Jones. *Equal Justice under Law: The Supreme Court in American Life*. Washington, DC: Foundation of the Federal Bar Association, 1965.

155. Harris, Lawrence T. "Guardians of the Constitution." *American Law Review* 57 (March/April 1923): 183-219.

156. Harris, William F. "Bonding Word and Polity: The Logic of American Constitutionalism." *American Political Science Review* 76 (March 1982): 34-45.

157. Hart, Henry M., Jr., and Herbert Wechsler. *The Federal Courts and the Federal System*. Brooklyn, NY: Foundation Press, 1953.

158. Haskins, George L. "Prejudice and Promise in the Early Years of the Federal Judiciary." *Maine Law Review* 37 (July 1985): 301-311.

159. Henderson, Dwight F. *Courts for a New Nation*. Washington, DC: Public Affairs Press, 1971.

160. Henderson, Gerard C. *The Position of Foreign Corporations in American Constitutional Law: A Contribution to the History and Theory of Juristic Persons in Anglo American Law*. Cambridge: Harvard University Press, 1918.

161. Hendricks, Thomas A. "The Supreme Court of the United States and the Influences That Have Contributed to Make It the Greatest Judicial Tribunal in the World." *Chicago Legal News* 17 (July 18, 1885): 380-382.

162. Henry, John M. *Nine above the Law: Our Supreme Court*. Pittsburgh: R. T. Lewis Company, 1936.

163. Herbert, Hilary A. "The Supreme Court of the United States and Its Functions." *Pennsylvania Bar Association Re-*

port of the Third Annual Meeting 3 (1897): 155-178.

164. Hodder-Williams, Richard. *The Politics of the U.S. Supreme Court*. London: Allen and Unwin, 1980.

165. Hoffman, Richard J. "Classics in the Courts of the United States." *American Journal of Legal History* 22 (January 1978): 55-84.

166. Hogan, Harry J. "The Supreme Court and Natural Law." *American Bar Association Journal* 54 (June 1968): 570-573.

167. Holst, Herman E. *The Constitutional and Political History of the United States*. 8 vols. Chicago: Callaghan, 1876-1892.

168. Holt, Wythe, ed. *Essays in Nineteenth-Century American Legal History*. Westport, CT: Greenwood Press, 1976.

169. Honnold, Arthur B. *Supreme Court Law*. St. Paul, MN: West Publishing Company, 1933.

170. Honnold, John, ed. *The Life of the Law: Readings on the Growth of Legal Institutions*. New York: Free Press, 1964.

171. Howe, Mark D., ed. *Readings in American Legal History*. Cambridge: Harvard University Press, 1949.

172. Howes, Roy F. "The Social Significance of the Supreme Court of the United States." *Florida State Bar Association Law Journal* 6 (April 1933): 568-572.

173. Hughes, Graham. *The Conscience of the Courts: Laws and Morals in American Life*. Garden City, NY: Doubleday, 1975.

174. Hume, F. Charles. "The Supreme Court of the United States." *American Law Review* 33 (September/October 1899): 641-664.

175. Hurst, James W. *The Growth of American Law: The Law Makers*. Boston: Little, Brown, 1950.

176. Hyman, Harold, and Stuart Bruchey, eds. *American Legal and Constitutional History*. New York: Garland Publishing, 1989.

177. Hyneman, Charles S. *The Supreme Court on Trial*. New York: Atherton Press, 1963.

178. Hyneman, Charles S., and George W. Carey. *A Second Federalist*. New York: Appleton-Century-Crofts, 1967.

179. Jackson, Percival E. *The Wisdom of the Supreme Court*. Norman: University of Oklahoma Press, 1962.

180. Jacob, Herbert. *Justice in America*. Boston: Little, Brown, 1965.

181. Jacob, Herbert, ed. *Law, Politics, and the Federal Courts*. Boston: Little, Brown, 1967.

182. Jacobs, Clyde E. *Law Writers and the Courts: The Influence of Thomas P. Cooley, Christopher G. Tiedeman, and John F. Dillon upon American Constitutional Law*. Berkeley: University of California Press, 1954.

183. James, Leonard F. *The Supreme Court in American Life*. 2d ed. Glenview, IL: Scott, Foresman, 1971.

184. Jameson, J. Franklin. "The Predecessor of the Supreme Court." In *Essays in the Constitutional History of the United States in the Formative Period, 1775-1789*, edited by J. Franklin Jameson, 1-45. Boston: Houghton Mifflin, 1889.

185. Jaros, Dean, and Robert T. Roper. "The U.S. Supreme Court: Myth, Diffuse Support, Specific Support, and Legitimacy." *American Politics Quarterly* 8 (January 1980): 85-105.

186. Johnson, Gerald W. *The Supreme Court*. New York: Morrow, 1961.

187. Johnston, Richard E. "Some Comparative Statistics on U.S. Chief Justice Courts." *Rocky Mountain Social Science Journal* 9 (January 1972): 89-100.

188. Jordan, Christine R. "Last of the

Jacksonians." *Supreme Court Historical Society Yearbook* 1980 (1980): 78-88.

189. Kauper, Paul G. *The Supreme Court: Hybrid Organ of State.* Dallas: Southern Methodist University School of Law, 1967.

190. Keefe, Arthur J. "Inside the Supreme Court." *American Bar Association Journal* 61 (December 1975): 1509-1512.

191. Kennedy, Cornelius B., and Harry J. Haynsworth. "Preserving the Supreme Court's Heritage." *American Bar Association Journal* 71 (November 1985): 162.

192. Kent, James. *Commentaries on American Law.* New York: James Kent, 1840.

193. Kerr, Charles. "The Thirty Years' Wars on the Supreme Court." *Vanderbilt Law Review* 17 (May 1931): 629-652.

194. Knopf, Alfred. *The Supreme Court in the American System of Government.* Cambridge: Harvard University Press, 1955.

195. Krislov, Samuel. *The Supreme Court in the Political Process.* New York: Macmillan, 1965.

196. Kurland, Philip B. "Public Policy, the Constitution, and the Supreme Court." *Northern Kentucky Law Review* 12 (Spring 1985): 181-200.

197. Kurland, Philip B. "The Role of the Supreme Court in American History: A Lawyer's Interpretation." *Bucknell Review* 14 (December 1966): 16-26.

198. Kurland, Philip B. *The Supreme Court and the Judicial Function.* Chicago: University of Chicago Press, 1976.

199. Kurland, Philip B. "Toward a Political Supreme Court." *University of Chicago Law Review* 37 (Autumn 1969): 19-46.

200. Kutler, Stanley I., ed. *The Supreme Court and the Constitution: Readings in American Constitutional History.* 3d ed.

New York: W. W. Norton, 1984.

201. Lankevich, George J. *The Federal Court, 1789-1901.* Millwood, NY: Associated Faculty Press, 1986.

202. Lankevich, George J., and Howard B. Furer. *The Supreme Court in American Life.* Millwood, NY: Associated Faculty Press, 1986.

203. Lawton, Alexander R. "The Supreme Court in United States History." *Georgia Historical Quarterly* 7 (December 1923): 289-312.

204. Lee, Carol F. "Sovereign Immunity and the Eleventh Amendment: The Uses of History." *Urban Lawyer* 18 (Summer 1986): 519-550.

205. Lee, Howard B. *The Story of the Constitution.* Charlottesville, VA: Michie Company, 1932.

206. Lerner, Max. "The Supreme Court and American Capitalism." *Yale Law Journal* 42 (February 1933): 668-701.

207. Levi, Edward H. *An Introduction to Legal Reasoning.* Chicago: University of Chicago Press, 1948.

208. Levy, Leonard W., ed. *Essays on the Making of the Constitution.* New York: Oxford University Press, 1969.

209. Lewis, Anthony. "The Changing Role of the Supreme Court of the United States of America." *New York State Bar Journal* 34 (December 1962): 416-427.

210. Lieberman, Jethro K. *Milestones: 200 Years of American Law: Milestones in Our Legal History.* New York: Oxford University Press, 1976.

211. Lindsay, James K. "Council and Court: The Handbill Ordinances, 1889-1939." *Michigan Law Review* 39 (February 1941): 561-596.

212. Lippmann, Walter. *The Supreme Court, Independent or Controlled?* New York: Harper and Brothers, 1937.

213. Liston, Robert A. *Tides of Justice: The Supreme Court and the Constitution in Our Time*. New York: Delacorte Press, 1966.

214. Loreh, Robert S. "The South and the Supreme Court." *Mid-American* 40 (July 1958): 131-162.

215. Lowry, Stephen M. "A Small Group Study of the Supreme Courts of the United States, 1803-1971." Ph.D. diss., University of Pennsylvania, 1974.

216. Lowry, Walker. "The Supreme Court in 1848 and 1948: Review of Two Terms." *Southern California Law Review* 23 (July 1950): 459-472.

217. Luck, Barbara Ann. "Reassessing the Dynamics of Public Support for the U.S. Supreme Court." Ph.D. diss., Washington University, 1984.

218. McCann, Michael W., and Gerald L. Houseman. *Judging the Constitution: Critical Essays on Judicial Lawmaking*. Glenview, IL: Scott, Foresman, 1989.

219. McClain, Emlin. *Constitutional Law in the United States*. New York: Longmans, Green, 1905.

220. McClennen, Edward F. "The Supreme Court." *Law Society Journal* 7 (May 1937): 784-805.

221. McCloskey, Robert G. *The American Supreme Court*. Chicago: University of Chicago Press, 1960.

222. McCloskey, Robert G. *The Modern Supreme Court*. Cambridge: Harvard University Press, 1972.

223. Macdonell, John. "The Supreme Court of the United States." *Nineteenth Century and After* 50 (August 1901): 327-338.

224. McGowan, Carl. "The Supreme Court in the American Constitutional System: The Problem in Historical Perspective." *Notre Dame Lawyer* 33 (August 1958): 527-547.

225. McLaughlin, Kenneth F. *Color Me Justice: An Analysis and Collection of the Leading Supreme Court Cases of Our Time*. Washington, DC: Equity, 1969.

226. Maier, Pauline. *From Resistance to Revolution: Colonial Radicals and the Development of American Opposition to Britain, 1765-1776*. New York: Knopf, 1972.

227. Marcus, Maeva, and James R. Perry, eds. *The Documentary History of the Supreme Court of the United States, 1789-1800*. Vol. 2, *Justice on Circuit, 1790-1794*. New York: Columbia University Press, 1985-1988.

228. Marke, Julius J. *Vignettes of Legal History*. South Hackensack, NJ: Fred B. Rothman, 1965.

229. Marquardt, Dorothy A. *A Guide to the Supreme Court*. Indianapolis: Bobbs-Merrill, 1977.

230. Marshall, Thomas R. "Public Opinion, Representation, and the Modern Supreme Court." *American Politics Quarterly* 16 (July 1988): 296-316.

231. Mason, Alpheus T. *The Supreme Court from Taft to Burger*. 3d ed. Baton Rouge: Louisiana State University Press, 1979.

232. Mason, Alpheus T. *The Supreme Court: Palladium of Freedom*. Ann Arbor: University of Michigan Press, 1962.

233. Mason, Alpheus T. "The Supreme Court: Temple and Forum." *Yale Review* 48 (Summer 1959): 524-540.

234. Mason, Alpheus T., and William M. Beaney. *The Supreme Court in a Free Society*. Englewood Cliffs, NJ: Prentice Hall, 1960.

235. Mason, Alpheus T., and Gerald Garvey, eds. *American Constitutional History: Essays by Edward S. Corwin*. New York: Harper and Row, 1964.

236. Mason, Alpheus T., William M.

Beaney, and Donald G. Stevenson, Jr. *American Constitutional Law: Introductory Essays and Selected Cases.* 8th ed. Englewood Cliffs, NJ: Prentice-Hall, 1986.

237. Masterson, William E. "Supreme Court of the United States and American Political History." *Institute of World Affairs Proceedings* 13 (1935): 155-169.

238. Maverick, Maury. *In Blood and Ink.* New York: Modern Age Books, 1939.

239. Mayers, Lewis. *The American Legal System: The Administration of Justice in the United States by Judicial, Administrative, Military, and Arbitral Tribunals.* New York: Harper and Brothers, 1955.

240. Mayo, Bernard. *Myths and Men: Patrick Henry, George Washington, and Thomas Jefferson.* Athens: University of Georgia Press, 1959.

241. Meigs, William M. "The Relief of the Supreme Court of the United States." *American Law Register* 32 (June 1884): 360-370.

242. Mendelson, Wallace. *Capitalism, Democracy, and the Supreme Court.* New York: Appleton, 1960.

243. Mendelson, Wallace. "Sectional Politics and the Rise of Judicial Supremacy." *Journal of Politics* 9 (May 1947): 255-272.

244. Mendelson, Wallace. *The Supreme Court: Law and Discretion.* Indianapolis: Bobbs-Merrill, 1967.

245. Mendelson, Wallace. *The Supreme Court Statecraft: The Rule of Law and Men.* Ames: Iowa State University Press, 1985.

246. Merkel, Philip L. "The Origins of an Expanded Federal Court Jurisdiction: Railroad Development and the Ascendancy of the Federal Judiciary." *Business History Review* 58 (Autumn 1984): 336-358.

247. Michelman, Frank. "Bringing the Law to Life: A Plea for Disenchantment." *Cornell Law Review* 74 (January 1989): 256-269.

248. Miller, Arthur S. *The Supreme Court: Myth and Reality.* Westport, CT: Greenwood Press, 1978.

249. Miller, Charles A. *The Supreme Court and the Uses of History.* Cambridge: Harvard University Press, 1969.

250. Miller, David H. "Some Early Cases in the Supreme Court of the United States." *Virginia Law Review* 8 (December 1921): 108-120.

251. Miller, Perry, ed. *The Legal Mind in America: From Independence to the Civil War.* Garden City, NY: Doubleday, 1962.

252. Montgomery, H. H. "Some Miscellanea of History of the Supreme Court." *Oklahoma State Bar Journal* 8 (April 1937): 15-21.

253. Morley, Felix. "The Supreme Court and the Republic." *Fortune* 70 (August 1964): 102, 220-224.

254. Muller, William H. *Early History of the Federal Supreme Court.* Boston: Chipman Law Publishing, 1922.

255. Murphy, Walter F., and C. Herman Pritchett. *Courts, Judges, and Politics: An Introduction to the Judicial Process.* 2d ed. New York: Random House, 1974.

256. Murphy, Walter F., James E. Fleming, and William F. Harris, II. *Constitutional Interpretation.* Mineola, NY: Foundation Press, 1986.

257. Myers, Gustavus. *History of the Supreme Court of the United States.* Chicago: C. H. Kerr, 1925.

258. Nagel, Stuart S. "Court-Curbing Periods in American History." *Vanderbilt Law Review* 18 (June 1965): 925-1044.

259. Nagel, Thomas. "Supreme Court and Political Philosophy." *New York University Law Review* 56 (May/June 1981): 519-524.

260. Noel, Francis R. "Vestiges of a Supreme Court among the Colonies and under the Articles of Confederation." *Columbia Historical Society Records* 37/38 (1937): 123-143.

261. Nolan, Dennis R. "Sir William Blackstone and the New American Republic: A Study in Intellectual Impact." *New York University Law Review* 51 (November 1976): 731-768.

262. North, Arthur H. *The Supreme Court: Judicial Process and Judicial Politics*. New York: Appleton-Century-Crofts, 1906.

263. O'Brien, David M. "The Supreme Court: A Co-Equal Branch of Government." *Supreme Court Historical Society Yearbook* 1984 (1984): 90-105.

264. O'Brien, David M. "The Supreme Court: From Warren to Burger to Rehnquist." *PS* 20 (Winter 1987): 12-20.

265. Pace, Thomas A. "A 'Lost' Supreme Court Decision: Historical 'Nuggets v. Gold Brick' Indexes." *American Bar Association Journal* 45 (March 1958): 264-267, 305-307.

266. Paddock, Frank. "American Democracy and the Supreme Court." *Temple Law Quarterly* 14 (February 1940): 210-227.

267. Page, William H. "Full Faith and Credit: The Discarded Constitutional Provision." *Wisconsin Law Review* 1948 (May 1948): 265-329.

268. Palmer, William J. *The Court v. the People*. Chicago: Hallberg, 1969.

269. Patterson, C. Perry. "The Supreme Court as a Constituent Convention." *Tulane Law Review* 23 (June 1949): 431-451.

270. Paul, Julius. "The American Supreme Court: Mirror of the American Conscience." *American Journal of Economics and Sociology* 19 (October 1959): 1-15.

271. Peabody, Robert L. *Cases in American Politics*. New York: Praeger, 1976.

272. Peeler, A. J. *A Treatise on Law and Equity as Distinguished and Enforced in the Courts of the United States*. Austin, TX: Swindells Printing House, 1883.

273. Pei, Mario. "The Case for a Constitutional Convention." *Modern Age* 12 (Winter 1967/1968): 8-13.

274. Peterson, Arnold. *The Supreme Court*. New York: New York Labor News, 1971.

275. Peterson, Helen S. *The Supreme Court in America's Story*. Champaign, IL: Garrard, 1976.

276. Pfeffer, Leo. *This Honorable Court: A History of the United States Supreme Court*. New York: Octagon Books, 1978.

277. Phelps, Edward J. "The Supreme Court of the United States." *Juridical Review* 2 (1890): 122-130.

278. Phillips, Michael J. "Thomas Hill Green, Positive Freedom and the United States Supreme Court." *Emory Law Journal* 25 (Winter 1976): 63-114.

279. Phillips, Nathaniel. "Historic Supreme Court Battles." *American Mercury* 66 (January 1948): 95-101.

280. Phillips, Nathaniel. "Historic Supreme Court Battles." *Case and Comment* 53 (May/June 1948): 3-11.

281. Pierson, Charles W. "*The Federalist* in the Supreme Court." *Yale Law Journal* 33 (May 1924): 728-735.

282. Pollock, Frederick. "The Supreme Court of the United States." *Law Quarterly Review* 8 (April 1892): 162-164.

283. Pollock, Paul K. "The Political Scientist and Supreme Court History." *Polity* 5 (Winter 1972): 260-266.

284. Pomeroy, John N. "The Use of the

Supreme Court to the Union." *Nation* 6 (February 20, 1868): 146-147.

285. Pound, Roscoe. "The Supreme Court and Responsible Government: 1864-1930." *Nebraska Law Review* 40 (1960): 16-34.

286. Powell, E. P. "The Supreme Court in History." *Arena* 23 (March 1900): 271-283.

287. Powell, Thomas R. "From Philadelphia to Philadelphia." *American Political Science Review* 32 (February 1938): 1-27.

288. Pritchett, C. Herman, and Alan F. Westin. *The Third Branch of Government: Eight Cases in Constitutional Politics.* New York: Harcourt, Brace, and World, 1963.

289. Rabkin, Jeremy. "The Judiciary in the Welfare State." *Public Interest* 71 (Spring 1983): 62-84.

290. Ratcliffe, Robert H., ed. *Great Cases of the Supreme Court.* Boston: Houghton Mifflin, 1971.

291. Reidenger, Paul. "Six Cases That Shaped America." *American Bar Association Journal* 73 (September 1987): 56-60.

292. Remington, Frank. "The Role of the Supreme Court." *Current History* 60 (June 1971): 353-356, 370.

293. Riley, Jim L. "The Future of Limited Government." *Rocky Mountain Social Science Journal* 11 (January 1974): 53-69.

294. Roche, John P. *Courts and Rights: The American Judiciary in Action.* New York: Random House, 1966.

295. Roche, John P., and Leonard W. Levy. *The Judiciary.* New York: Harcourt, Brace, and World, 1964.

296. Rodell, Fred. *Nine Men: A Political History of the Supreme Court of the United States from 1790-1955.* New York: Random House, 1955.

297. Roe, Gilbert E. *Our Judicial Oligarchy.* New York: Huebsch, 1912.

298. Rostow, Eugene V. *The Sovereign Prerogative: The Supreme Court and the Quest for Law.* New Haven, CT: Yale University Press, 1962.

299. Rostow, Eugene V. "The Supreme Court and the People's Will." *Notre Dame Lawyer* 33 (August 1958): 573-596.

300. Rothman, Edwin. "Individualism, Indecision, and Indifference: The Supreme Court and the Popular Will, 1870-1949." *Marquette Law Review* 35 (Winter 1951/1952): 219-228.

301. Rottschaefer, Henry. *The Supreme Court and Socio-Economic Change.* Ann Arbor: University of Michigan, 1948.

302. Sager, Lawrence G. "What's a Nice Court Like You Doing in a Democracy Like This?" *Stanford Law Review* 36 (April 1984): 1087-1105.

303. Salomon, Leon I. *The Supreme Court.* New York: H. W. Wilson Company, 1969.

304. Saylor, J. R. "Creation of the Federal Judiciary." *Baylor Law Review* 8 (Summer 1956): 257-282.

305. Scanlan, Alfred L. "The Roosevelt Court Becomes the Truman Court." *Notre Dame Lawyer* 26 (Winter 1951): 214-267.

306. Schmidhauser, John R. *The Supreme Court: Its Politics, Personality, and Procedures.* New York: Holt, Rinehart, and Winston, 1960.

307. Schubert, Glendon A. *Human Jurisprudence: Public Law as Political Science.* Honolulu: University of Hawaii, 1975.

308. Schubert, Glendon A. "A Solution to the Intermediate Factorial Resolution of Thurstone and Degan's Study of the Supreme Court." *Behavioral Science* 7 (October 1962): 448-458.

309. Schultz, Dorothy C. "The Making of

the Modern Court System." Ph.D. diss., University of Arizona, 1978.

310. Schwartz, Bernard. *A Basic History of the United States Supreme Court.* Princeton, NJ: D. Van Nostrand Company, 1968.

311. Schwartz, Bernard. "The Changing Role of the United States Supreme Court." *Canadian Bar Review* 28 (January 1950): 48-61.

312. Scigliano, Robert, ed. *The Courts: A Reader in the Judicial Process.* Boston: Little, Brown, 1962.

313. Shamon, Elias F. *Does the U.S. Supreme Court Govern the United States?* Boston: Old South Book Company, 1969.

314. Shapiro, Martin M. "The Supreme Court and Constitutional Adjudication: Of Politics and Neutral Principles." *George Washington Law Review* 31 (March 1963): 587-606.

315. Shapiro, Martin M. "The Supreme Court from Warren to Burger." In *The New American Political System,* edited by Anthony King, 48-72. Washington, DC: American Enterprise Institute, 1978.

316. Sheldon, Charles H. *The American Judicial Process: Models and Approaches.* New York: Dodd, Mead, 1974.

317. Shnayerson, Robert. *The Illustrated History of the Supreme Court of the United States.* New York: Abrams, 1986.

318. Smalley, E. V. "The Supreme Court of the United States." *Century Magazine* 25 (December 1882): 163-181.

319. Smith, James A. *The Growth and Decadence of Constitutional Government.* New York: Holt, 1930.

320. Smith, James A. *The Spirit of American Government: A Study of the Constitution; Its Origin, Influence, and Relation to Democracy.* New York: Macmillan, 1907.

321. Smith, Joseph H. "An Independent Judiciary: The Colonial Background."

University of Pennsylvania Law Review 124 (May 1976): 1104-1156.

322. Snee, Joseph M. "*Leviathan* at the Bar of Justice." In *Government under Law: A Conference Held at Harvard Law School on the Occasion of the Bicentennial of John Marshall,* edited by Arthur E. Sutherland, 101-132. Cambridge: Harvard University Press, 1956.

323. Snow, Alpheus H. "The Position of the Judiciary in the United States." *Annals of the American Academy of Political and Social Science* 43 (September 1912): 286-310.

324. Speak, David M. "Living Law: The Transformation of American Jurisprudence in the Early Twentieth Century." Ph.D. diss., University of North Carolina, 1979.

325. Steamer, Robert J. *The Supreme Court in Crisis: A History of Conflict.* Amherst: University of Massachusetts Press, 1971.

326. Stephenson, D. Grier, Jr. "On Review: Recent Books about the Supreme Court, the Justices, and the Constitution." *Supreme Court Historical Society Yearbook* 1984 (1984): 127-143.

327. Stickney, Albert. *A True Republic.* New York: Harper and Brothers, 1879.

328. Swiggett, Howard. *Forgotten Leaders of the Revolution.* New York: Doubleday, 1955.

329. Swindler, William F. "Of Revolution, Law, and Order." *Supreme Court Historical Society Yearbook* 1976 (1976): 16-24.

330. Swisher, Carl B. *Historic Decisions of the Supreme Court.* 2d ed. New York: Van Nostrand Reinhold, 1979.

331. Swisher, Carl B. *The Supreme Court in Modern Role.* Rev. ed. New York: New York University Press, 1965.

332. Taggart, William A. "Court Clerks, Court Administrators, and Judges: Con-

flict in Managing the Courts." *Journal of Criminal Justice* 14 (January/February 1986): 1-7.

333. Taggart, William A., and Matthew R. DeZee. "A Note on Substantive Access Doctrine in the U.S. Supreme Court: A Comparative Analysis of the Warren and Burger Courts." *Western Political Quarterly* 38 (March 1985): 84-93.

334. Teiser, Sidney. "The Genesis of the Supreme Court." *Virginia Law Review* 25 (February 1939): 398-421.

335. Thomas, Brook. "The Pioneers, on the Sources of American Legal History: A Critical Tale." *American Quarterly* 36 (Spring 1984): 86-111.

336. Thomason, Robert E. "The United States Supreme Court." *Southwestern Law Journal* 11 (Spring 1957): 131-138.

337. Tobriner, Matthew O. "Lawyers, Judges, and Watergate." *California State Bar Journal* 49 (March/April 1974): 111-116.

338. Tresolini, Rocco J. *Justice and the Supreme Court.* Philadelphia: Lippincott, 1963.

339. Tully, Andrew. *Supreme Court.* New York: Simon and Schuster, 1963.

340. Ulmer, S. Sidney. "Bricolage and Assorted Thoughts on Working in the Papers of Supreme Court Justices." *Journal of Politics* 35 (May 1973): 286-310.

341. Ulmer, S. Sidney. "Researching the Supreme Court in a Democratic Pluralist System: Some Thoughts on New Directions." *Law and Policy Quarterly* 1 (January 1979): 53-80.

342. U.S. National Archives and Records Service. *Preliminary Inventory of the Records of the Supreme Court of the United States, Record Group 267.* Washington, DC: National Archives and Records Service, General Services Administration, 1973.

343. Vale, V. "The Supreme Court Reconsidered: Least or Most Dangerous Branch? Some Recent Appraisals." *Political Studies* 16 (June 1968): 249-253.

344. Vanderzell, John H. *The Supreme Court and American Government.* New York: Crowell, 1968.

345. Veeder, Van Vechten. "A Century of Federal Judicature." *Green Bag* 15 (January 1903): 17-24; (February 1903): 71-80; (March 1903): 127-138; (April 1903): 181-191; (May 1903): 223-232; (June 1903): 281-289; (July 1903): 323-332; (August 1903): 377-385; (September 1903): 419-429.

346. Vose, Clement E. *Constitutional Change: American Politics and Supreme Court Litigation since 1900.* Lexington, MA: D. C. Heath, 1972.

347. Vose, Clement E. "Crosskey on Shenanigans v. Science." *Journal of Politics* 17 (August 1955): 448-452.

348. Wagner, W. Joseph. "The History and Role of a Supreme Court in a Federal System." *Montana Law Review* 20 (Spring 1959): 171-191.

349. Walker, Mary M. *The Evolution of the United States Supreme Court.* Morristown, NJ: General Learning Press, 1974.

350. Walsh, Anthony. " 'The People Who Own the Country Ought to Govern It': The Supreme Court, Hegemony, and Its Consequences." *Law and Inequality* 5 (January 1988): 431-451.

351. Warren, Charles. "The Early History of the Supreme Court of the United States in Connection with Modern Attacks on the Judiciary." *Massachusetts Law Quarterly* 8 (December 1922): 1-23.

352. Warren, Charles. *The Supreme Court and the World Court, 1832 and 1932: Record of Ratifications and Signatures to* *the Protocol of Signature of the World Court, the Optional Clause Recognizing the Court's Jurisdiction, the Protocol of Revision of the Statute, the Protocol of Accession of the United States.* Worcester, MA: Carnegie Endowment for International Peace, Division of Intercourse and Education, 1933.

353. Warren, Charles. *The Supreme Court in United States History.* Rev. ed. Littleton, CO: Fred B. Rothman, 1987.

354. Wasby, Stephen L. *The Supreme Court in the Federal Judicial System.* 3d ed. Chicago: Nelson-Hall, 1988.

355. Wechsler, Herbert. *Principles, Politics, and Fundamental Law: Selected Essays.* Cambridge: Harvard University Press, 1961.

356. Westin, Alan F. *An Autobiography of the Supreme Court: Off-the-Bench Commentary by the Justices.* New York: Macmillan, 1963.

357. Wheeler, Everett P. "The Supreme Court: A Coordinate Branch of the United States Government." *Yale Law Journal* 24 (February 1915): 300-315.

358. White, G. Edward. "Reflections on the Role of the Supreme Court: The Contemporary Debate and the 'Lessons' of History." *Judicature* 63 (October 1979): 162-173.

359. White, G. Edward. "The Supreme Court's Public and the Public's Supreme Court." *Virginia Quarterly Review* 52 (Summer 1976): 370-388.

360. Whitlock, Alice M. "In and Around the Supreme Court." *Green Bag* 9 (June 1897): 274-277.

361. Whitney, David C. *Founders of Freedom in America.* Chicago: Ferguson, 1964.

362. Wiecek, William M. "Clio as Hostage: The United States Supreme Court and the Uses of History." *California Western Law Review* 24 (1987-1988): 227-268.

363. Wiecek, William M. "The Imperial Judiciary in Historical Perspective." *Supreme Court Historical Society Yearbook 1984* (1984): 61-89.

364. Wiecek, William M. *Liberty under Law: The Supreme Court in American Life.* Baltimore, MD: Johns Hopkins Press, 1988.

365. Williams, Jerre S. *The Supreme Court Speaks.* Austin: University of Texas Press, 1956.

366. Willoughby, Westel W. *The Supreme Court of the United States: Its History and Influence in Our Constitutional System.* Baltimore, MD: Johns Hopkins Press, 1890.

367. Wills, Garry. *Inventing America: Jefferson's Declaration of Independence.* Garden City, NY: Doubleday, 1978.

368. Wilson, Margaret B. "American Judiciary in Historical Perspective." *Crisis* 89 (February 1982): 37-40.

369. Wilson, Woodrow. *Constitutional Government in the United States.* New York: Columbia University Press, 1908.

370. Wise, John S. *A Treatise on American Citizenship.* Long Island, NY: Edward Thompson Company, 1906.

371. Witt, Elder, ed. *The Supreme Court and Its Work.* Washington, DC: Congressional Quarterly, 1981.

372. Woodburn, James A. *The American Republic and Its Government, an Analysis of the Government of the United States, with a Consideration of Its Fundamental Principles and of Its Relations to the States and Territories.* New York: Putnam, 1903.

373. Wu, Ching-Hsiung. *The Art of Law and Other Essays Juridical and Literary.* Shanghai, China: Commercial Press, 1936.

374. Wyzanski, Charles E., Jr. *Whereas ... A Judge's Premises: Essays in Judgement, Ethics, and the Law.* Boston: Little, Brown, 1965.

375. Yankwich, Leon R. "The Background of the American Bill of Rights." *Georgetown Law Journal* 37 (November 1948): 1-28.

376. "Ye Difficulty of Gaining Admittance to Ye Bar of Ye Supreme Court of Ye United States in Ye Olden Time." *American Law Review* 34 (July/August 1900): 628-629.

1790-1800

377. Aumann, Francis R. "Some Problems of Growth and Development in the Formative Period of the American Legal System, 1775-1866." *University of Cincinnati Law Review* 13 (May 1939): 382-445.

378. Currie, David P. "The Constitution in the Supreme Court: 1789-1801." *University of Chicago Law Review* 48 (Fall 1981): 819-881.

379. Eisenberg, David. "A Consideration of Extra-Judicial Activities in the Pre-Marshall Era." *Supreme Court Historical Society Yearbook* 1985 (1985): 117-126.

380. Ellis, Richard E. *The Jeffersonian Crisis: Courts and Politics in the Young Republic.* New York: Oxford University Press, 1971.

381. Gatton, Douglas W. "A Study of the Roles of the State and Federal High Courts in the Law and Politics of Pennsylvania, 1787-1810." Ph.D. diss., University of Illinois, 1973.

382. Goebel, Julius, Jr. *Antecedents and Beginnings to 1801. The History of the Supreme Court of the United States,* edited by Paul A. Freund and Stanley N. Katz, vol 1. New York: Macmillan, 1971.

383. Haines, Charles G., and Foster H. Sherwood. *The Role of the Supreme Court in American Government and Politics, 1789-1835.* Berkeley: University of California Press, 1944.

384. Hicks, Xenophon. "The Beginnings of the Federal Judiciary." *Tennessee Law Review* 20 (December 1947): 21-32.

385. Horwitz, Morton J. "The Legacy of 1776 in Legal and Economic Thought." *Journal of Law and Economics* 19 (October 1976): 621-632.

386. Horwitz, Morton J. *The Transformation of American Law: 1780-1860.* Cambridge: Harvard University Press, 1977.

387. Marcus, Maeva, James R. Perry, James M. Buchanan, Christine R. Jordan, and Steven L. Tull. "It Is My Wish as Well as My Duty to Attend the Court: The Hardships of Supreme Court Service, 1790-1800." *Supreme Court Historical Society Yearbook* 1984 (1984): 118-126.

388. Mathis, Doyle. "Georgia before the Supreme Court: The First Decade." *American Journal of Legal History* 12 (April 1968): 112-121.

389. Mitchell, William D. "The Supreme Court in Washington's Time." *American Bar Association Journal* 18 (May 1932): 341-342.

390. Mowry, Don E. "Political and Party Aspects of the National Judiciary, 1801-1835." *American Historical Magazine* 3 (September 1908): 331-335, 471-492.

391. Nordham, George W. "President George Washington and the First Supreme Court." *Supreme Court Historical Society Yearbook* 1984 (1984): 7-11.

392. Surrency, Erwin C., ed. "The Minutes of the Supreme Court of the United States, 1789-1806." *American Journal of Legal History* 5 (January 1961): 67-86.

393. Surrency, Erwin C., ed. "The Minutes of the Supreme Court of the United States, 1789-1806." *American Journal of Legal History* 5 (April 1961): 166-196.

394. Surrency, Erwin C., ed. "The Minutes of the Supreme Court of the United States, 1789-1806." *American Journal of Legal History* 5 (October 1961): 369-384.

395. Surrency, Erwin C., ed. "Minutes of the Supreme Court of the United States, August Term, 1795." *American Journal of Legal History* 6 (January 1962): 71-81.

396. Surrency, Erwin C., ed. "Minutes of the Supreme Court of the United States, February Term, 1796." *American Journal of Legal History* 7 (January 1963): 63-82.

397. Surrency, Erwin C., ed. "Minutes of the Supreme Court of the United States, August Term, 1796." *American Journal of Legal History* 7 (April 1963): 165-175.

398. Surrency, Erwin C., ed. "Minutes of the Supreme Court of the United States, February Term, 1797 to August Term, 1798." *American Journal of Legal History* 7 (July 1963): 246-271.

399. Surrency, Erwin C., ed. "Minutes of the Supreme Court of the United States, February Term, 1799 to August Term, 1800." *American Journal of Legal History* 7 (October 1963): 340-355.

400. Surrency, Erwin C., ed. "Minutes of the Supreme Court of the United States, August Term, 1800." *American Journal of Legal History* 8 (January 1964): 72-77.

401. Swindler, William F. "Mr. Chisholm and the Eleventh Amendment." *Supreme Court Historical Society Yearbook* 1981 (1981): 14-18.

402. Teeter, Dwight L. "The Printer and the Chief Justice: Seditious Libel in 1782-1783." *Journalism Quarterly* 45 (Summer 1968): 235-242.

403. Treacy, Kenneth W. "The *Olmstead* Case, 1778-1809." *Western Political Quarterly* 10 (September 1957): 675-691.

404. Warren, Charles. "The First Decade of the Supreme Court of the United States." *University of Chicago Law Review* 7 (June 1940): 631-654.

405. Yarborough, Kemp P. "*Chisholm v. Georgia*: A Study of the Minority Opinion." Ph.D. diss., Columbia University, 1963.

1801-1835

406. Baxter, Maurice G. *Daniel Webster and the Supreme Court.* Amherst: University of Massachusetts Press, 1966.

407. Beirne, Francis F. *Shout Treason: The Trial of Aaron Burr.* New York: Hastings House, 1959.

408. Currie, David P. "Constitution in the Supreme Court: State and Congressional Powers, 1801-1835." *University of Chicago Law Review* 49 (Fall 1982): 887-975.

409. Currie, David P. "Constitution in the Supreme Court: The Powers of the Federal Courts, 1801-1835." *University of Chicago Law Review* 49 (Summer 1982): 646-724.

410. Dumbauld, Edward. "Olmstead's Claim: The Case of the Mutinous Mariner." *Supreme Court Historical Society Yearbook* 1977 (1977): 52-58, 69.

411. Farrand, Max. "The Judiciary Act of 1801." *American Historical Review* 5 (July 1900): 682-686.

412. Friendly, Henry J. *The* Dartmouth College *Case and the Public-Private Penumbra.* Austin: University of Texas Press, 1968.

413. Haines, Charles G. "Political Theories of the Supreme Court from 1789-1835." *American Political Science Review* 2 (February 1908): 221-244.

414. Haskins, George L. "Law Versus Politics in the Early Years of the Marshall Court." *University of Pennsylvania Law Review* 130 (November 1981): 1-27.

415. Jessup, Dwight W. *Reaction and Accommodation: The United States Supreme*

Court and Political Conflict, 1809-1835. New York: Garland, 1987.

416. Johnson, Eldon L. "The Dartmouth College Case: The Neglected Educational Meaning." *Journal of the Early Republic* 3 (Spring 1983): 45-67.

417. Klinkhamer, Marie C. "The Use of History in the Supreme Court, 1789-1835." *University of Detroit Law Journal* 36 (June 1959): 553-578.

418. Lewis, Walker. "Backstage at *Dartmouth College*." *Supreme Court Historical Society Yearbook* 1977 (1977): 29-37.

419. Magrath, C. Peter. *Yazoo: Law and Politics in the New Republic: The Case of* Fletcher v. Peck. Providence, RI: Brown University Press, 1966.

420. Mendelson, Wallace. "B. F. Wright on the Contract Clause: A Progressive Misreading of the Marshall-Taney Era." *Western Political Quarterly* 38 (June 1985): 262-275.

421. Mendelson, Wallace. "New Light on *Fletcher v. Peck* and *Gibbons v. Ogden*." *Yale Law Journal* 58 (March 1949): 567-573.

422. Mowry, Don E. "Political and Party Aspects of the National Judiciary, 1789-1801." *American Historical Magazine* 3 (January 1908): 83-97; (June 1908): 331-355; (September 1908): 471-492.

423. Nettles, Curtis. "The Mississippi Valley and the Federal Judiciary, 1807-1837." *Mississippi Valley Historical Review* 12 (September 1925): 202-216.

424. Newmyer, R. Kent. *The Supreme Court under Marshall and Taney.* New York: Crowell, 1968.

425. Porter, Mary C. A. "That Commerce Shall Be Free: A New Look at the Old Laissez-Faire Court." *Supreme Court Review* 1976 (1976): 135-159.

426. Powers, George M. "The Supreme Court of 1834." *Vermont Bar Association* 28 (October 2-3, 1934): 75-80.

427. Redlich, Norman. "The Supreme Court: 1833 Term." *New York University Law Review* 40 (January 1965): 1-11.

428. Roe, David B., and Russell K. Osgood. "United States Supreme Court, February Term 1824." *Yale Law Journal* 84 (March 1975): 770-808.

429. Roper, Donald M. "In Quest of Judicial Objectivity: The Marshall Court and the Legitimation of Slavery." *Stanford Law Review* 21 (February 1969): 532-549.

430. Roper, Donald M. "Judicial Unanimity and the Marshall Court: A Road to Reappraisal." *American Journal of Legal History* 9 (April 1965): 118-134.

431. Shirley, John M. *The* Dartmouth College *Causes and the Supreme Court of the United States.* New York: DaCapo Press, 1971.

432. Siegel, Adrienne. *The Marshall Court, 1801-1835.* Millwood, NY: Associated Faculty Press, 1987.

433. Steamer, Robert J. "Congress and the Supreme Court during the Marshall Era." *Review of Politics* 27 (July 1965): 364-385.

434. Stites, Francis. *Private Interest and Public Gain: The* Dartmouth College *Case, 1819.* Amherst: University of Massachusetts Press, 1972.

435. Strickland, Rennard J., and William R. Strickland. "The Court and the Trail of Tears." *Supreme Court Historical Society Yearbook* 1979 (1979): 20-30.

436. Summersell, Charles G. "Alabama and the Supreme Court: The First Case." *Alabama Review* 10 (July 1957): 163-175.

437. Surrency, Erwin C. "The Judiciary Act of 1801." *American Journal of Legal History* 2 (January 1958): 53-65.

438. Surrency, Erwin C., ed. "Minutes of the Supreme Court of the United States, February Term, 1801 to December Term, 1801." *American Journal of Legal History* 8 (October 1964): 326-344.

439. Swindler, William F. "The Trials of Aaron Burr." *Supreme Court Historical Society Yearbook* 1978 (1978): 18-24.

440. Turner, Kathryn. "Federalist Policy and the Judiciary Act of 1801." *William and Mary Quarterly* 22 (January 1965): 1-32.

441. Turner, Kathryn. "The Midnight Judges." *University of Pennsylvania Law Review* 109 (February 1961): 494-523.

442. White, G. Edward. "Art of Revising History: Revisiting the Marshall Court." *Suffolk University Law Review* 16 (Fall 1982): 659-685.

443. White, G. Edward. "The Working Life of the Marshall Court, 1815-1835." *Virginia Law Review* 70 (February 1984): 1-52.

444. Whitehead, John S. "How to Think about the *Dartmouth College* Case." *History of Education Quarterly* 26 (Fall 1986): 333-349.

445. Wiecek, William M. "A 'Peculiar Conservatism' and the Dorr Rebellion: Constitutional Clash in Jacksonian America." *American Journal of Legal History* 22 (July 1978): 237-253.

446. Wunder, John R. "Constitutional Oversight: *Clarke v. Baza Done* and the Territorial Supreme Court as Court of Last Resort." *Old Northwest* 4 (September 1978): 259-284.

447. Wyllie, Irvin G. "Search for an American Law of Charity, 1776-1844." *Mississippi Valley Historical Review* 46 (September 1959): 203-221.

1836-1864

448. Carpenter, Richard V. "Lincoln's First Supreme Court Case." *Illinois State Historical Society Journal* 4 (October 1911): 317-323.

449. Currie, David P. "The Constitution in the Supreme Court: Article IV and Federal Powers, 1836-1864." *Duke Law Journal* 1983 (Summer 1983): 695-747.

450. Dolan, Paul. "Dissent in the Taney Court." *Dickinson Law Review* 68 (Spring 1964): 281-306.

451. Fried, Joseph P. "The U.S. Supreme Court during the Civil War." *Civil War Times Illustrated* 1 (February 1963): 28-37.

452. Gordan, John D., III. "The Trial of the Officers and Crew of the Schooner 'Savannah.' " *Supreme Court Historical Society Yearbook* 1983 (1983): 31-45.

453. Haines, Charles G., and Foster H. Sherwood. *The Role of the Supreme Court in American Government and Politics, 1835-1864.* Berkeley: University of California Press, 1957.

454. Kutler, Stanley I. *Privilege and Creative Destruction: The* Charles River Bridge *Case.* Philadelphia: Lippincott, 1971.

455. McGinty, Brian. "War in the Court." *Civil War Times Illustrated* 19 (August 1980): 22-25, 39-41.

456. Monkkonen, Eric. "*Bank of Augusta v. Earle*: Corporate Growth v. States' Rights." *Alabama Historical Quarterly* 34 (Summer 1972): 113-130.

457. O'Brien, Joseph A. "The Use of History in the Supreme Court, 1864-1873." Master's thesis, Catholic University of America, 1950.

458. Peters, Richard. *Report of the Case of Edward Prigg against the Commonwealth* of Pennsylvania, Argued and Judged in the *Supreme Court of the United States at January Term, 1842*. Westport, CT: Negro Universities Press, 1970.

459. Randall, James G. *Constitutional Problems under Lincoln*. Urbana: University of Illinois Press, 1951.

460. Schmidhauser, John R. "Judicial Behavior and the Sectional Crisis of 1837-1860." *Journal of Politics* 23 (November 1961): 615-640.

461. Silver, David M. *Lincoln's Supreme Court*. Urbana: University of Illinois Press, 1957.

462. Silver, David M. "The Supreme Court during the Civil War." Ph.D. diss., University of Illinois, 1940.

463. Swisher, Carl B. *The Taney Period, 1835-1864. The History of the Supreme Court of the United States*, edited by Paul A. Freund and Stanley N. Katz, vol. 5. New York: Macmillan, 1974.

464. Tilger, Justine. "The Taney Court and the Legal Status of Corporations." Master's thesis, Indiana University, 1962.

465. Whatley, George C. "Jackson's Justices and the Federal System, 1830-1856." Ph.D. diss., University of Alabama, 1969.

1865-1873

466. Bates, Samuel P. "Edwin M. Stanton." In *Martial Deeds of Pennsylvania*, by Samuel P. Bates, 976-981. Philadelphia: T. H. Davis and Company, 1875.

467. Benjamin, Charles F. "Recollections of Secretary Stanton." *Century Magazine* 33 (March 1887): 758-768.

468. Carnegie, Andrew. *Edwin M. Stanton: An Address by Andrew Carnegie on Stanton Memorial Day at Kenyon College*. New York: Doubleday, Page, and Company, 1906.

469. Craven, Avery O. *Reconstruction: The Ending of the Civil War*. New York: Holt, Rinehart, and Winston, 1969.

470. Currie, David P. "The Constitution in the Supreme Court: Civil War and Reconstruction, 1865-1873." *University of Chicago Law Review* 51 (Winter 1984): 131-186.

471. Currie, David P. "The Constitution in the Supreme Court: Contracts and Commerce, 1836-1864." *Duke Law Journal* 1983 (June 1983): 471-513.

472. Dawes, Henry L. "Recollections of Stanton under Johnson." *Atlantic Monthly* 74 (October 1894): 494-504.

473. Dawes, Henry L. "Recollections of Stanton under Lincoln." *Atlantic Monthly* 73 (February 1894): 162-169.

474. Fairman, Charles. *Reconstruction and Reunion, 1864-1888, Part One. The History of the Supreme Court of the United States*, edited by Paul A. Freund and Stanley N. Katz, vol. 6. New York: Macmillan, 1971.

475. Fairman, Charles. *Reconstruction and Reunion, 1864-1888, Part Two. The History of the Supreme Court of the United States*, edited by Paul A. Freund and Stanley N. Katz, vol. 7. New York: Macmillan, 1971.

476. Franklin, Mitchell. "The Foundations and Meanings of the *Slaughter House Cases*." *Tulane Law Review* 18 (October 1943): 1-88; (December 1943): 218-262.

477. Freyer, Tony A. "The Federal Courts, Localism, and the National Economy, 1865-1900." *Business History Review* 53 (Autumn 1979): 343-363.

478. Fridlington, Robert. *The Reconstruction Court, 1864-1888*. Millwood, NY: Associated Faculty Press, 1988.

479. Godkin, E. L. "The Supreme Court Bills." *Nation* 6 (January 30, 1868): 85-86.

480. Parsons, R. C. "Sketch of the Bench and Bar of the Supreme Court of the United States in 1866." *Western Reserve Law Journal* 1 (March 1895): 43-51.

481. Rau, Donald. "*Cummings v. Missouri*: Three Cheers for Father Cummings." *Supreme Court Historical Society Yearbook* 1977 (1977): 20-28.

482. Scarborough, Jane L. "George W. Paschal, Texas Unionist and Scalawag Jurisprudent." Ph.D. diss., Rice University, 1972.

483. Smith, Bryant. "Neglected Evidence on an Old Controversy: *Bronson v. Rodes* as a Forecast of *Hepburn v. Griswold*." *American Historical Review* 34 (April 1929): 532-535.

484. "Supreme Court of the United States." *Albany Law Journal* 1 (March 12, 1870): 188-189.

485. Sutherland, Arthur E., Jr. *Apology for Uncomfortable Change, 1865-1965.* New York: Macmillan, 1965.

486. Wiecek, William M. "The Great Writ and Reconstruction: The *Habeas Corpus* Act of 1867." *Journal of Southern History* 36 (November 1970): 530-548.

487. Wiecek, William M. "The Reconstruction of Federal Judicial Power, 1863-1875." *American Journal of Legal History* 13 (October 1969): 333-359.

1874-1888

488. Bigelow, John. *The Supreme Court and the Electoral Commission: An Open Letter to the Hon. Joseph H. Choate.* New York: Putnam's, 1903.

489. Black, Jeremiah S. "Letters to Henry Wilson." In *Essays and Speeches*, edited by Jeremiah S. Black, 245-292. New York: Appleton and Company, 1885.

490. Clark, E. P. "Parties and the Supreme Court." *Nation* 44 (May 26, 1887): 442.

491. Fairman, Charles. *Five Justices and the Electoral Commission of 1877. The History of the Supreme Court of the United States*, edited by Paul A. Freund and Stanley N. Katz, supplement to vol. 7. New York: Macmillan, 1986.

492. Fairman, Charles. "Supreme Court in 1878." *American Bar Association Journal* 64 (July 1978): 1024-1034.

493. Garland, Augustus H. *Experience in the Supreme Court of the United States, with Some Reflections and Suggestions as to the Tribunal.* Washington, DC: Byrne, 1898.

494. Garraty, John A. *The New Commonwealth 1877-1890.* New York: Harper and Row, 1968.

495. Hawkins, Seth C. "Garfield at the Bar: An Architectonic Rhetorical Criticism of Selected Speeches by James A. Garfield before the U.S. Supreme Court." Ph.D. diss., Bowling Green State University, 1975.

496. Horan, Michael J. "Political Economy and Sociological Theory as Influences upon Judicial Policy-Making: The Civil Rights Cases of 1883." *American Journal of Legal History* 16 (January 1972): 71-86.

497. Westin, Alan. "Populism and the Supreme Court." *Supreme Court Historical Society Yearbook* 1980 (1980): 62-77.

1889-1920

498. Bickel, Alexander M., and Benno C. Schmidt, Jr. *The Judiciary and Responsible Government, 1910-1921. The History of the Supreme Court of the United States*, edited by Paul A. Freund and Stanley N. Katz, vol. 9. New York: Macmillan, 1984.

499. Bigelow, John. "Mr. John Bigelow on the United States Supreme Court." *Harper's Weekly* 47 (August 1, 1903): 1251-1252.

500. Bindler, Norman. *The Conservative Court, 1910-1930.* Millwood, NY: Associated Faculty Press, 1986.

501. Clark, E. P. "The Supreme Court Vacancy." *Nation* 61 (August 22, 1895): 129-130.

502. Currie, David P. "The Constitution in the Supreme Court: Full Faith and the Bill of Rights, 1889-1910." *University of Chicago Law Review* 52 (Fall 1985): 867-902.

503. Currie, David P. "The Constitution in the Supreme Court: 1910-1921." *Duke Law Journal* 1985 (December 1985): 1111-1162.

504. Currie, David P. "The Constitution in the Supreme Court: The Protection of Economic Interests, 1889-1910." *University of Chicago Law Review* 52 (Spring 1985): 324-388.

505. Furer, Howard B. *The Fuller Court, 1888-1910.* 9 vols. Millwood, NY: Associated Faculty Press, 1986.

506. Hill, Frederick T. "The Supreme Court and Coming Events." *Appleton's Magazine* 8 (July 1906): 9-15.

507. Hofstadter, Richard. *Social Darwinism in American Thought.* New York: George Braziller, 1959.

508. McClain, Emlin. "Decisions of the Supreme Court of the United States on Constitutional Questions, 1911-1914." *American Political Science Review* 9 (February 1915): 36-49.

509. McCurdy, Charles W. "The *Knight* Decision of 1895 and the Modernization of American Corporation Law, 1869-1903." *Business History Review* 53 (Autumn 1979): 304-342.

510. Noblitt, Harding C. "The Supreme Court and the Progressive Era, 1902-1921." Ph.D. diss., University of Chicago, 1956.

511. Paul, Arnold M. *Conservative Crisis and the Rule of Law: Attitudes of Bar and Bench, 1887-1895.* Rev. ed. New York: Harper and Row, 1969.

512. Paul, Arnold M. "Legal Progressivism, the Courts, and the Crisis of the 1890's." *Business History Review* 33 (Winter 1959): 495-509.

513. Phillips, Harry. "Tennessee and the U.S. Court of Appeals: The Sixth Circuit." *Tennessee Historical Quarterly* 33 (Spring 1954): 22-33.

514. Powell, Thomas R. "Decisions of the Supreme Court of the United States on Constitutional Questions, 1914-1917." *American Political Science Review* 12 (February 1918): 17-48; (August 1918): 427-457; (November 1918): 640-666.

515. Pratt, Walter F. "Rhetorical Styles on the Fuller Court." *American Journal of Legal History* 24 (July 1980): 189-220.

516. Rodes, Robert E., Jr. "Due Process and Social Legislation in the Supreme Court: A Post Mortem." *Notre Dame Lawyer* 33 (December 1957): 5-33.

517. Semonche, John E. *Charting the Future: The Supreme Court Responds to a Changing Society, 1890-1920.* Westport, CT: Greenwood Press, 1978.

518. Smith, Douglas C. "A West Virginia Dilemma: *Martin v. Board of Education,* 1896." *West Virginia History* 40 (Winter 1979): 158-163.

519. Thernstrom, Abigail M. "The Left against the Court: The Supreme Court and Its Critics, 1900-1937." Ph.D. diss., Harvard University, 1975.

520. Urofsky, Melvin I. "Myth and Reality: The Supreme Court and Protective Legislation in the Progressive Era." *Supreme Court Historical Society Yearbook* 1983 (1983): 53-72.

521. Warren, Charles. "The Progressiveness of the United States Supreme Court." *Columbia Law Review* 13 (April 1913): 294-313.

522. Westin, Alan F. "The Supreme Court, the Populist Movement, and the Campaign of 1896." *Journal of Politics* 15 (February 1953): 3-41.

523. Williams, George H. "Reminiscences of the United States Supreme Court." *Yale Law Journal* 8 (April 1899): 296-306.

1921-1940

524. Anderson, George C. "We Will Hear More on the Supreme Court." *Tennessee Law Review* 15 (February 1938): 112-115.

525. Biddle, Francis. "Past Term of the Supreme Court of the United States." *Federal Bar Association Journal* 4 (November 1941): 218-225.

526. Braeman, John. "Thomas Reed Powell on the Roosevelt Court." *Constitutional Commentary* 5 (Winter 1988): 143-157.

527. Carrott, M. Browning. "The Supreme Court and Law and Order in the 1920s." *Maryland Historian* 16 (Fall/Winter 1985): 12-26.

528. Castleberry, H. Paul. "Supreme Court and International Questions: 1917-1948." Ph.D. diss., University of Chicago, 1949.

529. Cathcart, Arthur M. "The Supreme Court and the New Deal." *Southern California Law Review* 9 (June 1936): 315-333.

530. Childs, Marquis. "Politics and the Supreme Court." In *Witness to Power*, by Marquis Childs, 30-52. New York: McGraw-Hill, 1975.

531. Childs, Marquis. "The Supreme Court Today." *Harper's* 176 (May 1938): 581-588.

532. Currie, David P. "The Constitution in the Supreme Court: 1921-1930." *Duke Law Journal* 1986 (February 1986): 65-144.

533. Currie, David P. "The Constitution in the Supreme Court: The New Deal, 1931-1940." *University of Chicago Law Review* 54 (Spring 1987): 504-555.

534. Cushman, Robert E. "Constitutional Law in 1923-1924: The Constitutional Decisions of the Supreme Court of the United States in the October Term, 1923." *American Political Science Review* 19 (February 1925): 51-68.

535. Cushman, Robert E. "Constitutional Law in 1924-1925: The Constitutional Decisions of the Supreme Court of the United States in the October Term, 1924." *American Political Science Review* 20 (February 1926): 80-100.

536. Cushman, Robert E. "Constitutional Law in 1925-1926: The Constitutional Decisions of the Supreme Court of the United States in the October Term, 1925." *American Political Science Review* 21 (February 1927): 71-97.

537. Cushman, Robert E. "Constitutional Law in 1926-1927: The Constitutional Decisions of the Supreme Court of the United States in the October Term, 1926." *American Political Science Review* 22 (February 1928): 70-107.

538. Cushman, Robert E. "Constitutional Law in 1927-1928: The Constitutional Decisions of the Supreme Court of the United States in the October Term, 1927." *American Political Science Review* 23 (February 1929): 78-101.

539. Cushman, Robert E. "Constitutional Law in 1928-1929: The Constitutional Decisions of the Supreme Court of the United States in the October Term, 1928." *American Political Science Review* 24 (February 1930): 67-103.

540. Cushman, Robert E. "Constitutional

Law in 1929-1930: The Constitutional
Decisions of the Supreme Court of the
United States in the October Term, 1929."
American Political Science Review 25
(February 1931): 73-102.

541. Cushman, Robert E. "Constitutional
Law in 1930-1931: The Constitutional
Decisions of the Supreme Court of the
United States in the October Term, 1930."
American Political Science Review 26
(April 1932): 256-284.

542. Cushman, Robert E. "Constitutional
Law in 1931-1932: The Constitutional
Decisions of the Supreme Court of the
United States in the October Term, 1931."
American Political Science Review 27
(February 1933): 39-57.

543. Cushman, Robert E. "Constitutional
Law in 1932-1933: The Constitutional
Decisions of the Supreme Court of the
United States in the October Term, 1932."
American Political Science Review 28
(February 1934): 40-64.

544. Cushman, Robert E. "Constitutional
Law in 1933-1934: The Constitutional
Decisions of the Supreme Court of the
United States in the October Term, 1933."
American Political Science Review 29
(February 1935): 36-59.

545. Cushman, Robert E. "Constitutional
Law in 1934-1935: The Constitutional
Decisions of the Supreme Court of the
United States in the October Term, 1934."
American Political Science Review 30
(February 1936): 51-89.

546. Cushman, Robert E. "Constitutional
Law in 1935-1936: The Constitutional
Decisions of the Supreme Court of the
United States in the October Term, 1935."
American Political Science Review 31
(April 1937): 253-279.

547. Cushman, Robert E. "Constitutional
Law in 1936-1937: The Constitutional
Decisions of the Supreme Court of the
United States in the October Term, 1936."

American Political Science Review 32
(April 1938): 278-310.

548. Cushman, Robert E. "Constitutional
Law in 1937-1938: The Constitutional
Decisions of the Supreme Court of the
United States in the October Term, 1937."
American Political Science Review 33
(April 1939): 234-266.

549. Cushman, Robert E. "Constitutional
Law in 1938-1939: The Constitutional
Decisions of the Supreme Court of the
United States in the October Term, 1938."
Amercian Political Science Review 34
(April 1940): 249-283.

550. Cushman, Robert E. "Constitutional
Law in 1939-1940: The Constitutional
Decisions of the Supreme Court of the
United States in the October Term, 1939."
American Political Science Review 35
(April 1941): 250-283.

551. Davis, Charles H. "Criticism of Supreme Court Decisions." *Lawyer and
Banker* 25 (May/June 1932): 166-175.

552. Dodd, Walter F. "The United States
Supreme Court, 1936-1946." *American
Political Science Review* 41 (February
1947): 1-11.

553. Duram, James C. "Press Attitudes
towards the Role of the Supreme Court in
the 1930s." Ph.D. diss., Wayne State University, 1969.

554. Farnham, Henry P. "Recent Decisions of the U.S. Supreme Court." *Case
and Comment* 32 (January/February/
March 1926): 3-5.

555. Field, Oliver P. "The Advisory Opinion: An Analysis." *Indiana Law Journal*
24 (Winter 1949): 203-230.

556. Fish, Peter G. "*Red Jacket* Revisited:
The Case That Unraveled John J.
Parker's Supreme Court Appointment."
Law and History Review 5 (Spring 1987):
199-240.

557. Fraenkel, Osmond K. "Constitutional

Issues in the Supreme Court, 1936 Term." *University of Pennsylvania Law Review* 86 (November 1937): 38-76.

558. Fraenkel, Osmond K. "Constitutional Issues in the Supreme Court, 1937 Term." *University of Pennsylvania Law Review* 87 (November 1938): 50-88.

559. Fraser, G. A. "Recent Constitutional Law in the Supreme Court." *Massachusetts Law Quarterly* 21 (July 1936): 3-16.

560. Freund, Paul A. "Recent Decisions of the Supreme Court of the United States." *Federal Bar Association Journal* 3 (April 1939): 341-343.

561. Freund, Paul A. "Recent Decisions of the Supreme Court." *Federal Bar Association Journal* 3 (November 1939): 389-392.

562. Galloway, Russell W., Jr. "The Taft Court." *Santa Clara Law Review* 25 (Winter 1985): 1-64.

563. Hagens, G. R. "The Supreme Court and the New Deal." *Wyoming State Bar Association* 1935-1937: 59-68.

564. Hankin, Gregory. "The New Deal in the Courts." *Editorial Research Reports* 2 (May 25, 1934): 347-362.

565. Hankin, Gregory. "Recent Trends in the Decisions of the Supreme Court of the United States." *George Washington Law Review* 8 (May 1940): 1001-1032.

566. Hankin, Gregory. "U.S. Supreme Court under New Act." *Journal of American Judicature Society* 12 (August 1928): 40-43.

567. Harrison, Robert. "The Breakup of the Roosevelt Supreme Court: The Contribution of History and Biography." *Law and History Review* 2 (Fall 1984): 165-221.

568. Hill, David J. "The Assault on the Constitution and the Courts." *Constitutional Review* 9 (January 1925): 12-18.

569. Hudson, David E. "Recent Decisions

of the Supreme Court of the United States." *Federal Bar Association Journal* 3 (April 1938): 149-152, 191-192.

570. Hudson, David E. "Recent Decisions of the Supreme Court of the United States." *Federal Bar Association Journal* 3 (November 1938): 217-220, 249.

571. Hudson, David E. "Recent Decisions of the United States Supreme Court." *Federal Bar Association Journal* 2 (March 1936): 279-284, 314.

572. Hudson, David E. "Recent Decisions of the United States Supreme Court." *Federal Bar Association Journal* 2 (October 1936): 337-340, 370.

573. Hudson, David E. "Reviews of Decisions of the Supreme Court of the United States: October 1936 to June 1937." *Federal Bar Association Journal* 3 (November 1937): 77-82, 116.

574. Kennedy, Walter B. "What Is Wrong with the Supreme Court?" *Catholic Charities Review* 7 (May 1923): 172-175.

575. Klare, Karl E. "Judicial Deradicalization of the Wagner Act and the Origins of Modern Legal Consciousness, 1937-1941." *Minnesota Law Review* 62 (March 1978): 265-339.

576. Lerner, Max. "The Great Constitutional War." *Virginia Quarterly Review* 18 (Autumn 1942): 530-545.

577. Leuchtenburg, William E. "Constitutional Revolution of 1937." In *The Great Depression*, edited by Victor Hoar, 31-83. Toronto: Copp Clark, 1969.

578. Lumpkin, Alva M. "Some Observations Concerning Recent Decisions of the Supreme Court of the United States." *South Carolina Bar Association* (1935): 85-104.

579. Marshall, Rembert. "A Study of the Supreme Court of the United States." *Georgia Bar Association Proceedings* 1930 (1930): 128-147.

580. Mason, Alpheus T. "Supreme Court: Instrument of Power or Revealed Truth, 1930-1937." *Boston University Law Review* 33 (June 1953): 279-336.

581. Mason, Alpheus T. *The Supreme Court: Vehicle of Revealed Truth or Power Groups, 1930-1937.* Boston: Boston University Press, 1953.

582. Mayer, Robert R. *The Court and the American Crisis, 1930-1952.* Millwood, NY: Associated Faculty Press, 1986.

583. Meador, Daniel J. "Alabama Cases in the Supreme Court of the United States, 1925-1953." *Alabama Lawyer* 16 (October 1955): 341-367.

584. Moore, Glenn E. "Recent Changes in the Supreme Court." *Federal Bar Association Journal* 3 (April 1939): 337-338, 346.

585. Moore, James W., and J. Benson Saks. "The Supreme Court: 1939 and 1940 Terms: Administrative Review and Pending Administrative Legislation." *Virginia Law Review* 27 (June 1941): 983-1050.

586. Moore, James W., and J. Benson Saks. "The Supreme Court: 1939 Term; Public Law." *Virginia Law Review* 27 (January 1941): 253-327.

587. Moore, James W., and Shirley Adelson. "The Supreme Court: 1938 Term." *Virginia Law Review* 26 (November 1939): 1-69; (April 1940): 697-758; (May 1940): 887-917.

588. Murphy, Paul L. *The Constitution in Crisis Times, 1918-1969.* New York: Harper and Row, 1972.

589. O'Brien, Kenneth B., Jr. "Education, Americanization, and the Supreme Court: The 1920s." *American Quarterly* 13 (Summer 1961): 161-171.

590. Oppenheimer, Reuben. "The Supreme Court and Administrative Law." *Columbia Law Review* 37 (January 1937): 1-42.

591. Oppenheimer, Reuben. "The Supreme Court and Administrative Law, 1936-1940." *Maryland Law Review* 5 (April 1941): 231-279.

592. Parrish, Michael E. "The Great Depression, the New Deal, and the American Legal Order." *Washington Law Review* 59 (September 1984): 723-750.

593. Phillips, Herbert S. "The Reaction of the Supreme Court to Emergency Legislation." *Florida Law Journal* 9 (January 1935): 223-232.

594. Pritchett, C. Herman. "Divisions of Opinion among Justices of the U.S. Supreme Court, 1939-1941." *American Political Science Review* 35 (October 1941): 890-897.

595. Rankin, J. Lee. "The Supreme Court, the Depression, and the New Deal: 1930-1941." *Nebraska Law Review* 40 (1961): 35-62.

596. Rankin, Robert S. "President Hoover and the Supreme Court." *South Atlantic Quarterly* 30 (October 1931): 427-438.

597. Schlesinger, Arthur M. *The Age of Roosevelt.* 3 vols. Boston: Houghton Mifflin, 1957-1960.

598. Sears, Kenneth C. "The Supreme Court and the New Deal: An Answer to Texas." *University of Chicago Law Review* 12 (February 1945): 140-178.

599. Spaulding, Thomas M. "The Supreme Court: 1937." *Michigan Quarterly Review* 2 (Winter 1963): 1-9.

600. Telford, George B. "The Supreme Court and the New Deal: An Analysis of Recent Supreme Court Decisions Affecting New Deal Legislation." Ph.D. diss., University of Iowa, 1938.

601. Tushnet, Mark V. "Sloppiness in the Supreme Court, October Term 1935-October Term 1944." *Constitutional Commentary* 3 (Winter 1986): 73-89.

602. Willis, Hugh E. "Constitution Making by the Supreme Court since March 29, 1937." *Indiana Law Journal* 15 (February 1940): 179-201.

603. Wolfe, Edwin P. "The Supreme Court: Then and Now." *St. John's Law Review* 15 (April 1941): 188-202.

604. Yarros, Victor S. "Progress and the Supreme Court." *American Federationist* 43 (June 1936): 616-619.

1941-1968

605. Acheson, Dean G. "Recollections of Service with the Federal Supreme Court." *Alabama Lawyer* 18 (October 1961): 355-366.

606. Barnum, David G. "The Supreme Court and Public Opinion: Judicial Decision Making in the Post-New Deal Period." *Journal of Politics* 47 (May 1985): 652-666.

607. Bartholomew, Paul C. "The Supreme Court of the United States, 1946-1956." *Southwestern Social Science Quarterly* 38 (December 1957): 195-205.

608. Bartholomew, Paul C. "The Supreme Court of the United States, 1952-1953." *Social Science* 29 (January 1954): 3-9.

609. Bartholomew, Paul C. "The Supreme Court of the United States, 1953-1954." *Social Science* 30 (January 1955): 9-16.

610. Bartholomew, Paul C. "The Supreme Court of the United States, 1954-1955." *Social Science* 31 (January 1956): 23-30.

611. Bartholomew, Paul C. "The Supreme Court of the United States, 1955-1956." *Social Science* 32 (January 1957): 21-31.

612. Bartholomew, Paul C. "The Supreme Court of the United States, 1956-1966." *American Bar Association Journal* 53 (August 1967): 729-731.

613. Bartholomew, Paul C. "The Supreme Court of the United States, 1956-1957." *Social Science* 33 (January 1958): 10-17.

614. Bartholomew, Paul C. "The Supreme Court of the United States, 1957-1958." *Social Science* 34 (January 1959): 15-23.

615. Bartholomew, Paul C. "The Supreme Court of the United States, 1959-1960." *Western Political Quarterly* 14 (March 1961): 5-16.

616. Bartholomew, Paul C. "The Supreme Court of the United States, 1960-1961." *Western Political Quarterly* 15 (March 1962): 33-45.

617. Bartholomew, Paul C. "The Supreme Court of the United States, 1961-1962." *Western Political Quarterly* 15 (December 1962): 652-660.

618. Bartholomew, Paul C. "The Supreme Court of the United States, 1962-1963." *Western Political Quarterly* 16 (December 1963): 757-770.

619. Bartholomew, Paul C. "The Supreme Court of the United States, 1963-1964." *Western Political Quarterly* 17 (December 1964): 595-607.

620. Bartholomew, Paul C. "The Supreme Court of the United States, 1964-1965." *Western Political Quarterly* 18 (December 1965): 741-754.

621. Bartholomew, Paul C. "The Supreme Court of the United States, 1965-1966." *Western Political Quarterly* 19 (December 1966): 705-718.

622. Bartholomew, Paul C. "The Supreme Court of the United States, 1966-1967." *Western Political Quarterly* 20 (December 1967): 841-855.

623. Bartholomew, Paul C. "The Supreme Court of the United States, 1967-1968." *Western Political Quarterly* 21 (December 1968): 570-576.

624. Bartholomew, Paul C. "The Supreme Court of the United States, 1968-1969."

Western Political Quarterly 23 (March 1970): 104-119.

625. Beaney, William M. "The Warren Court and the Political Process." *Michigan Law Review* 67 (December 1968): 343-352.

626. Beardsley, Charles A. "Address to the Supreme Court of the United States on the 150th Anniversary of Its First Session, February 1, 1940 at Washington, D.C." *Law Society Journal* 9 (February 1940): 15-17.

627. Berman, Daniel M. "Constitutional Issues and the Warren Court." *American Political Science Review* 53 (June 1959): 500-502.

628. Bickel, Alexander M. *Politics and the Warren Court.* New York: Harper and Row, 1965.

629. Bickel, Alexander M. "The Warren Court and the Idea of Progress." *Harvard Law School Bulletin* 21 (December 1969): 16-17.

630. Black, Charles L. "The Unfinished Business of the Warren Court." *Washington Law Review* 46 (October 1970): 3-45.

631. Bozell, L. Brent. *The Warren Revolution: Reflections on the Consensus Society.* New Rochelle, NY: Arlington House, 1966.

632. Brandwen, Maxwell. "U.S. Supreme Court: Current Criticism in Perspective." *Chitty's Law Journal* 8 (September/October 1958): 111-118, 120.

633. Cahill, Fred V., Jr. "United States Supreme Court, 1947-1948." *Oregon Law Review* 28 (December 1948): 26-53.

634. Chase, Harold W. "The Warren Court and Congress." *Minnesota Law Review* 44 (March 1960): 595-637.

635. Childress, Richard J. "The Supreme Court, 1961-1962: Analysis of the Principle Cases Adjudicated during the 1961-1962 Term." *Social Order* 12 (September 1962): 328-340.

636. Childress, Richard J., and John E. Dunsford. "The Supreme Court, 1957-1958." *Social Order* 8 (September 1958): 336-342.

637. Childress, Richard J., and John E. Dunsford. "The Supreme Court, 1958-1959." *Social Order* 9 (September 1959): 309-319.

638. Childress, Richard J., and John E. Dunsford. "The Supreme Court, 1959-1960." *Social Order* 10 (October 1960): 340-352.

639. Clark, Charles L., Jr. "The Unfinished Business of the Supreme Court." *University of Washington Law Review* 46 (October 1970): 3-45.

640. Cover, Robert M., and T. Alexander Aleinikoff. "Dialectical Federalism: *Habeas Corpus* and the Court." *Yale Law Journal* 86 (May 1977): 1035-1102.

641. Cox, Archibald. "Observations on the Supreme Court." *Harvard Law Record* 33 (November 16, 1961): 10-13.

642. Cox, Archibald. "The Supreme Court 1965 Term." *Harvard Law Review* 80 (November 1966): 91-272.

643. Cox, Archibald. *The Warren Court: Constitutional Decisions as an Instrument of Reform.* Cambridge: Harvard University Press, 1968.

644. Cranberg, Gilbert. "What Did the Supreme Court Say?" *Saturday Review* 50 (April 8, 1967): 90-92.

645. Currie, David P. "The Constitution in the Supreme Court: The Preferred-Position Debate, 1941-1946." *Catholic University Law Review* 37 (Fall 1987): 39-71.

646. Currie, David P. "The Constitution in the Supreme Court: The Second World War, 1941-1946." *Catholic University Law Review* 37 (Fall 1987): 1-37.

647. Cushman, Robert E. "Constitutional Law in 1940-1941: The Constitutional Decisions of the Supreme Court of the United States in the October Term, 1940." *American Political Science Review* 36 (April 1942): 263-289.

648. Cushman, Robert E. "Constitutional Law in 1941-1942: The Constitutional Decisions of the Supreme Court of the United States in the October Term, 1941." *American Political Science Review* 37 (April 1943): 263-289.

649. Cushman, Robert E. "Constitutional Law in 1942-1943: The Constitutional Decisions of the Supreme Court of the United States in the October Term, 1942." *American Political Science Review* 38 (April 1944): 266-288.

650. Cushman, Robert E. "Constitutional Law in 1943-1944: The Constitutional Decisions of the Supreme Court of the United States in the October Term, 1943." *American Political Science Review* 39 (April 1945): 392-398.

651. Cushman, Robert E. "Constitutional Law in 1944-1945: The Constitutional Decisions of the Supreme Court of the United States in the October Term, 1944." *American Political Science Review* 40 (April 1946): 231-255.

652. Cushman, Robert E. "Constitutional Law in 1945-1946: The Constitutional Decisions of the Supreme Court of the United States in the October Term, 1945." *American Political Science Review* 41 (April 1947): 248-270.

653. Cushman, Robert E. "Constitutional Law in 1946-1947: The Constitutional Decisions of the Supreme Court of the United States in the October Term, 1946." *American Political Science Review* 42 (June 1948): 469-485.

654. Cushman, Robert E., ed. "Ten Years of the Supreme Court, 1937-1947." *American Political Science Review* 41 (December 1947): 1142-1181.

655. Cushman, Robert E., ed. "Ten Years of the Supreme Court, 1937-1947." *American Political Science Review* 42 (February 1948): 32-67.

656. Daly, Charles B. "General Semantics and the Rule of *Stare Decisis* as Regards the Supreme Court of the United States since 1937." Ph.D. diss., New York University, 1953.

657. Daniels, Roger. *American Concentration Camps: A Documentary History of the Relocation and Incarceration of Japanese Americans, 1942-1946.* New York: Garland Publishing, 1989.

658. Dunsford, John E. "The Supreme Court, 1960-1961." *Social Order* 11 (October 1961): 356-370.

659. Dunsford, John E., and Richard J. Childress. "Attacks on the Supreme Court." *Social Order* 7 (December 1957): 453-459.

660. Fairman, Charles. "The Supreme Court 1955 Term." *Harvard Law Review* 70 (November 1956): 83-188.

661. Fellman, David. "Constitutional Law in 1947-1948: The Constitutional Decisions of the Supreme Court of the United States in the October Term, 1947." *American Political Science Review* 43 (April 1949): 275-308.

662. Fellman, David. "Constitutional Law in 1950-1951." *American Political Science Review* 46 (March 1952): 158-199.

663. Fellman, David. "Constitutional Law in 1951-1952." *American Political Science Review* 47 (March 1953): 126-170.

664. Fellman, David. "Constitutional Law in 1952-1953." *American Political Science Review* 48 (March 1954): 63-113.

665. Fellman, David. "Constitutional Law in 1953-1954." *American Political Science Review* 49 (March 1955): 63-106.

666. Fellman, David. "Constitutional Law

in 1954-1955." *American Political Science Review* 50 (March 1956): 43-100.

667. Fellman, David. "Constitutional Law in 1955-1956." *American Political Science Review* 51 (March 1957): 158-196.

668. Fellman, David. "Constitutional Law in 1956-1957." *American Political Science Review* 52 (March 1958): 140-191.

669. Fellman, David. "Constitutional Issues and the Warren Court." *American Political Science Review* 53 (June 1959): 500-502.

670. Fellman, David. "Constitutional Law in 1957-1958." *American Political Science Review* 53 (March 1959): 138-180.

671. Fellman, David. "Constitutional Law in 1958-1959 I." *American Political Science Review* 54 (March 1960): 167-199.

672. Fellman, David. "Constitutional Law in 1958-1959 II." *American Political Science Review* 54 (June 1960): 474-493.

673. Fellman, David. "Constitutional Law in 1959-1960." *American Political Science Review* 55 (March 1961): 112-135.

674. Foley, John P. *Natural Law, Natural Right, and the Warren Court.* Rome: Pontificia Studiorum Universitasa S. Thoma Aq., 1965.

675. Frank, John P. "United States Supreme Court, 1946-1947." *University of Chicago Law Review* 15 (Autumn 1947): 1-50.

676. Frank, John P. "United States Supreme Court: 1948-1949." *University of Chicago Law Review* 17 (Autumn 1949): 1-55.

677. Frank, John P. "United States Supreme Court: 1949-1950." *University of Chicago Law Review* 18 (Autumn 1950): 1-54.

678. Frank, John P. "United States Supreme Court: 1950-1951." *University of Chicago Law Review* 19 (Winter 1952): 165-236.

679. Frank, John P. "United States Supreme Court: 1951-1952." *University of Chicago Law Review* 20 (Autumn 1952): 1-68.

680. Frank, John P. *The Warren Court.* New York: Macmillan, 1964.

681. Franklin, Mitchell. "Contribution to an Explication of the Activity of the Warren Majority of the Supreme Court." *Buffalo Law Review* 24 (Spring 1975): 187-543.

682. Freund, Paul A. "Supreme Court under Attack." *University of Pittsburgh Law Review* 25 (October 1963): 1-7.

683. Friedman, W. "Property, Freedom, Security, and the Supreme Court of the United States." *Modern Law Review* 19 (September 1956): 461-477.

684. Friendly, Henry J. "Time and Tide in the Supreme Court." *Connnecticut Law Review* 2 (Winter 1969/1970): 213-221.

685. Galloway, Russell W., Jr. "The Early Years of the Warren Court: Emergence of Judicial Liberalism (1953-1957)." *Santa Clara Law Review* 18 (Summer 1978): 609-640.

686. Galloway, Russell W., Jr. "The Roosevelt Court: The Liberals Conquer (1937-1941) and Divide (1941-1946)." *Santa Clara Law Review* 23 (Spring 1983): 491-542.

687. Galloway, Russell W., Jr. "The Second Period of the Warren Court: The Liberal Trend Abates." *Santa Clara Law Review* 19 (Fall 1979): 947-984.

688. Galloway, Russell W., Jr. "Vinson Court: Polarization and Conservative Dominance." *Santa Clara Law Review* 22 (Spring 1982): 375-418.

689. Gibson, Dale. "And One Step Backward: The Supreme Court and Constitutional Law in the Sixties." *Canadian Bar Review* 53 (September 1975): 621-640.

690. Gimlin, Hoyt. "Challenging of Supreme Court." *Editorial Research Reports* 2 (October 1968): 741-760.

691. Glennon, Robert J. "Role of a Circuit Judge in Shaping Constitutional Law: Jerome Frank's Influence on the Supreme Court." *Arizona State Law Journal* 1978 (1978): 523-560.

692. Goodman, Elaine, and Walter Goodman. *The Rights of the People: The Major Decisions of the Warren Court.* New York: Farrar, Straus, and Giroux, 1971.

693. Griswold, Erwin N. "Fools Rush In." *New Jersey Law Journal* 82 (April 23, 1959): 1, 5-8.

694. Griswold, Erwin N. "The Supreme Court 1959 Term." *Harvard Law Review* 74 (November 1960): 81-94.

695. Groner, Samuel B. "Recent Supreme Court Decisions." *Federal Bar Journal* 12 (January 1952): 213-215.

696. Hanna, W. Clark. "An Attempted Appraisal of 'an Attempted Appraisal of the Warren Court'." *North Carolina Central Law Journal* 2 (Spring 1970): 110-114.

697. Harper, Fowler V. "Conflict of Laws: The 1946 Term of the Supreme Court of the United States." *Columbia Law Review* 47 (September 1947): 883-913.

698. Harris, Robert J. "Constitutional Law in 1948-1949." *American Political Science Review* 44 (March 1950): 23-46.

699. Harris, Robert J. "Constitutional Law in 1949-1950." *American Political Science Review* 45 (March 1951): 86-109.

700. Hayden, James J. "The Supreme Court: Newly Radical?" *Social Science* 39 (October 1964): 195-203.

701. Henkin, Louis. "Some Reflections on Current Constitutional Controversy." *University of Pennsylvania Law Review* 109 (March 1961): 637-662.

702. Henkin, Louis. "The Supreme Court, 1967 Term." *Harvard Law Review* 82 (November 1968): 63-92.

703. Henry, Samuel J., and Thomas O. Morris, Jr. "A Decade of Legislative History in the Supreme Court: 1950-1960." *Virginia Law Review* 46 (November 1960): 1408-1438.

704. Homire, James L., Mark H. Johnson, and Richard B. Allen. "Review of Recent Supreme Court Decisions." *American Bar Association Journal* 34 (June 1948): 497-502.

705. Howard, Robert L. "Constitutional Law Cases in the United States Supreme Court: 1941-1946." *Missouri Law Review* 11 (June 1946): 197-316.

706. "Image in the Mirror: The Functions of the Supreme Court Today as Reflected in Its Current Opinions." *Yale Law Journal* 56 (September 1947): 1356-1382.

707. Jacobs, Clyde E. "The Warren Court: After Three Terms." *Western Political Quarterly* 9 (December 1956): 937-954.

708. Johnson, Mark H., and Rowland L. Young. "Review of Recent Supreme Court Decisions." *American Bar Association Journal* 36 (May 1950): 398-403.

709. Kauper, Paul G. "A Look at the Burger Court and a Look Back at the Warren Court." *Law Quadrangle Notes* 17 (Winter 1973): 6-11.

710. Keefe, Arthur J. "Comments on the Supreme Court's Treatment of the Bill of Rights in the October 1956 Term." *Fordham Law Review* 26 (Autumn 1957): 468-505.

711. Kirkpatrick, Dick. *U.S. Supreme Court Upsets Tradition.* Washington, DC: U.S. Government Printing Office, 1967.

712. Kohlmeier, Louis M. *God Save This Honorable Court.* New York: Scribner's, 1972.

713. Kramer, Daniel C., and Robert Riga.

"The New York Court of Appeals and the United States Supreme Court, 1960-1976." *Publius* 8 (Fall 1978): 75-111.

714. Kurland, Gerald. *The Supreme Court under Warren.* Edited by D. Steve Rahmas. Charlotteville, NY: SamHar Press, 1973.

715. Kurland, Philip B. "Egalitarianism and the Warren Court." *Michigan Law Review* 68 (March 1970): 629-682.

716. Kurland, Philip B. "History and the Constitution: All or Nothing at All?" *Illinois Bar Journal* 75 (January 1987): 262-266.

717. Kurland, Philip B. *Politics, the Constitution, and the Warren Court.* Chicago: University of Chicago Press, 1970.

718. Kurland, Philip B. "The Supreme Court, 1963 Term." *Harvard Law Review* 78 (November 1964): 143-176.

719. Latham, Earl. *The Communist Controversy in Washington.* Cambridge: Harvard University Press, 1966.

720. Longaker, Richard P. "The Supreme Court: 1945 and 1960 Issues and Decisions." *Western Political Quarterly* 15 (September 1962): 44-45.

721. Losos, Joseph O. "The Supreme Court and Its Critics: Is the Court Moving Left?" *Review of Politics* 21 (July 1959): 495-510.

722. Lytle, Clifford M. *The Warren Court and Its Critics.* Tucson: University of Arizona Press, 1968.

723. McCloskey, Robert G. "Economic Due Process and the Supreme Court: An Exhumation and Reburial." *Supreme Court Review* 1962 (1962): 34-62.

724. McGrath, J. Howard. "Recent Decisions of the Supreme Court of the United States." *Arkansas Bar Association* 1946 (1946): 270-283.

725. Maidment, Richard A. "Policy in Search of Law: The Warren Court from *Brown* to *Miranda.*" *Journal of American Studies* 9 (December 1975): 301-320.

726. Meiklejohn, Donald. "Labels and Libertarians." *Ethics* 66 (October 1955): 51-60.

727. Mitau, G. Theodore. *Decade of Decision: The Supreme Court and the Constitutional Revolution, 1954-1964.* New York: Scribner's, 1967.

728. Moore, James W. "The Supreme Court: 1940, 1941 Terms; The Supreme Court and Judicial Administration." *Virginia Law Review* 28 (May 1942): 861-910.

729. Nolan, Jon D. "*Stare Decisis* and the Overruling of Constitutional Decisions in the Warren Years." *Utah Law Review* 4 (Fall 1969): 101-135.

730. Nutting, Charles B. "The New Court and the Spirit of Laws: A Clinical Study." *Georgetown Law Review* 30 (May 1942): 610-624.

731. Parrish, Michael E. "Cold War Justice: The Supreme Court and the Rosenbergs." *American Historical Review* 82 (October 1977): 805-842.

732. Parrish, Michael E. "The Hughes Court, the Great Depression, and the Historians." *Historian* 40 (February 1978): 286-308.

733. Pessen, Edward. "The *Rosenberg* Case Revisited: A Critical Essay on a Recent Scholarly Examination." *New York History* 65 (January 1984): 82-102.

734. Pickering, John W. "A Behavioral Analysis of the 1965 Term of the United States Supreme Court." *Southern Quarterly* 7 (April 1969): 323-344.

735. Pritchett, C. Herman. "The Coming of the New Dissent: The Supreme Court, 1942-1943." *University of Chicago Law Review* 11 (December 1943): 49-61.

736. Pritchett, C. Herman. *Congress Ver-*

sus the Supreme Court 1957-1960. Minneapolis: University of Minnesota Press, 1961.

737. Pritchett, C. Herman. "Dissent on the Supreme Court, 1943-1944." *American Political Science Review* 39 (February 1945): 42-54.

738. Pritchett, C. Herman. "The Divided Supreme Court, 1944-1945." *Michigan Law Review* 44 (December 1945): 427-442.

739. Pritchett, C. Herman. "The Supreme Court and Administrative Regulation, 1941-1944." *Iowa Law Review* 31 (November 1945): 103-123.

740. Pritchett, C. Herman. "The Warren Court: Turn to Liberalism." *Nation* 182 (July 14, 1956): 31-34.

741. Rice, Arnold. *The Warren Court, 1953-1969.* Millwood, NY: Associated Faculty Press, 1987.

742. Rodell, Fred. "The Warren Court...." *Frontier* 9 (November 1957): 11-12.

743. Rosenberg, Julius. *Supreme Court of the United States, October Term, 1951.* New York: Committee to Secure Justice for Morton Sobell, 1960.

744. Rosenwein, Samuel, et al. "Review of the 1960 Term." *Law in Transition* 21 (Fall 1961): 141-205; (Winter 1962): 219-249.

745. Rossman, George, ed. "Review of Recent Supreme Court Decisions." *American Bar Association Journal* 38 (October 1952): 848-856.

746. Rossman, George, ed. "Review of Recent Supreme Court Decisions." *American Bar Association Journal* 41 (September 1955): 845-853.

747. Rossman, George, ed. "Review of Recent Supreme Court Decisions." *American Bar Association Journal* 42 (September 1956): 856-859.

748. Rossman, George, ed. "Review of Recent Supreme Court Decisions." *American Bar Association Journal* 44 (September 1958): 881-886.

749. Rossman, George, ed. "Review of Recent Supreme Court Decisions." *American Bar Association Journal* 45 (September 1959): 963-970.

750. Rossman, George, ed. "Review of Recent Supreme Court Decisions." *American Bar Association Journal* 46 (September 1960): 1010-1015.

751. Sayler, Richard H., Barry B. Boyer, and Robert E. Gooding, Jr., eds. *The Warren Court: A Critical Analysis.* New York: Chelsea House, 1969.

752. Schlesinger, Arthur M., Jr. "The Supreme Court, 1947." *Fortune* 35 (January 1947): 73-79, 201-202, 204-212.

753. Schubert, Glendon A. "Civilian Control and *Stare Decisis* in the Warren Court." In *Judicial Decision-Making,* by Glendon A. Schubert, 55-77. New York: Free Press, 1963.

754. Schubert, Glendon A. "The 1960 Term of the Supreme Court: A Psychological Analysis." *American Political Science Review* 56 (March 1962): 90-107.

755. Schwartz, Bernard. *Inside the Warren Court.* Garden City, NY: Doubleday, 1983.

756. Schwartz, Bernard. "More Unpublished Warren Court Opinions." *Supreme Court Review* 1986 (1986): 889-926.

757. Schwartz, Bernard. "The Supreme Court: October 1956 Term." *New York University Law Review* 32 (November 1957): 1202-1241.

758. Schwartz, Bernard. "The Supreme Court: October 1957 Term." *Michigan Law Review* 57 (January 1959): 315-348.

759. Schwartz, Bernard. *The Unpublished Opinions of the Warren Court.* New York: Oxford University Press, 1985.

760. Schwartz, Bernard. "Warren Court: An Opinion." *New York Times Magazine* 106 (June 30, 1957): 10-11.

761. Silver, Isidore. "Warren Court Critics: Where Are They Now That We Need Them?" *Hastings Constitutional Law Quarterly* 3 (Spring 1976): 373-452.

762. Simmons, Stephen J. "The Warren Court and Civil Liberties." *Howard Law Journal* 18 (1975): 610-638.

763. Spaeth, Harold J. *The Warren Court: Cases and Commentary*. San Francisco: Chandler, 1966.

764. Starr, Isadore. *The Supreme Court and Contemporary Issues*. Chicago: Encyclopedia Britannica Educational Corporation, 1969.

765. Strong, Frank R. "Trends in Supreme Court Interpretation of Constitution and Statute." *Wayne Law Review* 6 (Summer 1960): 285-310.

766. Swartz, Barbara J. "Denaturalization of Nazi War Criminals after *Fedorenko*." *New York University Journal of International Law and Politics* 15 (Fall 1982): 169-194.

767. Swindler, William F. "The Warren Court: Completion of a Constitutional Revolution." *Vanderbilt Law Review* 23 (March 1970): 205-250.

768. Swisher, Carl B. "The Supreme Court and the South." *Journal of Politics* 10 (May 1948): 282-305.

769. Thompson, Dennis L. "The Kennedy Court: Left and Right of Center." *Western Political Quarterly* 26 (June 1973): 263-279.

770. Tipton, S. Victor. "Warren Court Versus the Burger Court." *Florida Bar Journal* 48 (August 1974): 560-563.

771. Tugwell, Rexford G. "Reflections on the Warren Court." *Center Magazine* 6 (January/February 1973): 59-64.

772. Watson, Harold F., and Rowland L. Young. "Review of Recent Supreme Court Decisions." *American Bar Association Journal* 37 (May 1951): 369-373.

773. Weissman, David L. "The Warren Court and Its Critics." *Progressive* 23 (May 1959): 21-24.

774. White, G. Edward. "The Mosaic of the Warren Court: Frankfurter, Black, Warren, and Harlan." In *The American Judicial Tradition*, by G. Edward White, 317-368. New York: Oxford University Press, 1988.

775. White, J. Patrick. "The Warren Court under Attack: The Role of the Judiciary in a Democratic Society." *Maryland Law Review* 19 (Summer 1959): 181-199.

776. Woolsey, Mark H. "Business and the Warren Court." *Fortune* 50 (October 1954): 129-211.

777. Woolsey, Mark H. " 'Business-Minded' Supreme Court?" *Ohio State Bar Association Report* 26 (October 19, 1953): 701-706.

778. Woolsey, Mark H. "The Supreme Court: 1950-1951." *Ohio Bar* 23 (December 4, 1950): 687-691.

779. Woolsey, Mark H. "United States Supreme Court: 1951-1952." *Ohio Bar* 24 (December 24, 1951): 783-788.

780. Wright, Benjamin F. "Rights of Majorities and of Minorities in the 1961 Term of the Supreme Court." *American Political Science Review* 57 (March 1963): 98-115.

781. Young, Rowland L. "Review of Recent Supreme Court Decisions." *American Bar Association Journal* 35 (June 1949): 494-497.

782. Young, Rowland L. "Review of Recent Supreme Court Decisions." *American Bar Association Journal* 38 (June 1952): 494-502.

783. Zlinkoff, Sergei S., and Robert C. Barnard. "The Supreme Court and a

Competitive Economy: 1946 Term." *Columbia Law Review* 47 (September 1947): 914-952.

1969-1980

784. Alschuler, Albert W. "Failed Pragmatism: Reflections on the Burger Court." *Harvard Law Review* 100 (April 1987): 1436-1456.

785. Anastaplo, George. "Legal Realism: The New Journalism and *The Brethren*." *Duke Law Journal* 1983 (November 1983): 1045-1074.

786. Association of American Law Schools. *The Burger Court: Reflections on the First Decade*. Durham, NC: School of Law, Duke University, 1980.

787. Bartholomew, Paul C. "The Supreme Court of the United States, 1969-1970." *Western Political Quarterly* 23 (December 1970): 854-869.

788. Bartholomew, Paul C. "The Supreme Court of the United States, 1970-1971." *Western Political Quarterly* 24 (December 1971): 687-701.

789. Bartholomew, Paul C. "The Supreme Court of the United States, 1971-1972." *Western Political Quarterly* 25 (December 1972): 761-788.

790. Bartholomew, Paul C. "The Supreme Court of the United States, 1972-1973." *Western Political Quarterly* 27 (March 1974): 164-181.

791. Bellow, Gary. "The Trouble with the Burger Court." *Working Papers for a New Society* 6 (September/October 1978): 16, 18, 21, 78-80.

792. Berns, Walter. "Has the Burger Court Gone Too Far?" *Commentary* 78 (October 1984): 27-33.

793. Blasi, Vincent, ed. *The Burger Court: The Counter-Revolution That Wasn't.*

New Haven, CT: Yale University Press, 1986.

794. Choper, Jesse H., Yale Kamisar, Laurence H. Tribe, and Dorothy Opperman, eds. *The Supreme Court: Trends and Developments, 1979-1980*. Minneapolis: National Practice Institute, 1981.

795. Currie, David P. "Supreme Court and Federal Jurisdiction: 1975 Term." *Supreme Court Review* 1976 (1976): 183-219.

796. Dellinger, Walter E., and Michael L. Chartan, eds. "The Burger Court: Reflections on the First Decade." *Law and Contemporary Problems* 43 (Summer 1980): 1-135.

797. Dorsen, Norman. "The United States Supreme Court: Trends and Prospects." *Harvard Civil Rights-Civil Liberties Law Review* 21 (Winter 1986): 1-26.

798. Eagleton, Thomas F. "Rights without Remedies: The Burger Court in Full Bloom." *Washington University Law Quarterly* 63 (Fall 1985): 365-376.

799. Eubank, William L. "The First Five Years of the Burger Court: Policies and Attitudes." Ph.D diss., University of Oregon, 1978.

800. Fein, Bruce E. *Significant Decisions of the Supreme Court: 1971-1972 Term*. Washington, DC: American Enterprise Institute for Public Policy Research, 1972.

801. Fein, Bruce E. *Significant Decisions of the Supreme Court: 1975-1976 Term*. Washington, DC: American Enterprise Institute for Public Policy Research, 1977.

802. Fein, Bruce E. *Significant Decisions of the Supreme Court: 1978-1979 Term*. Washington, DC: American Enterprise Institute for Public Policy Research, 1980.

803. Fein, Bruce E. *Significant Decisions of the Supreme Court: 1979-1980 Term*. Littleton, CO: Fred B. Rothman, 1985.

804. Fiscus, Ronald J. "Studying *The Brethren*: The Legal-Realist Bias of Investigative Journalism." *American Bar Foundation Research Journal* 1984 (Spring 1984): 487-503.

805. Flax, Karen H. "Liberty, Property, and the Burger Court: The Entitlement Doctrine in Transition." *Tulane Law Review* 60 (May 1986): 889-926.

806. Gabel, Peter. "The Mass Psychology of the New Federalism: How the Burger Court's Political Imagery Legitimizes the Privatization of Everyday Life." *George Washington Law Review* 52 (January 1984): 263-271.

807. Galloway, Russell W., Jr. "The Burger Court (1969-1986)." *Santa Clara Law Review* 27 (Winter 1987): 31-59.

808. Galub, Arthur. *The Burger Court, 1968-1984*. Millwood, NY: Associated Faculty Press, 1985.

809. Gazell, James A. "Federal District Court Caseloads in the Burger Era: Rearguard Tactics in a Losing War?" *Southwestern University Law Review* 13 (1983): 699-722.

810. Gelfand, M. David. "Burger Court and the New Federalism: Preliminary Reflections on the Roles of Local Government Actors in the Political Dramas of the 1980s." *Boston College Law Review* 21 (May 1980): 763-850.

811. Ginger, Ann F. "The Nixon-Burger Court and What to Do about It." *National Lawyer's Guild Practitioner* 33 (Fall 1976): 143-151.

812. Greene, Evalyn. "Chief Justice Burger's Administrative Agenda: A Chronology of His Speeches Made Available through Legal Publications and the Media, with Noteworthy Responses, 1969-1986." *Law Library Journal* 80 (Fall 1988): 665-684.

813. Gunther, Gerald. "Reflections on the Burger Court." *Stanford Lawyer* 19 (Spring 1985): 4-9.

814. Gunther, Gerald. "The Supreme Court, 1971 Term." *Harvard Law Review* 86 (November 1972): 1-49.

815. Handberg, Roger B., Jr. "The 1974 Term of the United States Supreme Court." *Western Political Quarterly* 29 (June 1976): 298-312.

816. Handberg, Roger B., Jr., and William S. Maddox. "Public Support for the Supreme Court in the 1970s." *American Politics Quarterly* 10 (July 1982): 333-346.

817. Higdon, Philip R. "Burger Court and the Media: A Ten Year Perspective." *Western New England Law Review* 2 (Spring 1980): 593-680.

818. Hodder-Williams, Richard. "Is There a Burger Court?" *British Journal of Political Science* 9 (April 1979): 173-200.

819. Hutchins, Robert M. "The New Supreme Court." *Center Magazine* 5 (September/October 1972): 12-23.

820. Jones, Urban L. "The Burger Court: A Behavioral Analysis." Ph.D. diss., University of Missouri, 1978.

821. Kelley, Dean M. "'Let Them Eat Cake', Says the Supreme Court." *Christian Century* 97 (August 27/September 3, 1980): 820-824.

822. Kupferberg, Seth. "Don't Blame the Court." *Washington Monthly* 9 (October 1977): 40-43.

823. Kurland, Philip B. "Enter the Burger Court: The Constitutional Business of the Supreme Court, October Term 1969." *Supreme Court Review* 1970 (1970): 1-92.

824. Kurland, Philip B. "1970 Term: Notes on the Emergence of the Burger Court." *Supreme Court Review* 1971 (1971): 265-295.

825. Kurland, Philip B. "1971 Term: The

Year of the Stewart-White Court." *Supreme Court Review* 1972 (1972): 181-203.

826. Kurland, Philip B., ed. *The Supreme Court Review, 1976*. Chicago: University of Chicago Press, 1977.

827. LaMorte, Michael W. "The Burger Court: Its Liberal/Conservative Attitude toward Educational Issues." *NOLPE School Law Journal* 7 (1977): 153-177.

828. Laughlin, Stanley K., Jr. "The Burger Court and the United States Territories." *University of Florida Law Review* 36 (Fall 1984): 755-816.

829. Lehmann, Michael P., and Mary C. Eklund. "Constitutional Review: Supreme Court 1976-1977 Term." *Hastings Constitutional Law Quarterly* 5 (Winter 1978): 61-419.

830. Levy, Martin L. "*The Brethren*: A Reader's Guide to the Innersanctums of the Supreme Court." *Texas Southern University Law Review* 6 (1981): 397-418.

831. Lukoff, Roger M. "Constitutional Scholars Appraise Supreme Court." *Trial* 20 (November 1984): 65-68.

832. Mason, Alpheus T. "The Burger Court in Historical Perspective." *New York State Bar Journal* 47 (February 1975): 87-91.

833. Mason, Alpheus T. "The Burger Court in Historical Perspective." *Political Science Quarterly* 89 (March 1974): 27-45.

834. Melone, Albert P. "A Political Scientist Writes in Defense of *The Brethren*." *Judicature* 64 (September 1980): 140-144.

835. Nolte, M. Chester. *Supreme Court Stabilizing, Moving Right*. Baton Rouge: Louisiana State University, 1974.

836. Nowak, John E. "Constitutional Review: Foreword: Evaluating the Work of the New Libertarian Supreme Court; Supreme Court Review: 1978-1979 Term." *Hastings Constitutional Law Journal* 7 (Winter 1980): 263-523.

837. Paulsen, Monrad G. "Some Insights into the Burger Court." *Oklahoma Law Review* 27 (Fall 1974): 677-684.

838. Regan, Richard J. "Supreme Court Roundup: 1978 Term." *Thought* 54 (December 1979): 393-404.

839. Rosenberg, Yale L. "Notes from the Underground: A Substantive Analysis of Summary Adjudication by the Burger Court: Part 1." *Houston Law Review* 19 (May 1983): 607-693.

840. Rosenberg, Yale L. "Notes from the Underground: A Substantive Analysis of Summary Adjudication by the Burger Court: Part 2." *Houston Law Review* 19 (July 1983): 831-897.

841. Saphire, Richard B. "Value of *The Brethren*: A Response to the Critics." *Texas Law Review* 58 (November 1980): 1475-1497.

842. Schultz, Marjorie S. "The Jury Redefined: A Review of Burger Court Decisions." *Law and Contemporary Problems* 43 (Autumn 1980): 8-23.

843. Schwartz, Herman. *The Burger Years: Rights and Wrongs in the Supreme Court 1969-1986*. New York: Penguin, 1988.

844. Sherrill, Robert. "Burger's Court Feathers Its Nest." *Nation* 226 (June 24, 1978): 750-753.

845. Simon, James F. *In His Own Image: The Supreme Court in Richard Nixon's America*. New York: David McKay, 1973.

846. Swindler, William F. "Burger Court, 1969-1979: Continuity and Contrast." *Kansas Law Review* 28 (Fall 1979): 99-110.

847. Taylor, Telford, Jack Greenberg, Harriet F. Pilpel, and Monrad G. Paulsen. "Burger Court and the Constitution: Fifteenth Annual Columbia Law

Symposium." *Columbia Journal of Law and Social Problems* 11 (Fall 1974): 35-71.

848. Tigar, Michael E. "The Supreme Court, 1969 Term, Foreword: Waiver of Constitutional Rights; Disquiet in the Citadel." *Harvard Law Review* 84 (November 1970): 1-29.

849. Tribe, Laurence H. "The Supreme Court, 1972 Term, Foreword: Toward a Model of Roles in the Due Process of Life and Law." *Harvard Law Review* 87 (November 1973): 1-54.

850. Tushnet, Mark V. "And Only Wealth Will Buy You Justice: Some Notes on the Supreme Court 1972 Term." *Wisconsin Law Review* 1974 (1974): 177-197.

851. Vieira, Norman. "Journalists in the Supreme Court: A Review of *The Brethren*." *Idaho Law Review* 16 (Spring 1980): 235-245.

852. Waltz, Jon R. "The Burger/Blackmun Court." *New York Times Magazine* 120 (December 6, 1970): 60-80.

853. Wasby, Stephen L. "Certain Conservatism or Mixed Surprise? Civil Liberties in the Burger Court, 1976-1977." *Civil Liberties Review* 4 (November/December 1977): 33-51.

854. Wasby, Stephen L. *Continuity and Change: From the Warren Court to the Burger Court.* Pacific Palisades, CA: Goodyear Publishing Company, 1976.

855. Wilber, Leon A. "Development of Constitutional Law in the Supreme Court, 1966 to 1971: Civil Aspects." *Southern Quarterly* 11 (July 1973): 317-344.

856. Woodward, Bob, and Scott Armstrong. *The Brethren: Inside the Supreme Court.* New York: Simon and Schuster, 1979.

857. Wright, J. Skelly. "Selected Topics: United States Supreme Court 1977-1978 Term." *American Criminal Law Review* 16 (Winter 1978): 1-2.

1981-1989

858. Bernstein, Sidney. "Supreme Court Review." *Trial* 19 (October 1983): 26.

859. Bernstein, Sidney. "Supreme Court Review." *Trial* 19 (November 1983): 20.

860. Bernstein, Sidney. "Supreme Court Review." *Trial* 21 (April 1985): 14-15.

861. Bernstein, Sidney. "Supreme Court Review." *Trial* 21 (November 1985): 103-104.

862. Blaze, Douglas A. "The Nomination of Robert Bork: Revisiting the Constitution." *Arizona State Law Journal* 19 (1987): 467-474.

863. Bushman, Dave. *Supreme Court Highlights, 1982.* St. Paul, MN: West Publishing Company, 1983.

864. Bushman, Dave. *Supreme Court Highlights, 1984: Cases Decided by the Court during the 1982-1983 Term.* St. Paul, MN: West Publishing Company, 1984.

865. Bushman, Dave. *Supreme Court Highlights, 1985: Cases Decided by the Court during the 1983-1984 Term.* St. Paul, MN: West Publishing Company, 1985.

866. Cover, Robert M. "The Supreme Court, 1982 Term, Foreword: *Nomos* and Narrative." *Harvard Law Review* 97 (November 1983): 31-306.

867. Dworkin, Ronald. "Reagan Justice (The Supreme Court)." *New York Review of Books* 17 (1984): 27-33.

868. Easterbrook, Frank H. "The Supreme Court, 1983 Term, Foreword: The Court and the Economic System." *Harvard Law Review* 98 (November 1984): 4-60.

869. Epstein, Richard A. "The Supreme Court, 1987 Term, Foreword: Unconstitutional Conditions, State Power, and the Limits of Consent." *Harvard Law Review* 102 (November 1988): 1-358.

870. Erickson, William H. "1981-1982 U.S. Supreme Court Decisions." *Trial* 18 (November 1982): 44-49.

871. Galloway, Russell W., Jr. "The October 1984 Term: A Courtwatcher's Perspective." *Santa Clara Law Review* 26 (Spring 1986): 355-379.

872. Goldstein, Steven M. "Selected Federal Litigation Concerns: The 1982-1983 Supreme Court Term." *Clearinghouse Review* 17 (January 1984): 1071-1079.

873. Kurland, Philip B., and Dennis J. Hutchinson. "The Business of the Supreme Court: October Term 1982." *University of Chicago Law Review* 50 (Spring 1983): 628-651.

874. Kurland, Philip B., Gerhard Casper, and Dennis J. Hutchinson. *The Supreme Court Review, 1985.* Chicago: University of Chicago Press, 1986.

875. McDowell, Gary L. "The Supreme Court in Review: 1981 Term." *Teaching Political Science* 10 (Winter 1982/1983): 70-76.

876. Meador, Daniel J. "American Courts in the Bicentennial Decade and Beyond." *Mississippi Law Journal* 55 (March 1985): 1-20.

877. Minow, Martha. "The Supreme Court, 1986 Term, Foreword: Justice Engendered." *Harvard Law Review* 101 (November 1987): 10-370.

878. Morley, Jay. "Reagan v. Walsh." *Nation* 246 (April 23, 1988): 546-557.

879. Owles, Derrick. "Term Report for the U.S. Supreme Court." *New Law Journal* 133 (December 23, 1983): 1137-1139.

880. Regan, Richard J. "Supreme Court Roundup: 1980 Term." *Thought* 56 (December 1981): 491-502.

881. Regan, Richard J. "Supreme Court Roundup: 1982 Term." *Thought* 58 (December 1983): 472-483.

882. Regan, Richard J. "Supreme Court Roundup, 1983 Term." *Thought* 60 (March 1985): 99-111.

883. Silas, Faye A. "Meese Rips Court: Charges Unclear Direction." *American Bar Association Journal* 71 (September 1985): 17.

884. Stephan, Paul B., III. *Significant Decisions of the Supreme Court, 1980-1981 Term.* Littleton, CO: Fred B. Rothman, 1985.

885. Stone, Geoffrey R. "October Term 1983 and the Era of Aggressive Majoritarianism: A Court in Transition." *Georgia Law Review* 19 (Fall 1984): 15-30.

886. Wald, Patricia M. "Some Observations on the Use of Legislative History in the 1981 Supreme Court Term." *Iowa Law Review* 68 (January 1983): 195-216.

887. White, Charles. "Courtly Manners: The Term in Review." *American Lawyer* 3 (October 1981): 66-67.

888. Young, Rowland L. "Final Decisions of 1980-1981 Term Deal with Specialties." *American Bar Association Journal* 67 (November 1981): 1524-1526.

Constitution and the Court

889. Agresto, John. *Supreme Court and Constitutional Democracy.* Ithaca, NY: Cornell University Press, 1984.

890. Albertsworth, E. F. "The Federal Supreme Court and the Superstructure of the Constitution." *American Bar Association Journal* 16 (September 1930): 565-571.

891. Alston, Robert C. "Development of

the Federal Constitution." *Georgia Bar Association Report* 31 (1914): 100-120.

892. Ames, Herman V. *The Proposed Amendments to the Constitution of the United States during the First Century of Its History*. Washington, DC: U.S. Government Printing Office, 1897.

893. Anderson, William. "The Intention of the Framers: A Note on Constitutional Interpretation." *American Political Science Review* 49 (June 1955): 340-352.

894. Armstrong, Robert G. "Reply to Herbert Wechsler's Holmes Lecture, towards Neutral Principles of Constitutional Law." *Phylon* 21 (Fall 1960): 211-224.

895. Arnold, Joseph I. "Historic Roots of the Constitution." *Constitutional Review* 11 (July 1927): 151-160.

896. Association of American Law Schools. *Selected Essays on Constitutional Law*. 4 vols. Chicago: Foundation Press, 1938.

897. Association of American Law Schools. *Selected Essays on Constitutional Law, 1938-1962*. St. Paul, MN: West Publishing Company, 1963.

898. Bailey, Hollis R. "Origin of the United States Constitution." *Boston University Law Review* 7 (June 1927): 171-180.

899. Bailey, Josiah W. "Supreme Court, the Constitution, and the People." *Law Journal* 19 (August 1954): 373-379.

900. Baker, Fred A. *The Fundamental Law of American Constitutions*. 3 vols. Washington, DC: J. Byrne, 1916.

901. Bancroft, George. *History of the Formation of the Constitution of the United States of America*. 2 vols. New York: Appleton and Company, 1882.

902. Barnes, William R., and Arthur W. Littlefield, eds. *The Supreme Court Issue and the Constitution: Comments Pro and Con by Distinguished Men*. New York: Barnes and Noble, 1937.

903. Barnett, Vincent M., Jr. "Constitutional Interpretation and Judicial Self-Restraint." *Michigan Law Review* 39 (December 1940): 213-237.

904. Barrett, C. Waller. "The Miracle of the Constitution." *Supreme Court Historical Society Yearbook* 1978 (1978): 97-102.

905. Bauer, Elizabeth. *Commentaries on the Constitution, 1790-1860*. New York: Columbia University Press, 1952.

906. Beard, Charles A. *An Economic Interpretation of the Constitution of the United States*. New York: Macmillan, 1913.

907. Beard, Charles A. *The Supreme Court and the Constitution*. Englewood Cliffs, NJ: Prentice-Hall, 1962.

908. Beck, James M. *The Constitution of the United States: A Brief Study of the Genesis, Formulation, and Political Philosophy of the Constitution of the United States*. New York: Doran, 1922.

909. Beck, James M. *The Constitution of the United States: Yesterday, Today, and Tomorrow*. New York: Doran, 1924.

910. Beck, James M. *May It Please the Court*. Edited by Ollie R. McGuire. Freeport, NY: Essay Index Reprint Service, 1930.

911. Becker, Carl. *The Declaration of Independence: A Study in the History of Political Ideas*. New York: Knopf, 1942.

912. Bellot, Hugh H. *Texts Illustrating the Constitution of the Supreme Court of the United States and the Permanent Court of International Justice*. London: Sweet and Maxwell, 1921.

913. Berch, Michael A. "An Essay on the Role of the Supreme Court in the Adjudication of Constitutional Rights." *Arizona State Law Journal* 1984 (1984): 283-304.

914. Beth, Loren P. *The Constitution, Politics, and the Supreme Court*. New York: Harper and Row, 1962.

915. Beth, Loren P. *The Development of the American Constitution, 1877-1917.* New York: Harper and Row, 1971.

916. Bickel, Alexander M. "Notes on the Constitution." *Commentary* 69 (August 1975): 53-57.

917. Biggs, A. W. Crawford. "The Supreme Court of the United States." In *The Report of the Thirty-ninth Annual Meeting of the Maryland State Bar Association, Held at Atlantic City, NJ, June 28, 29, and 30, 1934,* 160-183. Baltimore, MD: Daily Record Company, 1934.

918. Black, Charles L. *Perspectives in Constitutional Law.* Rev. ed. Englewood Cliffs, NJ: Prentice-Hall, 1970.

919. Black, Charles L. "The Proposed Amendment of Article V: A Threatened Disaster." *Yale Law Journal* 72 (April 1963): 957-968.

920. Black, Charles L. *Structure and Relationship in Constitutional Law.* Baton Rouge: Louisiana State University Press, 1969.

921. Blake, Harold R. "The Compromises in the Federal Constitution." *Confederation of Veterans* 25 (July 1917): 309-314.

922. Bonfield, Arthur E. "The Guarantee Clause of Article IV, Section 4: A Study in Constitutional Desuetude." *Minnesota Law Review* 46 (January 1962): 513-572.

923. Boston, Charles A. "One Hundred and Forty-two Years of Government under the Constitution of the United States." *American Bar Association Journal* 17 (November 1931): 705-714, 767-773.

924. Boutwell, George S. *The Constitution of the United States at the End of the First Century.* Boston: Heath, 1895.

925. Braden, George D. "The Search for Objectivity in Constitutional Law." *Yale Law Journal* 57 (February 1948): 571-594.

926. Brant, Irving. *The Bill of Rights: Its Origin and Meaning.* Indianapolis: Bobbs-Merrill, 1965.

927. Brant, Irving. *Storm over the Constitution.* Indianapolis: Bobbs-Merrill, 1936.

928. Breckenridge, Ralph W. "The Constitution, the Court, and the People." *Yale Law Journal* 22 (January 1913): 181-202.

929. Bridwell, Randall, and Ralph U. Whitten. *The Constitution and the Common Law: The Decline of the Doctrines of Separation of Powers and Federalism.* Lexington, MA: D. C. Heath, 1977.

930. Brown, Everett S. *Ratification of the Twenty-first Amendment to the Constitution of the United States.* Ann Arbor, MI: American Constitutional and Legal History Service, 1938.

931. Brown, George S. "The Supreme Court's Duty to Defend the Constitution." *Washington Law Review* 14 (July 1939): 202-209.

932. Brown, Robert E. *Reinterpretation of the Formation of the American Constitution.* Boston: Boston University Press, 1963.

933. Bryant, Edwin E. "The Judicial Power." In *The Constitution of the United States, with Notes of the Decisions of the Supreme Court Thereon, from the Organization of Court till October 1900,* by Edwin E. Bryant, 221-243. Madison, WI: Democrat Printing Company, 1901.

934. Bullitt, William M. "The Supreme Court and the Constitution." *Michigan State Bar Journal* 7 (March 1928): 135-148.

935. Burdick, Charles K. *The Law of the American Constitution: Its Origin and Development.* New York: Putnam, 1922.

936. Burkhart, James A. *The Constitution and Its Judges.* Englewood Cliffs, NJ: Prentice-Hall, 1958.

937. Butowsky, Harry A. *United States*

Constitution: A National Historic Landmark Theme Study. Washington, DC: U.S. Government Printing Office, 1986.

938. Call, Joseph L. "The Constitution v. the Supreme Court." *Baylor Law Review* 11 (Fall 1959): 383-412.

939. Caplan, Russell L. "The History and Meaning of the Ninth Amendment." *Virginia Law Review* 69 (March 1983): 223-268.

940. Carson, Hampton L. "The Phases of Our Constitutional Growth as Guarded by the Supreme Court of the United States." *Case and Comment* 25 (June 1918): 3-13.

941. Chamberlain, John D. "Our Constitution and Its Makers." *Case and Comment* 24 (October 1917): 349-354.

942. Chandler, Julian A. *Genesis and Birth of the Federal Constitution: Addresses and Papers in the Marshall-Wythe School of Government and Citizenship of the College of William and Mary.* New York: Macmillan, 1924.

943. Choate, Joseph H. "The Supreme Court of the United States: Its Place in the Constitution." In *Abraham Lincoln, and Other Addresses in England,* by Joseph H. Choate, 157-195. New York: Century, 1910.

944. Clark, Ramsey. "Enduring Constitutional Issues." *Tulane Law Review* 61 (April 1987): 1093-1095.

945. Clark, Walter. "Is the Supreme Court Constitutional?" *Independent* 63 (September 26, 1907): 723-726.

946. Clark, Walter. "The Next Constitutional Convention of the United States: Some Defects in the Constitution; Necessity for a Constitutional Convention to Revise It, Address Delivered before the University of Pennsylvania, at Philadelphia, April 27, 1906." *Albany Law Journal* 68 (May 1906): 145-153.

947. Cooley, Thomas M. "The Federal Supreme Court: Its Place in the American Constitutional System." In *Constitutional History of the United States as Seen in the Development of American Law,* edited by Thomas M. Cooley, 28-52. New York: Putnam's, 1889.

948. Cooley, Thomas M. *A Treatise on the Constitutional Limitations Which Rest upon the Legislative Power of the States of the American Union.* Boston: Little, Brown, 1868.

949. Corwin, Edward S. "The Basic Doctrine of American Constitutional Law." *Michigan Law Review* 12 (February 1914): 247-276.

950. Corwin, Edward S. *A Constitution of Powers in a Secular State: Three Lectures of the William H. White Foundation at the University of Virginia, April 1950, and an Additional Chapter.* Charlottesville, VA: Michie, 1951.

951. Corwin, Edward S. *The Constitution of the United States of America.* Washington, DC: U.S. Government Printing Office, 1953.

952. Corwin, Edward S. *Constitutional Revolution, Ltd.* Claremont, CA: Associated College, 1941.

953. Corwin, Edward S. "The Debt of American Constitutional Law to Natural Law Concepts." *Notre Dame Lawyer* 25 (Winter 1950): 258-284.

954. Corwin, Edward S. "The 'Higher Law' Background of American Constitutional Law." *Harvard University Law Review* 42 (December 1928): 149-185, 365-409.

955. Corwin, Edward S. "The Progress of Constitutional Theory between the Declaration of Independence and the Meeting of the Philadelphia Convention." *American Historical Review* 30 (April 1925): 511-536.

956. Corwin, Edward S. *The Twilight of the Supreme Court: A History of Our Con-*

stitutional Theory. New Haven, CT: Yale University Press, 1934.

957. Corwin, Edward S., and Mary L. Ramsey. "The Constitutional Law of Constitutional Amendment." *Notre Dame Lawyer* 26 (Winter 1951): 185-213.

958. Crosskey, William W. *Politics and the Constitution in the History of the United States.* Chicago: University of Chicago Press, 1953.

959. Cushman, Robert E. *Supreme Court and the Constitution.* Washington, DC: Public Affairs Committee, 1940.

960. Davenport, Frederick M. "The Supreme Court Makes the Constitution March." *Boston University Law Review* 14 (November 1934): 752-765.

961. Dodd, Walter F. "The United States Supreme Court as the Final Interpreter of the Federal Constitution." *Illinois Law Review* 6 (December 1911): 289-312.

962. Dorsen, Norman, ed. *The Evolving Constitution: Essays on the Bill of Rights and the United States Supreme Court.* Middletown, CT: Wesleyan University Press, 1987.

963. Dowling, Noel T. *Cases on Constitutional Law.* 6th ed. Brooklyn, NY: Foundation Press, 1959.

964. Dumbauld, Edward. *The Constitution of the United States.* Norman: University of Oklahoma Press, 1964.

965. Durham, James A. "Congress, the Constitution, and Crosskey." *Indiana Law Journal* 29 (Spring 1954): 355-366.

966. Durham, James A. "Crosskey on the Constitution: An Essay Review." *California Law Review* 41 (Summer 1953): 209-229.

967. Eckhardt, Bob, and Charles L. Black. *The Tides of Power: Conversations on the American Constitution.* New Haven, CT: Yale University Press, 1976.

968. Elfenbein, Donald. "The Myth of Conservatism as a Constitutional Philosophy." *Iowa Law Review* 71 (January 1986): 401-488.

969. Evans, Medford. "The Court Versus the Constitution." *American Opinion* 16 (June 1973): 39-48.

970. Farrand, Max. *The Framing of the Constitution of the United States.* New Haven, CT: Yale University Press, 1913.

971. Fenn, Percy T. *The Development of the Constitution.* New York: Appleton and Company, 1948.

972. Ford, Paul L. *Essays on the Constitution of the United States.* New York: Burt Franklin, 1970.

973. Ford, Paul L., ed. *Pamphlets on the Constitution of the United States.* New York: Da Capo Press, 1968.

974. Forkosch, Morris D. "The Alternative Amending Clause in Article V: Reflections and Suggestions." *Minnesota Law Review* 51 (1967): 1053-1085.

975. Fraenkel, Osmond K. "What Can Be Done about the Constitution and the Supreme Court." *Columbia Law Review* 37 (February 1937): 212-226.

976. Freund, Paul A., Arthur E. Sutherland, Jr., Mark H. De Wolfe, and J. Brown. *Constitutional Law: Cases and Other Problems.* 2 vols. Boston: Little, Brown, 1954.

977. Friedman, Lawrence M. "The American Constitution: A Double Life." *University of Arkansas at Little Rock Law Journal* 10 (1987/1988): 257-274.

978. Friendly, Fred W., and Martha J. Elliott. *The Constitution, That Delicate Balance.* New York: Random House, 1984.

979. Gaugush, Bill. "Principles Governing the Interpretation and Exercise of Article 5 Powers." *Western Political Quarterly* 35 (June 1982): 212-221.

980. Goedecke, Robert. "What Are the

Principles of American Constitutional Law?" *Ethics* 78 (October 1967): 17-31.

981. Goldstein, Nathaniel L. "That Most Remarkable Work: The Constitution of the United States." *Notre Dame Lawyer* 28 (Winter 1953): 199-218.

982. Grinnell, Frank W. "Constitutional Amendments Proposed Relative to the Supreme Court of the United States." *Massachusetts Law Quarterly* 34 (October 1949): 33-38.

983. Guthrie, William D. "The Eleventh Article of Amendment to the Constitution of the United States." *Columbia Law Review* 8 (March 1908): 183-207.

984. Hall, Kermit L. *United States Constitutional and Legal History.* 20 vols. New York: Garland, 1989.

985. Hand, Learned. *The Bill of Rights.* Cambridge: Harvard University Press, 1958.

986. Harmon, M. Judd. *Essays on the Constitution of the United States.* Port Washington, NY: Kennikat Press, 1978.

987. Hendrick, Burton J. *Bulwark of the Republic: A Biography of the Constitution.* Boston: Little, Brown, 1937.

988. Henkin, Louis. *Foreign Affairs and the Constitution.* New York: W. W. Norton, 1972.

989. Hillhouse, James. *Proposition for Amending the Constitution of the United States Providing for the Election of President and Vice-President, and Guarding against the Undue Exercise of Executive Influence, Patronage, and Power.* Washington, DC: Gales and Seaton, 1830.

990. Hirsch, Robert S. *The Constitution and the Court: The Development of the Basic Law through Judicial Interpretation.* New York: Random House, 1963.

991. Hitchcock, Henry. "The Supreme Court and the Constitution." *Advocate* 2 (February 18, 1890): 77-82.

992. Hitchcock, Henry. "The Supreme Court and the Constitution." In *The Supreme Court of the United States*, part 2, by Hampton L. Carson, 626-664. Philadelphia: A. R. Keller Company, 1892.

993. Hockett, Homer C. *The Constitutional History of the United States.* 2 vols. New York: Macmillan, 1939.

994. Hofstadter, Richard. "Beard and the Constitution: The History of an Idea." *American Quarterly* 2 (Fall 1950): 195-213.

995. Howard, A. E. Dick. "Making It Work." *Wilson Quarterly* 11 (Summer 1987): 122-133.

996. Hunting, Warren B. *The Obligation of Contracts Clause of the United States Constitution.* Westport, CT: Greenwood Press, 1976.

997. Jameson, J. Franklin, ed. *Essays in the Constitutional History of the United States in the Formative Period, 1775-1789.* Boston: Houghton Mifflin, 1889.

998. Jennings, Newell. "The Constitution of the United States." *Connecticut Bar Journal* 9 (April 1935): 65-85.

999. Jensen, Merrill. *The Making of the American Constitution.* New York: Van Nostrand Reinhold, 1964.

1000. Jensen, Merrill, ed. *The Documentary History of the Ratification of the Constitution.* Madison: State Historical Society of Wisconsin, 1976.

1001. Jones, Alan. "Thomas M. Cooley and 'Laissez-Faire Constitutionalism': A Reconsideration." *Journal of American History* 53 (March 1967): 751-771.

1002. Jones, Walter B. "The American Constitution, Its Establishment and Purposes." *Alabama Lawyer* 9 (January 1948): 64-80.

1003. Kasson, John A. *The Evolution of the Constitution of the United States of*

America and History of the Monroe Doctrine. Boston: Houghton Mifflin, 1904.

1004. Katz, Arthur S. "The Philosophy of the First Ten Amendments: An Appraisal and a Plea." *Southern California Law Review* 25 (December 1951): 22-35.

1005. Katz, Stanley N. "The Origins of American Constitutional Thought." *Perspectives in American History* 3 (1969): 474-490.

1006. Kauper, Paul G. "The First Ten Amendments." *American Bar Association Journal* 37 (October 1951): 717-720, 780-784.

1007. Kelly, Alfred H., Winfred A. Harbison, and Herman Belz. *The American Constitution: Its Origins and Development.* 6th ed. New York: W. W. Norton, 1982.

1008. Kelsey, Rayner W. "The Constitution and the Supreme Court." *Nation* 98 (February 1914): 183.

1009. Konvitz, Milton R. *Bill of Rights Reader.* 5th ed. Ithaca, NY: Cornell University Press, 1973.

1010. Kurland, Philip B. *The Supreme Court and the Constitution: Essays in Constitutional Law from the Supreme Court Review.* Chicago: University of Chicago Press, 1965.

1011. Landon, Judson S. *The Constitutional History and Government of the United States.* 2d ed. Boston: Houghton Mifflin, 1905.

1012. Landynski, Jacob W. "The Making of Constitutional Law." *Social Research* 31 (Spring 1964): 23-44.

1013. Latham, Earl. *The Declaration of Independence and the Constitution.* Lexington, MA: D. C. Heath, 1964.

1014. Latham, Earl. "The Supreme Court and the Supreme People." *Journal of Politics* 16 (May 1954): 207-235.

1015. Lawther, Harry P. "The Making of

the Federal Constitution." *Texas Law Review* 11 (December 1932): 67-79.

1016. Lay, Donald P. "The Constitution, the Supreme Court, and Mr. Meese: *Habeas Corpus* and the Doctrine of Original Intent." *Detroit College of Law Review* 1986 (Winter 1986): 983-1002.

1017. Lee, Rex E. "The Provinces of Constitutional Interpretation." *Tulane Law Review* 61 (April 1987): 977-1095.

1018. Lerner, Max. "Constitution and Court as Symbols." *Yale Law Journal* 46 (June 1937): 1290-1319.

1019. Levinson, Sanford. "Could Meese Be Right This Time?" *Tulane Law Review* 61 (April 1987): 977-1095.

1020. Levy, Leonard W. *Judgements: Essays on American Constitutional History.* Chicago: Quadrangle Books, 1972.

1021. Levy, Leonard W., ed. *American Constitutional Law: Historical Essays.* New York: Harper and Row, 1966.

1022. Lewis, Leon R. *Democracy and the Law.* Washington, DC: Public Affairs Press, 1963.

1023. Llewellyn, Karl N. "The Constitution as an Institution." *Columbia Law Review* 34 (January 1934): 1-40.

1024. Lodge, Henry C. "The Constitution and Its Makers." *North American Review* 196 (July 1912): 20-57.

1025. Lodge, Henry C. *The Constitution and Its Makers: An Address Delivered before the Literary and Historical Association of North Carolina at Raleigh, NC, November 28, 1911.* Washington, DC: U.S. Government Printing Office, 1911.

1026. McArthur, John B. "Abandoning the Constitution: The New Wave in Constitutional Theory." *Tulane Law Review* 59 (December 1984): 280-334.

1027. McCloskey, Robert G., ed. *Essays in*

Constitutional Law. New York: Knopf, 1957.

1028. McDonald, Forrest. *We the People: The Economic Origins of the Constitution.* Chicago: University of Chicago Press, 1958.

1029. McDonald, Laughlin. "Has the Supreme Court Abandoned the Constitution?" *Saturday Review* 4 (May 28, 1977): 10-12.

1030. McLaughlin, Andrew C. *The Confederation and the Constitution 1783-1789.* New York: Harper and Brothers, 1907.

1031. McLaughlin, Andrew C. *A Constitutional History of the United States.* New York: Appleton-Century, 1936.

1032. McLaughlin, Andrew C. *The Foundations of American Constitutionalism.* New York: Peter Smith, 1932.

1033. Main, Jackson T. *The Antifederalists: Critics of the Constitution, 1781-1788.* Chapel Hill: University of North Carolina Press, 1961.

1034. Maltbie, William M. "Our Attitude to the Constitution." *Law Library Journal* 23 (July 1930): 104-111.

1035. Martin, Philip L. "Madison's Precedent of Legislative Ratification for Constitutional Amendments." *American Philosophical Society Proceedings* 109 (February 18, 1965): 47-52.

1036. Martineau, Robert J., Jr. "Interpreting the Constitution: The Use of International Human Rights Norms." *Human Rights Quarterly* 5 (February 1983): 87-107.

1037. Meese, Edwin. "The Law of the Constitution." *Tulane Law Review* 61 (April 1987): 977-1095.

1038. Meigs, William M. *The Growth of the Constitution in the Federal Convention of 1787, an Effort to Trace the Origin and Development of Each Separate Clause from Its Suggestion in That Body to the Form Finally Approved, Containing Also a Fascimile of a Heretofore Unpublished Manuscript of the First Draft of the Instrument Made for Use in the Committee of Detail.* Philadelphia: Lippincott, 1900.

1039. Meigs, William M. *The Relation of the Judiciary to the Constitution.* New York: Da Capo Press, 1971.

1040. Melvin, Frank E. "The Judicial Bulwark of the Constitution." *American Political Science Review* 8 (May 1914): 167-203.

1041. Miller, Arthur S. "Bill of Rights to Protect Our Liberties?" *Political Quarterly* 47 (April 1976): 137-148.

1042. Miller, Arthur S. *Politics, Democracy, and the Supreme Court: Essays on the Frontier of Constitutional Theory.* Westport, CT: Greenwood Press, 1985.

1043. Miller, Arthur S. *Social Change and Fundamental Law: America's Evolving Constitution.* Westport, CT: Greenwood Press, 1979.

1044. Miller, Arthur S. *The Supreme Court and the Living Constitution.* Washington, DC: Lerner Law Book Company, 1969.

1045. Mitchell, Broadus, and Louise P. Mitchell. *A Biography of the Constitution of the United States.* New York: Oxford University Press, 1964.

1046. Miyakawa, Masuji. *Powers of the American People, Congress, President and Courts, According to Evolution of Constitutional Construction.* Washington, DC: Wilkens-Sheiry Company, 1906.

1047. Monaghan, Henry P. "Professor Jones and the Constitution." *Vermont Law Review* 4 (Spring 1979): 87-93.

1048. Monroe, Alan H. "Supreme Court and the Constitution." *American Political Science Review* 18 (November 1924): 737-759.

1049. Mott, Kenneth F. *The Supreme*

Court and the Living Constitution. Lanham, MD: University Press of America, 1981.

1050. Murphy, Walter F. "The Constitution: Interpretation and Intent." *American Bar Association Journal* 45 (June 1958): 592-595.

1051. Murphy, Walter F. "Constitutional Interpretation: The Art of the Historian, Magician, or Statesman?" *Yale Law Journal* 87 (July 1978): 1752-1771.

1052. Nagel, Robert F. "A Comment on Democratic Constitutionalism." *Tulane Law Review* 61 (April 1987): 977-1095.

1053. Nichol, Gene R. "Ripeness and the Constitution." *University of Chicago Law Review* 54 (Winter 1987): 153-183.

1054. Nowak, John E. "The Scope of Congressional Power to Create Causes of Action against State Governments and the History of the Eleventh and Fourteenth Amendments." *Columbia Law Review* 75 (December 1975): 1413-1469.

1055. O'Hara, Barratt, and Marie Crowe. *Who Made the Constitution? With the Authority for the Charge of Usurpation by the Judges.* Chicago: privately published, 1936.

1056. Ostrom, Vincent. "The American Contribution to a Theory of Constitutional Choice." *Journal of Politics* 38 (August 1976): 56-78.

1057. Palfrey, John G. "The Constitution and the Courts." *Harvard Law Review* 26 (April 1913): 507-530.

1058. Papenfuse, Edward C. "An Undelivered Defense of a Winning Cause: Charles Carroll of Carrollton's 'Remarks on the Proposed Federal Constitution'." *Maryland Historical Magazine* 71 (Summer 1976): 220-251.

1059. Paschal, George W. *The Constitution of the United States Defined and Carefully Annotated.* 3d ed. Washington, DC: William H. Morrison, 1882.

1060. Patterson, C. Perry. "The Evolution of Constitutionalism." *Minnesota Law Review* 32 (April 1948): 427-457.

1061. Patterson, C. Perry. "The General Welfare Clause." *Minnesota Law Review* 20 (January 1946): 43-67.

1062. Patterson, C. Perry. *The Supreme Court and the Constitution.* Dallas: George F. and Ora Nixon Arnold Foundation, Southern Methodist University, 1936.

1063. Patterson, Christopher S. *The United States and the States under the Constitution.* 2d ed. Philadelphia: I. and J. W. Johnson, 1904.

1064. Peltason, Jack W. *Understanding the Constitution.* 4th ed. New York: Holt, Rinehart, and Winston, 1959.

1065. Pittman, Robert C. "The Law of the Land." *Journal of Public Law* 6 (Fall 1957): 444-454.

1066. Pollak, Louis H. *The Constitution and the Supreme Court: A Documentary History.* 2 vols. Cleveland: World Publishing, 1966.

1067. Pomeroy, John N. *An Introduction to the Constitution Law of the United States.* 9th ed. Boston: Houghton Mifflin, 1886.

1068. Powell, Thomas R. "Some Aspects of American Constitutional Law." *Harvard Law Review* 53 (February 1940): 529-553.

1069. Powell, Thomas R. "The Supreme Court and the Constitution, 1919-1920." *Political Science Quarterly* 35 (September 1920): 411-439.

1070. Powell, Thomas R. *The Supreme Court's Construction of the Federal Constitution in 1921.* Ann Arbor: Michigan Law Review Association, 1922.

1071. Powell, Thomas R. *Vagaries and*

Varieties in Constitutional Interpretation. New York: Columbia University Press, 1956.

1072. Prescott, Arthur T. *Drafting the Federal Constitution.* Baton Rouge: Louisiana State University Press, 1941.

1073. Pritchett, C. Herman. *The American Constitution.* 3d ed. New York: McGraw-Hill, 1977.

1074. Pritchett, C. Herman. *The Federal System in Constitutional Law.* Englewood Cliffs, NJ: Prentice-Hall, 1978.

1075. Rabkin, Jeremy. "Constitutional Roulette: Original Intent is Not the Issue." *American Spectator* 19 (May 1986): 14-16.

1076. Rawle, William. *A View of the Constitution of the United States of America.* 2d ed. Philadelphia: Philip H. Nicklin, 1829.

1077. Read, Conyers, ed. *The Constitution Reconsidered.* Rev. ed. New York: Harper and Row, 1968.

1078. Roche, John P. "The Founding Fathers: A Reform Caucus in Action." *American Political Science Review* 55 (December 1961): 799-816.

1079. Rodell, Fred. *Fifty-five Men.* New York: Telegraph, 1936.

1080. Rogers, A. K. "Constitutionalism." *International Journal of Ethics* 40 (April 1930): 289-304.

1081. Rosenblum, Victor G., and A. Didrick Castberg. *Cases on Constitutional Law: Political Roles of the Supreme Court.* Homewood, IL: Dorsey, 1973.

1082. Rossum, Ralph A. "Government and Ethics: The Constitutional Foundation." *Teaching Political Science* 11 (Spring 1984): 100-105.

1083. Rubin, W. B. "Constitution and the Supreme Court." *American Federationist* 29 (September 1922): 675-680.

1084. Russel, Robert R. "Constitutional Doctrine with Regard to Slavery in the Territories." *Journal of Southern History* 32 (1966): 466-486.

1085. Saphire, Richard B. "Constitutional Theory in Perspective: A Response to Professor Van Alstyne." *Northwestern University Law Review* 78 (February 1984): 1435-1462.

1086. Sargent, Noel. " 'Signers' and the Constitution." *Central Law Journal* 85 (December 7, 1917): 406-419.

1087. Scheiber, Harry N. "American Constitutional History and the New Legal History: Complementary Themes in Two Modes." *Journal of American History* 68 (September 1981): 337-350.

1088. Scheips, Paul J. "The Significance and Adoption of Article V of the Constitution." *Notre Dame Lawyer* 26 (Fall 1950): 46-67.

1089. Schmidhauser, John R. *Constitutional Law in American Politics.* Monterey, CA: Brooks and Cole, 1984.

1090. Schmidhauser, John R., ed. *Constitutional Law in the Political Process.* Chicago: Rand McNally, 1963.

1091. Schouler, James. *Constitutional Studies: State and Federal.* New York: Dodd, Mead, 1897.

1092. Schram, Glenn. "Critique of Contemporary Constitutionalism." *Comparative Politics* 11 (July 1979): 483-495.

1093. Schubert, Glendon A. *The Constitutional Polity.* Boston: Boston University Press, 1970.

1094. Schwartz, Bernard. *A Commentary on the Constitution of the United States.* 5 vols. New York: Macmillan, 1963-1968.

1095. Schwartz, Bernard. *From Confederation to Nation: The American Constitution, 1835-1877.* Baltimore: Johns Hopkins University Press, 1973.

1096. Schwartz, Bernard. *The Great*

Rights of Mankind: A History of the American Bill of Rights. New York: Oxford University Press, 1977.

1097. Schwartz, Bernard. *The Reins of Power: A Constitutional History of the United States.* New York: Hill and Wang, 1963.

1098. Schwartz, Bernard. *The Supreme Court: Constitutional Revolution in Retrospect.* New York: Ronald Press, 1957.

1099. Shaffer, Thomas I. "First Amendment: History and the Courts." *Review of Politics* 40 (April 1978): 271-279.

1100. Shalope, Robert E. "The Ideological Origins of the Second Amendment." *Journal of American History* 69 (December 1982): 599-614.

1101. Shapiro, Martin M. *The Supreme Court and Constitutional Rights: Readings in Constitutional Law.* Atlanta: Scott, Foresman, 1967.

1102. Shattuck, Charles E. "The True Meaning of the Term 'Liberty' in Those Clauses in the Federal and State Constitutions Which Protect Life, Liberty, and Property." *Harvard Law Review* 4 (March 15, 1891): 365-392.

1103. Siegan, Bernard. *The Supreme Court's Constitution.* New York: Transaction Books, 1987.

1104. Simon, Larry G. "The Authority of the Constitution and Its Meaning: A Preface to a Theory of Constitutional Interpretation." *Southern California Law Review* 58 (January 1985): 603-646.

1105. Simon, Larry G. "The Authority of the Framers of the Constitution: Can Originalist Interpretation Be Justified?" *California Law Review* 73 (October 1985): 1482-1539.

1106. Simson, Gary J. "The Role of History in Constitutional Interpretation: A Case Study." *Cornell Law Review* 70 (January 1985): 253-270.

1107. Smith, David G. *The Convention and the Constitution: The Political Ideas of the Founding Fathers.* New York: St. Martin's Press, 1965.

1108. Smith, F. Dumont. "Decisive Battles of Constitutional Law." *American Bar Association Journal* 9 (February 1923): 109-111; (March 1923): 165-167; (April 1923): 234-236; (May 1923): 315-317; (June 1923): 385-387; (July 1923): 446-448; (August 1923): 527-528; (October 1923): 649-652; (November 1923): 711-712; (December 1923): 807-810.

1109. Smith, Page. *The Constitution: A Documentary and Narrative History.* New York: Morrow, 1978.

1110. Stevens, C. Ellis. *Sources of the Constitution of the United States Considered in Relation to Colonial and English History.* New York: Macmillan, 1894.

1111. Stevens, J. Morgan. "The Constitution of the United States." *Mississippi Law Journal* 7 (April 1935): 338-350.

1112. Stimson, Frederic J. *The American Constitution: The National Powers, the Rights of the States, the Liberties of the People.* New York: Scribner's, 1908.

1113. Strong, Frank R. "Court v. Constitution: Disparate Distortions of the Indirect Limitations in the American Constitutional Framework." *North Carolina Law Review* 54 (January 1976): 125-172.

1114. Sunderland, Lane V. "Constitutional Theory and the Role of the Court: An Analysis of Contemporary Constitutional Commentary." *Wake Forest Law Review* 21 (1986): 855-900.

1115. Sutherland, Arthur E., Jr. *Constitutionalism in America: Origin and Evolution of Its Fundamental Ideas.* New York: Blaisdell, 1965.

1116. Sutherland, William A. *Notes on the Constitution of the United States Showing the Construction and Operation of the Constitution as Determined by the Federal Su-*

preme Court. San Francisco: Bancroft-Whitney Company, 1904.

1117. Swaney, W. B. "The Federal Constitution and First Ten Amendments." *Virginia Law Review* 11 (January 1924): 210-221.

1118. Swindler, William F. *Court and Constitution in the Twentieth Century: The Modern Interpretation.* Indianapolis: Bobbs-Merrill, 1974.

1119. Swindler, William F. *Court and Constitution in the Twentieth Century: The New Legality.* Indianapolis: Bobbs-Merrill, 1954.

1120. Swindler, William F. *Court and Constitution in the Twentieth Century: The Old Legality, 1889-1932.* Indianapolis: Bobbs-Merrill, 1970.

1121. Swindler, William F. "The Selling of the Constitution." *Supreme Court Historical Society Yearbook* 1980 (1980): 49-54.

1122. Swisher, Carl B. *The Growth of the Constitutional Power in the United States.* Chicago: University of Chicago Press, 1946.

1123. Taylor, Hannis. "The 125th Anniversary of the Drafting of the Constitution of the United States, 1787-1912." *Georgetown Law Journal* 1 (November 1912): 1-16.

1124. Taylor, John. *Construction Construed and Constitutions Vindicated.* Richmond, VA: Sheperd and Pollard, 1820.

1125. Taylor, John. *New Views of the Constitution of the United States.* Washington, DC: Way and Gideon, 1823.

1126. Thayer, James B. "The Origin and Scope of the American Doctrine of Constitutional Law." *Harvard Law Review* 7 (October 25, 1893): 129-156.

1127. Thorpe, Francis N. *The Constitutional History of the United States.* 3 vols. Chicago: Callaghan, 1901.

1128. Tiffany, Joel. *A Treatise on Government and Constitutional Law.* Albany, NY: W. C. Little, 1867.

1129. Towle, Nathaniel C. *A History and Analysis of the Constitution of the United States.* 3d ed. Boston: Little, Brown, 1871.

1130. Townsend, Edward W. *Our Constitution: Why and How It Was Made, Who Made It, and What It Is.* New York: Moffat, Yard, 1906.

1131. Trautman, Bertrand C. "Natural Law Concepts in the Decisions of the Supreme Court of the United States." Ph.D. diss., Harvard University, 1957.

1132. Tucker, John R. *The Constitution of the United States: A Critical Discussion of Its Genesis, Development, and Interpretation.* 2 vols. Chicago: Callaghan, 1899.

1133. Tugwell, Rexford G. *The Compromising of the Constitution: Early Departures.* Notre Dame, IN: University of Notre Dame, n.d.

1134. Tweed, Harrison. "Provisions of the Constitution Concerning the Supreme Court of the United States: Address." *Boston University Law Review* 31 (January 1951): 1-46.

1135. Van Alstyne, William W. "Notes on a Bicentennial Constitution: Part II, Antinomial Choices and the Role of the Supreme Court." *Iowa Law Review* 72 (July 1987): 1281-1299.

1136. Van Doren, Carl C. *The Great Rehearsal: The Story of the Making and Ratifying of the Constitution of the United States.* New York: Viking Press, 1948.

1137. Ward, Bernard J. "A Symposium: The Role of the Supreme Court." *American Bar Association Journal* 44 (June 1958): 534-537.

1138. Warren, Charles. *The Making of the Constitution.* Boston: Little, Brown, 1929.

1139. Wechsler, Herbert. *The Courts and*

the Constitution. Athens: University of Georgia School of Law, 1965.

1140. Wechsler, Herbert. "Courts and the Constitution." *Columbia Law Review* 65 (May 1965): 1001-1014.

1141. Wechsler, Herbert. "Toward Neutral Principles of Constitutional Law." *Harvard Law Review* 73 (November 1959): 1-35.

1142. Wechsler, Herbert, and Henry M. Hart, Jr., eds. *The Federal Courts and the Federal System*. Brooklyn: Foundation Press, 1953.

1143. Wham, Benjamin. "Jefferson Wins over Hamilton: Historical Explanation of Constitutional Changes." *American Bar Association Journal* 35 (January 1949): 23-26, 86-87.

1144. Wheeler, B. K. "The Constitution and the Supreme Court." *Bar Briefs* 15 (December 1938): 71-75.

1145. Willis, Hugh E. "Capitalism, the United States Constitution and the Supreme Court." *Kentucky Law Journal* 22 (March 1934): 343-370; (May 1934): 515-542.

1146. Willis, Hugh E. "Some Conflicting Decisions of United States Supreme Court." *Virginia Law Review* 13 (January 1927): 155-174; (February 1927): 278-299.

1147. Willoughby, Westel W. *The Constitutional Law of the United States*. 3 vols. 2d ed. New York: Baker, Voorhis, 1929.

1148. Wilson, Fred T. *Our Constitution and Its Makers*. New York: Revell, 1937.

1149. Wolfe, Christopher. "Theory of U.S. Constitutional History." *Journal of Politics* 43 (May 1981): 292-316.

1150. Woodburn, James A. *The Making of the Constitution, a Syllabus of "Madison's Journal of the Constitutional Convention" Together with a Few Outlines Based on "The Federalist"*. Chicago: Scott, Foresman, 1908.

1151. Wright, Benjamin F. "The Early History of Written Constitutions in America." In *Essays in History and Political Theory in Honor of Charles Howard McIlwain*, edited by Carl Wittke, 341-371. Cambridge: Harvard University Press, 1936.

1152. Wright, Benjamin F. *The Growth of American Constitutional Law*. Chicago: University of Chicago Press, 1967.

1153. Young, Alfred, ed. *The Debate over the Constitution, 1787-1789*. Chicago: Rand McNally, 1965.

II. The Court and the Federal Government

General Studies

1154. Andrews, William G. *Coordinate Magistrates: Constitutional Law by Congress and President.* New York: Van Nostrand Reinhold, 1969.

1155. Aranson, Peter H. "Judicial Control of the Political Branches: Public Purpose and Public Law." *Cato Journal* 4 (Winter 1985): 719-782.

1156. Barker, Lucius J. "The Supreme Court as Policy-Maker: The Tidelands Oil Controversy." *Journal of Politics* 24 (May 1962): 350-366.

1157. Berger, Raoul. "The President, Congress, and the Courts." *Yale Law Journal* 83 (May 1974): 1111-1153.

1158. Berle, Adolf A. *Three Faces of Power.* New York: Harcourt, Brace, and World, 1967.

1159. Choper, Jesse H. "The Supreme Court and the Political Branches: Democratic Theory and Practice." *University of Pennsylvania Law Review* 122 (April 1974): 810-858.

1160. Cox, Archibald. "The Supreme Court and the Federal System." *California Law Review* 50 (December 1962): 800-820.

1161. Davis, Horace A. *American Constitutions: The Relations of the Three Departments as Adjusted by a Century.* Baltimore: Johns Hopkins University, 1885.

1162. Dorsen, Norman, and John H. F. Shattuck. "Executive Privilege, the Congress, and the Court." *Ohio State Law Journal* 35 (1974): 1-40.

1163. Ellis, Overton G. "Dual Sovereignty and the Supreme Court." *Washington Law Review* 1 (June 1925): 1-8.

1164. Fein, Bruce E. "Is the Supreme Court the President's Sole Preserve? A Proper Check on the Supreme Court." *American Bar Association Journal* 71 (August 1985): 36-40.

1165. Fisher, Louis. *A Constitution between Friends: Congress, the President, and the Law.* New York: St. Martin's Press, 1978.

1166. Freund, Paul A. "Umpiring the Federal System." *Columbia Law Review* 54 (April 1954): 561-578.

1167. Gewirtz, Paul. "The Courts, Congress, and Executive Policy Making: Notes on Three Doctrines." *Law and Contemporary Problems* 10 (Summer 1976): 46-85.

1168. Jantzen, Steven. *The Presidency, Congress, and the Supreme Court.* New York: Scholastic, 1977.

1169. Joyner, Conrad, and John F. Kozlowicz. "The Supreme Court and the Electoral Process." *Arizona Law Review* 8 (Spring 1967): 260-275.

1170. Kurland, Philip B. "Equal in Origin and Equal in Title to the Legislative and Executive Branches of the Government." *Harvard Law Review* 68 (November 1968): 145-176.

1171. MacCorkle, Stuart A. "Alas, Poor Jefferson! The Executive, Congress, and the Courts." *Sewanee Review* 44 (April 1936): 135-144.

1172. Mearns, Edward A., Jr. "Check-reins upon Government." *Virginia Law Review* 44 (November 1958): 1117-1127.

1173. Mills, Jon, and William G. Munselle. "Unimpoundment: Politics and the Courts in the Release of Impounded Funds." *Emory Law Journal* 24 (Spring 1975): 313-353.

1174. Moeller, John. "Alexander M. Bickel: Toward a Theory of Politics." *Journal of Politics* 47 (February 1985): 113-139.

1175. Murray, William H. *The Presidency, the Supreme Court, and Seven Senators.* Boston: Meador Publishing Company, 1939.

1176. Pierce, Franklin. *Federal Usurpation.* New York: D. Appleton, 1908.

1177. Pritchett, C. Herman. *Constitutional Law of the Federal System.* Englewood Cliffs, NJ: Prentice-Hall, 1984.

1178. Strong, Frank R. "President, Congress, Judiciary: One Is More Equal Than the Others." *American Bar Association Journal* 60 (September 1974): 1050-1052.

1179. Sutherland, William A. "Politics and the Supreme Court." *American Law Review* 48 (May 1914): 390-402.

1180. Swindler, William F. "The Supreme Court, the President, and Congress." *International and Comparative Law Quarterly* 19 (October 1970): 671-692.

1181. Tapia, Raul R., John P. James, and Robert Levine. "Congress versus the Executive: The Role of the Courts." *Harvard Journal on Legislation* 11 (February 1974): 352-413.

Separation of Powers

1182. Babu, B. Ramesh. "The Ephemeral and the Eternal in *The Federalist.*" *Indian Journal of American Studies* 9 (January 1979): 3-14.

1183. Berger, Raoul. "Bills of Attainder: A Study of Amendment by the Court." *Cornell Law Review* 63 (March 1978): 355-404.

1184. Braveman, Daan. "*Chadha*: The Supreme Court as Umpire in Separation of Powers Disputes." *Syracuse Law Review* 35 (Spring 1984): 735-748.

1185. Brent, Robert A. "The Myth of Separation of Powers." *Southern Quarterly* 7 (July 1969): 433-442.

1186. Carpenter, William S. "Separation of Powers in the Eighteenth Century." *American Political Science Review* 22 (February 1928): 32-44.

1187. Chemerinsky, Erwin. "A Paradox without a Principle: A Comment on the Burger Court's Jurisprudence in Separation of Powers Cases." *Southern California Law Review* 60 (May 1987): 1083-1111.

1188. Clark, A. Inglis. "The Supremacy of the Judiciary under the Constitution of the United States, and under the Constitution of the Commonwealth of Australia." *Harvard Law Review* 17 (November 1903): 1-19.

1189. Clark, Walter. "Judicial Supremacy." *Arena* 39 (February 1908): 148-155.

1190. Clark, Walter. "Judicial Veto Wholly without Authority in the Constitution." *American Federationist* 28 (September 1921): 723-726.

1191. Curtis, Charles P. "A Natural Law for Today and the Supreme Court as Its Prophet, Gaspar G. Bacon Lectures, 1958." *Boston University Law Review* 39 (Winter 1959): 1-51.

1192. Day, L. B. "The Independence of the Judiciary." *Nebraska Law Bulletin* 15 (July 1936): 60-68.

1193. Diamond, Ann S. "The Zenith of the Separation of Powers Theory: The Federal Convention of 1787." *Publius* 8 (Summer 1978): 45-70.

1194. Edwards, George. "The President, the Media, and the First Amendment." *Presidential Studies Quarterly* 12 (Winter 1982): 42-47.

1195. Ervin, Samuel J., Jr. "Separation of Powers: Judicial Independence." *Law and Contemporary Problems* 35 (Winter 1970): 108-128.

1196. Fellman, David. "The Separation of Powers and the Judiciary." *Review of Politics* 37 (January 1975): 357-376.

1197. Field, Oliver P. "Ten Years of the Supreme Court: 1937-1947, II: Separation and Delegation of Powers." *American Political Science Review* 41 (December 1947): 1142-1181.

1198. Fisher, Louis. "The Administrative World of *Chadha* and *Bowsher*." *Public Administration Review* 47 (May/June 1987): 213-219.

1199. Fisher, Louis. "Judicial Misjudgments about the Lawmaking Process: The Legislative Veto Case." *Public Administration Review* 45 (November 1985): 705-711.

1200. Gazell, James A., and Darrell L. Pugh. "Voiding the Legislative Veto: Possible Impacts for the Administrative State." *Glendale Law Review* 7 (1985): 1-38.

1201. Giunta, Joseph J. "Standing, Separation of Powers, and the Demise of the Public Citizen." *American University Law Review* 24 (Spring 1975): 835-876.

1202. Glasser, Eli A. "The Supreme Court Issue in Retrospect." *Law Society Journal* 7 (August 1937): 930-933.

1203. Hochenberger, Ruth. "Supreme Court to Decide Case of Separation of Powers: High Court Opens New Term." *New York Law Journal* 186 (October 1981): 1.

1204. Jefferson, Bernard S. "Supreme Court and State Separation and Delegation of Powers." *Columbia Law Review* 44 (January 1944): 1-33.

1205. Kurland, Philip B. "New Supreme Court." *John Marshall Journal of Practice and Procedure* 7 (Fall 1973): 1-14.

1206. Lee, William P. "LFPMA's Legislative Veto Provisions and *INS v. Chadha*: Who Controls the Federal Lands?" *Boston College Environmental Affairs Law Review* 12 (Summer 1985): 791-821.

1207. Leventhal, Harold. "Courts and Political Thickets." *Columbia Law Review* 77 (April 1977): 345-387.

1208. Lofgren, Charles A. "*United States v. Curtiss-Wright*: An Historical Assessment." *Yale Law Journal* 83 (November 1973): 1-32.

1209. Lowden, Frank O. "An Independent Judiciary: The Bulwark of the People's Liberties." *Commercial Law Journal* 42 (August 1937): 227-230.

1210. Mamlet, Alfred. "Reconsideration of Separation of Powers and the Bargaining Game: Limiting the Policy Discretion of Judges and Plaintiffs in Institutional Suits." *Emory Law Journal* 33 (Summer 1984): 685-732.

1211. Mason, Alpheus T. *Security through Freedom*. Ithaca, NY: Cornell University Press, 1955.

1212. Matteson, David M. *The Organization of the Government under the Constitution*. New York: Da Capo Press, 1970.

1213. Miller, Arthur S. "An Inquiry into the Relevance of the Intentions of the Founding Fathers, with Special Emphasis upon the Doctrine of Separation of Powers." *Arkansas Law Review* 27 (Winter 1973): 583-602.

1214. Moynihan, Daniel P. "Imperial Government." *Commentary* 65 (June 1978): 25-32.

1215. Parker, Reginald. "The Historic Basis of Administrative Law: Separation of Powers and Judicial Supremacy." *Rutgers Law Review* 12 (Spring 1958): 449-481.

1216. Parker, Reginald. "Separation of Powers Revisited: Its Meaning to Administrative Law." *Michigan Law Review* 49 (May 1951): 1009-1038.

1217. Ray, Ben F. "The Supreme Court: An Independent Department of Government." *Alabama Lawyer* 7 (October 1946): 450-455.

1218. Reinstein, Robert, and Harvey Silvergate. "Legislative Privilege and the Separation of Powers." *Harvard Law Review* 86 (May 1973): 1113-1183.

1219. Rodell, Fred. "Conflict over the Court." *Progressive* 22 (December 1958): 11-13.

1220. Shaffer, Helen B. "Separation of Powers." *Editorial Research Reports* 2 (September 12, 1973): 691-708.

1221. Sharp, Malcolm P. "The Classical American Doctrine of Separation of Powers." *University of Chicago Law Review* 2 (April 1935): 385-436.

1222. Shevlin, Matthew J. "The Supreme Court: Checks and Balances." *Queen's Bar Bulletin* 32 (October 1968): 29-36.

1223. Shirley, William A. "Resolving Challenges to Statutes Containing Unconstitutional Legislative Veto Provisions." *Columbia Law Review* 85 (December 1985): 1808-1832.

1224. Smolla, Rodney A. "The Supreme Court and the Temple of Doom: A Short Story." *Constitutional Commentary* 2 (Winter 1985): 41-68.

1225. Spahr, Margaret. "When the Supreme Court Subordinates Judicial Reason to Legislation." In *Rational Decision*, edited by Carl S. Friedrich, 160-173. New York: Atherton Press, 1964.

1226. Stauss, James H. "The Supreme Court and the Architects of Economic Legislation." *Journal of Political Economy* 56 (April 1948): 138-156.

1227. Strum, Philippa. *The Supreme Court and Political Questions: A Study in Judicial Evasion.* University: University of Alabama Press, 1974.

1228. Swisher, Carl B. "The Supreme Court in a Changing Role." *University of Kansas City Law Review* 20 (December 1951/February 1952): 1-14.

1229. Taylor, Hannis. "Independence of the Federal Judiciary." *American Law Review* 40 (July/August 1906): 481-495.

1230. Vandenberg, Arthur H. "A Layman Looks at the Court." *Case and Comment* 42 (Spring 1936): 4-6.

1231. Vile, M. J. C. *Constitution and the Separation of Powers.* London: Oxford University Press, 1967.

1232. Wolkinson, Herman. "Demand of Congressional Committees for Executive Papers." *Federal Bar Journal* 10 (April/October 1949): 103-150.

1233. Younger, Irving. "Congressional Investigations and Executive Secrecy: A Study in Separation of Powers." *University of Pittsburgh Law Review* 20 (June 1959): 755-784.

The Court and Congress

General Studies

1234. Abraham, Henry J. "A 'Self-Inflicted Wound'?" *Judicature* 65 (October 1981): 178-184.

1235. Anderson, Carl A. "Government of Courts: The Power of Congress under Article III." *American Bar Association Journal* 68 (June 1982): 686-690.

1236. Anderson, Martin. "The Sophistry That Made Urban Renewal Possible." *Law and Contemporary Problems* 30 (Winter 1965): 199-211.

1237. Appleman, Irving. "The Supreme Court on Expatriation: An Historical Review." *Federal Bar Journal* 23 (Fall 1963): 351-373.

1238. "Association's Views on the Supreme Court Issue Presented to Senate Committee." *American Bar Association Journal* 23 (May 1937): 315-318.

1239. Ball, Howard. "The U.S. Supreme Court's Glossing of the Federal Tort Claims Act: Statutory Construction and Veterans' Tort Actions." *Western Political Quarterly* 41 (September 1988): 529-552.

1240. Barber, Sotirios A. *The Constitution and the Delegation of Congressional Power.* Chicago: University of Chicago Press, 1975.

1241. Berg, Larry L. "The Supreme Court and Congress: Conflict and Interaction, 1947-1968." Ph.D. diss., University of California, 1972.

1242. Berger, Raoul. *Congress versus the Supreme Court.* Cambridge: Harvard University Press, 1969.

1243. Blake, William J. "The Supreme Court Interprets the Speech and Debate Clause." *University of Cincinnati Law Review* 48 (Fall 1979): 1015-1026.

1244. Bolton, John, and Kevin Abrams.

"The Judicial and Congressional Response to the Invalidation of the Legislative Veto." *Journal of Law and Politics* 1 (Spring 1984): 299-356.

1245. Bowman, Harold M. "Congress and the Supreme Court." *Political Science Quarterly* 25 (March 1910): 20-34.

1246. Brabner-Smith, John W. "Congress vs. the Supreme Court: A Constitutional Amendment?" *Virginia Law Review* 22 (April 1936): 665-675.

1247. Brady, David W., John Schmidhauser, and Larry Berg. "House Lawyers and Support for the Supreme Court." *Journal of Politics* 35 (August 1973): 724-729.

1248. Brant, Irving. "Appellate Jurisdiction: Congressional Abuse of the Exception Clause." *Oregon Law Review* 53 (Fall 1973): 3-28.

1249. Braveman, Daan. "The Standing Doctrine: A Dialogue between the Court and Congress." *Cardozo Law Review* 2 (Fall 1980): 31-69.

1250. Breckenridge, Adam C. *Congress against the Court.* Lincoln: University of Nebraska Press, 1970.

1251. Brown, Douglas W. "The Proposal to Give Congress the Power to Nullify the Constitution." *American Law Review* 57 (March/April 1923): 161-181.

1252. Butler, George B. "Congress and the Supreme Court." *Harper's New Monthly Magazine* 36 (April 1868): 657-662.

1253. Celler, Emanuel. "The Supreme Court Survives a Barrage (of Criticism)." *Reporter* 19 (November 27, 1958): 31-33.

1254. Clark, Walter. "Where Does the Governing Power Reside?" *American Law Review* 52 (September 1918): 687-694.

1255. Cox, Paul N. "Ruminations on Statutory Interpretation in the Burger Court." *Valparaiso University Law Review* 19 (Winter 1985): 287-395.

1256. Dilliard, Irving. "Senator Thomas C. Hennings, Jr. and the Supreme Court." *Missouri Law Review* 26 (November 1961): 429-439.

1257. Dorsen, Norman. "Senator Eastland's Attack on the United States Supreme Court: An Analysis and Response." *University of Pennsylvania Law Review* 111 (April 1963): 693-707.

1258. Ervin, Samuel J., Jr. "The *Gravel* and *Brewster* Cases: An Assault on Congressional Independence." *Virginia Law Review* 59 (February 1973): 175-195.

1259. Ettrude, Dormin J., ed. *The Power of Congress to Nullify Supreme Court Decisions*. New York: H. W. Wilson, 1924.

1260. Faust, George H. "Congressional Control of U.S. Supreme Court Jurisdiction." *Cleveland-Marshall Law Review* 7 (September 1958): 513-523.

1261. Forkosch, Morris D. "The Expectations and Regulations Clause of Article III and a Person's Constitutional Rights: Can the Latter Be Limited by Congressional Power under the Former?" *West Virginia Law Review* 72 (April 1970): 807-813.

1262. Frank, Theodore D. *A Footnote to a Dialogue: Some Reflections on Congressional Power and the Supreme Court's Appellate Jurisdiction*. Cambridge: Harvard Law School, 1969.

1263. Ginsberg, Benjamin. "*Berman v. Parker*: Congress, the Court, and the Public Purpose." *Polity* 4 (Autumn 1971): 48-74.

1264. Gonzalez, Raymond B. "Expatriation: Congress versus the Court." *Southern Quarterly* 7 (July 1969): 443-469.

1265. Gordon, Irving A. "Nature and Uses of Congressional Power under Section 5 of the 14th Amendment to Overcome Decisions of Supreme Court." *Northwestern University Law Review* 72 (November/December 1977): 656-705.

1266. Green, Frederick. "The Judicial Censorship of Legislation." *American Law Review* 47 (January/February 1913): 90-110.

1267. Green, Justin J., John R. Schmidhauser, and Larry L. Berg. "Variations in Congressional Responses to the Warren and Burger Courts." *Emory Law Journal* 23 (Summer 1974): 725-744.

1268. Grinnell, Frank W. "Shall Congress Take Over Powers of the Supreme Court?" *Massachusetts Law Quarterly* 8 (February 1923): 66-75.

1269. Hall, Kermit L. "The Taney Court in the Second Party System: The Congressional Response to the Federal Judicial Reform." Ph.D. diss., University of Minnesota, 1972.

1270. Halper, Thomas. "Supreme Court Responses to Congressional Threats: Strategy and Tactics." *Drake Law Review* 19 (May 1970): 292-326.

1271. Harris, Robert J. *The Quest for Equality: The Constitution, Congress, and the Supreme Court*. Baton Rouge: Louisiana State University Press, 1960.

1272. Harvard Law School Students. "Congressional Access to the Federal Courts." *Harvard Law Review* 90 (June 1977): 1632-1655.

1273. Henschen, Beth M. "Statutory Interpretations of the Supreme Court: Congressional Response." *American Politics Quarterly* 11 (October 1983): 441-458.

1274. Henschen, Beth M. "Supreme Court-Congressional Interaction in the Interpretation of Statutes." Ph.D. diss., Ohio State University, 1980.

1275. Hibschman, Harry. "Power to Regulate Court Procedure: Is It a Legislative or a Judicial Function?" *United States Law Review* 71 (November 1937): 618-644.

1276. Horack, Frank E., Jr. "Congressional Silence: A Tool of Judicial Supremacy." *Texas Law Review* 25 (January 1947): 247-261.

1277. Hurst, James W. "The Legislative Branch and the Supreme Court." *University of Arkansas at Little Rock Law Journal* 5 (1982): 487-518.

1278. Ingersoll, Edward. *An Abridgment of the Acts of Congress Now in Force, Excepting Those of Private and Local Application: With Notes of Decisions Giving Construction to the Same in the Supreme Court of the United States.* Philadelphia: Towar and Hogan, 1825.

1279. Kauper, Paul G. "The *Steel Seizure Case*: Congress, the President, and the Supreme Court." *Michigan Law Review* 51 (December 1952): 141-182.

1280. Klubock, Daniel. "Expatriation and the Constitution." *Law in Transition Quarterly* 1 (Winter 1964): 25-48.

1281. Konop, Thomas F. "Congress and the Supreme Court." *Notre Dame Lawyer* 1 (January 1926): 67-76; (February 1926): 115-121.

1282. Langran, Robert W. "Congress versus the Court." *Supreme Court Historical Society Yearbook* 1978 (1978): 91-96.

1283. Lanier, Alexander S. "Congress and the Supreme Court." *North American Review* 218 (November 1923): 577-588.

1284. Lansing, Paul, and John S. Zieser. "The Liability of 'Street-Level' Officials' Societal Objectives: Congress and the Supreme Court." *Southern University Law Review* 8 (Spring 1982): 231-254.

1285. Lawson, James F. *The General Welfare Clause: A Study of the Power of Congress under the Constitution of the United States.* Washington, DC: published by author, 1934.

1286. Lenoir, James J. "Congressional Control over the Appellate Jurisdiction of the Supreme Court." *University of Kansas Law Review* 5 (October 1956): 16-41.

1287. Lincoln, Alexander. "The Supreme Court as Arbiter between Congress and the States." *Virginia Law Review* 24 (April 1938): 613-641.

1288. Lippe, Emil. "Uneasy Partnership: The Balance of Power between Congress and the Supreme Court in Interpretation of the Civil War Amendments." *Akron Law Review* 7 (Fall 1978): 49-60.

1289. McCarthy, Martha M. "The 'Equal Access' Law: A Potential Conflict between Congress and the Supreme Court." *Educational Horizons* 63 (Spring 1985): 96-97.

1290. McConnell, Michael W., and Laurence H. Tribe. *The Senate, the Courts, and the Constitution: A Debate.* Washington, DC: Center for National Policy, 1986.

1291. Margulies, Herbert F. "The Senate and the World Court." *Capitol Studies* 4 (Fall 1976): 37-51.

1292. Martig, Ralph R. "Congress and the Appellate Jurisdiction of the Supreme Court." *Michigan Law Review* 34 (March 1936): 650-670.

1293. Martin, Philip L. "Hatch Act in Court: Some Recent Developments." *Public Administration Review* 33 (September 1973): 443-447.

1294. Melone, Albert P. "System Support Politics and the Congressional Court of Appeals." *North Dakota Law Review* 51 (Spring 1975): 597-613.

1295. Mitchell, Clarence. "The Warren Court and Congress: A Civil Rights Partnership." *Nebraska Law Review* 48 (November 1968): 91-130.

1296. Moore, James W., and Helen I. Bendix. "Congress, Evidence and Rulemaking." *Yale Law Journal* 84 (November 1974): 9-38.

1297. Morgan, Donald G. *Congress and the Constitution: A Study of Responsibility.* Cambridge: Harvard University Press, 1966.

1298. Muir, Gerald A. "U.S. Supreme Court and Congress." *Bi-Monthly Law Review* 10 (March/April 1927): 153-157.

1299. Murphy, Walter F. *Congress and the Court: A Case Study in the American Political Process.* Chicago: University of Chicago Press, 1962.

1300. Nagel, Robert F. "The Legislative Veto, the Constitution, and the Courts." *Constitutional Commentary* 3 (Winter 1986): 61-72.

1301. Nathanson, J. Edmond. "Congressional Power to Contradict the Supreme Court's Constitutional Decisions: Accommodation of Rights in Conflict." *William and Mary Law Review* 27 (Winter 1986): 331-370.

1302. Nichols, Egbert R., ed. *Congress or the Supreme Court: Which Shall Rule America? Containing the Principal Arguments Both for and against the Proposition: Resolved That Congress Should Have the Power to Override, by a Two-thirds Majority Vote, Decisions of the Supreme Court Declaring Laws Passed by Congress Unconstitutional.* New York: Noble and Noble, 1935.

1303. Norris, William A., and Julian Burke. "Congress and the Supreme Court's Appellate Jurisdiction." *Los Angeles Bar Bulletin* 35 (May 1960): 212-215, 229-231.

1304. Pedrick, Willard H. "From Congress to the Court of Appeals." *Northwestern University Law Review* 49 (March/April 1954): 54-61.

1305. Power, John, John D. O'Neill, and Arthur M. Diamond. "An Examination of Congressional Vesting of Federal Courts with Authority to Deal with State Matters." *Notre Dame Lawyer* 20 (March 1945): 306-311.

1306. Ransom, William L. *Majority Rule and the Judiciary: An Examination of Current Proposals for Constitutional Change Affecting the Relation of Courts to Legislation.* New York: Charles Scribner's Sons, 1912.

1307. Rashid, Baddia J. "Congressional Reaction to Recent Supreme Court Decisions in Taxation and Criminal Law." *Georgetown Law Journal* 36 (November 1947): 48-65.

1308. Ratner, Leonard G. "Congressional Power over the Appellate Jurisdiction of the Supreme Court." *University of Pennsylvania Law Review* 109 (December 1960): 157-202.

1309. Rauh, Joseph L., Jr. "The Truth about Congress and the Court." *Progressive* 22 (November 1958): 30-33.

1310. Redlich, Norman. "Rights of Witnesses before Congressional Committees: Effects of Recent Supreme Court Decisions." *New York University Law Review* 36 (June 1961): 1126-1156.

1311. Rusher, William A. "Can Congressional Investigations Survive *Watkins,* A Former Counsel to the Senate Internal Security Subcommittee Explains Why the *Watkins* Case Cripples Congress in a New and Peculiarly Deadly Way." *National Review* 4 (September 7, 1957): 201-203.

1312. Sager, Lawrence G. "Supreme Court, 1980 Term, Foreword: Constitutional Limitations on Congress' Authority to Regulate the Jurisdiction of the Federal Courts." *Harvard Law Review* 95 (November 1981): 17-345.

1313. Schmidhauser, John R., and Larry L. Berg. *The Supreme Court and Congress: Conflict and Interaction, 1945-1968.* New York: Free Press, 1972.

1314. Schoenberg, David. "The Delegation Doctrine: Could the Court Give It Substance?" *Michigan Law Review* 83 (April 1985): 1223-1290.

1315. Schwartz, Herman. "The Senate Can Play Too." *American Bar Association Journal* 71 (August 1985): 36-39.

1316. Semerjian, Evan Y. "The Right of Confrontation." *American Bar Association Journal* 55 (February 1969): 152-156.

1317. Shipley, Carl L. "Legislative Control of Judicial Behavior." *Law and Contemporary Problems* 35 (Winter 1970): 178-201.

1318. Sirotkin, Phillip L. "The Supreme Court and the Legislative Process: Two Case Studies in Policy." Ph.D. diss., University of Chicago, 1952.

1319. Smith, Mortimer. "Senator Paul H. Douglas." *American Mercury* 71 (July 1950): 25-32.

1320. Smith, Young B. "Statement on the Proposal Regarding the Supreme Court before the Senate Judiciary Committee." *American Bar Association Journal* 23 (April 1937): 261-264.

1321. Strickland, Stephen P. "Congress, the Supreme Court, and Public Policy: Activism, Restraint, and Interplay." *American University Law Review* 18 (March 1969): 267-298.

1322. Strong, Frank R. "Courts, Congress, Judiciary: One Is More Equal Than the Others." *American Bar Association Journal* 60 (October 1974): 1203-1206.

1323. Stumpf, Harry P. "The Congressional Reversal of Supreme Court Decisions, 1957-1961." Ph.D. diss., Northwestern University, 1964.

1324. Stumpf, Harry P. "Political Efficacy of Judicial Symbolism." *Western Political Quarterly* 19 (June 1966): 293-303.

1325. Sutherland, Arthur E., Jr. "Reasons in Retrospect: Reflections on the Labor Laws of 1947 and on the Doctrine That Judges Should Not Meddle with Social and Economic Arrangements Made by Legislators." *Cornell Law Journal* 33 (September 1947): 1-39.

1326. Swaney, Charles B. "Congress and the Supreme Court." *Social Science* 12 (April 1937): 176-180.

1327. Trickett, William. "The Great Usurpation." *American Law Review* 40 (May/June 1906): 356-376.

1328. Turck, Charles J. "Keeping the Supreme Court Supreme." *Tennessee Law Review* 4 (November 1925): 15-23.

1329. Van Nuys, Frederick. "The Work of the Senate Judiciary Committee." *Federal Bar Association Journal* 4 (December 1942): 338, 356-357.

1330. Velvel, Lawrence R. "Supreme Court Tramples *Gravel*." *Kentucky Law Journal* 61 (Winter 1972/1973): 525-537.

1331. Vold, Lauriz. "The Supreme Court, Congress, and the Constitution." *Quarterly Journal of the University of North Dakota* 15 (May 1925): 314-359.

1332. Walsh, Richard L. "Congress Cannot Give Federal District Courts Outside District of Columbia Jurisdiction." *Georgetown Law Journal* 36 (January 1948): 251-253.

1333. Warren, Charles. *Congress, the Constitution, and the Supreme Court.* Rev. ed. Boston: Little, Brown, 1935.

1334. Weeks, Kent M. *Adam Clayton Powell and the Supreme Court.* New York: Dunellen Publishing Company, 1971.

1335. Winter, Bill. "Can Congress Curtail Federal Court Power?" *American Bar Association Journal* 67 (September 1981): 1095.

1336. Wolff, Irving M. "Congressional Consideration of the Supreme Court Quorum." *Georgetown Law Journal* 32 (March 1944): 293-307.

1337. Yackle, Larry W. "Burger Court, 'State Action', and Congressional Enforcement of the Civil War Amendments." *Alabama Law Review* 27 (Fall 1975): 479-574.

1338. Yarwood, Dean L., and Bradley C.

Canon. "On the Supreme Court's Annual Trek to the Capitol." *Judicature* 63 (February 1980): 322-327.

1339. Zahniser, Marvin R., ed. "John W. Bricker Reflects upon the Fight for the Bricker Amendment." *Ohio History* 87 (Summer 1978): 322-333.

Commerce Power

1340. Baxter, Maurice G. *The Steamboat Monopoly:* Gibbons v. Ogden, *1824*. New York: Knopf, 1972.

1341. Benson, Paul R., Jr. *The Supreme Court and the Commerce Clause: 1937-1970*. New York: Dunellen, 1970.

1342. Corwin, Edward S. *The Commerce Power versus State Power*. Princeton, NJ: Princeton University Press, 1936.

1343. Culberson, Charles A. "The Supreme Court and Interstate Commerce." *American Law Review* 24 (January/February 1890): 25-63.

1344. Fallon, Perlie P. "The Commerce Clause from the *Schechter* Case through the 1944-1945 Term." *Temple Law Quarterly* 19 (September 1945): 421-448.

1345. Farber, Daniel A. "State Regulation and the Dormant Commerce Clause." *Urban Law* 18 (Summer 1986): 483-705.

1346. Finneran, Daniel V. "State Taxation of Interstate Commerce: The Supreme Court's Balancing Role." Ph.D. diss., New School for Social Research, 1968.

1347. Ganoe, John T. "The Roosevelt Court and the Commerce Clause." *New Jersey Law Journal* 68 (September 6, 1945): 297, 299, 303-304.

1348. Gavit, Bernard C. *The Commerce Clause of the United States Constitution*. Bloomington, IN: Principia Press, 1932.

1349. Kirshen, Himy B. "The Commerce Clause, the Supreme Court, and Nationalism." Ph.D. diss., University of Wisconsin, 1937.

1350. Maltz, Earl M. "The Burger Court, the Commerce Clause, and the Problem of Differential Treatment." *Indiana Law Journal* 54 (Winter 1979): 165-183.

1351. Mann, W. Howard. "The Marshall Court: Nationalization of Private Rights and Personal Liberty from the Authority of the Commerce Clause." *Indiana Law Journal* 38 (Winter 1963): 117-238.

1352. Regan, Donald H. "The Supreme Court and State Protectionism: Making Sense of the Dormant Commerce Clause." *Michigan Law Review* 84 (May 1986): 1091-1287.

1353. Stern, Robert L. "The Commerce Clause and the National Economy, 1933-1946." *Harvard Law Review* 59 (May 1946): 645-693; (July 1946): 884-947.

1354. Tushnet, Mark V. "Rethinking the Dormant Commerce Clause." *Wisconsin Law Review* 1979 (1979): 125-165.

1355. Whitman, Douglas F. "The Commerce Clause since *National League of Cities*." *Business Law Review* 10 (Fall 1977): 46-53.

Foreign Policy

1356. Baldwin, Simeon E. "The Supreme Court and the *Insular Cases*." *Yale Review* 10 (August 1901): 129-143.

1357. Boutwell, George S. "The Supreme Court and the Dependencies." *North American Review* 173 (August 1901): 154-160.

1358. Burgess, John W. "The Decisions of the Supreme Court in the *Insular Cases*." *Political Science Quarterly* 16 (September 1901): 486-504.

1359. Cooper, Joseph. "Postscript on the Congressional Veto: Is There Life after

Chadha?" Political Science Quarterly 98 (Fall 1983): 427-429.

1360. Franck, Thomas M., and Clifford A. Bob. "The Return of Humpty-Dumpty: Foreign Relations Law after the *Chadha* Case." *American Journal of International Law* 79 (October 1985): 912-960.

1361. Haffer, Louis P. "Personal Jurisdiction over Foreign Corporations as Defendants in the United States Supreme Court." *Boston University Law Review* 17 (April 1937): 639-669.

1362. Horan, Michael J. "On Train Wrecks, Time Bombs, and Skinned Cats: The Congressional Response to the Fall of the Legislative Veto." *Journal of Legislation* 13 (1986): 22-47.

1363. Kerr, James E. *The* Insular Cases*: The Role of the American Judiciary in American Expansionism.* Port Washington, NY: Kennikat Press, 1981.

1364. MacIver, Kenneth F., Jr., Beverly M. Wolfe, and Leonard B. Locke. "The Supreme Court as Arbitrator in the Conflict between Presidential and Congressional War-Making Power." *Boston University Law Review* 50 (Spring 1970): 78-116.

1365. Pilchen, Saul M. "Politics v. the Cloister: Deciding When the Supreme Court Should Defer to Congressional Factfinding under the Post-Civil War Amendments." *Notre Dame Law Review* 59 (1984): 337-398.

1366. Rodriguez, Raquel A. "Holding Foreign Government Corporations Liable for the Wrongs of the Government: A Clash among Competing Policies." *University of Miami Law Review* 39 (June 1985): 341-368.

1367. Rowe, L. S. "The Supreme Court and the *Insular Cases.*" *Annals of the American Academy of Political and Social Science* 18 (September 1901): 226-250.

1368. Stebbins, Phillip E. "A History of

the Role of the United States Supreme Court in Foreign Policy." Ph.D. diss., Ohio State University, 1966.

1369. Vose, Clement E. "State against Nation: The Conservation Case of *Missouri v. Holland.*" *Prologue* 16 (Winter 1984): 233-247.

Investigations

1370. Alfange, Dean, Jr. "Congressional Investigation and the Fickle Court." *University of Cincinnati Law Review* 30 (Spring 1961): 113-171.

1371. Cohen, Nachman S. "Legislative Investigations, Due Process: *John T. Watkins v. United States.*" *Boston University Law Review* 37 (Fall 1957): 515-518.

1372. Dembitz, Nanette. "The Supreme Court's New Look at Investigations of Subversion." *Association of the Bar of the City of New York Record* 18 (November 1963): 574-577.

1373. Fleishmann, Hartly. "*Watkins v. U.S.* and Congressional Power of Investigation." *Hastings Law Journal* 9 (February 1958): 145-166.

1374. McKay, Robert B. "Congressional Investigations and the Supreme Court." *California Law Review* 51 (May 1963): 267-295.

1375. Newman, Frank C. "The Supreme Court, Congressional Investigations, and Influence Peddling." *New York University Law Review* 33 (June 1958): 796-810.

1376. O'Reilly, Kenneth. "Stamler Challenge: Congressional Investigative Power and the First Amendment." *Congressional Studies* 7 (Spring 1979): 57-72.

Judicial Review

1377. Abraham, Henry J. "Machtkampf: The Supreme Court of the U.S. in the Political Process." *Parliamentary Affairs* 13 (Autumn 1960): 424-441.

1378. Adamany, David. "Legitimacy, Realigning Elections, and the Supreme Court." *Wisconsin Law Review* 1973 (1973): 790-846.

1379. Albertsworth, E. F. "Judicial Review of Administrative Action by the Federal Supreme Court." *Harvard Law Review* 35 (December 1921): 127-153.

1380. Attansio, John B. "Everyman's Constitutional Law: A Theory of the Power of Judicial Review." *Georgetown Law Journal* 72 (August 1984): 1665-1723.

1381. Auchampaugh, Philip G. "James Buchanan, the Court, and the *Dred Scott* Case." *Tennessee History Magazine* 9 (January 1928): 231-240.

1382. Aumann, Francis R. "The Doctrine of Judicial Review." *Kentucky Law Journal* 20 (March 1932): 276-303.

1383. Baker, Richard C. "Legislating Judicially: Should the Power of Judicial Review Be Curbed?" *American Bar Association Journal* 35 (July 1949): 555-556.

1384. Bander, Edward J. "The *Dred Scott* Case and Judicial Statesmanship." *Villanova Law Review* 6 (Summer 1961): 514-524.

1385. Bates, Henry M. "The Courts and Unconstitutional Legislation: A Suggested Aid in Work of Judicial Review." *Nebraska Law Bulletin* 5 (July 1926): 101-119.

1386. Beard, Charles A. "The Supreme Court: Usurper or Grantee?" *Political Science Quarterly* 27 (March 1912): 1-35.

1387. Bermann, George A. "Comments II." *American Journal of Comparative Law* 27 (Fall 1979): 583-587.

1388. Beth, Loren P. "The Supreme Court and the Future of Judicial Review." *Political Science Quarterly* 76 (March 1961): 11-23.

1389. Beth, Loren P. "The Supreme Court Reconsidered: Opposition and Judicial Review in the United States." *Political Studies* 16 (June 1968): 243-249.

1390. Beveridge, Albert J. "The Supremacy of the Supreme Court." In *The State of the Nation*, edited by Albert J. Beveridge, 245-270. Indianapolis: Bobbs-Merrill, 1924.

1391. Black, Charles L. *The People and the Court: Judicial Review in a Democracy.* New York: Macmillan, 1960.

1392. Bobbitt, Philip. "Constitutional Fate." *Texas Law Review* 58 (April 1980): 695-775.

1393. Brown, William H. "Judicial Review of Congressional Investigative Powers with Special Reference to the Period 1945-1957." Ph.D. diss., American University, 1959.

1394. Bruff, Harold H. "Judicial Review and the President's Statutory Powers." *Virginia Law Review* 68 (January 1982): 1-61.

1395. Bullitt, William M. "The Supreme Court and Unconstitutional Legislation." *American Bar Association Journal* 10 (June 1924): 419-425.

1396. Burns, Edward M. "Madison's Theory of Judicial Review." *Kentucky Law Journal* 24 (May 1936): 412-423.

1397. Burr, Charles H. "Unconstitutional Laws and the Federal Judicial Power." *University of Pennsylvania Law Review* 60 (June 1912): 624-642.

1398. Call, Joseph L. "Judicial Review vs. Judicial Supremacy." *Dickinson Law Review* 62 (October 1957): 71-83.

1399. Cappelletti, Mauro. "Judicial Review in Comparative Perspective." *California Law Review* 58 (October 1970): 1017-1053.

1400. Cappelletti, Mauro. *Judicial Review in the Contemporary World*. Indianapolis: Bobbs-Merrill, 1971.

1401. Carey, George W. "The Supreme Court, Judicial Review, and *Federalist 78*." *Modern Age* 18 (Fall 1974): 356-369.

1402. Carpenter, Charles E. "Constitutionality of the National Industrial Recovery Act and the Agricultural Adjustment Act." *Southern California Law Review* 7 (January 1934): 125-143.

1403. Carr, Robert K. *The Supreme Court and Judicial Review*. New York: Farrar and Rinehart, 1942.

1404. Carson, Hampton L. "The Historic Relation of Judicial Power to Unconstitutional Legislation." *University of Pennsylvania Law Review* 60 (October 1912): 687-699.

1405. Catton, Bruce. "Black Pawn on a Field of Peril." *American Heritage* 15 (December 1963): 66-71.

1406. Choper, Jesse H. *Judicial Review and the National Political Process: A Functional Reconsideration of the Role of the Supreme Court*. Chicago: University of Chicago Press, 1980.

1407. Choper, Jesse H. "On the Warren Court and Judicial Review." *Catholic University of America Law Review* 17 (Fall 1967): 20-43.

1408. Choper, Jesse H. "Too Much Judicial Review May Be Injudicious." *Center Magazine* 14 (July/August 1981): 29-38.

1409. Clark, Charles E. "Supreme Court or People?" *American Scholar* 6 (Spring 1937): 201-213.

1410. Claunch, John M., ed. *The Politics of Judicial Review, 1937-1957: A Symposium*. Dallas: Southern Methodist University Press, 1957.

1411. Conkle, Daniel O. "Nonoriginalist Constitutional Rights and the Problem of Judicial Finality." *Hastings Constitutional Law Quarterly* 13 (Fall 1985): 9-56.

1412. Cooper, Charles P. *The Power of the Supreme Court of the United States to Declare Acts of Congress Void: Did the Framers of the Constitution and the American People Intend to Confer Such Power? Discussions of the Judicial Power, by the Delegates to the Constitutional Conventions*. Jacksonville, FL: Cooper Press, 1935.

1413. Corwin, Edward S. *Court over Constitution: A Study of Judicial Review as an Instrument of Popular Government*. Princeton, NJ: Princeton University Press, 1938.

1414. Corwin, Edward S. "Curbing the Court." *American Labor Legislation Review* 26 (June 1936): 85-88.

1415. Corwin, Edward S. "Curbing the Court." *Annals of the American Academy of Political and Social Science* 185 (May 1936): 45-55.

1416. Corwin, Edward S. *The Doctrine of Judicial Review, Its Legal and Historical Basis, and Other Essays*. Princeton, NJ: Princeton University Press, 1914.

1417. Corwin, Edward S. "The *Dred Scott* Decision in Light of Contemporary Legal Doctrines." *American Historical Review* 17 (October 1911): 52-69.

1418. Corwin, Edward S. "The Establishment of Judicial Review." *Michigan Law Review* 9 (December 1910): 102-125; (February 1911): 283-316.

1419. Corwin, Edward S. "*Marbury v. Madison* and the Doctrine of Judicial Review." *Michigan Law Review* 12 (May 1914): 538-572.

1420. Corwin, Edward S. "The Supreme Court and Unconstitutional Acts of Congress." *Michigan Law Review* 4 (June 1906): 616-630.

1421. Coxe, Brinton. *An Essay on Judicial Power and Unconstitutional Legislation, Being a Commentary on Parts of the Con-*

stitution of the United States. Philadelphia: Kay and Brother, 1893.

1422. Culp, Maurice S. "A Survey of the Proposals to Limit or Deny the Power of Judicial Review by the Supreme Court of the United States." *Indiana Law Journal* 4 (March 1929): 386-398; (April 1929): 474-490.

1423. Curtice, Lawrence L. "Judicial Review of Selective Service Action: A Need for Reform." *California Law Review* 56 (April 1968): 448-465.

1424. Davis, Horace A. "Annulment of Legislation by the Supreme Court." *American Political Science Review* 7 (November 1913): 541-587.

1425. Davis, Horace A. *The Judicial Veto.* Boston: Houghton Mifflin, 1914.

1426. Davis, Kenneth C. "Ripeness of Governmental Action for Judicial Review." *Harvard Law Review* 68 (May 1955): 1122-1153; (June 1955): 1326-1373.

1427. Davis, Michael H. "The Law/Politics Distinction, the French Conseil Constitutional, and the U.S. Supreme Court." *American Journal of Comparative Law* 34 (Winter 1986): 45-92.

1428. Dean, Howard E. *Judicial Review and Democracy.* New York: Random House, 1967.

1429. Dean, Howard E. "Judicial Review, Judicial Legislation, and Judicial Oligarchy." *Oregon Law Review* 34 (December 1954): 20-32.

1430. Deener, David. "Judicial Review in Modern Constitutional Systems." *American Political Science Review* 46 (December 1952): 1067-1099.

1431. Destler, I. M. "Dateline Washington: Life after the Veto." *Foreign Policy* 52 (Fall 1983): 181-186.

1432. Dimond, Paul R. *The Supreme Court and Judicial Choice: The Role of*

Provisional Review in a Democracy. Ann Arbor: University of Michigan Press, 1989.

1433. Doar, W. T. "The Power of the Courts to Declare Laws Unconstitutional." *Wisconsin Bar Association Proceedings* 23 (1933): 15-34.

1434. Doolittle, James R. "The Veto Power of the Supreme Court." *Chicago Law Times* 1 (April 1887): 177-186.

1435. Drone, Eaton S. "The Power of the Supreme Court." *Forum* 8 (February 1890): 653-664.

1436. Edgerton, Henry W. "The Incidence of Judicial Control over Congress." *Cornell Law Quarterly* 22 (April 1937): 299-348.

1437. Ehrlich, Walter. "Was the *Dred Scott* Case Valid?" *Journal of American History* 55 (September 1968): 256-265.

1438. Elliot, William Y. "The Supreme Court as Censor." In *The Need for Constitutional Reform: A Program for National Security*, by William Y. Elliot, 147-159. New York: McGraw-Hill, 1935.

1439. Elliott, Sheldon D. "The Supreme Court in the American Constitutional System: Court Curbing Proposals in Congress, 1935-1958." *Notre Dame Lawyer* 33 (August 1958): 597-616.

1440. Ely, John H. *Democracy and Distrust: A Theory of Judicial Review.* Cambridge: Harvard University Press, 1980.

1441. Eschweiler, F. C. "The Veto Power of the Judiciary." *Marquette Law Review* 7 (December 1922): 5-27.

1442. Esterline, Blackburn. "Acts of Congress Declared Unconstitutional by the Supreme Court of the United States." *American Law Review* 38 (January/February 1904): 21-43.

1443. Estreicher, Samuel. "Platonic Guardians of Democracy: John Hart Ely's Role for the Supreme Court in the Constitution's Open Texture." *New York University Law Review* 56 (May/June 1981): 547-582.

1444. Ewing, Albert W. *Legal and Historical Status of the* Dred Scott *Decision: A History of the Case and an Examination of the Opinion Delivered by the Supreme Court of the United States, March 6, 1857.* Washington, DC: Cobden, 1909.

1445. Farber, William O. "Judicial Self-Limitation: A Study of Those Limitations Imposed by the United States Supreme Court on Its Exercise of the Power of Judicial Review." Ph.D. diss., University of Wisconsin, 1936.

1446. Fay, Michael M. "The Pluralization of the Supreme Court: Inciting an Interpretive Battle with the Non-Political Branch." *Journal of Law and Politics* 4 (Summer 1987): 165-205.

1447. Field, Oliver P. *The Effect of an Unconstitutional Statute.* Minneapolis: University of Minnesota Press, 1935.

1448. Field, Oliver P. "Unconstitutional Legislation by Congress." *American Political Science Review* 39 (February 1945): 54-61.

1449. Forte, David F., ed. *The Supreme Court in American Politics: Judicial Activism and Judicial Restraint.* Lexington, MA: D. C. Heath, 1972.

1450. Fraenkel, Osmond K. "Judicial Review and Civil Liberties." *Brooklyn Law Review* 6 (May 1937): 409-422.

1451. Frey, John P. "Shall the People or the Supreme Court Be the Final Voice in Legislation?" *American Federationist* 29 (September 1922): 629-635.

1452. Friedelbaum, Stanley H. "Reprise or Denouement: Deference and the New Dissonance in the Burger Court." *Emory Law Journal* 26 (Spring 1977): 337-378.

1453. Gangi, William. "The Supreme Court: An Intentionist's Critique of Non-Interpretive Review." *Catholic Lawyer* 28 (Autumn 1983): 253-314.

1454. Gardner, James A. "The Supreme Court and Philosophy of Law." *Villanova Law Review* 5 (Winter 1960): 181-205.

1455. Giddings, Franklin H. "Supreme Court Government." *American Federationist* 15 (February 1908): 94-96.

1456. Gilbert, Wilfred C. *Provisions of Federal Law Held Unconstitutional by the Supreme Court of the United States.* Washington, DC: Congressional Research Service, 1975.

1457. Grant, J. A. C. "*Marbury v. Madison* Today." *American Political Science Review* 23 (August 1929): 673-681.

1458. Grey, Thomas C. "Do We Have an Unwritten Constitution?" *Stanford Law Review* 27 (February 1975): 703-718.

1459. Gunther, Gerald. "The Subtle Vices of the Passive Virtues: A Comment on Principle and Expediency in Judicial Review." *Columbia Law Review* 64 (January 1964): 1-25.

1460. Haines, Charles G. "Judicial Review of Acts of Congress and the Need for Constitutional Reform." *Yale Law Journal* 45 (March 1936): 816-856.

1461. Haines, Charles G. "Judicial Review of Legislation in the United States and the Doctrine of Vested Rights." *Texas Law Review* 2 (April 1924): 257-290, 387-421; 3 (June 1924): 1-43.

1462. Hall, Kermit L. *The Supreme Court and Judicial Review in American History.* Washington, DC: American Historical Association, 1985.

1463. Handberg, Roger B., Jr., and Harold F. Hill. "Court Curbing, Court Reversals, and Judicial Review: The Supreme Court versus Congress." *Law and Society Review* 14 (Winter 1980): 309-322.

1464. Harris, Luther. "Judicial Review in the United States of America: 1777-1865."

Dickinson Law Review 56 (January 1952): 177-200.

1465. Harris, Robert J. "The Decline of Judicial Review." *Journal of Politics* 10 (February 1948): 1-19.

1466. Harris, Robert J. "Judicial Review: Vagaries and Varieties." *Journal of Politics* 38 (August 1976): 173-208.

1467. Hart, Henry M., Jr. "Professor Crosskey and Judicial Review." *Harvard Law Review* 67 (June 1954): 1456-1486.

1468. Hatcher, John H. "The Power of Federal Courts to Declare Acts of Congress Unconstitutional." *West Virginia Law Quarterly* 42 (February 1936): 96-109.

1469. Hill, J. H. "Before *Marbury v. Madison.*" *Oklahoma State Bar Journal* 9 (July 1938): 129-132; (August 1938): 158-163.

1470. Hodder, Frank H. "Some Phases of the *Dred Scott* Case." *Mississippi Valley Historical Review* 16 (June 1929): 3-22.

1471. Hopkins, Vincent C. *Dred Scott's Case.* New York: Atheneum, 1967.

1472. Howard, Benjamin C. *A Report of the Decision of the Supreme Court of the United States and the Opinions of the Judges Thereof, in the Case of Dred Scott vs. John F. A. Sandford, December Term, 1856.* New York: D. Appleton, 1857.

1473. Jaffe, Louis L. "Judicial Review: Constitutional and Jurisdictional Fact." *Harvard Law Review* 70 (April 1961): 953-985.

1474. Jaffe, Louis L. "Judicial Review: Substantial Evidence on the Whole Record." *Harvard Law Review* 64 (June 1951): 1233-1261.

1475. Jaffe, Louis L. "The Right to Judicial Review." *Harvard Law Review* 71 (January/March 1958): 769-814.

1476. Jaffe, Louis L. "Standing to Secure Judicial Review: Public Actions." *Harvard Law Review* 74 (May 1961): 1265-1314.

1477. Johnsen, Julia E., ed. *Limitation of the Power of the Supreme Court to Declare Acts of Congress Unconstitutional.* New York: H. W. Wilson, 1935.

1478. Johnson, George R., Jr. "Two Hundred Years of Judicial Review: Delivering the Promise of America." *George Mason University Law Review* 9 (Summer 1987): 223-244.

1479. Kadish, Sanford H. "Judicial Review in the United States Supreme Court. . . . " *Texas Law Review* 37 (November 1958): 1-32.

1480. Ketcham, Ralph L. "James Madison and Judicial Review." *Syracuse Law Review* 8 (Spring 1957): 158-165.

1481. Killian, Johnny H. *The 18-Year-Old Vote Case: The Voting Rights Act Amendments of 1970 and Its Age Reduction, Residency Changes, and Literacy Test Suspension in the Supreme Court.* Washington, DC: Congressional Research Service, 1975.

1482. Kline, M. A. "The United States Supreme Court and the Federal Constitution." *Wyoming State Bar Association* (1935-1937): 80-95.

1483. Kolson, Kenneth P. " 'Voluntary Relinquishment' of American Citizenship: A Proposed Definition." *Cornell Law Review* 53 (January 1968): 325-336.

1484. Kommers, David P. "Judicial Review: Its Influence Abroad." *Annals of the American Academy of Political and Social Science* 428 (November 1976): 52-64.

1485. Kramer, Daniel C. "Courts, Legislatures, and Social Reform." *Comparative Politics* 4 (January 1972): 251-268.

1486. Kreamer, John H. "Judicial Review of Orders of the Interstate Commerce Commission." *ICC Practitioners Journal* 18 (March 1951): 496-507.

1487. Krislov, Samuel. "Jefferson and Judicial Review: Refereeing Cahn, Commager, and Mendelson." *Journal of Public Law* 9 (Fall 1960): 374-381.

1488. Kutler, Stanley I., ed. *The* Dred Scott *Decision: Law or Politics?* Boston: Houghton Mifflin, 1967.

1489. Levinson, Joseph L. "Limiting Judicial Review by Act of Congress." *California Law Review* 23 (September 1935): 591-601.

1490. Levy, Leonard W., ed. *Judicial Review and the Supreme Court: Selected Essays.* New York: Harper and Row, 1967.

1491. Lewinson, Joseph L. *Limiting Judicial Review.* Los Angeles: Parker, Stone, and Baird, 1937.

1492. Lewis, Anthony. "A Newspaperman's View: The Role of the Supreme Court." *American Bar Association Journal* 45 (September 1959): 911-914.

1493. London, Meyer. "Veto Power of the Supreme Court." *American Federationist* 30 (March 1923): 224-231.

1494. Long, Joseph R. "Unconstitutional Acts of Congress." *Virginia Law Review* 1 (March 1914): 417-444.

1495. Lusky, Louis. "For Preservation of Judicial Review." *Journal of Law and Politics* 3 (Spring 1987): 597-623.

1496. McBain, Howard L. "Some Aspects of Judicial Review." *Boston University Law Review* 16 (June 1936): 525-538.

1497. MacCallum, Gerald C., Jr. "Judicial Review by the United States Supreme Court: An Analysis of Some Controversies in Accounts of a Judicial Activity." Ph.D. diss., University of California, Berkeley, 1961.

1498. McCormac, Eugene I. "The Supreme Court and Unconstitutional Laws." *California Law Review* 25 (July 1937): 552-563.

1499. Mace, George. "Anti-Democratic Character of Judicial Review." *California Law Review* 60 (June 1972): 1140-1149.

1500. McGowan, Carl. "Regulatory Analysis and Judicial Review." *Ohio State Law Journal* 42 (Fall 1981): 627-637.

1501. McLaughlin, Andrew C. "*Marbury vs. Madison* Again." *American Bar Association Journal* 14 (March 1928): 155-159.

1502. Mahoney, Edward A., Jr. "Right of United States Supreme Court to Declare Act of Congress Unconstitutional: Historical Study." *Notre Dame Lawyer* 16 (May 1941): 379-386.

1503. Marshall, Geoffrey. "The Supreme Court and the Dilemma of Judicial Review." *Political Studies* 24 (December 1976): 502-509.

1504. Mason, Alpheus T. "Has the Supreme Court Abdicated?" *North American Review* 238 (October 1934): 353-360.

1505. Mendelson, Wallace. "Judicial Review and Party Politics." *Vanderbilt Law Review* 12 (March 1959): 447-457.

1506. Moore, Blaine F. "Judicial Veto and Political Democracy." *American Political Science Review* 10 (November 1916): 700-709.

1507. Moore, Blaine F. *The Supreme Court and Unconstitutional Legislation.* New York: Columbia University, 1913.

1508. Moschzisker, Robert von. *Judicial Review of Legislation: A Consideration of the Warrants for and Merits of Our American System of Judicially Reviewing Legislation to Ascertain Its Constitutional Validity.* Washington, DC: National Association for Constitutional Government, 1923.

1509. Murray, Craig C. "Chief Justice Gibson of the Pennsylvania Supreme Court and Judicial Review." *University of Pittsburgh Law Review* 32 (Winter 1970): 127-166.

1510. Palmer, Ben W. "Judicial Review: Usurpation or Abdication?" *American Bar*

Association Journal 46 (August 1960): 881-888.

1511. Peake, James F. "Power of the Supreme Court to Nullify Acts of Congress." *Constitutional Review* 8 (April 1934): 83-97.

1512. Peck, Darrell L. "Justices and the Generals: The Supreme Court and Judicial Review of Military Activities." *Military Law Review* 70 (Fall 1975): 1-81.

1513. Peck, Epaphroditus. "The Power of the Courts of the United States to Hold Statutes Void as Not Authorized by the Constitution." *Connecticut Bar Journal* 10 (July 1936): 192-205.

1514. Pennoyer, Sylvester. "The Case of *Marbury v. Madison.*" *American Law Review* 30 (March/April 1986): 188-202.

1515. Pennoyer, Sylvester. "The Income Tax Decision and the Power of the Court to Nullify Acts of Congress." *American Law Review* 29 (July/August 1895): 550-558.

1516. Plous, Harold J., and Gordon Baker. *McCulloch v. Maryland*: Right Principle, Wrong Case." *Stanford Law Review* 9 (1957): 710-731.

1517. Prygoski, Philip J. "Supreme Court Review of Congressional Action in the Federalism Area." *Duquesne Law Review* 18 (Winter 1980): 197-223.

1518. Ralston, Jackson H. "Judicial Control over Legislatures as to Constitutional Questions." *American Law Review* 54 (January/March 1920): 1-38, 193-230.

1519. Raymar, Robert S. "Judicial Review of Credentials Contests: The Experience of the 1972 Democratic National Convention." *George Washington Law Review* 42 (November 1972): 1-39.

1520. Richter, A. W. "A Legislative Curb on the Judiciary." *Journal of Political Economy* 21 (April 1913): 281-295.

1521. Rostow, Eugene V. "The Democratic Character of Judicial Review." *Harvard Law Review* 66 (December 1952): 193-224.

1522. Sargent, Noel. "The American Judicial Veto." *American Law Review* 51 (September 1917): 663-710.

1523. Saylor, J. R. "Judicial Review Prior to *Marbury v. Madison.*" *Southwestern Law Journal* 7 (Winter 1953): 88-96.

1524. Senior, Mildred R., comp. *The Supreme Court: Its Power of Judicial Review with Respect to Congressional Legislation.* Washington, DC: Division of Library Science, George Washington University, 1937.

1525. Shapiro, Martin M. "Judicial Review: Political Reality and Legislative Purpose: The Supreme Court's Supervision of Congressional Investigations." *Vanderbilt Law Review* 15 (March 1962): 535-557.

1526. Shapiro, Martin M. "The Supreme Court and Government Planning: Judicial Review and Policy Formation." *George Washington Law Review* 35 (December 1966): 329-344.

1527. Shearer, Alan K. "The Political Unity of Judicial Review." *University of Missouri-Kansas City Law Review* 2 (May 1954): 381-392.

1528. Sky, Theodore. "Judicial Review of Congressional Investigations: Is There an Alternative to Contempt?" *George Washington Law Review* 31 (December 1962): 399-430.

1529. Squiers, Mary P. "Restricted Judicial Review Provisions of the Clean Air Act: Denial of Due Process or Indispensable to Efficient Administration?" *Boston College Environmental Affairs Law Review* 8 (1979): 119-151.

1530. Stenberg, Richard R. "Some Political Aspects of the *Dred Scott* Case." *Mississippi Valley Historical Review* 19 (March 1933): 571-577.

1531. Stern, Robert L. "Separability and Separability Clauses in the Supreme Court." *Harvard Law Review* 51 (November 1937): 76-128.

1532. Swindler, William F. "Reviewing Judicial Review. A Note in Constitutional History." *St. Louis University Law Journal* 6 (Summer 1960): 121-149.

1533. Swisher, Carl B. "*Dred Scott*: One Hundred Years After." *Journal of Politics* 19 (May 1957): 167-183.

1534. Thompson, Bradley M. "Justice Afloat: Political and Judicial Review of the Famous *Dred Scott* Case." *Lawyer and Banker* 10 (December 1917): 381-386.

1535. Tiedeman, Christopher G. "The Income Tax Decisions as an Object Lesson in Constitutional Construction." *Annals of the American Academy of Political and Social Science* 6 (September 1895): 268-279.

1536. Timbers, William H., and David A. Wirth. "Private Rights of Action and Judicial Review in Federal Environmental Law." *Cornell Law Review* 70 (March 1985): 403-417.

1537. Trickett, William. "Judicial Nullification of Acts of Congress." *North American Review* 185 (August 16, 1907): 848-856.

1538. Trickett, William. "*Marbury v. Madison*: A Critique." *American Law Review* 53 (September 1919): 737-748.

1539. Trieber, Jacob. "Review of Act of Congress of February 13, 1925, Defining the Jurisdiction of the Circuit Courts of Appeals and of the Supreme Court." *American Law Review* 59 (May 1925): 321-333.

1540. Trombetas, Thomas P. "The U.S. Supreme Court and the Federal Constitutional Court of Germany." *Revue Hellennique de Droit Internationale* 17 (December 1964): 281-291.

1541. Turner, Jesse. "Four Fugitive Cases from the Realm of American Constitutional Law." *American Law Review* 49 (November 1915): 818-857.

1542. Ulmer, S. Sidney. "Judicial Review as Political Behavior: Temporary Check on Congress." *Administrative Science Quarterly* 4 (March 1960): 426-445.

1543. U.S. Library of Congress. *Provisions of the Federal Law Held Unconstitutional by the Supreme Court of the U.S.* Washington, DC: U.S. Government Printing Office, 1936.

1544. Valuri, John T. "Constitutional Theodicy: The Antimony of Finality and Fallibility in Judicial Review." *St. Louis University Law Journal* 29 (March 1985): 245-292.

1545. Van Alstyne, William W. "A Critical Guide to *Marbury v. Madison*." *Duke Law Journal* 1969 (January 1969): 1-47.

1546. Van Alstyne, William W. "The Idea of the Constitution as Hard Law." *North Carolina State Bar Quarterly* 34 (Spring 1987): 4-9.

1547. Warren, Charles. "Legislative and Judicial Attacks on the Supreme Court of the United States: A History of the Twenty-fifth Section of the Judiciary Act." *American Law Review* 47 (January 1913): 1-34; (March 1913): 161-189.

1548. Warren, Charles. "New Light on the History of the Federal Judiciary Act of 1789." *Harvard Law Review* 37 (November 1923): 49-132.

1549. West, Robin L. "In the Interest of the Governed: A Utilitarian Justification for Substantive Judicial Review." *Georgia Law Review* 18 (Spring 1984): 469-528.

1550. Wheeler, Everett P. "Judicial Power to Declare Legislation Unconstitutional." *American Bar Association Journal* 10 (January 1924): 29-30.

1551. Wilson, Charles M. *The* Dred Scott *Decision*. Philadelphia: Auerbach Publishers, 1973.

1552. Wolfson, Richard F. "Extraordinary Writs in the Supreme Court since *Ex parte Peru*." *Columbia Law Review* 51 (December 1951): 977-992.

1553. Yates, Robert. "The Letters of Brutus." In *Court over Constitution: A Study of Judicial Review as an Instrument of Popular Government*, edited by Edward S. Corwin, 231-262. Princeton, NJ: Princeton University Press, 1938.

1554. Young, G. C. "Some Observations on the Supreme Court and Its Decisions." *Kansas City Law Review* 4 (June 1936): 122-125.

Monetary Powers

1555. Dolan, Michael W. "Congress, the Executive, and the Court: The Great Resale Price Maintenance Affair of 1983." *Public Administration Review* 45 (November 1985): 718-722.

1556. Howard, Robert L. "The Supreme Court, the Constitution, and the A.A.A." *Kentucky Law Journal* 25 (May 1937): 291-320.

1557. Rauch, Jonathan. "The Thickening Fog: The Supreme Court's Decision Striking Down the Balanced Budget Act's Automatic Mechanism for Cutting Spending Has Added to Congress's Budgetary Uncertainty." *National Journal* 18 (July 12, 1986): 1721-1724.

1558. Wales, Robert W. "Legislative Aspects of Ten Years of Federal Income Tax Opinions of the Supreme Court." *Tax Law Review* 4 (November 1948): 73-87.

The Court and the President

General Studies

1559. Alsop, Joseph W., and Turner Catledge. *The 168 Days*. Garden City, NY: Doubleday, Doran, 1938.

1560. Anderson, James J. "The President's Supreme Court Proposal: A Study in Presidential Leadership and Public Opinion." Ph.D. diss., Cornell University, 1941.

1561. Baker, Leonard. *Back to Back: The Duel between FDR and the Supreme Court*. New York: Macmillan, 1967.

1562. Barondess, Benjamin. "Buchanan and the *Dred Scott* Justices." *Manuscripts* 10 (Winter 1958): 2-9.

1563. Basler, Roy P. "Beef! Beef! Beef! Lincoln and Judge Robertson." *Abraham Lincoln Quarterly* 6 (September 1951): 400-407.

1564. Braden, George D. "Umpire to the Federal System." *University of Chicago Law Review* 10 (October 1942): 27-48.

1565. Brudner, Helen G. "A Study and Analysis of the Role of the Supreme Court of the United States as Interpreter of the Powers of the President as the Commander in Chief." Ph.D. diss., New York University, 1973.

1566. Busch, D. Carolyn, and Lee E. Hartman, Jr. "*Jefferson v. Hackney*: Charting the Direction of the Nixon Court." *Public Welfare* 31 (Spring 1973): 55-63.

1567. "Candidates Answer." *American Bar Association Journal* 70 (November 1984): 52-57.

1568. Cannon, Mark W. "Administrative Change and the Supreme Court." *Judicature* 57 (March 1974): 334-341.

1569. Carpenter, Charles E. "President and the Court: Should the President Be Given the Power to Appoint Additional Justices to the Supreme Court?" *U.S. Law Review* 71 (March 1937): 139-149.

1570. Carrington, Paul D. "Political Questions: The Judicial Check on the Executive." *Virginia Law Review* 42 (February 1956): 175-201.

1571. Casey, Gregory. "The Theory of Presidential Association: A Replication." *American Journal of Political Science* 19 (February 1975): 19-25.

1572. Chapin, Leland T. "President Roosevelt and the United States Supreme Court." *Scots Law Times* 1937 (December 4, 1937): 249-251.

1573. Cope, Alfred H., and Fred Krinsky, eds. *Franklin D. Roosevelt and the Supreme Court.* Rev. ed. Lexington, MA: D. C. Heath, 1969.

1574. Corwin, Edward S. *The President: Office and Powers, 1787-1957.* 4th ed. New York: New York University Press, 1957.

1575. Corwin, Edward S. "The *Steel Seizure Case*: A Judicial Brick without Straw." *Columbia Law Review* 53 (January 1953): 53-66.

1576. Crouch, Barry A. "Dennis Chavez and Roosevelt's 'Court-Packing Plan'." *New Mexico Historical Review* 42 (October 1967): 261-280.

1577. Cummings, Homer S., and Carl McFarland. *Federal Justice: Chapters in the History of Justice and the Federal Executive.* New York: Macmillan, 1937.

1578. Dause, Charles A. "An Analysis of the 1937 Public Debate over Franklin D. Roosevelt's Court Reform Proposal." Ph.D. diss., Wayne State University, 1969.

1579. Davenport, Frederick M. "Executive Intimidation of the Judiciary." *Outlook* 86 (July 13, 1907): 553-555.

1580. Dilliard, Irving. "Lincoln Remakes the Supreme Court." In *Lincoln for the Ages*, edited by Ralph G. Newman, 301-306. Garden City, NY: Doubleday, 1960.

1581. Dilliard, Irving. "Mr. Roosevelt and the Supreme Court: The Observations of a Citizen." *Survey Graphic* 26 (February 1937): 93-96.

1582. Dionisopoulos, P. Allan. "New Patterns in Judicial Control of the Presidency: 1950s to 1970s." *Akron Law Review* 10 (Summer 1976): 1-38.

1583. Dixon, Lawrence W. "Attitude of Thomas Jefferson toward the Judiciary." *Southwestern Social Science Quarterly* 28 (June 1947): 13-19.

1584. Drew, Elizabeth. "Washington: The Nixon Court." *Atlantic* 230 (November 1972): 6-10.

1585. Duane, Morris. *The New Deal in Court.* Philadelphia: G. T. Bisel, 1935.

1586. Dumbauld, Edward. *Thomas Jefferson and the Law.* Norman: University of Oklahoma Press, 1978.

1587. Duram, James C. "Supreme Court Packing and the New Deal: The View from Southwestern Michigan." *Michigan History* 52 (Spring 1968): 13-27.

1588. Duram, James C., and Eleanor A. Duram. "Congressman Clifford Hope's Correspondence with His Constituents: A Conservative View of the Court-Packing Fight of 1937." *Kansas Historical Quarterly* 37 (Spring 1971): 64-80.

1589. Eizenstat, Stuart E. "White House and Justice Department after Watergate." *American Bar Association Journal* 68 (February 1982): 175-177.

1590. Ellingwood, Albert R. "The New Deal and the Constitution." *Illinois Law Review* 28 (February 1934): 729-751.

1591. Eriksson, Erik M. *The Supreme Court and the New Deal: A Study of Recent Constitutional Interpretation.* Los Angeles: Lymanhouse, 1941.

1592. Fehrenbacher, Don E. "Lincoln and Judicial Supremacy: A Note on the Galena Speech of July 23, 1856." *Civil War History* 16 (September 1970): 197-204.

1593. Flynn, John T. "The President and the Supreme Court." *Southern Review* 3 (Summer 1937): 1-14.

1594. Galloway, Russell W., Jr. "The Court That Challenged the New Deal." *Santa Clara Law Review* 24 (Winter 1984): 65-109.

1595. Gardner, Robert W. "Roosevelt and Supreme Court Expansion." *Connecticut Review* 3 (October 1969): 58-68.

1596. Garvey, Gerald. "Scholar in Politics: Edward S. Corwin and the 1937 Court-Packing Battle." *Princeton University Library Chronicle* 31 (Autumn 1969): 1-11.

1597. Genovese, Michael A. "The Supreme Court as a Check on Presidential Power." *Presidential Studies Quarterly* 6 (Winter/Spring 1976): 40-44.

1598. Genovese, Michael A. *The Supreme Court, the Constitution, and Presidential Power.* Lanham, MD: University Press of America, 1980.

1599. Gressley, Gene M. "Joseph C. O'Mahoney, FDR, and the Supreme Court." *Pacific Historical Review* 40 (May 1971): 183-202.

1600. Grigoroff, Catherine S. "A Study of the Political Strategy and Techniques Employed in the Court Reorganization Fight of 1937." Master's thesis, University of Illinois, 1949.

1601. Grinnell, Frank W. "The Supreme Court and the Presidency." *Massachusetts Law Quarterly* 40 (May 1955): 22-24.

1602. Gunther, Gerald. "The Reagan Impact on the Supreme Court May Not Be What We're Expecting or Fearing: A Noted Constitutional Expert Explains Why." *Student Lawyer* 14 (October 1985): 11-13.

1603. Gustafson, Milton O. "The Supreme Court and Kissinger's Telephone Records." *Society for History of American Foreign Relations Newsletter* 11 (1980): 18-22.

1604. Habibuddin, Syed M. "Theodore Roosevelt's Attitude toward the Judi-

ciary." *Indian Journal of Politics* 9 (1975): 20-32.

1605. Hoar, George F. *The Charge against President Grant and Attorney General Hoar of Packing the Supreme Court of the United States, to Secure the Reversal of the Legal Tender Decision by the Appointment of Judges Bradley and Strong, Refuted: Letter to the Boston Herald.* Worcester, MA: C. Hamilton, 1896.

1606. Hunter, Robert M. "Shall the Supreme Court Have New Blood?" *Ohio State University Law Journal* 3 (March 1937): 125-141.

1607. Ifshin, David M., and Roger E. Warin. "Litigating the 1980 Presidential Election." *American University Law Review* 31 (Spring 1982): 485-550.

1608. Ireton, Robert E. "Jefferson and the Supreme Court." *Boston University Law Review* 17 (January 1937): 81-89.

1609. Jacobson, Gary J. "Abraham Lincoln on This Question of Judicial Authority: The Theory of Constitutional Aspiration." *Western Political Quarterly* 36 (March 1983): 52-70.

1610. John, Arthur M. "Theodore Roosevelt and the Bureau of Corporations." *Mississippi Valley Historical Review* 45 (March 1945): 571-590.

1611. Kauper, Paul G. "Judicial Review and 'Strict Construction' of the Constitution: President Nixon and the Supreme Court of the United States." *Zeitschrift für Auslandisches Offentliches Recht und Volkerrecht* 30 (December 1970): 631-645.

1612. Klaus, Samuel, ed. *The Milligan Case.* New York: Knopf, 1929.

1613. Kurland, Philip B. *Watergate and the Constitution.* Chicago: University of Chicago Press, 1978.

1614. Lamb, Karl. "Opposition Party as Secret Agent: Republicans and the Court Fight, 1937." *Michigan Academy of Sci-*

ence, Arts and Letters, Papers 46 (1961): 539-550.

1615. Langran, Robert W. "Presidents vs. the Court." *Supreme Court Historical Society Yearbook* 1977 (1977): 70-78.

1616. Latham, Frank B. *FDR and the Supreme Court Fight, 1937.* London: F. Watts, 1972.

1617. Lawrence, David. *Supreme Court or Political Puppets? Shall the Supreme Court Be Free or Controlled by a Supreme Executive?* New York: D. Appleton, 1937.

1618. Lecher, Louis A. "President's Supreme Court Plan." *American Bar Association Journal* 23 (April 1937): 242-246.

1619. Lee, Frederic P. "The Origins of Judicial Control of Federal Executive Action." *Georgetown Law Journal* 36 (March 1948): 287-309.

1620. Leek, L. H. "Packing the Court." *American Federationist* 44 (April 1937): 378-387.

1621. Lees, John D. *The President and the Supreme Court: New Deal to Watergate.* Durham, NC: British Association for American Studies, 1980.

1622. Leuchtenburg, William E. "FDR's Court-Packing Plan: A Second Life, A Second Death." *Duke Law Journal* 1985 (June/September 1985): 673-689.

1623. Leuchtenburg, William E. "Franklin D. Roosevelt's Supreme Court Packing Plan." In *Essays on the New Deal*, edited by Harold Hollingsworth and William F. Holmes, 69-115. Austin: University of Texas Press, 1969.

1624. Leuchtenburg, William E. "The Origins of Franklin D. Roosevelt's 'Court-Packing' Plan." *Supreme Court Review* 1966 (1966): 347-400.

1625. Longaker, Richard P. "Andrew Jackson and the Judiciary." *Political Science Quarterly* 71 (September 1956): 341-364.

1626. Lowitt, Richard. "Only God Can Change the Supreme Court." *Capitol Studies* 5 (Spring 1977): 9-24.

1627. McBain, Howard L. "The Constitution and the New Deal." *Yale Review* 25 (September 1935): 114-130.

1628. MacColl, E. Kimbark. "The Supreme Court and Public Opinion: A Study of the Court Fight of 1937." Ph.D. diss., University of California, 1953.

1629. McConnell, Grant. *The President Seizes the Steel Mills.* Montgomery: University of Alabama Press, 1960.

1630. Maddox, Robert J. "Roosevelt vs. the Court." *American History Illustrated* 4 (November 1969): 4-11.

1631. Mangan, Robert M. "Judicial Administrative Relationships: Old Wine or a New Brew?" *Georgetown Law Journal* 36 (May 1948): 589-601.

1632. Marcus, Maeva. "The *Steel Seizure Case* of 1952." Ph.D. diss., Columbia University, 1975.

1633. Marcus, Maeva. *Truman and the Steel Seizure Case: The Limits of Presidential Power.* New York: Columbia University Press, 1977.

1634. Mason, Alpheus T. "Politics and the Supreme Court: President Roosevelt's Proposal." *University of Pennsylvania Law Review* 85 (May 1937): 659-677.

1635. Miller, William I. "Dorothy Thompson and the Court Packing Plan: Of Muse and Men." *Houston Law Review* 19 (May 1982): 695-711.

1636. Morgan, Donald G. "The Origin of Supreme Court Dissent." *William and Mary Quarterly* 10 (July 1953): 353-377.

1637. Morrison, Rodney J. "Franklin D. Roosevelt and the Supreme Court: An Example of the Use of Probability Theory in Political History." *History and Theory* 16 (May 1977): 137-146.

1638. Murphy, Jay. "Some Observations

on the *Steel* Decisions." *Alabama Law Review* 4 (Spring 1952): 214-231.

1639. Nelson, Michael. "The President and the Court: Reinterpreting the Court-Packing Episode of 1937." *Political Science Quarterly* 103 (Summer 1988): 267-293.

1640. Niedziela, Theresa A. "Franklin D. Roosevelt and the Supreme Court." *Presidential Studies Quarterly* 6 (Fall 1976): 51-57.

1641. O'Brien, Francis W. "Bicentennial Reflections on Herbert Hoover and the Supreme Court." *Iowa Law Review* 61 (December 1975): 397-417.

1642. Patenaude, Lionel V. "Garner, Sumners, and Connally: The Defeat of the Roosevelt Court Bill in 1937." *Southwestern Historical Quarterly* 74 (July 1970): 36-51.

1643. Patterson, C. Perry. "The President over the Judiciary." *Brooklyn Law Review* 11 (October 1941): 1-29; (April 1942): 155-186.

1644. Pepper, George W. "Plain Speaking: The President's Case against the Supreme Court." *American Bar Association Journal* 23 (April 1937): 247-251.

1645. Phelps, Bernard F. "A Rhetorical Analysis of the 1937 Addresses of Franklin D. Roosevelt in Support of Court Reform." Master's thesis, Ohio State University, 1957.

1646. Pollitt, Daniel H. "A Dissenting View: The Executive Enforcement of Judicial Decrees." *American Bar Association Journal* 45 (June 1959): 600-603, 606.

1647. Pritchett, C. Herman. "President and the Supreme Court." *Journal of Politics* 11 (February 1949): 80-92.

1648. Pusey, Merlo J. "FDR vs. the Supreme Court." *American Heritage* 9 (April 1958): 24-27, 105-107.

1649. Putney, Bryant. "The President, the Constitution, and the Supreme Court." *Editorial Research Reports* 1 (June 19, 1935): 451-470.

1650. Raffel, Burton. "Presidential Removal Power: The Role of the Supreme Court." *University of Miami Law Review* 13 (Fall 1958): 69-80.

1651. Ratner, Sidney. "Was the Supreme Court Packed by President Grant?" *Political Science Quarterly* 50 (September 1935): 343-358.

1652. Roche, John P. "Executive Power and Domestic Emergency: The Quest for Prerogative." *Western Political Quarterly* 5 (December 1952): 592-618.

1653. Roosevelt, Theodore. "Judges and Progress." *Outlook* 100 (January 6, 1912): 40-48.

1654. Rossiter, Clinton L. *Supreme Court and the Commander in Chief.* Rev. ed. Ithaca, NY: Cornell University Press, 1976.

1655. Sachs, Stephen M. "The Supreme Court and National Emergency." Ph.D. diss., University of Chicago, 1968.

1656. Saylor, J. R. "Court Packing Prior to FDR." *Baylor Law Review* 20 (Spring 1968): 147-165.

1657. Schubert, Glendon A. "Judicial Review of the Subdelegation of Presidential Power." *Journal of Politics* 12 (November 1950): 668-693.

1658. Schubert, Glendon A. *The Presidency in the Courts.* Minneapolis: University of Minnesota Press, 1957.

1659. Schubert, Glendon A. "The *Steel* Case: Presidential Responsibility and Judicial Irresponsibility." *Western Political Quarterly* 6 (March 1953): 61-77.

1660. Schwartz, Bernard. "Bad Presidents Make Hard Law: Richard M. Nixon in the Supreme Court." *Rutgers Law Review* 31 (May 1978): 22-38.

1661. Schwartz, Bernard. "The Papers of

the Executive Branch." *American Bar Association Journal* 45 (May 1958): 467-470, 525-526.

1662. Scigliano, Robert. *The Supreme Court and the Presidency.* New York: Free Press, 1971.

1663. Sharp, James R. "Andrew Jackson and the Limits of Presidential Power." *Congressional Studies* 7 (Winter 1980): 63-80.

1664. Sirevag, Torbjorn. "Rooseveltian Ideas and the 1937 Court Fight: A Neglected Factor." *Historian* 33 (August 1971): 578-595.

1665. Smith, Charles W., Jr. "President Roosevelt's Attitude toward the Courts." *Kentucky Law Journal* 31 (May 1943): 301-315.

1666. Stephenson, D. Grier, Jr. "The Mild Magistracy of the Law: *U.S. versus Richard Nixon.*" *Intellect* 103 (February 1975): 288-292.

1667. Stinchfield, Frederick H. "The American Bar and the Supreme Court Proposal." *Washington Law Review* 12 (April 1937): 164-165.

1668. Stinchfield, Frederick H. "The Proposals as to the Supreme Court." *Florida Law Journal* 11 (April 1937): 135-141.

1669. Tanenhaus, Joseph. "The Supreme Court and Presidential Power." *Annals of the American Academy of Political and Social Science* 307 (September 1956): 106-113.

1670. Turner, Lynn W. "The Impeachment of John Pickering." *American Historical Review* 54 (April 1949): 485-507.

1671. Vieg, John A. "Supreme Court and Its Social Obligations." *American Federationist* 44 (August 1937): 835-843.

1672. Wallach, H. G. Peter. "Restraint and Self-Restraint: The Presidency and the Courts." *Capital University Law Review* 7 (Winter 1977): 59-74.

1673. Wasby, Stephen L. "The Presidency before the Courts." *Capital University Law Review* 6 (Winter 1976): 35-73.

1674. Wilkinson, Ignatius M. "The President's Plan Respecting the Supreme Court." *Fordham Law Review* 6 (May 1937): 179-189.

Executive Powers

1675. DeFuniak, W. Q. "The United States Supreme Court and the *Wiener* Case." *Notre Dame Lawyer* 23 (November 1947): 28-46.

1676. Dumbrell, John W., and John D. Lees. "Presidential Pocket-Veto Power: A Constitutional Anachronism?" *Political Studies* 28 (March 1980): 109-116.

1677. Eaton, William D. "Constitutional Guarantees and the *Steel* Decision." *Rocky Mountain Law Review* 25 (February 1953): 220-223.

1678. Galloway, George B. "Consequences of the *Myers* Decision." *American Law Review* 61 (July 1927): 481-508.

1679. Hart, James. "American Government and Politics: Bearing of *Myers v. United States* upon the Independence of Federal Administrative Tribunals." *American Political Science Review* 23 (August 1929): 657-672.

1680. Horn, Robert A. "The Warren Court and the Discretionary Power of the Executive." *Minnesota Law Review* 44 (March 1960): 639-672.

1681. Leuchtenburg, William E. "The Case of the Contentious Commissioner: *Humphrey's Executor v. U.S.*" In *Freedom and Reform: Essays in Honor of Henry Steele Commager*, edited by Harold M. Hyman and Leonard W. Levy, 276-312. New York: Harper and Row, 1967.

1682. Max Planck Institute. *Judicial Pro-*

tection against the Executive. 3 vols. Dobbs Ferry, NY: Oceana, 1970-1971.

1683. Milligan, Lambdin P. *The* Milligan *Case.* New York: Da Capo Press, 1970.

1684. Rosenberg, Morton. "Beyond the Limits of Executive Power: Presidential Control of Agency Rulemaking under Executive Order 12291." *Michigan Law Review* 80 (December 1981): 193-247.

1685. Ross, Russell M., and Fred Schwengel. "An Item Veto for the President." *Presidential Studies Quarterly* 12 (Winter 1982): 66-79.

1686. Stidham, Ronald, Robert A. Carp, and C. K. Rowland. "Patterns of Presidential Influence on the Federal District Courts: An Analysis of the Appointment Process." *Presidential Studies Quarterly* 14 (Fall 1984): 548-560.

Foreign Policy

1687. Belknap, Michael R. "The New Deal and the Emergency Powers Doctrine." *Texas Law Review* 62 (August 1983): 67-109.

1688. Bigel, Alan I. *The Supreme Court on Emergency Powers, Foreign Affairs, and Protection of Civil Liberties, 1935-1975.* Lanham, MD: University Press of America, 1986.

1689. Bigel, Alan I. "The Supreme Court on Presidential and Congressional Powers Relating to Foreign Affairs, War Powers, and Internal Security, 1935-1980." Ph.D. diss., New School for Social Research, 1984.

1690. Bricker, John W. "Constitutional Insurance for a Safe Treaty-Making Policy (1787-1955)." *Dickinson Law Review* 60 (January 1956): 103-120.

1691. Chirico, Guy W. "The Right to Travel and Presidential Emergency Authority: The Supreme Court Lowers the

Standard of Review in *Regan v. Wald.*" *Albany Law Review* 49 (Summer 1985): 1001-1031.

1692. D'Amato, Anthony A., and Robert O'Neil. *Judiciary and Vietnam.* New York: St. Martin's Press, 1972.

1693. Dickinson, Edwin D. "Supreme Court Interprets the Liquor Treaties." *American Journal of International Law* 21 (July 1927): 505-509.

1694. Edwards, James M. "The Erie Doctrine in Foreign Affairs Cases." *New York University Law Review* 42 (October 1967): 674-693.

1695. Emerson, Thomas I. "Controlling the Spies." *Center Magazine* 12 (January 1979): 60-74.

1696. Holman, Frank E. "Need for a Constitutional Amendment on Treaties and Executive Agreements." *Washington University Law Quarterly* 1955 (December 1955): 340-354.

1697. Hyde, Charles C. "Interpretation of Treaties by the Supreme Court of the United States." *American Journal of International Law* 23 (October 1929): 824-828.

1698. Hyde, Charles C. "The Supreme Court of the United States as an Expositor of International Law." *British Year Book of International Law* 18 (1937): 1-16.

1699. Jessup, Philip C. "Has the Supreme Court Abdicated One of Its Functions?" *American Journal of International Law* 40 (January 1946): 168-172.

1700. Lenoir, James J. "Conclusions Derived from Treaty Cases Decided by the United States Supreme Court." *Mississippi Law Journal* 7 (April 1935): 401-405.

1701. Lenoir, James J. "International Law in the Supreme Court of the United States." *Mississippi Law Journal* 7 (April 1935): 327-337.

1702. Lenoir, James J. "The Interpretation by the Supreme Court of the United States of Certain Phrases of International Law." Ph.D. diss., University of Illinois, Champaign-Urbana, 1934.

1703. Lenoir, James J. "Treaties and the Supreme Court." *University of Chicago Law Review* 1 (March 1934): 602-622.

1704. Lowenfeld, Andreas F. "Act of State and Department of State: *First National City Bank v. Banco Nacional de Cuba.*" *American Journal of International Law* 66 (October 1972): 795-814.

1705. McAllister, Breck P. "Influence of Supreme Court Decisions on the Conduct of American Foreign Affairs." *Institute of World Affairs Proceedings* 15 (1937): 157-161.

1706. Mashburn, Thomas M. "*Regan v. Wald*: The Supreme Court Defers to Presidential Authority in Matters of Foreign Policy by Upholding Travel Restrictions to Cuba." *Georgia Journal of International and Comparative Law* 15 (Winter 1985): 83-110.

1707. Mikva, Abner J., and Gerald L. Neuman. "Hostage Crisis and the 'Hostage Act'." *University of Chicago Law Review* 49 (Spring 1982): 292-354.

1708. Miller, Arthur S. "*Dames and Moore v. Regan*: A Political Decision by a Political Court." *UCLA Law Review* 29 (June/August 1982): 1104-1128.

1709. Millett, Stephen M. "The Constitutionality of Executive Arguments: An Analysis of *United States v. Belmont.*" Ph.D. diss., Ohio State University, 1972.

1710. Newton, Ernest L. "Termination of a War." *Wyoming Law Journal* 4 (Winter 1949): 115-120.

1711. Powell, Nancy E. "The Supreme Court as Interpreter of Executive Foreign Affairs Powers." *Connecticut Journal of International Law* 3 (Fall 1987): 161-203.

1712. Reveley, W. Taylor, III. "Presiden-

tial War-Making: Constitutional Prerogative or Usurpation?" *Virginia Law Review* 55 (November 1969): 1243-1305.

1713. Riesenfeld, Stefan A. "Doctrine of Self-Executing Treaties in *U.S. v. Postal*: Win at Any Price?" *American Journal of International Law* 74 (October 1980): 829-904.

1714. Sandler, Michael. "Foreign Policy in the Courtroom: The Iranian Litigation." *Litigation* 8 (Fall 1981): 10-13, 55-56.

1715. Stinson, Joseph W. "The Supreme Court and Treaties." *University of Pennsylvania Law Review* 73 (November 1924): 1-18.

1716. Tennant, John S. "Judicial Process of Treaty Interpretation in the United States Supreme Court." *Michigan Law Review* 30 (May 1932): 1016-1039.

1717. Thomas, Ann V., and A. J. Thomas, Jr. "Presidential War-Making Power: A Political Question?" *Southwestern Law Journal* 35 (November 1981): 879-898.

1718. Timbers, Edwin. "The Supreme Court and the President as Commander in Chief." *Presidential Studies Quarterly* 16 (Spring 1986): 224-236.

1719. Vance, William R. *The Supreme Court of the United States as an International Tribunal.* Baltimore: American Society for Judicial Settlement of International Disputes, 1915.

1720. Webster, Sidney. *Two Treaties of Paris and the Supreme Court.* New York: Harper and Brothers, 1901.

1721. Wechsler, Herbert. "Appellate Jurisdiction of the Supreme Court: Reflections on the Law and the Logistics of Direct Review." *Washington and Lee Law Review* 34 (Fall 1977): 1043-1064.

1722. Young, Rowland L. "Iranian Treaty, Passport Issues Dominate End of 1980 Term." *American Bar Association*

Journal 67 (September 1981): 1184-1186, 1190-1198.

Privilege and Immunity

1723. Berger, Raoul. *Executive Privilege: A Constitutional Myth*. Cambridge: Harvard University Press, 1974.

1724. Berger, Raoul. "Executive Privilege in Light of *United States v. Nixon*." *Maryland Historian* 6 (April 1975): 67-78.

1725. Freund, Paul A. "The Supreme Court, 1973 Term, Foreword: On Presidential Privilege." *Harvard Law Review* 88 (November 1974): 13-39.

1726. Friedman, Leon, ed. United States v. Nixon: *The President before the Supreme Court*. New York: Chelsea House, 1974.

1727. Kramer, Robert, and Herman Marcuse. "Executive Privilege: A Study of the Period 1953-1960." *George Washington Law Review* 29 (April 1961): 623-717; (June 1961): 827-916.

1728. Schultz, L. Peter. "The Constitution, the Court, and Presidential Immunity: A Defense of *Nixon vs. Fitzgerald*." *Presidential Studies Quarterly* 16 (Spring 1986): 247-257.

The States and the Court

General Studies

1729. Bloch, Beate, and Joyce H. Benjamin. "State and Local Legal Center at Five: A Few Thoughts." *Urban Lawyer* 20 (Spring 1988): 233-238.

1730. Catalano, Michael W. "How State and Local Government Fared in the United States Supreme Court for the Past Five Terms." *Urban Lawyer* 20 (Spring 1988): 341-352.

1731. Choper, Jesse H. "The Scope of National Power Vis-à-Vis the States: The Dispensability of Judicial Review." *Yale Law Journal* 86 (July 1977): 1552-1621.

1732. Easley, Allen K. "The Supreme Court and the Eleventh Amendment: Mourning the Last Opportunity to Synthesize Conflicting Precedents." *Denver University Law Review* 64 (Spring 1988): 485-527.

1733. Garvey, John H. "Child, Parent, State, and the Due Process Clause: An Essay on the Supreme Court's Recent Work." *Southern California Law Review* 51 (July 1978): 769-822.

1734. Haber, David. "*Arizona v. California*: A Brief Review." *Natural Resources Journal* 4 (May 1964): 17-28.

1735. Holsinger, M. Paul. "*Wyoming v. Colorado* Revisited: The United States Supreme Court and the Laramie River Controversy: 1911-1922." *Annals of Wyoming* 42 (April 1970): 47-56.

1736. Jackson, Vicki C. "The Supreme Court, the Eleventh Amendment, and State Sovereign Immunity." *Yale Law Journal* 98 (November 1988): 1-126.

1737. Laskowski, Anna. "Effect of State and Federal Decisions: United States Supreme Court Ruling Treated as Advisory." *University of Detroit Law Journal* 9 (January 1946): 106-109.

1738. Long, Hamilton A. *The Constitution Betrayed: Usurpers, Foes of Free Men*. Philadelphia: Your Heritage Books, 1971.

1739. McDermott, John T. "Personal Jurisdiction: The Hidden Agendas in the Supreme Court Decisions." *Vermont Law Review* 10 (Spring 1985): 1-54.

1740. Mathis, Doyle. "*Chisholm v. Georgia*: Background and Settlement." *Journal of American History* 54 (June 1967): 19-29.

1741. Mitchell, Lawrence E. "Mandate: Effect of Mandate of Supreme Court of

United States Directed to Supreme Court of State." *George Washington Law Review* 14 (February 1946): 379-382.

1742. Parker, John J. "Dual Sovereignty and the Federal Courts." *Northwestern University Law Review* 51 (September/October 1956): 407-423.

1743. Pierson, William W. "*Texas v. White.*" *Southwestern Historical Quarterly* 18 (April 1915): 341-367.

1744. Pierson, William W. "*Texas v. White.*" *Southwestern Historical Quarterly* 19 (July 1915): 1-36.

1745. Pierson, William W. "*Texas v. White.*" *Southwestern Historical Quarterly* 19 (October 1915): 142-158.

1746. Porter, Mary C. A. "State Supreme Courts and the Legacy of the Warren Court: Some Inquiries for a New Situation." *Publius* 8 (Fall 1978): 55-74.

1747. Powell, Thomas R. "The Supreme Court and State Police Power, 1922-1930." *Virginia Law Review* 17 (April 1931): 529-556; (May 1931): 653-675; (June 1931): 765-799.

1748. Scott, James B. *Judicial Settlement of Controversies between States of the American Union: An Analysis of Cases Decided in the Supreme Court of the United States.* Oxford: Clarendon Press, 1919.

1749. Scott, James B. "The Role of the Supreme Court of the United States in the Settlement of Interstate Disputes." *Georgetown Law Journal* (January 1927): 146-167.

1750. Scott, Robert D. "*Kansas v. Colorado* Revisited." *American Journal of International Law* 52 (July 1958): 432-454.

1751. Sullivan, Harold J. "Privatization of Public Services: A Growing Threat to Constitutional Rights." *Public Administration Review* 47 (November/December 1987): 461-467.

1752. Warren, Charles. "A Bulwark to the State Police Power: The United States Supreme Court." *Columbia Law Review* 13 (December 1913): 667-695.

1753. Warren, Charles. "Earliest Cases of Judicial Review of State Legislation by Federal Courts." *Yale Law Review* 32 (November 1922): 15-28.

Federalism

1754. Alexander, C. H. "How the States Have Fared during the Last Decade in the Supreme Court of the United States." *Chicago Legal News* 41 (September 21, 1908): 41-43.

1755. Allen, Ethan P. "Appeals from the Supreme Court of Iowa to the Supreme Court of the United States." *Iowa Journal of History* 31 (April 1933): 211-273.

1756. Allen, Francis A. "Federalism and the Fourth Amendment: A Requiem for *Wolf.*" *Supreme Court Review* 1961 (1961): 1-48.

1757. Baird, Zoe. "State Empowerment after *Garcia.*" *Urban Lawyer* 18 (Summer 1986): 491-518.

1758. Baker, Stewart A. "*Garcia* Costs States More Than Wages." *State Government News* 28 (May 1985): 23-25.

1759. Baker, Thomas, and James C. Hill. "Dam Federal Jurisdiction!" *Emory Law Journal* 32 (Winter 1983): 3-87.

1760. Balkin, J. M. "Ideology and Counter-Ideology from *Lochner* to *Garcia.*" *University of Missouri at Kansas City Law Review* 54 (Winter 1986): 175-214.

1761. Barnes, William S. "Suits between States in the Supreme Court." *Vanderbilt Law Review* 7 (June 1954): 494-520.

1762. Barrett, George B. "The State of Georgia and the Supreme Court of the United States." *Georgia Bar Journal* 3 (August 1940): 34-45.

1763. Bartow, Robert J. "Safeguarding

Federalism: Changing Conceptions of the Judicial Role from *National League of Cities v. Usery* to *Equal Employment Opportunity Commission v. Wyoming.*" *Temple Law Quarterly* 55 (1982): 889-944.

1764. Beck, James M. "Nullification by Indirection." *Harvard Law Review* 23 (April 1910): 441-455.

1765. Benedict, Michael L. "Preserving Federalism: Reconstruction and the Waite Court." *Supreme Court Review* 1978 (1978): 39-79.

1766. Bergman, G. Merle. "Reappraisal of Federal Question Jurisdiction." *Michigan Law Review* 46 (November 1947): 17-46.

1767. Bingham, Joseph W. "The American Law Institute v. the Supreme Court in the Matter of *Haddock v. Haddock.*" *Cornell Law Quarterly* 21 (April 1936): 393-433.

1768. Birkby, Robert H. "Politics of Accommodation: The Origin of the Supremacy Clause." *Western Political Quarterly* 19 (March 1966): 123-135.

1769. Blackmar, Charles B. "Radical Surgery for the Constitution? A Response to Chief Justice Donnelly's State of the Judiciary Message." *Journal of the Missouri Bar* 38 (April/May 1982): 150-156.

1770. Bogaard, William J. "The Act of State Doctrine after *Sabbatino.*" *Michigan Law Review* 63 (January 1965): 528-542.

1771. Bogert, George G. "Decision of the Supreme Court in the West Virginia Compact Case." *State Government* 24 (June 1951): 162-164.

1772. Bozeman, Robert M. "The Supreme Court and Migratory Divorce: A Reexamination of an Old Problem." *American Bar Association Journal* 37 (February 1951): 107-110, 168-171.

1773. Brilmayer, Leo, and Ronald D. Lee. "State Sovereignty and the Two Faces of Federalism: A Comparative Study of Federal Jurisdiction and the Conflict of Laws." *Notre Dame Law Review* 60 (1985): 833-861.

1774. Brown, George D. "State Sovereignty under the Burger Court: How the Eleventh Amendment Survived the Death of the Tenth: Some Broader Implications of *Atascadero State Hospital v. Scanlon.*" *Georgetown Law Journal* 74 (December 1985): 363-394.

1775. Burke, Joseph C. "What Did the *Prigg* Decisions Really Decide?" *Pennsylvania Magazine of History and Biography* 93 (January 1969): 73-85.

1776. Castro, Dayton C., Jr. "The Doctrinal Development of the Tenth Amendment." *West Virginia Law Quarterly* 51 (June 1949): 227-249.

1777. Catterall, Helen T. "Some Antecedents of the *Dred Scott* Case." *American Historical Review* 30 (October 1924): 56-71.

1778. Cherubin, David M. "*Garcia v. San Antonio Metropolitan Transit Authority*: The Fall of *National League of Cities.*" *Albany Law Review* 49 (Summer 1985): 967-1000.

1779. Chiaraviglio, Ida M. "The Supreme Court, the National Government, and States' Rights: An Analysis of Georgia Cases." Ph.D. diss., Emory University, 1962.

1780. Clark, John A. "Supreme Court Rules on When State Court Decisions Will Bind Federal Courts." *Journal of Taxation* 27 (August 1967): 82-85.

1781. Clarke, Charles H. "Supreme Court Assault upon the Constitutional Settlement of the New Deal: *Garcia* and *National League of Cities.*" *Northern Illinois University Law Review* 6 (Winter 1986): 39-80.

1782. Cohn, Morris M. "The *Dred Scott* Case in the Light of Later Events." *American Law Review* 46 (July 1912): 548-557.

1783. Collins, Ronald K. "Plain Statements: The Supreme Court's New Requirement." *American Bar Association Journal* 70 (March 1984): 92-94.

1784. Conference of Chief Justices. *Report of the Committee on Federal-State Relationships as Affected by Judicial Decisions, August, 1958.* Richmond: Virginia Commission on Constitutional Government, 1958.

1785. "Constitutional Law: The New Standard of Independent and Adequate State Grounds: A Presumption of Reviewability." *Thurgood Marshall Law Review* 10 (Spring 1985): 506-521.

1786. Cooper, Charles J. "The Demise of Federalism." *Urban Law* 20 (Spring 1988): 239-284.

1787. Corley, Roger W. "The United States Supreme Court and State Economic Power, 1932-1937: An Evolution." Ph.D. diss., University of Kansas, 1973.

1788. Corwin, Edward S. *National Supremacy: Treaty Power versus State Power.* New York: Holt, 1913.

1789. Corwin, Edward S. "The Passing of Dual Federalism." *Virginia Law Review* 36 (February 1950): 1-24.

1790. Cox, Archibald. "Federalism and Individual Rights under the Burger Court." *Northwestern University Law Review* 73 (March/April 1978): 1-25.

1791. Cramton, Roger C. "*Pennsylvania v. Nelson*: A Case Study in Federal Preemption." *University of Chicago Law Review* 26 (Autumn 1958): 85-108.

1792. Currie, David P. "The Constitution in the Supreme Court: Limitations on State Power, 1865-1873." *University of Chicago Law Review* 51 (Spring 1984): 329-365.

1793. Dean, Benjamin S. "The Betrayal of a Sacred Trust." *Lawyer and Banker* 24 (May/June 1931): 122-137.

1794. Dexter, William D. "Analysis of Supreme Court's *United States Steel* Decision Upholding Multistate Tax Compact." *Journal of Taxation* 48 (June 1978): 368-371.

1795. *'Dred Scott' Case.* Freeport, NY: Books for Libraries Press, 1973.

1796. Dunn, William R. "An Attorney General Goes to Jail." *Virginia Cavalcade* 21 (Autumn 1971): 28-39.

1797. Dunne, Gerald T. *Monetary Decisions of the Supreme Court.* New Brunswick, NJ: Rutgers University Press, 1960.

1798. Earle, Valerie A., ed. *Federalism: Infinite Variety in Theory and Practice.* Itasca, IL: F. E. Peacock, 1968.

1799. Easterbrook, Frank H. "Antitrust and the Economics of Federalism." *Journal of Law and Economics* 26 (April 1983): 23-50.

1800. Elazar, Daniel J. *American Federalism: A View from the States.* New York: Harper and Row, 1984.

1801. Elison, Larry M., and Dennis N. Simmons. "Federalism and State Constitutions: The New Doctrine of Independent and Adequate State Grounds." *Montana Law Review* 45 (Summer 1984): 177-214.

1802. Engahl, David E. "Construction of Interstate Compacts: A Questionable Federal Question." *Virginia Law Review* 51 (October 1965): 987-1049.

1803. Falk, Richard A. "The Complexity of *Sabbatino*." *American Journal of International Law* 58 (October 1964): 935-951.

1804. Farnum, George R. "State's Rights, Nationalism, and the Supreme Court." *Commercial Law Journal* 42 (January 1937): 23-26.

1805. Fein, Bruce E. "The Waning and Waxing of Federalism." *American Bar Association Journal* 72 (January 1986): 118-124.

1806. Fellman, David. "Federalism and

the Commerce Clause, 1937-47." *Journal of Politics* 10 (February 1948): 155-167.

1807. Fellman, David. "Ten Years of the Supreme Court, 1937-1947: Federalism." *American Political Science Review* 40 (December 1947): 1142-1160.

1808. Field, Martha A. "Comment: *Garcia v. San Antonio Metropolitan Transit Authority*: The Demise of a Misguided Doctrine." *Harvard Law Review* 99 (November 1985): 84-119.

1809. Field, Oliver P. "States versus Nation, and the Supreme Court." *American Political Science Review* 28 (April 1934): 233-245.

1810. Freilich, Robert H. "State and Local Government at the Crossroads: A Bitterly Divided Supreme Court Reevaluates Federalism in the Bicentennial Year of the Constitution." *Urban Law* 19 (Fall 1987): 791-865.

1811. Freilich, Robert H., Madeline Montello, and James J. Mueth. "The Supreme Court and Federalism on the Eve of the Bicentennial of the Constitution: A Review of the 1985-1986 Term." *Urban Lawyer* 18 (Fall 1986): 779-861.

1812. Freilich, Robert H., Russell J. Greenhagen, and Marcia J. Lamkin. "The Demise of the Tenth Amendment: An Analysis of Supreme Court Decisions Affecting Constitutional Federalism." *Urban Lawyer* 17 (Fall 1985): 651-732.

1813. Freund, Paul A. "The Supreme Court Crisis." *New York State Bar Bulletin* 31 (February 1959): 66-80.

1814. Friedelbaum, Stanley H. "The Warren Court and American Federalism: A Preliminary Appraisal." *University of Chicago Law Review* 28 (Autumn 1960): 53-87.

1815. Gabel, Peter. "The Mass Psychology of the New Federalism: How the Burger Court's Political Imagery Legitimizes the Privatization of Everyday Life."

George Washington Law Review 52 (January 1984): 263-271.

1816. "*Garcia v. San Antonio Metropolitan Transit Authority* and the Manifest Destiny of Congressional Power." *Harvard Journal of Law and Public Policy* 8 (Summer 1985): 745-765.

1817. Griswold, Erwin N. "The Long View Speech at Annual Dinner in Honor of Judiciary under Auspices of the ABA Section of Judicial Administration, Miami Beach." *American Bar Association Journal* 51 (November 1965): 1017-1022.

1818. Halberstam, Malvina. "*Sabbatino* Resurrected: The Act of State Doctrine in the Revised Restatement of U.S. Foreign Relations Law." *American Journal of International Law* 79 (January 1985): 68-91.

1819. Hellerstein, Walter. "State Income Taxation of Multijurisdictional Corporations and the Supreme Court." *National Tax Journal* 35 (December 1982): 401-425.

1820. Hellerstein, Walter. "State Taxation and the Supreme Court: Toward a More Unified Approach to Constitutional Adjudication?" *Michigan Law Review* 75 (June 1977): 1426-1455.

1821. Hellerstein, Walter. "State Taxation of Interstate Business and Supreme Court 1974 Term: Standard Pressed Steel and Colonial Pipeline." *Virginia Law Review* 62 (February 1976): 149-192.

1822. Henkin, Louis. "The Foreign Affairs Power of the Federal Courts: *Sabbatino.*" *Columbia Law Review* 64 (May 1964): 805-832.

1823. Howard, A. E. Dick. "*Garcia* and the Values of Federalism: On the Need for a Recurrence to Fundamental Principles." *Georgia Law Review* 19 (Summer 1985): 789-798.

1824. Howard, A. E. Dick. "State Courts and Constitutional Rights in the Day of the Burger Court." *Virginia Law Review* 62 (June 1976): 873-944.

1825. Hutson, James H. "Country, Court, and Constitution: Antifederalism and the Historians." *William and Mary Quarterly* 38 (July 1981): 337-368.

1826. Iams, Leslie A. "Constitutional Federalism Revisited." *Akron Law Review* 19 (Summer 1985): 141-155.

1827. Johnston, Richard E., and John T. Thompson. "The Burger Court and Federalism: A Revolution in 1976?" *Western Political Quarterly* 33 (June 1980): 197-216.

1828. Kann, Carol A. "Supreme Court Review of State Court Cases: Principled Federalism or Selective Bias?" *Emory Law Journal* 36 (Fall 1987): 1277-1311.

1829. Kincaid, John. "The State of American Federalism—1986." *Publius* 17 (Spring 1987): 1-33.

1830. Kurland, Philip B. "The A.L.I. Proposed Division of Jurisdiction between State and Federal Courts." *University of Chicago Law School Record* 12 (Autumn 1964): 9-13.

1831. Kutler, Stanley I. *Judicial Power and Reconstruction Politics.* Chicago: University of Chicago Press, 1968.

1832. Kutler, Stanley I. "Reconstruction and the Supreme Court: The Numbers Game Reconsidered." *Journal of Southern History* 32 (February 1966): 42-58.

1833. Lantry, Terry L. "*Stare Decisis* Eroded: A Redefinition of Rights of States." *American Business Law Journal* 24 (Spring 1986): 129-137.

1834. Laselva, Samuel V. "Federalism and Unanimity: The Supreme Court and Constitutional Amendment." *Canadian Journal of Political Science* 16 (December 1983): 757-770.

1835. LeBel, Paul A. "Legal Positivism and Federalism: The Certification Experi-

ence." *Georgia Law Review* 19 (Summer 1985): 999-1040.

1836. Lee, Carol F. "The Political Safeguard of Federalism? Congressional Responses to Supreme Court Decisions on State and Local Liability." *Urban Lawyer* 20 (Spring 1988): 301-340.

1837. Lieberman, Joseph I. "Modern Federalism: Altered States." *Urban Lawyer* 20 (Spring 1988): 285-299.

1838. Lynch, Joseph M. "*Garcia v. San Antonio Metropolitan Transit Authority*: An Alternative Opinion." *Seton Hall Law Review* 16 (1986): 74-100.

1839. MacChesney, Brunson. "Full Faith and Credit: A Comparative Study." *Illinois Law Review* 44 (July/August 1949): 298-314.

1840. McCoy, Candace. "New Federalism, Old Remedies, and Corrections Policymaking." *Policy Studies Review* 2 (November 1982): 271-278.

1841. McFeeley, Neil D. "The Supreme Court and the Federal System: Federalism from Warren to Burger." *Publius* 8 (Fall 1978): 5-36.

1842. McGovney, Dudley O. "A Supreme Court Fiction: Corporations in the Diverse Citizenship Jurisdiction of the Federal Courts." *Harvard Law Review* 56 (May 1943): 853-898; (June 1943): 1090-1124; (July 1943): 1225-1260.

1843. McKeage, Everett C. "Judicial Supergovernment and States' Rights." *Public Utilities Fortnightly* 64 (September 24, 1959): 486-494.

1844. McLarty, Robert A., Jr., and S. Catherine Wilson. "Federal Jurisdiction, Original Jurisdiction of Supreme Court in Suit between States." *Georgia Bar Journal* 2 (November 1939): 57-58.

1845. Miles, Edwin A. "After John Marshall's Decision: *Worcester v. Georgia* and the Nullification Crisis." *Journal of Southern History* 39 (November 1973): 519-544.

1846. Miller, Louise B. "The Burger Court's View of Federalism." *Policy Studies Journal* 13 (March 1985): 576-583.

1847. Miller, Louise B. "The Burger Court's View of the Relationship between the States and Their Municipalities." *Publius* 17 (Spring 1987): 85-92.

1848. Mister, James F. "Professor Pomeroy and the United States Supreme Court: His Arraignment of It Not Justified." *American Law Review* 17 (November/December 1883): 933-947.

1849. Moss, Larry E. "Federal Water Development: Imperial Edict or Federal State Partnership?" *Publius* 9 (Winter 1979): 127-140.

1850. Munro, James. "Supreme Court and the Marginal Sea." *Wyoming Law Journal* 4 (Spring 1950): 181-191.

1851. Murchison, Kenneth M. "Waivers of Intergovernmental Immunity in Federal Environmental Statutes." *Virginia Law Review* 62 (November 1976): 1177-1209.

1852. Murphy, William P. "Supreme Court Review of Abstract State Court Decisions on Federal Law: A Justiciability Analysis." *St. Louis University Law Journal* 25 (June 1981): 473-499.

1853. Oberst, Paul. "The Supreme Court and States' Rights." *Kentucky Law Journal* 48 (Fall 1959): 63-102.

1854. Overton, Elvin E. "State Decisions in Conflict of Laws and Review by the United States Supreme Court under the Due-Process Clause." *Oregon Law Review* 22 (February 1943): 109-181.

1855. Overton, Elvin E. "State Decisions in Conflict of Laws and Review by the United States Supreme Court under the Due-Process Clause." Ph.D. diss., Harvard University, 1950.

1856. Partridge, Dennis J. "The *Dred Scott* Case: The Justices and the Decision and an Analysis of the March 4th, 1858 Speech of William H. Seward and of the March 11th, 1858 Speech of Judah P. Benjamin in Terms of Personal Attacks and Their Defense." Master's thesis, Florida State University, 1977.

1857. Paul, Roland A. "The Act of State Doctrine: Revived but Suspended." *University of Pennsylvania Law Review* 113 (March 1965): 691-713.

1858. Persil, Herbert G. "The Supreme Court and the Scope of State Activity, 1870-1906." Ph.D. diss., University of Chicago, 1964.

1859. Peterson, Merrill D., ed. *Democracy, Liberty, and Property: The State Constitutional Conventions of the 1820s.* Indianapolis: Bobbs-Merrill, 1966.

1860. Plouffe, William L. "Forty Years after *First Iowa*: A Call for Greater State Control of River Resources." *Cornell Law Review* 71 (May 1986): 833-849.

1861. Pomeroy, John N. "The Supreme Court and Its Theory of Nationality." *Nation* 12 (June 29, 1871): 445-446.

1862. Pomeroy, John N. "The Supreme Court and State Repudiation: The Virginia and Louisiana Cases." *American Law Review* 17 (September/October 1883): 684-734.

1863. Powell, Thomas R. "Supreme Court Decisions on the Commerce Clause and State Police Power, 1910-1914." *Columbia Law Review* 21 (December 1921): 737-756; 22 (January 1922): 28-49.

1864. Rashid, Baddia J. "The Full Faith and Credit Clause: Collateral Attack of Jurisdictional Issues." *Georgetown Law Journal* 36 (January 1948): 154-181.

1865. Redish, Martin H. "Supreme Court Review of State Court 'Federal' Decisions: A Study in Interactive Federalism." *Georgia Law Review* 19 (Summer 1985): 861-916.

1866. Reese, Willis L. M., and Vincent A. Johnson. "The Scope of Full Faith and Credit to Judgements." *Columbia Law Review* 49 (February 1949): 153-179.

1867. Richards, Eric L., and Douglas F. Whitman. "*Louisiana Power and Light*: Examining the State Action Immunity." *American Business Law Journal* 17 (Fall 1979): 386-404.

1868. Riker, William H. *Federalism: Origin, Operation, and Significance.* Boston: Little, Brown, 1964.

1869. Roettinger, Ruth L. *The Supreme Court and State Police Power: A Study in Federalism.* Washington, DC: Public Affairs Press, 1957.

1870. Romm, Jeff, and Sally K. Fairfax. "The Backwaters of Federalism: Receding Reserved Water Rights and the Management of National Forests." *Policy Studies Review* 5 (November 1985): 413-430.

1871. Rose, Winfield H. "Public Sector Labor Relations, the Supreme Court, and the New Federalism." *Journal of Collective Negotiations in the Public Sector* 13 (1984): 281-289.

1872. Ross, Douglas. "Safeguarding our Federalism: Lessons for the States from the Supreme Court." *Public Administration Review* 45 (November 1985): 723-731.

1873. Rudenstine, David. "Judicially Ordered Social Reform: Neo-Federalism and Neo-Nationalism and the Debate over Political Structure." *Southern California Law Review* 59 (March 1986): 449-494.

1874. Sandalow, Terrance, ed. *Courts and Free Markets: Perspectives from the United States and Europe.* New York: Oxford University Press, 1982.

1875. Scheiber, Harry N. "Federalism and the American Economic Order, 1789-1910." *Law and Society Review* 10 (Fall 1975): 57-118.

1876. Schlueter, David A. "Federalism and Supreme Court Review of Expansive State Court Decisions: A Response to Unfortunate Impressions." *Hastings Constitutional Law Quarterly* 71 (Summer 1984): 523-550.

1877. Schlueter, David A. "Judicial Federalism and Supreme Court Review of State Court Decisions: A Sensible Balance Emerges." *Notre Dame Law Review* 59 (Fall 1984): 1079-1117.

1878. Schmidhauser, John R. " 'States' Rights' and the Origin of the Supreme Court's Power as Arbiter in Federal-State Relations." *Wayne Law Review* 4 (Spring 1958): 101-114.

1879. Schmidhauser, John R. *The Supreme Court as Final Arbiter in Federal-State Relations, 1789-1957.* Chapel Hill: University of North Carolina Press, 1958.

1880. Schoenfeld, Benjamin N. "American Federalism and the Abstention Doctrine in the Supreme Court." *Dickinson Law Review* 73 (Summer 1969): 605-637.

1881. Schofield, Henry. "The Supreme Court of the United States and the Enforcement of State Law by State Courts." *Illinois Law Review* 3 (November 1908): 195-217.

1882. Schofield, William. "Uniformity of Law in the Several States as an American Ideal." *Harvard Law Review* 21 (June 1908): 583-594.

1883. Shearn, Clarence J., Jr. "Split Decisions in the Supreme Court in Invalidating Federal and State Enactments and Attempted Exercises of Power, 1933-1937." *American Bar Association Journal* 23 (May 1937): 329-334.

1884. Shuman, Samuel I., comp. *The Future of Federalism.* Detroit: Wayne State University Press, 1968.

1885. Simmonds, K. R. "The *Sabbatino* Case and the Act of State Doctrine." *International and Comparative Law Quarterly* 14 (April 1965): 452-492.

1886. Snow, Alpheus H. *The Development of the American Doctrine of Jurisdiction of Courts over States*. Baltimore: American Society for Judicial Settlement of International Disputes, 1911.

1887. Soloman, Benna R., and Joyce H. Benjamin. "Foreword: Federalism—Making the Case for State and Local Governments." *Urban Lawyer* 18 (Summer 1986): 483-490.

1888. Spears, James W. "Supreme Court February Sextet: *Younger v. Harris* Revisited." *Baylor Law Review* 26 (Winter 1974): 1-67.

1889. Sprague, John D. *Voting Patterns of the United States Supreme Court: Cases in Federalism, 1889-1959*. Indianapolis: Bobbs-Merrill, 1968.

1890. Stephenson, D. Grier, Jr., and Barry M. Levine. "Vicarious Federalism: The Modern Supreme Court and the Tenth Amendment." *Urban Lawyer* 19 (Summer 1987): 683-700.

1891. Stevenson, John R. "State Department and *Sabbatino*: 'Even Victors Are by Victories Undone'." *American Journal of International Law* 58 (July 1964): 707-711.

1892. Stevenson, Julie V. "Exclusive Original Jurisdiction of the United States Supreme Court: Does It Still Exist?" *Brigham Young University Law Review* 1982 (Summer 1982): 727-751.

1893. Stewart, Richard B. "Federalism and Rights." *Georgia Law Review* 19 (Summer 1985): 917-980.

1894. Swisher, Carl B. "The Supreme Court and the Forging of Federalism: 1789-1864." *Nebraska Law Review* 40 (1961): 3-15.

1895. Talbot, Earl A. "The Due-on-Sale Clause Revisited: The United States Supreme Court Dabbles in Mortgage Law." *Appraisal Journal* 50 (October 1982): 603-606.

1896. Treacy, Kenneth W. "The Collisions of the Supreme Court of the United States and the States: The Marshall Court, 1801-1835." Ph.D. diss., University of Utah, 1958.

1897. Tribe, Laurence H. "Unraveling *National League of Cities*: The New Federalism and Affirmative Rights to Essential Government Services." *Harvard Law Review* 90 (April 1977): 1065-1104.

1898. Trickett, William. "The Newest Neologism of the Supreme Court." *American Law Review* 41 (September/October 1907): 729-739.

1899. Tushnet, Mark V. "Federalism and the Traditions of American Political Theory." *Georgia Law Review* 20 (Summer 1985): 981-998.

1900. U.S. Library of Congress. *United States Supreme Court Cases Declaring State Laws Unconstitutional, 1912-1938*. Washington, DC: U.S. Government Printing Office, 1938.

1901. Versfelt, David S. "The Effect of the Twenty-first Amendment on State Authority to Control Intoxicating Liquors." *Columbia Law Review* 75 (December 1975): 1578-1610.

1902. Vile, M.J.C. *The Structure of America's Federalism*. London: Oxford University Press, 1961.

1903. Wall, Julia R. "The United States Supreme Court Upholds Federal Use of State Resources to Further National Goals." *Natural Resources Journal* 23 (July 1983): 725-734.

1904. Warren, Charles. *The Supreme Court and the Sovereign States*. Princeton, NJ: Princeton University Press, 1924.

1905. Weinberg, Lee S. "*Askew v. American Waterway Operators Inc.*: The Emerging New Federalism." *Publius* 8 (Fall 1978): 37-53.

1906. Weinberg, Louise. "A New Judicial

Federalism?" *Daedalus* 107 (Winter 1978): 129-142.

1907. Weinberg, Louise. "The New Judicial Federalism." *Stanford Law Review* 29 (July 1977): 1191-1244.

1908. Weinberg, Louise. "The New Judicial Federalism: Where We Are Now." *Georgia Law Review* 19 (Summer 1985): 1075-1096.

1909. Weisberg, Morris L. "Supreme Court Review of State Court Decisions Involving Multiple Questions." *University of Pennsylvania Law Review* 95 (June 1947): 764-781.

1910. Wells, Lloyd M. "Interposition and the Supreme Court." *Southwestern Review* 41 (Autumn 1956): 305-313.

1911. Welsh, Robert C. "Whose Federalism? The Burger Court's Treatment of State Civil Liberties Judgements." *Hastings Constitutional Law Quarterly* 10 (Summer 1983): 819-875.

1912. Wendell, Mitchell. *Relations between Federal and State Courts.* New York: Columbia University Press, 1949.

1913. White, Jeffrey. "State Constitutional Guarantees as Adequate State Ground: Supreme Court Review and Problems of Federalism." *American Criminal Law Review* 13 (Spring 1976): 737-778.

1914. Wilcox, Thomas. *States' Rights v. the Supreme Court.* Boston: Little, Brown, 1960.

1915. Wilkes, Donald E., Jr. "The New Federalism in Criminal Procedure: State Court Evasion of the Burger Court." *Kentucky Law Journal* 62 (1973/1974): 421-451.

1916. Wilkes, Donald E., Jr. "The New Federalism in Criminal Procedure: State Court Evasion of the Burger Court, More on the New Federalism in Criminal Procedure." *Kentucky Law Journal* 63 (1974/1975): 873-894.

1917. Wilkins, Raymond S. "Federal-State Relationships." *Massachusetts Law Quarterly* 48 (September 1963): 297-301.

1918. Winkle, John W., III. "Dimensions of Judicial Federalism." *Annals of the American Academy of Political and Social Science* 416 (November 1974): 67-76.

1919. Woodward, C. Vann. *Reunion and Reaction: The Compromise of 1877 and the End of Reconstruction.* Boston: Little, Brown, 1951.

1920. Young, Scott A. "The Right of Autonomy: Constitutional Limit to Plenary Federal Power." *Journal of Criminal Law and Criminology* 68 (March 1977): 56-69.

1921. Zeller, M. R. "Preemption Issues Draw the Court's Attention." *Employee Relations Today* 12 (Autumn 1985): 195-202.

Taxation

1922. Blasi, Ronald W., and C. James Judson. "Supreme Court Provides Guideline for Taxing of Federal Securities by States." *Journal of Taxation* 64 (January 1986): 42-45.

1923. Coppola, Andrew J. "The Supreme Court and Multiple State Taxation of Intangibles." Ph.D diss., New York University, 1943.

1924. DuMars, Charles T. "Evaluating Congressional Limits on a State's Severance Tax Equity Interest in Its Natural Resources: An Essential Responsibility for the Supreme Court." *Natural Resources Journal* 22 (July 1982): 673-687.

1925. Fraenkel, Osmond K. "Supreme Court and the Taxing Power of the States." *Illinois Law Review* 28 (January 1934): 621-635.

1926. Freeman, Brian M. "State Power to Tax Trust Income on Basis of Settlor's or

Grantor's Residence or Domicile." *Taxes* 53 (April 1975): 237-244.

1927. Hellerstein, Walter. "Commerce Clause Restraints on State Taxation: Purposeful Economic Protectionism and Beyond." *Michigan Law Review* 85 (February 1987): 758-769.

1928. Hellerstein, Walter. "State's Power to Tax Foreign Commerce Dominates Supreme Court's 1978 Agenda." *Journal of Taxation* 51 (August 1979): 106-111.

1929. Hellerstein, Walter, and Ruurd Leegstra. "Supreme Court in *Metropolitan Life* Strikes Down Discriminatory State Insurance Tax." *Journal of Taxation* 63 (August 1985): 108-111.

1930. Jennings, Karen L. "Supreme Court Opens Door to More State Revenues from Mined Resources." *Natural Resources Journal* 23 (January 1983): 213-218.

1931. Lathrop, Robert G. "*Armco*: A Narrow and Puzzling Test for Discriminatory State Taxes under the Commerce Clause." *Taxes* 63 (August 1985): 551-561.

1932. Peters, James H. "Constitutional Limitations on State Taxation Redefined by Supreme Court." *Journal of Taxation* 49 (October 1978): 240-244.

1933. Peters, James H. "Supreme Court Hands Down Many Important New Decisions in State and Local Tax Area." *Journal of Taxation* 43 (September 1975): 174-176.

1934. Peters, James H. "Supreme Court in *Container*, Upholds State's Broad Power under Unitary Taxation Method." *Journal of Taxation* 59 (November 1983): 300-307.

1935. Peters, James H. "Supreme Court Requires Unitary Relationship before States Can Tax Investment Income." *Journal of Taxation* 57 (November 1982): 314-318.

1936. Peters, James H. "Supreme Court

Says California Sales Tax Is Subject to Federal Immunity." *Journal of Taxation* 45 (August 1976): 116-117.

1937. Peters, James H. "Supreme Court Sets New Test for Local Taxation of Imports in *Michelin Tire*." *Journal of Taxation* 44 (April 1976): 244-245.

1938. Spahr, Margaret. "The Supreme Court on the Incidence and Effects of Taxation, an Analysis of Economic Theory Embedded in the Constitutional Law Derived from the Explicit Tax Clauses." Ph.D. diss., Columbia University, 1926.

Administrative Law

1939. Cortner, Richard C. *The Bureaucracy in Court: Commentaries and Case Studies in Administrative Law*. Port Washington, NY: Kennikat Press, 1982.

1940. Crowley, Donald W. "Judicial Review of Administrative Agencies: Does the Type of Agency Matter?" *Western Political Quarterly* 40 (June 1987): 265-283.

1941. Davis, Kenneth C. "Standing to Challenge and to Enforce Administrative Action." *Columbia Law Review* 49 (June 1949): 759-795.

1942. Dickinson, John. *Administrative Justice and the Supremacy of Law in the United States*. New York: Russell and Russell, 1955.

1943. Fuchs, Ralph F. "Administrative Determinations and Personal Rights in the Present Supreme Court." *Indiana Law Journal* 24 (Winter 1949): 163-194.

1944. Funston, Richard Y. "Judicialization of the Administrative Process." *American Politics Quarterly* 2 (January 1974): 38-60.

1945. Handberg, Roger B., Jr. "Supreme Court and Administrative Agencies: 1965-

1978." *Journal of Contemporary Law* 6 (Winter 1979): 161-176.

1946. Hiestand, O. S., Jr., and William C. Parler. "The Disputes Procedure under Government Contracts: The Role of the Appeals Board and the Courts." *Boston College Industrial and Commercial Law Review* 8 (Fall 1966): 1-27.

1947. Layton, Robert, and Ralph I. Fine. "The Draft and Exhaustion of Administrative Remedies." *Georgetown Law Journal* 56 (December 1967): 315-335.

1948. Minor, Robert W. "The Administrative Court: Here It Comes Again." *I.C.C. Practitioner's Journal* 24 (May 1961): 807-815.

1949. Minor, Robert W. "The Administrative Court: Variations on a Theme." *Ohio State Law Journal* 19 (Summer 1958): 380-399.

1950. Price, M. Donna. "Administering Public Assistance: The Burger Court Perspective." Ph.D. diss., Claremont Graduate School, 1980.

1951. Rabkin, Jeremy. "Judiciary in the Administrative State." *Public Interest* 71 (Spring 1983): 62-84.

1952. Raedy, Raymond. "The Supreme Court Decision: A Judicial Breakthrough? A Procedural History of the *ADAPSO* Case." *National Public Accountant* 15 (May 1970): 4-6.

1953. Rosenbloom, David H. "Public Administrators' Official Immunity and the Supreme Court: Developments during the 1970's." *Public Administration Review* 40 (March 1980): 166-173.

1954. Schwartz, Bernard. "Administrative Law and the Burger Court." *Hofstra Law Review* 8 (Winter 1980): 325-401.

1955. Schwartz, Bernard. "*Gray vs. Powell* and the Scope of Review." *Michigan Law Review* 54 (November 1955): 1-70.

1956. Shapiro, Martin M. *The Supreme Court and Administrative Agencies.* New York: Free Press, 1968.

1957. Sherwood, Foster H. "Judicial Control of Administrative Discretion, 1932-1952." *Western Political Quarterly* 6 (December 1953): 750-761.

1958. Simon, Karla W. "Supreme Court Limits Ability of Third Parties to Sue Agencies Such as the IRS." *Journal of Taxation* 61 (December 1984): 400-402.

1959. Sovern, Michael I. "The Function of the Supreme Court in the Development and Acquisition of Powers by Administrative Agencies." *Minnesota Law Review* 42 (December 1957): 271-291.

1960. Tanenhaus, Joseph. "Supreme Court Attitudes toward Federal Administrative Agencies." *Journal of Politics* 22 (August 1960): 502-524.

1961. White, G. Edward. "Allocating Power between Agencies and Courts: The Legacy of Justice Brandeis." *Duke Law Journal* 1974 (April 1974): 195-244.

III. The Organization of the Court

General Studies

1962. Bullitt, William G. "Organization of the Judicial Department." In *Review of the Constitution of the United States: Including Changes by Interpretation and Amendment: For Lawyers and Those Not Learned in the Law,* by William G. Bullitt, 236-267. Cincinnati: R. Clarke, 1899.

1963. Conkling, Alfred. *A Treatise on the Organization, Jurisdiction, and Practice of the Courts of the United States.* 5th ed. Albany, NY: W. C. Little, 1870.

1964. Handberg, Roger B., Jr. "Longitudinal Look at Court Structure, 1916-1969." *Capital University Law Review* 7 (1978): 385-396.

1965. Jones, Harry W. "Extrinsic Aids in the Federal Courts." *Iowa Law Review* 25 (May 1940): 737-764.

1966. Kales, Albert M. "The Place of Oral Arguments in the Work of the Supreme Court." *Illinois Law Review* 2 (April 1908): 594-600.

1967. Peltason, Jack W. *Federal Courts in the Political Process.* New York: Random House, 1955.

1968. Pound, Roscoe. *Organization of Courts.* Boston: Little, Brown, 1940.

1969. Simonton, Charles H. *The Federal Courts: Their Organization, Jurisdiction, and Procedure, Lectures before the Richmond Law School, Richmond College, Virginia.* Richmond, VA: B. F. Johnson Publishing Company, 1896.

1970. Zvetina, John A. "The Judiciary Act of 1789: A Stepping Stone in National Development." *Mid-America* 18 (January 1936): 48-66; (April 1936): 125-132.

Supporting Facilities

1971. Clarke, Oscar D. "The Library of the Supreme Court of the United States." *Law Library Journal* 31 (May 1938): 89-102.

1972. "Cornerstone of New Home of Supreme Court of the United States Is Laid." *American Bar Association Journal* 18 (November 1932): 723-729.

1973. Elliott, Richard N. "New Home for Highest Court." *Federal Bar Association Journal* 1 (September 1931): 12-13, 31-35.

1974. "Exhibit on the U.S. Supreme Court and the Law Library of Congress Opens." *Library of Congress Information Bulletin* 44 (January 7, 1985): 3-4.

1975. Field, Frank H. "A New Building for the Supreme Court of the United States." *American Law Review* 34 (November/December 1900): 924-926.

1976. Galloway, Gail. "Art in the Supreme Court Building." *Federal Bar News and Journal* 30 (January 1983): 37-38.

1977. Greenberg, Alan, and Stephen Kieran. "The United States Supreme Court Building, Washington, DC." *Magazine Antiques* 128 (October 1985): 760-769.

1978. Hudon, Edward G. "The Library Facilities of the Supreme Court of the United States: A Historical Study." *University of Detroit Law Journal* 34 (November 1965): 181-203, 317-332.

1979. Hudon, Edward G. "The Supreme Court of the United States: A History of Its Books and Libraries." *Federal Bar Journal* 19 (April 1959): 185-199.

1980. Lord, Margaret P. "Supreme Courthouse (United States Supreme Court Building as an Architectural Masterpiece)." *Connoisseur* 214 (July 1984): 60-67.

1981. Manton, Martin T. "Historical Fragments Pertaining to the United States Supreme Court: Observations Suggested by the Announcement That the Court Is to Have a New Home." *United States Law Review* 66 (October 1932): 538-548.

1982. Mason, David. "Supreme Court's Bronze Doors." *American Bar Association Journal* 63 (October 1977): 1395-1399.

1983. Reeder, Robert P. "First Homes of the Supreme Court of the United States." *American Philosophical Society Proceedings* 76 (1936): 543-596.

1984. Skefos, Catherine H. "The Supreme Court Gets a Home." *Supreme Court Historical Yearbook* 1976 (1976): 25-36.

1985. Snyder, Paul S. "Supreme Court On-line." *American Bar Association Journal* 72 (August 1986): 80.

1986. U.S. Senate. Commission on Art and Antiquities. *The Supreme Court Chamber, 1810-1860.* Washington, DC: Senate Commission on Art and Antiquities, 1981.

1987. Von Euler, Mary. "Meeting the Court's New Research Needs." *Education and Urban Society* 9 (May 1977): 277-302.

1988. Waggaman, Thomas E. "The Supreme Court: Its Homes Past and Present." *American Bar Association Journal* 27 (May 1941): 283-289.

1989. "When the Supreme Court Was in the Capitol." *American Bar Association Journal* 61 (August 1975): 949-954.

Supporting Personnel

1990. Abrams, Floyd. "Trivializing the Supreme Court." *Fortune* 101 (March 10, 1980): 129-130.

1991. Alschuler, Albert W. "Supreme Court, the Defense Attorney, and the Guilty Plea." *University of Colorado Law Review* 47 (Fall 1975): 1-71.

1992. Baker, Elizabeth F. *Henry Wheaton, 1785-1848.* Philadelphia: University of Pennsylvania Press, 1937.

1993. Cummings, Homer S. *Selected Papers of Homer Cummings, Attorney General of the United States, 1933-1939.* Edited by Carl B. Swisher. New York: Da Capo Press, 1972.

1994. Davis, Kenneth C. "Judicial, Legislative, and Administrative Lawmaking: A Proposed Research Service for the Supreme Court." *Minnesota Law Review* 71 (October 1986): 1-18.

1995. Denniston, Lyle. "Play 'Em Again, Counsel (Lois De Julio before the Supreme Court and Other Cases)." *American Lawyer* 6 (December 1984): 110-111.

1996. Dunne, Gerald T. "Proprietors, Sometimes Predators: Early Court Reporters." *Supreme Court Historical Society Yearbook* 1976 (1976): 61-72.

1997. Frank, John P. "The Supreme Court: The Muckrakers Return." *American Bar Association Journal* 66 (February 1980): 160-164.

1998. Griswold, Erwin N. "The Office of

the Solicitor General: Representing the Interests of the United States before the Supreme Court." *Missouri Law Review* 34 (Fall 1969): 527-536.

1999. Hills, Roderick M. "Law Clerk at the Supreme Court of the United States." *Los Angeles Bar Bulletin* 33 (September 1958): 333-338.

2000. Joyce, Craig. "The Rise of the Supreme Court Reporter: An Institutional Perspective on Marshall Court Ascendancy." *Michigan Law Review* 83 (April 1985): 1291-1391.

2001. Joyce, Craig. "*Wheaton v. Peters*: The Untold Story of the Early Reporters." *Supreme Court Historical Society Yearbook* 1985 (1985): 35-92.

2002. Lerner, Max. "Personnel of the Supreme Court: Some Recent Literature." *National Lawyers Guild Quarterly* 2 (April 1939): 9-16.

2003. Lilly, Linus A. "Organization and Personnel of the Supreme Court." *Law Student* 4 (October 1, 1926): 11-14.

2004. McGurn, Barret. "Law Clerks: A Professional Elite." *Supreme Court History Society Yearbook* 1980 (1980): 98-101.

2005. Marcosson, Isaac F. "Attorney General Moody and His Work." *World's Work* 13 (November 1906): 8190-8194.

2006. O'Connor, Karen, and Lee Epstein. "*Amicus Curiae* Participation in U.S. Supreme Court Litigation: An Appraisal of Hakman's 'Folklore'." *Law and Society Review* 16 (1981/1982): 311-320.

2007. Putzel, Henry, and Paul R. Baier. " 'Double Revolving Peripatetic Nitpicker.' " *Supreme Court Historical Society Yearbook* 1980 (1980): 10-24.

2008. Williams, Richard L. "Supreme Court of the United States: The Staff That Keeps It Operating." *Smithsonian* 7 (January 1977): 39-49.

Reform of the Court

2009. Ashley, James M. "Should the Supreme Court Be Reorganized and Proportional Representation Be Demanded for the Election of Representatives in Congress?" *Arena* 14 (October 1895): 221-227.

2010. Baker, Thomas, and Douglas McFarland. "The Need for a New National Court." *Harvard Law Review* 100 (April 1987): 1400-1416.

2011. Beeley, Arthur L., and John S. Boyden. "A Ministry of Justice: The Pound-Cardozo Concept Embodied in a Utah State Council." *Utah Law Review* 8 (Winter 1963/1964): 328-337.

2012. Bickel, Alexander M. *The Caseload of the Supreme Court, and What, If Anything, to Do about It.* Washington, DC: American Enterprise Institute for Public Policy Research, 1973.

2013. Black, Charles L. "The National Court of Appeals: An Unwise Proposal." *Yale Law Journal* 83 (April 1974): 883-899.

2014. Blumstein, James F. "Supreme Court's Jurisdiction: Reform Proposals, Discretionary Review, and Writ Dismissals." *Vanderbilt Law Review* 26 (October 1973): 895-938.

2015. Brand, James T. "Statement in Behalf of the Oregon State Bar Relative to the Proposal to Increase the Number of Justices of the Supreme Court, Respectfully Submitted to the Judiciary Committee of the United States." *Oregon State Bar Bulletin* 2 (June 1937): 141-148.

2016. Bridge, William J., and C. Arthur Diamond. "The National Court of Appeals: A Qualified Concurrence." *Georgetown Law Journal* 62 (February 1974): 881-912.

2017. Buell, Raymond L. "Reforming the

Supreme Court." *Nation* 114 (June 12, 1922): 714.

2018. Carpenter, William S. "The Repeal of the Judiciary Act of 1801." *American Political Science Review* 9 (August 1915): 519-528.

2019. Casper, Gerhard, and Richard A. Posner. "Caseload of Supreme Court: 1975 and 1976 Terms." *Supreme Court Review* 1977 (1977): 87-98.

2020. Casper, Gerhard, and Richard A. Posner. "Study of the Supreme Court's Caseload." *Journal of Legal Studies* 3 (June 1974): 339-375.

2021. Casper, Gerhard, and Richard A. Posner. *The Workload of the Supreme Court.* Chicago: American Bar Foundation, 1976.

2022. Chilton, Jan T. "Appellate Court Reform: The Premature Scalpel." *California State Bar Journal* 48 (July 1973): 393-397; (July/August 1973): 462-475.

2023. Clark, Grenville. "The Supreme Court Issue." *Yale Review* 26 (Summer 1937): 669-688.

2024. Cohen, Richard E. "Reformers Revise Plans for New National Appeals Court." *National Journal Reports* 7 (January 25, 1975): 144-146.

2025. Commission on Revision of the Federal Court Appellate System. *Structure and Internal Procedures: Recommendations for Change.* Washington, DC: Commission on Revision of the Federal Court Appellate System, 1975.

2026. Coxe, Alfred C. "Relief for the Supreme Court." *Forum* 6 (February 1889): 567-578.

2027. Cronin, E. David. "A Southern Progressive Looks at the New Deal." *Journal of Southern History* 24 (May 1958): 151-176.

2028. Davis, Polly. "Court Reform and Alben W. Barkley's Election as Majority

Leader." *Southern Quarterly* 15 (October 1976): 15-31.

2029. Deutsch, Eberhard P. "The National Court of Appeals: Another Dissent." *Judicature* 59 (November 1975): 164-183.

2030. Estreicher, Samuel, and John E. Sexton. "A Managerial Theory of the Supreme Court's Responsibilities: An Empirical Study." *New York University Law Review* 59 (October 1984): 681-822.

2031. Federal Judicial Center. *Case Load of the Supreme Court: A Report of the Study Group.* Washington, DC: Administrative Office of U.S. Courts, 1972.

2032. Finley, Robert C. "Judicial Administration: What Is This Thing Called Legal Reform?" *Columbia Law Review* 65 (March 1965): 569-592.

2033. Fish, Peter G. "Crises, Politics, and Federal Judicial Reform: The Administrative Office Act of 1939." *Journal of Politics* 32 (August 1970): 599-627.

2034. Freund, Paul A. "Storm over the American Supreme Court." *Modern Law Review* 21 (July 1958): 345-358.

2035. Freund, Paul A. "Storms over the Supreme Court." *American Bar Association Journal* 69 (October 1983): 1474-1480.

2036. Freund, Paul A. "Why We Need the National Court of Appeals." *American Bar Association Journal* 59 (March 1973): 247-252.

2037. Gazell, James A. "The National Court of Appeals Controversy: An Emergency Negative Consensus." *Northern Illinois University Law Review* 6 (Winter 1986): 1-37.

2038. Ginsburg, Ruth B., and P. W. Huber. "The Intercircuit Committee." *Harvard Law Review* 100 (April 1987): 1417-1435.

2039. Good, I. J., and Gordon Tullock. "Judicial Errors and a Proposal for Reform." *Journal of Legal Studies* 13 (June 1984): 289-298.

2040. Green, Theodore. "Proposed Supreme Court Changes." *Law Society Journal* 7 (May 1937): 806-814.

2041. Gressman, Eugene. "The Constitution v. the Freund Report." *Washington Law Review* 41 (July 1973): 951-970.

2042. Grippando, James M. "The U.S. Supreme Court's Workload and Intercircuit Conflicts: Reform through Existing Judicial Authority." *Florida Bar Journal* 60 (June 1986): 13-17.

2043. Griswold, Erwin N. "Helping the Supreme Court by Reducing the Flow of Cases into the Courts of Appeals." *Judicature* 67 (August 1983): 28-67.

2044. Hellman, Arthur D. "Caseload, Conflicts, and Decisional Capacity: Does the Supreme Court Need Help?" *Judicature* 67 (June/July 1983): 28-48.

2045. Hellman, Arthur D. "How Not to Help the Supreme Court." *American Bar Association Journal* 69 (June 1983): 750-754.

2046. Hellman, Arthur D. "The Proposed Intercircuit Tribunal: Do We Need It? Will It Work?" *Hastings Constitutional Law Quarterly* 11 (Spring 1984): 375-456.

2047. Holtzoff, Alexander. "Judicial Procedure Reform: Leadership of the Supreme Court." *American Bar Association Journal* 43 (March 1957): 215-218.

2048. Horsky, Charles A. "Law Day: Some Reflections on Current Proposals to Curtail the Supreme Court." *Minnesota Law Review* 42 (May 1958): 1105-1011.

2049. Hruska, Roman L. "Commission Recommends New National Court of Appeals." *American Bar Association Journal* 61 (July 1975): 819-824.

2050. Huggins, William L. "The New Attack upon the Independence of the Judiciary." *Law and Labor* 6 (March 1924): 56-62; (April 1924): 86-92; (May 1924): 118-124.

2051. Huston, Luther A. "The Supreme Court and Its Critics." *Nieman Reports* 11 (June 1961): 19-22.

2052. Johnsen, Julia E. *Reorganization of the Supreme Court.* New York: H. W. Wilson, 1937.

2053. Keefe, Arthur J. "Mini Supreme Court or a Maxi Appeals Court." *American Bar Association Journal* 59 (1973): 182-184.

2054. Komar, Borris M. "On the Reform of Appellate Procedures of the United States Supreme Court." *Chicago-Kent Law Review* 44 (Spring 1967): 28-38.

2055. Konop, Thomas F., and William M. Cain. "Reorganization of the Federal Judiciary." *Notre Dame Lawyer* 12 (May 1937): 347-360.

2056. Lawson, Steven F. "Progressives and the Supreme Court: A Case for Judicial Reform in the 1920s." *Historian* 42 (May 1980): 419-436.

2057. Lay, Donald P. "Why Rush to Judgement: Some Second Thoughts on the Proposed National Court of Appeals." *Judicature* 59 (November 1975): 164-183.

2058. Levin, A. Leo, and Arlene Fickler. "A New Proposal for a National Court of Appeals." *Judicature* 59 (November 1975): 164-183.

2059. Lewin, Nathan. "A Caustic Look at the Freund Report." *Student Lawyer* 1 (May 1973): 12-17.

2060. Lunt, Dudley C. "The Proposals to Curb the Supreme Court: An Old Question Bobs Up Once More." *Public Utilities Fortnightly* 17 (June 4, 1936): 717-724.

2061. McCree, Wade H., Jr. "To Preserve an Endangered Species." *University of Cincinnati Law Review* 52 (Fall 1983): 986-993.

2062. McCrory, C. B. "Congress Has

Constitutional Authority to Reorganize Court." *Oklahoma State Bar Journal* 8 (April 1937): 8-12.

2063. McEnerney, Garrett W. *The Proposal to Add Six Additional Judges to the Supreme Court of the United States.* San Francisco: The Recorder, 1937.

2064. McGovney, Dudley O. "Reorganization of the Supreme Court." *California Law Review* 25 (May 1937): 389-412.

2065. McLeese, Roy W. "Disagreement in DC: The Relationship between the Supreme Court and the DC Circuit and Its Implications for a National Court of Appeals." *New York University Law Review* 59 (November 1984): 1048-1077.

2066. Maury, William A. *The Supreme Court of the United States: A Discussion of Its Wants and the Remedy for Them, with the Draught of a Statute Embodying a Plan of Relief.* Washington, DC: William H. Morrison, 1881.

2067. Maxwell, Samuel. "Relief of the United States Supreme Court." *American Law Review* 23 (November/December 1889): 958-964.

2068. Maynard, Fred A., and Everett P. Wheeler. "Five to Four Decision of the Supreme Court of the United States: Reply." *American Law Review* 54 (July/August 1920): 481-514; (November/December 1920): 921-928.

2069. Mayne, Wiley E. "No Relief in Sight for a Beleaguered Supreme Court." *Litigation News* 9 (Spring 1984): 3-5.

2070. Morgan, John T. "Partisanship in the Supreme Court." *North American Review* 132 (February 1881): 176-186.

2071. Nathanson, Nathaniel L. "Proposals for an Administrative Appellate Court." *Administrative Law Review* 25 (Winter 1973): 85-96.

2072. Nugent, W. L. "Delay of Business in the Supreme Court of the United States: Another Suggestion." *Central Law Journal* 2 (August 20, 1875): 545.

2073. Olney, Warren. "President's Proposal to Add Six New Members to the Supreme Court." *American Bar Association Journal* 23 (April 1937): 237-241, 264.

2074. Orth, John V. "A Reverie on Medieval Judges, Milton Friedman, and the Supreme Court's Workload." *American Bar Association Journal* 69 (October 1983): 1454-1483.

2075. Parker, Alan. "The Tenth Justice." *Trial* 21 (March 1985): 11.

2076. Patterson, Kirby W. "Thinning the Judicial Thicket: Further Possible Steps to Meet the Continuing Caseload Problem." *Federal Rules Decisions* 74 (1977): 477-496.

2077. Perrigo, Lynn I. "The Federal Judiciary: An Analysis of Proposed Revisions." *Minnesota Law Review* 21 (April 1937): 481-511.

2078. Phelps, Edward J., et al. "Relief of the Supreme Court." *Albany Law Journal* 25 (May 13, 1882): 370-372.

2079. Poe, Douglas A., John R. Schmidt, and Wayne W. Whalen. "A National Court of Appeals: A Dissenting View." *Northwestern University Law Review* 67 (January/February 1973): 842-856.

2080. Pollitt, Basil H. "What Is Wrong with the Supreme Court of the United States." *Florida Law Journal* 25 (July 1951): 233-235.

2081. Pugh, James T. "The Unconstitutional Aspect of the Proposal to Enlarge the Supreme Court." *Massachusetts Law Quarterly* 22 (April/June 1937): 25-29.

2082. Pusey, Merlo J. "The 'Judges' Bill after Half a Century." *Supreme Court Historical Society Yearbook* 1976 (1976): 73-81.

2083. Pusey, Merlo J. *The Supreme Court*

Crisis. New York: Macmillan Company, 1937.

2084. Rice, George P., Jr. "Shall We Curb the U.S. Supreme Court? Arguments For and Against." *Armenian Review* 12 (February 1960): 33-38.

2085. Rodino, Peter J. "Legislative Proposals to Curtail the Jurisdiction of the Federal Courts." *Catholic Lawyer* 29 (Spring 1984): 137-145.

2086. Rosenburg, Maurice. "Enlarging the Federal Courts' Capacity to Settle the National Law." *Gonzaga Law Review* 10 (Spring 1975): 709-730.

2087. Sedgwick, A. G. "The Plans for the Relief of the Supreme Court." *Nation* 34 (May 18, 1882): 418-419.

2088. Severance, Cardenio A. "The Proposal to Make Congress Supreme." *American Bar Association Journal* 8 (August 1922): 459-464.

2089. Siferd, Willis S. "Proposals to Limit the Power of the Supreme Court in the Seventy-Fourth Congress." *George Washington Law Review* 4 (March 1936): 381-390.

2090. Smith, Sylvester C., Jr. "Critical Stage in Supreme Court Fight." *American Bar Association Journal* 23 (July 1937): 491-495.

2091. Sommer, Frank H. *Reforming the Supreme Court.* New York: New York University School of Law, 1937.

2092. Steamer, Robert J. "Statesmanship or Craftsmanship: Current Conflict over the Supreme Court." *Western Political Quarterly* 11 (June 1958): 265-277.

2093. Stokes, Isaac N. P. "National Court of Appeals: An Alternative Proposal." *American Bar Association Journal* 60 (February 1974): 179-181.

2094. Stolz, Preble. "Federal Review of State Court Decisions of Federal Questions: The Need for Additional Appellate

Capacity." *California Law Review* 64 (July 1976): 943-983.

2095. Sumner, Charles. "Remodelling of the Supreme Court of the United States, Remarks in the Senate, on the Bill to Reorganize the Judiciary of the United States, April 12, 1866." In *Complete Works,* vol. 14, by Charles Sumner, 30-32. Boston: Lee and Shepard, 1900.

2096. "Supreme Court of the U.S.: Amendments of the Constitution Are Proposed." *American Bar Association Journal* 34 (January 1948): 1-3.

2097. Thompson, Seymour D., and John F. Dillon, eds. "Supreme Court of the United States." *Central Law Journal* 2 (January 22, 1875): 55-56.

2098. Thompson, Todd E. "Increasing Uniformity and Capacity in the Federal Appellate System." *Hastings Constitutional Law Quarterly* 11 (Spring 1984): 457-504.

2099. Trieber, Jacob. "Further Relief for United States Supreme Court." *American Bar Association Journal* 12 (March 1926): 167.

2100. Ulmer, S. Sidney. "Revising the Jurisdiction of the Supreme Court: Mere Administrative Reform or Substantive Policy Change?" *Minnesota Law Review* 58 (November 1973): 121-155.

2101. Ulmer, S. Sidney, and John A. Stookey. "How Is the Ox Being Gored: Toward a Theory of Docket Size and Innovation in the U.S. Supreme Court." *University of Toledo Law Review* 7 (Fall 1975): 1-28.

2102. Vale, Ruby R. "Observations on the Proposals of the President to Change the Personnel of the Judges." *Dickinson Law Review* 41 (June 1937): 195-200.

2103. Wiggins, Charles. "National Court of Appeals." *Trial* 13 (November 1977): 36-39.

2104. Williams, Ira J. "The Attack upon the Supreme Court." *Constitutional Review* 7 (July 1923): 143-153.

2105. Winters, Glenn R. "Shall We 'Curb' the Supreme Court?" *Massachusetts Law Quarterly* 42 (October 1957): 51-54.

2106. Winters, Glenn R., ed. *Selected Readings, Court Congestion and Delay.* Chicago: American Judicature Society, 1971.

IV. The Work of the Court

Power of the Court

2107. Bass, Stanley A. *United States Supreme Court Decisions during the Last Decade: Has the Court Exceeded Its Powers?* Chicago: American Bar Foundation, 1964.

2108. Beale, Sara S. "Reconsidering Supervisory Power in Criminal Cases: Constitutional and Statutory Limits on the Authority of the Federal Courts." *Columbia Law Review* 84 (October 1984): 1433-1522.

2109. Billikoph, David M. *The Exercise of Judicial Power, 1789-1864.* New York: Vantage Press, 1973.

2110. Coleman, Jimmy R. "Supreme Oligarchy." *Engage/Social Action* 6 (August 1928): 4-8.

2111. Dornan, Robert K., and Csaba Vedlik, Jr. *Judicial Supremacy: The Supreme Court on Trial.* Marlborough, NH: Plymouth Rock Foundation, 1986.

2112. Evans, DeLavan P. "An Analysis of the Use of the Concept of Inherent Federal Powers by the United States Supreme Court." Ph.D diss., University of California, Berkeley, 1951.

2113. Fowler, Robert L. "The Origin of the Supreme Judicial Power in the Federal Constitution." *American Law Review* 29 (September/October 1895): 711-725.

2114. Glazer, Nathan. "Towards an Imperial Judiciary." *Public Interest* 41 (Fall 1975): 104-123.

2115. Graglia, Lino A. "The Power of Congress to Limit Supreme Court Jurisdiction." *Harvard Journal of Law and Public Policy* 7 (Winter 1984): 23-29.

2116. Haines, Charles G. *The American Doctrine of Judicial Supremacy.* Berkeley: University of California Press, 1932.

2117. Hallam, Oscar. "Judicial Power to Declare Legislative Acts Void." *American Law Review* 48 (January 1914): 85-114; (March 1914): 225-273.

2118. Harris, Robert J. *The Judicial Power of the United States.* Baton Rouge: Louisiana State University Press, 1940.

2119. Herriott, Maxwell H. "Has Congress the Power to Modify the Effect of *Erie Railroad Co. v. Tompkins?*" *Marquette Law Review* 26 (December 1941): 1-10.

2120. Hook, Sidney, Alan F. Westin, John R. Schmidhauser, and Mark D. Howe. "Four Briefs on the U.S. Supreme Court." *Saturday Review* 43 (April 30, 1960): 19-21.

2121. Kilgore, Carol D. *Judicial Tyranny.* Nashville, TN: Thomas Nelson, 1977.

2122. Kutler, Stanley I. "*Ex Parte McCardle*: Judicial Impotence?" *American Historical Review* 72 (April 1967): 835-851.

2123. Lasser, William. *The Limits of Judicial Power: The Supreme Court in American Politics.* Chapel Hill: University of North Carolina Press, 1988.

2124. Lerner, Max. "Minority Rule and the Constitutional Tradition." In *Ideas Are Weapons: The History and Uses of Ideas*, edited by Max Lerner, 461-477. New York: Viking Press, 1939.

2125. Lerner, Max. "The Supreme Court and American Capitalism." In *Ideas Are Weapons: The History and Uses of Ideas*, edited by Max Lerner, 425-460. New York: Viking Press, 1939.

2126. Levi, Edward H. "The Sovereignty of the Courts." *University of Chicago Law Review* 50 (Spring 1983): 679-700.

2127. Lewis, Anthony. "Enforcing Our Rights." *George Washington Law Review* 50 (March 1982): 414-429.

2128. Lusky, Louis. *By What Right? A Commentary on the Supreme Court's Power to Revise the Constitution.* Charlottesville, VA: Michie, 1975.

2129. Lusky, Louis. "Public Trial and Public Right: The Missing Bottom Line." *Hofstra Law Review* 8 (Winter 1980): 273-323.

2130. McAffee, Thomas B. "Berger v. the Supreme Court: The Implications of His Exceptions—Clause Odyssey." *University of Dayton Law Review* 9 (Winter 1984): 219-273.

2131. McBain, Howard L. "Constitutional Power and Social Desirability." *American Labor Legislation Review* 26 (March 1936): 35-44.

2132. McDonough, James B. "The Alleged Usurpation of Power by the Federal Courts." *American Law Review* 46 (January/February 1912): 45-59.

2133. McGowan, Carl. *The Organization of Judicial Power in the United States.* Evanston, IL: Northwestern University Press, 1969.

2134. McKeage, Everett C. "The Supreme Law of the Land: A Decision of the Supreme Court of the United States Can Hardly Be Considered the Supreme Law of the Land for Such a Decision Is Too Transitory and Mutable." *Public Utilities Fortnightly* 65 (March 3, 1960): 301-311.

2135. Malick, Clay P. "The Supreme Court Adds a Footnote to Sovereignty." *Western Political Quarterly* 12 (June 1959): 576-577.

2136. Meigs, William M. "Some Recent Attacks on the American Doctrine of Judicial Power." *American Law Review* 40 (September/October 1906): 641-670.

2137. Mendelson, Wallace. "The Politics of Judicial Supremacy." *Journal of Law and Economics* 4 (October 1961): 175-185.

2138. Menez, Joseph F. "A Brief in Support of the Supreme Court." *Northwestern University Law Review* 54 (March/April 1959): 30-59.

2139. Meyer, Erwin F. "Debates of the Constitutional Convention on the Jurisdiction of the Supreme Court." *Rocky Mountain Law Review* 5 (April 1933): 168-175.

2140. Miller, Arthur S., and Alan W. Sheflin. "The Power of the Supreme Court in the Age of the Positive State." *Duke Law Journal* 2 (April 1967): 273-320; 3 (June 1967): 522-551.

2141. Moran, James. "Judicial Supremacy as an American Doctrine." *Indiana State Bar Association Proceedings* 1924 (1924): 48-68.

2142. Mosby, Thomas S. "The Court Is King." *Arena* 36 (August 1906): 118-120.

2143. Murphy, Walter F. "Lower Court Checks on Supreme Court Power." *American Political Science Review* 53 (December 1959): 1017-1031.

2144. Orth, John V. "The Interpretation of the Eleventh Amendment, 1798-1908: A Case Study of Judicial Power." *University of Illinois Law Review* 1983 (1983): 423-455.

2145. Parker, Junius. "The Supreme

Court and Its Constitutional Duty and Power.'' *American Law Review* 30 (May/June 1896): 357-364.

2146. Percy, Billups P. "The Judicial Power: The Cement That Holds the Republic Together." *Judicature* 71 (August/September 1987): 65-67.

2147. Potter, William W. "Judicial Power in the United States." *Michigan Law Review* 27 (November 1928/January 1929): 1-22, 167-190, 285-313.

2148. Ramsay, David. *An Enquiry into the Constitutional Authority of the Supreme Federal Court, over the Several States, in Their Political Capacity; Being an Answer to Observations upon the Government of the State of Massachusetts by a Citizen of South Carolina.* Charleston: W. P. Young, Broadstreet, 1792.

2149. Rindler, Milton. "The Supreme Court Is Supreme." *Taxes* 20 (August 1942): 486-491, 509.

2150. Seckendorff, M. G. "The Enormous Power of the Supreme Court." *Munsey's Magazine* 43 (September 1910): 766-770.

2151. Sharp, Wilson W. "A Court Supreme: Arkansas Bar President Points Out Dangers." *American Bar Association Journal* 34 (September 1948): 788-790.

2152. Simons, Charles C. "Judicial Powers: Their Exercise without Constitutional Safeguards." *American Bar Association Journal* 34 (October 1948): 907-909, 977.

2153. Stebbins, Albert K. " 'Vested' Powers of the United States Supreme Court." *Marquette Law Review* 10 (June 1926): 204-211.

2154. Sunderland, Edson R. "Character and Extent of the Rule-Making Power Granted U.S. Supreme Court and Methods of Effective Exercise." *American Bar Association Journal* 21 (July 1935): 404-409, 458-460.

2155. Sunderland, Edson R. "Grant of Rule-Making Power to the Supreme Court of the United States." *Michigan Law Review* 32 (June 1934): 1116-1129.

2156. Sunderland, Edson R. "Implementing the Rule-Making Power." *New York University Law Review* 25 (January 1950): 27-41.

2157. Swisher, Carl B. "The Supreme Court: Need for Re-evaluation." *Virginia Law Review* 40 (November 1954): 837-851.

2158. Taylor, Telford. "Is the Supreme Court Supreme?" *New York Times Magazine* 108 (October 5, 1958): 10, 80-82.

2159. Tigar, Michael E. "Judicial Power, the 'Political Question Doctrine', and Foreign Relations." *UCLA Law Review* 17 (June 1970): 1135-1179.

2160. Van Alstyne, William W. "A Critical Guide to *Ex Parte McCardle*." *Arizona Law Review* 15 (1973): 229-269.

2161. Vining, Joseph. *The Authoritative and the Authoritarian.* Chicago: University of Chicago Press, 1986.

2162. Westin, Alan F. "Liberals and the Supreme Court: Making Peace with the 'Nine Old Men'." *Commentary* 22 (July 1956): 20-26.

2163. Willis, Hugh E. "The Doctrine of the Supremacy of the Supreme Court." *Indiana Law Journal* 6 (January 1931): 224-258.

2164. Willis, Hugh E. "The Part of the United States Constitution Made by the Supreme Court." *Iowa Law Review* 23 (January 1938): 165-214.

2165. Wiseman, Laurence E. "The New Supreme Court Commentators: The Principled, the Political, and the Philosophical." *Hastings Constitutional Law Quarterly* 10 (Winter 1983): 315-431.

Jurisdiction

General Studies

2166. Appelbaum, Paul S. "The Empirical Jurisprudence of the United States Supreme Court." *American Journal of Law and Medicine* 13 (Summer/Fall 1987): 153-364.

2167. Bailey, William F. *The Law of Jurisdiction, Including Impeachment of Judgements, Liability for Judicial Acts, and Special Remedies.* 2 vols. Chicago: T. H. Flood, 1899.

2168. Brown, Timothy. *Commentaries on the Jurisdiction of Courts.* 2d ed. Chicago: Callaghan, 1901.

2169. Brunet, Edward J. "Limiting Long-Arm Jurisdiction: The Burger Court and the Minimum Contact Test." *California State Bar Journal* 56 (August 1981): 318-322.

2170. Bunn, Charles W. "The New Appellate Jurisdiction in Federal Courts." *Minnesota Law Review* 9 (March 1925): 309-313.

2171. Carter, Howard M. *The Jurisdiction of Federal Courts, As Limited by the Citizenship and Resistance of the Parties.* Boston: Little, Brown, 1899.

2172. Clark, Charles E. "Power of the Supreme Court to Make Rules of Appellate Procedure." *Harvard Law Review* 49 (June 1936): 1303-1321.

2173. Clark, Charles E., and James W. Moore. "A New Federal Civil Procedure." *Yale Law Review* 44 (January 1935): 387-435; (June 1935): 291-323.

2174. Clark, Homer. "The Supreme Court and the Amending Process." *Virginia Law Review* 39 (June 1953): 621-652.

2175. Clayton, F. Brittin, III. "*Ohio v. Johnson*: The Continuing Demise of the Adequate and Independent State Ground Rule." *University of Colorado Law Review* 57 (Winter 1986): 395-417.

2176. Countryman, Edwin. *The Supreme Court of the United States, with a Review of Certain Decisions Relating to Its Appellate Power under the Constitution.* Albany, NY: M. Bender, 1913.

2177. Dabney, Walter D. *Outlines of Federal Jurisdiction and Law Procedure.* Charlottesville, VA: George W. Oliver, 1897.

2178. Dobie, Armistead M. "The Federal Rules of Civil Procedure." *Virginia Law Review* 25 (January 1939): 261-315.

2179. DuPonceau, Peter S. *A Dissertation on the Nature and Extent of the Jurisdiction of the Courts of the United States.* Philadelphia: Abraham Small, 1824.

2180. Eaton, James S. "Power of Congress to Limit the Jurisdiction of District Courts." *Mississippi Law Journal* 7 (April 1935): 405-411.

2181. Fischer, James M. "Concept of Mandatory Jurisdiction." *Ohio State Law Journal* 41 (Winter 1980): 861-904.

2182. Fischer, Thomas C. "*DeFunis* in the Supreme Court: Is That All There Is?" *Journal of Law and Education* 4 (July 1975): 487-509.

2183. Flaherty, Donald W. "The Role of the United States Supreme Court in the Settlement of Inter-Sovereign Disputes." Ph.D. diss., Syracuse University, 1954.

2184. Foster, Roger. *A Treatise on Federal Practice, Including Practice in Bankruptcy, Admiralty, Patent Cases, Foreclosure of Railway Mortgages, Suits upon Claims against the U.S., Equity Pleading and Practice, Receivers and Injunctions in the State Courts.* 3d ed. 2 vols. Chicago: Callaghan, 1901.

2185. Fowler, Robert L. "A Theory of Sovereignty under the Federal Constitution." *American Law Review* 21 (May/June 1887): 399-417.

2186. Friendly, Henry J. *Federal Jurisdiction: A General View.* New York: Columbia University Press, 1973.

2187. Gangi, William. "Judicial Expansionism: An Evaluation of the Ongoing Debate." *Ohio Northern University Law Review* 8 (January 1981): 1-68.

2188. Hart, Henry M., Jr. "The Power of Congress to Limit the Jurisdiction of Federal Courts: An Exercise in Dialectic." *Harvard Law Review* 66 (June 1953): 1362-1402.

2189. Hawes, Horace. *The Law Relating to the Subject of Jurisdiction of Courts.* San Francisco: Sumner Whitney, 1886.

2190. Heady, C. Ferrel, Jr. "Suits by States within the Original Jurisdiction of the Supreme Court." *Washington University Law Quarterly* 26 (December 1940): 61-83.

2191. Hooper, William S. "Supreme Court Has Original Jurisdiction to Disbar Attorneys, Not Merely Deferring to Statutory Regulations as Matter of Comity." *Wisconsin Law Review* 5 (April 1929): 181-184.

2192. Hughes, Robert M. *Handbook of Jurisdiction and Procedure in the United States Courts.* St. Paul, MN: West Publishing Company, 1904.

2193. Hughes, William L. "The New Federal Appellate Jurisdiction Act." *Georgetown Law Journal* 13 (March 1925): 266-274.

2194. Inger, Sarah S. "Congress vs. the Supreme Court in 1868 and 1957: A Reexamination of *Ex Parte McCardle.*" Ph.D. diss., University of Chicago, 1963.

2195. Johnson, J. Altheus. "Jurisdiction and Authority of the State Supreme Courts and of the Supreme Court of the United States." *Law Student's Helper* 15 (October 1907): 291-295.

2196. Karlen, Delmar. "The Highest Tribunal: The Supreme Court of the United States." In *Appellate Courts in the United States and England,* by Delmar Karlen, 57-79. New York: New York University Press, 1963.

2197. Karlen, Delmar. "The Supreme Court of the United States." *International and Comparative Law Quarterly* 11 (October 1962): 976-996.

2198. Kling, Edward L. "Greater Certainty in International Transactions through Choices of Forum?" *American Journal of International Law* 69 (April 1975): 366-374.

2199. Lawton, Alexander R. *Judicial Controversies on Federal Appellate Jurisdiction.* Savannah, GA: Private Print, 1921.

2200. Levy, Adrian F., Jr. "Jurisdiction of the Supreme Court to Issue *Mandamus* to a State Court." *Texas Law Review* 20 (January 1942): 358-366.

2201. McAnally, Charles W. "Original Jurisdiction of Supreme Court, Claims against the State." *North Carolina Law Review* 6 (June 1928): 486-488.

2202. Mayers, Lewis. "The *Habeas Corpus* Act of 1867: The Supreme Court as Legal Historian." *University of Chicago Law Review* 33 (Autumn 1965): 31-59.

2203. Merry, Henry J. "Scope of the Supreme Court's Appellate Jurisdiction: Historical Basis." *Minnesota Law Review* 47 (December 1962): 53-69.

2204. Mickenburg, Ira. "Abusing the Exceptions and Regulations Clause: Legislative Attempts to Divest the Supreme Court of Appellate Jurisdiction." *American University Law Review* 32 (Winter 1983): 497-542.

2205. Morse, Howard N. "A Study in the Significance of Constitutional Word-

Omission *Ex industria.*" *Kentucky Law Journal* 37 (November 1948): 78-80.

2206. O'Connell, Thomas J. "Arbitration and Forum Selection Clauses in International Business: The Supreme Court Takes an Internationalist View." *Fordham Law Review* 43 (December 1974): 424-440.

2207. Pepper, George W. *The Border Land of Federal and State Decisions.* Philadelphia: T. and J. W. Johnson, 1889.

2208. Phillips, Philip. *The Statutory Jurisdiction and Practice of the Supreme Court of the United States Together with Forms of Process and Rules Established for the Supreme Court, the Court of Claims, the Courts of Equity, and the Courts of Admiralty.* 5th ed. New York: Banks and Brothers, 1887.

2209. Pittman, Robert C. "Judicial Supremacy in America: Its Colonial and Constitutional History." *Georgia Bar Journal* 16 (November 1953): 148-165.

2210. Pittman, Robert C. "The Supremacy of the Judiciary: A Study in Pre-constitutional History." *American Bar Association Journal* 40 (May 1954): 389-393.

2211. Rearick, Francis G. "Supreme Court of United States: Original Jurisdiction." *Illinois Law Review* 20 (March 1926): 724.

2212. Reese, Willis L. M. "The Supreme Court Supports Enforcement of Choice-of-Forum Clauses." *International Lawyer* 7 (July 1973): 530-540.

2213. Robertson, Reynolds. *Jurisdiction of the Supreme Court of the United States.* St. Paul, MN: West Publishing Company, 1936.

2214. Rooks, Harry S. "Effect of the United States Supreme Court Decision in *Erie Railroad v. Tompkins.*" *Missouri Bar Journal* 9 (June 1938): 108-109, 121, 123.

2215. Rubin, Seymour J., and Sidney H.

Willner. "Obligatory Jurisdiction of the Supreme Court: Appeals from State Courts under Section 237(a) of the Judicial Code." *Michigan Law Review* 37 (February 1939): 540-563.

2216. Sedler, Robert A. "Limitations on the Appellate Jurisdiction of the Supreme Court." *University of Pittsburgh Law Review* 20 (Fall 1958): 99-115.

2217. Siegel, David D. "The Federal Rules in Diversity Cases: *Erie* Implemented, Not Retarded." *American Bar Association Journal* 54 (February 1968): 172-176.

2218. Simpson, John M. "Turning over the Reins: The Abolition of the Mandatory Appellate Jurisdiction of the Supreme Court." *Hastings Constitutional Law Quarterly* 6 (Fall 1978): 297-343.

2219. Snider, Clifford R. "Important Changes in Federal Appellate Jurisdiction." *West Virginia Law Quarterly* 31 (February 1925): 127-130.

2220. Spear, Samuel T. *The Law of the Federal Judiciary: A Treatise on the Provisions of the Constitution, the Laws of Congress, and the Judicial Decisions Relating to the Jurisdiction of, and Practice and Pleading in the Federal Courts.* New York: Baker, Voorhis, 1883.

2221. Stavton, John W. "Jurisdiction of the Supreme Court, Constitutionality of Statute Allowing Certified Questions from the District Court." *Texas Law Review* 12 (February 1934): 206-210.

2222. Steamer, Robert J. "The Legal and Political Genesis of the Supreme Court." *Political Science Quarterly* 77 (December 1962): 546-568.

2223. Stern, Robert L., Stephen M. Shapiro, and Eugene Gressman. "Epitaph for Mandatory Jurisdiction." *American Bar Association Journal* 74 (December 1988): 66-70.

2224. Stevens, Francis B. "Appeal and Error: Jurisdiction of the United States Supreme Court to Consider Errors Not Raised in State Court." *Mississippi Law Journal* 21 (March 1950): 278-280.

2225. Strong, Frank R. "The Time Has Come to Talk of Major Curtailment in the Supreme Court's Jurisdiction." *North Carolina Law Review* 48 (December 1969): 1-31.

2226. Taylor, Hannis. *Jurisdiction and Procedure of the Supreme Court of the United States.* Rochester, NY: Lawyers Co-Operative Publishing Company, 1905.

2227. Thatcher, Erastus. *A Digest of Statutes, Rules, and Decisions Relative to the Jurisdiction and Practice of the Supreme Court of the United States.* 2d ed. Boston: Little, Brown, 1893.

2228. Thayer, Amos M. *Jurisdiction of the Federal Courts.* St. Louis: W. W. Brewer Company, 1895.

2229. Tushnet, Mark V. "Mandatory Judisdiction of Supreme Court: Some Recent Developments." *University of Cincinnati Law Review* 46 (Spring 1977): 347-371.

2230. Wagner, W. Joseph. "Original Jurisdiction of National Supreme Courts." *St. John's Law Review* 33 (May 1959): 217-248.

2231. Wagner, Wienczslaw. "The Original and Exclusive Jurisdiction of the United States Supreme Court." *St. Louis University Law Journal* 2 (Fall 1952): 111-155.

2232. Wells, John C. *A Treatise on the Jurisdiction of Courts.* 2 vols. St. Paul, MN: West Publishing Company, 1880.

2233. Wells, Michael. "Why Professor Redish Is Wrong about Abstention." *Georgia Law Review* 19 (Summer 1985): 1097-1133.

2234. Whaley, Otis. "Interstate Boundary Disputes before the United States Supreme Court." Ph.D. diss., Duke University, 1935.

2235. Wiener, Frederick B. "Wanna Make a Federal Case Out of It? Litigation in Which There May Be a Question Arising under the Constitution or Law of the United States." *American Bar Association Journal* 48 (January 1962): 59-62.

2236. Wolfson, Richard F., and Philip B. Kurland. "Appeals to the United States Supreme Court under 28 U.S.C. 1252 and 28 U.S.C. 1254(2)." *New York University Law Review* 25 (January 1950): 100-111.

2237. Wolfson, Richard F., and Philip B. Kurland. *Jurisdiction of the Supreme Court of the United States.* Rev. ed. Albany, NY: Bender, 1951.

2238. Yohe, Susan A. "Supreme Court Says No to Pendent Parties: At Least This Time." *University of Pittsburgh Law Review* 38 (Winter 1976): 395-416.

Admiralty Law

2239. Arsenault, Richard J., and Richard W. Beard. "Bringing Pleasure Boat Accidents under the Admiralty Forum." *Trial* 18 (October 1982): 66-71.

2240. Arsenault, Richard J., and Richard W. Beard. "Maritime Personal Injury on Foreign Waters." *Trial* 20 (June 1984): 72-76.

2241. Baer, Herbert R. *Admiralty Law of the Supreme Court.* 3d ed. Charlottesville, VA: Michie, 1975.

2242. Baer, Herbert R. *Admiralty Law of the Supreme Court: Cumulative Supplement.* 3d ed. Charlottesville, VA: Michie, 1981.

2243. Dickinson, Edwin D., and William S. Andrew, Jr. "A Decade of Admiralty in the Supreme Court of the United States."

California Law Review 36 (June 1948): 169-222.

2244. Farwell, Raymond F. "The Supreme Court Speaks." *U.S. Naval Institute Proceedings* 67 (August 1941): 1088-1097.

2245. Hogan, Leila A. "Jurisdiction over Foreign Merchant Vessels in American Waters and Ports: Territorial Jurisdiction and Law of the Flag in Selected Decisions of the United States Supreme Court, 1900-1970." Ph.D. diss., University of Maryland, 1979.

2246. Kerr, J. Ernest. *Imprint of the Maritimes*. Boston: Christopher Publishing House, 1959.

2247. Shalowitz, A. L. "Navigability, a New Supreme Court Interpretation." *U.S. Naval Institute Proceedings* 67 (July 1941): 932-934.

2248. Walz, Kathleen L. "United States Supreme Court and Article VII of the 1958 Convention on the Territorial Sea and Contiguous Zone." *University of San Francisco Law Review* 11 (Fall 1976): 1-51.

Military Law

2249. Fairman, Charles. "The Supreme Court on Military Jurisdiction: Martial Rule in Hawaii and the *Yamashita* Case." *Harvard Law Review* 59 (July 1946): 833-882.

2250. Kaczynski, Stephen J. "From *O'Callahan* to *Chappell*: The Burger Court and the Military." *University of Richmond Law Review* 18 (Winter 1984): 235-299.

2251. Lieber, G. Norman. "The Supreme Court on the Military Status." *American Law Review* 31 (May/June 1897): 342-362.

2252. Ries, John C., and Owen S. Nibley. "Justice, Juries, and Military Depen-

dents." *Western Political Quarterly* 15 (September 1962): 438-448.

2253. Silliman, Scott L. "Supreme Court and Its Impact on the Court of Military Appeals." *Air Force Law Review* 18 (Summer 1976): 81-93.

2254. Swisher, Carl B. "The Supreme Court and Conscription." *Current History* 54 (June 1968): 351-357.

Operations and Procedures

2255. Abraham, Henry J. "Effectiveness of Government Operations." *Annals of the American Academy of Political and Social Science* 426 (July 1976): 81-115.

2256. Aikin, Charles. "*Stare Decisis*, Precedent, and the Constitution." *Western Political Science Quarterly* 9 (March 1956): 87-92.

2257. Albertsworth, E. F. "Advisory Functions in Federal Supreme Court (A Realistic Study in Judicial Administration)." *Georgetown Law Journal* 23 (May 1935): 643-670.

2258. American Bar Association. *Report of Some Members of the Committee of the American Bar Association on the Subject of Delays Incident to the Determination of Suits in the United States Supreme Court*. New Haven, CT: Tuttle, Morehouse, and Taylor, 1882.

2259. American Bar Association. Advisory Committee on the Prosecution and Defense Functions. *Standards Relating to Providing Defense Services Recommended by the Advisory Committee on the Prosecution and Defense Functions*. New York: Institute of Judicial Administration, 1967.

2260. "Appellate Jurisdiction of the Supreme Court: Application of Non-Federal Ground Rule; Causes Continued for Clarification by State Court." *University* *of Pennsylvania Law Review* 94 (January 1946): 251-253.

2261. "Appellate Procedure of U.S. Supreme Court and Circuit Courts of Appeals." *American Bar Association Journal* 11 (March 1925): 145-151.

2262. Bannan, Rosemary S. "Briefing the Court: Dialectic as Methodological Perspective." *Journal of Contemporary Law* 10 (1984): 121-139.

2263. Beach, Charles F., Jr. *Modern Pleading and Practice in Equity in the Federal and State Courts of the United States, with Particular Reference to the Federal Practice, Including Numerous Forms and Precedents.* 2 vols. Cincinnati: W. H. Anderson and Company, 1900.

2264. Beckwith, Edmund R., and Rudolf Sobernheim. "*Amicus Curiae*: Minister of Justice." *Fordham Law Review* 17 (March 1948): 38-62.

2265. Blair, Paxton. "Federal Appellate Procedure as Affected by the Act of February 13, 1925." *Columbia Law Review* 25 (April 1925): 393-407.

2266. Bond, James E. *The Art of Judging.* New Brunswick, NJ: Transaction Books, 1987.

2267. Bordwell, Percy. "The Function of the Judiciary." *Columbia Law Review* 7 (May 1907): 337-343; (November 1907): 520-528.

2268. Boskey, Bennett. "The Supreme Court's 'Miscellaneous' Docket." *Harvard Law Review* 59 (April 1946): 604-606.

2269. Butler, Charles H. "Customs, Courtesies, and Ceremonies." *Supreme Court Historical Society Yearbook* 1978 (1978): 79-90.

2270. Cannon, Mark W. "Judicial Administration to the 21st Century." *Public Administration Review* 45 (November 1985): 679-685.

2271. Cardozo, Michael H. "Preview

Helps Reporters Cover the Supreme Court." *Judicature* 68 (February/March 1985): 297-299.

2272. "Caseload Crisis in U.S. Supreme Court (LawPoll)." *American Bar Association Journal* 70 (April 1984): 50.

2273. Cohen, Benjamin G. "Wading through the Procedural Marshes of Original Jurisdiction Guided by the *Tidelands* Cases: A Trial before the United States Supreme Court." *American Journal of Trial Advocacy* 11 (Summer 1987): 65-81.

2274. Coleman, William T., Jr. "The Supreme Court of the United States: Managing Its Caseload to Achieve Its Constitutional Purposes." *Fordham Law Review* 52 (October 1983): 1-36.

2275. Corr, John B. "Supreme Court Doctrine in the Trenches: The Case of Collateral Estoppel." *William and Mary Law Review* 27 (Fall 1985): 35-89.

2276. Cunningham, H. E. "The Problem of the Supreme Court Quorum." *George Washington Law Review* 12 (February 1944): 175-189.

2277. Denniston, Lyle. "Beguiling the Court with Analogy." *American Lawyer* 7 (April 1985): 137-138.

2278. Denniston, Lyle. "Dubious Controversy and Innovative Argument." *American Lawyer* 7 (March 1985): 114-115.

2279. Denniston, Lyle. "Fumbling in the End Zone." *American Lawyer* 6 (June 1984): 122-123.

2280. Dwyer, John W. *The Law and Procedure of United States Courts.* Ann Arbor, MI: G. Wahr, 1901.

2281. Eckler, John. "Historical Review." *Annals of the American Academy of Political and Social Science* 328 (March 1960): 1-6.

2282. Federal Judicial Center. *Report of the Study Group on the Caseload of the Su-*

preme Court. Washington, DC: Federal Judicial Center, 1972.

2283. Fey, John T. "The Supreme Court: An Operational Survey." *Catholic Lawyer* 4 (Winter 1958): 64-76.

2284. Finkelstein, Maurice. "A Study in Administrative Procedure: The Case of the Red Sea Charters." *St. John's Law Review* 31 (May 1956): 216-237.

2285. Fish, Peter G. *The Politics of Federal Judicial Administration.* Princeton, NJ: Princeton University Press, 1973.

2286. Friedenthal, Jack H. "A Divided Supreme Court Adopts Discovery Amendments to the Federal Rules of Civil Procedure." *California Law Review* 69 (May 1981): 806-820.

2287. Gallas, Edward C., and Nest M. Gallas, eds. "Symposium: Judicial Administration." *Public Administration Review* 31 (March/April 1971): 111-149.

2288. Garland, Augustus H., Robert Ralston, and John J. Ingham. *A Treatise on the Constitution and Jurisdiction of the U.S. Courts, on Pleading, Practice, and Procedure Therein and on the Powers and Duties of the U.S. Commissioners, with Rules of the Court and Forms.* 2 vols. Philadelphia: J. W. Johnson, 1898.

2289. Gressman, Eugene. "Supreme Court Practices: An Amendment to 1980 Rules." *American Bar Association Journal* 66 (December 1980): 1530-1531.

2290. Gressman, Eugene. "Supreme Court Practices circa 1980." *American Bar Association Journal* 66 (November 1980): 1385-1390.

2291. Handler, Milton. "What to Do with the Supreme Court's Burgeoning Calendars?" *Cardozo Law Review* 5 (Winter 1984): 249-286.

2292. Hart, Henry M., Jr., and Herbert Wechsler. *The Judicial Code and Rules of Procedure in the Federal Courts.* Mineola, NY: Foundation Press, 1971.

2293. Hodder-Williams, Richard. "The Workload of the Supreme Court: A Comment on the Freund Report." *Journal of American Studies* 10 (August 1976): 215-239.

2294. Johnson, John W. "Dimensions of Non-Legal Evidence in the American Judicial Process: The Supreme Court's Use of Extra-Legal Materials in the Twentieth Century." Ph.D. diss., University of Minnesota, 1974.

2295. Johnson, Milton E., and Stanley E. Harper. "Supreme Court Time Charts and Group Decisions." *University of Cincinnati Law Review* 31 (Summer 1962): 241-265.

2296. Kramer, Paul R. *Jury Trials before the Supreme Court of the United States.* Washington, DC: n.p., 1961.

2297. Landers, Jonathan M., James A. Martin, and Stephen C. Yeazell, eds. *Federal Rules of Civil Procedure: With Selected Statutes, 1988.* Boston: Little, Brown, 1988.

2298. Levin, A. Leo, and Arthur D. Hellman. "Many Roles of the Supreme Court and the Constraints of Time and Caseload." *University of Toledo Law Review* 7 (Winter 1976): 399-430.

2299. Lewis, Anthony. *The Supreme Court: Process and Change.* Iowa City: College of Law, State University of Iowa, 1963.

2300. Little, Joseph W. "Workload of the United States Supreme Court: Ruling the Pen with the Tongue." *Journal of Legal Profession* 6 (1981): 51-73.

2301. Long, Thomas J. "Deciding Whether Conflicts with Supreme Court Precedent Warrant *Certiorari.*" *New York University Law Review* 59 (November 1984): 1104-1119.

2302. McCorkle, J. M. "The Delay of

Business in the Supreme Court of the United States." *Central Law Journal* 2 (August 6, 1875): 512-513.

2303. McLauchlan, William P. "Exploratory Analysis of the Supreme Court's Caseload from 1880-1976." *Judicature* 64 (June/July 1980): 32-42.

2304. Maury, William A. *Federal Jurisdiction and Procedure, as Modified by the Acts of Congress of March 3, 1891, and March 3, 1887, Corrected by the Act of August 13, 1888.* Washington, DC: W. H. Loudermilk, 1896.

2305. May, Heber J. *A Treatise on the Practice and Procedure of the United States Supreme Court, Common Law, Equity, Admiralty, Criminal Law, Court of Claims, Interstate Commerce Commission, with Rules and Forms.* Washington, DC: J. Byrne, 1899.

2306. Moore, Richter H., Jr. "Justices View Supreme Court Workload: A Subjective Appraisal." *Air Force Law Review* 17 (Fall 1975): 31-40.

2307. Moore, Russell F. *Stare Decisis: Some Trends in British and American Application of the Doctrine.* New York: Simmons-Boardman, 1958.

2308. O'Brien, David M. "Managing the Business of the Supreme Court." *Public Administration Review* 45 (November 1985): 667-678.

2309. O'Brien, David M. *Storm Center: The Supreme Court in American Politics.* New York: W. W. Norton, 1986.

2310. Prettyman, E. Barrett, Jr. "The Supreme Court's Use of Hypothetical Questions at Oral Argument." *Catholic University Law Review* 33 (Spring 1984): 555-591.

2311. Puro, Steven. "The Role of the *Amicus Curiae* in the United States Supreme Court: 1920-1966." Ph.D. diss., State University of New York at Buffalo, 1971.

2312. Robertson, Reynolds. *Practice and Procedure in the Supreme Court of the United States.* Rev. ed. New York: Prentice-Hall, 1929.

2313. Rose, Walter M. *A Code of Federal Procedure Embodying Enactments of Congress, Constitutional Provisions, Established Principles, and Court Rules, in Force December 1, 1906, and the Bankruptcy Act of 1898, with Amendments and Orders, Together with a Collection of Forms and Precedents.* 3d ed. San Francisco: Bancroft-Whitney Company, 1907.

2314. Rothstein, Paul F. "The Proposed Amendments to the Federal Rules of Evidence." *Georgetown Law Journal* 62 (October 1973): 125-173.

2315. Scott, Austin W., and Robert B. Kent. *Cases and Other Materials on Civil Procedure.* Boston: Little, Brown, 1967.

2316. Shapiro, Stephen M. "Oral Argument in the Supreme Court: The Felt Necessities of the Time." *Supreme Court Historical Society Yearbook* 1985 (1985): 22-34.

2317. Simkins, William S. *A Suit in Equity in the Federal Courts.* Austin, TX: Von-Boickman-Jones Company, 1904.

2318. Sloss, Frank H. "*Mandamus* in the Supreme Court since the Judiciary Act of 1925." *Harvard Law Review* 46 (November 1932): 91-124.

2319. Stern, Robert L., and Eugene Gressman. *Supreme Court Practice: For Practice in the Supreme Court of the United States.* 6th ed. Washington, DC: Bureau of National Affairs, 1986.

2320. Swisher, Carl B. "Supreme Court and the Moment of Truth." *American Political Science Review* 54 (December 1960): 879-886.

2321. Thompson, Seymour D. "Three Courts." *American Law Review* 34 (May/June 1900): 401-408.

2322. Thompson, Seymour D., and John

D. Lawson. "United States Supreme Court: When Causes Will Be Taken Up Out of Their Order." *Central Law Journal* 3 (November 17, 1876): 732.

2323. Vernon, J. Michael. "Contracts Clause and the Court: A View of Precedent and Practice in Constitutional Adjudication." *Tulane Law Review* 54 (December 1979): 117-162.

2324. Westin, Alan F. *The Anatomy of a Constitutional Law Case.* New York: Macmillan, 1958.

2325. Williams, Richard L. "Justices Run 'Nine Little Law Firms' at Supreme Court." *Smithsonian* 7 (February 1977): 84-93.

2326. Winters, Glenn R. *The Jury: Selected Readings.* Chicago: American Judicature Society, 1971.

2327. Wright, Lloyd. "The Advantages of a Report to Congress by the Chief Justice of the United States." *American Bar Association Journal* 41 (April 1955): 329-331.

Rules of the Court

2328. Boskey, Bennett, and Eugene Gressman. "The Supreme Court Bids Farewell to Mandatory Appeals." *Federal Rules Decisions* 121 (October 1988): 81-99.

2329. Boskey, Bennett, and Eugene Gressman. "Supreme Court's New Rules for the Eighties." *Federal Rules Decisions* 85 (June 1980): 487-519.

2330. Boskey, Bennett, and Eugene Gressman. "Supreme Court's 1980 Rules: The First Addendum." *Federal Rules Decisions* 87 (December 1980): 513-517.

2331. Clark, Charles E. "Proper Function of the Supreme Court's Federal Rules Committee." *American Bar Association Journal* 28 (August 1942): 521-525.

2332. Clark, Charles E. "The Role of the Supreme Court in Federal Rule-Making." *Journal of the American Judicature Society* 46 (April 1963): 250-258.

2333. Dewhurst, William W., ed. *The Rules of Practice in the United States Courts, Annotated.* New York: Banks Law Publishing, 1907.

2334. Friedenthal, Jack H. "The Rulemaking Power of the Supreme Court: A Contemporary Crisis." *Stanford Law Review* 27 (February 1975): 673-686.

2335. Gillers, Stephen. "Access to the Federal Courts: The Supreme Court Rewrites the Rules." *Record of the Association of the Bar of the City of New York* 32 (November 1977): 603-610.

2336. Gillers, Stephen. "Conflicts: Risky New Rules: If the American Law Institute Has Its Way, a Conflict of Interest Will Lurk around Every Corner, Waiting to Snare the Well-Meaning Lawyer." *American Lawyer* 11 (September 1989): 39-41.

2337. Gressman, Eugene, and Robert L. Stern. *Supreme Court Rules: The 1980 Revisions.* Washington, DC: Bureau of National Affairs, 1980.

2338. Jacobs, Randall M. "Supreme Court's 1986 Summary Judgement Trilogy: A Proposed Analytical Model." *Defense Counsel Journal* 54 (October 1987): 502-510.

2339. Levy, Herbert M. *How to Handle an Appeal.* New York: Practising Law Institute, 1968.

2340. Moore, James W. *Moore's Federal Practice, 1975.* New York: M. Bender, 1975.

2341. O'Connor, Karen, and Lee Epstein. "Court Rules and the Workload: A Case Study of Rules Governing *Amicus Curiae* Participation." *Justice System Journal* 8 (Spring 1983): 35-45.

2342. Paul, Charles H. "The Rule-Making Power of the Court." *Washington Law*

Review 1 (February 1926): 163-181; (May 1926): 223-242.

2343. Pound, Roscoe. "Senator Walsh on Rule-Making Power on Law Side of Federal Practice." *American Bar Association Journal* 13 (February 1927): 84-86.

2344. "Supreme Court Adopts Rules for Civil Procedure in Federal District Courts." *American Bar Association Journal* 24 (February 1938): 97-104.

2345. Wickes, Joseph A. "New Rule-Making Power of the United States Supreme Court." *Texas Law Review* 13 (December 1934): 1-32.

2346. Wiener, Frederick B. "The New Supreme Court Practice: A Summary of the New Rules." *American Bar Association Journal* 40 (August 1954): 659-662.

2347. Wiener, Frederick B. "The Supreme Court's New Rules." *Harvard Law Review* 68 (November 1954): 20-95.

Reviewing of Cases

2348. Armstrong, Virginia C. "A New Perspective on U.S. Supreme Court *Certiorari* Behavior: Cues vs. Attitudes." Ph.D. diss., Texas Tech University, 1979.

2349. Armstrong, Virginia C., and Charles A. Johnson. "*Certiorari* Decisions by the Warren and Burger Courts: Is Cue Theory Time Bound?" *Polity* 15 (Fall 1982): 141-150.

2350. Atwood, Barbara A. "Domestic Relations Cases in Federal Court: Toward a Principled Exercise of Jurisdiction." *Hastings Law Journal* 35 (March 1984): 571-628.

2351. Austern, David. "Legal and Judicial Ethics and the Supreme Court." *Trial* 22 (July 1986): 22-23.

2352. Baker, Stewart A. "A Practical

Guide to *Certiorari*." *Catholic University Law Review* 33 (Spring 1984): 611-632.

2353. *Bankruptcy Code, Rules, and Forms: Including Federal Rules of Civil Procedure and Federal Rules of Evidence.* Rev. ed. St. Paul, MN: West Publishing Company, 1984.

2354. Banoff, Grace. "The Declaratory Judgement in the United States Supreme Court." *Intramural Law Review* 1 (September 1945): 16-24.

2355. Berlage, Derick P. "Pleas of the Condemned: Should *Certiorari* Petitions from Death Row Receive Enhanced Access to the Supreme Court?" *New York University Law Review* 59 (November 1984): 1120-1149.

2356. Boskey, Bennett. "Mechanics of the Supreme Court's *Certiorari* Jurisdiction." *Columbia Law Review* 46 (March 1946): 255-265.

2357. Boskey, Bennett, and Eugene Gressman. "The Supreme Court's New *Certiorari* Jurisdiction over Military Appeals." *Federal Rules Decisions* 102 (October 1984): 329-337.

2358. Brenner, Saul. "New *Certiorari* Game." *Journal of Politics* 41 (May 1979): 649-655.

2359. "Competency of Supreme Court to Reverse Decision on Question of Fact: *Certiorari*." *Tulane Law Review* 18 (December 1943): 324-329.

2360. Compter, R. C. "Jurisdiction of the United States Supreme Court to Review by Writ of Error the Judgment of a State Court Upholding the Validity of Municipal Ordinance." *University of Pennsylvania Law Review* 77 (February 1929): 542-543.

2361. Conner, James C. "Supreme Court *Certiorari* Policy and the Federal Employers' Liability Act." *Cornell Law Quarterly* 43 (Spring 1958): 451-468.

2362. Dodd, E. Merrick. "Power in the

Supreme Court to Review State Decisions in the Field of Conflict of Laws." *Harvard Law Review* 39 (March 1926): 533-562.

2363. Earp, Stephen W. "Sovereign Immunity in Supreme Court: Using *Certiorari* Process to Avoid Decisionmaking." *Virginia Journal of International Law* 16 (Summer 1976): 903-929.

2364. Estreicher, Samuel, and John E. Sexton. "Improving the Process: Case Selection by the Supreme Court." *Judicature* 70 (June/July 1986): 41-47.

2365. Estreicher, Samuel, and John E. Sexton. *Redefining the Supreme Court's Role: A Theory of Managing the Federal Judicial Process.* New Haven, CT: Yale University Press, 1986.

2366. Fraenkel, Osmond K. "Discretionary Review by United States Supreme Court." *Lawyers Guild Review* 11 (Winter 1951): 31-35.

2367. Gibbs, Robert W. "*Certiorari*: Its Diagnosis and Cure." *Hastings Law Journal* 6 (February 1954): 131-170.

2368. Griswold, Erwin N. "Rationing Justice: The Supreme Court's Caseload and What the Court Does Not Do." *Cornell Law Review* 60 (March 1975): 335-354.

2369. Halpern, Stephen C., and Kenneth N. Vines. "Institutional Disunity, the Judges' Bill and the Role of the U.S. Supreme Court." *Western Political Quarterly* 30 (December 1977): 471-483.

2370. Hankin, Gregory. "United States Supreme Court: Problems." *Journal of American Judicature Society* 13 (October 1929): 92-94.

2371. Harper, Fowler V., and Alan S. Rosenthal. "What the Supreme Court Did Not Do in the 1949 Term: An Appraisal of *Certiorari*." *University of Pennsylvania Law Review* 99 (December 1950): 293-325.

2372. Harper, Fowler V., and Arnold Leibowitz. "What the Supreme Court Did Not Do during the 1952 Term." *University of Pennsylvania Law Review* 102 (February 1954): 427-463.

2373. Harper, Fowler V., and Edwin D. Etherington. "What the Supreme Court Did Not Do during the 1950 Term." *University of Pennsylvania Law Review* 100 (December 1951): 354-409.

2374. Harper, Fowler V., and George C. Pratt. "What the Supreme Court Did Not Do during the 1951 Term." *University of Pennsylvania Law Review* 101 (January 1953): 439-479.

2375. Hellman, Arthur D. "The Business of the Supreme Court under the Judiciary Act of 1925: The Plenary Docket in the 1970s." *Harvard Law Review* 91 (June 1978): 1709-1803.

2376. Hellman, Arthur D. "Case Selection in the Burger Court: A Preliminary Inquiry." *Notre Dame Law Review* 60 (Fall 1985): 947-1055.

2377. Hellman, Arthur D. "Error Correction, Lawmaking, and the Supreme Court's Exercise of Discretionary Review." *University of Pittsburgh Law Review* 44 (Summer 1983): 795-877.

2378. Hellman, Arthur D. "Granted, Vacated, and Remanded: Shedding Light on a Dark Corner of Supreme Court Practice." *Judicature* 67 (March 1984): 389-401.

2379. Hellman, Arthur D. "The Supreme Court and Statutory Law: The Plenary Docket in the 1970s." *University of Pittsburgh Law Review* 40 (Fall 1978): 1-46.

2380. Hellman, Arthur D. "The Supreme Court, the National Law, and the Selection of Cases for the Plenary Docket." *University of Pittsburgh Law Review* 44 (Spring 1983): 521-634.

2381. Hellman, Arthur D. "The Supreme Court's Second Thoughts: Remands for Reconsideration and Denials of Review in Cases Held for Plenary Decisions." *Has-*

tings Constitutional Law Quarterly 11 (Fall 1983): 5-41.

2382. Kadans, Joseph M. "The Definition of a Substantial Federal Question." *Utah Bar Journal* 12 (Spring/Summer 1984): 27-32.

2383. Leahy, Edward R. "The Ten Commandments of *Certiorari*." *American Bar Association Journal* 71 (October 1985): 78-82.

2384. Leiman, Joan M. "The Rule of Four." *Columbia Law Review* 57 (November 1957): 975-992.

2385. Levine, Rosemary T. "Federal Courts—Obligatory Appeals—Supreme Court Summary Disposition Upholding Lower Court Held Controlling in Second Circuit." *Fordham Law Review* 43 (December 1974): 476-484.

2386. Lewis, David C. "Is the Supreme Court Creating Unknown and Unknowable Law? The Insubstantial Federal Question Dismissal." *Nova Law Journal* 5 (Fall 1980): 11-29.

2387. Lipshitz, Fannie. "Federal Jurisdiction, Section 266 Judicial Code, Three Judge Court, Supreme Court Review of Decision of Three Judge Court." *George Washington Law Review* 8 (December 1939): 231-232.

2388. Locher, Ralph S. "A Supreme Court Justice's Perspective on Discretionary Appeals." *Ohio Northern University Law Review* 12 (Summer 1985): 301-305.

2389. *New Amendments to the Federal Rules of Civil Procedure.* New York: Law and Business, 1983.

2390. Pacelle, Richard L., Jr. "The Supreme Court Agenda across Time: Dynamics and Determinants of Change." Ph.D. diss., Ohio State University, 1985.

2391. Palmer, Jan. "An Econometric Analysis of the U.S. Supreme Court's *Cer-*

tiorari Decisions." *Public Choice* 39 (1982): 387-398.

2392. Prettyman, E. Barrett, Jr. "Opposing *Certiorari* in the United States Supreme Court." *Virginia Law Review* 61 (February 1975): 197-209.

2393. Priest, George L. "Regulating the Content and Volume of Litigation: An Economic Analysis." *Supreme Court Economic Review* 1 (1982): 163-184.

2394. Provine, Doris M. *Case Selection in the United States Supreme Court.* Chicago: University of Chicago Press, 1980.

2395. Provine, Doris M. "Deciding What to Decide: How the Supreme Court Sets Its Agenda." *Judicature* 64 (February 1981): 320-333.

2396. Revesz, Richard L., and Pamela S. Karlan. "Nonmajority Rules and the Supreme Court." *University of Pennsylvania Law Review* 136 (April 1988): 1067-1133.

2397. Rosenfield, Harry N. "The Supreme Court in Crisis: A Proposed Solution." *Federal Bar News and Journal* 30 (June 1983): 343-344.

2398. Shenberg, Michael S. "Identification, Tolerability, and Resolution of Intercircuit Conflicts: Reexamining Professor Feeney's Study of Conflicts in Federal Law." *New York University Law Review* 59 (November 1984): 1007-1047.

2399. Smith, Steven D. "Courts, Creativity, and the Duty to Decide a Case." *University of Illinois Law Review* 1985 (Summer 1985): 573-634.

2400. Songer, Donald R. "Concern for Policy Outputs as a Cue for Supreme Court Decisions on *Certiorari*." *Journal of Politics* 41 (November 1979): 1185-1194.

2401. Spaeth, Harold J. "Supreme Court Disposition of Federal Circuit Court Decisions." *Judicature* 68 (December/January 1984-1985): 245-250.

2402. Specter, Howard A. "Supreme Court: Workload Relief Preservation of Rights." *Trial* 19 (June 1983): 6.

2403. Stewart, David O. "An Inside Peek at How the Court Picks Its Cases." *American Bar Association Journal* 7 (February 1985): 110-115.

2404. Stockmeyer, N. O. "Rx for the *Certiorari* Crisis." *American Bar Association Journal* 59 (August 1973): 846-850.

2405. Strauss, Peter L. "One Hundred Fifty Cases per Year: Some Implications of the Supreme Court's Limited Resources for Judicial Review of Agency Action." *Columbia Law Review* 87 (October 1987): 1093-1136.

2406. Teger, Stuart H., and Douglas Kosinski. "The Cue Theory of Supreme Court *Certiorari* Jurisdiction: A Reconsideration." *Journal of Politics* 42 (August 1980): 834-846.

2407. Ulman, Francis J., and Frank H. Spears. "Dismissed for Want of a Substantial Federal Question." *Boston University Law Review* 20 (June 1940): 501-532.

2408. Ulmer, S. Sidney. "Conflict with Supreme Court Precedent and the Granting of Plenary Review." *Journal of Politics* 45 (May 1983): 474-478.

2409. Ulmer, S. Sidney. "Selecting Cases for Supreme Court Review: An Underdog Model." *American Political Science Review* 72 (September 1978): 902-910.

2410. Ulmer, S. Sidney. "The Supreme Court's *Certiorari* Decisions: Conflict as a Predictive Variable." *American Political Science Review* 78 (December 1984): 901-911.

2411. Whittaker, William L. "Differentiated Case Management in Appellate Courts." *Judicature* 56 (March 1973): 324-328.

2412. Wiener, Frederick B. "Federal Regional Courts: A Solution for the *Certio-* *rari* Dilemma." *American Bar Association Journal* 49 (December 1963): 1169-1174.

2413. Willey, Harold B. "Jurisdictional Statements on Appeals to U.S. Supreme Court." *American Bar Association Journal* 31 (May 1945): 239-240.

2414. Winter, Bill. "Odds against Hearing by U.S. Supreme Court." *American Bar Association Journal* 67 (November 1981): 1435.

2415. Woodlock, Douglas P. "Exploding Caseload Sets Off Debate over How Supreme Court Handles Its Work." *National Journal* 5 (April 28, 1973): 595-610.

2416. Woolsey, Mark H. "Supreme Court Docket." *Ohio Bar* 26 (January 12, 1953): 13-20.

2417. Yendes, Doris M. "A Proposed Plan for Commissioners for the United States Supreme Court." *University of Kansas City Law Review* 25 (September 1957): 178-199.

2418. Zimmerman, Niel T. "The Decision to Decide: A Statistical Analysis of the Preliminary Decision-Making Process of the United States Supreme Court." Ph.D. diss., University of California, Riverside, 1970.

Decisionmaking of the Justices

2419. Alito, Samuel A. "The 'Released Time' Cases Revisited: A Study of Group Decision Making by the Supreme Court." *Yale Law Journal* 83 (May 1974): 1202-1236.

2420. Allen, Ronald J. "Rationality and Accuracy in the Criminal Process: A Discordant Note on the Harmonizing of the Justices' Views on Burdens of Persuasion in Criminal Cases." *Journal of Criminal Law and Criminology* 74 (Winter 1983): 1147-1170.

2421. Allen, Ronald J., and John P.

Ratnaswamy. "*Heath v. Alabama*: A Case Study of Doctrine and Rationality in the Supreme Court." *Journal of Criminal Law and Criminology* 76 (Winter 1985): 801-831.

2422. Appelbaum, Paul S. "The Supreme Court Looks at Psychiatry." *American Journal of Psychiatry* 141 (July 1984): 827-835.

2423. Arledge, Paula C. "The Supreme Court and Administrative Agencies: An Examination of Agency Success before the Burger Court." Ph.D. diss., University of New Orleans, 1983.

2424. Atkinson, David N., and Dale A. Neuman. "Toward a Cost Theory of Judicial Alignment: The Case of the Truman Bloc." *Midwest Journal of Political Science* 13 (May 1969): 271-283.

2425. Barnett, Vincent M., Jr. "Political Philosophy of the New Supreme Court." *Journal of Social Philosophy* 7 (January 1942): 101-126.

2426. Bartee, Alice F. *Cases Lost, Causes Won: The Supreme Court and the Judicial Process*. New York: St. Martin's Press, 1984.

2427. Berger, Raoul. "A Response to D.A.J. Richard's Defense of Freewheeling Constitutional Adjudication." *Industrial Law Journal* 59 (Summer 1984): 203-223.

2428. Bernard, Jessie L. "Dimensions and Axes of Supreme Court Decisions: A Study in the Sociology of Conflict." *Social Forces* 34 (October 1955): 19-27.

2429. Berns, Walter. "Voting Rights and Wrongs." *Commentary* 73 (March 1982): 31-36.

2430. Bernstein, Neil N. "The Supreme Court and Secondary Source Material: 1965 Term." *Georgetown Law Journal* 57 (October 1968): 55-80.

2431. Bersoff, Donald N. "Social Science Data and the Supreme Court: *Lockhart* as a Case in Point." *American Psychologist* 42 (January 1987): 52-68.

2432. Bickel, Alexander M. "The New Supreme Court: Prospects and Problems." *Tulane Law Review* 45 (February 1971): 229-244.

2433. Birkby, Robert H. "Supreme Court Libertarians and the First Amendment: An Analysis of Voting and Opinion Agreement, 1956-1964." *Social Science Quarterly* 48 (March 1968): 586-599.

2434. Bolner, James, Arnold Feldman, and John Gates. "A New Method of Bloc Analysis of Judicial Voting." *Political Methodology* 7 (1981): 109-130.

2435. Bradley, Craig M. "The Uncertainty Principle in the Supreme Court." *Duke Law Journal* 1986 (February 1986): 1-64.

2436. Brams, Steven J., and Douglas Muzzio. "Unanimity in the Supreme Court: A Game-Theoretic Explanation of the Decision in the White House Tapes Case." *Public Choice* 32 (Winter 1977): 67-83.

2437. Brenner, Saul. "Fluidity on the Supreme Court: 1956-1967." *American Journal of Political Science* 26 (May 1982): 388-390.

2438. Brenner, Saul. "Fluidity on the United States Supreme Court: A Reexamination." *American Journal of Political Science* 24 (August 1980): 526-535.

2439. Brest, Paul. *Process of Constitutional Decisionmaking: Cases and Materials*. Boston: Little, Brown, 1975.

2440. Caldeira, Gregory A. "The United States Supreme Court and Criminal Cases, 1935-1976: Alternative Models of Agenda Building." *British Journal of Political Science* 11 (October 1981): 449-470.

2441. Carra, Jorge L., and Andrew R. Brann. "Use of Legislative Histories by the United States Supreme Court: A Statistical Analysis." *Journal of Legislation* 9 (Summer 1982): 282-303.

2442. Carrott, M. Browning. "Expansion of the Fourteenth Amendment to Include Personal Liberties, 1920-1941." Ph.D. diss., Northwestern University, 1957.

2443. Carter, Lief H. " 'Die Meistersinger von Nurnberg' and the United States Supreme Court: Aesthetic Theory in Constitutional Jurisprudence." *Polity* 18 (Winter 1985): 272-294.

2444. Carter, Lief H. *Reason in Law.* 2d ed. Boston: Little, Brown, 1984.

2445. Coles, Walter D. "Politics and the Supreme Court of the United States." *American Law Review* 27 (March/April 1893): 182-208.

2446. Cook, Beverly B. "Public Opinion and Federal Judicial Policy." *American Journal of Political Science* 21 (August 1977): 567-600.

2447. Daly, John J. *The Use of History in the Decisions of the Supreme Court: 1900-1930.* Washington, DC: Catholic University of America Press, 1954.

2448. Danelski, David J. "Conflict and Its Resolution in the Supreme Court." *Journal of Conflict Resolution* 11 (March 1967): 71-86.

2449. Daniels, Wes. "Far beyond the Law Reports: Secondary Source Citations in United States Supreme Court Opinions, October Terms 1900, 1940, and 1978." *Law Library Journal* 76 (Winter 1983): 1-47.

2450. Davidson, Norman, III. "Supreme Court Decision Making: The Ability to Decide and the Duty to Explain." *Loyola University of Los Angeles Law Review* 12 (March 1979): 335-355.

2451. Davis, Abraham L. *The United States Supreme Court and the Uses of So-cial Science Data.* New York: MSS Information Corporation, 1973.

2452. Davis, Abraham L. "The Utilization of Sociological Data in Judicial Decision-Making at the Supreme Court Level." Ph.D. diss., Ohio University, 1969.

2453. Davis, Kenneth C. "Facts in Lawmaking." *Columbia Law Review* 80 (June 1980): 931-942.

2454. Deutsch, Jan G. "Precedent and Adjudication." *Yale Law Journal* 83 (July 1974): 1553-1584.

2455. Easterbrook, Frank H. "Agreement among the Justices: An Empirical Note." *Supreme Court Review* 1984 (1984): 389-409.

2456. Easterbrook, Frank H. "Method, Result, and Authority: A Reply." *Harvard Law Review* 98 (January 1985): 622-629.

2457. Easterbrook, Frank H. "Ways of Criticizing the Court." *Harvard Law Review* 95 (February 1982): 802-833.

2458. Ellis, T. S. "In Defense of *In Pari Delicto*." *American Bar Association Journal* 56 (April 1970): 346-349.

2459. Ely, John H. "Supreme Court, 1977 Term, Foreword: Discovering Fundamental Values." *Harvard Law Review* 92 (November 1978): 5-55.

2460. Ewing, Cortez A. "Geography and the Supreme Court." *Southwestern Political and Social Science Quarterly* 11 (June 1930): 26-46.

2461. Festa, Linda, and Leo D. Vichules. "Cliques on the Supreme Court: Myth or Reality." *Sociological Quarterly* 9 (Autumn 1968): 540-554.

2462. Frank, Arthur Q., and Lloyd Shapley. *The Distribution of Power in the U.S. Supreme Court.* Santa Monica, CA: Rand, 1981.

2463. Gibson, James L. "The Role Concept in Judicial Research." *Law and Policy Quarterly* 3 (July 1981): 291-312.

2464. Giles, Michael W. "Equivalent versus Minimum Winning Opinion Coalition Size: A Test of Two Hypotheses." *American Journal of Political Science* 21 (May 1977): 405-408.

2465. Goldberg, Louis P., and Eleanore Levenson. *Lawless Judges.* New York: Da Capo Press, 1970.

2466. Golding, M. P. "Principled Decision-Making and the Supreme Court." *Columbia Law Review* 63 (January 1963): 35-58.

2467. Goldman, Sheldon. *Constitutional Law and Supreme Court Decision-Making: Cases and Essays.* New York: Harper and Row, 1982.

2468. Gonzalez, Raymond B. "The Warren Court's Adjudication on Denationalization: A Case Study of Judicial Consensus and Cleavage." Ph.D. diss., University of Massachusetts, 1975.

2469. Gow, David J. "Scale Fitting in the Psychometric Model of Judicial Decision Making." *American Political Science Review* 73 (June 1979): 430-441.

2470. Grofman, Bernard. "Jury Decision Making Models and the Supreme Court: The Jury Cases from *Williams v. Florida* to *Ballew v. Georgia*." *Journal of Social and Political Studies* 8 (Spring 1980): 749-772.

2471. Grossman, Joel B. "Social Backgrounds and Judicial Decisions: Notes for a Theory." *Journal of Politics* 29 (May 1967): 334-351.

2472. Grunbaum, Werner F. "Quantitative Analysis of the Presidential Ballot Case." *Journal of Politics* 34 (February 1972): 223-243.

2473. Haas, Kenneth C. "The Comparative Study of State and Federal Judicial Behavior Revisited." *Journal of Politics* 44 (August 1982): 721-746.

2474. Haines, Dennis. "Rolling Back the Top on Chief Justice Burger's Opinion Assignment Desk." *University of Pittsburgh Law Review* 38 (Summer 1977): 631-695.

2475. Handberg, Roger B., Jr. "Decision-Making in a Natural Court, 1916-1921." *American Politics Quarterly* 4 (July 1976): 357-378.

2476. Hassett, Joseph M. "Should Supreme Court Justices Deliberate More before They Begin to Write?" *Judicature* 63 (April 1980): 414-415, 458.

2477. Henschen, Beth M. "Judicial Use of Legislative History and Intent in Statutory Interpretation." *Legislative Studies Quarterly* 10 (August 1985): 353-371.

2478. Herasimchuk, Cathleen C. "The Burger Court Limits of *Habeas Corpus* Review: Which Path to Follow—Procedural Hurdles or Fundamental Fairness?" *Houston Law Review* 20 (October 1983): 1417-1446.

2479. Hogan, Harry J. "The Supreme Court and the Crisis in Liberalism." *Journal of Politics* 33 (May 1971): 257-292.

2480. "How the Judges of the Supreme Court of the United States Consult." *American Law Review* 30 (November/December 1896): 903-905.

2481. Howard, J. Woodford, Jr. "On the Fluidity of Judicial Choice." *American Political Science Review* 62 (March 1968): 43-56.

2482. Hoyer, R. W., Lawrence S. Mayer, and Joseph L. Bernd. "Some Problems in Validation of Mathematic and Stochastic Models of Political Phenomena: The Case of the Supreme Court." *American Journal of Political Science* 21 (May 1977): 381-403.

2483. Hundley, Norris, Jr. "Clio Nods: *Arizona v. California* and the Boulder Canyon Act: A Reassessment." *Western Historical Quarterly* 3 (January 1972): 17-52.

2484. Huston, Luther A. "United States Supreme Court: How It Reaches a Decision." *New Zealand Law Journal* 30 (July 20, 1954): 229-230.

2485. James, Dorothy. "Role Theory and the Supreme Court." *Journal of Politics* 30 (February 1968): 160-186.

2486. Jameson, William J. "Current Problems Affecting the Judicial Branch of the Government." *Western Political Quarterly* 11 (September 1958): 713-723.

2487. Johnson, Charles A. "Citations to Authority in Supreme Court Opinions." *Law and Policy* 7 (October 1985): 509-523.

2488. Johnson, Charles A. "Content-Analytic Techniques and Judicial Research." *American Politics Quarterly* 15 (January 1987): 147-168.

2489. Johnson, Charles A. "Follow-up Citations in the U.S. Supreme Court." *Western Political Quarterly* 39 (September 1986): 538-547.

2490. Johnston, Richard E. "Some Comparative Statistics on Chief Justice Opinion Writing." *Western Political Quarterly* 26 (September 1973): 453-460.

2491. LaFave, Wayne R. " 'Case by Case Adjudication' versus 'Standardized Procedures': The *Robinson* Dilemma." In *Supreme Court Review, 1974*, 127-163. Chicago: University of Chicago Press, 1974.

2492. Leathers, John R. "Supreme Court Voting Patterns Related to Jurisdictional Issues." *Washington Law Review* 62 (October 1987): 631-680.

2493. Leavitt, Donald C. "Attitude Change on the Supreme Court, 1910-1920." *Michigan Academician* 4 (Summer 1971): 53-66.

2494. Leavitt, Donald C. "Attitudes and Ideology on the White Supreme Court, 1910-1920." Ph.D. diss., Michigan State University, 1970.

2495. Leeper, Roy V. "Political Theory, Legal Theory, and Supreme Court Decisions." Ph.D. diss., University of Missouri, 1983.

2496. LeVar, C. Jeddy. "The Nixon Court: A Study of Leadership." *Western Political Quarterly* 30 (December 1977): 484-492.

2497. McGinley, G.P.J. "The Search for Unity: The Impact of Consensus Seeking Procedures in Appellate Courts." *Adelaide Law Review* 11 (December 1987): 203-214.

2498. Makau, Josina M. "The Supreme Court and Reasonableness." *Quarterly Journal of Speech* 70 (November 1984): 379-396.

2499. Marsh, James M. " 'Supreme Coort': Mr. Dooley Should Take Another Look." *Oklahoma Bar Association Journal* 24 (July 1953): 1329-1332.

2500. Marshall, William P. "Unprecedential Analysis and Original Intent." *William and Mary Law Review* 27 (Special Issue 1985/1986): 925-931.

2501. Meier, Kenneth J. "Ode to Patronage: A Critical Analysis of Two Recent Supreme Court Decisions." *Public Administration Review* 41 (September/October 1981): 558-563.

2502. Mendelson, Wallace. "Untroubled World of Jurimetrics." *Journal of Politics* 22 (November 1964): 27-28.

2503. Menez, Joseph F. *Decision Making in the Supreme Court of the United States: A Political and Behavioral View*. Lanham, MD: University Press of America, 1984.

2504. Murphy, Walter F. *Elements of Judicial Strategy*. Chicago: University of Chicago Press, 1964.

2505. Nathanson, Nathaniel L. "The Court, the Constitution, and the Changing of the Guard." *Social Science* 48 (Spring 1973): 97-106.

2506. Novak, L. "The Precedential Value of Supreme Court Plurality Decisions." *Columbia Law Review* 80 (May 1980): 756-781.

2507. Pacelle, Richard L., Jr. "Simulating Supreme Court Decisionmaking." *Political Science Teacher* 2 (Spring 1989): 8-10.

2508. Pound, Roscoe. "Runaway Courts in the Runaway World." *University of California at Los Angeles Law Review* 10 (1963): 729-738.

2509. Pritchett, C. Herman. "Politics and Value Systems: The Supreme Court, 1945-1946." *Journal of Politics* 8 (November 1946): 499-519.

2510. Pritchett, C. Herman. *The Roosevelt Court: A Study in Judicial Politics and Values, 1937-1947.* New York: Macmillan, 1948.

2511. Pritchett, C. Herman. "The Roosevelt Court: Votes and Values, 1937-1947." *American Political Science Review* 42 (February 1948): 53-67.

2512. Pritchett, C. Herman. "Ten Years of Supreme Court Voting: A Comment in Retrospect." *Social Science Quarterly* 50 (June 1970): 983-984.

2513. Pritchett, C. Herman. "Ten Years of Supreme Court Voting, 1931-1941." *Southwestern Social Science Quarterly* 24 (June 1943): 12-22.

2514. Pritchett, C. Herman. "Voting Behavior of the Supreme Court, 1941-1942." *Journal of Politics* 4 (November 1942): 491-506; 5 (February 1943): 65-66.

2515. Rathjen, Gregory J., and Harold J. Spaeth. "Denial of Access and Ideological Preferences: An Analysis of the Voting Behavior of the Burger Court Justices, 1969-1976." *Western Political Quarterly* 36 (March 1983): 71-87.

2516. Renstrom, Peter G. "The Dimensionality of Decision Making of the 1941-1945 Stone Court: A Computer Dependent Analysis of Supreme Court Behavior." Ph.D. diss., Michigan State University, 1972.

2517. Riggs, Robert E. "Supreme Court Voting Behavior: 1986 Term." *Brigham Young University Journal of Public Law* 2 (1988): 15-34.

2518. Robbins, Jan C. "Social Science Information and First Amendment Freedoms: An Aid to Supreme Court Decision Making." Ph.D. diss., University of Minnesota, 1970.

2519. Roche, John P. "The Expatriation Cases: 'Breathes There the Man, with Soul So Dead . . . ?'" *Supreme Court Review* 1963 (1963): 325-356.

2520. Roche, John P. "Expatriation Decisions: A Study in Constitutional Improvisation and the Uses of History." *American Political Science Review* 58 (March 1964): 72-80.

2521. Roche, John P. "Political Science and Science Fiction." *American Political Science Review* 52 (December 1958): 1026-1029.

2522. Rohde, David W. "Policy Goals and Opinion Coalitions in the Supreme Court." *Midwest Journal of Political Science* 16 (May 1972): 208-224.

2523. Rohde, David W. "Policy Goals, Strategic Choice, and Majority Opinion Assignments in the U.S. Supreme Court." *American Journal of Political Science* 16 (November 1972): 652-682.

2524. Rohde, David W. "Some Clarifications Regarding a Theory of Supreme Court Coalition Formation." *American Journal of Political Science* 21 (May 1977): 409-413.

2525. Rohde, David W. "Strategy and Ideology: The Assignment of Majority Opinions in the United States Supreme Court." Ph.D. diss., University of Rochester, 1971.

2526. Rohde, David W., and Harold J.

Spaeth. *Supreme Court Decision Making.* San Francisco: W. H. Freeman, 1976.

2527. Rosen, Dan. "Democracy and Demographics: The Inevitability of a Class-Bound Interpretation." *University of Dayton Law Review* 10 (Fall 1984): 37-96.

2528. Sager, Alan M. "A Simulation of Judicial Behavior in the United States Supreme Court." Ph.D. diss., Northwestern University, 1971.

2529. Scali, Louis J. "Prediction Making in the Supreme Court: The Granting of Stays by Individual Justices." *UCLA Law Review* 32 (June 1985): 1020-1059.

2530. Schmidhauser, John R., and David Gold. "Scaling Supreme Court Decisions in Relation to Social Background." *PROD* 1 (May 1958): 6-7.

2531. Schubert, Glendon A. "Judicial Attitudes and Voting Behavior: The 1961 Term of the U.S. Supreme Court." *Law and Contemporary Problems* 28 (Winter 1963): 100-143.

2532. Schubert, Glendon A. *Judicial Behavior: A Reader in Theory and Research.* Chicago: Rand McNally, 1964.

2533. Schubert, Glendon A., ed. *Judicial Decision-Making.* New York: Free Press, 1963.

2534. Schubert, Glendon A. "A Psychometric Model of the Supreme Court." *American Behavioral Scientist* 5 (November 1961): 14-18.

2535. Schubert, Glendon A. *Quantitative Analysis of Judicial Behavior.* Glencoe, IL: Free Press, 1959.

2536. Schubert, Glendon A. "Simulating the Supreme Court: An Extension of the Tenth Man Game." *Case Western Reserve Law Review* 23 (Spring 1972): 451-500.

2537. Schubert, Glendon A. "The Study of Judicial Decision-Making as an Aspect of Political Behavior." *American Political Science Review* 52 (December 1958): 1007-1025.

2538. Schultz, William B., and Phillip K. Howard. "Myth of Swing Voting: An Analysis of Voting Patterns on the Supreme Court." *New York University Law Review* 50 (October 1975): 798-868.

2539. Scruggs, Charles E. "Influences of Rights of Property upon Educational Cases Decided by the Supreme Court between 1789 and 1962." Ph.D. diss., Case Western Reserve University, 1964.

2540. Segal, Jeffrey A. "Measuring Change on the Supreme Court: Examining Alternative Models." *American Journal of Political Science* 29 (August 1985): 461-479.

2541. Shaman, Jeffrey M. "Constitutional Fact: The Perception of Reality by the Supreme Court." *University of Florida Law Review* 35 (Spring 1983): 236-253.

2542. Shaman, Jeffrey M. "Interpreting the Constitution: the Supreme Court's Proper and Historical Function." *Judicature* 71 (August/September 1987): 80-82.

2543. Shapiro, Martin M. *Law and Politics in the Supreme Court: New Approaches to Political Jurisprudence.* New York: Free Press, 1964.

2544. Slotnick, Elliot E. "Chief Justices and Self-Assignment of Majority Opinions: A Research Note." *Western Political Quarterly* 31 (June 1978): 219-225.

2545. Slotnick, Elliot E. "The Equality Principle and Majority Opinion Assignment on the United States Supreme Court." *Polity* 12 (Winter 1979): 318-332.

2546. Slotnick, Elliot E. "Judicial Career Patterns and Majority Opinion Assignment on the Supreme Court." *Journal of Politics* 41 (May 1979): 640-648.

2547. Slotnick, Elliot E. "On Conventional Wisdom, Context, and Judicial Career Patterns: A Response to Professor

Rathjen." *Journal of Politics* 42 (November 1980): 1173-1175.

2548. Slotnick, Elliot E. "Who Speaks for the Court? Majority Opinion Assignment from Taft to Burger." *American Journal of Political Science* 23 (February 1969): 60-77.

2549. Smith, Dale P. "Interstate Extradition: A Case Study in Constitutional Interpretation." Ph.D. diss., University of Georgia, 1984.

2550. Snyder, Eloise C. "Political Power and the Ability to Win Supreme Court Decisions." *Social Forces* 39 (October 1960): 36-40.

2551. Snyder, Eloise C. "A Quantitative Analysis of Supreme Court Opinions from 1921 to 1953: A Study of the Responses of an Institution Engaged in Resolving Social Conflict." Ph.D. diss., Pennsylvania State University, 1956.

2552. Snyder, Eloise C. "The Supreme Court as a Small Group." *Social Forces* 36 (March 1958): 232-238.

2553. Snyder, Eloise C. "Uncertainty and the Supreme Court's Decisions." *American Journal of Sociology* 65 (November 1959): 241-245.

2554. Spaeth, Harold J. "Distributive Justice: Majority Opinion Assignments in the Burger Court." *Judicature* 67 (December/January 1984): 299-304.

2555. Spaeth, Harold J. *An Introduction to Supreme Court Decision Making.* San Francisco: Chandler, 1965.

2556. Spaeth, Harold J. "Judicial Power as a Variable Motivating Supreme Court Behavior." *Midwest Journal of Political Science* 6 (February 1962): 54-82.

2557. Spaeth, Harold J. "Warren Court Attitudes toward Business: The 'B' Scale." In *Judicial Decision-Making*, edited by Glendon A. Schubert, 79-108. New York: Free Press, 1963.

2558. Spaeth, Harold J., and David J. Peterson. "The Analysis and Interpretation of Dimensionality: The Case of Civil Liberties Decision Making." *Midwest Journal of Political Science* 15 (August 1971): 415-441.

2559. Spaeth, Harold J., and Michael F. Altfeld. "Influence Relationships within the Supreme Court: A Comparison of the Warren and Burger Courts." *Western Political Quarterly* 38 (March 1985): 70-83.

2560. Spaeth, Harold J., and Michael F. Altfeld. "Measuring Power on the Supreme Court: An Alternative to the Power Index." *Jurimetrics Journal* 26 (Fall 1985): 48-75.

2561. Spritzer, Ralph S. "Multiple-Issue Cases and Multi-member Courts: Observations on Decision Making by Discordant Minorities." *Jurimetrics Journal* 28 (Winter 1988): 139-146.

2562. Stumpf, Samuel E. "The Moral Element in Supreme Court Decisions." *Vanderbilt Law Review* 6 (December 1952): 41-65.

2563. Tanke, Elizabeth D., and Tony J. Tanke. "Getting Off a Slippery Slope: Social Science in the Judicial Process." *American Psychologist* 34 (December 1979): 1130-1138.

2564. Tate, C. Neal. "Personal Attribute Models of the Voting Behavior of U.S. Supreme Court Justices: Liberalism in Civil Liberties and Economic Decisions, 1946-1978." *American Political Science Review* 75 (June 1981): 355-367.

2565. Tetlock, Philip E., Jane Bernzweig, and Jack L. Gallant. "Supreme Court Decision Making: Cognitive Style as a Predictor of Ideological Consistency of Voting." *Journal of Personality and Social Psychology* 48 (May 1985): 1227-1239.

2566. Thurstone, L. L., and J. W. Degan. "Factorial Study of the Supreme Court." *National Academy of Science Proceedings* 37 (September 1951): 628-635.

2567. Ulmer, S. Sidney. "The Analysis of Behavior Patterns on the United States Supreme Court." *Journal of Politics* 22 (November 1960): 629-653.

2568. Ulmer, S. Sidney. "Are Social Background Models Time-Bound?" *American Political Science Review* 80 (September 1986): 957-967.

2569. Ulmer, S. Sidney. "The Dimensionality of Judicial Voting Behavior." *Midwest Journal of Political Science* 13 (August 1969): 471-483.

2570. Ulmer, S. Sidney. "Dissent Behavior and the Social Background of Supreme Court Justices." *Journal of Politics* 32 (August 1970): 580-598.

2571. Ulmer, S. Sidney. "Homeostatic Tendencies in the United States Supreme Court." In *Introductory Reading in Political Behavior*, edited by S. Sidney Ulmer, 167-188. Chicago: Rand McNally, 1961.

2572. Ulmer, S. Sidney. "Polar Classification of Supreme Court Justices." *South Carolina Law Quarterly* 12 (Spring 1960): 407-417.

2573. Ulmer, S. Sidney. "Quantitative Analysis of Judicial Processes: Some Practical and Theoretical Applications." *Law and Contemporary Problems* 28 (Winter 1963): 164-184.

2574. Ulmer, S. Sidney. "Social Background as an Indicator to the Votes of Supreme Court Justices in Criminal Cases." *American Journal of Political Science* 17 (August 1973): 622-630.

2575. Ulmer, S. Sidney. "Supreme Court Behavior in Racial Exclusion Cases: 1935-1960." *American Political Science Review* 56 (June 1962): 325-330.

2576. Ulmer, S. Sidney. "Toward a Theory of Sub-group Formation in the United States Supreme Court." *Journal of Politics* 27 (Fall 1965): 133-152.

2577. Ulmer, S. Sidney, and John A. Stookey. "Nixon's Legacy to the Supreme Court: A Statistical Analysis of Judicial Behavior." *Florida State University Law Review* 3 (Summer 1975): 331-347.

2578. Walker, Thomas G., Lee Epstein, and William S. Dixon. "On the Mysterious Demise of Consensual Norms in the United States Supreme Court." *Journal of Politics* 50 (May 1988): 361-389.

2579. Walzer, Michael. "Courts, the Elections, and the People." *Dissent* 28 (Spring 1981): 153-155.

2580. Weaver, Michael R. "Cumulative Scaling as a Method for Analyzing Judicial Behavior: A Critique and an Example." *North Carolina Central Law Journal* 1969 (Spring 1969): 15-26.

2581. Westin, Alan F. *The Supreme Court: Views from the Inside.* New York: W. W. Norton, 1961.

2582. Whitaker, Steve. "Role-Playing Simulation of United States Supreme Court." *Teaching Political Science* 1 (1973): 47-58.

2583. Williams, P. M. "The Supreme Court and Politics." *Oxford Journal of Legal Studies* 5 (Spring 1985): 91-112.

2584. Wilson, James G. "The Most Sacred Text: The Supreme Court's Use of *The Federalist Papers.*" *Brigham Young University Law Review* 1985 (Winter 1985): 65-135.

2585. Woodford, Howard J. "Judicial Biography and the Behavioral Persuasion." *American Political Science Review* 65 (September 1971): 704-715.

2586. Zobell, Karl M. "Division of Opinion in the Supreme Court: A History of Judicial Disintegration." *Cornell Law Quarterly* 44 (Winter 1959): 186-214.

Opinions of the Court

2587. Aikin, Charles. "The Role of Dissenting Opinions in American Courts." *Politico* 33 (June 1968): 262-269.

2588. Alderman, Sidney S. "Chips from the Supreme Court's Workshop." *Tennessee Law Review* 23 (December 1954): 502-518.

2589. Aumann, Francis R. "The Supreme Court and the Advisory Opinion." *Ohio State Law Journal* 4 (December 1937): 21-55.

2590. Bezanson, Randall P. "Abstention: The Supreme Court and Allocation of Judicial Power." *Vanderbilt Law Review* 27 (November 1974): 1107-1151.

2591. Blandford, Linda A., and Patricia R. Evans, eds. *Supreme Court of the United States, 1789-1980: An Index to Opinions Arranged by Justice.* Millwood, NY: Kraus International Publications, 1983.

2592. Blaustein, Albert P., and Andrew H. Field. " 'Overruling' Opinions in the Supreme Court." *Michigan Law Review* 57 (December 1958): 151-194.

2593. Blum, Walter J. "Dissenting Opinions by Supreme Court Justices in Federal Income Tax Controversies." *Michigan Law Review* 82 (December 1983): 431-460.

2594. Boner, Marian. "Index to Chambers Opinions of Supreme Court Justices." *Law Library Journal* 65 (1972): 213-220.

2595. Bosmajian, Haig. "The Metaphoric Marketplace of Ideas and the Pig in the Parlor (Legal Metaphors and Figures of Speech in Supreme Court Opinions)." *Midwest Quarterly* 26 (Autumn 1984): 44-62.

2596. Brenner, Saul. "Is Competence Related to Majority Opinion Assignment on the Supreme Court?" *Capital University Law Review* 15 (Fall 1985): 35-41.

2597. Brenner, Saul. "Issue Specialization as a Variable in Opinion Assignment in the U.S. Supreme Court." *Journal of Politics* 46 (November 1984): 1217-1225.

2598. Brenner, Saul. "Minimum Winning Coalitions on the U.S. Supreme Court: A Comparison of the Original Vote on the Merits with the Opinion Vote." *American Politics Quarterly* 7 (July 1979): 384-392.

2599. Brenner, Saul. "Reassigning the Majority Opinion on the United States Supreme Court." *Justice System Journal* 11 (Fall 1986): 186-195.

2600. Brenner, Saul. "Strategic Choice and Opinion Assignment on the U.S. Supreme Court: A Reexamination." *Western Political Quarterly* 35 (June 1982): 204-211.

2601. Brenner, Saul, and Harold J. Spaeth. "Ideological Position as a Variable in the Authoring of Dissenting Opinions on the Warren and Burger Courts." *American Politics Quarterly* 16 (July 1988): 317-328.

2602. Brenner, Saul, and Harold J. Spaeth. "Issue Specialization in Majority Opinion Assignment on the Burger Court." *Western Political Quarterly* 39 (September 1986): 520-527.

2603. Brenner, Saul, and Harold J. Spaeth. "Majority Opinion Assignments and the Maintenance of the Original Coalition on the Warren Court." *American Journal of Political Science* 32 (February 1988): 72-81.

2604. Brenner, Saul, and Theodore S. Arrington. "Some Effects of Ideology and Threat upon the Size of Opinion Coalitions on the United States Supreme Court." *Journal of Political Science* 8 (Fall 1980): 49-58.

2605. "Burdens of a U.S. Chief Justice: Dissents and Disruptive Forces." *U.S. News and World Reports* 20 (May 3, 1946): 22.

2606. Casper, Gerhard. *Landmark Briefs and Arguments of the Supreme Court of the U.S.: Constitutional Law.* Vols. 134-142. Frederick, MD: University Publications of America, 1984.

2607. Chidsey, Charles E. "Some Epochal Decisions of United States Supreme Court and Dissenting Opinions Marking Critical Eras in Nation's History." *Lawyer and Banker* 19 (July/August 1926): 278-291.

2608. Colby, Paul L. "Two Views on the Legitimacy of Nonacquiescence in Judicial Opinions." *Tulane Law Review* 61 (April 1987): 1041-1069.

2609. Davis, John F., and William L. Reynolds. "Juridical Cripples: Plurality Opinions in Supreme Court." *Duke Law Journal* 1974 (March 1974): 59-85.

2610. *Digest of the United States Supreme Court Reports, Annotated with Case Annotations, Dissenting and Separate Opinions since 1900, Collateral References.* Rochester, NY: Lawyers Co-Operative Publishing Company, 1948.

2611. Fraenkel, Osmond K. "Opinions of United States Supreme Court for the 1934 Term, General Issues." *Fordham Law Review* 4 (November 1935): 416-455.

2612. Jackson, Percival E. *Dissent in the Supreme Court: A Chronology.* Norman: University of Oklahoma Press, 1969.

2613. Johnson, Marion M., Elaine C. Everly, and Toussaint L. Prince. *Index to the Manuscript and Revised Printed Opinions of the Supreme Court of the United States in the National Archives, 1808-73.* Washington, DC: National Archives Publication, 1965.

2614. Kelman, Maurice. "The Forked Path of Dissent." *Supreme Court Review* 1985 (1985): 227-298.

2615. Lashly, Jacob M., and Paul B. Rava. "The Supreme Court Dissents." *Washington University Law Quarterly* 28 (Summer 1943): 191-220.

2616. McLauchlan, William P. "Research Note: Ideology and Conflict in Supreme Court Opinion Assignment, 1946-1962." *Western Political Quarterly* 25 (March 1972): 16-27.

2617. Monaghan, Henry P. "Taking Supreme Court Opinions Seriously." *Maryland Law Review* 39 (1979): 1-26.

2618. Musmanno, Michael A. "Dissenting Opinions." *University of Kansas Law Review* 6 (May 1958): 407-420.

2619. Palmer, Ben W. "Dissension in the Court: *Stare Decisis* or 'Flexible Logic'?" *American Bar Association Journal* 34 (October 1948): 887-890.

2620. Palmer, Ben W. "Dissensions in the Court: 'Undefined and Shifting Lines' Cause Uncertainty." *American Bar Association Journal* 34 (November 1948): 1000-1004.

2621. Palmer, Ben W. "Dissents and Overrulings: A Study of Developments in the Supreme Court." *American Bar Association Journal* 34 (July 1948): 554-558.

2622. Palmer, Ben W. "Supreme Court of the United States: Analysis of Alleged and Real Causes of Dissents." *American Bar Association Journal* 34 (September 1948): 761-765.

2623. Peterson, Steven A. "Dissent in American Courts." *Journal of Politics* 43 (May 1981): 412-434.

2624. Rathjen, Gregory J. "An Analysis of Separate Opinion Writing Behavior as Dissonance Reduction." *American Politics Quarterly* 2 (October 1974): 393-411.

2625. Rathjen, Gregory J. "Conventional Wisdom Don't Die Easily: Judicial Career Patterns and the Context of Majority Opinion Assignment." *Journal of Politics* 42 (November 1980): 1170-1172.

2626. Rathjen, Gregory J. "Policy Goals, Strategic Choice, and Majority Opinion Assignments in the U.S. Supreme Court: A

Replication." *American Journal of Political Science* 18 (November 1974): 713-724.

2627. Rathjen, Gregory J. "Time and Dissension on the United States Supreme Court." *Ohio Northern University Law Review* 7 (April 1980): 227-258.

2628. Reynolds, William L. "The Supreme Court Rules for the Reporting of Opinions: A Critique." *Ohio State Law Journal* 46 (Spring 1985): 313-352.

2629. Reynolds, William L., and Gordon G. Young. "Equal Divisions in the Supreme Court: History, Problems, and Proposals." *North Carolina Law Review* 62 (October 1983): 29-56.

2630. Riordan, Dennis P. "Silence in the Court." *California Lawyer* 5 (January 1985): 14-16, 73.

2631. Stringham, Raymond B. *Pollution of the Law: A Decade of Dissension in the Supreme Court of the United States.* Salem, OR: n.p., 1970.

2632. Teitelbaum, Gene. "The Supreme Court's Edifice Complex." *Law Office Economics and Management* 26 (Fall 1985): 368-370.

Decisions of the Court

2633. Bernhardt, Charlotte C. "Supreme Court Reversals on Constitutional Issues." *Cornell Law Quarterly* 34 (September 1948): 55-70.

2634. Bernstein, Sidney. "*Ex Parte* Communication." *Trial* 20 (April 1984): 42-45.

2635. Black, Charles L. *Decisions According to Law.* New York: W. W. Norton, 1981.

2636. Bland, Randall W. *Constitutional Law in the United States: A Systematic Inquiry into the Change and Relevance of Supreme Court Decisions.* Minneapolis: Burgess, 1976.

2637. Brigham, John. *Constitutional Language: An Interpretation of Judicial Decision.* Westport, CT: Greenwood Press, 1978.

2638. Cahill, Edward. "Historical Lights from Judicial Decisions." *Michigan Pioneer and Historical Society: Historical Collection* 38 (1912): 118-130.

2639. Carrington, Paul D. "The Supreme Court: The Problem of Minority Decisions." *American Bar Association Journal* 44 (February 1958): 137-140.

2640. Chaplin, Herman W. *Principles of the Federal Law as Presented in Decisions of the Supreme Court, Citing Something over 3,500 Cases: 2 Dallas—241 U.S.* Washington, DC: J. Byrne, 1917.

2641. Coxe, Richard S. *A Digest of the Decisions in the Supreme Court, Circuit Courts, and District Courts of the United States.* Philadelphia: P. H. Nicklin, 1829.

2642. Cushman, Robert E. "Constitutional Decisions by a Bare Majority of the Court." *Michigan Law Review* 19 (June 1921): 771-803.

2643. Cushman, Robert F., and Robert E. Cushman. *Leading Constitutional Decisions.* 17th ed. New York: Appleton-Century-Crofts, 1987.

2644. Davis, J. C. Bancroft. *Appendix to the Reports of the United States, from September 24, 1789, to the End of October Term, 1888.* New York: Banks and Brothers, 1889.

2645. Ernst, Morris L. *The Great Reversals: Tales of the Supreme Court.* New York: Weybright and Talley, 1973.

2646. Fisher, Franklin M. "The Mathematical Analysis of Supreme Court Decisions: The Use and Abuse of Quantitative Methods." *American Political Science Review* 52 (June 1958): 321-338.

2647. *Great Supreme Court Decisions as Reported in* The New York Times. New

York: Microfilming Corporation of America, 1981.

2648. Griffin, G. Edward. *A Memorandum on Supreme Court Decisions.* Belmont, MA: n.p., 1968.

2649. Guenther, Nancy A. *United States Supreme Court Decisions: An Index to Their Locations.* Metuchen, NJ: Scarecrow Press, 1983.

2650. Handler, Milton. "The Supreme Court's Footnote Addiction." *New York State Bar Journal* 58 (December 1986): 18-20.

2651. Joseph, Joel D. *Black Mondays: Worst Decisions of the U.S. Supreme Court.* Bethesda, MD: National Printers, 1987.

2652. Kennedy, Walter B. " 'Five to Four' Decisions of the Supreme Court." *Catholic Charities Review* 7 (November 1923): 328-331.

2653. Kurland, Philip B., and Gerhard Casper. *Landmark Briefs and Arguments of the Supreme Court of the United States' Constitutional Law.* 80 vols. Arlington, VA: University Publications of America, 1975.

2654. Machen, Arthur W. "Dissent and *Stare Decisis* in the Supreme Court." *Maryland State Bar Association* 1940 (1940): 79-98.

2655. Mason, Alpheus T. "Myth and Reality in Supreme Court Decisions." *Virginia Law Review* 48 (December 1962): 1385-1406.

2656. "Modification of Consent Decrees in Institutional Reform Litigation." *Harvard Law Review* 99 (March 1986): 1020-1039.

2657. Nelson, Dorothy W. *Cases and Materials on Judicial Administration and the Administration of Justice.* St. Paul, MN: West Publishing Company, 1974.

2658. Nixon, Milton A. "Repeal by Implication: Recent Inconsistencies of the Supreme Court." *Georgetown Law Journal* 30 (June 1942): 776-780.

2659. Norton, Thomas J. "The Supreme Court's Five to Four Decisions." *American Bar Association Journal* 9 (July 1923): 417-420.

2660. Norton, Thomas J. "What Damage Have Five to Four Decisions Done?" *American Bar Association Journal* 9 (November 1923): 721-727.

2661. Putney, Albert H. "Five to Four Constitutional Law Decisions." *Yale Law Journal* 24 (April 1915): 460-470.

2662. Rose, Walter M. *Digest of the United States Reports from the Beginning to the October Term, 1902. Volume 1 to 186 United States, Inclusive with Table of Cases, Table of Citations of All Nonfederal Cases Cited by the Supreme Court, Table of Citations of Constitutional and Statutory Provisions, State and Federal, and the Equity, Admiralty, and General Rules of the Supreme Court.* 3 vols. San Francisco: Bancroft-Whitney Company, 1903.

2663. Rose, Walter M. *Notes on the United States Reports: A Brief Chronological Digest of All Points Determined in the Decisions of the Supreme Court, with Notes Showing the Influence, Following and Present Authority of Each Case, as Disclosed by the Citations Comprising All Citing Cases in That Court, the Intermediate and Inferior Federal Courts, and the Courts of Last Resort of All the States.* 13 vols. San Francisco: Bancroft-Whitney Company, 1899-1901.

2664. Savidge, Frank R. "Five to Four Supreme Court Decisions." *North American Review* 219 (April 1924): 460-473.

2665. Schaefer, Walter V. "The Control of *Sunburst:* Techniques of Prospective

Overruling." *New York University Law Review* 42 (October 1967): 631-646.

2666. Scheid, Dan, Juliann J. Sitoski, and Christine C. Parker. "United States Supreme Court Decisions." *Denver Law Journal* 58 (Spring 1981): 531-539.

2667. Sgroi, Peter. *The Living Constitution: Landmark Supreme Court Decisions.* New York: Messner, 1987.

2668. Sharp, Malcolm P. "Movement in Supreme Court Adjudication: A Study of Modified and Overruled Decisions." *Harvard Law Review* 46 (January/March 1933): 361-403, 593-637, 795-811.

2669. *Shepard's United States Citations: Cases. A Compilation of Citations to United States Supreme Court Cases.* New York: F. Shepard Company, 1982.

2670. Shivers, Lyda G. "Five to Four Decisions of the United States Supreme Court." *Mississippi Law Journal* 2 (February 1930): 334-338.

2671. Slane, Alton. *Major Supreme Court Decisions in American Government.* Washington, DC: University Press of America, 1981.

2672. Spaeth, Harold J. *Classic and Current Decisions of the United States Supreme Court.* San Francisco: Freeman, 1978.

2673. Streifford, Howard I. "An Axiological Analysis of the Rhetorical Implications in Selected Supreme Court Decisions." Ph.D. diss., Southern Illinois University, 1967.

2674. Thompson, Charles L. *Notes on the United States Supreme Court Reports, Supplementary to Rose's Notes on United States Reports, Showing the Present Authority of Each Case as Disclosed by the Citations as Found in All the Reports Both Federal and State from the Publication of Rose's Notes up to and Including July 1, 1904, with Parallel References to American State Reports and the Reporter Sys-* tem. 5 vols. San Fransisco: Bancroft-Whitney Company, 1904-1909.

2675. Von Haast, H. F. "Split Decisions in the Court of Appeal and in the Supreme Court of the United States." *New Zealand Law Journal* 19 (May 18, 1943): 107.

2676. Wheeler, Everett P. "Five to Four Decisions of the Supreme Court." *American Law Review* 54 (November/December 1920): 921-928.

Litigants, Groups, Attorneys

General Studies

2677. Abraham, Henry J., and Robert R. Benedetti. "The State Attorney General: A Friend of the Court." *University of Pennsylvania Law Review* 117 (April 1969): 795-828.

2678. Beardsley, Charles A. "The American Lawyer's Part in the Supreme Court Controversy." *Journal of the Kansas Bar Association* 5 (May 1937): 326-328.

2679. Benett, Edward J. "*Eisen v. Carlisle and Jacquelin*: Supreme Court Calls for Revamping of Class Action Strategy." *Wisconsin Law Review* 1974 (1974): 801-832.

2680. Brisbin, Richard A., Jr. "The Supreme Court and the Power of the Legal Profession." *Polity* 13 (Spring 1981): 505-523.

2681. Caldeira, Gregory A., and John R. Wright. "Organized Interests and Agenda Setting in the U.S. Supreme Court." *American Political Science Review* 82 (December 1988): 1109-1128.

2682. Canon, Bradley C., and Michael W. Giles. "Recurring Litigants: Federal Agencies before the Supreme Court." *Western Political Quarterly* 25 (June 1972): 183-191.

2683. Davis, Julia. "A Feisty Schoolmarm

Made the Lawyers Sit Up and Take Notice." *Smithsonian* 11 (March 1981): 133-150.

2684. Denniston, Lyle. "Three Poor Performances by Government Lawyers." *American Lawyer* 8 (April 1986): 135.

2685. Epstein, Lee. *Conservatives in Court.* Knoxville: University of Tennessee Press, 1985.

2686. Galloway, Russell W., Jr. "Taking It to the Supreme Court." *California Lawyer* 6 (June 1986): 13-15.

2687. Hakman, Nathan. "Lobbying the Supreme Court: An Appraisal of 'Political Science Folklore'." *Fordham Law Review* 35 (October 1966): 15-50.

2688. Harper, Fowler V., and Edwin D. Etherington. "Lobbyists before the Court." *University of Pennsylvania Law Review* 101 (June 1953): 1172-1177.

2689. Hine, Darlene C. "NAACP and Supreme Court: W. F. White, and Defeat of Judge J. J. Parker, 1930." *Negro History Bulletin* 40 (September/October 1977): 753-757.

2690. Jaffe, Louis L. "The Citizen as Litigant in Public Actions: The Non-Hohfeldian or Ideological Plaintiff." *University of Pennsylvania Law Review* 116 (April 1968): 1033-1047.

2691. Jaffe, Louis L. "Standing Again." *Harvard Law Review* 84 (January 1971): 633-638.

2692. Jaffe, Louis L. "Standing to Secure Judicial Review: Private Actions." *Harvard Law Review* 75 (December 1961): 255-305.

2693. Jung, William F. "Effective Appellate Advocacy: Lessons Learned at the U.S. Supreme Court." *Florida Bar Journal* 60 (July/August 1986): 17-19.

2694. Klonoski, James R. "The Influence of Government Counsel on Supreme Court Decisions Involving the Commerce

Power." Ph.D. diss., University of Michigan, 1958.

2695. Kolsrud, Russell A. "Preparing for a Supreme Court Argument ... Do What Your Mother Told You." *American Bar Association Journal* 66 (July 1980): 855-858.

2696. Levitsky, Ronald, and George Steffen. "Supreme Court Simulation Game." *Social Studies* 74 (March/April 1983): 89-92.

2697. McGinty, Brian. "Belva Lockwood, Woman in a Man's World." *American History Illustrated* 20 (April 1985): 36-37.

2698. Mann, Jim. "Missed Signals at the High Court." *American Lawyer* 6 (May 1984): 102-103.

2699. Mann, Jim. "The See-No-Evil Defense." *American Lawyer* 6 (March 1984): 142-143.

2700. Matza, Michael. "Preparing to Argue before the Supreme Court Is Hard, Especially When Your Case Might Make History." *Student Lawyer* 12 (May 1984): 24-31.

2701. Miller, Arthur S., and Jerome A. Barron. "Supreme Court, the Adversary System, and the Flow of Information to the Justices: A Preliminary Inquiry." *Virginia Law Review* 61 (October 1975): 1187-1245.

2702. Newland, Chester A. "Legal Periodicals and the United States Supreme Court." *Midwest Journal of Political Science* 3 (February 1959): 58-74.

2703. Newland, Chester A. "Legal Periodicals and the United States Supreme Court." Ph.D. diss., University of Kansas, 1959.

2704. Newland, Chester A. "The Supreme Court and Legal Writing: Learned Journals as Vehicles of an Anti-Antitrust Lobby?" *Georgetown Law Journal* 48 (Fall 1958): 105-143.

2705. O'Connor, Karen, and Lee Epstein. "Beyond Legislative Lobbying: Women's Rights Groups and the Supreme Court." *Judicature* 67 (September 1983): 134-143.

2706. O'Connor, Karen, and Lee Epstein. "Bridging the Gap between Congress and the Supreme Court: Interest Groups and the Erosion of the Attorney's Fees." *Western Political Quarterly* 38 (June 1985): 238-249.

2707. O'Connor, Karen, and Lee Epstein. "A Legal Voice for the Chicano Community: The Activities of the Mexican American Legal Defense and Education Fund, 1968-1982." *Social Science Quarterly* 65 (June 1984): 245-256.

2708. O'Connor, Karen, and Lee Epstein. "The Rise of Conservative Interest Groups Litigation." *Journal of Politics* 45 (May 1983): 479-489.

2709. O'Donnell, Alice L. "A Long Way, Baby: Women and Other Strangers before the Bar." *Supreme Court Historical Society Yearbook* 1977 (1977): 59-62, 114.

2710. Orren, Karen. "Standing to Sue: Interest Group Conflict in the Federal Courts." *American Political Science Review* 70 (September 1976): 723-741.

2711. Perlman, Philip B. "Some Maryland Lawyers in Supreme Court History." *Maryland Historical Magazine* 43 (September 1948): 180-196.

2712. Perry, James R., and James M. Buchanan. "Admission to the Supreme Court Bar, 1790-1800: A Case Study of Institutional Change." *Supreme Court Historical Society Yearbook* 1983 (1983): 11-16.

2713. Raymond, John M., and Barbara J. Frischolz. "Lawyers Who Established International Law in the United States, 1776-1914." *American Journal of International Law* 76 (October 1982): 802-829.

2714. Rhyne, Charles S. "United States Supreme Court and the Local Government Lawyer." *Florida Bar Journal* 52 (November 1978): 708-714.

2715. Roady, Joe G. "A Supreme Effort." *Litigation* 10 (Summer 1984): 49-50, 70.

2716. Robert, Joseph C. "The Many-Sided Attorney General." *Supreme Court Historical Society Yearbook* 1976 (1976): 51-60.

2717. Ronwin, Edward. "Edward Ronwin Replies." *American Lawyer* 6 (July/August 1984): 4.

2718. Scheingold, Stuart A. *The Politics of Rights: Lawyers, Public Policy, and Political Change.* New Haven, CT: Yale University Press, 1974.

2719. Schopler, Ernest H. "Every Lawyer Should Have U.S. Supreme Court Cases at Hand." *Case and Comment* 58 (November/December 1953): 12-16.

2720. Shapiro, Stephen M. "Oral Argument in the Supreme Court of the United States." *Catholic University Law Review* 33 (Spring 1984): 529-553.

2721. Sharpe, Allen. "Social Security Disability Cases." *American Bar Association Journal* 55 (February 1969): 141-143.

2722. Sorauf, Frank J. "Winning in the Courts: Interest Groups and Constitutional Change." *This Constitution* 4 (Fall 1984): 4-10.

2723. Springer, James V. "Some Suggestions on Preparing Briefs on the Merits in the Supreme Court of the United States." *Catholic University Law Review* 33 (Spring 1984): 593-602.

2724. Taylor, William L. "Litigation as an Empowerment Tool." *Social Policy* 16 (Spring 1986): 31-36.

2725. Tucker, K. Gregory. "Disbarment and the Supreme Court of the United States." *Federal Bar Journal* 37 (Spring 1978): 37-55.

2726. Twiss, Benjamin R. *Lawyers and*

the Constitution: *How Laissez-Faire Came to the Supreme Court.* Princeton, NJ: Princeton University Press, 1942.

2727. Uelmen, Gerald F. "The Influence of the Solicitor General upon the Supreme Court Disposition of Federal Circuit Court Decisions: A Closer Look at the Ninth Circuit Record." *Judicature* 69 (April/May 1986): 360-366.

2728. Ulmer, S. Sidney. "Governmental Litigants, Underdogs, and Civil Liberties in the Supreme Court: 1903-1968 Terms." *Journal of Politics* 47 (August 1985): 899-909.

2729. Vose, Clement E. "Interest Groups before the Supreme Court: The Restrictive Covenant Cases of 1948." Ph.D. diss., University of Wisconsin, 1953.

2730. Vose, Clement E. "Litigation as a Form of Pressure Group Politics." *Annals of the American Academy of Political and Social Science* 319 (September 1958): 20-31.

2731. Wasby, Stephen L. "The Functions of Oral Arguments in the U.S. Supreme Court." *Quarterly Journal of Speech* 62 (December 1976): 410-422.

2732. Wasby, Stephen L., Anthony A. D'Amato, and Rosemary Metrailer. "The Functions of Oral Argument in the U.S. Supreme Court." *Quarterly Journal of Speech* 62 (December 1976): 410-422.

2733. Yarbrough, Tinsley E. "Litigant Access Doctrine and the Burger Court." *Vanderbilt Law Review* 31 (January 1978): 33-70.

Amicus Curiae Briefs and Other Supporting Writings

2734. Bradley, Robert C., and Paul Gardner. "Underdogs, Upperdogs, and the Use of the *Amicus* Brief: Trends and Explanations." *Justice System Journal* 10 (Spring 1985): 78-96.

2735. Ennis, Bruce. "Effective *Amicus* Briefs." *Catholic University Law Review* 33 (Spring 1984): 603-609.

2736. Krislov, Samuel. "The *Amicus Curiae* Brief: From Friendship to Advocacy." *Yale Law Journal* 72 (March 1963): 694-721.

2737. Segal, Jeffrey A. "*Amicus Curiae* Briefs by the Solicitor General during the Warren and Burger Courts: A Research Note." *Western Political Quarterly* 41 (March 1988): 135-144.

2738. Shapiro, Stephen M. "*Amicus* Briefs in the Supreme Court." *Litigation* 10 (Spring 1984): 21-24.

Policymaking by the Court

General Studies

2739. "Abusing Standing: Furthering the Conservative Agenda." *William and Mary Law Review* 29 (Winter 1988): 387-414.

2740. Adamany, David, and Joel B. Grossman. "Support for the Supreme Court as a National Policymaker." *Law and Policy Quarterly* 5 (October 1983): 405-437.

2741. Alfange, Dean. "The Supreme Court Battle in Retrospect." *U.S. Law Review* 71 (September 1937): 497-502.

2742. Baas, Larry R., and Dan Thomas. "The Supreme Court and Policy Legitimation: Experimental Tests." *American Politics Quarterly* 12 (July 1984): 335-360.

2743. Ball, Howard. *Judicial Craftsmanship or Fiat? Direct Overturn by the United States Supreme Court.* Westport, CT: Greenwood Press, 1978.

2744. Bartholomew, Paul C. "Our Legislative Courts." *Southwestern Social Science Quarterly* 46 (June 1965): 11-19.

2745. Baum, Lawrence. "Measuring Policy Change in the U.S. Supreme Court." *American Political Science Review* 82 (September 1988): 905-912.

2746. Beaney, William M. "The Judiciary: Interpreter of the Constitution or Policymaker?" *Colorado Lawyer* 16 (September 1987): 1557-1562.

2747. Birkby, Robert H. *The Court and Public Policy.* Washington, DC: Congressional Quarterly Press, 1983.

2748. Brown, Henry B. "Development of International Law by Judicial Decisions in the United States: The Supreme Court." *Proceedings of the American Society of International Law* 1909 (1909): 166-188.

2749. Bruce, Andrew A. *The American Judge.* New York: Macmillan, 1924.

2750. Burris, William C. "John J. Parker and Supreme Court Policy: A Case Study in Judicial Control." Ph.D. diss., University of North Carolina, 1965.

2751. Carter, Lief H. "Limits of Traditional Jurisprudence: A Critique of *Agresto.*" *Georgia Law Review* 15 (Spring 1981): 667-679.

2752. Casper, Jonathan D. "The Supreme Court and National Policy Making." *American Political Science Review* 70 (March 1976): 50-63.

2753. Childress, Steven A. "A New Era for Summary Judgement: Recent Shifts at the Supreme Court." *Federal Rules Decisions* 116 (September 1987): 183-194.

2754. Dahl, Robert A. "Decision-Making in a Democracy: The Supreme Court as a National Policy-Maker." *Journal of Public Law* 6 (Fall 1957): 279-295.

2755. Dalton, John M. "United States Supreme Court: Evolution in Revolution." *Missouri Law Review* 23 (April 1958): 180-189.

2756. Dodd, Walter F. "Social Legislation and the Courts." *Political Science Quarterly* 28 (March 1913): 1-17.

2757. Dressler, Joshua. "A Lesson in Incaution, Overwork, and Fatigue: The Judicial Miscraftsmanship of *Segura v. United States.*" *William and Mary Law Review* 26 (Spring 1985): 375-422.

2758. Ducat, Craig R., and Robert L. Dudley. "Dimensions Underlying Economic Policymaking in the Early and Later Burger Courts." *Journal of Politics* 49 (May 1987): 521-539.

2759. Dudley, Robert L., and Craig R. Ducat. "The Burger Court and Economic Liberalism." *Western Political Quarterly* 39 (June 1986): 236-249.

2760. Ervin, Samuel J., and Ramsey Clark. *Role of the Supreme Court: Policymaker or Adjudicator?* Washington, DC: American Enterprise Institute for Public Policy Research, 1970.

2761. Eubank, William L. "Quasi-Experimental Approaches to Judicial Policy-Making." *Policy Studies Journal* 4 (Winter 1975): 171-174.

2762. Everson, David, ed. *The Supreme Court as Policy-Maker: Three Studies on the Impact of Judicial Decisions.* 2d ed. Carbondale: Public Affairs Research Bureau, Southern Illinois University, 1972.

2763. Fein, Bruce E. "Does the High Court Have the Low-Down on Election Results?" *District Law* 6 (September/October 1981): 42-48.

2764. Fleming, Macklin. *The Price of Perfect Justice: The Adverse Consequences of Current Legal Doctrine on the American Courtroom.* New York: Basic Books, 1974.

2765. Fletcher, R. V. "The Supreme Court as a Legislative Body." *Illinois Bar Journal* 31 (June 1943): 378-381, 428-431.

2766. Florentino, Tonianne. "Emerging Jurisdictional Doctrines of the Burger

Court: A Doctrine of Convenience." *St. John's Law Review* 59 (Winter 1985): 316-347.

2767. Floyd, C. Douglas. "The Justiciability Decisions of the Burger Court." *Notre Dame Law Review* 60 (1985): 862-946.

2768. Fluno, Robert Y. "How Deep Is the Supreme Court in Politics?" *Western Political Quarterly* 10 (June 1957): 459-461.

2769. Forrester, Ray. "Are We Ready for Truth in Judging? The Supreme Court Has Become Our Legiscourt." *American Bar Association Journal* 63 (September 1977): 1212-1216.

2770. Forrester, Ray. "Truth in Judging: Supreme Court Opinions as Legislative Drafting." *Vanderbilt Law Review* 38 (April 1985): 463-477.

2771. Fuchs, Ralph F. "The United States Supreme Court: Pioneer in Social Policy." *Indian Year Book of International Affairs* 11 (1962): 88-102.

2772. Funston, Richard Y. "The Burger Court: New Directions in Judicial Policy-Making." *Emory Law Journal* 23 (Summer 1974): 643-656.

2773. Funston, Richard Y. *Constitutional Counterrevolution: The Warren Court and the Burger Court: Judicial Policy Making in Modern America.* New York: Halsted Press, 1977.

2774. Gates, John B. "The American Supreme Court and Electoral Realignment: A Critical Review." *Social Science History* 8 (Summer 1984): 267-290.

2775. Gates, John B. "The American Supreme Court, Critical Elections, and the Invalidation of State and Federal Policies, 1837-1964: Supreme Court Policy-Making during Periods of Major Change in the Political Party System." Ph.D. diss., University of Maryland, 1985.

2776. Gates, John B. "Partisan Realignment, Unconstitutional State Policies, and

the U.S. Supreme Court, 1837-1964." *American Journal of Political Science* 31 (May 1987): 259-280.

2777. Gleicher, Jules. "The Straying of the Constitution: Raoul Berger and the Problem of Legal Continuity." *Continuity* 1 (Fall 1980): 99-123.

2778. Gordon, Walter R. "A Quiet Revolution." *Justice Magazine* 1 (March/April 1972): 12-13.

2779. Gordon, Walter R. "The Supreme Court, a Quiet Revolution." *California Trial Lawyers Association Journal* 11 (Fall 1972): 61-71.

2780. Graglia, Lino A. " 'Constitutional Theory': The Attempted Justification for the Supreme Court's Liberal Political Program." *Texas Law Review* 65 (March 1987): 789-798.

2781. Graham, Barbara L. "Supreme Court Policymaking in Civil Rights Cases: A Study of Judicial Discretion in Statutory Interpretation." *St. Louis University Public Law Review* 7 (Fall 1988): 401-421.

2782. Green, Justin J. "Judicial Policy-Making, 1973-1974." *Western Political Quarterly* 28 (March 1975): 167-192.

2783. Green, Wendell E. "*Stare Decisis* and the Supreme Court of the United States." *National Bar Journal* 4 (September 1946): 191-207.

2784. Grinnell, Frank W. "*Stare Decisis* and the Supreme Court of the United States." *American Judicature Society Journal* 27 (April 1944): 183-184.

2785. Grossman, Joel B. "Supreme Court and Social Change: A Preliminary Inquiry." *American Behavioral Scientist* 13 (March 1970): 535-551.

2786. Grossman, Joel B., and Richard S. Wells, eds. *Constitutional Law and Judicial Policy Making.* New York: Wiley, 1972.

2787. Handler, Milton. "Is Antitrust's

Centennial a Time for Obsequies or for Renewed Faith in Its National Policy?" *Cardozo Law Review* 10 (June 1989): 1933-1946.

2788. Henkin, Louis. "Is There a Political Question Doctrine?" *Yale Law Journal* 85 (April 1976): 597-625.

2789. Hiers, Richard. "Normative Analysis in Judicial Determination of Public Policy." *Journal of Law and Religion* 3 (Winter 1985): 77-115.

2790. Horowitz, Donald L. *The Courts and Social Policy*. Washington, DC: Brookings Institution, 1977.

2791. Howard, A. E. Dick. "From Warren to Burger: Activism and Restraint." *Wilson Quarterly* 1 (Spring 1977): 109-120.

2792. Jacobsohn, Gary J. "Constitutional Adjudication and Judicial Statesmanship: Principle, Fact, and Doctrine." *Emory Law Journal* 23 (Winter 1974): 137-150.

2793. Jacobsohn, Gary J. "Pragmatism and the Supreme Court." Ph.D. diss., Cornell University, 1972.

2794. Jacobsohn, Gary J. *Pragmatism, Statesmanship, and the Supreme Court*. Ithaca, NY: Cornell University Press, 1977.

2795. Jacobsohn, Gary J. *The Supreme Court and the Decline of Constitutional Aspiration*. Totowa, NJ: Rowman and Littlefield, 1986.

2796. Johnston, Forney. "Results of the Supreme Court's Reversal of Constitutional Theory." *Virginia State Bar Association* 1939 (1939): 266-299.

2797. Kelly, Joseph I. *Has the Supreme Court Committed Us to Socialism?* Baton Rouge, LA: Times Publishing Company, 1906.

2798. Kennedy, Walter B. "The Supreme Court and Social Legislation." *Catholic Charities Review* 7 (June 1923): 208-212.

2799. Krislov, Samuel. "The Supreme Court since 1937: Nine Judges in Search of a Role." Ph.D. diss., Princeton University, 1955.

2800. Kunin, Edward F. "Failure of the Supreme Court as a Constitutional Institution." *Connecticut Bar Journal* 50 (September 1976): 323-334.

2801. Kurland, Philip B. "*Auria Regis*: Some Comments on the Divine Rights of Kings and Courts 'to Say What the Law Is'." *Arizona Law Review* 23 (1981): 581-597.

2802. Kurland, Philip B. "Government by Judiciary." *Modern Age* 20 (Fall 1976): 358-371.

2803. Lamb, Charles M. "Judicial Policy-Making and Information Flow to the Supreme Court." *Vanderbilt Law Review* 29 (January 1976): 45-124.

2804. Landes, William M., and Richard A. Posner. "Independent Judiciary in an Interest-Group Perspective." *Journal of Law and Economics* 18 (December 1975): 875-891.

2805. Lasser, William. "Crisis and the Supreme Court: Judicial Politics in Periods of Critical Realignment." Ph.D. diss., Harvard University, 1983.

2806. Lasser, William. "The Supreme Court in Periods of Critical Realignment." *Journal of Politics* 47 (November 1985): 48-53.

2807. Latham, Earl. "The Supreme Court as a Political Institution." *Minnesota Law Review* 31 (February 1947): 205-231.

2808. Leflar, Robert. "The Task of the Appellate Court." *Notre Dame Lawyer* 33 (August 1958): 548-572.

2809. Lerner, Ralph. "The Supreme Court as Republican Schoolmaster." *Supreme Court Review* 1967 (1967): 127-180.

2810. Levinson, Sanford. "The Supreme

Court: Does It Have an Innovative Role?" *Harvard Review* 3 (Fall/Winter 1965): 1-23.

2811. Mabbutt, Fred R. "The Constitution and the Nixon Court." *Colorado Quarterly* 22 (Autumn 1973): 149-165.

2812. McDermott, Edwin J. *Modern Federal Contract Law: Modern Digest of Decisions of United States Court of Claims and of Supreme Court of the United States.* Philadelphia: n.p., 1969.

2813. McDermott, Edwin J. *Modern Federal Law: Carriers, Congressional Reference, Eminent Domain, Indian Claims, Patents, Miscellany; Modern Digest of Decisions of United States Court of Claims and of Supreme Court of United States.* Philadelphia: n.p., 1970.

2814. McDermott, Edwin J. *Modern Federal Military Pay Law: Modern Digest of Decision of U.S. Court of Claims and of Supreme Court of U.S.* Philadelphia: n.p., 1969.

2815. McDowell, Gary L. "Equal, Equitable, or Egalitarian? The Supreme Court, the Constitution, and the Equity Power." Ph.D. diss., University of Virginia, 1979.

2816. McDowell, Gary L. *The Supreme Court, the Constitution, and the Equity Power.* Chicago: University of Chicago Press, 1982.

2817. McKay, Robert B. "Supreme Court as an Instrument of Law Reform." *St. Louis University Law Journal* 13 (Spring 1969): 387-402.

2818. McWhinney, Edward. "The Supreme Court and the Dilemma of Judicial Policy-Making." *Minnesota Law Review* 39 (June 1955): 837-851.

2819. McWhinney, Edward. *Supreme Courts and Judicial Lawmaking: Constitutional Tribunals and Constitutional Review.* Boston: Nijhoff, 1986.

2820. Malick, Clay P. "The Supreme Court as Moral Force." *Midwest Quarterly* 1 (April 1960): 271-283.

2821. Maltz, Earl M. "Some Thoughts on the Death of *Stare Decisis* in Constitutional Law." *Wisconsin Law Review* 1980 (1980): 467-496.

2822. Mandell, Daniel R. "Compelling a Public Timberlands Policy: *United States v. Briggs*, 1850." *Journal of Forest History* 26 (July 1982): 140-147.

2823. Marshall, Thomas R. "The Supreme Court as an Opinion Leader: Court Decisions and the Mass Public." *American Politics Quarterly* 15 (January 1987): 147-168.

2824. Mason, Alpheus T. "Understanding the Warren Court: Judicial Self-Restraint and Judicial Duty." *Political Science Quarterly* 81 (December 1966): 523-563.

2825. Meacham, William S. "Supreme Court and the Sociological Proteus." *Virginia Quarterly Review* 35 (Fall 1959): 553-559.

2826. Meese, Edwin. "The Attorney General's View of the Supreme Court: Toward a Jurisprudence of Original Intention." *Public Administration Review* 45 (November 1985): 701-704.

2827. Mendelson, Wallace. "The Neo-behavioral Approach to the Judicial Process: A Critique." *American Political Science Review* 57 (September 1963): 593-603.

2828. Merritt, Walter G. "Judicial Legislation: Two Federal Legislatures?" *American Bar Association Journal* 30 (July 1944): 379-384.

2829. Miller, Arthur S. "Politics of the American Judiciary." *Political Quarterly* 49 (April 1978): 200-207.

2830. Miller, Arthur S. "Social Justice and the Warren Court: A Preliminary Examination." *Pepperdine Law Review* 11 (March 1984): 473-498.

2831. Miller, Arthur S. "Supreme Court

in a New Role from Negative Naysayer to Affirmative Commander." *Nova Law Journal* 6 (Fall 1981): 1-36.

2832. Minor, Berkley, Jr. "U.S. Supreme Court and Rulemaking Power." *American Bar Association Journal* 13 (March 1927): 165.

2833. Moeller, John. "The Supreme Court's Quest for Fair Politics." *Constitutional Commentary* 1 (Summer 1984): 203-223.

2834. Moore, James W., and Robert S. Oglebay. "The Supreme Court: *Stare Decisis* and Law of the Case." *Texas Law Review* 21 (May 1934): 514-553.

2835. Morgan, John A., Jr. "Judicial Freedom in Statutory Interpretation: The Use of the Concept of Congressional Intent in United States Supreme Court Opinions during the 1958, 1959, and 1960 terms." Ph.D. diss., Duke University, 1963.

2836. Morrison, Alan B. "Rights without Remedies: The Burger Court Takes the Federal Courts Out of the Business of Protecting Federal Rights." *Rutgers Law Review* 30 (Summer 1974): 841-862.

2837. Moynihan, Daniel P. "Social Science and the Courts." *Public Interest* 54 (Winter 1979): 12-31.

2838. Murphy, Walter F., and Joseph Tanenhaus. *The Study of Public Law.* New York: Random House, 1972.

2839. Nagel, Robert F. "The Formulaic Constitution." *Michigan Law Review* 84 (November 1985): 165-212.

2840. Nagel, Robert F. "Plague of Judges: The Burger Court's Secret Plan for America." *Washington Monthly* 12 (November 1980): 20-24.

2841. Neuborne, Burt. "The Binding Quality of Supreme Court Precedent." *Tulane Law Review* 61 (April 1987): 991-1002.

2842. Neuborne, Burt. "Procedural As-sault on the Warren Legacy: A Study in Repeal by Indirection." *Hofstra Law Review* 5 (Spring 1977): 545-580.

2843. Nutting, Charles B. "Policy Making by the Supreme Court." *University of Pittsburgh Law Review* 9 (December 1947): 59-73.

2844. Patterson, C. Perry. "The Supreme Court: Declarer or Amender? The Adaptation of the Constitution by the Supreme Court." *Brooklyn Law Review* 10 (October 1940): 48-75.

2845. Paul, Charles H. "The Supreme Court of the United States and National Policy." *Oregon Law Review* 21 (December 1941): 23-36.

2846. Peitzman, Larry. "The Supreme Court and the Credentials Challenge Cases: Ask a Political Question, You Get a Political Answer." *California Law Review* 62 (July/September 1974): 1344-1376.

2847. Perry, Michael J. "The Authority of Text, Tradition, and Reason: A Theory of Constitutional Interpretation." *Southern California Law Review* 58 (January 1985): 551-602.

2848. Perry, Michael J. *The Constitution, the Courts, and Human Rights: An Inquiry into the Legitimacy of Constitutional Policy-Making by the Judiciary.* New Haven, CT: Yale University Press, 1984.

2849. Philipps, T. L., Jr. "Precedential Effect of Summary Affirmances and Dismissals for Want of a Substantial Federal Question by Supreme Court after *Hicks v. Miranda* and *Mandel v. Bradley.*" *Virginia Law Review* 64 (February 1978): 117-143.

2850. Pollak, Louis H. "The Making of Law: Hierarchies of Courts and Hierarchies of Values." *American Philosophical Society Proceedings* 129 (1985): 82-89.

2851. Post, Charles G. ... *The Supreme*

Court and Political Questions. Baltimore: Johns Hopkins Press, 1936.

2852. Powell, Burnele V. "Sitting and Standing in the Supreme Court: *Warth* Standing and the Problem of Distributive Justice." *DePaul Law Review* 33 (Spring 1984): 429-464.

2853. Ramaswamy, M. *The Creative Role of the Supreme Court of the United States.* New York: Russell and Russell, 1970.

2854. Rathjen, Gregory J., and Harold J. Spaeth. "Access to the Federal Courts: An Analysis of Burger Court Policy Making." *American Journal of Political Science* 23 (May 1979): 360-382.

2855. Reich, Donald. "Supreme Court and Public Policy." *Phi Delta Kappan* 48 (September 1966): 29-32.

2856. Ribble, F.D.G. "The Development of the Supreme Court as Center of Controversy in the United States." *South Texas Law Journal* 4 (Spring 1959): 149-159.

2857. Ribble, F.D.G. "A Look at the Policy Making Powers of the United States Supreme Court and the Position of the Individual." *Washington and Lee Review* 14 (1957): 167-185.

2858. Richberg, Donald R. "Social Welfare and the Constitution." *American Labor Legislation Review* 27 (March 1937): 5-10.

2859. Riga, Peter J. "The Supreme Court, the Adversary System, and Some Moral Dilemmas." *Catholic Lawyer* 23 (Spring 1978): 97-107.

2860. Rohde, David W. "Policy Goals and Opinion Coalitions in the Supreme Court." *Midwest Journal of Political Science* 16 (May 1972): 208-224.

2861. Rosen, Paul L. "Judicial Interpretation and Extralegal Facts: An Analysis of the Supreme Court's Use of Social Science." Ph.D. diss., New School for Research, 1971.

2862. Rosen, Paul L. *The Supreme Court and Social Science.* Urbana: University of Illinois Press, 1972.

2863. Rowland, C. K. "A Longitudinal Study of Party Effects on Federal District Court Policy Propensities." *American Journal of Political Science* 24 (May 1980): 291-305.

2864. Rumble, Wilfrid E., Jr. *American Legal Realism: Skepticism, Reform, and the Judicial Process.* Ithaca, NY: Cornell University Press, 1968.

2865. Ryan, John P. *The Supreme Court in American Politics: Policy through Law.* Washington, DC: American Political Science Association, 1975.

2866. Schauer, Frederick. "Refining the Lawmaking Function of the Supreme Court." *University of Michigan Journal of Law Reform* 17 (Fall 1983): 1-24.

2867. Schubert, Glendon A. *Judicial Policy Making: The Political Role of the Courts.* Rev. ed. Glenview, IL: Scott, Foresman, 1974.

2868. Scott, Kenneth E. "Standing in Supreme Court: Functional Analysis." *Harvard Law Review* 86 (February 1973): 645-692.

2869. Sedler, Robert A. "Standing and the Burger Court: An Analysis and Some Proposals for Legislative Reform." *Rutgers Law Review* 30 (Summer 1977): 863-886.

2870. Seitz, Reynolds C. "Supreme Court Use of Non-Legal Materials." *Catholic Lawyer* 4 (Winter 1958): 71-76.

2871. Shapiro, Martin M. *The Supreme Court and Public Policy.* Glenview, IL: Scott, Foresman, 1969.

2872. Sherry, Suzanna. "Issue Manipulation by the Burger Court: Saving the Community from Itself." *Minnesota Law Review* 70 (February 1986): 611-663.

2873. Smith, Herbert A. *The American Supreme Court as an International Tribu-*

nal. New York: Oxford University Press, 1920.

2874. Spaeth, Harold J. *Supreme Court Policy Making: Explanation and Prediction.* San Francisco: W. H. Freeman, 1979.

2875. Spence, Paulsen. "Get the Supreme Court Out of Politics." *American Mercury* 85 (October 1957): 23-28.

2876. Spitz, David. "Freedom, Virtue, and the New Scholasticism: The Supreme Court as Philosopher-Kings." *Commentary* 28 (October 1959): 313-321.

2877. Stephenson, D. Grier, Jr. "Supreme Court and Constitutional Change: *Lochner v. New York* Revisited." *Villanova Law Review* 21 (January 1976): 217-243.

2878. Stick, John. "He Doth Protest Too Much: Moderating Meese's Theory of Constitutional Interpretation." *Tulane Law Review* 61 (April 1987): 1079-1091.

2879. Swinton, Katherine. "Judicial Policy Making: American and Canadian Perspectives." *Canadian Review of American Studies* 10 (Spring 1979): 89-94.

2880. TenBrock, Jacobus. "Admissibility and Use by the United States Supreme Court of Extrinsic Aids in Constitutional Construction." *California Law Review* 26 (March 1938): 287-308; 27 (January 1939): 157-181.

2881. TenBrock, Jacobus. "Use by the United States Supreme Court of Extrinsic Aids in Constitutional Construction." *California Law Review* 27 (May/September 1938): 437-454, 664-681.

2882. Thurman, Samuel D., Jr. "The Coming Test of the Supreme Court." *California State Bar Journal* 22 (January/February 1947): 21-37.

2883. Tribe, Laurence H. "Constitutional Calculus: Equal Justice or Economic Efficiency?" *Harvard Law Review* 98 (January 1985): 592-621.

2884. Tribe, Laurence H. "Seven Deadly Sins of Straining through a Pseudo-Scientific Sieve." *Hastings Law Journal* 36 (November 1984): 155-172.

2885. Trope, Roland L. "Double Standard in *Stare Decisis*: Should *Stare Decisis* Be Less Applicable in Constitutional Cases Than in Statutory Cases?" *Journal of the Beverly Hills Bar Association* 20 (Spring 1986): 85-102.

2886. Tushnet, Mark V. "The Supreme Court as Communicator: Carter's *Contemporary Constitutional Lawmaking.*" *American Bar Foundation Research Journal* 1987 (Winter 1987): 225-231.

2887. Tushnet, Mark V. "The Supreme Court, the Supreme Law of the Land, and Attorney General Meese: A Comment." *Tulane Law Review* 61 (April 1987): 977-1095.

2888. Ulmer, S. Sidney. *Supreme Court Policymaking and Constitutional Law.* New York: McGraw-Hill, 1986.

2889. Valente, William D. "On Eccentric Constitutional Jurisprudence." *Catholic Lawyer* 21 (Summer 1975): 235-243.

2890. Whitesel, William E., and Matthew Kamens. "Bank Expansion: Politics of Supreme Court Decisions." *Banking Law Journal* 91 (September 1974): 748-763.

2891. Worsnop, Richard L. "Supreme Court: Legal Storm Center." *Editorial Research Reports* 2 (September 1966): 701-720.

Activism and Restraint

2892. Agresto, John. "Limits of Judicial Supremacy: A Proposal for 'Checked Activism'." *Georgia Law Review* 14 (Spring 1980): 471-495.

2893. Atkinson, Thomas E., III. "Who's in Charge Here: Judicial Activism and the

Practicing Attorney." *Land and Water Law Review* 19 (Winter 1984): 169-185.

2894. Batey, Robert. "Strict Construction of Firearms Offenses: The Supreme Court and the Gun Control Act of 1968." *Law and Contemporary Problems* 49 (Winter 1986): 163-198.

2895. Bean, Ralph J., Jr. "The Supreme Court and the Political Question: Affirmation or Abdication?" *West Virginia Law Review* 71 (February 1967): 97-134.

2896. Bennett, Robert W. "Judicial Activism and the Concept of Original Intent: Instead of Trying to Figure Out the 'Original Intention' of the Framers of the Constitution in Deciding Cases Today, Judicial Decisionmakers Should Accommodate Change within a Framework of Stability Provided by Precedent and Accepted Patterns of Societal Interaction." *Judicature* 69 (December 1985/January 1986): 219-223.

2897. Bennett, Thomas J., and Quentin L. Quade. "The Court as Legislator: A Crucial Symptom." *St. Louis University Law Journal* 10 (Fall 1965): 92-108.

2898. Berger, Raoul. "The Activist Legacy of the New Deal Court." *Washington Law Review* 59 (September 1984): 751-793.

2899. Berger, Raoul. *Government by Judiciary: The Transformation of the Fourteenth Amendment.* Cambridge: Harvard University Press, 1977.

2900. Berger, Raoul. "Insulation of Judicial Usurpation: A Comment on Lawrence Sager's Court-Stripping Polemic." *Ohio State Law Journal* 44 (Fall 1983): 611-647.

2901. Brant, Jonathan. "*Pennhurst, Romeo,* and *Rogers*: The Burger Court and Mental Health Law Reform Litigation." *Journal of Legal Medicine* 4 (Summer 1983): 323-348.

2902. Bridwell, Randall. "Federal Judiciary: America's Recently Liberated Mi-

nority." *South Carolina Law Review* 30 (June 1979): 467-483.

2903. Buchanan, G. Sidney. "Judicial Supremacy Re-examined: A Proposed Alternative." *Michigan Law Review* 70 (June 1972): 1279-1322.

2904. Carter, John D. *The Warren Court and the Constitution: A Critical View of Judicial Activism.* Gretna, LA: Pelican, 1973.

2905. Catterall, Ralph T. "Judicial Self-Restraint: The Obligation of the Judiciary." *American Bar Association Journal* 42 (September 1956): 829-855.

2906. Choper, Jesse H. "The Burger Court: Misperceptions Regarding Judicial Restraint and Insensitivity to Individual Rights." *Syracuse Law Review* 30 (Summer 1979): 767-788.

2907. Cover, Robert M. "Origins of Judicial Activism in the Protection of Minorities." *Yale Law Journal* 91 (June 1982): 1287-1316.

2908. Cox, Archibald. "Dilemma of the Supreme Court." *Trial* 4 (June/July 1968): 12-16.

2909. Cox, Archibald. "The New Dimensions of Constitutional Adjudication." *Massachusetts Historical Society Proceedings* 88 (January 1976): 60-79.

2910. Cox, Archibald. "New Dimensions of Constitutional Adjudication." *Washington Law Review* 51 (October 1976): 791-829.

2911. Cox, Archibald. "The Role of the Supreme Court: Judicial Activism or Self-Restraint?" *Maryland Law Review* 47 (Fall 1987): 118-138.

2912. Dennison, George M. "The *Dorr* War and Political Questions." *Supreme Court Historical Yearbook* 1979 (1979): 45-62.

2913. Dennison, George M. "The *Dorr* War and the Triumph of Institutionalism." *Social Science Journal* 15 (April 1978): 39-58.

2914. Denvir, John. "Professor Dworkin and an Activist Theory of Constitutional Adjudication." *Albany Law Review* 45 (Fall 1980): 13-56.

2915. Eastland, Terry. "The Burger Court and the Founding Fathers: Are We All Activists Now?" *Policy Review* 28 (Spring 1984): 14-19.

2916. Faulkner, Robert K. "Bickel's Constitution: The Problem of Moderate Liberalism." *American Political Science Review* 72 (September 1978): 925-940.

2917. Finkelstein, Maurice. "Judicial Self-Limitation." *Harvard Law Review* 37 (January 1924): 338-364.

2918. Finkelstein, Maurice. "Judicial Self-Limitation." *Harvard Law Review* 39 (December 1925): 221-244.

2919. Fite, Katharine B., and Louis B. Rubenstein. "Curbing the Supreme Court: State Experiences and Federal Proposals." *Michigan Law Review* 35 (March 1937): 762-787.

2920. Friedelbaum, Stanley H. "Deference in Disarray: Conflict and Vacillation in the Burger Court." *Dickinson Law Review* 91 (Fall 1986): 187-212.

2921. Funston, Richard Y. "Supreme Court and Critical Elections." *American Political Science Review* 69 (September 1975): 795-811.

2922. Graglia, Lino A. "How the Constitution Disappeared." *Commentary* 81 (February 1986): 19-27.

2923. Grossman, Joel B. "The 'Roots' of 'Rootless Activism'." *American Bar Foundation Research Journal* 1985 (Winter 1985): 147-156.

2924. Halpern, Stephen C., and Charles M. Lamb, eds. *Supreme Court Activism and Restraint.* Lexington, MA: Lexington Books, 1982.

2925. Handberg, Roger B., Jr., and Harold F. Hill. "Judicial Activism and Restraint on the United States Supreme Court: A Political-Behavioral Analysis." *California Western Law Review* 20 (Winter 1984): 173-186.

2926. Holland, Kenneth M. "Judicial Activism vs. Restraint: McDowell, Miller, and Perry Reconsider the Debate." *American Bar Foundation Research Journal* 1983 (Summer 1983): 705-717.

2927. Holland, Maurice J. "American Liberals and Judicial Activism: Alexander Bickel's Appeal from the New to the Old." *Indiana Law Journal* 51 (Summer 1976): 1025-1050.

2928. Jaffe, Louis L. *English and American Judges as Lawmakers.* Oxford: Clarendon Press, 1969.

2929. Jenkins, Iredele. "Judicial Activism and Constitutional Government." *American Journal of Jurisdiction* 29 (1984): 169-197.

2930. Kim, Richard C. "The Supreme Court: Oracle without Truth." *Rocky Mountain Social Science Journal* 4 (October 1967): 131-139.

2931. Lamb, Charles M. "Judicial Restraint Reappraised." *Catholic University Law Review* 31 (Winter 1982): 181-199.

2932. Lamb, Charles M., and Mitchell S. Lustig. "Burger Court, Exclusionary Zoning, and the Activist-Restraint Debate." *University of Pittsburgh Law Review* 40 (Winter 1979): 169-226.

2933. Leedes, Gary C. "The Supreme Court Mess." *Texas Law Review* 57 (November 1979): 1361-1444.

2934. Lehne, Richard, and John Reynolds. "The Impact of Judicial Activism on Public Opinion." *American Journal of Political Science* 22 (November 1978): 896-904.

2935. McCloskey, Robert G. "Reflections on the Warren Court: 'Judicial Activism'."

Virginia Law Review 51 (November 1965): 1229-1270.

2936. McDowell, Gary L. "Modest Remedy for Judicial Activism." *Public Interest* 67 (Spring 1982): 3-20.

2937. McMahon, Paul J., and Gerald J. Rodos. "Judicial Implication of Private Causes of Action: Reappraisal and Retrenchment." *Dickinson Law Review* 80 (Winter 1976): 167-192.

2938. McWhinney, Edward. "The Great Debate: Activism and Self-Restraint and Current Dilemmas in Judicial Policy-Making." *New York University Law Review* 33 (June 1958): 775-795.

2939. Mason, Alpheus T. "Judicial Activism: Old and New." *Virginia Law Review* 55 (April 1969): 385-426.

2940. Mason, Alpheus T. "Judicial Restraint and Judicial Duty: An Historical Dichotomy." *New York State Bar Journal* 38 (June 1966): 216-231.

2941. Mason, Alpheus T. "Whence and Whither the Burger Court? Judicial Self-Restraint: A Beguiling Myth." *Review of Politics* 41 (January 1979): 3-37.

2942. Meese, Edwin. "The Supreme Court of the United States: Bulwark of a Limited Constitution." *South Texas Law Review* 27 (Fall 1986): 455-466.

2943. Melvin, Edward J. "Judicial Activism: The Violation of an Oath." *Catholic Lawyer* 27 (Autumn 1982): 283-300.

2944. Mendelson, Wallace. "Politics of Judicial Activism." *Emory Law Journal* 24 (Winter 1975): 43-66.

2945. Mendelson, Wallace. "A Response to Professor Goldman." *Journal of Politics* 39 (February 1977): 159-165.

2946. Mendelson, Wallace. "Separation, Politics, and Judicial Activism." *Indiana Law Journal* 52 (Winter 1977): 313-322.

2947. Miller, Arthur S. *Toward Increased Judicial Activism: The Political Role of the Supreme Court.* Westport, CT: Greenwood Press, 1982.

2948. Millet, Thomas. "The Supreme Court Political Questions and Article V: A Case for Judicial Restraint." *Santa Clara Law Review* 23 (Summer 1983): 745-768.

2949. Nagel, Robert F. "A Comment on the Burger Court and 'Judicial Activism'." *University of Colorado Law Review* 52 (Winter 1981): 223-245.

2950. O'Brien, David M. " 'The Imperial Judiciary:' Of Paper Tigers and Socio-Legal Indicators." *Journal of Law and Politics* 2 (Spring 1985): 1-56.

2951. Palmer, Ben W. "Causes of Dissents: Judicial Self-Restraint of Abdication?" *American Bar Association Journal* 34 (September 1948): 761-765.

2952. Pennybacker, John M. " 'Activism' v. 'Restraint': The DC Circuit, the FCC, and the Supreme Court." *Journal of Broadcasting* 28 (Spring 1984): 149-166.

2953. Pritchett, C. Herman. "The Supreme Court Today: Constitutional Interpretation and Judicial Self-Restraint." *South Dakota Law Review* 3 (Spring 1958): 51-79.

2954. Ribble, F.D.G. "Some Aspects of Judicial Self-Restraint." *Virginia Law Review* 26 (June 1940): 981-998.

2955. Roche, John P. "Judicial Self-Restraint." *American Political Science Review* 49 (September 1955): 762-772.

2956. Rodell, Fred. "Judicial Activists, Judicial Self-Deniers, Judicial Review, and the First Amendment.... " *Georgetown Law Journal* 47 (Spring 1959): 483-490.

2957. Roper, Robert T. "Measuring the Simulated Impact of Judicial Policy Making: The United States Supreme Court and the Jury's Operating Structure." Ph.D. diss., University of Kentucky, 1978.

2958. Rudko, Frances H. *Truman's Court: A Study in Judicial Restraint*. Westport, CT: Greenwood Press, 1988.

2959. Schubert, Glendon A. *Constitutional Politics: The Political Behavior of Supreme Court Justices and the Constitutional Policies That They Make*. New York: Holt, Rinehart, and Winston, 1960.

2960. Sherain, Howard. "Thayer, Judicial Self-Restraint, and Watergate." *Albany Law Review* 38 (January 1973): 52-65.

2961. Sherain, Howard. "The United States Supreme Court: Studies in Judicial Self-Restraint." Ph.D. diss., University of California, Berkeley, 1969.

2962. Silverstein, Mark, and Benjamin Ginsberg. "The Supreme Court and the New Politics of Judicial Power." *Political Science Quarterly* 102 (Fall 1987): 371-388.

2963. Steamer, Robert J. *The Supreme Court: Constitutional Revision and the New "Strict Constructionism"*. Minneapolis: Burgess Publishing Company, 1973.

2964. Vetter, George M., Jr. "Who Is Supreme: People, Court, or Legislature? Role of Supreme Court in the History of Judicial Supremacy." *American Bar Association Journal* 45 (October 1959): 1051-1055.

2965. Wright, J. Skelly. "Professor Bickel, the Scholarly Tradition, and the Supreme Court." *Harvard Law Review* 84 (February 1971): 768-805.

2966. Wright, J. Skelly. "The Role of the Supreme Court in a Democratic Society: Judicial Activism or Restraint?" *Cornell Law Review* 54 (November 1968): 1-28.

Capacity

2967. Barnett, Vincent M., Jr. "The Supreme Court and the Capacity to Govern." *Political Science Quarterly* 63 (September 1948): 342-367.

2968. Lay, George C. "The Power of the Supreme Court to Enforce Its Decrees." *American Law Review* 41 (July/August 1907): 515-526.

2969. Neier, Aryeh. *Only Judgment: The Limits of Litigation in Social Change*. Middleton, CT: Wesleyan University Press, 1982.

V. The Court and Civil Liberties

General Studies

2970. Abraham, Henry J. *Freedom and the Court: Civil Rights and Liberties in the United States*. 5th ed. New York: Oxford University Press, 1988.

2971. Abraham, Henry J. "Human Rights vs. 'Property' Rights: A Comment on the 'Double Standard'." *Political Science Quarterly* 90 (Summer 1975): 261-292.

2972. Abraham, Henry J. "Of Myths, Motives, Motivations, and Morality: Some Observations on the Burger Court's Record in Civil Rights and Liberties." *Notre Dame Lawyer* 52 (October 1976): 77-86.

2973. Ansell, Frederick S. "Property versus Civil Rights: An Alternative to the Double Standard." *Northern Kentucky Law Review* 11 (Winter 1984): 51-129.

2974. Antieau, Chester J. "The Limitation of Liberty." *Southern California Law Review* 24 (April 1951): 238-251.

2975. Bachrach, Peter. "The Supreme Court, Civil Liberties, and the Balance of Interest Doctrine." *Western Political Quarterly* 14 (June 1961): 391-399.

2976. Balcerzak, Stephanie E. "Qualified Immunity for Government Officials: The Problem of Unconstitutional Purpose in Civil Rights Litigation." *Yale Law Journal* 95 (November 1985): 126-147.

2977. Barker, Lucius J., and Twilley Barker. *Civil Liberties and the Constitu-tion: Cases and Commentaries*. 4th ed. Englewood Cliffs, NJ: Prentice-Hall, 1985.

2978. Bartholomew, Paul C. "The Supreme Court and Civil Liberties, 1973-1974." *Emory Law Journal* 23 (Fall 1974): 905-942.

2979. Bartholomew, Paul C. "The Supreme Court and Civil Liberties, 1974-1975." *Emory Law Journal* 24 (Fall 1975): 937-958.

2980. Baum, Lawrence. "Explaining the Burger Court's Support for Civil Liberties." *Political Science* 20 (Winter 1987): 21-28.

2981. Belknap, Michael R. "Supreme Court Goes to War: The Meaning and Implications of the Nazi Saboteur Case." *Military Law Review* 89 (Summer 1980): 59-95.

2982. Bell, Derrick A., Jr. "The Supreme Court, 1984 Term: The Civil Rights Chronicles." *Harvard Law Review* 99 (November 1985): 1-329.

2983. Bender, Paul. "The Reluctant Court." *Civil Liberties Review* 2 (Fall 1975): 86-103.

2984. Beth, Loren P. "The Case of Judicial Protection of Civil Liberties." *Journal of Politics* 17 (February 1955): 100-112.

2985. Beth, Loren P. "Civil Liberties and the American Supreme Court." *Political Studies* 6 (June 1958): 134-146.

2986. Beth, Loren P. "The Supreme

Court and State Civil Liberties." *Western Political Quarterly* 14 (December 1961): 825-838.

2987. Blum, Jeffrey, et al. "Cases That Shock the Conscience: Reflections on Criticism of the Burger Court." *Harvard Civil Rights-Civil Liberties Law Review* 15 (Winter 1980): 713-751.

2988. Brigham, John. *Civil Liberties and American Democracy.* Washington, DC: Congressional Quarterly Press, 1984.

2989. Cahn, Edmond N. *Can the Supreme Court Defend Civil Liberties?* New York: Sidney Hillman Foundation, 1956.

2990. Caracappa, Joseph P. "Section 1983 and the New Supreme Court: Cutting the Civil Rights Act Down to Size." *Duquesne University Law Review* 15 (Fall 1976): 49-96.

2991. Carrott, M. Browning. "The Supreme Court and Minority Rights in the 1920s." *Northwest Ohio Quarterly* 41 (Fall 1969): 144-156.

2992. Casper, Jonathan D. *Lawyers before the Warren Court: Civil Liberties and Civil Rights, 1957-1966.* Urbana: University of Illinois Press, 1972.

2993. Chafee, Zechariah, Jr. *The Blessings of Liberty.* Philadelphia: Lippincott, 1956.

2994. Cohen, Marshall. "Civil Disobedience in a Constitutional Democracy." *Massachusetts Review* 10 (Spring 1969): 211-226.

2995. Cortner, Richard C. *The Supreme Court and Civil Liberties Policy.* Palo Alto, CA: Mayfield, 1975.

2996. Cortner, Richard C. *The Supreme Court and the Second Bill of Rights: The Fourteenth Amendment and the Nationalization of Civil Liberties.* Madison: University of Wisconsin Press, 1981.

2997. Countryman, Vern. "Even-Handed Justice." *Harvard Civil Rights-Civil Liberties Law Review* 11 (Spring 1976): 229-242.

2998. Currie, David P. "The Constitution in the Supreme Court: Civil Rights and Liberties, 1930-1941." *Duke Law Journal* 1987 (November 1987): 800-830.

2999. Cushman, Robert E. *Civil Liberties in the United States.* Ithaca, NY: Cornell University Press, 1956.

3000. Cushman, Robert F. *Cases in Civil Liberties.* 5th ed. Englewood Cliffs, NJ: Prentice-Hall, 1989.

3001. Day, Drews. "Racial Justice." In *Our Endangered Rights: The ACLU Report on Civil Liberties Today*, edited by Norman Dorsen, 75-97. New York: Pantheon Books, 1984.

3002. Deakin, George R. "The Burger Court and the Public Schools." Ph.D. diss., University of North Carolina, Greensboro, 1978.

3003. Detlefsen, Robert R. "Civil Rights, the Courts, and the Reagan Justice Department." *Journal of Contemporary Studies* 8 (Spring/Summer 1985): 91-115.

3004. Donohúe, William. *The Politics of the American Civil Liberties Union.* New Brunswick, NJ: Transaction Books, 1985.

3005. Dorsen, Norman. "The Court of Some Resort: CLR Survey: The Supreme Court, 1972-1973." *Civil Liberties Review* 1 (Winter/Spring 1974): 82-104.

3006. Dorsen, Norman, ed. *Our Endangered Rights: The ACLU Report on Civil Liberties Today.* New York: Pantheon Books, 1984.

3007. Edmund, Sterling E. "Mining and Sapping Our Bill of Rights." *Virginia Law Review* 16 (November 1929): 1-39.

3008. Emerson, Thomas I., and David Haber. *Political and Civil Rights in the United States.* Buffalo, NY: Dennis, 1958.

3009. Emerson, Thomas I., and Robert M.

Hutchins. *Political and Civil Rights in the United States: A Collection of Legal and Related Materials.* 2d ed. 2 vols. Buffalo, NY: Dennis, 1958.

3010. Fellman, David. "Recent Tendencies in Civil Liberties Decisions of the Supreme Court." *Cornell Law Quarterly* 34 (Spring 1949): 331-351.

3011. Fordham, Jefferson B. "Present Supreme Court, Social Legislation, and the Judicial Process." *West Virginia Law Quarterly* 37 (February 1931): 167-208.

3012. Fraenkel, Osmond K. "Civil Liberties Decisions of the Supreme Court, 1941 Term." *University of Pennsylvania Law Review* 91 (August 1942): 1-28.

3013. Fraenkel, Osmond K. "Civil Rights: The 1946 Term of the Supreme Court of the United States." *Columbia Law Review* 47 (September 1947): 953-978.

3014. Fraenkel, Osmond K. *The Supreme Court and Civil Liberties: How the Court Has Protected the Bill of Rights.* 2d ed. New York: Oceana Publications, 1963.

3015. Fraenkel, Osmond K., et al. "Civil Liberties and the Supreme Court, October Term 1957: Annual Review." *Lawyers Guild Review* 18 (Fall 1958): 93-134.

3016. Frantz, Laurent B. "New Supreme Court Decisions on Federal Civil Rights Statutes." *Lawyers Guild Review* 11 (Summer 1951): 142-150.

3017. Freeman, Harrop A. "Civil Liberties: Acid Test of Democracy . . . Survey of the United States Supreme Court Decisions Dealing with Civil Liberties Suggestions for Future Court Policy." *Minnesota Law Review* 43 (January 1959): 511-530.

3018. Freund, Paul A. "Judicial Process in Civil Liberties Cases." *University of Illinois Law Forum* 1975 (1975): 493-501.

3019. Freund, Paul A. "The Supreme Court and Civil Liberties." *Vanderbilt Law Review* 4 (April 1951): 533-554.

3020. Friedman, Leon. "Up against the Burger Court: Conference Report." *Civil Liberties Review* 1 (Fall 1973): 156-161.

3021. Gellhorn, Walter. *American Rights: The Constitution in Action.* New York: Macmillan, 1960.

3022. Gillers, Stephen. "Organizing to Beat the Lawyers." *Civil Liberties Review* 1 (Fall 1974): 121-124.

3023. Ginger, Ann F. *The Law, the Supreme Court, and the People's Rights.* Woodbury, NY: Barron's Educational Series, 1974.

3024. Ginger, Thomas J. "Justice, Discrete and Insular Minorities, and Safety Values: The Supreme Court Refines Our Sense of Justiciability." *Nova Law Journal* 10 (Fall 1985): 29-87.

3025. Glazer, Nathan. "Interests and Passions." *Public Interest* 81 (Fall 1985): 17-30.

3026. Gordon, Rosalie M. *Nine Men against America: The Supreme Court and Its Attack on American Liberties.* 4th ed. Boston: Western Islands, 1965.

3027. Green, John R. "The Supreme Court, the Bill of Rights, and the States." *University of Pennsylvania Law Review* 97 (April 1949): 608-640.

3028. Greenawalt, Kenneth W. "Legal Aspects of Civil Liberties in the United States and Recent Developments." *International Commission of Jurists Review* 2 (Spring/Summer 1959): 81-144.

3029. Halpern, Stephen C. "Assessing the Litigative Role of ACLU Chapters." *Policy Studies Journal* 4 (Winter 1975): 157-161.

3030. Harris, Robert J. "Impact of the Cold War upon Civil Liberties." *Journal of Politics* 18 (February 1956): 3-16.

3031. Hennings, Thomas C., Jr. "The United States Supreme Court: The Ultimate Guardian of Our Freedom." *Ameri-*

can Bar Association Journal 44 (March 1958): 213-215.

3032. Holzer, Henry M. *Sweet Land of Liberty? The Supreme Court and Individual Rights.* Costa Mesa, CA: Common Sense Press, 1983.

3033. Holzer, Phyllis T., and Henry M. Holzer. "Liberty or Equality? How the Court Chose Equality." *Modern Age* 8 (Spring 1964): 134-142.

3034. Kauper, Paul G. *Civil Liberties and the Constitution.* Ann Arbor: University of Michigan Press, 1962.

3035. Konvitz, Milton R. *Expanding Liberties: Freedom's Gains in Postwar America.* New York: Viking Press, 1966.

3036. Latham, Earl. "The Supreme Court and Civil Liberty." *American Government Annual* 1958/1959 (1959): 1-26.

3037. Latham, Earl. "The Supreme Court's Crusade for Freedom: Balancing the Interests of Society and the Individual." *Commentary* 28 (August 1959): 108-117.

3038. Leahy, James E. "Tinkling Cymbals and Sounding Brass: 'Liberty' and 'Justice' in the Supreme Court Adjudication." *California Western Law Review* 8 (Winter 1972): 189-234.

3039. Lee, Francis G., ed. *Neither Conservative nor Liberal: The Burger Court on Civil Rights and Liberties.* Malabar, FL: R. E. Krieger Publishing Company, 1983.

3040. Lee, Rex E. "The Supreme Court's 1983 Term: Individual Rights, Freedom, and the Statue of Liberty." *Georgia Law Review* 19 (Fall 1984): 1-13.

3041. Loeb, Louis S. "Judicial Blocs and Judicial Values in Civil Liberties Cases Decided by the Supreme Court and the United States Court of Appeals for the District of Columbia." *American University Law Review* 14 (June 1965): 146-177.

3042. Loper, Merle W. "Court of Chief Justice Hughes: Contributions to Civil Liberties." *Wayne Law Review* 12 (Spring 1966): 535-595.

3043. Lyons, Thomas. *The Supreme Court and Individual Rights in Contemporary Society.* Menlo Park, CA: Addison-Wesley, 1975.

3044. McCloskey, Robert G. "Deeds without Doctrines: Civil Rights in the 1960 Term of the Supreme Court." *American Political Science Review* 56 (March 1962): 71-89.

3045. McCloskey, Robert G. "The Supreme Court Finds a Role: Civil Liberties in the 1955 Term." *Virginia Law Review* 42 (October 1956): 735-760.

3046. McCloskey, Robert G. "Tools, Stumbling Blocks, and Stepping Stones: Civil Liberties in the 1957 Term of the Supreme Court." *Virginia Law Review* 44 (November 1958): 1029-1055.

3047. McCloskey, Robert G. "Useful Toil or the Paths of Glory? Civil Liberties in the 1956 Term of the Supreme Court." *Virginia Law Review* 43 (October 1957): 803-855.

3048. Macey, Robert L. *Our American Leviathan Unbound: The Judicial Perversion of American Freedom.* Brooklyn, NY: Gaus, 1974.

3049. MacKenzie, John P. "Lost Court." *Civil Liberties Review* 3 (October/November 1976): 36-53.

3050. Mason, Alpheus T. "The Warren Court and the Bill of Rights." *Yale Review* 56 (December 1966): 197-211.

3051. Morgan, Donald G. "The Marshall Court and Civil Liberties." In *Aspects of Liberty: Essays Presented to Robert E. Cushman,* edited by Milton R. Konvitz and Clinton Rossiter, 163-178. Ithaca, NY: Cornell University Press, 1958.

3052. Morgan, Richard E. "The Right to

Know." *Policy Studies Journal* 4 (Winter 1975): 141-145.

3053. Murphy, Walter F. "Deeds under a Doctrine: Civil Liberties in the 1963 Term." *American Political Science Review* 59 (March 1965): 64-79.

3054. O'Brian, John L. "New Encroachments on Individual Freedom." *Harvard Law Review* 66 (November 1952): 1-27.

3055. Oddo, Gilbert L. *Freedom and Equality: Civil Liberties and the Supreme Court.* Santa Monica, CA: Goodyear Publishing Company, 1979.

3056. Pfeffer, Leo. *The Liberties of an American: The Supreme Court Speaks.* Boston: Beacon Press, 1963.

3057. Pollitt, Daniel H. "Should the Supreme Court Be 'Curbed'? A Presentation of Civil Liberties Decisions in the 1957-1958 Term." *North Carolina Law Review* 37 (December 1958): 17-57.

3058. Porter, Paul A. "The Supreme Court and Individual Liberties since 1952." *Kentucky Law Journal* 48 (Fall 1959): 48-62.

3059. Pritchett, C. Herman. *Civil Liberties and the Vinson Court.* Chicago: University of Chicago Press, 1954.

3060. Pritchett, C. Herman. *Constitutional Civil Liberties.* Englewood Cliffs, NJ: Prentice-Hall, 1984.

3061. Pritchett, C. Herman. "Libertarian Motivations on the Vinson Court." *American Political Science Review* 47 (June 1953): 321-336.

3062. Robison, Joseph B. "The Civil Rights and Civil Liberties Decisions of the United States Supreme Court for the 1965-1966 Term." *Law in Transition Quarterly* 3 (Fall 1966): 236-251.

3063. Selakovich, Daniel. *The Supreme Court: Does It Protect or Limit Our Freedoms?* Boston: Allyn and Bacon, 1976.

3064. Spaeth, Harold J. "Burger Court Review of State Court Civil Liberties Decisions." *Judicature* 68 (February/March 1985): 285-291.

3065. Spicer, George W. *Supreme Court and Fundamental Freedoms.* 2d ed. New York: Prentice-Hall, 1967.

3066. Steamer, Robert J. "Contemporary Supreme Court Directions in Civil Liberties." *Political Science Quarterly* 92 (Fall 1977): 425-442.

3067. Stockham, John R. "Summary of Civil Liberties Cases in the 1945 Term of the Supreme Court of the United States." *National Bar Journal* 4 (December 1946): 287-344.

3068. Thomas, William R. *The Burger Court and Civil Liberties.* Brunswick, OH: Kings Court Communications, 1976.

3069. Ulmer, S. Sidney. "Supreme Court Behavior and Civil Rights." *Western Political Quarterly* 13 (June 1960): 288-311.

3070. Witt, Elder. *The Supreme Court and Individual Rights.* 2d ed. Washington, DC: Congressional Quarterly, 1988.

First Amendment and Substantive Rights

General Studies

3071. Arons, Stephen. "The Separation of School and State: *Pierce* Reconsidered." *Harvard Educational Review* 46 (February 1976): 76-104.

3072. Bell, Barry R. "Prisoners' Rights, Institutional Needs, and the Burger Court." *Virginia Law Review* 72 (February 1986): 161-193.

3073. Berkby, Robert H. "Supreme Court Libertarians and the First Amendment: An Analysis of Voting and Opinion Agreement, 1956-1964." *Social Science Quarterly* 48 (March 1968): 586-594.

3074. Bernard, Burton C. "Avoidance of

Constitutional Issues in the United States Supreme Court: Liberties of the First Amendment." *Michigan Law Review* 50 (December 1951): 261-296.

3075. Berns, Walter. *The First Amendment and the Future of American Democracy*. New York: Basic Books, 1976.

3076. Berns, Walter. *Freedom, Virtue, and the First Amendment*. Baton Rouge: Louisiana State University Press, 1957.

3077. Bogen, David S. *Bulwark of Liberty: The Court and the First Amendment*. Millwood, NY: Associated Faculty Press, 1984.

3078. Bogen, David S. "First Amendment Ancillary Doctrines." *Maryland Law Review* 37 (Fall 1978): 679-738.

3079. Bonnicksen, Andrea L. *Civil Rights and Liberties*. Palo Alto, CA: Mayfield, 1982.

3080. Brady, Joseph H. *Confusion Twice Confounded: The First Amendment and the Supreme Court, A Historical Study*. South Orange, NJ: Seton Hall University Press, 1955.

3081. Burr, Steven J. "Immigration and the First Amendment." *California Law Review* 73 (December 1985): 1889-1928.

3082. Cole, David. "Agon at Agora: Creative Misreadings in the First Amendment Tradition." *Yale Law Journal* 95 (April 1986): 857-905.

3083. Cooper, Phillip J. "The Supreme Court, the First Amendment, and Freedom of Information." *Public Administration Review* 46 (November/December 1986): 622-628.

3084. Cover, Robert M. "Left, the Right, and the First Amendment: 1918-1928." *Maryland Law Review* 40 (Summer 1981): 349-388.

3085. Easton, Earnest L. "Licensing, Public Policy, and the Supreme Court." Ph.D. diss., Cornell University, 1978.

3086. Elkins, Bettye S. "Constitutional Problems of Population Control." *Journal of Law Reform* 4 (Fall 1970): 63-84.

3087. Emerson, Thomas I. "Colonial Intention and Current Realities of the First Amendment." *University of Pennsylvania Law Review* 125 (April 1977): 737-760.

3088. Emerson, Thomas I. "First Amendment Doctrine and the Burger Court." *California Law Review* 68 (May 1980): 422-481.

3089. Falls, Harold N., Jr. "Amendment Vagueness and Overbreadth: Theoretical Revisions by the Burger Court." *Vanderbilt Law Review* 31 (April 1978): 609-637.

3090. Fellman, David, ed. *The Supreme Court and Education*. New York: Teacher's College, Columbia University, 1969.

3091. Flygare, Thomas J. "Supreme Court Agrees to Reconsider First Amendment Rights of Students." *Phi Delta Kappan* 67 (December 1985): 312-313.

3092. Freeman, Brian A. "The Supreme Court and First Amendment Rights of Students in the Public School Classroom: A Proposed Model of Analysis." *Hastings Constitutional Law Quarterly* 12 (Fall 1984): 1-70.

3093. Gard, Stephen W. "The Flag Salute Cases and the First Amendment." *Cleveland State Law Review* 31 (Summer 1982): 419-453.

3094. Gibbs, Annette, and Graylord Crisp. "Question of First Amendment Rights vs. Mandatory Student Activity Fees." *Journal of Law and Education* 8 (April 1979): 185-196.

3095. Gibbs, Annette, and Miriam Jernigan. "Commercial Activity on Campus: Where Does It End?" *National Association of Student Personnel Administration Journal* 18 (Summer 1980): 28-32.

3096. Haiman, Franklyn S., and Martin H. Redish. "Comments on Martin

Redish's 'The Warren Court, the Burger Court, and the First Amendment Overbreadth Doctrine'." *Northwestern University Law Review* 78 (December 1983): 1031-1070, 1071-1076.

3097. Hemmer, Joseph J., Jr. *The Supreme Court and the First Amendment.* New York: Praeger, 1986.

3098. Hill, Alfred. "Defamation and Privacy under the First Amendment." *Columbia Law Review* 76 (December 1976): 1205-1313.

3099. Horn, Robert A. *Groups and the Constitution.* Stanford, CA: Stanford University Press, 1965.

3100. Hughes, Gregory L. "The Supreme Court's Limiting of First Amendment Protection for Defendants in Defamation Cases." *North Carolina Central Law Journal* 16 (1986): 171-206.

3101. Hughes, Michael H. "*CIA v. Sims*: Supreme Court Deference to Agency Interpretation of FOIA Exemption Three." *Catholic University Law Review* 35 (Fall 1985): 279-306.

3102. Hunter, Howard O. "Problems in Search of Principles: The First Amendment in the Supreme Court from 1791-1930." *Emory Law Journal* 35 (Winter 1986): 59-137.

3103. Irons, Peter. *The Courage of Their Convictions: Sixteen Americans Who Fought Their Way to the Supreme Court.* New York: Free Press, 1988.

3104. Johnson, Dennis W. "Friend of the Court: The United States Department of Justice as *Amicus Curiae* in Civil Rights Cases before the Supreme Court, 1947-1971." Ph.D. diss., Duke University, 1972.

3105. Johnson, Ralph H., and Michael Altman. "Communists in the Press: A Senate Witch-Hunt of the 1950s Revisited." *Journalism Quarterly* 55 (March 1978): 487-493.

3106. Johnson, Raymond T. "Post-War Protection of Freedom of Opinion: A Study of Supreme Court Attitudes." *Washington and Lee Law Review* 1 (Spring 1940): 192-214.

3107. Kaus, Robert M. "Zbig for Life." *Washington Monthly* 12 (June 1980): 25-32.

3108. Keele, Robert L. "The Supreme Court, Totalitarianism, and the National Security of Democratic America, 1941-1960." Ph.D. diss., Emory University, 1960.

3109. Leahy, James E. "The Public Employee and the First Amendment: Must He Sacrifice His Civil Rights to Be a Civil Servant?" *California Western Law Review* 4 (Spring 1968): 1-17.

3110. Levin-Epstein, Eve. "Rhetoric of the Supreme Court: A Dramatic Analysis of First Amendment Dissenting Opinions." Ph.D. diss., Temple University, 1978.

3111. Lucie, Patricia. "On Being a Free Person and a Citizen by Constitutional Amendment." *Journal of American Studies* (Great Britain) 12 (December 1978): 343-358.

3112. Ludlow, William L. *The American Constitution.* New Concord, OH: Radcliffe Press, 1941.

3113. Meiklejohn, Alexander. *Political Freedom: The Constitutional Powers of the People.* New York: Harper and Row, 1960.

3114. Melton, Gary B. "Child Witnesses and the First Amendment: A Psychological Dilemma." *Journal of Social Issues* 40 (Summer 1984): 109-123.

3115. Murphy, Paul L. *World War I and the Origin of Civil Liberties.* New York: W. W. Norton, 1979.

3116. Murphy, Walter F. "Civil Liberties and the Japanese American Cases: A Study in the Uses of *Stare Decisis*." *West-*

ern Political Quarterly 11 (March 1958): 3-13.

3117. Nathanson, Nathaniel L. "The Communist Trial and the Clear and Present Danger Test." *Harvard Law Review* 63 (May 1950): 1167-1175.

3118. Peterson, Walfred H. "Courts and Freedom of Conscience." *Religion in Life* 40 (Summer 1971): 247-256.

3119. Rabban, David M. "The First Amendment and Its Forgotten Years." *Yale Law Review* 90 (January 1981): 514-595.

3120. Redish, Martin H. "The Warren Court, the Burger Court, and the First Amendment Overbreadth Doctrine." *Northwestern University Law Review* 78 (December 1983): 1031-1070.

3121. Selvar, Drew K. "Legal Thinking in Six Selected Civil Liberties Decisions of the Warren Court." Ph.D. diss., Southern Illinois University, 1973.

3122. Shapiro, Martin M. "The Supreme Court and the First Amendment." Ph.D. diss., Harvard University, 1961.

3123. Sickal, James D. "Legal Tests to Determine the Constitutionality of Statutes Restricting First Amendment Freedoms." *Missouri Law Review* 26 (November 1961): 471-500.

3124. Spaeth, Edmund B., Jr. "Where Is the High Court Heading?" *Judges Journal* 24 (Summer 1985): 10-13.

3125. Van Alstyne, William W. *Interpretations of the First Amendment.* Durham, NC: Duke University Press, 1984.

3126. Weber, Paul J. "Excessive Entanglement: A Wavering First Amendment Standard." *Review of Politics* 46 (October 1984): 483-501.

3127. Wirin, A. L. "The Progress of Freedom in the Supreme Court." *Boston University Law Review* 15 (April 1935): 249-259.

3128. Zashin, Elliot. "The Progress of Black Americans in Civil Rights: The Past Two Decades Assessed." *Daedalus* 107 (Winter 1978): 239-262.

Association

3129. Abernathy, Glenn. *The Right of Assembly and Association.* Columbia: University of South Carolina Press, 1961.

3130. American Civil Liberties Union. *The Smith Act and the Supreme Court.* New York: American Civil Liberties Union, 1952.

3131. Benton, Fred. *Studies in Campus Law: The Legal Issues of* Pratz v. Louisiana State Board of Education. Baton Rouge, LA: Eagle Press, 1971.

3132. Bontecou, Eleanor. *The Federal Loyalty-Security Program.* Ithaca, NY: Cornell University Press, 1953.

3133. Boudin, Louis B. " 'Seditious Doctrines' and 'Clear and Present Danger' Rule." *Virginia Law Review* 38 (February 1952): 143-186; (April 1952): 315-356.

3134. Brown, Ralph S., Jr. *Loyalty and Security: Employment Tests in the United States.* New Haven, CT: Yale University Press, 1958.

3135. Celada, Raymond J., and Charles V. Dale. *Cases Related to Subversive Activities Appealed to the Supreme Court of the United States.* Washington, DC: Congressional Research Service, 1975.

3136. Chapin, Bradley. *The American Law of Treason: Revolutionary and Early American Origins.* Seattle: University of Washington Press, 1964.

3137. Chase, Harold W. *Security and Liberty: The Problem of Native Communists, 1947-1955.* Garden City, NJ: Doubleday, 1954.

3138. Cord, Robert L. *Protest, Dissent,*

and the Supreme Court. Cambridge, MA: Winthrop, 1971.

3139. Corwin, Edward S. "Bowing Out 'Clear and Present Danger'." *Notre Dame Lawyer* 27 (Spring 1952): 325-359.

3140. Cramton, Roger C. "The Supreme Court and State Power to Deal with Subversion and Loyalty." *Minnesota Law Review* 43 (May 1959): 1025-1082.

3141. Fraenkel, Osmond K. "The Smith Act Reconsidered." *Lawyers Guild Review* 16 (Winter 1956): 149-154.

3142. Fraenkel, Osmond K. "The Supreme Court and National Security." *Washington Law Review* 33 (Winter 1958): 343-363.

3143. Gellhorn, Walter. *Security, Loyalty, and Science.* Ithaca, NY: Cornell University Press, 1950.

3144. Gellhorn, Walter. *The States and Subversion.* Ithaca, NY: Cornell University Press, 1952.

3145. Gorfinkel, John A., and Julian W. Mack, III. "*Dennis v. United States* and the Clear and Present Danger Rule." *California Law Review* 39 (December 1951): 475-501.

3146. Herbert, Paul B., and Kathryn A. Young. "Political Association under the Burger Court: Fading Protection." *U.C. Davis Law Review* 15 (Fall 1981): 53-93.

3147. McTernan, John T. "*Schware, Konigsberg*, and Independence of the Bar: The Return to Reason." *Lawyers Guild Review* 17 (Summer 1957): 48-53.

3148. Markowitz, Gerald E., and Michael Meerpol. "The 'Crime of the Century' Revisited: David Greenglass' Scientific Evidence in the *Rosenberg* Case." *Science and Society* 44 (Spring 1980): 1-26.

3149. Mendelson, Wallace. "The Degradation of the Clear and Present Danger

Rule." *Journal of Politics* 15 (August 1953): 349-355.

3150. Neier, Aryeh. "Protest Movements among the Disenfranchised." *Civil Liberties Review* 1 (Fall 1973): 49-74.

3151. Ober, Frank B. "Communism and the Court: An Examination of Recent Developments." *American Bar Association Journal* 44 (January 1958): 35-38.

3152. Raggi, Reena. "An Independent Right to Freedom of Association." *Harvard Civil Rights-Civil Liberties Law Review* 12 (Winter 1977): 1-30.

3153. Rice, Charles E. "Sit-Ins: Proceed with Caution." *Missouri Law Review* 29 (Winter 1964): 39-70.

3154. Robinson, Marvin S. "Constitutional Law: Administrative Law: Statutory Construction; Relation of the Supreme Court and the Executive in the Federal Loyalty Program; *Peters v. Hobby.*" *Cornell Law Quarterly* 42 (Fall 1956): 90-99.

3155. Ruja, Harry. "The Communist Menace, the Supreme Court, and Academic Freedom." *Western Political Quarterly* 14 (September 1961): 715-726.

3156. Schaar, John H. *Loyalty in America.* Berkeley: University of California Press, 1957.

3157. Schmandt, Henry J. "The Clear and Present Danger Doctrine ... A Reappraisal in the Light of *Dennis v. U.S.*" *St. Louis University Law Journal* 1 (Winter 1951): 265-276.

3158. Schofield, Daniel L. "The Constitutionality of Organizational Limitations on the Associational Freedom of Law Enforcement Employees." *FBI Law Enforcement Bulletin* 55 (August 1986): 23-30.

3159. Somerville, John. "Law, Logic, and Revolution: The Smith Act." *Western Political Quarterly* 14 (December 1961): 839-849.

3160. Strong, Frank R. "Fifty Years of 'Clear and Present Danger': From *Schenck* to *Brandenburg* and Beyond." *Supreme Court Review* 1969 (1969): 41-80.

3161. Unger, John. "Subversion and the Warren Court." *American Mercury* 90 (January 1960): 48-57.

3162. Wham, Benjamin. "The Blind Goddess Balances Her Scales: The Supreme Court and Internal Security." *American Bar Association Journal* 46 (March 1960): 271-273.

3163. Williams, Jerre S. "National Security and the Supreme Court." *Texas Quarterly* 1 (Summer/Autumn 1958): 10-26.

Expression

3164. Alfange, Dean, Jr. "The Role of the Supreme Court in the Protection of Freedom of Expression in the United States." Ph.D diss., Cornell University, 1967.

3165. Aranson, Peter H., and Kenneth A. Shepsle. "The Compensation of Public Officials as a Campaign Issue: An Economic Analysis of *Brown v. Hartlage.*" *Supreme Court Economic Review* 2 (1983): 213-276.

3166. Bedi, Ajit S. *Freedom of Expression and Security: A Comparative Study of the Function of the Supreme Courts of the United States of America and India.* Bombay: Asia Publishing House, 1966.

3167. Bickel, Alexander M. *The Morality of Consent.* New Haven, CT: Yale University Press, 1974.

3168. Bork, Robert H. "First Amendment Does Not Give Greater Freedom to the Press Than to Speech." *Center Magazine* 12 (March 1979): 28-34.

3169. Burdette, Robert B. *Buckley v. Valeo: The Opinion of the United States Supreme Court in the Election Campaign Case; Summary and Commentary.* Washington, DC: Congressional Research Service, 1975.

3170. Carmen, Ira H. *Movies, Censorship, and the Law.* Ann Arbor: University of Michigan Press, 1966.

3171. Carrafiello, Vincent A. "Weighing the First Amendment on the Scales of the Balancing Test: The Choice of Safety before Liberty." *Southern University Law Review* 8 (Spring 1982): 255-300.

3172. Cohn, Roy M., and Thomas A. Bolan. "The Supreme Court and the A.B.A. Report and Resolutions." *Fordham Law Review* 28 (Summer 1958): 233-286.

3173. Cox, Archibald. "The Supreme Court, 1979 Term: Freedom of Expression in the Burger Court." *Harvard Law Review* 94 (November 1980): 1-73.

3174. Downs, Donald A. *Nazis in Skokie: Freedom, Community, and the First Amendment.* Notre Dame, IN: University of Notre Dame Press, 1985.

3175. Ehrmann, Henry W. "Zeitgeist and the Supreme Court." *Antioch Review* 11 (December 1951): 424-436.

3176. Emerson, Thomas I. *The System of Freedom of Expression.* New York: Random House, 1970.

3177. Fisher, Louis. "Supreme Court on Defamation." *Nation* 223 (November 1976): 485-487.

3178. Fleener-Marzec, Nickieann. "D. W. Griffith's the *Birth of a Nation*: Suppression, and the First Amendment as It Applies to Filmic Expression, 1915-1973." Ph.D. diss., University of Wisconsin, 1977.

3179. Fraenkel, Osmond K. "War, Civil Liberties, and the Supreme Court, 1941-1946." *Yale Law Journal* 55 (June 1946): 715-734.

3180. Gibson, Michael T. "The Supreme Court and Freedom of Expression from 1791-1917." *Fordham Law Review* 55 (December 1986): 263-333.

3181. Gordon, Charles. "Denaturalization in the Supreme Court." *Federal Bar Association Journal* 8 (January 1947): 172-189.

3182. Graham, Fred P. "The Supreme Court and the Flag." *Art in America* (March/April 1971): 27-30.

3183. Haight, Anne L. *Banned Books, 387 B.C. to 1978 A.D.* 4th ed. New York: R. R. Bowker, 1978.

3184. Haiman, Franklyn S. "Nonverbal Communication and the First Amendment: The Rhetoric of the Streets Revisited." *Quarterly Journal of Speech* 68 (November 1982): 371-383.

3185. Hale, Frank D. "Freedom of Expression: The Warren and Burger Courts." *Communications and the Law* 9 (December 1987): 3-21.

3186. Hannigan, Thomas H., Jr. "First Amendment Theory Applied to the Right of Publicity." *Boston College Law Review* 19 (January 1978): 277-294.

3187. Heck, Edward V., and Albert C. Ringelstein. "The Burger Court and the Primacy of Political Expression." *Western Political Quarterly* 40 (September 1987): 413-426.

3188. Hudon, Edward G. "The Evolution of First Amendment Doctrines in the Supreme Court: An Historical Study of Cases on Freedom of Expression." Ph.D. diss., George Washington University, 1962.

3189. Hurwitz, Leon. *Historical Dictionary of Censorship in the United States.* Westport, CT: Greenwood Press, 1985.

3190. Kerr, Baine. "*Bates v. State Bar of Arizona*: A Consumers' Rights Interpretation of the First Amendment Ends Bans on Legal Advertising." *Denver Law Journal* 55 (Winter 1978): 103-155.

3191. Kimmell, James, Jr. "Politics and the Non-Civil Service Public Employee: A Categorical Approach to First Amendment Protection." *Columbia Law Review* 85 (April 1985): 558-581.

3192. Konvitz, Milton R. *Fundamental Liberties of a Free People: Religion, Speech, Press, Assembly.* Ithaca, NY: Cornell University Press, 1957.

3193. Kreiter, Robert B. "Judicial Review of Student First Amendment Claims: Assessing the Legitimacy-Competency Debate." *Missouri Law Review* 50 (Winter 1985): 25-84.

3194. Krislov, Samuel. *The Supreme Court and Political Freedom.* New York: Free Press, 1968.

3195. LaMarche, Gara. "After Skokie: New Directions for Civil Liberties." *New York Affairs* 6 (1980): 84-91.

3196. Leffler, Keith B. "Prohibition of Billboard Advertising: An Economic Analysis of the Metromedia Decision." *Supreme Court Economic Review* 1 (1982): 113-134.

3197. Lynn, Conrad. "We Must Disobey." *New York University Law Review* 43 (October 1968): 648-650.

3198. Nagy, Alex. "Federal Censorship of Communist Political Propaganda and the First Amendment: 1941-1961." Ph.D. diss., University of Wisconsin, 1973.

3199. Neier, Aryeh. *Defending My Enemy: American Nazis, the Skokie Case, and the Risks of Freedom.* New York: Dutton, 1979.

3200. Nimmer, Melville B. "The Constitutionality of Official Censorship of Motion Pictures." *University of Chicago Law Review* 25 (Summer 1958): 625-657.

3201. Parker, J. Wilson. "Free Expression and the Function of the Jury." *Boston University Law Review* 65 (May 1985): 483-557.

3202. Pritchett, C. Herman. *The Political Offender and the Warren Court.* Boston: Boston University Press, 1958.

3203. Puner, Nicholas W. "Civil Disobedience: An Analysis and Rationale." *New York University Law Review* 43 (October 1968): 648-720.

3204. Quick, Albert T. "What Johnny Can't Read: The Supreme Court Book Removal." *Journal of Law and Education* 12 (January 1983): 116-126.

3205. Richards, Eric L. "In Search of a Consensus on the Future of Campaign Finance Laws: *California Medical Association v. Federal Election Commission.*" *American Business Law Journal* 20 (Summer 1982): 243-267.

3206. Rosenthal, Albert J. "Constitution and Campaign Finance Regulation after *Buckley v. Valeo.*" *Annals of the American Academy of Political and Social Science* 425 (May 1976): 124-133.

3207. Rudman, Norman G., and Richard C. Solomon. "Who Loves a Parade: *Walker v. City of Birmingham.*" *Law in Transition Quarterly* 4 (December 1967): 185-219.

3208. Smith, Don L. "The Right to Petition for Redress of Grievances: Constitutional Development and Interpretation." Ph.D. diss., Texas Tech University, 1971.

3209. Sorauf, Frank J. "Caught in a Political Thicket: The Supreme Court and Campaign Finance." *Constitutional Commentary* 3 (Winter 1986): 97-121.

3210. Starr, Isadore. "Recent Supreme Court Decisions: Censorship of Films." *Social Education* 26 (January 1962): 19-22.

3211. Stephens, Ronald W. "Study of U.S. Supreme Court Decisions from 1970 to 1977 as the Basis for Developing Policy for Censorship of Curriculum Materials by American Public Schools." Ph.D. diss., University of Nebraska, 1978.

3212. Stine, Alan C. "Base Access and the First Amendment: The Rights of Civilians on Military Installations." *Air Force Law Review* 18 (Fall 1976): 18-32.

3213. Strauber, Ira L. "Transforming Political Rights into Legal Ones." *Polity* 16 (Fall 1983): 72-95.

3214. Westin, Alan F., and Barry Mahoney. *The Trial of Martin Luther King.* New York: Crowell, 1975.

3215. Wright, J. Skelly. "Politics and the Constitution: Is Money Speech?" *Yale Law Journal* 85 (July 1976): 1001-1021.

3216. Yarbrough, Tinsley E. "Burger Court and the Freedom of Expression." *Washington and Lee Law Review* 33 (Winter 1976): 37-90.

Obscenity

3217. Bruce, William R. *The Bruce Resolution Debate.* Glen Rock, NJ: Microfilming Corporations of America, 1976.

3218. Burgess, Wells D. "Obscenity Prosecution: Artistic Value and the Concept of Immunity." *New York University Law Review* 39 (December 1964): 1063-1086.

3219. Byrne, Edward T. "Government Seizures of Imported Obscene Matter: Section 305 of Tariff Act of 1930 and Recent Supreme Court Obscenity Decisions." *Columbia Journal of Transnational Law* 13 (Winter 1974): 114-142.

3220. Coupe, Bradford. "The *Roth* Test and Its Corollaries." *William and Mary Law Review* 8 (Fall 1966): 121-132.

3221. Curtis, Michael K. "Obscenity: The Justices' (Not So) New Robes." *Campbell Law Review* 8 (Summer 1986): 387-419.

3222. Daniels, Stephen. "Supreme Court and Obscenity: An Exercise in Empirical Constitutional Policy-Making." *San Diego Law Review* 17 (July 1980): 757-799.

3223. Devol, Kenneth S. "The *Ginzburg* Decision: Reactions in California." *Journalism Quarterly* 45 (Summer 1968): 271-278.

3224. Driver, Tom F. "Obscenity and the

Court." *Christianity and Crisis* 26 (May 2, 1966): 81-82.

3225. Fahringer, Herald P. "Censorship and Pornography: Interview." *Humanist* 37 (July 1977): 30-33.

3226. Fahringer, Herald P., and Michael J. Brown. "The Rise and Fall of *Roth*: A Critique of the Recent Supreme Court Obscenity Decisions." *Kentucky Law Journal* 62 (1973/1974): 731-768.

3227. Fahringer, Herald P., and Michael J. Brown. "The Rise and Fall of *Roth*: Critique of the Recent Supreme Court Obscenity Decisions." *Criminal Law Bulletin* 10 (November 1974): 785-826.

3228. Fields, Howard. "Supreme Court May Redefine Obscenity." *Publisher's Weekly* 227 (March 8, 1985): 37-38.

3229. Fields, Howard. "Supreme Court Upholds New York Kiddieporn Law." *Publisher's Weekly* 222 (July 23, 1982): 66-68.

3230. Friedman, Leon. "The *Ginzburg* Decision and the Law." *American Scholar* 36 (Winter 1966/1967): 71-91.

3231. Friedman, Leon, ed. *Obscenity: The Complete Oral Arguments before the Supreme Court in the Major Obscenity Cases.* New York: Chelsea House, 1981.

3232. Friedman, Mel. "Judicial Ticket: Supreme Court and Obscenity." *Nation* 225 (August 1977): 110-113.

3233. Funston, Richard Y. "Pornography and Politics: The Court, the Constitution, and the Commission." *Western Political Quarterly* 24 (December 1971): 635-652.

3234. George, B. James, Jr. "Obscenity Litigation: An Overview of Current Legal Controversies." *National Journal of Criminal Defense* 3 (Fall 1977): 189-217.

3235. Grunes, Rodney A. "Obscenity Law and the Justices: Reversing Policy on the Supreme Court." *Seton Hall Law Review* 9 (1978): 403-473.

3236. Harris, Albert W., Jr. "Movie Censorship and the Supreme Court: What Next?" *California Law Review* 42 (Spring 1954): 122-138.

3237. Hayes, John C. "Survey of a Decade of Decisions on the Law of Obscenity." *Catholic Lawyer* 8 (Spring 1962): 93-109.

3238. Heishman, Stanley. "Obscenity and the Supreme Court." *Censorship Today* 1 (1968): 4-13.

3239. Israel, Jerold H., and Rita A. Burns. "Juvenile Obscenity Statutes: A Proposal and Analysis." *University of Michigan Journal of Law Reform* 9 (Spring 1976): 415-527.

3240. Kamp, John. "Obscenity and the Supreme Court: A Communication Approach to a Persistent Judicial Problem." *Communications and the Law* 2 (Summer 1980): 1-42.

3241. Kobylka, Joseph F. "A Court-Created Context for Group Litigation: Libertarian Groups and Obscenity." *Journal of Politics* 49 (November 1987): 1061-1078.

3242. Leventhal, Harold. "Confusion Worse Confounded: The Supreme Court and Obscenity Law." *New York University Law Review* 52 (October 1977): 820-859.

3243. Leventhal, Harold. "The 1973 Round of Obscenity-Pornography Decisions." *American Bar Association Journal* 59 (November 1973): 1261-1266.

3244. Levine, George D. "Sexual Sensationalism and the First Amendment: The Supreme Court's Questionable Regime of Obscenity Adjudication." *New York State Bar Journal* 42 (April 1970): 193-206.

3245. Levine, Stephen. "Pornography and Law: Latest U.S. Developments." *New Zealand Law Journal* 1973 (November 20, 1973): 497-502.

3246. Lockhart, William B., and Robert C. McClure. "Censorship of Obscenity:

The Developing Constitutional Standard." *Minnesota Law Review* 45 (November 1960): 5-121.

3247. Milligan, William W. "Obscenity: *Malum in Se* or Only in Context? The Supreme Court's Long Ordeal." *Capital University Law Review* 7 (Fall 1978): 631-645.

3248. Monaghan, Henry P. "Obscenity, 1966: The Marriage of Obscenity *Per Se* and Obscenity *Per Quod*." *Yale Law Journal* 76 (November 1966): 127-157.

3249. Morreale, Justin P. "Obscenity: An Analysis and Statutory Proposal." *Wisconsin Law Review* 1969 (1969): 421-468.

3250. Mott, Kenneth F., and Christine Kellett. "Obscenity, Community Standards, and the Burger Court: From Deference to Disarray." *Suffolk University Law Review* 13 (Winter 1979): 14-26.

3251. Murphy, Terrence J. "Some Constitutional Questions Involved in the Governmental Control of Obscenity, Their Historical Developments, and Their Present Status as Indicated in Recent Decisions of the United States Supreme Court." Ph.D. diss., Georgetown University, 1959.

3252. Nagel, Stuart S., and Marian Neef. "Judicial Behavior in Pornography Cases." *Journal of Urban Law* 52 (August 1974): 1-23.

3253. "Obscenity 1973: Something Old, a Little Bit New, Quite a Bit Borrowed, but Nothing Blue." *Maryland Law Review* 33 (1973): 421-460.

3254. Pearce, W. Barnett, and Dwight L. Teeter, Jr. "OBSC*N*TY: Historical and Behavioral Perspectives." *Intellect* 104 (November 1975): 166-170.

3255. Pilpel, Harriet F., and Marjorie T. Parsons. "Dirty Business in Court." *Civil Liberties Review* 1 (Fall 1974): 30-41.

3256. Proviser, Norman W. "Of Lines and Men: The Supreme Court, Obscenity, and the Issue of the Avertable Eye." *Tulsa Law Journal* 13 (1977): 52-81.

3257. Ragsdale, J. Donald. "Last Tango in Paris, et al. v. the Supreme Court: The Current State of Obscenity Law." *Quarterly Journal of Speech* 61 (October 1975): 279-287.

3258. Randall, Richard S. "Obscenity: Denationalization and the Conflict of Cosmopolitan and Local Popular Values." *Policy Studies Journal* 14 (Winter 1975): 151-156.

3259. Roberts, H. Buswell. "Supreme Court Takes Another Look at Obscenity." *University of Toledo Law Review* 5 (Fall 1973): 113-132.

3260. Rogge, O. John. "High Court of Obscenity, I." *University of Colorado Law Review* 41 (1968): 1-59.

3261. Rogge, O. John. "The Obscenity Terms of the Court." *Villanova Law Review* 17 (February 1972): 393-462.

3262. Rosenblum, Robert. "Judicial Politics of Obscenity." *Pepperdine Law Review* 3 (Winter 1975): 1-25.

3263. Schnall, Marc. "United States Supreme Court: Definitions of Obscenity." *Crime and Delinquency* 18 (January 1972): 59-67.

3264. Semonche, John E. "Definitional and Contextual Obscenity: The Supreme Court's New and Disturbing Accommodation." *UCLA Law Review* 13 (August 1966): 1173-1213.

3265. Serebnick, Judith. "The 1973 Court Rulings on Obscenity: Have They Made a Difference?" *Wilson Library Bulletin* 50 (December 1975): 304-310.

3266. Sunderland, Lane V. *Obscenity: The Court, the Congress, and the President's*

Commission. Washington, DC: American Enterprise Institute for Public Policy Research, 1975.

3267. Tedford, Thomas. "What Every Teacher Should Know about Supreme Court Obscenity Decisions." *English Journal* 63 (October 1974): 20-21.

3268. Wallace, Paul S. *Regulation of Obscenity: A Compilation of Federal and State Statutes and Analysis of Selected Supreme Court Opinions.* Washington, DC: Congressional Research Service, 1975.

3269. Wilson, W. Cody. "Pornography: The Emergence of a Social Issue and the Beginning of Psychological Study." *Journal of Social Issues* 29 (1978): 7-18.

Press

3270. Ablard, Charles D. "Obscenity, Advertising, and Publishing: The Impact of *Ginzburg* and *Mishkin*." *George Washington Law Review* 35 (October 1966): 85-92.

3271. Abrams, Floyd. "The Supreme Court Turns a New Page in Libel." *American Bar Association Journal* 70 (August 1984): 89-91.

3272. Adair, Donald R. "Free Speech and Defamation of Public Persons: The Expanding Doctrine of *New York Times Co. v. Sullivan*." *Cornell Law Quarterly* 52 (Winter 1967): 419-432.

3273. Allen, Richard B. "Validity of Restrictive Order of Prior Restraint Pending for Decision by Supreme Court." *American Bar Association Journal* 62 (June 1976): 770-772.

3274. Ashdown, Gerald G. "*Gertz* and *Firestone*: A Study of Constitutional Policy Making." *Minnesota Law Review* 61 (1977): 645-690.

3275. Berney, Arthur L. "Libel and the First Amendment: A New Constitutional Privilege." *Virginia Law Review* 51 (January 1965): 1-58.

3276. Berney, Arthur L. "*New York Times Co. v. Sullivan*: The Scope of a Privilege." *Virginia Law Review* 51 (January 1965): 106-120.

3277. Berns, Walter. "Freedom of the Press and the Alien and Sedition Laws: A Reappraisal." *Supreme Court Review* 1970 (1970): 109-160.

3278. Bertelsman, William O. "The First Amendment and Protection of Reputation and Privacy: *New York Times Co. v. Sullivan* and How It Grew." *Kentucky Law Journal* 56 (Summer 1967/1968): 718-756.

3279. Bertelsman, William O. "Libel and Public Men: Revolution in the Law of Defamation That Was Wrought by the Supreme Court's Decision in *New York Times Co. v. Sullivan*: Some Cases That Have Arisen Since." *American Bar Association Journal* 52 (July 1966): 657-662.

3280. Bezanson, Randall P. "The New Free Press Guarantee." *Virginia Law Review* 63 (June 1977): 731-788.

3281. Bliss, Robert M. "Development of Fair Comment as a Defense to Libel." *Journalism Quarterly* 44 (Winter 1967): 627-637.

3282. Boisseau, Merribeth. "*Time Inc. v. Firestone*: The Supreme Court's Restrictive New Libel Ruling." *San Diego Law Review* 14 (March 1977): 435-457.

3283. Bolback, Cynthia J. "Access to Information: Affirming the Press's Right." *Christian Century* 97 (September 24, 1980): 879-883.

3284. Bollinger, Lee C., Jr. "Freedom of the Press and Public Access: Toward a Theory of Partial Regulation of the Mass Media." *Michigan Law Review* 75 (November 1976): 1-42.

3285. Bowers, Michael. "*Zurcher v. Stan-

ford Daily: The Supreme Court and the Limits of the First Amendment." Ph.D. diss., University of Arizona, 1983.

3286. "Broadcasters Gain Other Allies in Campaign to Cover Courts." *Broadcasting* 93 (November 28, 1977): 49-50.

3287. Cohen, Dorothy. "Advertising and the First Amendment." *Journal of Marketing* 42 (July 1978): 59-68.

3288. Denniston, Lyle. "Allies Waver on Access." *Quill* 70 (September 1982): 16-19.

3289. Denniston, Lyle. "Ball's in Burger's Court." *Quill* 71 (May 1983): 19-20.

3290. Denniston, Lyle. "The Law Giveth, the Law Taketh Away." *Quill* 72 (November 1984): 46-49.

3291. Devol, Kenneth S., ed. *Mass Media and the Supreme Court: The Legacy of the Warren Years*. 3d ed. New York: Hastings House, 1982.

3292. Drechsel, Robert E., and Deborah Moon. "Corporate Libel Plaintiffs and the News Media: An Analysis of the Public-Private Figure Distinction after *Gertz*." *American Business Law Journal* 21 (Summer 1983): 127-156.

3293. Eaton, Joel D. "The American Law of Defamation through *Gertz v. Robert Welch Inc.* and Beyond: An Analytical Primer." *Virginia Law Review* 61 (November 1975): 1349-1451.

3294. Epstein, Richard A. "Was *New York Times v. Sullivan* Wrong?" *University of Chicago Law Review* 53 (Summer 1986): 782-818.

3295. "Freedom, the Courts, and the Media." *Center Magazine* 12 (March 1979): 28-45.

3296. Freund, Paul A. "Political Libel and Freedom of the Press." *American Philosophical Society Proceedings* 112 (April 15, 1968): 117-120.

3297. Gertz, Elmer. "Gertz on *Gertz*: Re-flections on the Landmark Libel Case." *Trial* 21 (October 1985): 66-75.

3298. Gutman, Howard A. "Attempt to Develop an Appropriate Standard of Liability for the Defamation of Public and Private People: The Supreme Court and the Federalization of Libel Law." *North Carolina Central Law Journal* 10 (Spring 1979): 201-226.

3299. Hachten, William A. *The Supreme Court on the Press: Decisions and Dissents*. Ames: Iowa State University Press, 1968.

3300. Hixon, Richard F. *Mass Media and the Constitution: An Encyclopedia of Supreme Court Decisions*. New York: Garland, 1989.

3301. Hudon, Edward G. "Supreme Court of the United States and the Law of Libel: A Review of Decided Cases." *Les Cahiers de Droit* 20 (December 1979): 833-854.

3302. Hurd, Joanne. "The Press' Right of Access to Criminal Trials: *Globe Newspaper Company v. Superior Court*." *Washington University Journal of Urban and Contemporary Law* 26 (1984): 177-192.

3303. Hurst, William S. "Has *Branzburg* Buried the Underground Press?" *Harvard Civil Rights-Civil Liberties Law Review* 8 (January 1973): 181-197.

3304. Ladenson, Robert F. "Freedom of the Press: A Jurisprudential Inquiry." *Social Theory and Practice* 6 (Summer 1980): 163-185.

3305. Lashner, Marilyn A. "Privacy and the Public's Right to Know." *Journalism Quarterly* 53 (Winter 1976): 679-688.

3306. Lawhorne, Clifton O. *The Supreme Court and Libel*. Carbondale: Southern Illinois University Press, 1981.

3307. Lee, William E. "Supreme Court on Privacy and the Press." *Georgia Law Review* 12 (Winter 1978): 215-247.

3308. Leeper, Roy V. "*Richmond Newspapers Inc. v. Virginia* and the Emerging

Right of Access." *Journalism Quarterly* 61 (Autumn 1984): 615-622.

3309. Levy, Leonard W. *Legacy of Suppression: Freedom of Speech and Press in Early American History.* Cambridge: Harvard University Press, 1960.

3310. Litwack, Thomas R. "The Doctrine of Prior Restraint." *Harvard Civil Rights-Civil Liberties Law Review* 12 (Summer 1977): 519-558.

3311. "Long Arm Jurisdiction over Publishers: To Chill a Mocking Word." *Columbia Law Review* 67 (February 1967): 342-365.

3312. McCarthy, William O. "How State Courts Have Responded to *Gertz* in Setting Standards of Fault." *Journalism Quarterly* 56 (Autumn 1979): 531-539.

3313. MacKenzie, John P. "The Warren Court and the Press." *Michigan Law Review* 67 (December 1968): 303-316.

3314. Mason, Robert. "Supreme Court and Press Fashions." *William and Mary Law Review* 22 (Winter 1980): 259-279.

3315. Mauney, Connie. "The First Amendment and the Supreme Court: Expansion and Restriction of Media Communication." *Delta Kappa Gamma Bulletin* 52 (Winter/Spring 1986): 49-54.

3316. Meeske, Milan D. "Broadcasting and the Law of Defamation." *Journal of Broadcasting* 15 (Summer 1971): 331-346.

3317. Meeske, Milan D. "Broadcasting in the Public Interest: The Supreme Court and the First Amendment." Ph.D. diss., University of Denver, 1968.

3318. Merin, Jerome L. "Libel and the Supreme Court." *William and Mary Law Review* 11 (Winter 1964): 371-423.

3319. Minnick, Wayne C. "United States Supreme Court on Libel." *Quarterly Journal of Speech* 68 (November 1982): 384-396.

3320. Murphy, William P. "Prior Re-

straint Doctrine in Supreme Court Re-evaluation." *Notre Dame Lawyer* 51 (July 1976): 898-918.

3321. Nejelski, Paul, and Kurt Finsterbusch. "The Prosecutor and the Researcher: Present and Prospective Variations on the Supreme Court's *Branzburg* Decision." *Social Problems* 21 (Summer 1973): 3-21.

3322. Nelson, Harold L., ed. *Freedom of the Press from Hamilton to the Warren Court.* Indianapolis: Bobbs-Merrill, 1967.

3323. New York Times. *The New York Times Company v. United States: A Documentary History of the Pentagon Papers Litigation.* New York: Arno Press, 1971.

3324. Nielsen, Richard P. "Court Ruling Gives Edge to Nonprofit Broadcasters." *Journalism Quarterly* 54 (Summer 1977): 385-387.

3325. O'Brien, David M. "Opening the Courthouse Doors: The First Amendment as the Key." *University of Virginia News Letter* 61 (May 1985): 51-55.

3326. O'Brien, David M. *The Public's Right to Know: The Supreme Court and the First Amendment.* New York: Praeger, 1981.

3327. Pember, Don R. "The *Pentagon Papers* Decision: More Questions Than Answers: The Supreme Court's 6-3 Decision Upholding the *New York Times* and *Washington Post*." *Journalism Quarterly* 48 (Autumn 1971): 403-411.

3328. Pember, Don R. "Privacy and the Press: The Defense of Newsworthiness." *Journalism Quarterly* 45 (Spring 1968): 14-24.

3329. Pfaff, Daniel W. "Race, Libel, and the Supreme Court." *Columbia Journalism Review* 8 (Summer 1969): 23-26.

3330. Pilpel, Harriet F., and Laurie R. Rockett. "Supreme Court Libel Ruling in *Firestone* Case Is a New Danger to Press

Freedom." *Publisher's Weekly* 209 (March 29, 1976): 39-40.

3331. Pullen, Ricky D. "A Comparison and Contrast of the Libertarian and Social Responsibility Theories of the Press Based on United States Supreme Court Decisions." Ph.D. diss., Southern Illinois University, 1973.

3332. Rutland, Robert A. "Freedom of the Press and the First Amendment." *Virginia Cavalcade* 32 (Winter 1983): 134-142.

3333. Schwartz, Thomas A. "A Reconceptualization of the First Amendment: The Burger Court and Freedom of the Press, 1969-1980." Ph.D. diss., Southern Illinois University, 1981.

3334. Solimine, Michael E. "Constitutionality of Congressional Legislation to Overrule *Zurcher v. Stanford Daily.*" *Journal of Criminal Law and Criminology* 71 (Summer 1980): 147-162.

3335. Sorenson, Gail P. "Removal of Books from School Libraries, 1972-1982: *Board of Education v. Pico* and Its Antecedents." *Journal of Law Education* 12 (July 1983): 417-441.

3336. Stempel, Guido H. "Guttman Scale Analysis of the Burger Court's Press Decisions." *Journalism Quarterly* 9 (Summer 1982): 256-258; 64 (Winter 1987): 860-861.

3337. Stephenson, D. Grier, Jr. "Can Judges Stop the Presses?" *Intellect* 105 (December 1976): 171-173.

3338. Stephenson, D. Grier, Jr. "Fair Trial—Free Press: Rights in Continuing Conflict." *Brooklyn Law Review* 46 (Fall 1979): 39-66.

3339. Stonecipher, Harry W., and Robert Trager. "The Impact of *Gertz* on the Law of Libel." *Journalism Quarterly* 53 (Winter 1976): 609-618.

3340. Ungar, Sanford J. *The Papers and the Papers: An Account of the Legal and Political Battle over the Pentagon Papers.* New York: Columbia University Press, 1989.

3341. Velvel, Lawrence R. "The Supreme Court Stops Presses." *Catholic University Law Review* 22 (Winter 1973): 324-343.

3342. Walden, Ruth C. "State Action and Media: Applicability of State Action Doctrine to Newspapers, Radio, and Television." Ph.D. diss., University of Wisconsin, 1981.

3343. Warnock, Frank H. "The *New York Times* Rule: The Awakening Giant of First Amendment Protections." *Kentucky Law Journal* 62 (1973/1974): 824-843.

3344. Weisberger, Joseph R. "Supreme Court and the Press: Is Accommodation Possible?" *Judges Journal* 19 (Winter 1980): 14-15.

3345. Weisberger, Joseph R. "Tale of Two Privileges." *Suffolk University Law Review* 15 (April 1981): 191-216.

3346. Wells, J. Kendrick, III. "Individual Rights in the Urban Law Context: *Board of Education v. Pico* and Other U.S. Supreme Court Decisions from October 1981 Term." *Urban Lawyer* 14 (Fall 1982): 771-780.

3347. Whitman, Douglas, and Clyde Stoltenberg. "Evolving Concepts of Lawyer Advertising: The Supreme Court's Latest Clarification." *Indiana Law Review* 19 (Spring 1986): 497-560.

3348. Zobin, Joseph. "Gag Orders and the First Amendment: The Legal Path to *Nebraska Press Association v. Stuart.*" Ph.D. diss., University of Wisconsin, 1978.

Privacy

3349. Apasu-Gbotso, Yao, et al. "Survey on the Constitutional Right to Privacy in the Context of Homosexual Activity." *University of Miami Law Review* 40 (January 1986): 521-657.

3350. Beaney, William M. "The Constitutional Right to Privacy in the Supreme Court." *Supreme Court Review* 1962 (1962): 212-251.

3351. Beaney, William M. "The *Griswold* Case and the Expanding Right to Privacy." *Wisconsin Law Review* 1966 (Fall 1966): 979-995.

3352. Borchard, Edwin. "The Supreme Court and Private Rights." *Yale Law Journal* 47 (May 1938): 1051-1078.

3353. Coffee, Melvin A. "Supreme Court's *Couch* Decision Signals New Directions in Guarding Clients' Records." *CPA Journal* 43 (July 1973): 603-608.

3354. Coffee, Melvin A. "Supreme Court's *Couch* Decision Signals New Directions in Guarding Clients' Records." *Journal of Taxation* 38 (May 1973): 258-261.

3355. Cohan, A. S. "Obstacles to Equality: Government Responses to the Gay Rights Movement in the United States." *Political Studies* 30 (March 1982): 59-76.

3356. Curran, William J. "Uncertainty in Prognosis of Violent Conduct: The Supreme Court Lays Down the Law." *New England Journal of Medicine* 310 (June 21, 1984): 1651-1652.

3357. Fiscus, Ronald J. "Before the Velvet Curtain: The Connecticut Contraceptive Cases as a Study in Constitutional Law and Supreme Court Behavior." Ph.D. diss., University of Wisconsin, 1983.

3358. Goodman, Irv S. "The Bedroom Should Not Be within the Province of the Law." *California Western Law Review* 4 (Spring 1968): 115-131.

3359. Greenawalt, Kent. "Burger Court and Claims of Privacy." *Hastings Center Report* 6 (August 1976): 19-20.

3360. Hart, Mary J. "Privacy and Media Encroachment." Ph.D. diss., University of Denver, 1976.

3361. Hutton, E. Jeremy. *The Constitutional Right of Privacy: Supreme Court Decisions and Congressional Action in Brief.* Washington, DC: Congressional Research Service, 1975.

3362. Katin, Ernest. "*Griswold v. Connecticut*: The Justices and Connecticut's 'Uncommonly Silly Law'." *Notre Dame Lawyer* 42 (June 1967): 680-706.

3363. Knowles, John H. "Health System and Supreme Court Decision an Affirmative Response." *Family Planning Perspectives* 5 (Spring 1973): 113-116.

3364. Levin, Hannah A., and Frank Askin. "Privacy in the Court: Law and Social Reality." *Journal of Social Issues* 33 (Summer 1977): 138-153.

3365. Lusky, Louis. "Invasion of Privacy: A Clarification of Concepts." *Columbia Law Review* 72 (April 1972): 693-710.

3366. Malmquist, Carl. "United States Supreme Court and Psychiatry: A Critical Look." *Journal of Psychiatry and Law* 13 (Spring/Summer 1986): 137-164.

3367. Nimmer, Melville B. "Tort Invasions of Privacy." *Center Magazine* 15 (September/October 1982): 46-47.

3368. Pollack, Harriet. "An Uncommonly Silly Law: The Connecticut Birth Control Cases in the U.S. Supreme Court." Ph.D. diss., Columbia University, 1967.

3369. Posner, Richard A. "The Uncertain Protection of Privacy by the Supreme Court." *Supreme Court Review* 1979 (1979): 173-216.

3370. Pray, Francis X. "A Bank Customer Has No Reasonable Expectation of Privacy of Bank Records: *United States v. Miller*." *San Diego Law Review* 14 (March 1977): 414-434.

3371. Robinson, David, Jr. "Sodomy and the Supreme Court." *Commentary* 82 (October 1986): 57-61.

3372. Schofield, Daniel L. "Constitutional Rights to Privacy and Regulations Affecting the Sexual Activity of Law Enforcement Employees." *FBI Law Enforcement Bulletin* 51 (October 1982): 24-31.

3373. Trubow, George R. "Fighting Off the New Technology." *Human Rights* 10 (Fall 1982): 26-29.

3374. Westin, Alan F. *Privacy and Freedom.* New York: Atheneum, 1967.

3375. Zinner, E. S. "Twenty-first Century Law: Supreme Court Ruling Supports Right to Suicide." *Death Education* 8 (1984): 137-151.

Privacy—Abortion

3376. Annas, George J. "Abortion and the Supreme Court: Round Two." *Hastings Center Report* 6 (October 1976): 15-17.

3377. Annas, George J. "Checkmating the *Baby Doe* Regulations." *Hastings Center Report* 16 (August 1986): 29-31.

3378. Annas, George J. "The Impact of Medical Technology on the Pregnant Woman's Right to Privacy." *American Journal of Law and Medicine* 13 (Summer/Fall 1987): 213-232.

3379. Annas, George J. "*Roe v. Wade* Reaffirmed." *Hastings Center Report* 13 (August 1983): 21-22.

3380. Annas, George J. "*Roe v. Wade* Reaffirmed Again." *Hastings Center Report* 16 (October 1986): 26-27.

3381. Annas, George J. "The Supreme Court and Abortion: The Irrelevance of Medical Judgement." *Hastings Center Report* 10 (October 1980): 23-24.

3382. Bennett, Robert W. "Abortion and Judicial Review: Of Burdens and Benefits, Hard Cases, and Some Bad Law." *Northwestern University Law Review* 75 (February 1981): 978-1017.

3383. Blake, Judith. "The Supreme Court's Abortion Decisions and Public

Opinion in the United States." *Population and Development Review* 3 (March/June 1977): 45-62.

3384. Blank, Robert H. "Judicial Decision Making and Biological Fact: *Roe v. Wade* and the Unresolved Question of Fetal Viability." *Western Political Quarterly* 37 (December 1984): 584-602.

3385. Bodenheimer, Edar. "Birth Control Legislation and the United States Supreme Court." *University of Kansas Law Review* 14 (1966): 453-460.

3386. Brady, David W., and Kathleen A. Kemp. "The Supreme Court's Abortion Rulings and Social Change." *Social Science Quarterly* 57 (December 1976): 535-546.

3387. Byrn, Robert M. "An American Tragedy: The Supreme Court on Abortion." *Fordham Law Review* 41 (March 1973): 807-862.

3388. Callahan, Daniel. "Abortion and Medical Ethics." *Annals of the American Academy of Political and Social Science* 437 (May 1978): 116-127.

3389. Callahan, Sidney. "The Court and a Conflict of Principles." *Hastings Center Report* 7 (August 1977): 7-8.

3390. Cunningham, Paige. "Revising *Roe vs. Wade.*" *Christianity Today* 29 (September 20, 1985): 20-22.

3391. Dellapenna, Joseph W. "Nor Piety nor Wit: Supreme Court on Abortion." *Columbia Human Rights Law Review* 6 (Fall/Winter 1974-1975): 379-413.

3392. Dembitz, Nanette. "The Supreme Court and a Minor's Abortion Decision." *Columbia Law Review* 80 (October 1980): 1251-1263.

3393. Destro, Robert A. "Abortion and the Constitution: The Need for a Life-Protective Amendment." *California Law Review* 63 (September 1975): 1250-1351.

3394. Duffy, Mary A. "Abortion Decisions: How Will the United States Supreme Court Define 'Necessary'?" *Women Lawyers Journal* 64 (Winter 1978): 3-16, 39.

3395. Friedman, Barbara W. "Indigent Women: What Right to Abortion?" *New York Law School Law Review* 23 (1978): 709-741.

3396. Granberg, Donald. "Abortion Controversy: An Overview." *Humanist* 41 (July/August 1981): 28-38.

3397. Granberg, Donald. "The United States Senate Votes to Uphold *Roe v. Wade.*" *Population Research and Policy Review* 4 (June 1985): 115-131.

3398. Hall, Robert E. "Supreme Court Decision on Abortion." *American Journal of Obstetrics and Gynecology* 116 (May 1, 1973): 1-8.

3399. Harrison, Stanley M. "Supreme Court and Abortional Reform: Means to an End." *New York Law Forum* 19 (Winter 1974): 685-701.

3400. Hogan, Timothy D. "An Intervention Analysis of the Effects of Legalized Abortion upon U.S. Fertility." *Population Research and Policy Review* 3 (October 1984): 201-218.

3401. Kemp, Kathleen A., Robert A. Carp, and David W. Brady. "Supreme Court and Social Change: Case of Abortion." *Western Political Quarterly* 31 (March 1978): 19-31.

3402. Klassel, Dara, and Andrea Lewin. "Minor's Right to Abortion and Contraception: Prospects for Invalidating Less Than Absolute Restrictions." *Women's Rights Law Reporter* 4 (Spring 1978): 165-183.

3403. Loewy, Arnold H. "Abortive Reasons and Obscene Standards: A Comment on the Abortion and Obscenity Cases." *North Carolina Law Review* 52 (December 1973): 223-243.

3404. Mathie, William. "Reason, Revela-

tion, and Liberal Justice: Reflections on George Grant's Analysis of *Roe vs. Wade.*" *Canadian Journal of Political Science* 19 (September 1986): 443-466.

3405. Matthews, Nathan. "Effect of the Recent Decisions of the Supreme Court on Reproduction Cost as a Test of Value." *Harvard Law Review* 37 (February 1924): 431-463.

3406. Mears, Judith M. "The Doctors as Abortion Ally." *Civil Liberties Review* 1 (Summer 1974): 134-136.

3407. Mechanic, David. "The Supreme Court and Abortion: Sidestepping Social Realities." *Hastings Center Report* 10 (December 1980): 17-19.

3408. Melton, Gary B., and Nancy F. Russo. "Adolescent Abortion: Psychological Perspectives on Public Policy." *American Psychologist* 42 (January 1987): 69-72.

3409. Melvin, Edward J. *The Legal Principles of the Founding Fathers and the Supreme Court.* Jenkintown, PA: Pro Life Coalition of Pennsylvania, 1977.

3410. Mendelson, June E., and Serena Domolky. "Courts and Elective Abortions under Medicaid." *Social Service Review* 54 (March 1980): 124-134.

3411. Neef, Marian H. "Policy Formation and Implementation in the Abortion Field." Ph.D. diss., University of Illinois, Urbana-Champaign, 1979.

3412. Neuhaus, Richard J. "Hyde and Hysteria: The Liberal Banner Has Been Planted on the Wrong Side of the Abortion Debate." *Christian Century* 97 (September 10-17, 1980): 849-852.

3413. Nicholson, Jeanne B., and Debra W. Stewart. "The Supreme Court, Abortion Policy, and State Response: A Preliminary Analysis." *Publius* 8 (Winter 1978): 159-178.

3414. Noonan, John T., Jr. "The Supreme Court and Abortion: Upholding Constitutional Principles." *Hastings Center Report* 10 (December 1980): 14-16.

3415. Palley, Howard A. "Abortion Policy: Ideology, Political Cleavage, and the Policy Process." *Policy Studies Journal* 7 (November 1978): 224-233.

3416. Perry, Michael J. "Abortion Funding Cases: A Comment on the Supreme Court's Role in American Government." *Georgetown Law Journal* 66 (June 1978): 1191-1245.

3417. Perry, Michael J. "Why the Supreme Court Was Plainly Wrong in the Hyde Amendment Case: A Brief Comment on *Harris v. McRae*." *Stanford Law Review* 32 (July 1980): 1113-1128.

3418. Plutzer, Eric, and Barbara Ryan. "Notifying Husbands about an Abortion: An Empirical Look at Constitutional and Policy Dilemmas." *Sociology and Social Research* 71 (April 1987): 183-189.

3419. Pollack, John C., Mary C. Murray, and J. L. Robinson. "Media Agendas and Human-Rights: Supreme Court Decision on Abortion." *Journalism Quarterly* 55 (Autumn 1978): 544-548.

3420. Putka, John S. "Supreme Court and Abortion: The Socio-Political Impact of Judicial Activism." Ph.D. diss., University of Cincinnati, 1979.

3421. Rhoden, Nancy K. "Trimesters and Technology: Revamping *Roe v. Wade*." *Yale Law Journal* 95 (March 1986): 639-697.

3422. Rigdon, Evelyn E. *Abortion on Demand: Why and How the Rockefellers Influenced the Supreme Court to Legalize Abortion.* Los Angeles: Reality Publishing Company, 1980.

3423. Robbins, John C., and Robert G. Stewart. "The Supreme Court and Legitimate State Interest: The Abortion Decision." *Ripon Forum* 9 (April 1973): 8-11.

3424. Robertson, John A. "Gestational Burdens and Fetal Status: Justifying *Roe v. Wade*." *American Journal of Law and Medicine* 13 (Summer/Fall 1987): 153-364.

3425. Robertson, Leon S. "Abortion and Infant-Mortality before and after the 1973 United States Supreme Court Decision on Abortion." *Journal of Biosocial Science* 13 (July 1980): 275-280.

3426. Rust, Mark G. "The Abortion Cases." *American Bar Association Journal* 72 (Fall 1986): 50-53.

3427. Sargent, John D. *Analysis of the United States Supreme Court Decisions Regarding Abortions:* Roe v. Wade, *No. 70-18, and* Doe v. Bolton, *No. 70-40, Decided January 22, 1973.* Washington, DC: Congressional Research Service, 1975.

3428. Segers, Mary C. "Abortion and the Supreme Court: Some Are More Equal Than Others." *Hastings Center Report* 7 (August 1977): 5-6.

3429. Sendor, Benjamin B. "Medical Responsibility for Fetal Survival under *Roe* and *Doe*." *Harvard Civil Rights-Civil Liberties Law Review* 10 (Spring 1975): 444-471.

3430. Sernett, Milton C. "The Efficacy of Religious Participation in the National Debates over Abolitionism and Abortion." *Journal of Religion* 64 (April 1984): 205-220.

3431. Sernett, Milton C. "The Rights of Personhood: The *Dred Scott* Case and the Question of Abortion." *Religion in Life* 49 (Winter 1980): 461-476.

3432. Spring, Beth. "Harsh Days at the High Court: Abortion Decision Devastates Right-to-Life Movements." *Christianity Today* 27 (July 5, 1983): 30-31.

3433. Stanley, John. "Right to Privacy: The Abortion Issue." *Bureaucrat* 16 (Summer 1987): 6.

3434. Swan, George S. "Article III, Section 2—14th Amendment; Section 5: Congressional Responses to *Roe*; *Roe* From Lincoln's *Dred Scott* Viewpoint." *Lincoln Law Review* 16 (Winter 1985): 63-89.

3435. Swan, George S. "Article III, Section 2—14th Amendment; Section 5: *Roe* Responses; *Roe* from Lincoln's *Dred Scott* Viewpoint." *Lincoln Law Review* 15 (Winter 1984): 23-44.

3436. Tatalovich, Raymond, and Byron W. Daynes. "The Limits of Judicial Intervention in Abortion Politics." *Christian Century* 99 (January 6-13, 1982): 16-20.

3437. Verhey, Allen. "Learning from *Roe v. Wade*." *Reformed Journal* 33 (April 1983): 3-4.

3438. Wardle, Lynn D. "Gap between Law and Moral Order: An Examination of the Legitimacy of the Supreme Court Abortion Decisions." *Brigham Young University Law Review* 1980 (1980): 811-835.

3439. Watt, Robert L., III. "A New Constitutional Right to an Abortion." *North Carolina Law Review* 51 (October 1973): 1573-1584.

3440. Weinstoc, Edward, et al. "Legal Abortions in United States since 1973 Supreme Court Decisions." *Family Planning Perspectives* 7 (January/February 1975): 23-31.

3441. Welch, Charles E., III. "The Regulation of American Fertility: Facts and Misconceptions." *International Journal of Women's Studies* 7 (May/June 1984): 273-281.

Privacy—Family

3442. Annas, George J. "Parents, Children, and the Supreme Court." *Hastings Center Report* 9 (October 1979): 21-23.

3443. Burt, Robert A. "Constitution of the Family." *Supreme Court Review* 1979 (1979): 329-395.

3444. Crutchfield, Charles F. "Medical Treatment for Minor Children: The Roles of Parents, the State, the Child, and the Supreme Court of the United States." *Family Relations* 30 (April 1981): 165-186.

3445. DeBettencourt, Kathleen B. "Parent, Child, and State: The Family in American Constitutional Law." Ph.D. diss., Catholic University of America, 1984.

3446. Rush, Sharon E. "The Warren and Burger Courts on State Parent and Child Conflict Resolution: A Comparative Analysis and Proposed Methodology." *Hastings Law Journal* 36 (March 1987): 461-513.

Religion

3447. Abraham, Henry J. "Status of the First Amendment's Religion Clauses: Some Reflections on Lines and Limits." *Journal of Church and State* 22 (Spring 1980): 215-231.

3448. Abrahams, Samuel. "Religion and Education: The Supreme Court Dilemma." *Midwest Journal* 2 (Summer 1950): 1-13.

3449. Abram, Morris B. "Is 'Strict Separation' Too Strict?" *Public Interest* 82 (Winter 1986): 81-90.

3450. Ackerman, David M. *Religious Activities in the Public Schools and the First Amendment: Judicial Decisions and the Congressional Response.* Washington, DC: Congressional Research Service, 1975.

3451. Ackerman, David M. *Supreme Court: Church-State Cases, October 1982 Term.* Washington, DC: Congressional Research Service, 1975.

3452. Allsberry, Gregory K. "Tax Deductions for Parochial School Tuition: *Mueller v. Allen*." *Washington University Journal of Urban and Contemporary Law* 26 (1984): 107-121.

3453. Arnold, Otto C. *Religious Freedom on Trial*. Valley Forge, PA: Judson Press, 1978.

3454. Bailey, Joseph R. "History of the Child-Benefit Doctrine as a Means for Providing Governmental Financial Aid to Non-Public Education." Ph.D. diss., University of Massachusetts, 1979.

3455. Baker, Richard C. "The Supreme Court and the Freedom of Religion Melange: The United States Supreme Court, Applying the First Amendment to the States via the Fourteenth, Has Created a Perplexing and Unacceptable Mishmash of Law in the Field of Church-State Relations." *American Bar Association Journal* 49 (May 1963): 439-443.

3456. Barnhard, William J. "Previous Decision of Supreme Court Held Not Binding on Lower Federal Court." *Georgetown Law Journal* 31 (November 1942): 85-88.

3457. Bedsole, Adolph. *Supreme Court Decision on Bible Reading and Prayers: America's Black Letter Day*. Grand Rapids, MI: Baker House Book, 1964.

3458. Bennett, John C. "Absolutism in the Supreme Court." *Christianity and Crisis* 22 (August 6, 1962): 135-136.

3459. Benway, Michael P. "The Church-State Relationship: A Historical and Legal Perspective." *Contemporary Education* 54 (Spring 1983): 201-207.

3460. Beth, Loren P. *The American Theory of Church and State*. Gainesville: University of Florida Press, 1958.

3461. Beth, Loren P. "The Wall of Separation and the Supreme Court." *Minnesota Law Review* 38 (February 1954): 215-227.

3462. BeVier, Lillian R. "The Free Exercise Clause: A View from the Public Forum." *William and Mary Law Review* 27 (Special Issue 1985/1986): 963-974.

3463. Birkby, Robert H. "The Supreme Court and the Bible Belt: Tennessee Reaction to the *Schempp* Decision." *Midwest Journal of Political Science* 10 (August 1966): 304-319.

3464. Black, Rutherford R. "Implications of Supreme Court Interpretations of the First Amendment to the Constitution for the Teaching of Religion in State Universities and Land-Grant Colleges in the United States." Ph.D. diss., University of Alabama, 1956.

3465. Blanshard, Paul. "The Big Decision." *Humanist* 23 (July/August 1963): 106-110.

3466. Blanton, Harry A. "The Entanglement Theory: Its Development and Some Implications for Future Aid to Church-Related Higher Education." *Journal of Law and Education* 7 (July 1978): 359-422.

3467. Boatti, Robert. "*Lynch v. Donnelly*: Supreme Court Approval of Publicly Sponsored Nativity Scene Displays Establishes an Unholy Alliance between Church and State." *Rutgers Law Review* 37 (Fall 1984): 103-136.

3468. Boggs, Timothy. "An Analysis of the Opinions in the United States Supreme Court Decisions of Religion and Education from 1948 through 1972." Ph.D. diss., University of Colorado, 1973.

3469. Boles, Donald E. "Burger Court and Parochial Schools: A Study in Law, Politics, and Educational Reality." *Valparaiso University Law Review* 9 (Spring 1975): 459-486.

3470. Boles, Donald E. "Church and State and the Burger Court: Recent Developments Affecting Parochial Schools." *Journal of Church and State* 18 (Winter 1976): 21-38.

3471. Boles, Donald E. "Church-State Conflicts: Public Policy Dilemmas of the School Administrator." *Journal of Church and State* 14 (Spring 1972): 297-317.

3472. Boles, Donald E. "Religion and the Public Schools in Judicial Review." *Journal of Church and State* 26 (Winter 1984): 55-71.

3473. Bolick, Ernest B., Jr. "A Historical Account of the Controversy over State Support of Church-Related Higher Education in the Fifty States." Ph.D. diss., University of North Carolina, Greensboro, 1978.

3474. Bowser, Anita. "Delimiting Religion in the Constitution: A Classification Problem." *Valparaiso University Law Review* 11 (Winter 1977): 163-226.

3475. Brickman, William W. "Supreme Court and Sectarian School." *Intellect* 102 (November 1973): 82-84.

3476. Brodie, Abner, and Harold P. Southerland. "Conscience, the Constitution, and the Supreme Court: The Riddle of *United States v. Seeger.*" *Wisconsin Law Review* 1966 (Spring 1966): 306-330.

3477. Buzzard, Lynn R., and Samuel Ericsson. "Public Aid to Private Schools: Ceasar Rendering to God." *Christianity Today* 27 (June 17, 1983): 20-23.

3478. Campbell, Bruce A. "*Dartmouth College* as a Civil Liberties Case: The Formation of Constitutional Policy." *Kentucky Law Journal* 70 (1981/1982): 3-18.

3479. Canavan, Francis. "The Impact of Recent Supreme Court Decisions on Religion in the United States." *Journal of Church and State* 16 (Spring 1974): 217-236.

3480. Canavan, Francis. "The Impact of Recent Supreme Court Decisions on Religion in the United States." *Social Studies: Irish Journal of Sociology* 3 (April 1974): 137-157.

3481. Capps, Kline, and Carl H. Esbeck. "The Use of Government Funding and Taxing Power to Regulate Religious Schools." *Journal of Law and Education* 14 (October 1985): 553-574.

3482. Carroll, William A. "The Constitution, the Supreme Court, and Religion." *American Political Science Review* 61 (September 1967): 657-674.

3483. Choper, Jesse H. "Church, State, and the Supreme Court: Current Controversy." *Arizona Law Review* 29 (Fall 1987): 551-561.

3484. Choper, Jesse H. "The Establishment Clause and Aid to Parochial Schools." *California Law Review* 56 (April 1968): 260-341.

3485. Choper, Jesse H. "The Free Exercise Clause: A Structural Overview and an Appraisal of Recent Developments." *William and Mary Law Review* 27 (Special Issue 1985/1986): 943-961.

3486. Clayton, James L. "The Supreme Court, Polygamy, and the Enforcement of Morals in Nineteenth Century America: An Analysis of *Reynolds v. United States.*" *Dialogue* 12 (Winter 1929): 46-61.

3487. Cochran, Bernard. "Tax Support for Church-Related Colleges: The Implications of the *Tilton* Decision." *Perspectives in Religious Studies* 2 (Spring 1975): 31-40.

3488. Conn, Joseph L. "*A. U. v. Bennett*: Defending the First Amendment." *Church and State* 38 (October 1985): 4-7.

3489. Conn, Joseph L. "Parochaid: Tax-Paid Teachers and Inspectors Are Halted at the Parochial School Door." *Church and State* 38 (July/August 1985): 4-5.

3490. Cord, Robert L. *Separation of Church and State: Historical Fact and Current Ficton.* New York: Lambeth, 1982.

3491. Cornelius, William J. "Church and State: The Mandate of the Establishment Clause, Wall of Separation, or Being in Neutrality?" *St. Mary's Law Journal* 16 (Winter 1984): 1-39.

3492. Corwin, Edward S. "The Supreme Court as a National School Board." *Law* *and Contemporary Problems* 14 (Winter 1949): 3-22.

3493. Crockenberg, Vincent A. "An Argument for the Constitutionality of Direct Aid to Religious Schools." *Journal of Law and Education* 13 (January 1984): 1-18.

3494. Curry, Patricia E. "James Madison and the Burger Court: Converging Views of Church-State Separation." *Indiana Law Journal* 56 (Summer 1981): 615-636.

3495. Denniston, Lyle. "Can Church and State Mix?" *California Lawyer* 5 (March 1985): 34-37, 40, 86.

3496. Devins, Neal. "Religious Symbols and the Establishment Clause." *Journal of Church and State* 27 (Winter 1985): 19-46.

3497. Devins, Neal. "The Supreme Court and Private Schools: An Update." *This World* 8 (Spring/Summer 1984): 13-26.

3498. Dillon, Michael R. "Religious Liberty, Common Law, and the Supreme Court." *Journal of Church and State* 14 (Spring 1972): 211-222.

3499. "Does the Constitution Allow Private School Students to Receive Public Assistance?" *Christianity Today* 29 (February 1985): 60-61.

3500. Dolbeare, Kenneth M., and Phillip E. Hammond. *The School Prayer Decisions: From Court Policy to Local Practice.* Chicago: University of Chicago Press, 1971.

3501. Donoghue, Daniel C. "Federal Constitutional Provisions with Respect to Religion." *American Catholic Historical Society Record* 39 (March 1928): 1-26.

3502. Drakeman, Donald L. "New Ruling on School Prayer." *Christian Century* 102 (June 19-26, 1985): 604-605.

3503. Drinan, Robert F. *Religion, the Courts, and Public Policy.* New York: McGraw-Hill, 1963.

3504. Drouin, Edmond G. "The United States Supreme Court and Religious Freedom in American Education in Its Decisions Affecting Church-Related Elementary and Secondary Schools during the First Three Quarters of the Twentieth Century." Ph.D. diss., Catholic University of America, 1980.

3505. Durland, William. "Case Denied: Christians Take Their War Tax Resistance to the Supreme Court." *Sojourners* 9 (March 1980): 8-10.

3506. Exton, Elaine. "Reactions of Congress to the Ruling on School Prayer." *American School Board Journal* 145 (September 1962): 66-70.

3507. Fahy, Charles. "Religion, Education, and the Supreme Court." *Law and Contemporary Problems* 14 (Winter 1949): 73-91.

3508. Fair, Daryl R. "The Church-State Policy Process." *Policy Studies Journal* 4 (Winter 1975): 117-122.

3509. Fair, Daryl R. "Remote from the Schoolhouse: The Passage of the New Jersey Parochial School Bus Bill." *New Jersey History* 99 (Spring/Summer 1981): 49-65.

3510. Fehr, Alex J. "Case Study of the Resistance of the Cornwall-Lebanon Suburban Joint School Directors to the United States Supreme Court Ban on Bible Reading in the Public Schools, 1963-1965." Ph.D. diss., Syracuse University, 1968.

3511. Fellman, David. *Religion in American Public Law.* Boston: Boston University Press, 1965.

3512. Fink, Nancy H. "Establishment Clause According to Supreme Court: The Mysterious Eclipse of Free Exercise Values." *Catholic University Law Review* 27 (Winter 1978): 207-262.

3513. Fisher, Barry A. "Comment on 'The Free Exercise Clause': A Structural Overview and an Appraisal of Recent Developments." *William and Mary Law Review* 27 (Special Issue 1985/1986): 975-984.

3514. Fisher, Joe A. "No National School Board: The United States Supreme Court, Religion, and Public Education." Ph.D. diss., University of Nebraska, 1966.

3515. Fishman, Ethan M. "School Prayer: Principle and Circumstance in American Politics." *Religious Education* 77 (May/June 1982): 269-278.

3516. Fister, J. Blaine. "Church and State in the U.S.A. and Canada: The U.S.A. Tradition." *Religious Education* 69 (May/June 1974): 365-372.

3517. Fitzpatrick, James K. *God, Country, and the Supreme Court.* Chicago: Regnery Books, 1985.

3518. Flowers, Ronald B. "Freedom of Religion versus Civil Authority in Matters of Health." *Annals of the American Academy of Political and Social Science* 446 (November 1979): 149-161.

3519. Flowers, Ronald B. "The 1960s: A Decisive Decade in American Church State Relationships." *Encounter* 40 (Summer 1979): 287-304.

3520. Flowers, Ronald B. "Supreme Court's Interpretation of the Free Exercise Clause." *Religion in Life* 49 (Fall 1980): 322-335.

3521. Flowers, Ronald B. "The Supreme Court's Three Tests of the Establishment Clause." *Religion in Life* 45 (Spring 1976): 41-52.

3522. Flowers, Ronald B. "What Is the Supreme Court Doing to the Establishment Clause?" *Lexington Theological Quarterly* 20 (July 1985): 79-90.

3523. Flygare, Thomas J. "Supreme Court Ducks Another Important Case." *Phi Delta Kappan* 67 (June 1986): 760-761.

3524. Flygare, Thomas J. "Supreme Court Reinforces the 'Wall of Separa-

tion'." *Phi Delta Kappan* 67 (October 1985): 157-158.

3525. Fordham, Jefferson B. "The Implications of the Supreme Court Decisions Dealing with Religious Practices in the Public Schools." *Journal of Church and State* 6 (Winter 1964): 44-60.

3526. Frasca, William R. "Confusion in the Supreme Court: History and the Confusion behind Three Church-State Decisions; the *Everson*, *McCollum*, and *Zorach* Cases." *Thought* 28 (Winter 1953/1954): 547-570.

3527. Freeman, Thomas J. "Opinions Expressed toward the United States Supreme Court Decisions on Bible Readings and Prayer." Ph.D. diss., Auburn University, 1978.

3528. Freund, Paul A. "Public Aid to Parochial Schools." *Harvard Law Review* 82 (June 1969): 1680-1692.

3529. Gaffney, Edward M., Jr. "Political Divisiveness along Religious Lines: The Entanglement of the Court in Sloppy History and Bad Public Policy." *St. Louis University Law Journal* 24 (September 1980): 205-236.

3530. Garrahan, John F. "Church-State Issues in Education as Seen in the Light of Selected Supreme Court Decisions." Ed.D. diss., University of Pennsylvania, 1969.

3531. Garrett, James L., Jr. "The 'Free Exercise' Clause of the First Amendment: Retrospect and Prospect." *Journal of Church and State* 17 (Autumn 1975): 393-398.

3532. Gedicks, Frederick M. "Motivation, Rationality, and Secular Purpose in Establishment Clause Review." *Arizona State Law Journal* 1985 (1985): 677-726.

3533. Giannella, Donald A. "*Lemon* and *Tilton*: The Bitter and the Sweet of Church-State Entanglement." *Supreme Court Review* 1971 (1971): 147-200.

3534. Golden, Cornelius J., Jr. "Education Vouchers: The Fruit of the Lemon Tree." *Stanford Law Review* 24 (April 1972): 687-711.

3535. Goldfarb, Ronald L. "Three Conscientious Objectors: Last Year the Supreme Court Decided the Cases of Three Young Men Who Claimed Exemption from the Draft on the Ground That They Were Conscientious Objectors: The Way the Court Resolved the Cases Leaves Draft Boards and Courts the Unwelcome Task of Deciding Some Hazy Questions." *American Bar Association Journal* 52 (June 1966): 564-567.

3536. Gordon, Glenn S. *"Lynch v. Donnelly*: Breaking Down the Barriers to Religious Displays." *Cornell Law Review* 71 (November 1985): 185-208.

3537. Gould, Diane B. "The First Amendment and the American Indian Religious Freedom Act: An Approach to Protecting Native American Religion." *Iowa Law Review* 71 (March 1986): 869-891.

3538. Greenawalt, Kent. "All or Nothing at All: The Defeat of Selective Conscientious Objection." *Supreme Court Review* 1971 (1971): 31-94.

3539. Gregory, David L. "The First Amendment Religion Clauses and Labor and Employment Law in the Supreme Court, 1984 Term." *New York Law School Law Review* 31 (1986): 1-36.

3540. Haddad, John. "Supreme Court Decisions: 'Wall of Separation between Church and State'?" Ed.D. diss., University of Pittsburgh, 1970.

3541. Hamilton, Howard D. "God in the Classroom: The New York Regents' Prayer Case Criticizes the Court's Opinion on Grounds of Public Policy and Federalism and Suggests Alternative Approaches." *Social Science* 38 (April 1963): 92-98.

3542. Hammond, Phillip E. "The Courts and Secular Humanism." *Society* 21 (May/June 1984): 11-16.

3543. Hammond, Phillip E. "The Shifting Meaning of a Wall of Separation: Some Notes on Church, State, and Conscience." *Sociological Analysis* 42 (Fall 1981): 227-234.

3544. Harder, Marvin. "The Supreme Court and the C. O." *Mennonite Life* 7 (October 1952): 185-187.

3545. Hartman, Paul. "Freedom of Religion and Speech and the United States Supreme Court." *Modern Law Review* 17 (May 1954): 220-228.

3546. Hastey, Stanley. "Supreme Court Decisions." *Fundamentalists Journal* 1 (October 1982): 56-58.

3547. Healey, Robert M. "Religious Freedom or Catch-22: The Private School Aid Issue." *Christian Century* 92 (April 23, 1975): 413-416.

3548. Henle, Robert J. "Dilemmas of the Prayer Decision." *Social Order* 13 (March 1963): 32-48.

3549. Herman, Donald H. "The Supreme Court and the Religion Clauses: 1982 and 1984 Terms." *Catholic Lawyer* 30 (Autumn 1986): 218-239.

3550. Holder, Angela R. "Old Wine in New Bottle? The Right of Privacy and Future School Prayer Cases." *Journal of Church and State* 12 (Spring 1970): 289-307.

3551. Howe, Mark D. *The Garden and the Wilderness: Religion and Government in American Constitutional History.* Chicago: University of Chicago Press, 1965.

3552. Hunt, Thomas C. "The Supreme Court, Religion, and the Temper of the Times." *Momentum* 17 (May 1986): 28-31.

3553. Johnson, Richard M. "Separation of Church and State: The Dynamics of Supreme Court Decision-Making." Ph.D diss., University of Illinois, 1965.

3554. Jones, John P. "A Comparative Analysis of Theories of Religion and Politics as Applied to Relevant Decisions of the United States Supreme Court." Ph.D. diss., Duke University, 1969.

3555. Jones, Richard H. "Accommodationist and Separationist Ideals in Supreme Court Establishment Clause Decisions." *Journal of Church and State* 28 (Spring 1986): 193-223.

3556. Kancelbaum, Joshua J. "Shifting Currents in the Narrow Channel of State Aid to Parochial Schools." *Ohio State Law Journal* 38 (1977): 757-782.

3557. Kannar, George. "The Devil and Warren Burger: *Grove City v. Bell*." *Christianity and Crisis* 44 (April 16, 1984): 126-128.

3558. Kantzer, Kenneth S. "The *Bob Jones* Decision: A Dangerous Precedent: You Don't Have to Be a Racist to Support BJU's Tax Exemption." *Christianity Today* 27 (September 2, 1983): 14-15.

3559. Katz, Ellis. "The Supreme Court in the Web of Government: The American Civil Liberties Union (ACLU), the Supreme Court, and the Bible." Ph.D. diss., Columbia University, 1966.

3560. Katz, Wilbur G., and Harold P. Southerland. "Religious Pluralism and the Supreme Court." *Daedalus* 96 (Winter 1967): 180-192.

3561. Kauper, Paul G. "Government and Religion: The Search for Absolutes." *Michigan Quarterly Review* 11 (Summer 1972): 197-207.

3562. Kauper, Paul G. "Prayer, Public Schools, and the Supreme Court." *Michigan Law Review* 61 (April 1963): 1031-1086.

3563. Kauper, Paul G. *Religion and the Constitution*. Baton Rouge: Louisiana State University Press, 1964.

3564. Kauper, Paul G. "Supreme Court and the Establishment Clause: Back to *Everson*?" *Case Western Reserve Law Review* (Fall 1974): 107-129.

3565. Kauper, Paul G. "The *Walz* Decision: More on the Religion Clauses of the First Amendment." *Michigan Law Review* 69 (December 1970): 179-210.

3566. Kauper, Paul G. "The Warren Court: Religious Liberty and Church-State Relations." *Michigan Law Review* 67 (December 1968): 269-288.

3567. Kelley, Dean M. "The Court and Conscience: Selective CO; Pandora's Box or Necessary Freedom?" *Christianity and Crisis* 31 (April 19, 1971): 68-74.

3568. Kelley, Dean M. "Religion, Education, and the Constitution." *Religious Education* 75 (November/December 1980): 619-630.

3569. Kelley, Dean M. "The Supreme Court Redefines Tax Exemption." *Society* 21 (May/June 1984): 23-28.

3570. Kendall, Willmoore. "American Conservatism and the 'Prayer' Decisions." *Modern Age* 8 (Summer 1964): 245-259.

3571. Kenneally, James J. "Catholicism and the Supreme Court Reorganization Proposal of 1937." *Journal of Church and State* 25 (Autumn 1983): 469-489.

3572. Kik, Jacob M. *The Supreme Court and Prayer in the Public Schools*. Philadelphia: Presbyterian and Reformed Publishing Company, 1963.

3573. Killilea, Alfred G. "Privileging Conscientious Dissents: Another Look at *Sherbert v. Verner*." *Journal of Church and State* 16 (Spring 1974): 197-215.

3574. Kim, Richard C. "The Constitution, the Supreme Court, and Religious Liberty." *Journal of Church and State* 6 (Autumn 1964): 333-343.

3575. Kim, Richard C. "The Constitutional Legacy of the Jehovah's Witnesses."

Southwestern Social Science Quarterly 45 (September 1964): 125-134.

3576. Kim, Richard C. "Jehovah's Witnesses and the Supreme Court: An Examination of the Cases Brought before the United States Supreme Court Involving the Rights Claimed by Jehovah's Witnesses from 1938 to 1960." Ph.D. diss., University of Oklahoma, 1963.

3577. Knudsen, Stephen T. "The Education of the Amish Child." *California Law Review* 62 (December 1974): 1506-1531.

3578. Kohler, Mark F. "Compromise and Interpretation: A Case Study of the Burger Court and the Religion Clauses." *Tulsa Law Journal* 23 (Spring 1988): 379-427.

3579. Korbel, Herbert J. "The State and Religion: Impartial Assistance and Absolute Non-Restraint." *New York State Bar Journal* 37 (October 1965): 405-410.

3580. Kurland, Philip B. *Church and State: The Supreme Court and the First Amendment.* Rev. ed. Chicago: University of Chicago Press, 1975.

3581. Kurland, Philip B. "Irrelevance of the Constitution: The Religion Clauses of the First Amendment and the Supreme Court." *Villanova Law Review* 24 (November 1978): 3-27.

3582. Kurland, Philip B. "Of Church and State and the Supreme Court." *University of Chicago Law Review* 29 (Autumn 1961): 1-96.

3583. Kurland, Philip B. *Religion and the Law of Church and State and the Supreme Court.* Chicago: Aldine, 1963.

3584. Kurland, Philip B. "The Religion Clauses and the Burger Court." *Catholic University Law Review* 34 (Fall 1984): 1-18.

3585. Kurland, Philip B. "Supreme Court, Compulsory Education, and First Amendments Religion Clauses." *West Virginia Law Review* 75 (April 1973): 213-245.

3586. Kurowski, Joan G. "An Analysis of the Opinions of Justices Casting Dissenting Votes on U.S. Supreme Court Cases on Schools and Religion." *Religious Education* 78 (Summer 1983) 422-423.

3587. Laubach, John H. *School Prayers: Congress, the Courts, and the Public.* Washington, DC: Public Affairs Press, 1965.

3588. Leary, John P. "Prayer and the Supreme Court." *Thought* 37 (Winter 1962): 485-491.

3589. Leavy, Edward N., and Eric A. Raps. "The Judicial Double Standard for State Aid to Church-Affiliated Educational Institutions." *Journal of Church and State* 21 (Spring 1979): 209-222.

3590. Ledbetter, Cal, Jr. "The Antievolution Law: Church and State in Arkansas." *Arkansas Historical Quarterly* 38 (Winter 1979): 299-327.

3591. Lee, Francis G. *Wall of Controversy: Church-State Conflict in America: The Justices and Their Opinions.* Malabar, FL: R. E. Krieger Publishing Company, 1986.

3592. Lee, Rex E. "Religion and the Burger Court." *Michigan Law Review* 84 (February/April 1986): 603-607.

3593. Levinson, Rosalie B. "Separation of Church and State: And the Wall Came Tumbling Down." *Valparaiso University Law Review* 18 (Summer 1984): 707-739.

3594. Levinson, Sanford. " 'Constitution' in American Civil Religion." *Supreme Court Review* 1979 (1979): 123-151.

3595. Liliemark, Randolph A. "Practices and Attitudes of Michigan Elementary School Teachers in the Light of the Supreme Court's Rulings on Prayer and Bible Reading in the Public Schools." Ed.D. diss., Wayne State University, 1973.

3596. Litka, Michael P., and Edward R. Trubac. "Aid to Private Schools: Legal and Economic Implications." *Momentum* 2 (February 1971): 4-9.

3597. Little, David. "Thomas Jefferson's Religious Views and Their Influence on the Supreme Court's Interpretation of the First Amendment." *Catholic Lawyer* 26 (Fall 1976): 57-72.

3598. Lorensen, Frederick H. "Evolution and Implications of *Tilton v. Richardson*: The First United States Supreme Court Test of the Constitutionality of Federal Grants to Religious-Affiliated Colleges and Universities." Ph.D. diss., University of Connecticut, 1979.

3599. McCarthy, Martha M. "Religion and Public Schools: Emerging Legal Standards and Unresolved Issues." *Harvard Educational Review* 55 (August 1985): 278-317.

3600. McCree, Wade H., Jr., and Rhonda Copelon. "Text of U.S. Supreme Court Decision: *Harris v. McRae*." *Journal of Church and State* 22 (Autumn 1980): 575-595.

3601. McGraw, James R. "Bible Lesson for the Court." *Christianity and Crisis* 37 (July 1977): 162-164.

3602. Malbin, Michael J. "The Supreme Court and the Definition of Religion." Ph.D. diss., Cornell University, 1973.

3603. Manwaring, David R. "Flag-Salute Case." In *The Third Branch of Government*, edited by C. Herman Pritchett and Alan F. Westin, 19-49. New York: Harcourt, Brace, and World, 1963.

3604. Manwaring, David R. *Render unto Caesar: The Flag-Salute Controversy*. Chicago: University of Chicago Press, 1962.

3605. Manzullo, Donald A. *Neither Sacred nor Profane: The Supreme Court and the Church*. Hicksville, NY: Exposition, 1973.

3606. Marshall, William P. " 'We Know It When We See It': The Supreme Court

and Establishment." *Southern California Law Review* 59 (March 1986): 495-550.

3607. Mead, Sidney E. "Religion, Constitutional Federalism, Rights, and the Court." *Journal of Church and State* 14 (Spring 1972): 191-209.

3608. Meiklejohn, Donald. "Religion in the Burger Court: The Heritage of Mr. Justice Black." *Indiana Law Review* 10 (1977): 645-674.

3609. Menefee, Samuel P. "Crowns and Crosses: The Problems of Politico-Religious Visits as They Relate to the Establishment Clause of the First Amendment." *Harvard Journal of Law and Public Policy* 3 (Summer 1980): 227-254.

3610. Michaelsen, Robert S. "Constitutions, Courts, and the Study of Religion." *Journal of the American Academy of Religion* 45 (Summer 1977): 291-308.

3611. Miller, Robert T., and Donald Flowers. *Toward Benevolent Neutrality: Church, State, and the Supreme Court*. Rev. ed. Waco, TX: Baylor University Press, 1982.

3612. Mitchell, Frederic. "The Supreme Court of the United States on Religion and Education." Ph.D. diss., Columbia University, 1959.

3613. Monkres, Peter. "Just-War Theology: Rejected by the Court." *Christian Century* 92 (May 28, 1975): 547-549.

3614. Morgan, Richard E. "The Establishment Clause and Sectarian Schools: A Final Installment?" *Supreme Court Review* 1973 (1973): 57-97.

3615. Morgan, Richard E. *The Supreme Court and Religion*. New York: Free Press, 1972.

3616. Morris, Edward A. "The Separation of Church and State Principle and the Use of Religious Music in the Public Schools." Ph.D. diss., University of Michigan, 1979.

3617. Morris, Richard B. "The Wall of

Separation: The Supreme Court and the Relationship between Church and State." *American Heritage* 35 (May 1984): 77-79.

3618. Mott, Kenneth F. "Religion, the State, and Education: The Supreme Court and Perspectives of Theory." Ph.D. diss., Brown University, 1967.

3619. Mott, Kenneth F. "The Supreme Court and the Establishment Clause: From Separation to Accommodation and Beyond." *Journal of Law and Education* 14 (April 1985): 111-145.

3620. Nagel, Stuart S., and Robert Erikson. "Editorial Reaction to Supreme Court Decisions on Church and State." *Public Opinion Quarterly* 30 (Winter 1966/1967): 647-655.

3621. Niebuhr, Reinhold. "The Regent's Prayer Decision." *Christianity and Crisis* 22 (July 23, 1962): 125-126.

3622. Nielson, Niels C., Jr. "The Advancement of Religion versus Teaching about Religion in the Public Schools." *Journal of Church and State* 26 (Winter 1984): 105-116.

3623. Nowak, John E. "The Supreme Court, the Religion Clause, and the Nationalization of Education." *Northwestern University Law Review* 70 (January/ February 1976): 883-909.

3624. Oaks, Dallin H. *Religious Freedom and the Supreme Court.* Washington, DC: Ethics and Public Policy Center, 1981.

3625. O'Brien, F. William. "The *Engel* Case from a Swiss Perspective." *Michigan Law Review* 61 (April 1963): 1031-1086.

3626. O'Brien, Stephen J., and Richard S. Vacca. *The Supreme Court and the Religion Education Controversy: A Tightrope to Entanglement.* Durham, NC: Moore, 1974.

3627. O'Donnell, Thomas F. "Religion, Basic Education, and the First Amendment: The Supreme Court from Fuller to

Warren." Ed.D. diss., Lehigh University, 1973.

3628. Paris, John J. "Toward an Understanding of the Supreme Court's Approach to Religion in Conscientious Objector Cases." Ph.D. diss., University of Southern California, 1972.

3629. Paulsell, William O., ed. "Church-State Issues." *Lexington Theological Quarterly* 20 (July 1985): 63-103.

3630. Paulsen, Michael A. "Religion, Equality, and the Constitution: An Equal Protection Approach to Establishment Clause Adjudication." *Notre Dame Law Review* 61 (1986): 311-371.

3631. Pear, R. H. "The U.S. Supreme Court and Religious Freedom." *Modern Law Review* 12 (April 1949): 167-182.

3632. Peterson, Walfred H. "The Baptist Joint Committee on Public Affairs and the *Amicus Curiae* Brief." *Mid-America* 60 (October 1984): 121-142.

3633. Peterson, Walfred H. "Confusion Confounded: Government Aid to Private Education in the Burger Court." *Christian Scholar's Review* 9 (1980): 195-214.

3634. Peterson, Walfred H. "The Thwarted Opportunity for Judicial Activism in Church-State Relations: Separation and Accommodation in Precarious Balance." *Journal of Church and State* 22 (Autumn 1980): 437-458.

3635. Pfeffer, Leo. "*Amici* in Church-State Litigation." *Law and Contemporary Problems* 44 (Spring 1981): 83-110.

3636. Pfeffer, Leo. *Church, State, and Freedom.* Rev. ed. Boston: Beacon Press, 1967.

3637. Pfeffer, Leo. "Current State of the Law in the United States and the Separationist Agenda." *Annals of the American Academy of Political and Social Science* 446 (November 1979): 1-9.

3638. Pfeffer, Leo. "The Deity in American Constitutional History." *Journal of Church and State* 23 (Spring 1981): 215-239.

3639. Pfeffer, Leo. *God, Caesar, and the Constitution: The Court as Referee of Church-State Confrontation.* Boston: Beacon Press, 1975.

3640. Pfeffer, Leo. "The New York Regent's Prayer Case." *Journal of Church and State* 4 (November 1962): 150-158.

3641. Pfeffer, Leo. *Religion, State, and the Burger Court.* Buffalo, NY: Prometheus Books, 1985.

3642. Pfeffer, Leo. "Sabbatarians and the Courts: Court Decisions over the Years Leave Religious Questions Unresolved." *Civil Rights Digest* 11 (Spring 1979): 28-33.

3643. Pfeffer, Leo. "The Supreme Court as Protector of Civil Rights: Freedom of Religion." *Annals of the American Academy of Political and Social Science* 275 (May 1951): 75-85.

3644. Pfeffer, Leo. "Workers' Sabbath: Religious Belief and Employment." *Civil Liberties Review* 4 (November/December 1977): 52-56.

3645. Pollak, Louis H. "Public Prayers in Public Schools." *Harvard Law Review* 77 (November 1963): 62-78.

3646. Proctor, William G., Jr. "The Unsystematic Theology of the United States Supreme Court." *Journal of Church and State* 9 (Winter 1967): 17-35.

3647. Pusey, Merlo J. "The 'Wall' between Church and State: United States Supreme Court's Decision in the School Prayer and Bible Reading Cases." *New York State Bar Journal* 37 (June 1965): 210-216.

3648. Rabin, Robert L. "When Is a Religious Belief Religious: *United States v. Seeger* and the Scope of Free Exercise: Recent Supreme Court Opinion Construing

the Exemption from Military Service for Conscientious Objectors." *Cornell Law Quarterly* 51 (Winter 1966): 231-249.

3649. Redlich, Norman. "Separation of Church and State: The Burger Court's Tortuous Journey." *Notre Dame Law Review* 60 (1985): 1094-1149.

3650. Regan, Richard J. *Private Conscience and Public Law: The American Experience.* New York: Fordham University Press, 1972.

3651. Regan, Richard J. "Regulating Cult Activities: The Limits of Religious Freedom." *Thought* 61 (June 1986): 185-196.

3652. Rice, Charles E. *The Supreme Court and Public Prayer: The Need for Restraint.* New York: Fordham University Press, 1964.

3653. Riga, Peter J. "*Yoder* and Free Exercise." *Journal of Law and Education* 6 (October 1977): 449-472.

3654. Royse, Phillip N. "The Warren Court: The Establishment of Religion and Schools." Ph.D. diss., University of Cincinnati, 1979.

3655. Schimmel, David. "Supreme Court: Silent Meditation OK, but No Transcendental Meditation in Schools." *American School Board Journal* 166 (March 1979): 32-33.

3656. Schmidt, Godfrey F. "Religious Liberty and the Supreme Court of the United States." *Fordham Law Review* 17 (November 1948): 173-199.

3657. Schram, Glenn N. "The Supreme Court on State Aid to Private Education: A Call for a Return to Older Criteria." *Currents in Theology and Mission* 6 (April 1979): 77-83.

3658. Schwartz, David F. "*Larkin v. Grendel's Den Inc.*: The Burger Court and the Establishment Clause Problem." *Houston Law Review* 21 (January 1984): 179-208.

3659. Sendor, Benjamin B. "Congress v. the Courts: Extracurricular Student Religious Groups." *School Law Bulletin* (University of North Carolina) 16 (Spring 1985): 1-5.

3660. Sheffer, Martin S. "The Supreme Court and the Free Exercise of Religion, the Judicial Development of Belief, Worship, and Proselytizing." Ph.D. diss., New School for Social Research, 1977.

3661. Sheffer, Martin S. "The U.S. Supreme Court and the Free Exercise Clause: Are Standards of Adjudication Possible?" *Journal of Church and State* 23 (Autumn 1981): 533-549.

3662. Sirico, Louis J., Jr. "The Secular Contribution of Religion to the Political Process: The First Amendment and School Aid." *Missouri Law Review* 50 (Spring 1985): 321-376.

3663. Smith, Michael E. "The Special Place of Religion in the Constitution." *Supreme Court Review* 1983 (1983): 83-123.

3664. Smith, Robert D. "The Supreme Court in the Political Process: The Impact of the *Engel* and *Schempp* Decisions." Ph.D. diss., Vanderbilt University, 1969.

3665. Sorauf, Frank J. *The Wall of Separation: The Constitutional Politics of Church and State.* Princeton, NJ: Princeton University Press, 1976.

3666. Sorauf, Frank J. "*Zorach v. Clausen*: The Impact of a Supreme Court Decision." *American Political Science Review* 53 (September 1959): 777-791.

3667. Spring, Beth. "The Ominous Implication of the *Bob Jones* Decision: Are Tax Exemptions Really Like Cash Grants from the Government." *Christianity Today* 11 (July 15, 1983): 32, 34-35.

3668. Spring, Beth. "Supreme Court Speaks Up for Religion in American Life: Nativity Scene at Pawtucket City Hall Not Unconstitutional." *Christianity Today* 28 (April 6, 1984): 68-69.

3669. Spring, Beth. "U.S. Supreme Court Restates Its Commitment to Separation of Church and State." *Christianity Today* 29 (August 9, 1985): 44-45.

3670. Spring, Beth. "Why High School Students Can't Discuss the Bible: The Supreme Court Turns Down the *Lubbock* Case." *Christianity Today* 4 (February 18, 1983): 34-35.

3671. Starr, Isadore. "Recent Supreme Court Decisions: Separation of Church and State." *Social Education* 26 (December 1962): 439-444.

3672. Stevens, John V., and John G. Julio. "Casenote: *United States v. Lee*, a Second Look." *Journal of Church and State* 26 (Autumn 1984): 455-472.

3673. Stone, Geoffrey R. "Constitutionally Compelled Exemptions and the Free Exercise Clause." *William and Mary Law Review* 27 (Special Issue 1985/1986): 985-996.

3674. Sturm, Douglas. "Constitutionalism and Conscientiousness: The Dignity of Objection to Military Service." *Journal of Law and Religion* 1 (Winter 1983): 265-277.

3675. Sturm, Douglas. "The Courts and the Church-State Tangle." *Christianity and Crisis* 44 (October 1984): 340-342.

3676. Sutherland, Arthur E., Jr. "Establishment According to *Engel*: Appraises the Widely Discussed School Prayer Case Decided by the Supreme Court Last Term." *Harvard Law Review* 76 (November 1962): 25-52.

3677. Tager, Evan M. "The Supreme Court, Effect Inquiry, and Aid to Parochial Education." *Stanford Law Review* 37 (November 1984): 219-251.

3678. Tarr, Curtis W. "Selective Service and Conscientious Objectors." *American Bar Association Journal* 57 (October 1971): 976-980.

3679. Taylor, Donald E. "Supreme Court

and a Definition of Religion." *Lexington Theological Quarterly* 13 (January 1978): 27-32.

3680. Teitel, Ruti G. "The Supreme Court's 1984-1985 Church-State Decisions: Judicial Paths of Least Resistance." *Harvard Civil Rights-Civil Liberties Law Review* 21 (Summer 1986): 651-688.

3681. Tushnet, Mark V. "Reflections on the Role of Purpose in the Jurisprudence of the Religion Clauses." *William and Mary Law Review* 27 (Special Issue 1985/1986): 997-1009.

3682. Tussman, Joseph. *The Supreme Court on Church and State.* New York: Oxford University Press, 1962.

3683. Underwood, James L. "Permissible Entanglement under the Establishment Clause." *Emory Law Journal* 25 (Winter 1976): 17-62.

3684. Van Alstyne, William W. "Constitutional Separation of Church and State: The Quest for a Coherent Position." *American Political Science Review* 57 (December 1963): 865-882.

3685. Van Alstyne, William W. "Trends in the Supreme Court: Mr. Jefferson's Crumbling Wall; A Comment on *Lynch v. Donnelly.*" *Duke Law Journal* 1984 (September 1984): 770-787.

3686. Vance, Donald F. "The Supreme Court and the Definition of Religion." Ph.D. diss., Indiana University, 1970.

3687. "Wages and Religion." *Christian Century* 102 (May 8, 1985): 464-465.

3688. Wall, James M. "A Wise Decision in a Complex Case." *Christian Century* 102 (July 17-24, 1985): 667-668.

3689. Warshaw, Thayer S. "The Bible as Textbook in Public Schools." *Religious Education* 77 (May/June 1982): 279-299.

3690. Way, H. Frank, Jr. "Survey Research on Judicial Decisions: The Prayer and Bible Reading Cases." *Western Political Quarterly* 21 (June 1968): 189-205.

3691. Weber, Paul J. "Building on Sand: Supreme Court Construction and Educational Tax Credits." *Creighton Law Review* 12 (Winter 1978-1979): 531-565.

3692. Weeks, Louis, and James C. Hickey. "Implied Trust for Connectional Churches: *Watson v. Jones* Revisited." *Journal of Presbyterian History* 54 (Winter 1976): 459-470.

3693. West, E. G. "An Economic Analysis of the Law and Politics of Non-Public School 'Aid'." *Journal of Law and Economics* 19 (April 1976): 79-101.

3694. West, Ellis M. "The Supreme Court and Religious Liberty in the Public Schools." *Journal of Church and State* 25 (Winter 1983): 87-112.

3695. West, Ellis M. "The Supreme Court and the Conflict between the Principles of Religious Liberty and Separation of Church and State." Ph.D. diss., Emory University, 1971.

3696. Whelan, Charles M. "Secular Education: Catholic Schools and the Supreme Court." *National Catholic Education Association Bulletin* 65 (November 1968): 8-12.

3697. Whitehead, John W. "Freedom in the Public Schools: Standing against the Tide of Secularism." *Fundamentalists Journal* 4 (September 1985): 17-19.

3698. Wilson, Bradford. "Enforcing the Fourth Amendment: The Original Understanding." *Catholic Lawyer* 28 (Summer 1983): 173-198.

3699. Wilson, Francis. "The Supreme Court's Civil Theology." *Modern Age* 13 (Summer 1969): 248-257.

3700. Wolfe, Christopher. "The Supreme Court and Catholic Social Thought." *American Journal of Jurisdiction* 29 (1984): 45-72.

3701. Wood, James E. "The Battle over the Public School." *Journal of Church and State* 28 (Winter 1985): 5-13.

3702. Wood, James E. "Legislating Prayer in the Public Schools." *Journal of Church and State* 23 (Spring 1981): 205-213.

3703. Wood, James E. "Parochiaid and the U.S. Supreme Court." *Journal of Church and State* 13 (Autumn 1971): 401-412.

3704. Worthing, Sharon L. "The State and the Church School: The Conflict over Social Policy." *Journal of Church and State* 26 (Winter 1984): 91-104.

3705. Young, David J. "Constitutional Validity of State Aid to Pupils in Church-Related Schools: Internal Tension between the Establishment and Free Exercise Clauses." *Ohio State Law Journal* 38 (1977): 783-805.

Speech

3706. Aptheker, Herbert. "Cold-War Court." *Masses and Mainstream* 3 (June 1950): 29-42.

3707. Baker, C. Edwin. "Commercial Speech: A Problem in the Theory of Freedom." *Iowa Law Review* 62 (October 1976): 1-56.

3708. Ball, Howard. "Careless Justice: The United States Supreme Court's Shopping Center Opinions, 1946-1976." *Polity* 11 (Winter 1978): 200-228.

3709. Berkman, Richard L. "Students in Court: Free Speech and the Functions of Schooling in America." *Harvard Educational Review* 40 (November 1970): 567-595.

3710. Bernheim, Emily. "Free Speech for Public Employees: The Supreme Court Strikes a New Balance." *School Law Bulletin* (University of North Carolina) 17 (Winter 1986): 8-17.

3711. Bogen, David S. "The Supreme Court's Interpretation of the Guarantee of Freedom of Speech." *Maryland Law Review* 35 (Fall 1976): 555-616.

3712. Bosmajian, Haig. "Restricting Stonley and Freedom of Speech." *Midwest Quarterly* 20 (Spring 1979): 228-240.

3713. Brockmeyer, Marta A. "The Warren Court First Amendment Decisions: Freedom of Expression Redefined for Students Enrolled in Public Institutions of Higher Education." Ph.D. diss., St. Louis University, 1982.

3714. Chafee, Zechariah, Jr. *Free Speech in the United States.* Cambridge: Harvard University Press, 1941.

3715. Child, Barbara. "Trends in the United States Supreme Court's Use of the Ripeness Doctrine in Free Speech and Association Cases: A Comparison with Canadian Trends." *Case Western Reserve Journal of International Law* 10 (Spring 1978): 415-468.

3716. Cohen, Jeremy. "*Schenck v. United States*: A Clear and Present Danger to the First Amendment." Ph.D. diss., University of Washington, 1983.

3717. Cortner, Richard C. "The Wobblies and *Fiske v. Kansas*: Victory Amid Disintegration." *Kansas History* 4 (Spring 1981): 30-38.

3718. Epstein, Edwin M. "Corporations and Labor Unions in Electoral Politics." *Annals of the American Academy of Political and Social Science* 425 (May 1976): 33-58.

3719. Farber, Daniel A., and John E. Nowak. "The Misleading Nature of Public Forum Analysis: Content and Context in First Amendment Adjudication." *Virginia Law Review* 70 (September 1984): 1219-1266.

3720. Gardner, George K. "Free Speech in Public Places." *Boston University Law Review* 36 (Spring 1956): 239-252.

3721. Gibson, James L., and Richard D. Bingham. *Civil Liberties and Nazis: The Skokie Free-Speech Controversy.* New York: Praeger, 1985.

3722. Gordon, William I. *Nine Men Plus: Supreme Court Opinions on Free Speech and Free Press: An Academic Game-Simulation.* Dubuque, IA: William C. Brown, 1971.

3723. Gray, John A. "Corporate Identity and Corporate Political Activities." *American Business Law Journal* 21 (Winter 1984): 439-461.

3724. Haiman, Franklyn S. *Speech and Law in a Free Society.* Chicago: University of Chicago Press, 1981.

3725. Hale, F. Dennis. "Comparison of Coverage of Speech and Press Verdicts of Supreme Court." *Journalism Quarterly* 56 (Spring 1979): 43-47.

3726. Hatano, Daryl G. "Should Corporations Exercise Their Freedom of Speech Rights?" *American Business Law Journal* 22 (Summer 1984): 165-187.

3727. Heberle, Klaus H. "From *Gitlow* to *Near*: Judicial Amendment by Absentminded Incrementalism." *Journal of Politics* 34 (May 1972): 458-483.

3728. Hentoff, Nat. *The First Freedom: The Tumultuous History of Free Speech in America.* New York: Delacorte, 1980.

3729. Holten, Ruth. "Acceptable Library Censorship: The Supreme Court's Guide." *Educational Forum* 50 (Fall 1985): 67-74.

3730. Hudon, Edward G. *Freedom of Speech and Press.* Washington, DC: Public Affairs Press, 1962.

3731. Johnson, Paul I. "Freedom of Speech Means Freedom to Teach: The Constitutional Battle in Nebraska, 1919-1923." *Concordia Historical Institute Quarterly* 52 (Fall 1979): 118-124.

3732. Kemerer, Frank R., and Stephanie A. Hirsh. "School Library Censorship Comes before the Supreme Court." *Phi Delta Kappan* 63 (March 1982): 444-448.

3733. Kipperman, Steven. "Civil Rights at Armageddon: The Supreme Court Steps Back: *Adderly v. Florida.*" *Law in Transition Quarterly* 3 (Fall 1966): 219-235.

3734. Konvitz, Milton R. "Free Speech for Naturalized Citizens: The Recent *Schneiderman* and *Baumgartner* Cases." *Common Ground* 5 (Spring 1945): 100-102.

3735. Kurland, Philip B. *Free Speech and Association: The Supreme Court and the First Amendment.* Chicago: University of Chicago Press, 1975.

3736. Latham, Earl. "Theory of the Judicial Concept of Freedom of Speech." *Journal of Politics* 12 (November 1950): 637-651.

3737. Levy, Leonard W. *Freedom of Speech and Press in Early American History: Legacy of Suppression.* New York: Harper and Row, 1963.

3738. Lieberman, Jethro K. *Free Speech, Free Press, and the Law.* New York: Lothrop, Lee, and Shepard, 1980.

3739. Linenthal, Eleanor. "Freedom of Speech and the Power of Courts and Congress to Punish for Contempt." Ph.D. diss., Cornell University, 1956.

3740. Lively, Donald E. "The Supreme Court's Emerging Vision of False Speech: A First Amendment Blind Spot." *Rutgers Law Review* 38 (Spring 1986): 479-499.

3741. Lusk, Louis B. "The Present Status of the 'Clear and Present Danger Test'." *Kentucky Law Journal* 45 (Summer 1957): 576-606.

3742. McChesney, Fred S. "Commercial Speech in the Professions: The Supreme Court's Unanswered Questions and Questionable Answers." *University of Pennsylvania Law Review* 134 (December 1985): 45-119.

3743. Marcus, Benjamin. "*FCC v. League of Women Voters*: Conditions on Federal Funding That Inhibits Speech and Subject Matter Restrictions on Speech." *Cornell Law Review* 71 (January 1986): 453-476.

3744. Meiklejohn, Donald. "Public Speech and the First Amendment." *Georgetown Law Journal* 55 (November 1966): 234-263.

3745. Meiklejohn, Donald. "Public Speech in the Supreme Court since *New York Times v. Sullivan*." *Syracuse Law Review* 26 (Summer 1975): 819-865.

3746. Miller, Arthur S. "On Politics, Democracy, and the First Amendment: A Commentary on *First National Bank v. Bellotti*." *Washington and Lee Law Review* 38 (Winter 1981): 21-41.

3747. Moore, John H. "The *Angelo Herndon* Case, 1932-1937." *Phylon* 32 (Spring 1971): 60-71.

3748. Moskowitz, Daniel B. "Lawyers Learn the Hard Sell and Companies Shudder." *Business Week* (June 10, 1985): 70-71.

3749. Murphy, Paul L. *The Meaning of Freedom of Speech: First Amendment Freedoms from Wilson to FDR*. Westport, CT: Greenwood Press, 1972.

3750. Nicholson, Marlene A. "*Buckley v. Valeo*: The Constitutionality of the Federal Election Campaign Act Amendments of 1974." *Wisconsin Law Review* 1977 (1977): 323-374.

3751. Nicholson, Marlene A. "The Supreme Court's Meandering Path in Campaign Finance Regulation and What It Portends for Future Reform." *Journal of Law and Politics* 3 (Winter 1987): 509-565.

3752. Nimmer, Melville B. "The Right to Speak from *Times* to *Time*: First Amendment Theory Applied to Libel and Misapplied to Privacy." *California Law Review* 56 (August 1968): 935-967.

3753. Nuchia, Sam M. "Freedom of Speech and Police Officers Public Criticism." *Police Chief* 51 (June 1984): 16-17.

3754. O'Brien, David M. "Freedom of Speech and Free Government: The First Amendment, the Supreme Court, and the Polity." *Virginia Cavalcade* 33 (Summer 1983): 30-37.

3755. Padgett, George E. "A Quantitative Analysis of United States Supreme Court Decision-Making Relative to First Amendment Issues of Free Speech and Free Press." Ph.D. diss., Ohio University, 1980.

3756. Porto, Brian L. "*Tinker* Decision and Native Americans: The Case for Expanding a Precedent." *Journal of Law and Education* 11 (January 1982): 65-77.

3757. Rentschler, Donald R. "The Tinker Test: An Analysis of the Judicial Interpretation of *Tinker v. Des Moines Independent Community School District*." Ph.D. diss., Duke University, 1981.

3758. Rice, George P., Jr. "The Supreme Court of the United States on Free Legal Speech." *Armenian Review* 10 (June 1957): 81-86.

3759. Richards, Eric L. "Raising the Banner of States' Rights to Prevent Private Abridgment of Speech." *American Business Law Journal* 23 (Summer 1985): 155-201.

3760. Richardson, Elliott L. "Freedom of Expression and the Function of Courts." *Harvard Law Review* 65 (November 1951): 1-54.

3761. Rogge, O. John. "Congress Shall Make No Law." *Michigan Law Review* 56 (January/February 1958): 331-374, 577-618.

3762. Roper, Robert T. "The Gag Order: Asphyxiating the First Amendment." *Western Political Quarterly* 34 (September 1981): 372-388.

3763. Rosenwein, Samuel. "The Supreme

Court and Freedom of Speech: *Terminiello v. City of Chicago.*" *Lawyers Guild Review* 9 (Spring 1949): 70-77.

3764. Rotfeld, Herbert J. "Regulation of the Free: Advertising and the First Amendment." *Policy Studies Review* 2 (February 1983): 474-483.

3765. Rotunda, Ronald D. "Commercial Speech Doctrine in Supreme Court." *University of Illinois Law Forum* 1976 (1976): 1080-1101.

3766. Rubin, Richard S. "When the Governed Criticize Their Governors: Parameters of Public Employees' Free-Speech Rights." *Employee Relations Law Journal* 10 (Summer 1984): 106-119.

3767. Rutzick, Mark C. "Offensive Language and the Evolution of First Amendment Protection." *Harvard Civil Rights-Civil Liberties Law Review* 9 (January 1974): 1-28.

3768. Sanford, Bruce W. "No Quarter from This Court." *Columbia Journalism Review* 18 (September 1979): 59-63.

3769. Schneider, Willys. "*Buckley v. Valeo*: Supreme Court and Federal Campaign Reform." *Columbia Law Review* 76 (June 1976): 852-891.

3770. Schoeman, Michael G. "The First Amendment and Restrictions on Advertising of Securities under the Securities Act of 1933." *Business Lawyer* 41 (February 1986): 377-392.

3771. Schofield, Lemuel B. "First Amendment Implications of Banning Alcoholic Beverage Ads on Radio and TV: Issue Has Been Dealt with Indirectly by Supreme Court: Indication Is That Such Legislation Would Not Violate First Amendment." *Journalism Quarterly* 62 (Autumn 1985): 533-539.

3772. Shapiro, Martin M. *Freedom of Speech: The Supreme Court and Judicial Review.* Englewood Cliffs, NJ: Prentice-Hall, 1966.

3773. Sheridan, David. "Commercial Speech: Supreme Court Sends Another Valentine to Advertisers." *Buffalo Law Review* 25 (Spring 1976): 737-751.

3774. Shockley, John S. "Direct Democracy, Campaign Finance, and the Courts: Can Corruption, Undue Influence, and Declining Voter Confidence Be Found?" *University of Miami Law Review* 39 (May 1985): 377-428.

3775. Siegel, Paul. "Protecting Political Speech: *Brandenburg vs. Ohio* Updated." *Quarterly Journal of Speech* 67 (February 1981): 69-80.

3776. Snyder, Franklin B. "Librarians and the Supreme Court." *American Libraries* 17 (March 1986): 205-206.

3777. Sterchi, Karen L. "Restraints on Alcoholic Beverage Advertising: A Constitutional Analysis." *Notre Dame Law Review* 60 (1985): 779-799.

3778. Stief, Erwin H. "The Supreme Court's Attitude toward Liberty of Contract and Freedom of Speech." *Yale Law Review* 41 (December 1931): 262-271.

3779. "Supreme Court Holds Lawyers May Advertise: But the Court Limits Its Decision and Rules That Some Restraints May Yet Be Exercised." *American Bar Association Journal* 63 (August 1977): 1092-1098.

3780. "Supreme Court Will Hear Lawyers Advertising Case from Arizona." *American Bar Association Journal* 62 (November 1976): 1422-1423.

3781. Tedford, Thomas. *Freedom of Speech in the United States.* New York: Random House, 1985.

3782. Trauth, Denise M., and John L. Huffman. "New U.S. Supreme Court Philosophy on Advertising Faces Opposition." *Journalism Quarterly* 56 (Autumn 1979): 540-545.

3783. "Utilities Win Free-Speech Cases at

Supreme Court." *Broadcasting* 98 (June 30, 1980): 66-67.

3784. Van Alstyne, William W. "The Specific Theory of Academic Freedom and the General Issue of Civil Liberties." *Annals of the American Academy of Political and Social Science* 404 (November 1972): 140-156.

3785. Vanderpool, William S., Jr. "The Rhetorical Principles Enunciated in Supreme Court Decisions Affecting Free Speech." Ph.D. diss., Louisiana State University, 1954.

3786. Vaughn, Stephen. "First Amendment Liberties and the Committee on Public Information." *American Journal of Legal History* 23 (April 1979): 95-119.

3787. Werhan, Keith. "The Supreme Court's Public Forum Doctrine and the Return of Formalism." *Cardozo Law Review* 7 (Winter 1986): 335-437.

3788. Wiener, Frederick B. "Are the General Military Articles Unconstitutionally Vague?" *American Bar Association Journal* 54 (April 1968): 357-364.

3789. Williams, Theodore R. "Educational Policy Implications of the U.S. Supreme Court Decision in the *Tinker v. Des Moines* Case." Ph.D. diss., University of Iowa, 1978.

3790. Yadlosky, Elizabeth. *The Supreme Court Decision on Campaign Financing, Buckley v. Valeo: A Discussion in Question and Answer Form.* Washington, DC: Congressional Research Service, 1975.

VI. The Court and Equal Rights

General Studies

3791. Andersen, Jill H. "Equal Protection during the 1984 Term: Revitalized Rational Basis Examination in the Economic Sphere." *Drake Law Review* 36 (1986/1987): 25-43.

3792. Bator, Paul. "Equality as a Constitutional Value." *Harvard Journal of Law and Public Policy* 9 (Winter 1986): 21-24.

3793. Berger, Morroe. *Equality by Statute: Legal Controls over Group Discrimination.* New York: Columbia University Press, 1952.

3794. Berger, Morroe. *Equality by Statute: The Revolution in Civil Rights.* Rev. ed. Garden City, NJ: Doubleday, 1968.

3795. Berger, Morroe. "The Supreme Court and Group Discrimination since 1937." *Columbia Law Review* 49 (February 1949): 201-230.

3796. Bischoff, Ralph F. "Constitutional Law and Civil Rights." *New York University Law Review* 31 (January 1956): 60-92.

3797. Blattner, J. H. "Supreme Court's 'Intermediate' Equal Protection Decisions: Five Imperfect Models of Constitutional Equality." *Hastings Constitutional Law Quarterly* 8 (Summer 1981): 777-842.

3798. Bolner, James. "The Burger Court and Equal Protection: Exercise in Legal Pragmatism." *Southern University Law Review* 10 (Spring 1984): 241-262.

3799. Boudin, Louis B. "The Supreme Court and Civil Rights." *Science and Society* 1 (Spring 1937): 273-309.

3800. Broderick, Albert. "Nature of the Constitutional Process: Equal Protection and the Burger Court." *North Carolina Central Law Journal* 12 (Spring 1981): 320-406.

3801. Carr, Robert K. *Federal Protection of Civil Rights.* Ithaca, NY: Cornell University Press, 1947.

3802. Clark, Elias. "Charitable Trusts, the Fourteenth Amendment, and the Will of Stephen Girard." *Yale Law Journal* 66 (June 1957): 979-1015.

3803. Collins, Charles W. "The Failure of the Fourteenth Amendment as a Constitutional Ideal." *South Atlantic Quarterly* 11 (April 1912): 101-115.

3804. Corwin, Edward S. "The Supreme Court and the Fourteenth Amendment." *Michigan Law Review* 7 (June 1909): 643-672.

3805. Davis, Sue. "Balancing, Weighing, and Measuring: The Supreme Court, the Fourteenth Amendment, and the Concept of State Action." Ph.D. diss., University of California, Santa Barbara, 1980.

3806. Dittman, Vance R., Jr. "Some Aspects of Procedural Due Process under the Fourteenth Amendment as Considered by the Supreme Court of the United States." *Dicta* 32 (July/August 1955): 263-274.

3807. Donovan, William J. "An Independent Supreme Court and the Protection of Minority Rights." *American Bar Association Journal* 23 (April 1937): 254-260, 295-296.

3808. Dunlap, Mary C. "Equal Rights Amendment and the Courts." *Pepperdine Law Review* 3 (Winter 1975): 42-81.

3809. Durchslag, Melvyn. "Constraints on Equal Access to Fundamental Liberties: Another Look at Professor Michelman's Theory of Minimum Protection." *Georgia Law Review* 19 (Summer 1985): 1041-1074.

3810. Ervin, Samuel J., Jr. "Civil Rights and Constitutional Wrongs." *Modern Age* 27 (Winter 1983): 25-35.

3811. Fairman, Charles. "Does the Fourteenth Amendment Incorporate the Bill of Rights: The Original Understanding." *Stanford Law Review* 2 (December 1949): 5-39.

3812. Fairman, Charles, and Stanley Morrison. *The Fourteenth Amendment and the Bill of Rights: The Incorporation Theory.* New York: De Capo, 1970.

3813. Fellman, David. "The Supreme Court as Protector of Civil Rights." *Annals of the American Academy of Political and Social Science* 275 (May 1951): 61-110.

3814. Flack, Horace E. *The Adoption of the Fourteenth Amendment.* Baltimore: Johns Hopkins Press, 1908.

3815. Fox, Randall. "Equal Protection Analysis: Laurence Tribe, the Middle Tier, and the Role of the Court." *University of San Francisco Law Review* 14 (Summer 1980): 525-570.

3816. Friendly, Henry J. *Some Equal Protection Problems of the 1970s.* New York: New York University School of Law, 1970.

3817. Funston, Richard Y. "The Double

Standard of Constitutional Protection in the Era of the Welfare State." *Political Science Quarterly* 90 (Summer 1975): 261-292.

3818. Gaffney, Edward M., Jr. "History and Legal Interpretation: The Early Distortion of the Fourteenth Amendment by the Gilded Age Court." *Catholic University Law Review* 25 (Winter 1976): 207-249.

3819. Goldstein, Robert D. " A Swann Song for Remedies: Equitable Relief in the Burger Court." *Harvard Civil Rights-Civil Liberties Law Review* 13 (Winter 1978): 1-80.

3820. Graham, Howard J. "The 'Conspiracy Theory' of the Fourteenth Amendment." *Yale Law Journal* 47 (January 1938): 371-403.

3821. Graham, Howard J. *Everyman's Constitution: Historical Essays on the Fourteenth Amendment, the "Conspiracy Theory," and Constitutionalism.* Madison: State Historical Society of Wisconsin, 1968.

3822. Graham, Howard J. "The Waite Court and the Fourteenth Amendment." *Vanderbilt Law Review* 17 (March 1964): 525-547.

3823. Graham, Robert L., and Jason H. Kravitt. "The Evolution of Equal Protection: Education, Municipal Services, and Wealth." *Harvard Civil Rights-Civil Liberties Law Review* 7 (January 1972): 105-213.

3824. Grano, Joseph. "Prophylactic Rules in Criminal Procedure: A Question of Article III Legitimacy." *Northwestern University Law Review* 80 (March 1985): 100-164.

3825. Green, John R. "The Bill of Rights, the Fourteenth Amendment, and the Supreme Court." *Michigan Law Review* 46 (May 1948): 869-910.

3826. Greenberg, Jack. "The Supreme

Court, Civil Rights, and Civil Dissonance." *Yale Law Journal* 77 (July 1968): 1520-1544.

3827. Griswold, Erwin N. *The Fifth Amendment Today: Three Speeches*. Cambridge: Harvard University Press, 1955.

3828. Griswold, Erwin N. "The Supreme Court's Case Load: Civil Rights and Other Problems." *University of Illinois Law Forum* 1973 (1973): 615-634.

3829. Gui, Janice. "Civil Rights in the Burger Court Era." *Akron Law Review* 10 (Fall 1976): 327-366.

3830. Gunther, Gerald. "Supreme Court, 1971 Term, Foreword: In Search of Evolving Doctrine on a Changing Court: A Model for a Newer Equal Protection." *Harvard Law Review* 86 (November 1972): 1-299.

3831. Guthrie, William D. *Lectures on the Fourteenth Article of Amendment to the Constitution of the United States, Delivered before the Dwight Alumni Association, New York, April-May 1898*. Boston: Little, Brown, 1898.

3832. Haddock, David, and Thomas D. Hall. "The Impact of Making Rights Inalienable: *Merrion v. Jicarilla Apache Tribe, Texaco Inc. v. Short, Fidelity Federal Savings and Loan Association v. de la Cuesta, and Ridgway v. Ridgway*." *Supreme Court Economic Review* 2 (1983): 1-42.

3833. Hellman, Arthur D. "Supreme Court and Civil Rights: The Plenary Docket in the 1970s." *Oregon Law Review* 58 (1979): 3-60.

3834. Henkin, Louis. "Constitutional Rights and Human Rights." *Harvard Civil Rights-Civil Liberties Law Review* 13 (Summer 1978): 593-632.

3835. Hogler, Raymond L. "Equal Pay, Equal Work, and the United States Supreme Court." *Labor Law Journal* 32 (November 1981): 737-744.

3836. Howard, Pendelton. "The Supreme Court and State Action Challenged under the Fourteenth Amendment: 1930-1931." *University of Pennsylvania Law Review* 80 (February 1932): 483-521.

3837. James, Joseph B. *The Framing of the Fourteenth Amendment*. Urbana: University of Illinois Press, 1956.

3838. Jones, Gary E. "Preferential Treatment and Individual Rights." *Pacific Philosophy Quarterly* 63 (July 1982): 289-295.

3839. Karst, Kenneth L. "Equal Citizenship under the Fourteenth Amendment." *Harvard Law Review* 91 (November 1977): 1-68.

3840. Kay, Richard S. "The Equal Protection Clause in the Supreme Court, 1873-1903." *Buffalo Law Review* 29 (Fall 1980): 667-725.

3841. Lamb, Charles M. "Legal Foundations of Civil Rights and Pluralism in America." *Annals of the American Academy of Political and Social Science* 454 (March 1981): 13-25.

3842. Lancaster, Robert S. "Limits of Judicial Intervention." *Sewanee Review* 67 (Winter 1959): 123-131.

3843. Landever, Arthur. "Perceptions of Judicial Responsibility: The Views of the Nine United States Supreme Court Justices as They Consider Claims in Fourteenth Amendment Non-Criminal Cases: A Post-*Bakke* Evaluation." *Wake Forest Law Review* 14 (December 1978): 1097-1156.

3844. Latham, Earl. "The Majoritarian Dilemma in the United States Supreme Court." *Confluence* 2 (December 1953): 22-36.

3845. Lobur, Connie L. "Equal Protection in the Burger Court: Egalitarian Impulse or Impasse?" Ph.D. diss., Rutgers University, State University of New Jersey, 1984.

3846. McCarrick, Earlean M. "Equality

v. Liberty: An Unresolved Constitutional Note." *Polity* 10 (Winter 1977): 241-260.

3847. McLaughlin, Andrew C. "The Court, the Cooperation, and Conkling." *American Historical Review* 46 (October 1940): 45-63.

3848. Martineau, Robert J., Jr. "Supreme Court and State Regulation of the Legal Profession." *Hastings Constitutional Law Quarterly* 8 (Winter 1981): 199-254.

3849. Mendelson, Wallace. "From Warren to Burger: The Rise and Decline of Substantive Equal Protection." *American Political Science Review* 66 (December 1972): 1226-1233.

3850. Mendelson, Wallace. "A Note on the Cause and Cure of the Fourteenth Amendment." *Journal of Politics* 43 (February 1981): 152-158.

3851. Meyer, Howard N. "Retrieving Self-Evident Truths: The Fourteenth Amendment." *This Constitution* 4 (Fall 1984): 11-16.

3852. Murphy, Brian M. "The American Ideology and the Supreme Court: The Quality of Equality." Ph.D. diss., Miami University, 1980.

3853. Mykkeltvedt, Roald Y. *The Nationalization of the Bill of Rights: Fourteenth Amendment, Due Process, and Procedural Rights.* Millwood, NY: Associated Faculty Press, 1983.

3854. Neighbor, Howard D. "The Case against Nonpartisanship: A Challenge from the Courts." *National Civic Review* 66 (October 1977): 447-452.

3855. Nelkin, Stuart M. "Cypres and the Fourteenth Amendment: A Discriminating Look at Very Private Schools and Not So Charitable Trusts." *Georgetown Law Journal* 56 (December 1967): 272-314.

3856. Nowak, John E. "Realigning the Standards of Review under the Equal Protection Guarantee: Prohibited, Neutral, and Permissive Classifications." *Georgetown Law Journal* 62 (March 1974): 1071-1122.

3857. O'Connell, Michael P. "Equal Protection: Modes of Analysis in the Burger Court." *Denver Law Journal* 53 (1976): 687-729.

3858. Pritchett, C. Herman. "Equal Protection and the Urban Majority." *American Political Science Review* 58 (December 1964): 869-875.

3859. Reid, Inez S. "Optimism Is Not Warranted: The Fate of Minorities and the Economically Poor before the Burger Court." *Howard Law Journal* 20 (1977): 346-373.

3860. Schwartz, David F. " 'New' Fourteenth Amendment: The Decline of State Action, Fundamental Rights, and Suspect Classifications under the Burger Court." *Chicago-Kent Law Review* 56 (Summer 1980): 865-892.

3861. Swindler, William F. "Equal Justice under Law." *American Bar Association Journal* 63 (August 1977): 1099-1104.

3862. Swindler, William F. "Roscoe Conkling and the Fourteenth Amendment." *Supreme Court Historical Society Yearbook* 1983 (1983): 46-52.

3863. Thigpen, Richard. "Application of Fourteenth Amendment Norms to Private Colleges and Universities." *Journal of Law and Education* 11 (April 1982): 171-208.

3864. Tussman, Joseph, and Jacobus TenBrock. "The Equal Protection of the Laws." *California Law Review* 37 (September 1949): 341-381.

3865. Winter, Arthur B. "The Changing Parameters of Substantive Equal Protection: From Warren to the Burger Era." *Emory Law Journal* 23 (Summer 1974): 657-700.

3866. Yarbrough, Tinsley E. "The Burger Court and Unspecified Rights: On Protecting Fundamental and Not-So-Fundamental 'Rights' or 'Interests' through a Flexible Conception of Equal Protection." *Duke Law Journal* 1977 (March 1977): 143-170.

Affirmative Action

3867. Ackerman, David M. *The Regents of the University of California v. Bakke: A Summary and Analysis.* Washington, DC: Congressional Research Service, 1975.

3868. Allen, Robert L. "The *Bakke* Case and Affirmative Action." *Black Scholar* 9 (November 1977): 9-16.

3869. Bakke, Allan P. *Allan Bakke versus Regents of the University of California.* Dobbs Ferry, NY: Oceana Publications, 1978.

3870. Bakke, Allan P. *Regents of the University of California v. Allan Bakke: Complete Case Record.* 3 vols. Englewood, CO: Information Handling Services, 1978.

3871. Beauchamp, Tom L. "Blackstone and the Problem of Reverse Discrimination." *Social Theory and Practice* 5 (Spring 1979): 227-238.

3872. Bennett, William J., and Terry Eastland. "Why *Bakke* Won't End Reverse Discrimination: 1." *Commentary* 66 (September 1978): 29-35.

3873. Bennett-Alexander, Dawn D. "Implications of the *Memphis Firefighters* Case." *Labor Law Journal* 36 (June 1985): 337-350.

3874. Berry, Stan. "Post-*Bakke* Assessment." *College and University* 54 (Winter 1979): 85-88.

3875. Bishop, David W. "The Affirmative Action Cases: *Bakke, Weber,* and *Fullilove.*" *Journal of Negro History* 67 (Fall 1982): 229-244.

3876. Broderick, Albert. "Constitutional Politics: Affirmative Action and Supreme Process." *North Carolina Central Law Journal* 16 (1987): 85-153.

3877. Choper, Jesse H. "Constitutionality of Affirmative Action: Views from the Supreme Court." *Kentucky Law Journal* 70 (1981/1982): 1-22.

3878. Clague, Monique W. "Voluntary Affirmative Action Plans in Public Education: Anticipating a Supreme Court Decision." *Journal of Law and Education* 14 (July 1985): 309-348.

3879. Finkin, Matthew W. "Some Thoughts on the Powell Opinion in *Bakke.*" *Academe* 65 (April 1979): 192-196.

3880. Flygare, Thomas J. "Supreme Court Confused by Reverse Discrimination." *Phi Delta Kappan* 68 (September 1986): 77-78.

3881. Flygare, Thomas J. "Supreme Court Holds That Section 504 Does Not Require Affirmative Action." *Phi Delta Kappan* 61 (September 1979): 63-64.

3882. Glazer, Nathan. "Why *Bakke* Won't End Reverse Discrimination: 2." *Commentary* 66 (September 1978): 36-41.

3883. Hsieh, An-Ping. "An Examination of Equal Protection Analysis in Construction Set-Aside Programs." *Boston College Third World Law Journal* 6 (January 1986): 57-83.

3884. Jacobson, Cardell K. "The *Bakke* Decision: White Reactions to the U.S. Supreme Court's Test of Affirmative Action Programs." *Journal of Conflict Resolution* 27 (December 1983): 687-705.

3885. Johnson, Ronald D. "Voluntary Affirmative Action in the Post-*Weber* Era: Issues and Answers." *Labor Law Journal* 32 (Spring 1981): 609-620.

3886. Johnson, Theresa. "The Future of Affirmative Action: An Analysis of the

Stotts Case." *Labor Law Journal* 36 (October 1985): 782-788.

3887. Jones, James E. "Reverse Discrimination in Employment: Judicial Treatment of Affirmative Action Programmes in the United States." *International Labour Review* 120 (July/August 1981): 453-472.

3888. Jones, Mack H. "The *Bakke* Case: The Logical Legacy of Atheoretical Protest Politics." *Freedomways* 18 (1978): 16-20.

3889. Kendrigan, G. M. "*Bakke* in Perspective: An Exercise in Judicial Wisdom." *Trial* 15 (August 1979): 48-50.

3890. Kilgore, Peter. "MBE Funding in the Construction Industry: A Constitutional Question of Reverse Discrimination." *Labor Law Journal* 30 (May 1979): 289-294.

3891. Lamber, Julia. "Observations on the Supreme Court's Recent Affirmative Action Cases." *Indiana Law Journal* 62 (Spring 1986/1987): 243-261.

3892. Lavinsky, Larry M. "Affirmative Action Trilogy and Benign Racial Classifications: Evolving Law in Need of Standards." *Wayne Law Review* 27 (Fall 1980): 1-34.

3893. Lincoln, C. Eric. "Beyond *Bakke, Weber,* and *Fullilove*: Peace from Our Sins: A Commentary on Affirmative Action." *Sound* 63 (Winter 1980): 361-380.

3894. McFeeley, Neil D. "*Weber* versus Affirmative Action?" *Personnel* 57 (January 1980): 38-51.

3895. Maguire, Daniel C. "Triumph of Unequal Justice." *Christian Century* 95 (September 27, 1978): 882-886.

3896. Maidment, Richard A. "U.S. Supreme Court and Affirmative Action: The Cases of *Bakke, Weber,* and *Fullilove.*" *Journal of American Studies* 15 (December 1981): 341-356.

3897. Manville, Richard, and Michael Siegal. "Supreme Court Struggles with Affirmative Action." *Police Chief* 54 (February 1987): 13.

3898. Mishkin, Paul J. "The Uses of Ambivalence: Reflections on the Supreme Court and the Constitutionality of Affirmative Action." *University of Pennsylvania Law Review* 131 (March 1983): 907-931.

3899. Novick, Melvin R., and Dorsey D. Ellis, Jr. "Equal Opportunity in Educational and Employment Selection." *American Psychology* 32 (May 1977): 306-320.

3900. Oats, William R., Jr. "Affirmative Action: A Question of Educational Deprivation." *Crisis* 85 (May 1978): 172-174.

3901. O'Neill, Timothy J. Bakke *and the Politics of Equality: Friends and Foes in the Classroom of Litigation.* Middletown, CT: Wesleyan University Press, 1985.

3902. Phillips, Michael J. "Neutrality in the Application of Strict Scrutiny: The Implications of *Bakke.*" *American Business Law Journal* 17 (Summer 1979): 230-246.

3903. Preer, Robert M. "We Have Reached a Common Destination: The Supreme Court, The Private Sector, and Affirmative Action." *Labor Law Journal* 38 (June 1987): 360-369.

3904. Rabkin, Peggy A. "Affirmative Action and Reverse Discrimination: The Implications of Herbert Hill's, 'Black Labor and the American Legal System', and William B. Gould's, 'Black Workers in White Unions'." *Afro-Americans in New York Life and History* 3 (July 1979): 69-78.

3905. Rasnic, Carol D. "The Supreme Court and Affirmative Action: An Evolving Standard or Compounded Confusion?" *Employee Relations Law Journal* 14 (Autumn 1988): 175-190.

3906. Reardan, Nancy B. "Reversal of Historical Discrimination: Is It Constitutional?" *Crisis* 84 (December 1977): 459-462.

3907. Robinson, William L., and Stephan

L. Spritz. "Did the *Stotts* Decision Really Spell the End of Race-Conscious Affirmative Action?" *New York Law School Human Rights Annual* 2 (Fall 1984): 1-17.

3908. Rossum, Ralph A. "Ameliorative Racial Preference and the Fourteenth Amendment: Some Constitutional Problems." *Journal of Politics* 38 (May 1976): 346-366.

3909. Rossum, Ralph A. "New Rights and Old Wrongs: The Supreme Court and the Problem of Retroactivity." *Emory Law Journal* 23 (Spring 1974): 381-420.

3910. Schnapper, Eric. "The Supreme Court and Affirmative Action: An Exercise in Judicial Restraint." *New Perspectives* 17 (Winter 1985): 12-15.

3911. Schwartz, Bernard. *Behind* Bakke: *Affirmative Action and the Supreme Court.* New York: New York University Press, 1988.

3912. Selig, Joel L. "Affirmative Action in Employment: The Legacy of a Supreme Court Majority." *Indiana Law Journal* 63 (Spring 1988): 301-368.

3913. Shapiro, Herbert. "The *Bakke* Decision: Illusion and Reality in the Supreme Court." *Crisis* 86 (February 1979): 62-66.

3914. Stephenson, D. Grier, Jr. "*Weber,* Affirmative Action, and Restorative Justice." *USA Today* 108 (May 1980): 48-50.

3915. Stewart, Debra W., and Charles V. Stewart. "*Bakke* and Beyond: Cooperation and Power Sharing in the Federal System." *Publius* 9 (Winter 1979): 141-159.

3916. Sullivan, Kathleen M. "Sins of Discrimination: Last Term's Affirmative Action Cases. . . . " *Harvard Law Review* 100 (November 1986): 1-311.

3917. Swanson, Stephen C. "Effect of the Supreme Court's Seniority Decisions." *Personnel Journal* 56 (December 1977): 625-627.

3918. Tatel, David S., and Elliot M. Mineberg. "The Supreme Court's Affirmative Decisions: Key Questions Remain Unanswered." *Public Management* 68 (October 1986): 19-21.

3919. Tatel, David S., and Elliot M. Mineberg. "The Supreme Court's 1987 Decision on Voluntary Affirmative Action." *Public Management* 69 (December 1987): 3-5.

3920. Watson, Denton L. "In the Wake of *Bakke.*" *Crisis* 86 (February 1979): 51-61.

3921. Woodside, Steven M., and Jan H. Marx. "Walking the Tightrope between Title VII and Equal Protection: Public Sector Voluntary Affirmative Action after *Johnson* and *Wygant.*" *Urban Lawyer* 20 (Spring 1988): 367-388.

3922. Wright, Bruce M. "Bangs and Whimpers: The Strange Case of Allan Bakke." *Freedomways* 18 (1978): 21-27.

Age

3923. Burt, Robert A. "Developing Constitutional Rights of, in, and for Children." *Law and Contemporary Problems* 39 (Summer 1975): 118-143.

3924. Corbin, A. Robert, and Anthony Walsh. "The U.S. Supreme Court and Value Legitimacy: An Experimental Approach with Older Americans." *Sociological Inquiry* 58 (February 1988): 75-86.

3925. Grant, Gerald. "Children's Rights and Adult Confusions." *Public Interest* 69 (Fall 1982): 83-99.

3926. Nathan, W. A. "Whose Rights Are They Anyway: The Supreme Court and the Rights of Juveniles." *Children and Youth Services Review* 6 (1984): 329-344.

3927. O'Neill, Robert M. "The Constitution, the Supreme Court, and Youth." *Social Education* 37 (May 1973): 397-399.

3928. Stern, Nat. "The Burger Court and

the Diminishing Constitutional Rights of Minors: A Brief Overview." *Arizona State Law Journal* 1985 (1985): 865-904.

3929. U.S. Library of Congress. Congressional Research Service. "Not for Adults Alone: Children Begin Pressing for Expansion of Constitutional Rights." *Civil Rights Digest* 11 (Winter 1979): 12-22.

Aliens

3930. Bembi, Bruno J. "Aliens and the Burger Court." *New York Law School Human Rights Annual* 4 (Spring 1987): 569-808.

3931. Berger, Andrew. "Alien Venue: Neither Necessary nor Constitutional." *New York University Journal of International Law and Politics* 9 (Fall 1976): 155-176.

3932. Carrott, M. Browning. "Prejudice Goes to the Court: The Japanese and the Supreme Court in the 1920s." *California History* 62 (Summer 1983): 122-138.

3933. Fragomen, Austin T. "Legislative and Judicial Developments: Alien Employment." *International Migration Review* 13 (Fall 1979): 527-531.

3934. Fragomen, Austin T. "Supreme Court Rules That States Can Prohibit Unauthorized Employment by Aliens." *International Migration Review* 10 (Summer 1976): 253-256.

3935. Guerrero, Manuel P. "Substantive Due Process for Resident Aliens." *Aztlan* 10 (Summer/Spring/Fall 1979): 31-52.

3936. Harvey, Gerald C., "Expatriation Law in the United States: The Confusing Legacy of *Afroyim* and *Bellei*." *Columbia Journal of Transnational Law* 13 (Fall 1974): 406-435.

3937. Henkin, Louis. "The Constitution as Compact and as Conscience: Individual Rights Abroad and at Our Gates." *William and Mary Law Review* 27 (Fall 1985): 11-34.

3938. Hull, Elizabeth A. "Resident Aliens and the Equal Protection Clause: The Burger Court's Retreat from *Graham v. Richardson*." *Brooklyn Law Review* 47 (Fall 1980): 1-42.

3939. Hull, Elizabeth A. "Resident Aliens, Public Employment, and the Political Community Doctrine." *Western Political Quarterly* 36 (June 1983): 221-240.

3940. Hutton, E. Jeremy. *Analysis of Supreme Court Decisions Relating to Extended Border Searches for Illegal Aliens.* Washington, DC: Congressional Research Service, 1975.

3941. Lesser, Jeff H. "Always Outsiders: Asians, Naturalization, and the Supreme Court." *Amerasia Journal* 12 (1985): 83-100.

3942. Liss, Jeffrey F. "*Schneiderman* Case: An Inside View of the Roosevelt Court." *Michigan Law Review* 74 (January 1976): 500-523.

3943. Loue, Sana. "Alien Rights and Government Authority: An Examination of the Conflicting Views of the Ninth Circuit Court of Appeals and the United States Supreme Court." *San Diego Law Review* 22 (September/October 1985): 1021-1073.

3944. Maltz, Earl M. "Burger Court and Alienage Classifications." *Oklahoma Law Review* 31 (Summer 1978): 671-691.

3945. Pelta, Eleanor. "*INS v. Phinpathya*: Literalist Statutory Interpretation in the Supreme Court." *San Diego Law Review* 23 (March/April 1986): 401-440.

3946. Piekarski, Victor J. "*Nyquist* and Public Aid to Private Education." *Marquette Law Review* 58 (1975): 247-267.

3947. Repa, Barbara K. "Decisions and Revisions: Is the Supreme Court Leading the Crackdown on Immigrants?" *Update* *on Law-Related Education* 8 (Fall 1984): 9-18.

3948. Schifter, Richard, and David Burgess. "The Supreme Court and a 'Well-Founded Fear of Persecution'." *Atlantic Community Quarterly* 25 (Summer 1987): 213-221.

3949. Scott, Margaret O. "Significant Developments in the Immigration Laws of the United States, 1983-1984." *San Diego Law Review* 22 (September/October 1985): 1101-1142.

3950. Smith, James M. *Freedom's Fetters: The Alien and Sedition Law and American Civil Liberties.* Ithaca, NY: Cornell University Press, 1956.

Disabled

3951. Baer, Judith A. "The Burger Court and the Rights of the Handicapped: The Case for Starting All Over Again." *Western Political Quarterly* 35 (September 1982): 339-358.

3952. Bernard, Jessie L. "Significance for Psychology of *O'Connor v. Donaldson*." *American Psychologist* 32 (December 1977): 1085-1088.

3953. Bradley, Valerie, and Gary Clarke, eds. *Paper Victories and Hard Realities: The Implementation of the Legal and Constitutional Rights of the Mentally Disabled; Selected Papers on the Supreme Court Decision,* O'Connor v. Donaldson. Washington, DC: Health Policy Center, Georgetown University, 1976.

3954. Connor, Susan M. "Zoning Discrimination Affecting Retarded Persons." *Washington University Journal of Urban and Contemporary Law* 29 (Winter 1985): 67-80.

3955. Cranford, Ronald E., and David R. Smith. "Consciousness: The Most Critical Moral (Constitutional) Standard for Human Personhood." *American Journal of Law and Medicine* 13 (Summer/Fall 1987): 233-248.

3956. Dismukes, Key. "Life Is Patently Not Human-Made." *Hastings Center Report* 10 (October 1980): 11-12.

3957. Ellis, James W. "Supreme Court and Institutions: A Comment on *Youngberg v. Romeo*." *Mental Retardation* 20 (October 1982): 197-200.

3958. Flaschner, Franklin N. "Constitutional Requirements in the Commitment of the Mentally Ill in the U.S.A.: Rights to Liberty and Therapy." *International Journal of Offender Therapy* 18 (1974): 283-301.

3959. Flygare, Thomas J. "Supreme Court Decides Attorney Fees Not Available in Special Education Cases." *Phi Delta Kappan* 66 (September 1984): 66-67.

3960. Flygare, Thomas J. "Twenty-five States Ask the Supreme Court to Decide Issues Involving Handicapped Students." *Phi Delta Kappan* 60 (February 1979): 456-457.

3961. Gangemi, Laura. "After *Rowley*: The Handicapped Child's Right to an Appropriate Education." *University of Miami Law Review* 38 (January 1984): 321-356.

3962. Grumet, Barbara R. "The Changing Role of the Federal and State Courts in Safeguarding the Rights of the Mentally Disabled." *Publius* 15 (Summer 1985): 67-80.

3963. Lauber, Daniel. "Mainstreaming Group Homes: A Recent U.S. Supreme Court Decision Put Some New Twists on Zoning for Group Homes." *Planning* 51 (December 1985): 14-18.

3964. McCarthy, Martha M. "The *Pennhurst* and *Rowley* Decisions: Issues and Implications." *Exceptional Children* 49 (April 1983): 517-522.

3965. McGarry, Barbara D. "Second Thoughts on Educating Handicapped Children: The Supreme Court's Ruling on the *Tatro* Case." *Journal of Visual Impairment and Blindness* 78 (September 1984): 328-330.

3966. Meisel, Alan. "The Rights of the Mentally Ill under State Constitutions." *Law and Contemporary Problems* 45 (Summer 1982): 7-40.

3967. Prettyman, E. Barrett, Jr., and Allen R. Snyder. "*Amicus Curiae* Brief in the *Donaldson* Case." *American Journal of Psychiatry* 132 (January 1975): 109-115.

3968. Schoenberg, Allen E. " 'Voluntary' Commitment of Mentally Ill or Retarded Children: Child Abuse by the Supreme Court." *University of Dayton Law Review* 7 (Fall 1981): 1-31.

3969. Tatro, Mary. "Related Services and the Supreme Court: A Family's Story." *Exceptional Parent* 14 (October/November 1984): 36-38, 40-41.

3970. Tucker, Bonnie P. "*Board of Education of the Hendrick Hudson Central School District v. Rowley*: Utter Chaos." *Journal of Law and Education* 12 (April 1983): 235-245.

Family

3971. Clark, Homer. "Supreme Court Faces the Family." *Children Today* 11 (November/December 1982): 18-21.

3972. Noonan, John T., Jr. "The Family and the Supreme Court." *Catholic University Law Review* 23 (Winter 1973): 255-274.

3973. Riga, Peter J. "Decision Making within the Family: Who Decides." *South Texas Law Journal* 23 (Winter 1982): 95-137.

3974. Riga, Peter J. "Supreme Court's View of Marriage and the Family: Tradition or Transition?" *Journal of Family Law* 18 (February 1980): 301-330.

3975. Rizzo, Mario J. "The Economics of Termination of Parental Rights: *Santosky v. Kramer*." *Supreme Court Economic Review* 2 (1983): 277-310.

3976. Rubin, Eva R. *The Supreme Court and the American Family: Ideology and Issues*. Westport, CT: Greenwood Press, 1986.

3977. Zigler, Edward, and Susan Hunsinger. "Supreme Court on Spanking: Upholding Discipline or Abuse?" *Young Children* 32 (Spring 1977): 14-15.

Gender

3978. Abuhoff, Daniel. "Title VII and the Appointment of Women Clergy: A Statutory and Constitutional Quagmire." *Columbia Journal of Law and Social Problems* 13 (Spring/Summer 1977): 256-302.

3979. Baer, Judith A. "Sexual Equality and the Burger Court." *Western Political Quarterly* 31 (December 1978): 470-491.

3980. Basch, Norma. "The Emerging Legal History of Women in the United States: Property, Divorce, and the Constitution." *Signs* 12 (Autumn 1986): 97-117.

3981. Berger, Margaret A. *Litigation on Behalf of Women: A Review for the Ford Foundation*. New York: The Foundation, 1980.

3982. Brown, Judith O., et al. "Equal Pay for Jobs of Comparable Worth: An Analysis of the Rhetoric." *Harvard Civil Rights-Civil Liberties Law Review* 21 (Winter 1986): 127-170.

3983. Cary, Eve. "Pregnancy without Penalty." *Civil Liberties Review* 1 (Fall 1973): 31-48.

3984. Cohen, Carl. "Justice Debased: The *Weber* Decision." *Commentary* 68 (September 1979): 43-53.

3985. Cook, Beverly B. "Sex Roles and the Burger Court." *American Politics Quarterly* 5 (July 1977): 353-394.

3986. Dalrymple, Candice. "Sexual Distinctions in the Law: Early Maximum Hour Decisions of the United States Supreme Court, 1905-1917." Ph.D. diss., University of Florida, 1979.

3987. Dow, Phyllis A. "Sexual Equality, the ERA, and the Court: A Tale of Two Failures." *New Mexico Law Review* 13 (Winter 1983): 53-97.

3988. Dubnoff, Caren. "Sex Discrimination and the Burger Court: A Retreat in Progress?" *Fordham Law Review* 50 (December 1981): 369-414.

3989. Eisler, Riane. "Thrusting Women Back into Their 1900 Roles: A Washington Theater of the Absurd." *Humanist* 42 (March/April 1982): 46-48.

3990. Erickson, Nancy S. "Women and the Supreme Court: Anatomy and Destiny." *Brooklyn Law Review* 41 (Fall 1974): 209-282.

3991. Estrich, Susan, and Virginia Kerr. "Sexual Justice." In *Our Endangered Rights*, edited by Norman Dorsen, 98-133. New York: Pantheon Books, 1984.

3992. Freedman, Ann E. "Sex Equality, Sex Differences, and Supreme Court." *Yale Law Journal* 92 (May 1983): 913-968.

3993. Gale, Mary E. "Unfinished Women: The Supreme Court and the Incomplete Transformation of Women's Rights in the United States." *Whittier Law Review* 9 (Fall 1987): 445-490.

3994. Ginsburg, Ruth B. "Gender in Supreme Court: 1973 and 1974 Terms." *Supreme Court Review* 1975 (1975): 1-24.

3995. Ginsburg, Ruth B. "Women, Equality, and the *Bakke* Case." *Civil Liberties Review* 4 (November/December 1977): 8-16.

3996. Goldstein, Leslie F. *The Constitutional Rights of Women: Cases in Law and Social Change.* 2d ed. Madison: University of Wisconsin, 1988.

3997. Goldstein, Leslie F. "The Constitutional Status of Women: The Burger Court and the Sexual Revolution in American Law." *Law and Policy Quarterly* 3 (January 1981): 5-28.

3998. Goldstein, Leslie F. "The Politics of the Burger Court toward Women." *Policy Studies Journal* 7 (February 1978): 213-218.

3999. Greenlaw, Paul S., and John P. Kohl. "Avoiding Sex Discrimination in Retirement Plans." *Cornell Hotel and Restaurant Administration Quarterly* 25 (May 1984): 19-21.

4000. Hamilton, Janice M., Janine S. Hiller, Joyce A. Naumann, and Barbara H. Vann. "Broadening Access to the Courts and Clarifying Judicial Standards: Sex Discrimination Cases in the 1978-1979 Supreme Court Term." *University of Richmond Law Review* 14 (Spring 1980): 515-584.

4001. Heen, Mary L. "Sex Discrimination in Pensions and Retirement Annuity Plans after *Arizona Governing Committee v. Norris*: Recognizing and Remedying Employer Non-Compliance." *Women's Rights Law Reporter* 8 (Summer 1985): 155-176.

4002. Hermanson, Roger H., and Tad D. Ransopher. "What the *Hishon* Case Means to CPA Firms: Partnership Selections and the Civil Rights Act." *Journal of Accountancy* 159 (Fall 1985): 78-80.

4003. Hill, Ann C. "Protection of Women

Workers and the Courts: A Legal Case History." *Feminist Studies* 5 (Summer 1979): 247-273.

4004. Johnston, John D., Jr. "Sex Discrimination and the Supreme Court, 1971-1974." *New York University Law Review* 49 (November 1974): 617-692.

4005. Johnston, John D., Jr. "Sex Discrimination and Supreme Court, 1975." *UCLA Law Review* 23 (December 1975): 235-265.

4006. Kelley, M. Page. "*Roberts v. United States Jaycees*: How Much Help for Women?" *Harvard Women's Law Journal* 8 (Spring 1985): 215-230.

4007. Kollar, Linda R. "Up or Out and Into the Supreme Court: A Forecast for *Hishon v. King and Spalding.*" *Pepperdine Law Review* 11 (January 1984): 391-419.

4008. Kopolow, Lewis E. "Review of Major Implications of the *O'Connor v. Donaldson* Decision." *American Journal of Psychiatry* 133 (April 1976): 377-383.

4009. Levine, Rebecca. "My Body, My Life, My Baby, My Rights." *Human Rights* 12 (Spring 1984): 26-35.

4010. Lewis, Karen J. *Sex Discrimination and the U.S. Supreme Court*. Washington, DC: Congressional Research Service, 1975.

4011. Linder, Douglas O. "Freedom of Association after *Roberts v. United States Jaycees.*" *Michigan Law Review* 82 (August 1984): 1878-1903.

4012. Lindsay, Cotton M., and Charles A. Shanor. "*County of Washington v. Gunther*: Legal and Economic Considerations for Resolving Sex-Based Wage Discrimination Cases." *Supreme Court Economic Review* 1 (1982): 185-234.

4013. Loewy, Arnold H. "Returned to the Pedestal: The Supreme Court and the Gender Classification Cases; 1980 Term." *North Carolina Law Review* 60 (October 1981): 87-101.

4014. Lorber, Lawrence Z., and J. Robert Kirk. "A Status Report on the Theory of Comparable Worth: Recent Developments in the Law of Wage Discrimination." *Public Personnel Management* 12 (Winter 1983): 332-344.

4015. Maltz, Earl M. "Sex Discrimination in the Supreme Court: A Comment on Sex Equality, Sex Differences, and the Supreme Court." *Duke Law Journal* 1985 (February 1985): 177-194.

4016. Mendelson, Wallace. "ERA, the Supreme Court, and Allegations of Gender Bias." *Missouri Law Review* 44 (Winter 1979): 1-10.

4017. Mezey, Susan G. "Gender Equality in Education: A Study of Policymaking by the Burger Court." *Wake Forest Law Review* 20 (Winter 1984): 793-817.

4018. Morrell, Marceil. "Waiting for the Other Shoe: *Wetzel* and *Gilbert* in Supreme Court." *Emory Law Journal* 25 (Winter 1976): 125-161.

4019. Morton, F. L. "The Supreme Court's Promotion of Sexual Equality: A Case Study of Institutional Capacity." *Polity* 16 (Spring 1984): 467-483.

4020. O'Connor, Karen. *Women's Organizations' Use of the Courts*. Lexington, MA: Lexington Books, 1980.

4021. O'Connor, Karen, and Lee Epstein. "Sex and the Supreme Court on Analysis of Judicial Support for Gender-Based Claims." *Social Science Quarterly* 64 (June 1983): 327-331.

4022. Scuro, Joseph E., Jr., and Lawrence J. Souza. "*Patsy v. Florida Board of Regents*: The Two-Edged Sword." *Police Chief* 49 (December 1982): 18-19.

4023. Segal, Jeffrey A., and Cheryl D. Reedy. "The Supreme Court and Sex Discrimination: The Role of the Solicitor

General." *Western Political Quarterly* 41 (September 1988): 553-568.

4024. Staley, Laura. "Suffrage Movement in St. Louis during the 1870s." *Gateway Heritage* 3 (Spring 1983): 34-41.

4025. Strum, Philippa. "The Supreme Court and Sexual Equality: A Case Study of Factors Affecting Judicial Policy-Making." *Policy Studies Journal* 4 (Winter 1975): 146-150.

4026. Tatel, David S., and Elliot Mineberg. "Supreme Court Decision Broadens Definition of Employment-Related Sexual Harassment." *Public Management* 68 (November 1988): 21.

4027. Taylor, Ann D. "Equal Justice under Law: Ascendent or Retrograde?" *Detroit College of Law Review* 1983 (Winter 1983): 1445-1449.

4028. Tevis, Martha. "Status of Women: The Path toward Legal Personhood." *Educational Horizons* 60 (Fall 1981): 11-15.

4029. Theiler, Patricia. "Power Plays: Over the Last Ten Years Working Women Have Made Important Inroads in Fighting Sexual Harassment; Some of Those Gains Are Now Being Challenged before the Supreme Court." *Common Cause* 12 (January/February 1986): 30-33.

4030. Van Alstyne, William W. "Equality for Individuals or Equality for Groups: Implications of Supreme Court Decision in *ManHart* Case." *American Association of University Professors Bulletin* 64 (May 1978): 150-155.

4031. Way, G. Darryl. "Japanese Employers and Title VII: *Sumitomo Shoji America Inc. v. Avagliano*." *New York University Journal of International Law and Policy* 15 (Spring 1983): 653-695.

4032. Wildman, Stephanie M. "The Legitimation of Sex Discrimination: A Critical Response to Supreme Court Jurisprudence." *Oregon Law Review* 63 (Spring 1984): 265-307.

4033. Williams, Wendy W. "Equality Crisis: Some Reflections on Culture, Courts, and Feminism." *Women's Rights Law Reporter* 7 (Spring 1982): 175-200.

4034. Wolf, Wendy A. "Sex-Discrimination in Pension Plans: The Problem of Incomplete Relief." *Harvard Women's Law Journal* 9 (Spring 1986): 83-103.

Indians

4035. Anderson, Steven B. "Native American Indian Law and the Burger Court: A Shift in Judicial Methods." *Hamline Law Review* 8 (October 1985): 671-712.

4036. Ball, Milner S. "Constitution, Court, Indian Tribes." *American Bar Foundation Research Journal* 1987 (Winter 1987): 1-140.

4037. Barsh, Russell L. "Is There Any Indian Law Left?" *Washington Law Review* 59 (September 1984): 863-893.

4038. Burke, Joseph C. "The Cherokee Cases: A Sudy in Law, Politics, and Morality." *Stanford Law Review* 21 (February 1969): 500-531.

4039. Cameron, George D., III. "Indian Taxation of Reservation Minerals: A Domestic OPEC in the Making?" *American Business Law Journal* 22 (Fall 1984): 429-438.

4040. Clinton, Robert N. "State Power over Indian Reservations: A Critical Comment on Burger Court Doctrine." *Cornell Law Review* 8 (June 1981): 8-13.

4041. Deloria, Vine, Jr. "Legislation and Litigation Concerning American Indians." *Annals of the American Academy of Political and Social Science* 436 (March 1978): 86-96.

4042. Hobbs, Charles A. "Indian Hunting and Fishing Rights." *George Washington Law Review* 37 (July 1969): 1251-1273.

4043. Johnson, Ralph W. "The States versus Indian Off-Reservation Fishing: A United States Supreme Court Error." *Washington Law Review* 47 (March 1972): 207-236.

4044. Lytle, Clifford M. "Supreme Court, Tribal Sovereignty, and Continuing Problems of State Encroachment into Indian Country." *American Indian Law Review* 8 (Summer 1980): 65-77.

4045. Neumann, Rita. "Taxation of Natural Resource Production on Tribal Lands." *Taxes* 63 (November 1985): 813-819.

4046. Pelcyger, Robert. "Justices and Indians: Back to Basics." *Oregon Law Review* 62 (Winter 1983): 29-47.

4047. Pilling, Arnold R. "Native American Religious Rights: Constitutional Considerations." *Indian Historian* 12 (Winter 1979): 13-19.

4048. Rodgers, Raymond S., and Phillip Lujan. "Natural Law, *Santa Clara*, and the Supreme Court." *Journal of Ethnic Studies* 9 (Fall 1981): 71-77.

4049. Rotenberg, Daniel L. "American States and Indian Tribes: Power Conflicts in the Supreme Court." *Dickinson Law Review* 92 (Fall 1987): 81-103.

4050. Schultz, Gregory. "The Federal Due Process and Equal Protection Rights of Non-Indian Civil Litigants in Tribal Courts after *Santa Clara Pueblo v. Martinez*." *Denver University Law Review* 62 (1985): 761-787.

4051. Slagle, Al L. "*Arizona v. California et al.*" *American Indian Culture and Research Journal* 7 (1983): 87-90.

4052. Walker, Jana L. "On-Reservation Treaty Hunting Rights: Abrogation v. Regulation by Federal Conservation Statutes—What Standard?" *Natural Resources Journal* 26 (Winter 1986): 187-196.

4053. Washburn, Wilcomb E. "The Supreme Court's Use and Abuse of History." *OAH Newsletter* 11 (August 1983): 7-9.

4054. Whiteing, Jeanne. "A Review of Indian Cases in the 1984-1985 Supreme Court Term." *Clearinghouse Review* 19 (January 1986): 982-987.

4055. Wilkinson, Charles F. *American Indians, Time, and the Law: Historical Rights at the Bar of the Supreme Court.* New Haven, CT: Yale University Press, 1987.

Poverty

4056. Areen, Judith, and Leonard Ross. "The *Rodriguez* Case: Judicial Oversight of School Finance." *Supreme Court Review* 1973 (1973): 33-55.

4057. Binion, Gayle. "The Burger Court and the Rights of the Poor." *Center Magazine* 15 (March/April 1982): 2-7.

4058. Binion, Gayle. "The Disadvantaged before the Burger Court: The Newest Unequal Protection." *Law and Policy Quarterly* 4 (January 1982): 37-70.

4059. Bolner, James, and Cecil L. Eubanks. "The Poverty of Justice: The Burger Court and the Poor." *Capital University Law Review* 7 (Summer 1978): 351-383.

4060. Buchanan, G. Sidney. "State Authorization, Class Discrimination, and the Fourteenth Amendment." *Houston Law Review* 21 (January 1984): 1-47.

4061. Canby, William C., Jr. "Burger Court and the Validity of Classifications in Social Legislation: Currents of Federalism." *Arizona State Law Journal* 1975 (1975): 1-30.

4062. Coven, Mark S., and Robert J. Fersh. "Equal Protection, Social Welfare

Litigation, the Burger Court." *Notre Dame Lawyer* 51 (July 1976): 873-897.

4063. Davidson, Kenneth M. "Welfare Cases and the 'New Majority': Constitutional Theory and Practice." *Harvard Civil Rights-Civil Liberties Law Review* 10 (Summer 1975): 513-574.

4064. Houseman, Alan W. "Equal Protection and the Poor." *Rutgers Law Review* 30 (Summer 1977): 887-906.

4065. Lagomarsino, Bartley A. "A Study of the California Public School Finance System: The Relation of the 1972-1973 and 1973-1974 School Years to Equalization and the *Serrano-Priest* Court Decisions." Ph.D. diss., Brigham Young University, 1977.

4066. Michelman, Frank I. "The Supreme Court, 1968 Term, Foreword: On Protecting the Poor through the Fourteenth Amendment." *Harvard Law Review* 83 (November 1969): 7-59.

4067. Porter, Mary C. A. "*Rodriguez*, the 'Poor', and the Burger Court: A Prudent Prognosis." *Baylor Law Review* 29 (Spring 1977): 199-242.

4068. Williams, Norman, Jr. "The Background and Significance of *Mount Laurel II*." *Washington University Urban and Contemporary Law* 26 (1984): 3-23.

4069. Woodward, David. "Affirmative Constitutional Overtones: Do Any Still Sound for the Poor?" *Human Rights Quarterly* 7 (August 1985): 268-333.

Race

General Studies

4070. Alexander, Raymond P. "Upgrading of the Negro's Status by Supreme Court Decisions." *Journal of Negro History* 30 (April 1945): 117-149.

4071. Baker, Liva. "With All Deliberate Speed." *American Heritage* 24 (February 1973): 42.

4072. Bannon, John. "Race Relations and Supreme Court Decision Making: Jurisprudential Reflections." *Notre Dame Lawyer* 51 (October 1975): 91-106.

4073. Bartley, Numan V. *The Rise of Massive Resistance: Race and Politics in the South during the 1950s*. Baton Rouge: Louisiana State University Press, 1969.

4074. Berger, Morroe. "Desegregation, Laws, and Social Science: What Was the Basis of the Supreme Court's Decision?" *Commentary* 23 (May 1957): 471-477.

4075. Bernstein, Barton J. "Case Law in *Plessy v. Ferguson*." *Journal of Negro History* 47 (July 1962): 192-198.

4076. Bernstein, Barton J. "*Plessy v. Ferguson*: Conservative Sociological Jurisprudence." *Journal of Negro History* 48 (July 1963): 196-205.

4077. Berry, Mary F. *Black Resistance/White Law: A History of Constitutional Racism in America*. New York: Appleton-Century-Crofts, 1971.

4078. Bestor, Arthur. "State Sovereignty and Slavery." *Illinois State Historical Society Journal* 59 (Summer 1961): 117-180.

4079. Bickel, Alexander M. "The Original Understanding and the Segregation Decision." *Harvard Law Review* 69 (November 1955): 1-65.

4080. Bishop, David W. "*Plessy v. Ferguson*: A Re-interpretation." *Journal of Negro History* 62 (April 1977): 125-133.

4081. Black, Charles L. "Lawfulness of the Segregation Decisions." *Yale Law Journal* 69 (January 1960): 421-430.

4082. Blackwood, Eileen M. "Race as a Factor in Custody and Adoption Disputes: *Palmore v. Sidoti*." *Cornell Law Review* 71 (November 1985): 209-226.

4083. Brest, Paul. "*Palmer v. Thompson*:

An Approach to the Problem of Unconstitutional Legislative Motive." *Supreme Court Review* 1971 (1971): 95-146.

4084. Brest, Paul. "Supreme Court, 1975 Term, Foreword: Defense of Anti-Discrimination Principle." *Harvard Law Review* 90 (November 1976): 1-275.

4085. Carmichael, Peter A. *The South and Segregation.* Washington, DC: Public Affairs Press, 1965.

4086. Carter, Robert L. "The Warren Court and Desegregation." *Michigan Law Review* 67 (December 1968): 237-248.

4087. Clark, Kenneth B. "Desegregation: An Appraisal of the Evidence." *Journal of Social Issues* 9 (1953): 1-76.

4088. Clarke, Mary M. "Our Constitution Is 'Color Blind'." *Catholic World* 180 (January 1955): 258-265.

4089. Cleveland, Len G. "Georgia Baptists and the 1954 Supreme Court Desegregation Decision." *Georgia Historical Quarterly* 59 (Supplement 1975): 107-117.

4090. Combs, Michael W. "Courts, Minorities, and the Dominant Coalition: Racial Policies in Modern America." Ph.D. diss., Washington University, 1978.

4091. Cox, Paul N. "Some Thoughts on the Future of Remedial Race and Gender Preferences under Title VII." *Valparaiso University Law Review* 19 (Summer 1985): 801-828.

4092. Cushing, John D. "The Cushing Court and the Abolition of Slavery in Massachusetts: More Notes on the *Quock Walker* Case." *American Journal of Legal History* 5 (April 1961): 118-144.

4093. David, C.W.A. "The Fugitive Slave Law of 1793." *Journal of Negro History* 9 (January 1924): 18-25.

4094. Davis, Michael. "Racial Quotas, Weights, and Real Possibilities: A Moral for Moral Theory." *Social Theory and Practice* 7 (Spring 1981): 49-84.

4095. Davis, Sue. "The Supreme Court: Finding State Action Sometimes." *Howard Law Journal* 26 (Fall 1983): 1395-1423.

4096. DeLacy, G. L. " 'Segregation Cases' Supreme Court." *Nebraska Law Review* (June 1959): 1017-1038.

4097. Drinan, Robert F. "The *Loving* Decision and the Freedom to Marry." *Ohio State Law Journal* 29 (Spring 1968): 358-398.

4098. Dymally, Mervyn M. "The Supreme Court and Civil Rights: Ten Cases." *Black Politician* 3 (Summer 1971): 96-100.

4099. Edwards, George. "Desegregation: A View from the Federal Bench." *Crisis* 83 (November 1976): 321-325.

4100. Ehrlich, Walter. *They Have No Rights: Dred Scott's Struggle for Freedom.* Westport, CT: Greenwood Press, 1979.

4101. Emerson, Thomas I. "Southern Justice in the Thirties." *Civil Liberties Review* 4 (May/June 1977): 70-74.

4102. Fairman, Charles. "The Attack on the Segregation Cases." *Harvard Law Review* 70 (November 1956): 83-94.

4103. Fehrenbacher, Don E. *The Dred Scott Case: Its Significance in American Law and Politics.* New York: Oxford University Press, 1978.

4104. Finkelman, Paul. "*Prigg v. Pennsylvania* and Northern State Courts: Anti-Slavery Use of a Pro-Slavery Decision." *Civil War History* 25 (March 1979): 5-35.

4105. Fletcher, John L. *The Segregation Case and the Supreme Court.* Boston: Boston University Press, 1958.

4106. Foley, William E. "Slave Freedom Suits before *Dred Scott*: The Case of Marie Jean Scypion's Descendants." *Missouri Historical Review* 79 (October 1984): 1-23.

4107. Frantz, Laurent B. "The School

Segregation Cases." *Lawyers Guild Review* 14 (Summer 1954): 13-18.

4108. Freeman, Alan D. "Legitimizing Racial Discrimination through Antidiscrimination Law: A Critical Review of Supreme Court Doctrine." *Minnesota Law Review* 62 (July 1978): 1049-1119.

4109. Gale, Mary E. "Relegating Minorities to the Back of the Courthouse." *Trial* 18 (October 1982): 40-45, 86-87.

4110. Gill, Robert L. "The Negro in the Supreme Court." *Negro History Bulletin* 28 (December 1964): 51-52.

4111. Gill, Robert L. "The Negro in the Supreme Court." *Negro History Bulletin* 28 (January 1965): 86-88.

4112. Gill, Robert L. "The Negro in the Supreme Court." *Negro History Bulletin* 28 (February 1965): 117-119.

4113. Gill, Robert L. "The Negro in the Supreme Court." *Negro History Bulletin* 28 (Summer 1965): 194-199.

4114. Grunbaum, Werner F. "Patterns of Differential Treatment of Minorities." *Policy Studies Journal* 4 (Winter 1975): 127-131.

4115. Hagan, Horace H. "The *Dred Scott* Decision." *Georgetown Law Journal* 15 (January 1927): 95-114.

4116. Hay, Logan. "Lincoln's Attitude toward the Supreme Court and the *Dred Scott* Decision." *Illinois State Bar Association* 1937 (1937): 90-100.

4117. Heafer, Dianne L. "A Historiographical Study of the Taney Court and the *Dred Scott* Decision." Ph.D. diss., University of Houston, 1983.

4118. Hewitt, Norman. "Legal Aspects of Desegregation in the United States." *Indian Journal of Social Research* 3 (January 1962): 145-149.

4119. Hirsch, Herbert, and Lewis Donohew. "A Note on Negro-White Differences in Attitudes toward the Supreme Court." *Social Science Quarterly* 53 (June 1972): 557-562.

4120. Howard, J. Woodford, Jr., and Cornelius Bushoven. "The *Screws* Case Revisited." *Journal of Politics* 29 (August 1967): 617-636.

4121. Hutchinson, Dennis J. "Unanimity and Desegregation: Decision-Making in the Supreme Court, 1948-1958." *Georgia Law Review* 68 (October 1979): 1-96.

4122. Irons, Peter. *Justice at War: The Story of the Japanese American Internment Cases.* New York: Oxford University Press, 1983.

4123. Jans, Ralph T. "Negro Civil Rights and the Supreme Court, 1865-1949." Ph.D. diss., University of Chicago, 1951.

4124. Johnson, Whittington B. "Vinson Court and Racial Segregation, 1946-1953." *Journal of Negro History* 63 (July 1978): 220-230.

4125. Jones, Sidney A., Jr. "The Supreme Court's Role in Jim Crow Transportation." *National Bar Journal* 3 (June 1945): 114-125.

4126. Kaiser, Ernest. "The Federal Government and the Negro, 1865-1955." *Science and Society* 20 (Winter 1956): 27-58.

4127. Kalven, Harry, Jr. *The Negro and the First Amendment.* Chicago: University of Chicago Press, 1966.

4128. Kaplan, John. "Equal Justice in an Unequal World: Equality for the Negro: The Problem of Special Treatment." *Northwestern University Law Review* 61 (July/August 1966): 363-410.

4129. Kelleher, Daniel T. "The Case of Lloyd Lionel Gaines: The Demise of the Separate but Equal Doctrine." *Journal of Negro History* 56 (October 1971): 262-271.

4130. Kelly, Alfred H. "The Fourteenth Amendment Reconsidered: The Segregation Question." *Michigan Law Review* 54 (June 1956): 1049-1086.

4131. Kennedy, Randall. "Race Relations Law and the Tradition of Celebration: The Case of Professor Schmidt." *Columbia Law Review* 86 (December 1986): 1622-1661.

4132. Kleber, Louis C. "*Dred Scott* Decision, 1857." *History Today* 22 (December 1972): 873-878.

4133. Kleven, Thomas. "Supreme Court, Race, and the Class Struggle." *Hofstra Law Review* 9 (Spring 1981): 795-858.

4134. Konvitz, Milton R. "The Courts Deal a Blow to Segregation: The 'Separate but Equal' Doctrine Begins to Crumble." *Commentary* 11 (February 1951): 158-166.

4135. Konvitz, Milton R., and Theodore Leskes. *A Century of Civil Rights, with a Study of State Law against Discrimination.* New York: Columbia University Press, 1961.

4136. Larson, Stephanie G. "How the *New York Times* Covered Discriminating Cases." *Journalism Quarterly* 62 (Winter 1985): 894-896.

4137. Latham, Frank B. *The* Dred Scott *Decision, March 6, 1857: Slavery and the Supreme Court's 'Self-Inflicted Wound'.* New York: F. Watts, 1968.

4138. Lusky, Louis. "National Policy and the Dead Hand: The Race Conscious Trust." *Trusts and Estates* 112 (August 1973): 554-557.

4139. Maidment, Richard A. "Changing Styles in Constitutional Adjudication: The United States Supreme Court and Racial Segregation." *Public Law* 1977 (Summer 1977): 168-186.

4140. Maynard, Robert C. "Blacks and the Burger Court: The Case of the Narrowing Path to Justice." *Black Enterprise* 8 (March 1978): 31-37.

4141. Mendelson, Wallace. "Clear and Present Danger: From *Schenck* to *Dennis*." *Columbia Law Review* 52 (March 1952): 313-333.

4142. Mendelson, Wallace. "The Court Must Not Be Curbed: A Reply to Mr. Byrnes." *Journal of Politics* 19 (February 1957): 81-86.

4143. Miller, Charles A. "Constitutional Law and the Rhetoric of Race." *Perspectives in American History* 5 (1971): 147-200.

4144. Miller, Loren. *The Petitioners: The Story of the Supreme Court of the United States and the Negro.* New York: Pantheon Books, 1966.

4145. Muskrat, Joe. "Assimilate: Or Starve!" *Civil Rights Digest* 5 (October 1972): 27-34.

4146. Nelson, Bernard H. *The Fourteenth Amendment and the Negro since 1920.* Washington, DC: Catholic University of America Press, 1946.

4147. Nelson, Bernard H. "The Negro before the Supreme Court." *Phylon* 8 (March 1947): 34-38.

4148. Newby, Idus A. *Challenge to the Court: Social Scientists and the Defense of Segregation, 1954-1966.* Baton Rouge: Louisiana State University Press, 1969.

4149. North, Arthur A. "The *Plessy* Doctrine: Rise and Demise, Death of the Doctrine 'Separate but Equal'." *Thought* 35 (September 1960): 365-392.

4150. Patton, William W. "The United States Supreme Court and the Civil Rights Act." *New Englander* 43 (January 1884): 1-19.

4151. Paul, Arnold M., comp. *Black Americans and the Supreme Court since Emancipation: Betrayal or Protection?* New York: Holt, Rinehart, and Winston, 1972.

4152. Phillips, Cyrus E., IV. "Miscegenation: The Courts and the Constitution." *William and Mary Law Review* 8 (Fall 1966): 133-142.

4153. Ransmeier, Joseph S. "The Fourteenth Amendment and the 'Separate but Equal' Doctrine." *Michigan Law Review* 50 (December 1951): 203-260.

4154. Richardson, Scovel. "Changing Concepts of the Supreme Court as They Affect the Legal Status of the Negro." *National Bar Journal* 1 (October 1941): 113-129.

4155. Rostow, Eugene V. "The Japanese American Cases: A Disaster." *Yale Law Journal* 54 (June 1945): 489-533.

4156. St. Antoine, Theodore J. "Color Blindness but Not Myopia: A New Look at State Action, Equal Protection, and 'Private' Racial Discrimination." *Michigan Law Review* 59 (May 1961): 993-1016.

4157. Saveth, Edward N. "The Supreme Court and Segregation." *Survey* 87 (July 1951): 314-317.

4158. Schmidt, Benno C., Jr. "Juries, Jurisdiction, and Race Discrimination: The Lost Promise of *Strauder v. West Virginia*." *Texas Law Review* 61 (May 1983): 1401-1499.

4159. Schmidt, Benno C., Jr. "Principle and Prejudice: The Supreme Court and Race in the Progressive Era: Part 1: The Heyday of Jim Crow." *Columbia Law Review* 82 (April 1982): 444-524.

4160. Schmidt, Benno C., Jr. "Principle and Prejudice: The Supreme Court and Race in the Progressive Era: Part 2: The Peonage Cases." *Columbia Law Review* 82 (May 1982): 646-718.

4161. Schmidt, Benno C., Jr. "Principle and Prejudice: The Supreme Court and Race in the Progressive Era: Part 3: Black Disfranchisement from the KKK to the Grandfather Clause." *Columbia Law Review* 82 (June 1982): 835-905.

4162. Shafer, Judith K. "The Long Arm of the Law: Slavery and the Supreme Court in Antebellum Louisiana, 1809-1862." Ph.D. diss., Tulane University, 1985.

4163. Sohn, Chang M. "Principle and Expediency in Judicial Review: Miscegenation Cases in the Supreme Court." Ph.D. diss., Columbia University, 1970.

4164. Spaeth, Harold J. "Race Relations and the Warren Court." *University of Detroit Law Journal* 43 (December 1965): 255-272.

4165. Spicer, George W. "The Federal Judiciary and Political Change in the South." *Journal of Politics* 26 (February 1964): 154-176.

4166. Spicer, George W. "The Supreme Court and Racial Discrimination." *Vanderbilt Law Review* 11 (June 1958): 821-852.

4167. Spitz, David. "Black Rights and Judicial Wrongs." *Dissent* 26 (Spring 1979): 194-203.

4168. "Supreme Court Equity Discretion: The Decrees in the Segregation Cases." *Yale Law Journal* 64 (November 1954): 124-136.

4169. "*Swain v. Alabama*: A Constitutional Blueprint for the Perpetuation of the All-White Jury." *Virginia Law Review* 52 (October 1966): 1157-1175.

4170. Taylor, Olive. "The Final Arbiter: A History of the Decisions Rendered by the Supreme Court of the United States Relative to the Negro Prior to the Civil War." *Negro History Bulletin* 43 (January/February/March 1980): 8-10.

4171. Tollett, Kenneth S. "Viability and Reliability of the U.S. Supreme Court as an Institution for Social Change and Progress Beneficial to Blacks." *Black Law Journal* 2 (Winter 1972): 197-219; 3 (Spring 1973): 5-50.

4172. Tussman, Joseph. *The Supreme*

Court on Racial Discrimination. New York: Oxford University Press, 1963.

4173. Van Alstyne, William W. "Rites of Passage: Race, the Supreme Court, and the Constitution." *University of Chicago Law Review* 46 (Summer 1979): 775-810.

4174. Waite, Edward F. "The Negro in the Supreme Court." *Minnesota Law Review* 30 (March 1946): 219-304.

4175. Waite, Edward F. "The Negro in the Supreme Court: Five Years More." *Minnesota Law Review* 35 (June 1951): 625-639.

4176. Westin, Alan F., and Barry Mahoney. "Martin Luther King, Jr., and the Supreme Court: On Protest and the First Amendment." *Civil Liberties Review* 3 (December 1976/January 1977): 9-46.

4177. Wiecek, William M. "Slavery and Abolition before the United States Supreme Court, 1820-1860." *Journal of American History* 65 (June 1978): 34-59.

4178. Wilder, Amos N. "Minorities and Professional Minorities." *Christianity and Crisis* 22 (August 6, 1962): 135-136.

4179. Wilkinson, J. Harvie. "Supreme Court: The Equal Protection Clause and the Three Faces of Constitutional Equality." *Virginia Law Review* 61 (June 1975): 945-1018.

4180. Woodson, Carter G. "Fifty Years of Negro Citizenship as Qualified by the United States Supreme Court." *Journal of Negro History* 6 (January 1921): 1-53.

4181. Wright, Claudia F. "Legitimation by the Supreme Courts of Canada and the United States: A Case Study of Japanese Exclusion." Ph.D. diss., Claremont Graduate School, 1973.

Education

4182. Adamo, Victor T. "Integration and the Burger Court: The New Boundaries of School Desegregation." *Intellect* 103 (March 1975): 378-390.

4183. Akers, Byron L., and Blaine E. Mercer. "A Legal Analysis of Segregation in Public Education." *Social Studies* 45 (February 1954): 43-51.

4184. Aldridge, Delores P. "Litigation and Education of Blacks: A Look at the U.S. Supreme Court." *Journal of Negro Education* 47 (Winter 1978): 96-112.

4185. Baldwin, Fletcher N., Jr. "*DeFunis v. Odegaard*: The Supreme Court and Preferential Law School Admissions; Discretion Is Sometimes Not the Better Part of Valor." *University of Florida Law Review* 27 (Winter 1975): 343-360.

4186. Bannon, John. "Legitimizing Segregation: The Supreme Court's Recent School Desegregation Decisions." *Civil Rights Digest* 9 (Summer 1977): 12-17.

4187. Baxter, Felix V. "Affirmative Duty to Desegregate Institutions of Higher Education: Defining the Role of the Traditionally Black College." *Journal of Law and Education* 11 (January 1982): 1-40.

4188. Bell, Derrick A., Jr. "Serving Two Masters: Integration Ideals and Client Interests in School Desegregation Litigation." *Yale Law Journal* 85 (March 1976): 470-516.

4189. Berman, Daniel M. *It Is So Ordered: The Supreme Court Rules on School Segregation*. New York: W. W. Norton, 1966.

4190. Blaustein, Albert P., and Clarence C. Ferguson. *Desegregation and the Law: The Meaning and Effect of the School Segregation Cases*. New Brunswick, NJ: Rutgers University Press, 1957.

4191. Bolmeier, Edward C. *Landmark Supreme Court Decisions on Public School Issues*. Charlottesville, VA: Michie, 1973.

4192. Bolner, James. "The Supreme Court and Racially Imbalanced Public

Schools in 1967." *Journal of Negro Education* 38 (Spring 1969): 125-134.

4193. Borinski, Ernst. "The Emerging Case Law in the Segregation Decisions of the Supreme Court of May 17, 1954 and May 31, 1955." *University of Pittsburgh Law Review* 17 (Spring 1956): 416-436.

4194. Borinski, Ernst. "A Legal and Sociological Analysis of the Segregation Decision of May 17, 1954." *University of Pittsburgh Law Review* 15 (Summer 1954): 622-634.

4195. Boyd, William M. "Second Emancipator." *Phylon* 16 (March 1955): 77-86.

4196. Breathett, George. "Black Educators and the United States Supreme Court Decision of May 17, 1954." *Journal of Negro History* 68 (Spring 1983): 201-208.

4197. Brown, Oliver. *Argument; Argument: The Oral Argument before the Supreme Court in* Brown v. Board of Education of Topeka, *1952-55.* Edited by Leon Friedman. New York: Chelsea House, 1969.

4198. Bullock, Charles S. "Federal Law and School Discrimination in the North." *Journal of Negro Education* 47 (Spring 1978): 113-131.

4199. Burns, Haywood. "From *Brown* to *Bakke* and Back: Race, Law, and Social Change in America." *Daedalus* 110 (Spring 1981): 219-231.

4200. Coates, Albert. *The School Segregation Decision: A Report to the Governor of North Carolina on the Decision of the Supreme Court of the United States on the 17th of May, 1954.* Littleton, CO: Fred B. Rothman, 1981.

4201. Coates, Albert, and James C. Paul. "A Report to the Governor of North Carolina on the Decision of the Supreme Court of the U.S. on the 17th of May, 1954." *Popular Government* 21 (September 1954): 1-29.

4202. Combs, Michael W. "The Federal Judiciary and Northern School Desegregation: Judicial Management Perspective." *Journal of Law and Education* 13 (July 1984): 345-399.

4203. Combs, Michael W. "The Supreme Court as a National Policy Maker: A History Legal Analysis of School Desegregation." *Southwestern Law Review* 8 (Spring 1982): 192-229.

4204. Cook, Eugene, and William I. Potter. "The School Segregation Cases: Opposing the Opinion of the Supreme Court." *American Bar Association Journal* 42 (April 1956): 313-317.

4205. Cook, Grant. "School Desegregation: To *Brown* and Back Again, The Great Circle." *Baylor Law Review* 23 (Summer 1971): 398-404.

4206. Cook, Stuart W. "Social Science and School Desegregation: Did We Mislead the Supreme Court?" *Personality and Social Psychology Bulletin* 5 (October 1979): 420-437.

4207. Cortes, Carlos E., and Van L. Perkins. "U.S. Supreme Court Decisions on Diversity." *Education Digest* 46 (February 1981): 21-24.

4208. Cox, Archibald. "After Twenty Years: Reflections upon the Constitutional Significance of *Brown vs. Board of Education.*" *Civil Rights Digest* 6 (Summer 1974): 38-45.

4209. Crowell, Judith. "Interdistrict School Desegregation: Remedies after *Milliken v. Bradley.*" *Boston University Law Review* 56 (March 1976): 357-378.

4210. DeFunis, Marco. *DeFunis v. Odegaard and the University of Washington: The University Admissions Case, The Record.* Dobbs Ferry, NY: Oceana, 1974.

4211. Demitchell, Todd A. "*Lau* Decision and Higher Education." *College Student Journal* 11 (Winter 1977): 344-345.

4212. Devins, Neal. "*Bob Jones University*

v. United States: A Political Analysis." *Journal of Law and Politics* 1 (Spring 1984): 403-421.

4213. Devins, Neal. "School Desegregation Law in the 1980s: The Court's Abandonment of *Brown v. Board of Education*." *William and Mary Law Review* 26 (Fall 1984): 7-43.

4214. Dunn, John C., Jr. "American Educational Jurisprudence: A Study of the Influence of State Statutes and Federal Courts on Public Schools and the Desegregation Process in the United States." Ph.D. diss., Ohio State University, 1978.

4215. Easterbrook, Gregg. "English, Si Spanish, No." *Washington Monthly* 12 (December 1980): 37-44.

4216. Edelman, Marian W. "Southern Schools Desegregation, 1954-1973: A Judicial-Political Overview." *Annals of the American Academy of Political and Social Science* 407 (May 1973): 32-42.

4217. Ethridge, Samuel B. "Impact of the 1954 *Brown v. Topeka Board of Education* Decision on Black Educators." *Education Digest* 45 (February 1980): 24-27.

4218. Ethridge, Samuel B. "Impact of the 1954 *Brown v. Topeka Board of Education* Decision on Black Educators." *Educational Review* 30 (October 1979): 217-232.

4219. Farber, Daniel A. "Supreme Court and the Rule of Law: *Cooper v. Aaron* Revisited." *University of Illinois Law Review* 1982 (Spring 1982): 387-412.

4220. Fierce, Milfred C. "Observations on *Bakke*: History, Issues, Implications." *Freedomways* 18 (1978): 9-15.

4221. Fisher, Marguerite J. "The Supreme Court and Negro Education." *Social Science* 29 (January 1954): 10-15.

4222. Flygare, Thomas J. "Supreme Court Hears Arguments on Tax Breaks for Racially Discriminatory Private

Schools." *Phi Delta Kappan* 64 (January 1983): 369.

4223. Fuerst, J. S., and Roy Petty. "Supreme Court and Quotas." *Christian Century* 94 (October 19, 1977): 948-952.

4224. Gahringer, Robert E. "Race and Class: The Basic Issue of the *Bakke* Case." *Ethics* 90 (October 1979): 97-114.

4225. Garfinkel, Herbert. "Social Science Evidence and the School Segregation Cases." *Journal of Politics* 21 (February 1959): 37-59.

4226. Garrow, David J. "The Federal Courts and School Desegregation in the 1970s." *Law and Society Review* 21 (1988): 879-884.

4227. George, John J., and James M. Collier. "Supreme Court and Racial Segregation in Education." *South Atlantic Quarterly* 48 (October 1949): 521-528.

4228. Giles, Michael W., and Thomas G. Walker. "Judicial Policy-Making and Southern School Segregation." *Journal of Politics* 37 (November 1975): 917-936.

4229. Gill, Robert L. "Defenders of Civil Liberties." *Quarterly Review of Higher Education among Negroes* 17 (January 1949): 1-19.

4230. Gill, Robert L. "The Shaping of Race Relations by the Federal Judiciary in Court Decisions." *Quarterly Review of Higher Education among Negroes* 28 (January 1960): 21-27.

4231. Gilmore, Henry F. "A Study of Attitudes of Negro Teachers toward the Supreme Court Decision and Other Issues of Desegregation in Education." Ph.D diss., Columbia University, 1958.

4232. Gittell, Marilyn. "School Desegregation and the Courts." *Social Policy* 6 (January/February 1976): 36-41.

4233. Glenn, Albert S. "State Court Desegregation Orders: Multi-District Busing, Supreme Court Review, and the Los Angeles School Case." *UCLA Law Review* 26 (June 1979): 1183-1230.

4234. Graglia, Lino A. *Disaster by Decree: The Supreme Court Decisions on Race and the Schools.* Ithaca, NY: Cornell University Press, 1976.

4235. Graham, Howard J. "The Fourteenth Amendment and School Segregation." *Buffalo Law Review* 3 (Winter 1953): 1-24.

4236. Grothaus, Larry. "The Inevitable Mr. Gaines: The Long Struggle to Desegregate the University of Missouri, 1936-1950." *Arizona and the West* 26 (Spring 1984): 21-42.

4237. Hanley, John W., Jr. "*Keyes v. School District No. 1*: Unlocking the Northern Schoolhouse Doors." *Harvard Civil Rights-Civil Liberties Law Review* 9 (January 1974): 124-155.

4238. Hawkins, John N. "Politics, Education, and Language Policy: The Case of the Japanese Language Schools in Hawaii." *Amerasia Journal* 5 (1978): 39-56.

4239. Henderson, Ronald D., and Mary Von Euler. "Metropolitan School Desegregation: Emerging Research Issues." *Urban Review* 10 (Summer 1978): 67-70.

4240. Hendrick, Irving G. "*Stare Decisis*, Federalism, and Judicial Self-Restraint: Concepts Perpetuating the Separate but Equal Doctrine in Public Education, 1849-1954." *Journal of Law and Education* 12 (October 1983): 561-585.

4241. Hobbs, E. H. "Negro Education and the Equal Protection of the Laws." *Journal of Politics* 14 (August 1952): 488-511.

4242. Hogan, John C. *The Schools, the Courts, and the Public Interest.* 2d ed. Lexington, MA: D. C. Heath, 1985.

4243. Horn, Robert. "National Constitutional Rights and the Desegregation Crisis." *Western Political Quarterly* 10 (June 1957): 463-465.

4244. Horton, Guy M. "Responses of Six Newspapers to Supreme Court Decisions Dealing with School Segregation." Ph.D. diss., University of Missouri, 1972.

4245. Howard, A. E. Dick. "Race and Education: The Road from *Brown*." *Wilson Quarterly* 3 (Spring 1979): 98-108.

4246. Hudgins, Herbert C. "Many Voices of the Burger Court and School Desegregation." *Phi Delta Kappan* 60 (November 1978): 165-168.

4247. Hudgins, Herbert C. *The Warren Court and the Public Schools: An Analysis of Landmark Supreme Court Decisions.* Danville, IL: Interstate Printers and Publishers, 1970.

4248. Jandura, Ronald M. "An Interpretation of United States Supreme Court Cases Since 1954 as They Affect School Segregation." Ed.D. diss., University of Alabama, 1970.

4249. Jones, Leon. "Desegregation and Social Reform since 1954." *Journal of Negro Education* 43 (Spring 1974): 155-171.

4250. Jones, Nathaniel R. "Anti-Black Strategy and Supreme Court." *Journal of Law and Education* 4 (January 1975): 203-208.

4251. Kauper, Paul G. "Segregation in Public Education: The Decline of *Plessy v. Ferguson*." *Michigan Law Review* 52 (June 1954): 1137-1158.

4252. Kinney, Bradford L. "Catalyst for a Revolution: A Rhetorical Analysis of the Oral Debates on School Segregation Leading to the Supreme Court Decision of 1954." Ph.D. diss., University of Pittsburgh, 1976.

4253. Kirp, David L. "School Desegregation and the Limits of Legalism." *Public Interest* 47 (Spring 1977): 101-128.

4254. Kirp, David L., and Mark G. Yudof. "*DeFunis* and Beyond." *Change* 9 (November 1974): 22-26.

4255. Kluger, Richard. *Simple Justice: The History of* Brown v. Board of Education *and Black America's Struggle for Equality.* New York: Random House, 1976.

4256. Knox, Robert F. "Interdistrict Desegregation: The Remaining Options." *Stanford Law Review* 28 (February 1976): 521-561.

4257. Kousser, J. Morgan. "Separate but Not Equal: The Supreme Court's First Decision on Racial Discrimination in Schools." *Journal of Southern History* 46 (February 1980): 17-44.

4258. Lerner, Barbara. "Supreme Court and the APA, AERA, NCME Test Standards: Past References and Future Possibilities." *American Psychologist* 33 (October 1978): 915-919.

4259. Lerner, Barbara. "War on Testing: *Detroit Edison* in Perspective." *Personnel Psychology* 33 (Spring 1980): 11-16.

4260. Levison, Gayle L. "The Rhetoric of the Oral Argument in the *Regents of the University of California v. Bakke.*" *Western Journal of Speech Communication* 43 (Fall 1979): 271-277.

4261. Logan, Rayford W. "The United States Supreme Court and the Segregation Issue." *Annals of the American Academy of Political and Social Science* 304 (March 1956): 10-16.

4262. McCain, R. Ray. "Reactions to the United States Supreme Court Segregation Decision of 1954." *Georgia Historical Quarterly* 52 (December 1968): 371-387.

4263. McCarthy, Martha M. "Is a New Standard of Discrimination Emerging? The Changing Judicial Interpretation of State Intent." *Journal of Law and Education* 8 (July 1979): 315-325.

4264. McCormack, Wayne. "Race and Politics in the Supreme Court: *Bakke* to Basics." *Utah Law Review* 1979 (1979): 491-545.

4265. Maidment, Richard A. "*Plessy v. Ferguson* Reexamined." *Journal of American Studies* (Great Britain) 7 (August 1973): 125-133.

4266. Marr, Warren, ed. "History of the Five School Cases." *Crisis* 86 (June/July 1979): 189-194.

4267. Mavrinak, Albert. "From *Lochner* to *Brown vs. Topeka*: The Court and Conflicting Concepts of the Political Process." *American Political Science Review* 52 (September 1958): 641-677.

4268. Mayer, Michael S. "With Much Deliberation and Some Speed: Eisenhower and the *Brown* Decision." *Journal of Southern History* 52 (February 1986): 43-76.

4269. Meador, Daniel J. "The Supreme Court and the School Segregation Cases." *American Review* 1 (Spring 1961): 10-26.

4270. Meyer, Howard N. "*Brown* and 'Big Fourteen'." *Crisis* 86 (June/July 1979): 223-225.

4271. Mishkin, Paul J. "Prophecy, Realism, and the Supreme Court: The Development of Institutional Unity." *American Bar Association Journal* 40 (August 1954): 680-683, 725-726.

4272. Muffler, John P. "Education and the Separate but Equal Doctrine." *Black Scholar* 17 (May/June 1986): 35-41.

4273. Murphy, Walter F. "Desegregation in Public Education: A Generation of Future Litigation." *Maryland Law Review* 15 (Summer 1955): 221-243.

4274. Muse, Benjamin. *Ten Years of Prelude: The Story of Integration since the Supreme Court's 1954 Decision.* New York: Viking Press, 1964.

4275. Ochoa, Victor-Alberto M. "Bilingual Desegregation: School Districts' Responses to the Spirit of the Law under the *Lau v. Nichols* Supreme Court Decision." Ed.D. diss., University of Massachusetts, 1978.

4276. O'Donnell, Denise E. "The Inequitable Burden of School Desegregation Remedies: Supreme Court Decisions on the Buffalo School Desegregation Case." *Buffalo Law Review* 29 (Fall 1980): 729-758.

4277. Peltason, Jack W. *Fifty-eight Lonely Men: Southern Federal Judges and School Desegregation.* New York: Harcourt, Brace, and World, 1961.

4278. Phillips, James E. "Legal Requirements of Intent to Segregate: Some Observations." *NOLPE School Law Journal* 7 (1977): 111-125.

4279. Rabb, Charles. "HEW, Justice Lawyers Draft Plans to Implement Supreme Court's Busing Decision." *National Journal* 3 (June 19, 1971): 1305-1313.

4280. Read, Frank T. "Judicial Evolution of the Law of School Integration since *Boston v. Board of Education.*" *Law and Contemporary Problems* 39 (Winter 1975): 7-49.

4281. Reams, Bernard D., and Paul E. Wilson, eds. *Segregation and the Fourteenth Amendment in the States: A Survey of State Segregation Laws, 1865-1953; Prepared by U.S. Supreme Court in re* Brown v. Board of Education of Topeka. Buffalo, NY: W. S. Hein, 1975.

4282. Reddick, L. D. "Great Decision." *Phylon* 15 (June 1954): 194-201.

4283. Redding, Louis L. "Desegregation in the Schools: Background, Developments, and Proposals." *Lawyers Guild Review* 14 (Winter 1954/1955): 163-168.

4284. Reid, Herbert O. "The Supreme Court Decision and Interposition." *Journal of Negro Education* 25 (Spring 1956): 109-117.

4285. Reid, Herbert O., and Frankie Foster-Davis. "State of the Art: The Law and Education since 1956." *Journal of Negro Education* 52 (Summer 1983): 234-269.

4286. Reid, Inez S. "The Burger Court and the Civil Rights Movement: The Supreme Court Giveth and the Supreme Court Taketh Away." *Rutgers Camden Law Journal* 3 (Spring 1972): 410-440.

4287. Reid, Inez S. "Cast Aside by the Burger Court: Blacks in Quest of Justice and Education." *Notre Dame Lawyer* 49 (October 1973): 105-121.

4288. Ribaudo, Anthony P. "Segregation in Education." *Boston University Law Review* 34 (November 1954): 463-478.

4289. Roche, John P. "Education, Segregation, and the United States Supreme Court, a Political Analysis." *University of Pennsylvania Law Review* 99 (May 1951): 949-959.

4290. Roche, John P. "The Future of Separate but Equal." *Phylon* 12 (1951): 219-226.

4291. Roche, John P. "*Plessy v. Ferguson: Requiescat in Pace?*" *University of Pennsylvania Law Review* 103 (October 1954): 44-58.

4292. Roman, Susan E. "Case Note: *Board of Education v. Harris*: Civil Rights: Impact over Intent—Changing the Rules for Antidiscrimination Funds." *NOLPE School Law Journal* 9 (1981): 171-184.

4293. Rossum, Ralph A. "*Plessy, Brown,* and the Reverse Discrimination Cases: Consistency and Continuity in Judicial Approach." *American Behavioral Scientist* 28 (July/August 1985): 705-806.

4294. Schwartz, Ruth E. "Descriptive Analysis of Oral Argument before the United States Supreme Court in the School Segregation Cases, 1952-1953." Ph.D. diss., University of Southern California, 1966.

4295. Schwartz, Ruth E., and Milton Dickens. "Oral Argument before the Supreme Court: *Marshall v. Davis* in the School Segregation Cases." *Quarterly Journal of Speech* 57 (February 1971): 32-42.

4296. Scott, James F. "*Brown* and *Bakke*: The Relation between Judicial Decisions and Socioeconomic Conditions." *Phylon* 41 (Fall 1980): 235-246.

4297. Sepaniak, Adrienne. "Bussing: A Permissible Tool of School Desegregation." *Journal of Urban Law* 49 (November 1971): 399-423.

4298. Shannon, Tom. "United States Supreme Court and Student Suspensions from School: Was *Goss v. Lopez* the Final Answer?" *Urban Lawyer* 7 (1975): 862-866.

4299. Spratlen, Thaddeus H. "*Bakke* Decision: Implications for Black Educational and Professional Opportunities." *Journal of Negro Education* 48 (Fall 1979): 449-456.

4300. Stockard, Robert M. "The United States Supreme Court and the Legal Aspects of Busing for Public School Desegregation." Ed.D. diss., University of North Carolina, 1978.

4301. Strickman, Leonard P. "School Desegregation at the Crossroads." *Northwestern University Law Review* 70 (November/December 1975): 725-769.

4302. Stumberg, George W. "The School Segregation Cases: Supporting the Opinion of the Supreme Court." *American Bar Association Journal* 42 (April 1956): 317-320.

4303. Sullivan, Harold J. "Intent Requirement in Desegregation Cases: The Inapplicability of *Washington v. Davis*." *Journal of Law and Education* 10 (July 1981): 325-333.

4304. Sutherland, Arthur E., Jr. "The Supreme Court and Private Schools: Reassurance for Some Worried Educators." *Harvard Educational Review* 25 (Summer 1955): 127-131.

4305. Sutherland, Arthur E., Jr. "The Supreme Court and the Public School: Significant Test Cases Concerning Such Critical Public Questions of Our Time as Loyalty Oaths for Teachers, Religious Instruction in the Public Schools, and the Constitutional Rights of the States to Maintain Separate Public Schools for Negro and White Children." *Harvard Educational Review* 24 (Spring 1954): 71-85.

4306. Taylor, William L. "Supreme Court and Recent School Desegregation Cases: The Role of Social Science in a Period of Judicial Retrenchment." *Law and Contemporary Problems* 42 (Autumn 1978): 37-56.

4307. Taylor, William L., John E. Benjes, and Eric E. Wright. "School Desegregation and the Courts." *Social Policy* 6 (January/February 1976): 32-35.

4308. Teitelbaum, Herbert, and Richard J. Hiller. "Bilingual Education: The Legal Mandate." *Harvard Educational Review* 47 (May 1977): 138-170.

4309. Tieszen, D. W. "The Black-Robed School Board." *American School Board Journal* 125 (November 1952): 29-30.

4310. Tisdale, James W. *A Southerner's Reflections about the 1954 Supreme Court Decision Concerning Racial Segregation in the Public Schools.* Asheville, NC: Jarrett's Press, 1956.

4311. Tollett, Kenneth S. "What Led to *Bakke*." *Center Magazine* 11 (January 1978): 2-10.

4312. Tollett, Kenneth S., Jeanette J. Leonard, and Portia P. James. "A Color-Conscious Constitution: The One Pervading Purpose *Redux*." *Journal of Negro Education* 52 (Summer 1983): 189-212.

4313. Tomberlin, Joseph A. "Florida and the School Desegregation Issue, 1957-1959: A Summary View." *Journal of Negro Education* 43 (Fall 1974): 457-467.

4314. Tyler, Ralph S. "School Desegregation in the Supreme Court: The Development of a Jurisprudence of Remedies for Complex Constitutional Cases." *Emory Law Journal* 28 (1979): 985-1032.

4315. Valenti, Jasper J., et al. "A Double

Revolution? The Supreme Court's Desegregation Decision." *Harvard Educational Review* 25 (Winter 1955): 1-17.

4316. Van Wright, Aaron, Jr. "Factors Relative to Job Selections in Music Faculties of the Original Negro Land-Grant Colleges since the 1954 Supreme Court Decision." Ed.D. diss., University of Oklahoma, 1965.

4317. Waite, Edward F. "Race Segregation in the Public Schools: Jim Crow at the Judgement Seat." *Minnesota Law Review* 38 (May 1954): 612-621.

4318. Wasby, Stephen L., Anthony A. D'Amato, and Rosemary Metrailer. *Desegregation from* Brown *to* Alexander: *An Exploration of Supreme Court Strategies.* Carbondale: Southern Illinois University Press, 1977.

4319. Weinstein, Allen, et al. "Part 1. Civil Rights since *Brown*: 1954-1984." *Center Magazine* 17 (May 1984): 2-10.

4320. Wiley, Walter E. "The Influence of the State and the United States Supreme Court Decisions on the Education of the Negro." Ph.D. diss., Ohio State University, 1951.

4321. Wilkinson, J. Harvie. *From* Brown *to* Bakke: *The Supreme Court and School Integration, 1954-1978.* New York, Oxford University Press, 1979.

4322. Wilkinson, J. Harvie. "Supreme Court and Southern School Desegregation, 1955-1970: A History and Analysis." *Virginia Law Review* 64 (May 1978): 485-559.

4323. Yudof, Mark G. "School Desegregation: Legal Realism, Reasoned Elaboration, and Social Science Research in the Supreme Court." *Law and Contemporary Problems* 42 (Autumn 1978): 57-110.

4324. Ziegler, Benjamin M. *Desegregation and the Supreme Court.* Lexington, MA: D. C. Heath, 1953.

Employment

4325. Camper, Diane. "And Justice for Whom?" *Black Enterprise* 15 (March 1985): 52-55.

4326. Chick, C. A. "Some Recent Supreme Court Decisions Affecting the Rights of Negro Workers." *Journal of Negro Education* 16 (Spring 1947): 172-179.

4327. Crowley, Donald W. "Selection Tests and Equal Opportunity: The Court and the EEOC." *Administration and Society* 17 (November 1985): 361-384.

4328. Gillepsie, J. David, and Michael L. Mitchell. "*Bakke, Weber*, and Race in Employment: Analysis of Informed Opinion." *Policy Studies Journal* 8 (Winter 1979): 383-391.

4329. Gould, William B. "Racial Equality in Jobs and Unions, Collective Bargaining, and the Burger Court." *Michigan Law Review* 68 (December 1969): 237-258.

4330. Jones, James E. "Title VII, Seniority and the Supreme Court: Clarification or Retreat?" *University of Kansas Law Review* 26 (Fall 1977): 1-60.

4331. Kilgore, Peter. "Racial Preferences in the Federal Grant Programs: Is There a Basis for Challenge after *Fullilove v. Klutznick?*" *Labor Law Review* 32 (May 1981): 306-314.

4332. Modjeska, Lee. "The Supreme Court and the Ideal of Equal Employment Opportunity." *Mercer Law Review* 36 (Spring 1985): 795-811.

4333. Phillips, Michael J. "Paradoxes of Equal Opportunity: Voluntary Racial Preferences and the *Weber* Case." *Business Horizons* 23 (August 1980): 41-47.

4334. Sendor, Benjamin B. "The High Court Splits on Race-Based Layoff Policies." *American School Board Journal* 173 (September 1986): 20, 47.

4335. Simba, Malik. "The Black Laborer, the Black Legal Experience, and the United States Supreme Court with Emphasis on the Neo-Concept of Equal Employment." Ph.D. diss., University of Minnesota, 1977.

4336. Singer, James W. "High Court Is Expected to Reverse Job Bias Ruling." *National Journal Reports* 7 (August 2, 1975): 1117.

4337. Sisneros, Antonio. "Early Application of Contemporary Race-Conscious Law in the Lower Federal Courts." *Labor Law Journal* 37 (May 1986): 282-290.

4338. Smith, Arthur B., Jr. "Economic Pressure in Support of Unlawful Employment Discrimination Claims." *Cornell Law Review* 61 (March 1976): 368-415.

4339. Summers, William C., and Christine D. Kleinke. "Employment Discrimination Focuses on Individuals Instead of Bottom Line." *Police Chief* 49 (November 1982): 18-19.

4340. Warren, William H. "*Albemarle v. Moody*: Where It All Began." *Labor Law Journal* 27 (October 1976): 609-613.

Housing

4341. Dale, Charles V. *An Analysis of the Supreme Court Ruling in* Village of Arlington Heights v. Metropolitan Housing Development Corporation: *Proving Racial Discrimination in Local Land Use Policies.* Washington, DC: Congressional Research Service, 1975.

4342. Dale, Charles V. *The Supreme Court and Exclusionary Zoning:* Village of Arlington Heights v. Metropolitan Housing Development Corporation. Washington, DC: Congressional Research Service, 1975.

4343. Groves, Harry E. "Judicial Interpretation of the Holdings of the United States Supreme Court in the Restrictive Covenant Cases." *Illinois Law Review* 45 (November/December 1950): 614-631.

4344. Haber, Gary M. "*Gladstone Realtors v. Village of Bellwood*: Expanding Standing under the Fair Housing Act." *Boston College Environmental Affairs Law Review* 8 (April 1980): 783-819.

4345. Miller, Barry A. "Proof of Racially Discriminatory Purpose under the Equal Protection Clause: *Washington v. Davis, Arlington Heights, Mt. Healthy, and Williamsburgh*." *Harvard Civil Rights-Civil Liberties Law Review* 12 (Summer 1977): 725-770.

4346. Pearlman, Kenneth. "The Closing Door: The Supreme Court and Residential Segregation." *Journal of the American Institute of Planners* 44 (April 1978): 160-169.

4347. Robison, Joseph B. "Fair Housing Restored in California." *New South* 22 (Fall 1967): 54-60.

4348. Sager, Lawrence G. "Questions I Wish I Had Never Asked: The Burger Court in Exclusionary Zoning." *Southwestern University Law Review* 1 (1979): 509-545.

4349. Seeley, James J. "The Public Referendum and Minority Group Legislation: Postscript to *Reitman v. Mulkey*." *Cornell Law Review* 55 (July 1970): 881-910.

4350. Thomas, Mark S. "Exclusionary Zoning and a Reluctant Supreme Court." *Wake Forest Law Review* 13 (Spring 1977): 107-138.

4351. Vose, Clement E. *Caucasians Only: The Supreme Court, the NAACP, and the Restrictive Covenant Cases.* Berkeley: University of California Press, 1959.

4352. Welfeld, Irving. "Courts and Desegregated Housing: The Meaning of the *Gautreaux* Case." *Public Interest* 45 (Fall 1976): 123-135.

Voting

4353. Beth, Loren P. "White Primary and the Judicial Function in the United States." *Political Quarterly* 29 (October 1958): 366-377.

4354. Bickel, Alexander M. "The Voting Rights Cases." *Supreme Court Review* 1966 (1966): 79-102.

4355. Bixby, David M. "The Roosevelt Court, Democratic Ideology, and Minority Rights: Another Look at *United States v. Classic*." *Yale Law Review* 90 (March 1981): 741-815.

4356. Claude, Richard. "Constitutional Voting Rights and Early U.S. Supreme Court Doctrine." *Journal of Negro History* 51 (April 1966): 114-124.

4357. Edgington, T. B. "The Repeal of the Fifteenth Amendment." *North American Review* 188 (July 1908): 92-100.

4358. Elliott, Ward E. "Ideology and Intervention: Supreme Court Intervention in Voting Rights Disputes from Taney to Warren." Ph.D. diss., Harvard University, 1969.

4359. Elliott, Ward E. *The Rise of Guardian Democracy: The Supreme Court's Role in Voting Rights Disputes, 1845-1969.* Cambridge: Harvard University Press, 1974.

4360. Engstrom, Richard L. "Post-Census Representational Districting: The Supreme Court, 'One Person, One Vote' and the Gerrymandering Issue." *Southern University Law Review* 7 (Spring 1981): 173-226.

4361. Engstrom, Richard L. "Racial Vote Dilution: Supreme Court Interpretations of Section 5 of the Voting Rights Act." *Southern University Law Review* 4 (Spring 1978): 139-164.

4362. Engstrom, Richard L. "Supreme Court and Equipopulous Gerrymandering: A Remaining Obstacle in the Quest for Fair and Effective Representation." *Arizona State Law Journal* 1976 (1976): 277-319.

4363. Fox, Russell H. "Achieving Fair Representation: The *Rome* and *Mobile* Decisions." *National Civic Review* 69 (November 1980): 555-565.

4364. Grantham, Dewey W., Jr. "White Primary and the Supreme Court." *South Atlantic Quarterly* 48 (October 1949): 529-538.

4365. Hine, Darlene C. "Blacks and the Destruction of the Democratic White Primary, 1935-1944." *Journal of Negro History* 62 (January 1977): 43-59.

4366. Jones, Sidney A., Jr. "The White Primary and the Supreme Court: Will *Smith v. Allwright* End Southern Disenfranchisement?" *National Bar Journal* 3 (March 1945): 10-28.

4367. Kozusko, Donald D., and Paul J. Lambert. "The Uncertain Impact of *Williams v. Rhodes* on Qualifying Minority Parties for the Ballot." *Harvard Journal on Legislation* 6 (January 1969): 236-253.

4368. McKay, Robert B. "Racial Discrimination in the Electoral Process." *Annals of the American Academy of Political and Social Science* 407 (May 1973): 102-118.

4369. Mathews, John M. *Legislative and Judicial History of the Fifteenth Amendment.* Baltimore: Johns Hopkins Press, 1909.

4370. Smith, C. Calvin. "Politics of Evasion: Arkansas' Reaction to *Smith v. Allwright*, 1944." *Journal of Negro History* 67 (Spring 1982): 40-51.

4371. Workman, W. D., Jr. "State Regulation of the Right to Vote: The Role of the Supreme Court in Civil Rights." *American Bar Association Journal* 35 (May 1949): 393-396, 439.

Reapportionment

4372. Auerbach, Carl A. "The Reapportionment Cases: One Person, One Vote; One Vote, One Value." *Supreme Court Review* 1964 (1964): 1-87.

4373. Bagger, Richard H. "The Supreme Court and Congressional Apportionment: Slippery Slope to Equal Representation Gerrymandering." *Rutgers Law Review* 38 (Fall 1985): 109-137.

4374. Baker, Gordon E. "One Man, One Vote, and Political Fairness: Or, How the Burger Court Found Happiness by Rediscovering *Reynolds v. Sims*." *Emory Law Journal* 23 (Summer 1974): 701-724.

4375. Baker, Gordon E. *The Reapportionment Revolution: Representation, Political Power, and the Supreme Court*. New York: Random House, 1966.

4376. Ball, Howard. *The Warren Court's Conceptions of Democracy: An Evaluation of the Supreme Court's Apportionment Opinions*. Rutherford, NJ: Fairleigh Dickinson University Press, 1971.

4377. Banzhaf, John F., III. "Multi-Member Electoral Districts: Do They Violate the 'One Man, One Vote' Principle?" *Yale Law Journal* 75 (July 1966): 1309-1338.

4378. Beiser, Edward N. "A Comparative Analysis of State and Federal Judicial Behavior: The Reapportionment Cases." *American Political Science Review* 62 (September 1968): 788-795.

4379. Bickel, Alexander M. "Reapportionment and Liberal Myths." *Commentary* 35 (June 1963): 483-491.

4380. Boyd, William J. "Apportionment Facts: Answers Given to Some Frequently Asked Questions Raised by Supreme Court's Apportionment Rulings." *National Civic Review* 53 (November 1964): 530-534.

4381. Clinton, Robert N. "Further Explorations in the Political Thicket: The Gerrymander and the Constitution." *Iowa Law Review* 59 (October 1973): 1-47.

4382. Cortner, Richard C. *The Apportionment Cases*. Knoxville: University of Tennessee Press, 1970.

4383. DeGrazia, Alfred. *Essay on Apportionment and Representative Government*. Washington, DC: American Enterprise Institute for Public Policy Research, 1963.

4384. Dixon, Robert G., Jr. *Democratic Representation: Reapportionment in Law and Politics*. New York: Oxford University Press, 1968.

4385. Dixon, Robert G., Jr. "Legislative Apportionment and the Federal Constitution." *Law and Contemporary Problems* 27 (Summer 1962): 100-142.

4386. Dixon, Robert G., Jr. "The Warren Court Crusade for the Holy Grail of 'One Man-One Vote'." *Supreme Court Review* 1969 (1969): 219-270.

4387. Feig, Douglas G. "Looking at Supreme Court Impact in Context: The Case of Reapportionment and State Spending." *American Politics Quarterly* 13 (April 1985): 167-187.

4388. Fordham, Jefferson B. "A Spur for the States: Reapportionment Decisions by U.S. Supreme Court Can Serve as Impetus for Legislative Improvement." *National Civic Review* 53 (October 1964): 474-478.

4389. Friedman, John A. "Beyond *Wesberry*: State Apportionment and Equal Protection." *New York University Law Review* 39 (April 1964): 264-289.

4390. Grofman, Bernard. "Alternatives to Single-Member Plurality Districts: Legal and Empirical Issues." *Policy Studies Journal* 9 (May 1980/1981): 875-898.

4391. Grofman, Bernard. "Reformers, Politicians, and the Courts: A Preliminary Look at U.S. Redistricting." *Political Ge-*

ography Quarterly 1 (October 1982): 303-316.

4392. Hamilton, Howard D. "Congressional Districting: A Landmark Decision of the Supreme Court." *Social Education* 29 (January 1965): 23-26.

4393. Hanson, Royce. *The Political Thicket: Reapportionment and Constitutional Democracy.* Englewood Cliffs, NJ: Prentice-Hall, 1966.

4394. Hill, A. Spencer. "Reapportionment Decisions: A Return to Dogma?" *Journal of Politics* 31 (February 1969): 186-213.

4395. Hofeller, Thomas B. "Mississippi Redistricting, 1977-1980." Ph.D. diss., Claremont Graduate School, 1979.

4396. Hyman, Harold M. *A More Perfect Union: The Impact of the Civil War and Reconstruction on the Constitution.* New York: Knopf, 1973.

4397. Katz, Ellis. "Apportionment and Majority Rule." *Publius* 1 (1971): 141-161.

4398. Kennedy, Cornelius B. "The Reapportionment Decisions: A Constitutional Amendment Is Needed [To Give] the People of the States the Right to Determine the Composition of Their Own Legislatures, Providing That One House Is Based on Population." *American Bar Association Journal* 51 (February 1965): 123-127.

4399. Lacy, Donald P., and Philip L. Martin. "Extraordinary Majority: The Supreme Court's Retreat from Voting Equity." *California Western Law Review* 10 (Spring 1974): 551-589.

4400. Larson, James E. *Reapportionment and the Court: A Survey of Recent Cases.* Birmingham: University of Alabama Press, 1962.

4401. Lee, Calvin B. *One Man, One Vote: WMCA and the Struggle for Equal Representation.* New York: Scribner's, 1967.

4402. Lucas, Jo D. "Legislative Apportionment and Representative Government:

The Meaning of *Baker v. Carr.*" *Michigan Law Review* 61 (February 1963): 711-804.

4403. McKay, Robert B. "Court, Congress, and Reapportionment." *Michigan Law Review* 63 (December 1964): 255-278.

4404. McKay, Robert B. "The Reapportionment Decisions, Retrospect and Prospect, Contend That the Equal Population Principle Announced by the Supreme Court in the Reapportionment Cases Is Sound Constitutional Doctrine. . . . " *American Bar Association Journal* 51 (February 1965): 128-133.

4405. McKay, Robert B. "Reapportionment: Success Story of the Warren Court." *Michigan Law Review* 67 (December 1968): 223-236.

4406. McKay, Robert B. *Reapportionment: The Law and Politics of Equal Representation.* New York: Twentieth Century Fund, 1965.

4407. McLaughlin, James A. "What Has the Supreme Court Taught? A Criticism on the United States Supreme Court by Way of a Critique of *Lance v. the Board of Education of Roane County.*" *West Virginia Law Review* 72 (December/February 1969/1970): 1-32.

4408. Martin, Philip L. "The Supreme Court and Local Government Reapportionment: The Second Phase." *Baylor Law Review* 21 (Winter 1969): 5-17.

4409. Martin, Philip L. "The Supreme Court and Local Reapportionment: The Third Phase." *George Washington Law Review* 39 (October 1970): 102-122.

4410. Martin, Philip L. "The Supreme Court and Local Reapportionment: Voter Inequality in Special-Purpose Units." *William and Mary Law Review* 15 (Spring 1974): 601-614.

4411. Martin, Philip L. "The Supreme Court and State Legislative Reapportionment: The Retreat from Absolutism." *Valparaiso University Law Review* 9 (Fall 1974): 31-54.

4412. Nash, Peter H., and Richard L. Strecker. "Legislative Reapportionment, Urban Planning, and the Supreme Court." *American Institute of Planners Journal* 28 (August 1962): 145-151.

4413. Neal, Phil C. "*Baker v. Carr*: Politics in Search of Law." *Supreme Court Review* 1962 (1962): 252-327.

4414. Neighbor, Howard D. "Equity in the Electoral/Representative Structure: Is the Supreme Court Leaving the Political Thicket?" *National Civic Review* 74 (April 1985): 169-177, 181.

4415. Noragon, Jack. "Congressional Redistricting and Population Composition, 1964-1970." *Midwest Journal of Political Science* 16 (May 1972): 295-302.

4416. Parkinson, Jerry R. "Reapportionment: A Call for a Consistent Quantitative Standard." *Iowa Law Review* 70 (March 1985): 663-692.

4417. Polsby, Nelson W., ed. *Reapportionment in the 1970s.* Berkeley: University of California Press, 1971.

4418. Quinlan, Patrick J. "Legislative Reapportionment: A Policy Emerges." *Baylor Law Review* 25 (Fall 1973): 660-673.

4419. Redenius, Charles M. "Representation, Reapportionment, and the Supreme Court." *Political Studies* 30 (December 1982): 515-532.

4420. Rogowski, Ronald. "Representation in Political Theory and in Law." *Ethics* 91 (April 1981): 395-430, 451-485.

4421. Scarrow, Howard A. "Partisan Gerrymandering: Invidious or Benevolent? *Gaffney v. Cummings* and Its Aftermath." *Journal of Politics* 44 (August 1982): 810-821.

4422. Schubert, Glendon A. *Reapportionment.* New York: Scribner's, 1965.

4423. Shapiro, Martin M. "Gerrymandering, Unfairness, and the Supreme Court." *University of California at Los Angeles Law Review* 33 (October 1985): 227-256.

4424. Shelley, Fred M. "A Constitutional Choice Approach to Electoral District Boundary Delineation." *Political Geography Quarterly* 1 (October 1982): 341-350.

4425. Wells, David I. "Con Affirmative Gerrymandering." *Policy Studies Journal* 9 (Special Issue 1980-1981): 863-874.

4426. Wells, David I. "The 1983 Redistricting Decisions: What People Think the Court Said . . . What the Court Really Said." *National Civil Review* 73 (April 1984): 181-188.

4427. Wingerd, Karen R. "Function of the Supreme Court as a Rhetorical Instrument in Reapportionment." Ph.D. diss., University of Denver, 1967.

Voting

4428. Buell, E. Rick, II. "*Katzenbach v. Morgan* and the 18 Year Old Vote." *Journal of Law Reform* 4 (Fall 1970): 149-160.

4429. Claude, Richard. *The Supreme Court and the Electoral Process.* Baltimore: Johns Hopkins University Press, 1970.

4430. Claude, Richard. "Supreme Court Policy-Making and Electoral Reform." *Policy Studies Journal* 2 (Summer 1974): 261-266.

4431. Earle, Valerie A., and Chester B. Earle. "The Supreme Court and the Electoral Process." *World Affairs* 140 (Summer 1977): 25-40.

4432. Hadley, Charles D. "The Nationalization of American Politics: Congress, the Supreme Court, and the National Political Parties." *Journal of Social and Political Studies* 4 (Winter 1979): 359-380.

4433. Kirby, James C., Jr. "The Constitutional Right to Vote." *New York University Law Review* 45 (November 1970): 995-1014.

4434. Montoya, Solomon. "The Formulation and Ratification of the Twenty-sixth Amendment." Ph.D. diss., New York University, 1973.

4435. Riker, William H. "Democracy and Representation: A Reconciliation of *Ball v. James* and *Reynolds v. Sims*." *Supreme Court Economic Review* 1 (1982): 39-68.

4436. Still, Jonathan W. "Political Equality and Election Systems." *Ethics* 91 (April 1981): 375-394, 452-485.

Other Rights

4437. Clune, William H., III. "Supreme Court's Treatment of Wealth Discrimination under the Fourteenth Amendment." *Supreme Court Review* 1975 (1975): 289-354.

4438. Hartstone, Eliot, Henry J. Steadman, and John Monahan. "*Vitek* and Beyond: The Empirical Context of Person-to-Hospital Transfers." *Law and Contemporary Problems* 45 (Summer 1982): 125-136.

4439. Lasiter, Susan S. "Can Louisiana's Succession Laws Survive in Light of the Supreme Court's Recent Recognition of Illegitimates' Rights?" *Louisiana Law Review* 39 (Summer 1979): 1132-1160.

4440. "Legal Status of the Illegitimate Child under Recent Supreme Court Decisions." *Interpreter Releases* 49 (July 18, 1972): 185-189.

4441. Leisy, Raymond. "Supreme Court Decision Regarding Out-of-State Tuition." *Journal of College Student Personnel* 15 (January 1974): 3-4.

4442. Raab, Jennifer J. "*Lehr v. Robertson*: Unwed Fathers and Adoption: How Much Process Is Due?" *Harvard Women's Law Journal* 7 (Spring 1984): 265-286.

4443. Rosenheim, Margaret K. "Constitutionality of Durational Residence Requirements." *Social Service Review* 44 (March 1970): 82-93.

4444. Rosenheim, Margaret K. "*Shapiro v. Thompson*: The Beggars Are Coming to Town." *Supreme Court Review* 1969 (1969): 303-346.

4445. Stenger, Robert L. "Supreme Court and Illegitimacy: 1968-1977." *Family Law Quarterly* 11 (Winter 1978): 365-405.

4446. Zingo, Martha T. "Equal Protection for Illegitimate Children: The Supreme Court's Standard for Discrimination." *Antioch Law Journal* 3 (Spring 1985): 59-97.

VII. The Court and Due Process

General Studies

4447. Adelstein, Richard P. "Informational Paradox and the Pricing of Crime: Capital Sentencing Standards in Economic Perspective." *Journal of Criminal Law and Criminology* 70 (Fall 1979): 281-298.

4448. Allen, Francis A. "Criminal." *University of Chicago Law Review* 31 (Winter 1964): 257-262.

4449. Allen, Francis A. "Judicial Quest for Penal Justice: The Warren Court and the Criminal Cases." *University of Illinois Law Forum* 1975 (1975): 518-542.

4450. Allen, Francis A. "The Supreme Court and State Criminal Justice." *Wayne Law Review* 4 (Summer 1958): 191-204.

4451. Allen, Ronald J. "*Mullaney v. Wilbur*, Supreme Court and Substantive Criminal Law: Examination of Limits of Legitimate Intervention." *Texas Law Review* 55 (January 1977): 269-301.

4452. Altman, Andrew, and Steven Lee. "Legal Entrapment." *Philosophy and Public Affairs* 12 (Winter 1983): 51-69.

4453. American Bar Association. Committee on Criminal Justice and Military. *Comparative Analysis: Federal Rules of Criminal Procedure and Military Practice and Procedure.* Washington, DC: American Bar Association, 1982.

4454. American Bar Association. Project on Standards for Criminal Justice. *Standards Relating to the Administration of Criminal Justice.* New York: Institute of Judicial Administration, 1974.

4455. Amsterdam, Anthony G. "A Selective Survey of Supreme Court Decisions in Criminal Law and Procedure." *Criminal Law Bulletin* 9 (June 1973): 389-406.

4456. Arenella, Peter. "Foreword: Rethinking the Functions of Criminal Procedure: The Warren and Burger Courts' Competing Ideologies." *Georgetown Law Journal* 72 (December 1983): 185-248.

4457. Baer, Harold, Jr. "Sequestering Witnesses: Does the Practice Interfere with the Defendant's Constitutional Rights?" *Trial* 22 (July 1986): 99-102.

4458. Baker, Thomas. "The Ambiguous Independent and Adequate State Ground in Criminal Cases: Federalism along a Mobius Strip." *Georgia Law Review* 19 (Summer 1985): 799-859.

4459. Barber, Susanna R. "*Chandler v. Florida*: The Supreme Court's Reluctance to Endorse Televised Trials." *Southern Speech Communication Journal* 48 (Summer 1983): 323-339.

4460. Barkin, Eugene N. "Legal Issues Facing Parole." *Crime and Delinquency* 25 (April 1979): 219-235.

4461. Batey, Robert. "Techniques of Strict Construction: The Supreme Court and the Gun Control Act of 1968." *American Journal of Criminal Law* 13 (Winter 1986): 123-156.

4462. Bazelon, David L. "The Morality of

Criminal Law: Rights of the Accused." *Journal of Criminal Law and Criminology* 72 (Winter 1981): 1143-1170.

4463. Beaird, J. Ralph. "In Their Own Image: The Reframing of the Due Process Clause by the United States Supreme Court." *Georgia Law Review* 13 (Winter 1979): 479-503.

4464. Beisel, Albert R., Jr. "Control over Illegal Enforcement of the Criminal Law: Role of the Supreme Court." *Boston University Law Review* 34 (November 1954): 413-448.

4465. Beisel, Albert R., Jr. "Control over Illegal Enforcement of the Criminal Law: Role of the Supreme Court." *Boston University Law Review* 35 (January 1955): 1-76.

4466. Bell, Richard S. "Decision Theory and Due Process: A Critique of the Supreme Court's Lawmaking for Burdens of Proof." *Journal of Criminal Law and Criminology* 78 (Fall 1987): 557-585.

4467. Bender, Louis, and Steven Bender. "Supreme Court in *Sells* and *Baggott*: Lays Down Tests for Disclosing Grand Jury Materials." *Journal of Taxation* 59 (September 1983): 138-141.

4468. Berger, Mark. "Withdrawal of Rights and Due Deference: The New Hands-Off Policy in Correctional Litigation." *University of Missouri at Kansas City Law Review* 47 (Fall 1978): 1-30.

4469. Berman, Bayard F. "Supreme Court Review of State Court 'Findings of Fact' in Certain Criminal Cases: The Fact-Law Dichotomy in a Narrow Area." *Southern California Law Review* 23 (April 1950): 334-343.

4470. Bernstein, H. Carol. "Psychotherapist-Patient Privilege under Federal Rule of Evidence 501." *Journal of Criminal Law and Criminology* 75 (Summer 1984): 388-412.

4471. Bernstein, Sidney, and Michael Ei-

senstein. "1981 Supreme Court Update: The Criminal Law." *Trial* 17 (October 1981): 54-60.

4472. Bernstein, Sidney, and Michael Eisenstein. "1982 Supreme Court Update: The Criminal Law." *Trial* 18 (September 1982): 45-50; (October 1982): 58-65.

4473. Beytagh, Francis X., Jr. "Ten Years of Non-Retroactivity: A Critique and a Proposal." *Virginia Law Review* 61 (December 1975): 1557-1625.

4474. Bilaisis, Vilija. "Harmless Error: Abettor of Courtroom Misconduct." *Journal of Criminal Law and Criminology* 74 (Summer 1983): 457-475.

4475. Bird, Francis W. "The Evolution of Due Process of Law in the Decision of the United States Supreme Court." *Columbia Law Review* 13 (January 1913): 37-50.

4476. Blakesley, Christopher L. "United States Jurisdiction over Extraterritorial Crime." *Journal of Criminal Law and Criminology* 73 (Fall 1982): 1109-1163.

4477. Boskey, Bennett, and John H. Pickering. "Federal Restrictions on State Criminal Procedure." *University of Chicago Law Review* 13 (April 1946): 266-299.

4478. Bowers, William J., and Glenn J. Pierce. "Arbitrariness and Discrimination under Post-*Furman* Capital Statutes." *Crime and Delinquency* 26 (October 1980): 563-635.

4479. Brockelbank, William J. "The Role of Due Process in American Constitutional Law (1787-1954)." *Cornell Law Quarterly* 39 (Summer 1954): 561-591.

4480. Brower, George D. "The Supreme Court and the Growth of Crime." Ph.D. diss., State University of New York at Buffalo, 1985.

4481. Brown, Ray A. "Due Process of Law, Police Power, and the Supreme Court." *Harvard Law Review* 40 (May 1927): 943-968.

4482. Brown, Ray A. "Police Power: Legislation for Health and Personal Safety." *Harvard Law Review* 42 (May 1929): 866-898.

4483. Caldwell, Robert G. "Supreme Court and Law Enforcement." *Journal of Police Science and Administration* 3 (June 1975): 222-237.

4484. Carlson, Ronald. *Criminal Justice Procedure.* 3d ed. Cincinnati: Anderson, 1985.

4485. Carter, Barry. "Effective Guaranty of a Speedy Trial for Convicts in Other Jurisdictions." *Yale Law Journal* 77 (March 1968): 767-788.

4486. Casey, Patrick S. "The Admissibility of Grand Jury Testimony under 804 (b)(5): A Two-Test Proposal." *Journal of Criminal Law and Criminology* 74 (Winter 1983): 1446-1470.

4487. Chase, Edward. "The Burger Court, the Individual, and the Criminal Process: Directions and Misdirections." *New York University Law Review* 52 (June 1977): 518-597.

4488. Cohen, Stanley. *A Law Enforcement Guide to United States Supreme Court Decisions.* Springfield, IL: Thomas, 1972.

4489. Cord, Robert L. "Neo-Incorporation: The Burger Court and the Due Process Clause of the Fourteenth Amendment." *Fordham Law Review* 44 (November 1975): 215-248.

4490. Cortner, Richard C. *A "Scottsboro" Case in Mississippi: The Supreme Court and* Brown vs. Mississippi. Jackson: University Press of Mississippi, 1986.

4491. Corwin, Edward S. "The Doctrine of Due Process of Law before the Civil War." *Harvard Law Review* 24 (March 1911): 366-385, 460-479.

4492. Criminal Law Reporter. *The Criminal Law Revolution and Its Aftermath,*
1960-1974. Washington, DC: Bureau of National Affairs, 1975.

4493. Criminal Law Reporter. *The Criminal Law Revolution and Its Aftermath, Supplements: 1977-1978; 1978-1979; 1979-1980.* Washington, DC: Bureau of National Affairs, 1979-1981.

4494. Curtis, Charles P. "A Modern Supreme Court in a Modern World." *Vanderbilt Law Review* 4 (April 1951): 427-445.

4495. Cutts, John A., III. "Procedural Due Process: A Haven for Judges." *American Bar Association Journal* 54 (December 1968): 1199-1208.

4496. Denniston, Lyle. "Supreme Court Agrees to Hear Many Appeals by Prosecutors." *Criminal Justice Newsletter* 16 (October 15, 1985): 1-3.

4497. Dressler, Thomas W. "Developments in the Manifest Necessity Rule." *Journal of Criminal Law and Criminology* 70 (Spring 1979): 63-67.

4498. Dubnoff, Caren. "Pretrial Publicity and Due Process in Criminal Proceedings." *Political Science Quarterly* 92 (Spring 1977): 89-108.

4499. Duker, William F. "The Fuller Court and State Criminal Process: Threshold of Modern Limitations on Government." *Brigham Young University Law Review* 1980 (1980): 275-293.

4500. Edelstein, Charles D. "And 'They Shall Beat Their Plowshares into Swords': Examination of Three United States Supreme Court Decisions." *Justice System Journal* 2 (1977): 284-292.

4501. Elliot, Ivan A., Jr. "Supervision of State Criminal Procedure by United States Supreme Court." *University of Illinois Law Forum* 1950 (Summer 1950): 240-248.

4502. Erickson, William H. "The Pronouncements of the Supreme Court of the

United States in the Criminal Law Field during the 1974-1975 Term." *National Journal of Criminal Defense* 1 (Fall 1975): 376-456.

4503. Erickson, William H. "The Pronouncements of the Supreme Court of the United States in the Criminal Law Field during the 1975-1976 Term." *National Journal of Criminal Defense* 2 (Fall 1976): 157-236.

4504. Erickson, William H. "The Pronouncements of the Supreme Court of the United States in the Criminal Law Field during the 1976-1977 Term." *National Journal of Criminal Defense* 3 (Spring 1977): 1-84.

4505. Erickson, William H. "Pronouncements of the United States Supreme Court Relating to the Criminal Law Field: 1978-1979." *National Journal of Criminal Defense* 5 (Spring 1979): 1-103.

4506. Erickson, William H. "Pronouncements of the United States Supreme Court Relating to the Criminal Law Field: 1979-1980." *National Journal of Criminal Defense* 5 (Fall 1979): 135-257.

4507. Erickson, William H. "Pronouncements of the United States Supreme Court Relating to the Criminal Law Field: 1980-1981." *National Journal of Criminal Defense* 7 (Fall 1981): 161-297.

4508. Erickson, William H. "Pronouncements of the United States Supreme Court Relating to the Criminal Law Field: 1982-1983." *Colorado Lawyer* 12 (September 1983): 1377-1444.

4509. Erickson, William H. "Pronouncements of the United States Supreme Court Relating to the Criminal Law Field: 1982-1983." *Federal Rules Decisions* 99 (January 1984): 345-464.

4510. Erickson, William H. "The Supreme Court's Impact on Criminal Law in the 1971-72 Term of Court." *Interna-tional Society of Barristers* 8 (January 1973): 35-58.

4511. Erickson, William H., and William D. Neighbors. "Pronouncements of the United States Supreme Court Relating to Criminal Law, 1984-1985 Term." *Prosecutor, Journal of the National District Attorneys Association* 19 (Fall 1985): 1-45.

4512. Erickson, William H., and William D. Neighbors. "Pronouncements of the United States Supreme Court Relating to the Criminal Law Field: 1983-1984." *Federal Rules Decisions* 103 (December 1984): 187-317.

4513. Erickson, William H., and William D. Neighbors. "Pronouncements of the U.S. Supreme Court Relating to the Criminal Law Field: 1983-1984." *Colorado Lawyer* 13 (September 1984): 1561-1566.

4514. Erickson, William H., et al. "Pronouncements of the U.S. Supreme Court Relating to the Criminal Law Field: 1985-1986." *Emory Law Journal* 35 (Winter 1986): 1553-1556.

4515. Erickson, William H., William D. Neighbors, and B. James George, Jr. "Pronouncements of the U.S. Supreme Court Relating to the Criminal Field: 1985-1986." *Colorado Lawyer* 15 (Spring 1986): 1553-1556.

4516. Erlinder, C. Peter. "*Mens Rea*, Due Process, and the Supreme Court: Toward a Constitutional Doctrine of Substantive Criminal Law." *American Journal of Criminal Law* 9 (July 1981): 163-192.

4517. Erlinder, C. Peter, and David C. Thomas. "Prohibiting Prosecutorial Discretion: Toward a Principled Resolution of a Due Process Dilemma." *Journal of Criminal Law and Criminology* 76 (Summer 1985): 341-438.

4518. Fellman, David. *The Defendant's Rights.* New York: Holt, Rinehart, and Winston, 1958.

4519. Fellman, David. *The Defendant's*

Rights Today. Madison: University of Wisconsin Press, 1976.

4520. Fellman, David. "The Supreme Court's Changing Views of Criminal Defendants' Rights." In *Crime in Urban Society*, edited by Barbara N. McLennan, 93-123. New York: Dunellen, 1970.

4521. Fort, William S. "*Gault*: Adversity or Opportunity?" *Judicature* 51 (August/September 1967): 53-57.

4522. Fraenkel, Osmond K. "The Supreme Court as Protector of Civil Rights: Criminal Justice." *Annals of the American Academy of Political and Social Science* 275 (May 1951): 86-100.

4523. Frankel, Marvin E., and Leonard Orland. "Fourteenth Annual Review of Criminal Procedure: United States Supreme Court and Courts of Appeals, 1983-1984 Project; Foreword: Sentencing Commissions and Guidelines." *Georgetown Law Journal* 73 (December 1984): 225-248.

4524. Frazer, Douglas H. "The Newsperson's Privilege in Grand Jury Proceedings: An Argument for Uniform Recognition and Application." *Journal of Criminal Law and Criminology* 75 (Summer 1984): 413-442.

4525. Frey, Richard G. "Supreme Court Limits on Non-Capital Punishment: The Politics of Proportionality." *Willamette Law Review* 21 (Spring 1985): 261-278.

4526. Friendly, Henry J. "The Bill of Rights as a Code of Criminal Procedure." *California Law Review* 53 (October 1965): 929-956.

4527. Fuerst, J. S., and Roy Petty. "Due Process: How Much Is Enough?" *Public Interest* 79 (Spring 1985): 96-110.

4528. Furlow, David A. "Civil RICO Comes to Texas: A Review of Civil RICO Jurisprudence in the Fifth Circuit and in the Federal District Courts of Texas." *Baylor Law Review* 37 (Fall 1985): 841-912.

4529. Galloway, John, ed. *Criminal Justice and the Burger Court*. New York: Facts on File, 1978.

4530. Galloway, John, ed. *The Supreme Court and the Rights of the Accused*. New York: Facts on File, 1973.

4531. Gangi, William. "O What a Tangled Web We Weave. . . ." *Prosecutor, Journal of the National District Attorneys Association* 19 (Spring 1986): 15-48.

4532. George, B. James, Jr. "From Warren to Burger to Chance: Future Trends in the Administration of Criminal Justice." *Criminal Law Bulletin* 12 (May/June 1976): 253-288.

4533. George, B. James, Jr. "Supreme Court Review, 1977 Foreword—Doctrinal Doldrums: The Supreme Court 1976 Term Criminal Law Decisions." *Journal of Criminal Law and Criminology* 68 (December 1977): 469-642.

4534. George, B. James, Jr. "United States Supreme Court 1979-1980 Term: Criminal Law Decisions." *New York Law School Law Review* 26 (Winter 1981): 99-220.

4535. George, B. James, Jr. "United States Supreme Court 1981-1982 Term: Criminal Law Decisions." *New York Law School Law Review* 29 (1985): 551-686.

4536. George, B. James, Jr. "United States Supreme Court 1982-1983 Term: Criminal Law Decisions." *New York Law School Law Review* 30 (1985): 229-383.

4537. George, B. James, Jr. "United States Supreme Court 1983-1984 Term: Highlights of Criminal Procedure." *New York Law School Law Review* 31 (1986): 61-132.

4538. George, B. James, Jr. "United States Supreme Court 1984-1985 Term: Criminal Law and Procedure Highlights." *Capital University Law Review* 16 (Winter 1986): 159-201.

4539. George, B. James, Jr. "United

States Supreme Court 1985-1986 Term: Criminal Law Decisions." *New York Law School Law Review* 31 (1986): 427-581.

4540. Ginsberg, Daniel L., and Steven M. Stein. "Due Process and the Tax Court." *Kentucky Law Journal* 53 (Winter 1964/1965): 336-359.

4541. Glanzer, Seymour, and Paul R. Taskier. "Attorneys before the Grand Jury: Assertion of the Attorney-Client Privilege to Protect a Client's Identity." *Journal of Criminal Law and Criminology* 75 (Winter 1984): 1070-1099.

4542. Goldberg, Steven H. "Harmless Error: Constitutional Sneak Thief." *Crime Law and Criminology* 71 (Winter 1980): 421-442.

4543. Goldman, Sheldon. "Criminal Justice in the Federal Courts." *Current History* 70 (June 1976): 257-271.

4544. Graham, Fred P. *The Due Process Revolution: The Warren Court's Impact on Criminal Law.* Rochelle Park, NJ: Hayden Book Company, 1970.

4545. Graham, Howard J. "Procedure to Substance: Extra-Judicial Rise of Due Process, 1830-1860." *California Law Review* 40 (Winter 1952/1953): 483-500.

4546. Grant, J.A.C. "Natural Law Background of Due Process." *Columbia Law Review* 31 (January 1931): 56-81.

4547. Greenfield, Beth. "Fourteenth Annual Review of Criminal Procedure: United States Supreme Court and Courts of Appeals, 1983-1984 Project." *Georgetown Law Journal* 73 (December 1984): 225-874.

4548. Greenhalgh, Ronald J. "Teachings of *Harlow v. Fitzgerald*." *Police Chief* 50 (May 1983): 20.

4549. Griffin, G. Edward. *The Great Prison Break: The Supreme Court Leads the Way.* Boston: Western Islands, 1968.

4550. Haddad, James B. "The Finality

Distinction in Supreme Court Retroactivity Analysis: An Inadequate Surrogate for Modification of the Scope of Federal *Habeas Corpus*." *Northwestern University Law Review* 79 (December 1984/February 1985): 1062-1079.

4551. Halberstam, Malvina. "Towards Neutral Principles in the Administration of Criminal Justice: A Critique of Supreme Court Decisions Sanctioning the Plea-Bargaining Process." *Journal of Criminal Law and Criminology* 73 (Spring 1982): 1-49.

4552. Hall, Livingston. *Modern Criminal Procedure: Cases, Comments, and Questions.* 3d ed. St. Paul, MN: West Publishing Company, 1969.

4553. Harris, Leslie J. "Constitutional Limits on Criminal Presumptions as an Expression of Changing Concepts of Fundamental Fairness." *Journal of Criminal Law and Criminology* 77 (Summer 1986): 308-357.

4554. Harrison, Katherine B., Harlan Cohen, Brian M. Colligan, and Ana Maria Martinez, eds. "Sixteenth Annual Review of Criminal Procedure: United States Supreme Court and Courts of Appeals, 1985-1986 Project." *Georgetown Law Journal* 75 (February 1987): 713-1340.

4555. Herman, Lawrence. "The Supreme Court and Restrictions on Police Interrogation." *Ohio State Law Journal* 25 (Fall 1964): 449-500.

4556. Hickey, Thomas J., Jr. "A Comparative Legal Analysis of Warren and Burger Court Decisions in Fourth, Fifth, and Sixth Amendment Cases." Ph.D. diss., Sam Houston State University, 1985.

4557. Hochman, Charles B. "The Supreme Court and the Constitutionality of Retroactive Legislation." *Harvard Law Review* 73 (Fall 1960): 692-727.

4558. Hofer, Stephen R. "The Fallacy of *Farber*: Failure to Acknowledge the Constitutional Newman's Privilege in Criminal Cases." *Journal of Criminal Law and Criminology* 70 (Fall 1979): 299-336.

4559. Holley, Dannye. " 'Plea Convictions': Documenting and Evaluating the Reasons the United States Supreme Court and State Supreme Courts Don't Require Proof of Guilt." *Thurgood Marshall Law Review* 11 (Spring 1986): 301-325.

4560. Israel, Jerold H. "Criminal Procedure, the Burger Court, and the Legacy of the Warren Court." *Michigan Law Review* 75 (June 1977): 1320-1425.

4561. Kales, Albert M. "New Methods in Due Process Cases." *American Political Science Review* 12 (May 1918): 241-250.

4562. Kamisar, Yale. *Modern Criminal Procedure: Cases, Comments, and Questions.* 5th ed. St. Paul: West Publishing Company, 1980.

4563. Kane, Peter E. *Murder, Courts, and the Press: Issues in Free Press/Fair Trial.* Carbondale: Southern Illinois University Press, 1986.

4564. Kennedy, Thomas F., Jr. "Constitutional Trends of Systematic Exclusion in Grand and Petit Juries." *National Journal of Criminal Defense* 3 (Fall 1977): 277-288.

4565. Kitch, Edmund W. "The Supreme Court's Code of Criminal Procedure: 1968-1969 Edition." *Supreme Court Review* 1969 (1969): 155-202.

4566. Kurland, Philip B. "The Supreme Court, the Due Process Clause, and the *In Personam* Jurisdiction of State Courts." *University of Chicago Law Review* 25 (Summer 1958): 569-624.

4567. Kurland, Philip B., and Richard F. Wolfson. "Direct Appeal to the Supreme Court by the United States in Criminal Cases." *Indiana Law Journal* 24 (Summer 1949): 547-565.

4568. Lane, Margaret J. "Eyewitnesses

Identification: Should Psychologists Be Permitted to Address the Jury?" *Journal of Criminal Law and Criminology* 75 (Winter 1984): 1321-1365.

4569. Lanza-Kaduce, Lonn. "Formality, Neutrality, and Goal-Rationality: The Legacy of *Weber* in Analyzing Legal Thought." *Journal of Criminal Law and Criminology* 73 (Summer 1982): 533-560.

4570. Lefstein, Norman. "*In re Gault*, Juvenile Courts and Lawyers." *American Bar Association Journal* 53 (September 1967): 811-814.

4571. Leonard, Vivian A. *The Police, the Judiciary, and the Criminal.* Springfield, IL: Charles C. Thomas, 1966.

4572. Lermack, Paul. *Rights on Trial: The Supreme Court and the Criminal Law.* Millwood, NY: Associated Faculty Press, 1983.

4573. Levy, Leonard W. *Against the Law: The Nixon Court and Criminal Justice.* New York: Harper and Row, 1974.

4574. Lewis, Peter W. *Criminal Procedure: The Supreme Court's View Cases.* St. Paul, MN: West Publishing Company, 1979.

4575. Lewis, Peter W. *The Supreme Court and the Criminal Process: Cases and Comments.* Philadelphia: Saunders, 1978.

4576. Lewis, Peter W. "United States Supreme Court Decisions on Criminal Cases with Opinions (1953-1971): An Empirical Analysis of the Warren and Burger Courts." Ph.D. diss., Florida State University, 1972.

4577. Lippe, Emil. *Cases on the Jury System in the United States.* New York: Western, 1971.

4578. Loewy, Arnold H. "The Warren Court as Defender of State and Federal Criminal Laws: A Reply to Those Who Believe That the Court Is Oblivious to the Needs of Law Enforcement." *George*

Washington Law Review 37 (July 1969): 1218-1250.

4579. Lytton, William B. "Grand Jury Secrecy: Time for a Reevaluation." *Journal of Criminal Law and Criminology* 75 (Winter 1984): 1110-1128.

4580. McFeeley, Neil D. "A Change of Direction: *Habeas Corpus* from Warren to Burger." *Western Political Quarterly* 32 (June 1979): 174-188.

4581. McFeeley, Neil D. "The Expansion of Federal Jurisdiction: *Habeas Corpus* and the Warren Court." Ph.D. diss., University of Texas, 1975.

4582. McFeeley, Neil D. "*Habeas Corpus* and Due Process: From Warren to Burger." *Baylor Law Review* 28 (Summer 1976): 533-561.

4583. McGehee, Lucius P. *Due Process of Law under the Federal Constitution*. Northport, NY: Edward Thompson Company, 1906.

4584. McGuiness, Robert L. "Probable Cause: Informant Information, Part 1." *FBI Law Enforcement Bulletin* 51 (November 1982): 23-30.

4585. McGuiness, Robert L. "Probable Cause: Informant Information, Part 2." *FBI Law Enforcement Bulletin* 51 (December 1982): 19-24.

4586. McKusick, Marshall M. "Administration of the Rules of Evidence in the Federal District Courts." *South Dakota Bar Journal* 17 (April 1949): 23-28.

4587. Maclin, Tracey. "*New York v. Class*: A Little-Noticed Case with Disturbing Implications." *Journal of Criminal Law and Criminology* 78 (Spring 1987): 1-86.

4588. McMahon, Richard J. "Recent Criminal Law Rulings from the Supreme Court: The Conservative Bloc Begins to Exercise Control." *Delaware Lawyer* 3 (Summer 1984): 49-55.

4589. McMillian, Theodore. "*Habeas Corpus* and the Burger Court." *St. Louis University Law Journal* 28 (February 1984): 11-16.

4590. McMorris, S. Carter. "Can We Punish for the Acts of Addiction?" *American Bar Association Journal* 54 (November 1968): 1081-1085.

4591. MacNamara, Donald E., and Edward Sagarin. "The Warren Court and the Administration of Criminal Justice." *Crime and Delinquency* 18 (January 1972): 49-58.

4592. Manak, James P. "New Constitutional Rule on Use of Deadly Force." *Police Chief* 52 (September 1985): 12.

4593. Marks, Thomas C., and Mary Greenwood. "Burger Court and Substantive Rights, an Analytical Approach." *University of Detroit Journal of Urban Law* 57 (Summer 1980): 751-775.

4594. Maslow, Robert M. *"Coddling Criminals" under the Warren Court*. Washington, DC: Coiner Publications, 1969.

4595. Maurer, Robert A. "Due Process and the Supreme Court: A Revaluation." *Georgetown Law Journal* 22 (May 1934): 710-749.

4596. Mays, George L. "Supreme Court Disengagement from State Criminal Procedure: The Case of *Stone vs. Powell*." Ph.D. diss., University of Tennessee, 1979.

4597. Menacker, Julius. "Review of Supreme Court Reasoning in Cases of Expression, Due Process, and Equal Protection." *Phi Delta Kappan* 63 (November 1981): 188-190.

4598. Mertens, William J., and Silas Wasserstrom. "Eleventh Annual Review of Criminal Procedure: United States Supreme Court and the Court of Appeals, 1980-1981." *Georgetown Law Journal* 70 (December 1981): 365-835.

4599. Meyerhoff, Albert H., and Jeffrey

A. Mishkin. "Application of *Goldberg v. Kelly* Hearing Requirements to Termination of Social Security Benefits." *Stanford Law Review* 26 (February 1974): 549-575.

4600. Michael, Richard A. "The 'New' Federalism and the Burger Court's Deference to the States in Federal *Habeas* Proceedings." *Iowa Law Review* 64 (January 1979): 233-273.

4601. Michelman, Frank I. "Supreme Court and Litigation Access Fees: Right to Protect One's Rights, Pt. I." *Duke Law Journal* 1973 (January 1973): 1153-1215.

4602. Michelman, Frank I. "Supreme Court and Litigation Access Fees: Right to Protect One's Rights, Pt. II." *Duke Law Journal* 1974 (August 1974): 527-570.

4603. Mishkin, Paul J. "The High Court, the Writ, and Due Process of Law." *Harvard Law Review* 79 (November 1965): 56-102.

4604. Mitchell, Linda M., ed. "Fifteenth Annual Review of Criminal Procedure: United States Supreme Court and Courts of Appeals, 1984-1985." *Georgetown Law Journal* 4 (February 1986): 499-997.

4605. Morris, Grant H. "The Supreme Court Examines Civil Commitment Issues: A Retrospective and Prospective Assessment." *Tulane Law Review* 60 (May 1986): 927-953.

4606. Mott, Rodney L. *Due Process of Law.* New York: Da Capo Press, 1973.

4607. National Judicial Conference on Criminal Justice Standards, 1972. *Proceedings at the National Judicial Conference on Standards for the Administration of Criminal Justice.* St. Paul, MN: West Publishing Company, 1973.

4608. Nedrud, Duane R. *The Supreme Court and the Criminal Law.* Philadelphia: L. E. Publishers, 1978.

4609. Neighbors, William D., and Wil-liam H. Erickson. "Pronouncements of the U.S. Supreme Court Relating to the Criminal Law Field: 1984-1985." *Colorado Lawyer* 14 (September 1985): 1541-1544.

4610. Northrop, Edward S. "The Supreme Court and Criminal Procedure." *Maryland Law Review* 26 (Winter 1966): 1-12.

4611. Nutting, Charles B. "The Supreme Court, the Fourteenth Amendment, and State Criminal Cases." *University of Chicago Law Review* 3 (Fall 1936): 244-260.

4612. Oaks, Dallin H. "The 'Original' Writ of *Habeas Corpus* in the Supreme Court." *Supreme Court Review* 1962 (1962): 153-211.

4613. O'Brien, Kevin J. "Plea Bargaining and the Supreme Court: The Limits of Due Process and Substantive Justice." *Hastings Constitutional Law Quarterly* 9 (Fall 1981): 109-151.

4614. O'Neill, Timothy P. "The Good, the Bad, and the Burger Court: Victim's Rights and a New Model of Criminal Review." *Journal of Criminal Law and Criminology* 75 (Summer 1984): 363-387.

4615. Orfield, Lester B. "A Résumé of Decisions of the United States Supreme Court on Federal Criminal Procedure." *Nebraska Law Review* 20 (September 1941): 251-303; 21 (March 1942) 1-24; (June 1942): 113-142.

4616. Orfield, Lester B. "A Résumé of Decisions of the United States Supreme Court on Federal Criminal Procedure." *Oregon Law Review* 22 (December 1942): 60-87.

4617. Orren, Karen. "Judicial Whipsaw: Interest Conflict, Corporate Business, and the Seventh Amendment." *Polity* 18 (Fall 1985): 70-97.

4618. Packer, Herbert L. "*Mens Rea* and the Supreme Court." *Supreme Court Review* 1962 (1962): 107-152.

4619. Padgett, Gregory L. "Racially Motivated Violence and Intimidation: Inadequate State Enforcement and Federal Civil Rights Remedies." *Journal of Criminal Law and Criminology* 75 (Spring 1984): 103-138.

4620. Parker, William C. "Arrest Warrants Don't Provide Officers Absolute Protection." *Police Chief* 53 (July 1986): 14.

4621. Parker, William L., Jr. "Police Interrogation Governed by Suspect, Not Attorney." *Police Chief* 53 (June 1986): 20.

4622. Pauley, Roger A. "The Emerging 'Victim Factor' in the Supreme Court's Criminal Jurisprudence: Should Victims' Interests Ever Prevent a Court from Overturning a Conviction and Ordering a Retrial?" *Indiana Law Journal* 61 (Spring 1986): 149-164.

4623. Perlin, Michael L. "The Supreme Court, the Mentally Disabled Criminal Defendant, and Symbolic Values: Random Decisions, Hidden Rationales, or 'Doctrinal Abyss'?" *Arizona Law Review* 29 (Winter 1987): 1-98.

4624. Perlin, Michael L. "The Supreme Court, the Mentally Disabled Criminal Defendant, Psychiatric Testimony in Death Penalty Cases, and the Power of Symbolism: Dulling the *Ake* in *Barefoot's* Achilles Heel." *New York Law School Human Rights Annual* 3 (Fall 1985): 91-169.

4625. Pidgeon, Mary Ann. "*Miller, Fisher,* and *Andresen*: Assistance for Investigations of White Collar Crime." *Criminal Justice Quarterly* 6 (Winter/ Spring 1978): 38-49.

4626. Plitt, Emory A., Jr. "Post-Termination Hearings without Pre-Termination Opportunity to Respond Violates Due Process." *Police Chief* 52 (June 1985): 15.

4627. Plitt, Emory A., Jr. "Remarks: Legal Issues Concerning Sobriety Checkpoints: The Maryland Experience." *Police Chief* 51 (March 1984): 82-85.

4628. Ponsoldt, James F. "A Due Process

Analysis of Judicially Authorized Presumptions in Federal Aggravated Bank Robbery Cases." *Journal of Criminal Law and Criminology* 74 (Summer 1983): 363-390.

4629. Powe, L. A., Jr. "Rehearsal for Substantive Due Process: The Municipal Bond Cases." *Texas Law Review* 53 (May 1975): 738-756.

4630. Powell, Thomas R. *The Supreme Court and State Police Power, 1922-1930.* Charlottesville, VA: Michie Company, 1932.

4631. Pratt, John E. *Robbery, Rape, Burglary, Riot, Murder, Arson, Bombings: The Earl Warren Supreme Court.* Columbus, OH: Bourke, 1970.

4632. Pye, A. Kenneth. "The Warren Court and Criminal Procedure." *Michigan Law Review* 67 (December 1968): 249-268.

4633. Redish, Martin, and Marshall Lawrence. "Adjudicatory Independence and the Values of Procedural Due Process." *Yale Law Journal* 95 (January 1986): 455-505.

4634. Robertson, John A. "Supreme Court and Limited Jurisdiction Courts: *Ward v. Village of Monroeville,* and *Shadwick v. City of Tampa. Justice System Journal* 1 (Winter 1974): 55-62.

4635. Robinson, W. S. "Bias, Probability, and Trial by Jury." *American Sociological Review* 15 (February 1950): 73-78.

4636. Rusin, Michael E. "Prosecutor's Duty of Disclose: From *Brady* to *Agurs* and Beyond." *Journal of Criminal Law and Criminology* 69 (Summer 1978): 197-225.

4637. Ryan, Mark J. "*Rose v. Lundy*: The Supreme Court Adopts the Total Exhaustion Rule for Review of Mixed *Habeas Corpus* Petitions." *Wisconsin Law Review* 1984 (1984): 859-892.

4638. Saari, David J. "The Criminal Jury

Faces Future Shock." *Judicature* 57 (June/July 1973): 12-17.

4639. Schmolesky, John M. "*County Court of Ulster County v. Allen* and *Sandstrom v. Montana*: The Supreme Court Lends an Ear But Turns Its Face." *Rutgers Law Review* 33 (Winter 1981): 261-316.

4640. Schofield, Henry. "Jury Trial in Original Proceedings for *Mandamus* in the Supreme Court." *Illinois Law Review* 3 (March 1909): 479-492.

4641. Schrader, George D. "United States Supreme Court Recent Decisions in Criminal and Criminal Law-Related Cases." *Alabama Lawyer* 42 (January 1981): 641-658.

4642. Scott, Austin W., Jr. "The Supreme Court's Control over State and Federal Criminal Juries." *Iowa Law Review* 34 (May 1949): 577-604.

4643. Seidman, Louis M. "Factual Guilt and the Burger Court: An Examination of Continuity and Change in Criminal Procedure." *Columbia Law Review* 80 (April 1980): 436-503.

4644. Serr, Brian J., and Mark Maney. "Racism, Peremptory Challenges, and the Democratic Jury: The Jurisprudence of a Delicate Balance." *Journal of Criminal Law and Criminology* 79 (Spring 1988): 1-65.

4645. Singer, Shelvin. "October 1974 Term of United States Supreme Court: Decisions of Importance to Police Personnel." *Police Law Quarterly* 5 (October 1975): 5-14.

4646. Singer, Shelvin. "United States Supreme Court Decisions of Importance to Law Enforcement Officers, 1975-1976 Term." *Police Law Quarterly* 6 (January 1977): 5-22.

4647. Singer, Shelvin. "United States Supreme Court Decisions of Importance to Law Enforcement Officers, 1976 Term." *Police Law Quarterly* 7 (October 1977): 5-18.

4648. Singer, Shelvin. "United States Supreme Court Decisions of Importance to Law Enforcement Officers, 1977 Term (Part I)." *Police Law Quarterly* 8 (October 1978): 5-12.

4649. Slovenko, Ralph. "Constitutional Limitations on the Rules of Evidence." *University of Cincinnati Law Review* 26 (Fall 1961): 493-536.

4650. Smith, Jim. "Federal *Habeas Corpus*: A Need for Reform." *Journal of Criminal Law and Criminology* 73 (Fall 1982): 1036-1050.

4651. Sokol, Ronald P. *Law-Abiding Policeman: A Guide to Recent Supreme Court Decisions.* Charlottesville, VA: Michie, 1966.

4652. Spritzer, Ralph S. "Criminal Waiver, Procedural Default, and the Burger Court." *University of Pennsylvania Law Review* 126 (January 1978): 473-514.

4653. Stephens, Otis H., Jr. "The Burger Court: New Dimensions in Criminal Justice." *Georgetown Law Journal* 60 (November 1971): 249-278.

4654. Stern, Robert L. "Attorney-Client Privilege: Supreme Court Repudiates the Control Group Test." *American Bar Association Journal* 67 (September 1981): 1142-1146.

4655. Tarlton, Charles D. "Mentally Ill in Criminal Cases: The Constitutional Issue." *Western Political Quarterly* 16 (September 1963): 525-540.

4656. Tauro, G. Joseph. "The Challenge to American Criminal Jurisprudence." *Judicature* 50 (February 1967): 188-193.

4657. Thompson, Mark. "Conservative Trend Is Seen in Supreme Court Decisions." *Criminal Justice Newsletter* 15 (August 1, 1984): 5-6.

4658. Tiedeman, Christopher G. *A Treatise on the Limitations of Police Power in the United States.* New York: Da Capo Press, 1971.

4659. Tish, Martin H. "Duplicate Statutes, Prosecutorial Discretion, and the Illinois Armed Violence Statute." *Journal of Criminal Law and Criminology* 71 (Fall 1980): 226-243.

4660. Van Alstyne, William W. "The Supreme Court Speaks to the Untenured: A Comment on *Board of Regents v. Roth* and *Perry v. Sinderman.*" *American Association of University Professors Bulletin* 58 (September 1972): 267-278.

4661. Vitiello, Michael. "Independent and Adequate State Grounds: A Stone Unturned by Louisiana's Criminal Defense Bar?" *Loyola Law Review* 25 (Fall 1979): 745-769.

4662. Wagner, Leslie. "Wavering over the Scope of Waiver: The Burger Court and Out-of-Court Waiver of Fourth, Fifth, and Sixth Amendment Rights." *National Journal of Criminal Defense* 6 (Spring 1980): 1-62.

4663. Wasby, Stephen L. "Communication of the Supreme Court's Criminal Procedure Decisions: A Preliminary Mapping." *Villanova Law Review* 18 (June 1973): 1086-1118.

4664. Way, H. Frank, Jr. *Criminal Justice and the American Constitution.* North Scituate, MA: Duxberry Press, 1980.

4665. Weihofen, Henry P. "Supreme Court Review of State Criminal Procedure." *American Journal of Legal History* 10 (July 1966): 189-200.

4666. Whalen, Frank J., Jr. "Punishment for Crime: The Supreme Court and the Constitution." *Minnesota Law Review* 35 (January 1951): 109-167.

4667. Whicher, John F. "The Eric Doctrine and the Seventh Amendment: A Suggested Resolution of Their Conflict." *Texas Law Review* 37 (May 1958): 549-563.

4668. Whitebread, Charles H. "The Burger Court's Counter-Revolution in Criminal Procedure: The Recent Criminal Decisions of the United States Supreme Court." *Washburn Law Journal* 24 (Spring 1985): 471-498.

4669. Whitebread, Charles H. "The Counterrevolution in Criminal Procedure." *Judges Journal* 24 (Fall 1985): 40-43.

4670. Whitebread, Charles H., and John Heilman. "The Counterrevolution Enters a New Era: Criminal Procedure Decisions during the Final Term of the Burger Court." *Puget Sound Law Review* 10 (Spring 1987): 571-590.

4671. Whitebread, Charles H., and John Heilman. "The Interpretation of Constitutional Rights: Reflections on the Burger Court's Counterrevolution in Criminal Procedure." *Detroit College of Law Review* 1986 (Winter 1986): 935-946.

4672. Wickersham, Cornelius W., Jr. "The Supreme Court and Federal Criminal Procedure." *Cornell Law Quarterly* 44 (Fall 1958): 14-26.

4673. Wilber, Leon A. "Development of Criminal Law in the Supreme Court, 1966 to 1971." *Southern Quarterly* 11 (July 1973): 121-146.

4674. Wilkinson, J. Harvie. "*Goss v. Lopez*: The Supreme Court as School Superintendent." *Supreme Court Review* 1975 (1975): 25-75.

4675. Winters, Glenn R. "The Supreme Court's Leadership in Judicial Administration." *Journal of the American Judicature Society* 46 (April 1963): 237-242, 258.

4676. Winters, Glenn R., ed. *Selected Readings: Fair Trial—Free Press.* Chicago: American Judicature Society, 1971.

4677. Wood, Virginia L. *Due Process of*

Law, 1932-1949: The Supreme Court's Use of a Constitutional Tool. Baton Rouge: Louisiana State University Press, 1951.

4678. Wright, Quincy. "Due Process and International Law." *American Journal of International Law* 40 (April 1946): 398-406.

4679. Yarborough, Michael K. "Availability of Federal Post-Conviction Relief in Light of a Subsequent Change in Law." *Journal of Criminal Law and Criminology* 66 (June 1975): 117-134.

4680. Zagel, James B. "Supreme Court Review 1973." *Journal of Criminal Law and Criminology* 64 (December 1973): 379-458.

4681. Zeisel, Hans. "The Waning of the American Jury." *American Bar Association Journal* 58 (April 1972): 367-370.

Cruel and Unusual Punishment

4682. Adlfinger, Kerry M. "The Court and Capital Punishment: A Study of the Supreme Court's Environments and Policy-Making." Ph.D. diss., University of California, Davis, 1974.

4683. Aked, Jonathan C. "*Solem v. Helm*: The Supreme Court Extends the Proportionality Requirement to Sentences of Imprisonment." *Wisconsin Law Review* 1984 (1984): 1401-1430.

4684. Alexander, Elizabeth. "New Prison Administrators and the Court: New Directions in Prison Law." *Texas Law Review* 56 (June 1978): 963-1008.

4685. Amsterdam, Anthony G. "In *Favorem Mortis*: The Supreme Court and Capital Punishment." *Human Rights* 14 (Winter 1987): 14-17.

4686. Azarian, David P. "An Examination of the Burger Court and Capital Punish-

ment." *Ohio Northern University Law Review* 11 (Fall 1984): 813-825.

4687. Bailey, William L., and Ruth D. Peterson. "Police Killings and Capital Punishment: The Post-*Furman* Period." *Criminology* 25 (February 1987): 1-25.

4688. Bedau, Hugo A. *The Courts, the Constitution, and Capital Punishment.* Lexington, MA: D. C. Heath, 1977.

4689. Bedau, Hugo A. "The Problem of Capital Punishment." *Current History* 71 (July/August 1976): 14-18, 34.

4690. Bedau, Hugo A., and Chester M. Pierce, eds. *Capital Punishment in the United States.* New York: AMS Press, 1976.

4691. Berger, Raoul. *Death Penalties: The Supreme Court's Obstacle Course.* Cambridge: Harvard University Press, 1982.

4692. Berkson, Larry C. "Cruel and Unusual Punishment: The Parameters of the Eighth Amendment." *Policy Studies Journal* 4 (Winter 1975): 131-136.

4693. Black, Charles L. *Capital Punishment: The Inevitability of Caprice and Mistake.* New York: W. W. Norton, 1974.

4694. Black, Charles L. "Objections to S. 1382, a Bill to Establish Rational Criteria for the Imposition of Capital Punishment." *Crime and Delinquency* 26 (October 1980): 441-452.

4695. Brinkmann, Beth S. "The Presumption of Life: A Starting Point for a Due Process Analysis of Capital Sentencing." *Yale Law Journal* 94 (December 1984): 351-373.

4696. Carrington, Frank G. *The Case for Capital Punishment: Neither Cruel nor Unusual.* New Rochelle, NY: Arlington House, 1978.

4697. Combs, Michael W. "Supreme Court and Capital Punishment: Uncertainty, Ambiguity, and Judicial Control."

Southern University Law Review 71 (Fall 1980): 1-41.

4698. Daniels, Stephen. "Social Science and Death Penalty Cases: Reflections on Change and the Empirical Justification of Constitutional Policy." *Law and Policy Quarterly* 1 (July 1979): 336-372.

4699. Dobbs, G. Bryon. "Murder in the Supreme Court: Appeals from the Hanging Judge." *Arkansas Law Review* 29 (Spring 1975): 47-70.

4700. Doyle, Charles. *Capital Punishment in the Supreme Court: Recent Developments.* Washington, DC: Congressional Research Service, 1975.

4701. Enslin, Morton S. "Capital Punishment: Cruel and Unusual?" *Religion in Life* 41 (Summer 1972): 254-258.

4702. Entin, Jonathan L. "Psychiatry, Insanity, and the Death Penalty: A Note on Implementing Supreme Court Decisions." *Journal of Criminal Law and Criminology* 79 (Spring 1988): 218-239.

4703. Gardner, Romaine L. "Capital Punishment: The Philosophers and the Court." *Syracuse Law Review* 29 (Fall 1978): 1175-1216.

4704. Geimer, William S. "Death at Any Cost: A Critique of the Supreme Court's Recent Retreat from Its Death Penalty Standards." *Florida State University Law Review* 12 (Winter 1985): 737-780.

4705. Greenwald, Helene B. "Capital Punishment for Minors: An Eighth Amendment Analysis." *Journal of Criminal Law and Criminology* 74 (Winter 1983): 1471-1517.

4706. Haney, Craig. "Juries and the Death Penalty: Readdressing the *Witherspoon* Question." *Crime and Delinquency* 26 (October 1980): 512-527.

4707. Jolly, Robert W., Jr., and Edward Sagarin. "The First Eight after *Furman*: Who Was Executed with the Return of the Death Penalty?" *Crime and Delinquency* 30 (October 1984): 610-623.

4708. Karge, Stewart W. "Capital Punishment: Death for Murder Only." *Journal of Criminal Law and Criminology* 69 (Summer 1978): 179-196.

4709. Kassekert, Rosemary, and Joseph L. Daly. "Bizarre Murder Case Resparks Controversy over Death Sentence." *Update* 8 (Spring 1984): 28-36.

4710. Knight, Barbara B. "Capital Punishment in the States: Prospects for the Future." *Virginia Social Science Journal* 12 (November 1977): 6-13.

4711. Manheim, Karl M. "Capital Punishment Cases: A Criticism of Judicial Method." *Loyola University of Los Angeles Law Review* 12 (December 1978): 85-134.

4712. Meagher, B. S. "Capital Punishment Review of Recent Supreme Court Decisions." *Notre Dame Lawyer* 52 (December 1976): 261-289.

4713. Meltsner, Michael. *Cruel and Unusual: The Supreme Court and Capital Punishment.* New York: Random House, 1973.

4714. Meltsner, Michael, and Marvin E. Wolfgang, eds. "Symposium on Current Death Penalty Issues." *Journal of Criminal Law and Criminology* 74 (Fall 1983): 659-1114.

4715. Murchison, Kenneth M. "Toward a Perspective on the Death Penalty Cases." *Emory Law Journal* 27 (Summer 1978): 469-555.

4716. Nathanson, Stephen, and E.V.D. Haag. "Does It Matter If the Death Penalty Is Arbitrarily Administered?" *Philosophy and Public Affairs* 14 (Spring 1985): 149-176.

4717. Nevares-Muniz, Dora. "The Eighth Amendment Revisited: A Model of Weighted Punishments." *Journal of Crim-*

inal Law and Criminology 75 (Spring 1984): 272-289; 76 (Spring 1985): 201-207.

4718. Poe, Douglas A. "Capital Punishment Statutes in the Wake of *United States v. Jackson*: Some Unresolved Questions." *George Washington Law Review* 37 (May 1969): 719-745.

4719. Polsby, Daniel D. "The Death of Capital Punishment? *Furman v. Georgia*." *Supreme Court Review* 1972 (1972): 1-40.

4720. Prettyman, E. Barrett, Jr. "The Chief Justice Should Address Congress." *American Bar Association Journal* 56 (May 1970): 441-446.

4721. Prettyman, E. Barrett, Jr. *Death and the Supreme Court*. New York: Harcourt, Brace, and World, 1961.

4722. Radelet, Michael L. "Racial Characteristics and the Imposition of the Death Penalty." *American Sociology Review* 46 (December 1981): 918-927.

4723. Rubin, Sol. "The Supreme Court, Cruel and Unusual Punishment, and the Death Penalty." *Crime and Delinquency* 15 (January 1969): 121-131.

4724. Schwartz, Charles W. "Eighth Amendment Proportionality Analysis and the Compelling Case of William Rummel." *Journal of Criminal Law and Criminology* 71 (Winter 1980): 378-420.

4725. Schwartz, Richard D. "The Supreme Court and Capital Punishment: A Quest for a Balance between Legal and Societal Morality." *Law and Policy Quarterly* 1 (July 1979): 285-335.

4726. Shelley, Marshall. "The Death Penalty: Two Sides of a Growing Issue; As More and More Executions Make the News, Here Are the Questions Christians Need to Face." *Christianity Today* 28 (March 2, 1984): 14-17.

4727. Silets, Harvey M., and Susan W. Brenner. "Commentary on the Prelimi-

nary Draft of the Sentencing Guidelines Issued by the United States Sentencing Commission in September 1986." *Journal of Criminal Law and Criminology* 77 (Winter 1986): 1069-1111.

4728. Tao, L. S. "The Constitutional Status of Capital Punishment: An Analysis of *Gregg, Jurek, Roberts*, and *Woodson*." *Journal of Urban Law* 54 (Winter 1977): 345-366.

4729. Urofsky, Melvin I. "A Right to Die: Termination of Appeal for Condemned Prisoners." *Journal of Criminal Law and Criminology* 75 (Fall 1984): 553-582.

4730. Weisberg, Robert. "Deregulating Death." *Supreme Court Review* 1983 (Annual 1983): 305-395.

4731. White, Welsh S. *The Death Penalty in the Eighties: An Examination of the Modern System of Capital Punishment*. Ann Arbor: University of Michigan, 1987.

4732. White, Welsh S. "Role of the Social Sciences in Determining the Constitutionality of Capital Punishment." *American Journal of Ortho Psychology* 45 (July 1975): 581-595.

4733. White, Welsh S. "Waiver and the Death Penalty: the Implications of *Estelle v. Smith*." *Journal of Criminal Law and Criminology* 72 (Winter 1981): 1522-1549.

4734. Wright, Ronald E., and Marc Miller. "In Your Court: State Judicial Federalism in Capital Cases." *Urban Lawyer* 8 (Summer 1986): 659-705.

Fifth Amendment

4735. Baker, Liva. Miranda: *Crime, Law, and Politics*. New York: Atheneum, 1983.

4736. Baum, Lawrence. "Police Response to Appellate Court Decisions: *Mapp* and

Miranda." *Policy Studies Journal* 7 (Special Issue 1978): 425-431.

4737. Berger, Mark. "Burdening the Fifth Amendment: Toward a Presumptive Barrier Theory." *Journal of Criminal Law and Criminology* 70 (Spring 1979): 27-41.

4738. Berger, Mark. *Taking the Fifth: The Supreme Court and the Privilege against Self-Incrimination.* Lexington, MA: Lexington Books, 1980.

4739. Brady, Steven G. "The 'Public Safety' Exception to the *Miranda* Warnings Requirement." *Police Chief* 51 (October 1984): 20.

4740. Burt, Robert A. "*Miranda* and Title II: A Morganatic Marriage." *Supreme Court Review* 1969 (1969): 81-134.

4741. Caginalp, O. A. "Fifth Amendment Privilege against Self-Incrimination and Compulsory Self-Disclosure under the Clean Air and Clean Water Acts." *Boston College Environmental Affairs Law Review* 9 (1980/1981): 359-395.

4742. Callahan, John M. "Entrapment, Due Process, and the U.S. Constitution." *FBI Law Enforcement Bulletin* 51 (February 1982): 25-31.

4743. Canon, Bradley C. "Organizational Contumacy in the Transmission of Judicial Policies: The *Mapp, Escobedo, Miranda,* and *Gault* Cases." *Villanova Law Review* 20 (November 1974): 50-79.

4744. Carr, Pitts, and Luther J. Carroll, III. "*Conboy* Decision and the Plaintiff's Antitrust Case." *Trial* 20 (March 10, 1984): 80-82.

4745. Caruso, Kenneth A. "Double Jeopardy and Government Appeals in Criminal Cases." *Columbia Journal of Law and Social Problems* 12 (Spring 1976): 295-350.

4746. Collins, Ronald K., and Robert Welsh. "*Miranda's* Fate in the Burger Court." *Center Magazine* 13 (September 1980): 43-52.

4747. Comisky, Ian M., and Matthew J. Comisky. "Supreme Court in *Doe* Limits Fifth Amendment Protection, but Uncertainty Remains." *Journal of Taxation* 61 (August 1984): 66-70.

4748. Corwin, Edward S. "The Supreme Court's Construction of the Self-Incrimination Clause." *Michigan Law Review* 29 (November 1930): 1-27, 29; (December 1930): 191-207.

4749. Cramer, Kevin D. "Back from the Brink: *Boyd's* Private Papers Protection and the Sole Proprietor's Business Records." *American Business Law Journal* 21 (Winter 1984): 367-401.

4750. Deutsch, Eadie F. "Judicial Rhetoric as Persuasive Communication: A Study of the Supreme Court Opinions in the *Escobedo* and *Miranda* Cases and the Responses in the California Press." Ph.D. diss., University of California, Los Angeles, 1970.

4751. Donigan, Robert L., and Edward C. Fisher. "Supreme Court Delineates New Confession Rules." *Traffic Digest and Review* 14 (August 1966): 14-22.

4752. Ennico, Clifford R. "Emerging Standards in Supreme Court Double Jeopardy Analysis." *Vanderbilt Law Review* 32 (March 1979): 609-640.

4753. "Fifth Amendment: Compulsory Production of Incriminating Business Records." *Journal of Criminal Law and Criminology* 71 (Spring 1980): 51-55.

4754. Foglia, Richard. "Developments in the Attachment of Jeopardy." *Journal of Criminal Law and Criminology* 70 (Spring 1979): 68-72.

4755. Franck, Michael. "The Myth of *Spevack v. Klein.*" *American Bar Association Journal* 54 (October 1968): 970-974.

4756. Fuqua, Ellis E. "United States Supreme Court Interpretation of Admissibility of Criminal Confessions." *Journal of*

Criminal Law and Criminology 36 (September 1945): 222-226.

4757. Gandara, Daniel. "Admissibility of Confessions in Federal Prosecutions: Implementation of Section 3501 by Law Enforcement Officials and the Courts." *Georgetown Law Journal* 63 (November 1974): 305-321.

4758. Gangi, William. "The Supreme Court, Confessions, and the Counter-Revolution in Criminal Justice." *Judicature* 58 (August/September 1974): 68-73.

4759. Graham, Fred P. *The Self-Inflicted Wound.* New York: Macmillan, 1970.

4760. Griswold, Erwin N. *The Fifth Amendment Today.* Cambridge: Harvard University Press, 1955.

4761. Herskovitz, Donald L. "Supreme Court Says *Miranda* Warning Does Not Apply to Non-Custodial Interviews." *Journal of Taxation* 45 (July 1976): 5-7.

4762. Holtz, Larry E. "*Miranda* in a Juvenile Setting: A Child's Right to Silence." *Journal of Criminal Law and Criminology* 78 (Fall 1987): 534-556.

4763. Inbau, Fred E. "Over-Reaction: The Mischief of *Miranda v. Arizona.*" *Journal of Criminal Law and Criminology* 73 (Summer 1982): 797-810.

4764. Kobey, Eugene F. "Confessions in the Supreme Court of United States." *Marquette Law Review* 34 (Summer 1950): 23-28.

4765. Lane, Alan N., and Richard D. Grossman. "*Miranda*: The Erosion of a Doctrine." *Chicago Bar Record* 62 (March/April 1981): 250-254, 256, 258-260, 262-264, 266-276.

4766. Levy, Leonard W. *Origins of the Fifth Amendment.* New York: Oxford University Press, 1968.

4767. Levy, Leonard W. "Right against Self-Incrimination: History and Judicial History." *Political Science Quarterly* 84 (March 1969): 1-29.

4768. Long, Richard W. "*Miranda* and the Police: The Impact of the *Miranda* Decision in Medium Size Missouri Cities." Ph.D. diss., University of Missouri, Columbia, 1973.

4769. Lowen, Robert G. "Confessions by the Accused: Does *Miranda* Relate to Reality?" *Kentucky Law Journal* 62 (1973/1974): 794-823.

4770. Lushing, Peter. "Testimonial Immunity and the Privilege against Self-Incrimination: A Study in Isomorphism." *Journal of Criminal Law and Criminology* 73 (Winter 1982): 1690-1739.

4771. Marcus, Paul. "The Supreme Court and the Privilege against Self-Incrimination: Has the Burger Court Retreated?" *Oklahoma Law Review* 38 (Winter 1985): 719-739.

4772. Mednick, Herbert S., and Richard G. Greiner. "Supreme Court Further Limits Scope of Privilege against Self-Incrimination." *Journal of Taxation* 41 (September 1974): 182, 187.

4773. Meltzer, Bernard D. "Privileges against Self-Incrimination and the Hit-and-Run Opinions." *Supreme Court Review* 1971 (1971): 1-30.

4774. Miller, Robert W. "The Supreme Court's Review of Hypothetical Alternatives in a State Confession Case." *Syracuse Law Review* 5 (Fall 1953): 53-61.

4775. O'Brien, David M. "Fifth Amendment: Fox Hunters, Old Women, Hermits, and the Burger Court." *Notre Dame Lawyer* 54 (October 1978): 26-72.

4776. Perkins, Walter M. "A Supreme Court Round Up: The Court Answers Questions Ranging from 'Can Life Be Patented?' to 'When Must *Miranda* Warnings Be Given?'" *Update* 4 (Fall 1980): 60-66.

4777. Picou, Cynthia. "*Miranda* and

Escobedo: Warren v. Burger Court Decisions of Fifth Amendment Rights." *Southern University Law Review* 4 (Spring 1978): 175-197.

4778. Pizzi, William T. "The Privilege against Self-Incrimination in a Rescue Situation." *Journal of Criminal Law and Criminology* 76 (Fall 1985): 567-607.

4779. Potts, C. S. "Unmerited Criticism of Federal Supreme Court." *St. Louis University Law Review* 12 (February 1927): 118-123.

4780. Prettyman, E. Barrett, Jr. "*Fikes v. Alabama*: The Unconstitutional Conviction of 'Baby'." *Supreme Court History Society Yearbook* 1978 (1978): 68-78.

4781. Quillian, Sally C. "*Ohio v. Johnson*: Prohibiting the Offensive Use of Guilty Pleas to Invoke Double Jeopardy Protection." *Georgia Law Review* 19 (Fall 1984): 159-188.

4782. Reeder, Robert H. "Double Jeopardy." *Traffic Digest and Review* 19 (January 1971): 15-21.

4783. Ritchie, Larry J. "Compulsion That Violates the Fifth Amendment: The Burger Court's Definition." *Minnesota Law Review* 61 (February 1977): 383-431.

4784. Ritholz, Jules, and Elliot Silverman. "Supreme Court's *Rylander* Decision Contains a Message for Corporate Record Custodians." *Journal of Taxation* 59 (July 1983): 16-17.

4785. Rogge, O. John. *The First and the Fifth: With Some Excursions into Others.* New York: Thomas Nelson and Sons, 1960.

4786. Rogge, O. John. "Of Pleas and Confessions: A Review of U.S. Supreme Court Decisions Excluding from Evidence Confessions Which Defendants Repudiate in Court." *Bar Bulletin* (New York County) 23 (1965/1966): 49-59.

4787. Scuro, Joseph E., Jr. "*Berkemer v.

McCarty: *Miranda* and the Routine Traffic Stop." *Police Chief* 51 (November 1984): 19.

4788. Scuro, Joseph E., Jr. "*Oregon v. Bradshaw*: Custodial Interrogation; Where Do We Go from Here?" *Police Chief* 50 (October 1983): 12.

4789. Sonenshein, David. "*Miranda* and the Burger Court: Trends and Countertrends." *Loyola University of Chicago Law Journal* 13 (Spring 1982): 405-462.

4790. Stephens, Otis H., Jr. "The Fourteenth Amendment and Confessions of Guilt: Role of the Supreme Court." *Mercer Law Review* 15 (Winter 1964): 309-335.

4791. Stephens, Otis H., Jr. "The Fourteenth Amendment and Confessions of Guilt: The Role of the Supreme Court." Ph.D. diss., Johns Hopkins University, 1963.

4792. Stephens, Otis H., Jr. *The Supreme Court and Confessions of Guilt.* Knoxville: University of Tennessee Press, 1973.

4793. Stone, Geoffrey R. "*Miranda* Doctrine in the Burger Court." *Supreme Court Review* 1977 (1977): 99-169.

4794. Tetu, Philip R. "*Miranda* Revisited." *Police Chief* 48 (December 1981): 44-46.

4795. Thomas, George C., III. "The Prohibition of Successive Prosecutions for the Same Offense: In Search of a Definition." *Iowa Law Review* 71 (January 1986): 323-399.

4796. Tilzer, Ira L. "Supreme Court Narrows Fifth Amendment Privilege for Records Held by Third Party." *Journal of Taxation* 45 (July 1976): 2-64.

4797. Watts, L. Poindexter. "In the Wake of *Miranda*." *Popular Government* 33 (November 1966): 1-8.

4798. Webb, Dan K., and James R. Ferguson. "*United States v. Doe*: The Su-

preme Court and the Fifth Amendment."
Loyola University of Chicago Law Journal
16 (Summer 1986): 729-756.

4799. Winnick, Pamela R. "Precedential
Weight of a Dismissal by Supreme Court
for Want of a Substantial Federal Ques-
tion: Some Implications of *Hicks v.
Miranda.*" *Columbia Law Review* 76
(April 1976): 508-533.

Juvenile

4800. Hopson, Dan, Jr. *The Juvenile Offender and the Law: A Symposium.* New
York: Da Capo Press, 1971.

4801. Rosenblum, Victor G. "School Children: Yes, Policemen: No: Some Thoughts
about the Supreme Court's Priorities Concerning the Right to a Hearing in Suspension and Removal Cases." *Northwestern
University Law Review* 72 (March/April
1977): 146-170.

4802. "Supreme Court and Pretrial Detention of Juveniles: A Principled Solution
to a Due Process Dilemma." *University of
Pennsylvania Law Review* 132 (1983): 95-
119.

4803. Weinstein, Noah. *Supreme Court
Decisions and Juvenile Justice.* Reno: Na-
tional Council of Juvenile and Family
Court Judges, University of Nevada,
Reno, 1979.

4804. "Where Have All the Children
Gone? The Supreme Court Finds Pretrial
Detention of Minors Constitutional."
DePaul Law Review 34 (Spring 1985):
733-756.

4805. Winslow, Robert W., ed. *Juvenile
Delinquency in a Free Society: Selections
from the President's Commission on Law
Enforcement and Administration of Justice.*
Encino, CA: Dickenson Publishing Com-
pany, 1972.

Prisoners

4806. Bronstein, Alvin. "Criminal Justice:
Prisons and Penology." In *Our Endangered Rights: The ACLU Report on Civil
Liberties,* edited by Norman Dorsen, 221-
234. New York: Pantheon Books, 1984.

4807. Calhoun, Emily. "Supreme Court
and the Constitutional Rights of Prisoners:
A Reappraisal." *Hastings Constitutional
Law Quarterly* 4 (Spring 1977): 219-247.

4808. Falkof, Bradley B. "Prisoner Representative Organizations, Prison Reform,
and *Jones v. North Carolina Prisoners' Labor Union:* An Argument for Increased
Court Intervention in Prison Administration." *Journal of Criminal Law and Criminology* 70 (Spring 1979): 42-56.

4809. Gardner, Martin R. "*Hudson v.
Palmer:* 'Bright Lines' but Dark Directions for Prisoner Privacy Rights." *Journal
of Criminal Law and Criminology* 76
(Spring 1985): 75-115.

4810. Herman, Susan N. "The New Liberty: The Procedural Due Process Rights
of Prisoners and Others under the Burger
Court." *New York University Law Review*
59 (June 1984): 482-575.

4811. Katz, Ellis. "Prisoner's Rights,
State's Rights, and the Bayh-Kastenmeier
'Institutions Bill'." *Publius* 8 (Winter
1978): 179-198.

4812. Prigmore, Charles S., and Richard
T. Crow. "Is the Court Remaking the
American Prison System? A Brief Overview of Significant Court Decisions." *Federal Probation* 40 (June 1976): 3-10.

4813. Robbins, Ira P. "Cry of *Wolfish* in
the Federal Courts: The Future of Federal
Judicial Intervention in Prison Administration." *Journal of Criminal Law and
Criminology* 71 (Fall 1980): 211-225.

4814. Rotman, Edgardo. "Do Criminal Of-
fenders Have a Constitutional Right to Re-

habilitation?" *Journal of Criminal Law and Criminology* 77 (Winter 1986): 1023-1068.

4815. Rubin, Sol. "Burger Court and the Penal System." *Church and Society* 62 (November/December 1971): 27-32.

4816. Sargentich, Thomas O. "Two Views of a Prisoner's Right to Due Process: *Meachum v. Fano.*" *Harvard Civil Rights-Civil Liberties Law Review* 12 (Spring 1977): 405-439.

Property Rights

General Studies

4817. Beck, James M., and Merle Thorpe. *Neither Purse nor Sword*. New York: Macmillan, 1936.

4818. Brigham, John. "Property and the Supreme Court: Do the Justices Make Sense?" *Polity* 16 (Winter 1983): 242-262.

4819. Brown, Robert C. "State Property Taxes and the Federal Supreme Court." *Indiana Law Journal* 14 (August 1939): 491-528.

4820. Cowles, Willard B. *Treaties and Constitutional Law: Property Interferences and Due Process of Law*. Washington, DC: American Council on Public Affairs, 1941.

4821. Ebright, Malcolm. "The San Joaquin Grant: Who Owned the Common Land? A Historical Legal Puzzle." *New Mexico Historical Review* 57 (January 1982): 5-26.

4822. Marke, Julius J. "The Banded Butchers and the Supreme Court: Herein of the *Slaughter House Cases.*" *New York University Law Center Bulletin* 12 (Spring 1964): 8-13, 18-19.

4823. Patterson, Elizabeth G. "Property Rights in the Balance: The Burger Court and Constitutional Property." *Maryland Law Review* 43 (Summer 1984): 518-570.

4824. Powell, Thomas R. "Protecting Property and Liberty, 1922-1924." *Political Science Quarterly* 40 (September 1925): 404-437.

4825. Ragsdale, John W., Jr. "A Synthesis and Integration of the Supreme Court Precedent Regarding the Regulatory Taking of Land." *University of Missouri-Kansas City Law Review* 55 (Winter 1987): 213-250.

4826. Ragsdale, John W., Jr., and Richard P. Sher. "The Court's Role in the Evolution of Power over Land." *Urban Lawyer* 7 (Winter 1975): 60-95.

4827. Shedd, Peter J. "Inverse Condemnation: Will the Supreme Court Allow It?" *Real Estate Law Journal* 9 (Spring 1981): 336-350.

4828. Walts, Brenda L. "Focus: A Forthcoming Decision." *Journal of Law and Education* 13 (April 1984): 302-308.

Contracts

4829. Hale, Robert L. "The Supreme Court and the Contract Clause." *Harvard Law Review* 57 (April 1944): 512-557, 621-674, 852-892.

4830. Phillips, Michael J. "The Life and Times of the Contract Clause." *American Business Law Journal* 20 (Summer 1982): 139-178.

4831. Phillips, Vivian. "The Supreme Court and Mortgage Moratorium Laws." *Kansas City Law Review* 2 (February 1934): 54-55.

4832. Strong, Frank R. "The Economic Philosophy of *Loehmer*: Emergence, Embrasure, Emasculation." *Arizona Law Review* 15 (1973): 419-455.

4833. Wright, Benjamin F. *The Contract Clause of the Constitution*. Cambridge: Harvard University Press, 1938.

Eminent Domain

4834. Ackerman, Bruce. *Private Property and the Constitution*. New Haven, CT: Yale University Press, 1977.

4835. Bechara, Dennis. "Eminent Domain and the Rule of Law." *Freeman* 35 (May 1985): 273-282.

4836. Dougan, Michael B. "The Doctrine of Creative Destruction: Ferry and Bridge Law in Arkansas." *Arkansas Historical Quarterly* 39 (Summer 1980): 136-158.

4837. Dunham, Allison. "*Griggs v. Allegheny County* in Perspective: Thirty Years of Supreme Court Expropriation Law." *Supreme Court Review* 1962 (1962): 63-106.

4838. Hancock, Scott. "Supreme Court Fails to Reach Inverse Condemnation Issue." *Natural Resources Journal* 21 (January 1981): 169-175.

4839. Levin, Murray S., and John W. Gergacz. "Open Space Zoning: *Agins v. City of Tiburon*." *American Business Law Journal* 19 (Winter 1982): 493-511.

4840. McNamara, Paul J. "The United States Supreme Court's Role in Local Land Law Issues." *Boston Bar Journal* 30 (July/August 1986): 7-9.

4841. Malone, Linda A. "The Future of Transferable Development Rights in the Supreme Court." *Kentucky Law Journal* 73 (1984/1985): 759-793.

4842. Sallet, Jonathan B. "Regulatory 'Takings' and Just Compensation: The Supreme Court's Search for a Solution Continues." *Urban Lawyer* 18 (Summer 1986): 635-658.

4843. Scheiber, Harry N. "The Road to *Munn*: Eminent Domain and the Concept of Public Purpose in the State Courts." *Perspectives in American History* 5 (1971): 329-402.

Right to Counsel

4844. Allison, Junius L., and Whitney N. Seymour. "The Supreme Court and the Doctrine of the Right of Counsel." *Journal of the American Judicature Society* 46 (April 1963): 259-266.

4845. Berger, Vivian O. "The Supreme Court and Defense Counsel: Old Roads, New Paths—A Dead End?" *Columbia Law Review* 86 (January 1986): 9-116.

4846. Blumer, Kenneth R. "The New Definition: A Fifth Amendment Right to Counsel." *UCLA Law Review* 14 (January 1967): 604-630.

4847. Buchwald, Don D. "Indigent Criminal Defendant's Constitutional Right to Compensated Counsel." *Cornell Law Quarterly* 52 (Winter 1967): 433-444.

4848. Carter, Dan T. *Scottsboro: A Tragedy of the American South*. Baton Rouge: Louisiana State University Press, 1969.

4849. Froyd, Paul B. "Is *Argersinger* a Shot in the Arm or a Coup de Grace?" *American Bar Association Journal* 62 (September 1976): 1154-1158.

4850. Heller, Francis H. *The Sixth Amendment to the Constitution of the United States*. Lawrence: University of Kansas Press, 1951.

4851. Israel, Jerold H. "*Gideon v. Wainwright*: The 'Art' of Overruling." *Supreme Court Review* 1963 (1963): 211-272.

4852. Jaeger, Richard. "The Right to Counsel during Police Interrogation: The Aftermath of *Escobedo*." *California Law Review* 53 (March 1965): 337-363.

4853. Ketcham, Orman W. "Guidelines from *Gault*: Revolutionary Requirements and Reappraisal." *Virginia Law Review* 53 (December 1967): 1700-1718.

4854. Kort, Fred. "Predicting Supreme Court Decisions Mathematically: A Quantitative Analysis of the Right to Counsel Cases." *American Political Science Review* 51 (March 1957): 1-12.

4855. Krantz, Sheldon, et al. *Right to Counsel in Criminal Cases: The Mandate of* Argersinger v. Hamlin. Cambridge, MA: Ballinger, 1976.

4856. Krash, Abe. "The Right to a Lawyer: The Implications to *Gideon v. Wainwright.*" *Notre Dame Lawyer* 39 (February 1964): 150-160.

4857. Krause, Marshall W. "Search and Seizure: Some Recent Developments and Issues." *Law in Transition Quarterly* 4 (September 1967): 157-162.

4858. Lester, R. David. "*Couch v. United States:* The Supreme Court Takes a Fresh Look at the Attorney-Client Privilege; Or Does It?" *Kentucky Law Journal* 62 (1973): 253-277.

4859. Lewis, Anthony. *Clarence Earl Gideon and the Supreme Court.* New York: Random House, 1967.

4860. Lewis, Anthony. *Gideon's Trumpet.* New York: Random House, 1964.

4861. Lewis, Anthony. *The Supreme Court and How It Works: The Story of the* Gideon *Case.* New York: Random House, 1966.

4862. Myers, Martee S. "Foul for a Client: Supreme Court Rules on Pro-se Right." *University of Pittsburgh Law Review* 37 (Winter 1975): 403-415.

4863. Tague, Peter W. "Federal *Habeas Corpus* and Ineffective Representation of Counsel: Supreme Court Has Work to Do." *Stanford Law Review* 31 (November 1978): 1-67.

4864. Turpen, Bernadyne W. "The Supreme Court and Reform in Local Criminal Justice Systems: The Impact of the Right-to-Counsel Cases." Ph.D. diss., University of New Mexico, 1977.

4865. Wertheimer, Alan. "Freedom, Mo-

rality, Plea Bargaining, and the Supreme Court." *Philosophy and Public Affairs* 8 (Spring 1979): 203-234.

Search and Seizure

4866. Aaronson, David E., and Rangeley Wallace. "A Reconsideration of the Fourth Amendment's Doctrine of Search Incident to Arrest." *Georgetown Law Journal* 64 (October 1975): 53-84.

4867. Abramowitz, Nancy S. "Searches Incident to Arrest, the Expanding Exception to the Warrant Requirement." *Georgetown Law Journal* 63 (October 1974): 223-240.

4868. Abrams, Norman. "Liberty at Bay: Supreme Court and Search and Seizure." *Center Magazine* 10 (January 1977): 16-20.

4869. Abrams, Sharon E. "Third Party Consent Searches, the Supreme Court, and the Fourth Amendment." *Journal of Criminal Law* 75 (Fall 1984): 963-994.

4870. Amsterdam, Anthony G. "Perspectives on the Fourth Amendment." *Minnesota Law Review* 58 (January 1974): 349-477.

4871. Antrobus, Louis A. "The Federal Exclusionary Rule in Relation to the Fourth Amendment as Applied and Interpreted by the United States Supreme Court." Ph.D. diss., University of Michigan, 1956.

4872. Arons, Stephen, and Ethan Katsh. "Reclaiming the Fourth Amendment in Massachusetts." *Civil Liberties Reviews* 2 (Winter 1975): 82-89.

4873. Barnett, Edward L., Jr. *Personal Rights, Property Rights, and the Fourth Amendment.* Chicago: University of Chicago Press, 1960.

4874. Bayh, Birch. "Search and Seizure:

Aftermath of *Stanford Daily.*" *Trial* 16 (August 1980): 30-33.

4875. Berch, Michael A. "Money Damages for Fourth Amendment Violations by Federal Officials: An Explanation of *Bivens v. Six Unknown Named Agents of the Federal Bureau of Narcotics.*" *Law and the Social Order* 1971 (1971): 43-63.

4876. Black, Forrest R. "The Supreme Court Plays at 'This Is the House That Jack Built'." *Notre Dame Lawyer* 6 (May 1931): 436-441.

4877. Bloodworth, James N. "Where Search and Seizure Is Today: An Outline of Fourth Amendment U.S. Supreme Court Decisions." *Alabama Lawyer* 39 (October 1978): 444-465.

4878. Bloom, Robert M. "The Supreme Court and Its Purported Preference for Search Warrants." *Tennessee Law Review* 50 (Winter 1983): 231-270.

4879. Bonaguro, Lester A. "Electronic Eavesdropping and Wiretapping: Constitutional Guidelines." *Traffic Digest and Review* 16 (March 1968): 16-22.

4880. Brubaker, Stanley C. "An Extravagance of Righteousness: Reconsidering Integrity and Dignity as Bases for the Exclusionary Rule." *Policy* 17 (Summer 1985): 715-735.

4881. Buchwald, Don D. "Eavesdropping, Informers, and the Right to Privacy: A Judicial Tightrope." *Cornell Law Quarterly* 52 (Summer 1967): 975-1001.

4882. Burkhoff, John M. "Court That Devoured the Fourth Amendment: The Triumph of an Inconsistent Exclusionary Doctrine." *Oregon Law Review* 58 (1979): 151-192.

4883. Campane, Jerome O., Jr. "*Michigan v. Summers*: Detention of Occupants during Search Warrant Execution." *FBI Law Enforcement Bulletin* 52 (January 1983): 25-31; (February 1983): 25-31.

4884. Campane, Jerome O., Jr. "Sobriety Checkpoints: A Historical Perspective." *Police Chief* 52 (March 1985): 122-125.

4885. Chardak, Sharon R. "Airport Drug Stops: Defining Reasonable Suspicion Based on the Characteristics of the Drug Courier Profile." *Boston College Law Review* 26 (May 1985): 693-726.

4886. Cohen, A. "Supreme Court Hears More Search Cases." *Police Magazine* 6 (January 1983): 8-9.

4887. Collins, John W., and Sandra N. Hurd. "Warrantless Administrative Searches: It's Time to Be Frank Again." *American Business Law Journal* 22 (Summer 1984): 189-208.

4888. Couleur, Terri M. "The Use of Illegally Obtained Evidence to Rebut the Insanity Defense: A New Exception to the Exclusionary Rule?" *Journal of Criminal Law and Criminology* 74 (Summer 1983): 391-427.

4889. Dall'Osoto, Raymond. "U.S. Supreme Court Attack on Fourth Amendment Law." *Wisconsin Bar Bulletin* 58 (September 1985): 25-26, 56.

4890. Davidson, Philip L. "The Warren Court and Its Impact on the Fourth Amendment Rights of College and University Students." Ph.D. diss., George Peabody College, 1981.

4891. "Defining a Fourth Amendment Search: A Critique of the Supreme Court's Post-*Katz* Jurisprudence." *Washington Law Review* 61 (January 1986): 191-216.

4892. Denniston, Lyle. "Supreme Court Takes Another Stab at the Rules for Auto Searches." *Police Magazine* 5 (May 1982): 45-50.

4893. Dershowitz, Alan M. "Wiretaps and National Security." *Commentary* 53 (January 1972): 56-61.

4894. Deutsch, Jan G. "The Jurisprudence of the Burger Court: A Reading of

Michigan v. Long." *Connecticut Bar Journal* 59 (January 1985): 220-235.

4895. Edelman, Sidney. "Search Warrants and Sanitation Inspection: The New Look in Enforcement." *American Journal of Public Health* 58 (May 1968): 930-937.

4896. Finer, Joel J. "*Gates* and the Compromise of Adjudicative Fairness: A Dialogue on Prejudicial Concurrences." *Cleveland State Law Review* 33 (1984/1985): 707-750.

4897. Finer, Joel J. "*Gates, Leon,* and the Compromise of Adjudicative Fairness (Part II): Of Aggressive Majoritarianism, Willful Deafness, and the New Exception to the Exclusionary Rule." *Cleveland State Law Review* 34 (1985/1986): 199-248.

4898. Flygare, Thomas J. "High Court Approves Searches of Students but Ducks Many Tough Issues." *Phi Delta Kappan* 66 (March 1985): 504-505.

4899. Flygare, Thomas J. "Supreme Court Ruling on Exclusion by Private Schools." *Phi Delta Kappan* 58 (November 1976): 279-280.

4900. Flygare, Thomas J. "U.S. Supreme Court Volunteers to Decide New Jersey Student Search and Seizure Case." *Phi Delta Kappan* 66 (December 1984): 294-295.

4901. Forkosch, Morris D. "In Defense of the Exclusionary Rule: What It Protects Are the Constitutional Rights of Citizens, Threatened by the Court, the Executive, and the Congress." *American Journal of Economics and Sociology* 41 (April 1982): 151-156.

4902. Fox, Karla H. "Right to Say No: The Fourth Amendment and Administrative Inspections." *American Business Law Journal* 17 (Fall 1979): 283-311.

4903. Franklin, David L. "Search and Seizure in Public Schools: The Supreme Court's Impact on School Security." *American School and University* 58 (September 1985): 42-50.

4904. Gammon, Timothy E. "The Exclusionary Rule and the 1983-1984 Term." *Marquette Law Review* 68 (Fall 1984): 1-25.

4905. Gammon, Timothy E. "The Fourth Amendment and Supreme Court Decision-Making: Some Thoughts While Awaiting *Sheppard.*" *North Dakota Law Review* 60 (1984): 693-715.

4906. Gardiner, Hilliard A. "OSHA and the Fourth Amendment: *Corruptissima Republic Plurimae Leges?*" *American Business Law Journal* 17 (Fall 1979): 405-413.

4907. Gardiner, Thomas G. "Consent to Search in Response to Police Threats to Seek or to Obtain a Search Warrant: Some Alternatives." *Journal of Criminal Law and Criminology* 71 (Summer 1980): 163-172.

4908. Gasque, Aubrey. "Wiretapping: A History of Federal Legislation and Supreme Court Decisions." *South Carolina Law Review* 15 (1963): 593-622.

4909. Gee, Donald. "The Independent Source Exception to the Exclusionary Rule: The Burger Court's Attempted Common Sense Approach and Resulting 'Cure-All' to Fourth Amendment Violations." *Howard Law Journal* 28 (1985): 1005-1049.

4910. George, B. James, Jr. "The Potent, the Omnipresent Teacher: The Supreme Court and Wiretapping." *Virginia Law Review* 47 (June 1961): 751-797.

4911. Gerstein, Robert, Sr. "Search and Seizure in the Supreme Court: A Legislative Problem in the Adjudicatory Context." Ph.D. diss., University of California, Los Angeles, 1967.

4912. Goldberger, P. "Consent, Expectations of Privacy, and the Meaning of Searches in the Fourth Amendment."

Journal of Criminal Law and Criminology 75 (Summer 1984): 319-362.

4913. Goldsmith, Michael. "Supreme Court and Title III: Rewriting the Law of Electronic Surveillance." *Journal of Criminal Law and Criminology* 74 (Spring 1983): 1-171.

4914. Greenawalt, Kent. "The Consent Problem in Wire-Tapping and Eavesdropping: Surreptitious Monitoring with the Consent of a Participant in a Conversation." *Columbia Law Review* 68 (February 1968): 189-240.

4915. Greenberg, Peter S. "Balance of Interests Theory and the Fourth Amendment: A Selective Analysis of Supreme Court Action since *Camara* and *See*." *California Law Review* 61 (June 1973): 1011-1047.

4916. Greene, Laurence. "U.S. Supreme Court and the Exclusionary Rule: Trimming the Branches of the 'Fruit of the Poisonous Tree Doctrine'." *Journal of the Beverly Hills Bar Association* 10 (November/December 1975): 10-29.

4917. Greig, William H., and Phillip S. Althoff. "The Constitutionality of Roadblocks: The Fourth Amendment on the Firing Line Again." *Trial* 22 (February 1986): 56-65.

4918. Griswold, Erwin N. *Search and Seizure: A Dilemma of the Supreme Court.* Lincoln: University of Nebraska Press, 1970.

4919. Hall, John C. "Motor Vehicle Exception to the Search Warrant Requirement." *FBI Law Enforcement Bulletin* 50 (November 1981): 24-31; (December 1981): 20-26.

4920. Hallworth, Gerald L. "The *Miranda* Decision: Was It Needed?" *Rocky Mountain Social Sciences Journal* 5 (April 1968): 109-118.

4921. Hamilton, John A. "The United States Supreme Court's Erosion of Fourth Amendment Rights: The Trend Continues." *South Dakota Law Review* 30 (Summer 1985): 574-598.

4922. Hartman, Marshall J., and Sidney Bernstein. "To *Leon* and Beyond: Two Commentators React." *Trial* 21 (January 1985): 50-56.

4923. Heck, Edward V. "Searching for the Elusive Balance between State Power and Individual Liberty: The Burger Court and Fourth Amendment." *Capital University Law Review* 15 (Fall 1985): 1-34.

4924. Hirschel, J. David. *Fourth Amendment Rights.* Lexington, MA: Lexington Books, 1979.

4925. Inbau, Fred E. "The Confession Dilemma in the United States Supreme Court." *Illinois Law Review* 43 (September/October 1948): 442-463.

4926. Irons, Robert S. "Burger Court: Discord in Search and Seizure." *University of Richmond Law Review* 8 (Spring 1974): 433-445.

4927. Iverson, William D. "Judicial Control of Secret Agents." *Yale Law Journal* 76 (April 1967): 994-1019.

4928. Jensen, D. Lowell, and Rosemary Hart. "Good Faith Restatement of the Exclusionary Rule." *Journal of Criminal Law and Criminology* 73 (Fall 1982): 916-938.

4929. Joseph, Paul R., and David Blumberg. "The Case for the Exclusionary Rule: The Case against the Exclusionary Rule." *Human Rights* 14 (Winter 1987): 38-48.

4930. Kamisar, Yale. "Mondale on *Mapp*." *Civil Liberties Review* 3 (February/March 1977): 62-64.

4931. Katz, Lewis R. "*United States v. Ross*: Evolving Standards for Warrantless Searches." *Journal of Criminal Law and Criminology* 74 (Spring 1983): 172-208.

4932. Kepner, Raymond R. "Subsequent Use of Electronic Surveillance Interceptions and the Plain View Doctrine: Fourth Amendment Limitations on the Omnibus Crime Control Act." *University of Michigan Journal of Law Reform* 9 (Spring 1976): 529-553.

4933. Kerr, Kenneth F. "An Analysis of Judicial Attitudes in the Conditions and Limitations of the Right to Search and Seizure Decisions of the Warren Court." *Southern Quarterly* 11 (October 1972): 91-105.

4934. LaFave, Wayne R. " 'Street Encounters' and the Constitution: *Terry, Sibron, Peters*, and Beyond." *Michigan Law Review* 67 (November 1968): 39-126.

4935. Landynski, Jacob W. *Search and Seizure and the Supreme Court*. Baltimore: Johns Hopkins Press, 1966.

4936. Landynski, Jacob W. "The Supreme Court's Search for Fourth Amendment Standards: The Problem of Stop and Frisk." *Connecticut Bar Journal* 45 (January 1971): 146-186.

4937. Landynski, Jacob W. "The Supreme Court's Search for Fourth Amendment Standards: The Warrantless Search." *Connecticut Bar Journal* 45 (March 1971): 2-39.

4938. Laskey, Lawrence A. "Misstating Exigency Rule: The Supreme Court v. the Exigency Requirement in Warrantless Automobile Searches." *Syracuse Law Review* 28 (Fall 1977): 981-1008.

4939. Lasson, Nelson B. *The History and Development of the Fourth Amendment to the United States Constitution*. Baltimore: Johns Hopkins Press, 1937.

4940. Laughlin, Gregory K. "The Return to Open Season for Police in the Open Field: *Oliver v. United States.*" *Missouri Law Review* 50 (Spring 1985): 425-437.

4941. Lewis, Peter W., Henry W. Mannle, and Harry E. Allen. "The Burger Court and Searches Incident to a Lawful Arrest: The Current Perspective." *Capital University Law Review* 7 (Winter 1977): 1-23.

4942. Lincoln, Eugene O. "Searches and Seizures: The U.S. Supreme Court's Decision on the Fourth Amendment." *Urban Education* 21 (October 1986): 254-262.

4943. Loewy, Arnold H. "Protecting Citizens from Cops and Crooks: An Assessment of the Supreme Court's Interpretation of the Fourth Amendment during the 1982 Term." *North Carolina Law Review* 62 (January 1984): 329-356.

4944. McAdams, Richard H. "Tying Privacy in *Knotts*: Beeper Monitoring and Collective Fourth Amendment Rights." *Virginia Law Review* 71 (March 1985): 297-341.

4945. Majestic, Ann L. "Search and Seizure in the Schools: Defending Reasonableness." *School Law Bulletin* (University of North Carolina) 16 (Summer 1985): 1-8.

4946. Manak, James P. "Good Faith Exception to the Exclusionary Rule: Is the Supreme Court Ready Now?" *Police Chief* 51 (April 1984): 20-21.

4947. Mandell, Leonard B., and L. Anita Richardson. "Surgical Search: Removing a Scar on the Fourth Amendment." *Journal of Criminal Law* 75 (Fall 1984): 525-552.

4948. Mathias, Charles M., Jr. "*Zurcher*: Judicial Dangers and Legislative Action." *Trial* 15 (January 1979): 40-43.

4949. Medalie, Richard J. *From* Escobedo *to* Miranda: *The Anatomy of a Supreme Court Decision*. Washington, DC: Lerner Law Book Company, 1966.

4950. Meese, Edwin. "*Mapp v. Ohio*: Micro-Managing the Police." *Police Chief* 54 (January 1987): 13.

4951. Miles John G., Jr. "The Ailing Fourth Amendment: A Suggested Cure." *American Bar Association Journal* 63 (March 1977): 364-371.

4952. Murchison, Kenneth M. "Prohibition and the Fourth Amendment: A New Look at Some Old Cases." *Journal of Criminal Law and Criminology* 73 (Summer 1982): 471-532.

4953. Murphy, Walter F. *Wiretapping on Trial: A Case Study in the Judicial Process.* New York: Random House, 1965.

4954. Oaks, Dallin H. "Studying the Exclusionary Rule in Searches and Seizures." *University of Chicago Law Review* 37 (Summer 1970): 665-757.

4955. Ramsey, Mary L. "Acquisition of Evidence of Search and Seizure." *Michigan Law Review* 47 (June 1949): 1137-1156.

4956. Reeder, Robert H. " 'Stop and Frisk': Approved by U.S. Supreme Court." *Traffic Digest and Review* 16 (September 1968): 17-23.

4957. Savarese, Anthony P., Jr. "Eavesdropping and the Law." *American Bar Association Journal* 46 (March 1960): 263-266.

4958. Schlag, Pierre J. "Assaults on the Exclusionary Rule: Good Faith Limitations and Damage Remedies." *Journal of Criminal Law and Criminology* 73 (Fall 1982): 875-915.

4959. Schlesinger, Steven R. *Exclusionary Injustice: The Problem of Illegally Obtained Evidence.* New York: Dekker, 1977.

4960. Schlesinger, Steven R. *The United States Supreme Court: Fact, Evidence, and Law.* Lanham, MD: United Press of America, 1983.

4961. Schmertz, John R. *Proposed Federal Rules of Evidence: With Supreme Court Advisory Committee's Notes, HR 5463, Judiciary Committee Report, and Amendments to Federal Rules of Civil and Criminal Procedure.* Chicago: Callaghan, 1974.

4962. Schnapper, Eric. "Unreasonable Searches and Seizures of Papers." *Virginia Law Review* 71 (September 1985): 869-931.

4963. Segal, Jeffrey A. "Predicting Supreme Court Cases Probabilistically: The Search and Seizure Cases, 1962-1981." *American Political Science Review* 78 (September 1984): 891-900.

4964. Segal, Jeffrey A. "Predicting Supreme Court Cases Probabilistically: The Search and Seizure Cases, 1962-1981." Ph.D. diss., Michigan State University, 1983.

4965. Segal, Jeffrey A. "Supreme Court Justices as Human Decision Makers: An Individual-Level Analysis of the Search and Seizure Cases." *Journal of Politics* 48 (November 1986): 938-955.

4966. Segal, Terry D. "Supreme Court: Fourth Amendment Does Not Bar Subpoena of Taxpayer's Bank Records." *Journal of Taxation* 45 (August 1976): 80-81.

4967. Sendor, Benjamin B. "That Heralded High Court Ruling on Student Searches Leaves Crucial Questions Unanswered." *American School Board Journal* 172 (April 1985): 24-25.

4968. Shapiro, Harry D., and Robert K. Briskin. "Supreme Court in G. M. Leasing, Restricts I.R.S. Property Seizures without Search Warrants." *Journal of Taxation* 46 (April 1977): 218-221.

4969. Shapiro, J. Irwin. "Searches, Seizures, and Line Ups: Evolving Constitutional Standards under the Warren and Burger Courts." *New York Law Forum* 20 (Fall 1974): 217-252.

4970. Singer, Richard. "The Aftermath of an Insanity Acquittal: The Supreme Court's Recent Decision in *Jones v. United States.*" *Annals of the American Academy of Political and Social Science* 477 (January 1985): 114-124.

4971. Smith, Steven R. "*United States v. Finazzo*: Sixth Circuit Position on Break-

Ins to Install Bugs Rejected by Supreme Court in *Dalia*." *University of Toledo Law Review* 10 (Spring 1979): 697-724.

4972. Stratton, Brent D. "The Attenuation Exception to the Exclusionary Rule: A Study in Attenuated Principle and Dissipated Logic." *Journal of Law and Criminology* 75 (Spring 1984): 139-165.

4973. Strickland, Ralph B., Jr. "*Stegald v. United States*: The Supreme Court Adopts a Search Warrant Rule for Entries of Third-Party Residences." *Police Chief* 48 (September 1981): 12-13.

4974. Summers, William C. "Good Faith Exception to the Exclusionary Rule." *Police Chief* 51 (December 1984): 18-19.

4975. Thompson, John D., Jr. "Eroding the Fourth Amendment: The Burger Court and the Warrantless Search Exception: Some Post-1970 Developments." Ph.D. diss., University of Nebraska, 1980.

4976. Trimble, E. G. "Search and Seizure under the Fourth Amendment as Interpreted by the United States Supreme Court." *Kentucky Law Journal* 42 (January 1954): 197-237; (March 1954): 423-454.

4977. Turley, Jonathan. "The Not-So-Noble Lie: The Nonincorporation of State Consensual Surveillance Standards in Federal Courts." *Journal of Criminal Law and Criminology* 79 (Spring 1988): 66-134.

4978. Vernon, D. E. "Supreme Court Simplifies the Rules for Auto Searches." *Police Magazine* 5 (September 1982): 47-48.

4979. Wagner, Allen E. "The Exclusionary Rule: Some Additional Thoughts." *Police Chief* 51 (May 1984): 28-30.

4980. Wagner, Allen E. "The Good Faith Exception to the Exclusionary Rule: Some Implications for the Police." *Journal of Criminal Justice* 15 (January/February 1987): 75-91.

4981. Wasserstrom, Silas J. "The Incredible Shrinking Fourth Amendment." *American Criminal Law Review* 21 (Winter 1984): 257-401.

4982. Watkins, William R. "The Supreme Court and Evidence." *Texas Law Review* 11 (April 1933): 339-346.

4983. Weeks, J. Devereux. "Public Employee Drug Testing under the Fourth and Fifth Amendments: Where Are We Now and Where Are We Going under Federal Decisions?" *Urban Lawyer* 20 (Spring 1988): 445-474.

4984. White, James B. "The Fourth Amendment as a Way of Talking about People: A Study of *Robinson* and *Matlock*." *Supreme Court Review* 1974 (1974): 165-232.

4985. Williamson, Richard A. "Supreme Court, Warrantless Searches, and Exigent Circumstances." *Oklahoma Law Review* 31 (Winter 1978): 110-147.

4986. Wilson, James Q. "Buggings, Break-Ins, and the FBI." *Commentary* 65 (June 1978): 52-58.

4987. Wolf, Robert. "Electronic Surveillance: Foreign Intelligence—Wiretapping of an Alien Spy for Foreign Intelligence Purposes Does Not Violate Communications Act of 1934 or Fourth Amendment." *New York University Journal of International Law and Politics* 8 (Winter 1976): 479-520.

4988. Yackle, Larry W. "Burger Court and the Fourth Amendment." *Kansas Law Review* 26 (Spring 1978): 336-437.

4989. Zirkel, Perry A., and Ivan B. Gluckman. "Student Searches Revisited: What Is the Proper Standard?" *NASSP Bulletin* 69 (May 1985): 117-120.

4990. Zirkel, Perry A., and Ivan B. Gluckman. "Student Searches Revisited." *Prinicpal* 64 (May 1985): 42-44.

Welfare as a Right

4991. Dembitz, Nanette. "The Good of the Child versus the Rights of the Parent: The Supreme Court Upholds the Welfare Home-Visit." *Political Science Quarterly* 86 (September 1971): 389-405.

4992. Hyman, Howard J. "Federal Judicial Review of State Welfare Programs: A Case Study of the Judicial Review of State Welfare Practices by the Warren and Burger Courts." Ph.D. diss., New School for Social Research, 1975.

4993. Krislov, Samuel. "American Welfare Policy and the Supreme Court." *Current History* 65 (July 1973): 33-36, 41-42.

4994. Kurland, Philip B. "Judicial Road to Social Welfare." *Social Service Review* 48 (December 1974): 481-493.

4995. Lourie, Norman V., and Stanley J. Brody. "Implications of Recent U.S. Supreme Court Decisions on Residence Re-quirements." *Public Welfare* 28 (January 1970): 45-51.

4996. O'Neill, Robert M. "Of Justice Delayed and Justice Denied: The Welfare Prior Hearing Cases." *Supreme Court Review* 1970 (1970): 161-214.

4997. Reiss, Howard R. "Due Process and Statutory Limitations on AFDC Recoupment Procedures." *Columbia Law Review* 74 (December 1974): 1464-1486.

4998. Simon, Peter N. "Liberty and Property in the Supreme Court: A Defense of *Roth* and *Perry*." *California Law Review* 71 (January 1983): 146-192.

4999. Wasby, Stephen L. "The Supreme Court as Enunciation of Welfare Policy." *Policy Studies Journal* 2 (Spring 1974): 205-209.

5000. Wasby, Stephen L. "Welfare Policy and Supreme Court: Era of Uncertainty." *Public Welfare* 30 (Fall 1972): 16-27.

VIII. The Court and Regulation

General Studies

5001. Boulton, William R. "Government Control: Business Strikes Back." *Business Horizons* 22 (August 1979): 61-66.

5002. Brown, Ray A. "The Constitution, the Supreme Court, and the N.I.R.A." *Oregon Law Review* 13 (February 1934): 102-121.

5003. Carlin, Edward A. "The Relationships between the Major Economic Philosophies since Adam Smith and Those Expressed by the Supreme Court, through Opinions Rendered in Cases Affecting the Governmental Control of Business Corporations from 1930-1940." Ph.D. diss., New York University, 1950.

5004. Christoffel, Tom. "The Supreme Court and Airbags." *American Journal of Public Health* 74 (March 1984): 269-270.

5005. Cooke, Morris L. "Taking Stock of Regulation in the State of New York." *Yale Law Journal* 40 (November 1930): 17-33.

5006. D'Andrade, Hugh A. "DESI and Supreme Court." *Food and Drug Cosmetic Law Journal* 28 (July 1973): 486-492.

5007. Elliot, William Y. "The Judicial Fate of the NRA." In *The Need for Constitutional Reform: A Program for National Security,* by William Y. Elliot, 160-181. New York: McGraw-Hill, 1935.

5008. Finkelstein, Maurice. *The Dilemma of the Supreme Court: Is the N.R.A. Constitutional?* New York: John Day, 1933.

5009. Gardner, Judy. "Supreme Court Rule on Ineffective Drugs Gives FDA Sweeping Regulatory Powers." *National Journal* 5 (June 30, 1973): 963.

5010. Greer, Edward H. "OSHA's Cotton Dust Standard Deregulation Fever Hits the Supreme Court." *Nation* 231 (December 1980): 666-668.

5011. Guzzardi, Walter, Jr. "What the Supreme Court Is Really Telling Business: Out of the Welter of Conflicting Judicial Pronouncements, an Underlying Message Is Beginning to Emerge." *Fortune* 95 (January 1977): 146-154.

5012. Hale, Robert L. "Valuation and Rate Making, the Conflicting Theories of the Wisconsin Railroad Commission, 1905-1917, with a Chapter on U.S. Supreme Court Decisions." Ph.D. diss., Columbia University, 1918.

5013. Heineman, Benjamin W., Jr. and Carter B. Phillips. "Federal Preemption: A Comment on Regulatory Preemption after *Hillsborough County.*" *Urban Lawyer* 18 (Summer 1986): 589-606.

5014. Hutt, Peter B. "View on Supreme Court FDA Decisions." *Food, Drug, Cosmetic Law Journal* 28 (November 1973): 662-675.

5015. Krier, James E. "The Regulation Machine." *Supreme Court Economic Review* 1 (1982): 1-38.

5016. Lawrence, Nathaniel S. "Regulatory Takings: Beyond the Balancing Test." *Urban Lawyer* 20 (Spring 1988): 231-474, 389-444.

5017. Leffler, Keith B. *"Arizona v. Maricopa County Medical Society*: Maximum Price Agreements in Markets with Insured Buyers." *Supreme Court Economic Review* 2 (1983): 187-212.

5018. McDermott, Edwin J. *Modern Federal Civilian Pay Law: Modern Digest of Decisions of United States Court of Claims and of Supreme Court of United States.* Philadelphia: n.p., 1969.

5019. McDermott, John T. "Supreme Court's Changing Attitude toward Consumer Protection and Its Impact on Montana Prejudgment Remedies." *Montana Law Review* 36 (Summer 1975): 165-188.

5020. McDermott, John T. "Supreme Court's Still Changing Attitude toward Consumer Protection and Its Impact on the Integrity of the Court." *Montana Law Review* 37 (Winter 1976): 27-38.

5021. Maidment, Richard A. "Law and Economic Policy in the United States: The Judicial Response to Governmental Regulation of the Economy." *Journal of Legal History* 7 (September 1986): 196-211.

5022. Miller, Arthur S. *The Supreme Court and American Capitalism.* New York: Free Press, 1968.

5023. Mussati, James. *New Deal Decisions of the United States Supreme Court.* Los Angeles: California Publication, 1936.

5024. Nelson-Horchler, Joani. "Business Year in Court a Disappointment." *Industry Week* 210 (July 13, 1981): 19-20.

5025. Pepper, George W. "Recent Development of Corporation Law by the Supreme Court of the United States." *American Law Register* 2 (May 1895): 296-313; (July 1895): 448-459.

5026. Powe, L. A., Jr. "Economic Make-Believe in the Supreme Court." *Constitutional Commentary* 3 (Summer 1986): 385-393.

5027. Rezmak, Scott M. "Constitutionality of Business Regulations in the Burger Court: Revival and Restraint." *Hastings Law Journal* 33 (September 1981): 1-102.

5028. Richberg, Donald R. "Supreme Court Discusses Value." *Harvard Law Review* 37 (January 1924): 289-300.

5029. Temin, Peter. "The Origin of Compulsory Drug Prescriptions." *Journal of Law and Economics* 22 (April 1979): 91-106.

5030. Tolman, Edgar B. "Review of Recent Supreme Court Decisions." *American Bar Association Journal* 31 (November 1945): 577-580.

5031. Vig, Norman J., and Patrick S. Bruer. "The Courts and Risk Assessment." *Policy Studies Review* 1 (May 1982): 716-727.

5032. Williams, Gardner S. "The *Sanitary District of Chicago* in the Supreme Court of the United States." *Michigan Law Review* 28 (November 1929): 1-25.

5033. Yannacone, Victor J., Jr. "Supreme Court Bails Grandma Out of Local Jail: A Review and Preview of Key Land Use Cases." *National Real Estate Investor* 19 (December 1977): 32-33.

Antitrust

5034. Adelman, Martin J. "The Supreme Court, Market Structure, and Innovation: *Chakrabarty, Rohm,* and *Haas.*" *Antitrust Bulletin* 27 (Summer 1982): 457-479.

5035. Allison, John R. "Arbitration of Private Antitrust Claims in International Trade: A Study in the Subordination of National Interests to the Demands of a World Market." *New York University*

Journal of International Law and Politics 18 (Winter 1986): 361-439.

5036. Asch, Peter. "Public Merger, Policy, and the Meaning of 'Competition'." *Quarterly Review of Economics and Business* 6 (Winter 1966): 53-64.

5037. Baker, Tyler A. "Supreme Court and the *Per Se* Tying Rule: Cutting the Gordian Knot." *Virginia Law Review* 66 (November 1980): 1235-1319.

5038. Barnes, Gary H. "New Twists on Old Wrinkles: Primary Jurisdiction and Regulatory Accommodation with the Antitrust Laws." *Boston College Industrial and Commercial Law Review* 15 (November 1973): 80-118.

5039. Bauer, Joseph P. "Challenging Conglomerate Mergers under Section 7 of the Clayton Act: Today's Law and Tomorrow's Legislation." *Boston University Law Review* 58 (March 1978): 199-245.

5040. Baxter, William F. "Vertical Restraints and Resale Price Maintenance: A 'Rule of Reason' Approach." *Antitrust Law and Economics Review* 14 (Fall 1982): 13-36.

5041. Bemis, Edward W. "Going Value in Rate Cases in the Supreme Court." *Columbia Law Review* 27 (May 1927): 530-546.

5042. Bienstock, Robert E. "Municipal Antitrust Liability: Beyond Immunity." *California Law Review* 73 (December 1985): 1829-1888.

5043. Boatwright, John W. "The Evolution of the Doctrines of Restraint of Trade and Unlawful Monopoly as Expressed by the Supreme Court in the Interpretation of the Sherman Anti-Trust Act." Ph.D. diss., Northwestern University, 1932.

5044. Bock, Betty. *Antitrust and the Supreme Court: An Economic Exploration.* New York: Conference Board, 1980.

5045. Bock, Betty. "Conglomerate Merg-

ers, Joint Ventures, and Potential Competition: What the Supreme Court's Action in the *Penn-Olin* Case Suggests." *Conference Board Records* 5 (February 1968): 2-6.

5046. Bock, Betty. "Mergers and Reciprocity: The Supreme Court Considers a Merger's Effects on Distribution." *Conference Board Records* 2 (July 1965): 27-36.

5047. Bock, Betty. "Rediscovering Economic Realism in Defining Competition." *Conference Board Records* 11 (June 1974): 6-12.

5048. Bringhurst, Bruce. *Antitrust and the Oil Monopoly: The Standard Oil Cases, 1890-1911.* Westport, CT: Greenwood Press, 1979.

5049. Brunet, Edward J. "Streamlining Antitrust Litigation by 'Facial Examination' of Restraints: The Burger Court and the *Per Se* Rule of Reason Distinction." *Washington Law Review* 60 (December 1984): 1-32.

5050. Campbell, Thomas J. "Supreme Court Developments." *Antitrust Law Journal* 55 (1986): 449-461.

5051. Conant, Michael. "The Paramount Decrees Reconsidered." *Law and Contemporary Problems* 44 (August 1981): 79-107.

5052. Dam, Kenneth W. "*Fortner Enterprises v. United States Steel*: Neither a Borrower nor a Lender Be." *Supreme Court Review* 1969 (1969): 1-40.

5053. Dana, William R. "The Supreme Court and the Sherman Anti-Trust Act." *Harvard Law Review* 16 (January 1903): 178-185.

5054. Doherty, Anthony N. "Buyer Liability under the Price Discrimination Law: An Economic Analysis." *Antitrust Law and Economic Review* 1 (Winter 1967): 59-86.

5055. Dreiser, Theodore. "The Supreme

Court as a Corporate-Minded Institution." In *Tragic America*, by Theodore Dreiser, 129-153. New York: Horace Liveright, 1931.

5056. Duggan, Michael A. *Antitrust and the U.S. Supreme Court, 1829-1980: A Compendium of Supreme Court Decisions Dealing with Restraint of Trade and Monopoly and Supplementary Material.* New York: Federal Legal Publications, 1981.

5057. Duggan, Michael A. *Antitrust and the U.S. Supreme Court, 1980-1982: Supplement.* Washington, DC: Federal Legal Publications, 1983.

5058. Elzinga, Kenneth G., and Thomas F. Hogarty. "*Utah Pie* and the Consequences of Robinson Patman." *Journal of Law and Economics* 21 (October 1978): 427-434.

5059. Fairbanks, Philip. "Antitrust and Consumer Interest: Can Section 4 of Clayton Act Survive Current Supreme Court?" *Catholic University Law Review* 27 (Fall 1977): 81-113.

5060. Ferleger, David A. "Anti-Institutionalization and the Supreme Court." *Rutgers Law Journal* 14 (Spring 1983): 595-636.

5061. Fox, Eleanor M. "Antitrust, Mergers, and Supreme Court: The Politics of Section 7 of the Clayton Act." *Mercer Law Review* 26 (Spring 1975): 389-425.

5062. Fox, William, Jr. "*Mitsubishi v. Soler* and Its Impact on International Commercial Arbitration." *Journal of World Trade Law* 19 (November/December 1985): 579-591.

5063. Gamboni, Ciro A. "Unfair Competition Protection after *Sears* and *Compco*." *New York University Law Review* 40 (January 1965): 101-153.

5064. Garvey, Edward R. "From Chattel to Employee: The Athlete's Quest for Freedom and Dignity." *Annals of the American Academy of Political and Social Science* 445 (September 1979): 91-101.

5065. Graham, Fred P. "Supreme Court: What Can Business Expect?" *Duns Review* 90 (September 1967): 29-31.

5066. Guzzardi, Walter, Jr. "A Search for Sanity in Antitrust." *Fortune* 97 (January 30, 1978): 72-75.

5067. Hale, G. E., and Rosemary D. Hale. "The *Otter Tail Power* Case: Regulation by Commission or Antitrust Laws." *Supreme Court Review* 1973 (1973): 99-122.

5068. Hale, Robert L. "The Supreme Court's Ambiguous Use of 'Value' in Rate Cases." *Columbia Law Review* 18 (March 1918): 208-229.

5069. Hamlin, Ross, J. "Application of the Sherman Act State Exemption to Municipal Environmental Regulations: A Case for Broader Local Discretion." *Boston College Environmental Affairs Review* 11 (April 1984): 609-664.

5070. Handler, Milton. "Antitrust Review—1988." *New York Law Journal* 200 (December 15, 1988): 1-9.

5071. Handler, Milton. "Changing Trends in Antitrust Doctrines: An Unprecedented Supreme Court Term, 1977." *Columbia Law Review* 77 (November 1977): 979-1028.

5072. Handler, Milton. "Industrial Mergers and the Anti-Trust Laws." *Columbia Law Review* 32 (February 1932): 179-276.

5073. Handler, Milton. "Labor and Antitrust: A Bit of History." *Antitrust Law Journal* 40 (April 1971): 233-241.

5074. Handler, Milton. "Nineteenth Annual Review of Recent Antitrust Developments, 1966." *Association of the Bar of the City of New York Record* 21 (November 1966): 539-580.

5075. Handler, Milton. "The Supreme Court and the Antitrust Laws." *Antitrust Law Journal* 34 (April 1967): 21-41.

5076. Handler, Milton. "Through the Antitrust Looking Glass: Twenty-first Annual Antitrust Review." *California Law Review* 57 (January 1969): 182-217.

5077. Hopkins, Thomas A. "The Speech That Validated the Sherman Anti-Trust Act of 1890: Philander Chase Knox's Address to the Supreme Court." *Quarterly Journal of Speech* 48 (February 1962): 51-58.

5078. Hyman, Jacob D., and Nathaniel L. Nathanson. "Judicial Review of Price Control: The Battle of the Meat Regulations." *Illinois Law Review* 42 (November/December 1947): 584-634.

5079. Jenkins, William O., Jr. "The Role of the Supreme Court in National Merger Policy: 1950-1973." Ph.D. diss., University of Wisconsin, 1975.

5080. Jones, Bryce J. "The New Thrust of the Antimerger Act: The *Brown Shoe* Decision." *Notre Dame Lawyer* 38 (April 1963): 229-243.

5081. Jones, Mary C. "Analysis of the Sources of Argument and Strategies Used in Briefs Presented to the Supreme Court in Selected Antitrust Cases: 1967-1977." Ph.D. diss., Wayne State University, 1978.

5082. Jones, Mary G. "The Growth and Importance of Franchising and the Role of Law." *Antitrust Bulletin* 12 (Fall 1967): 717-747.

5083. Kauper, Thomas E. "The 'Warren Court' and the Antitrust Laws: Of Economics, Populism, and Cynicism." *Michigan Law Review* 67 (December 1968): 325-342.

5084. Keck, Robert C. "The *Schwinn* Case." *Business Lawyer* 23 (April 1968): 669-687.

5085. Kirkpatrick, Miles W., and Stephen Mahinka. "Supreme Court and the 'New Economic Realism' of Section 7 of the Clayton Act." *Southwestern University Law Journal* 30 (Fall 1976): 821-837.

5086. Kirkpatrick, W. Wallace. "Antitrust to the Supreme Court: The Expediting Act." *George Washington Law Review* 37 (May 1969): 746-787.

5087. Kitch, Edmund W. "The *Yellow Cab* Antitrust Case." *Journal of Law and Economics* 15 (October 1972): 327-336.

5088. Kittelle, Sumner S. "Territorial and Customer Restrictions through Consignment or Agency: *Schwinn* or Sin?" *Antitrust Bulletin* 12 (Winter 1967): 1007-1031.

5089. Kittelle, Sumner S. "Trade Associations and Small Business." *Antitrust Law Journal* 16 (April 1960): 61-72.

5090. Klebaner, Benjamin J. "The Lexington Merger Decision and Its Significance for Commercial Banking." *Antitrust Bulletin* 11 (September/December 1966): 897-923.

5091. Kovaleff, Theodore P. "Divorce American Style: The *DuPont-General Motors* Case." *Delaware History* 18 (January 1978): 28-42.

5092. Kramer, Victor H. "The Antitrust Division and the Supreme Court, 1890-1953." *Virginia Law Review* 40 (May 1954): 433-463.

5093. Kramer, Victor H. "The Supreme Court and Trying Arrangements: Antitrust as History." *Minnesota Law Review* 69 (May 1985): 1013-1070.

5094. Lee, Rex E. "Resale Price Fixing and the Supreme Court: Petition to Reverse the *Per Se* Rule." *Antitrust Law and Economic Review* 14 (Fall 1982): 37-44.

5095. Lehrman, Kenneth F., III. "Trying to Explain the Sherman Act and Warren Court Antitrust Policy: Excursion into Political Theory and Values Involved in the Economic Decision-Making Process of the Supreme Court, 1958-1969." Ph.D. diss., University of Oregon, 1983.

5096. Lifland, William T. "Responding to

Local Competition: The *Utah Pie* Case." *Antitrust Bulletin* 12 (Fall 1967): 805-817.

5097. Loevinger, Lee. "The Morality of Mergers: The Antitrust Trip from Economics to Ecclesiastes and Back." *Mergers and Acquisitions* 10 (Spring 1975): 16-30.

5098. Lurie, Howard R. "Mergers under the Burger Court: An Anti-Antitrust Bias and Its Implications." *Villanova Law Review* 23 (January 1978): 213-283.

5099. McGee, Glenn W. "Burger Court Looks at the Antitrust Laws: A New Approach?" *Law Notes for the General Practitioner* 11 (Winter 1975): 1-9.

5100. McIlnay, Bruce A. "*Arizona v. Maricopa County Medical Society*: Supreme Court Refuses to Immunize Doctors against Sting of Sherman Act Section 1." *Wisconsin Law Review* 1983 (1983): 1203-1230.

5101. Malina, Michael. "Supreme Court Review: 1987." *Antitrust Law Journal* 56 (Summer 1987): 289-301.

5102. Malina, Michael. "Supreme Court Update: 1985." *Antitrust Law Journal* 54 (1985): 289-302.

5103. Marcus, Philip. "The Supreme Court and the Antitrust Laws, 1947-1948." *Georgetown Law Journal* 37 (March 1949): 341-369.

5104. Marcus, Sumner. "New Weapons against Bigness Are Being Forged from Judiciary Attitudes and Supreme Court Decisions." *Harvard Business Review* 43 (January 1965): 100-108.

5105. Marinelli, Arthur J. "Judicial Reexamination of Section 7 of the Clayton Act." *American Business Law Journal* 20 (Summer 1982): 203-221.

5106. Martin, David D. "The *Brown Shoe* Case and the New Antimerger Policy." *American Economic Review* 53 (June 1963): 340-358.

5107. Maurer, Virginia G. "*Blue Shield of*

Virginia v. McCready: The Limits of the Antitrust Injury Doctrine." *American Business Law Journal* 22 (Spring 1984): 67-91.

5108. Metzger, Michael B. "*Schwinn's* Swan Song." *Business Horizons* 21 (April 1978): 52-56.

5109. Miles, Jeff, and John Russell. "Economic Competition and the Supreme Court: Decisions in the 1977 Term." *University of Richmond Law Review* 13 (Fall 1978): 1-68.

5110. Page, William H. "The Scope of Liability for Antitrust Violations." *Stanford Law Review* 37 (July 1985): 1445-1512.

5111. Pettit, William. "Rate Cases, Value, and the Supreme Court." *Mississippi Law Journal* 8 (June 1936): 467-475.

5112. Pollock, Earl E. "Antitrust, the Supreme Court, and the Spirit of 1976." *Northwestern University Law Review* 72 (November/December 1977): 631-655.

5113. Posner, Richard A. "Antitrust Policy and Supreme Court: An Analysis of the Restricted Distribution, Horizontal Merger, and Potential Competition Decisions." *Columbia Law Review* 75 (March 1975): 282-327.

5114. Posner, Richard A. "Supreme Court and Antitrust Policy: A New Direction?" *Antitrust Law Journal* 44 (Spring 1975): 141-149.

5115. Reed, Thomas J., and Henry S. Allen. "The United States Supreme Court Looks at Hospital Physician Relationships: The *Hyde* Decision." *Hospital and Health Services Administration* 29 (May/June 1984): 36-49.

5116. Richman, Sheldon B. "Setbacks to Private Antitrust Enforcement: A Review of the Supreme Court's 1976-1977 Term." *Harvard Law Journal* 21 (Summer 1978): 727-747.

5117. Riesenfeld, Stefan A. "Antitrust Decisions of the Supreme Court during Its 1968/1969 Term." *Business Lawyer* 25 (July 1970): 1337-1354.

5118. Riley, Thomas. "The Act of State Doctrine: Antitrust Conspiracies to Induce Foreign Sovereign Acts." *New York University Journal of International Law and Politics* 10 (Winter 1978): 495-534.

5119. Robinson, Glen O. "The Sherman Act as a Home Rule Charter: *Community Communications Co. v. City of Boulder.*" *Supreme Court Economic Review* 2 (1983): 131-164.

5120. Robinson, Stanley D. "Antitrust Developments, 1973." *Columbia Law Review* 74 (March 1974): 163-206.

5121. Rose, Stanley D. "Your Right to Lower Your Prices." *Harvard Business Review* 29 (September 1951): 90-98.

5122. Rosett, Arthur. "Supreme Court versus the District Court in Antitrust Cases." *Mercer Law Review* 26 (Spring 1975): 795-811.

5123. Seligman, Joel. "The Application of the Federal Antitrust Laws to Municipal Taxicab Regulation." *Washington University Journal of Urban and Contemporary Law* 26 (1984): 25-68.

5124. Shniderman, Harry L. "The Robinson-Patman Act and the Supreme Court." *Antitrust Bulletin* 31 (Fall 1986): 665-708.

5125. Sichel, Werner. "The *Proctor and Gamble-Clorox* Decision and the Economics of Conglomerate Mergers." *Antitrust Bulletin* 12 (November 1967): 1081-1089.

5126. Slesinger, Reuben E. "The du Pont Divestiture: An Example of Economic Regulation." *University of Missouri Business and Government Review* 4 (September/Ocotber 1963): 9-17.

5127. Solo, Robert. "The New Look in the Constitutional Structure of Public Regulation." *Antitrust Bulletin* 4 (July/August 1959): 503-511.

5128. Steuer, Richard M. "Special Issue on Distribution after *Monsanto.*" *Antitrust Bulletin* 30 (Spring 1985): 1-256.

5129. Stigler, George J. "*United States v. Loew's Inc.*: A Note on Block-Booking." *Supreme Court Review* 1963 (1963): 152-157.

5130. Stone, Ralph T., Jr. "United States Supreme Court Directives on Corporate Mergers under the Antitrust Laws." Ph.D. diss., University of Tennessee, 1975.

5131. Susman, Stephen D. "Standing in Private Antitrust Cases: Where Is the Supreme Court Going?" *Antitrust Law Journal* 52 (August 1983): 465-477.

5132. Tone, Philip W. "U.S. Supreme Court Shows New Trends in Antitrust." *Illinois Bar Journal* 42 (August 1954): 896-901.

5133. Van Cise, Jerrold G. *The Supreme Court and the Anti-Trust Laws, 1966-1967.* New York: Practising Law Institute, 1967.

5134. Van Cise, Jerrold G. "The Supreme Court and the Anti-Trust Laws: 1971-1972." *Antitrust Bulletin* 17 (Winter 1972): 975-995.

5135. Van Cise, Jerrold G. "The Supreme Court and the Antitrust Laws: 1972-1973." *Antitrust Bulletin* 18 (Winter 1973): 691-714.

5136. Waller, James M. "The Social Philosophy and Economic Theory of the Supreme Court in Sherman Act Cases on Single-Firm Expansion, 1919-1954." Ph.D. diss., University of North Carolina, 1957.

5137. Willacy, Aubrey B., and Hazel M. Willacy. "Conglomerate Bank Mergers and Clayton: Is Potential Competition the Answer?" *Banking Law Journal* 93 (February 1976): 148-195.

5138. Williams, Larry L. "New Dimensions to Bank, Merger Law: The Supreme

Court in the Mid-Seventies." *Antitrust Bulletin* 20 (Winter 1975): 699-711.

5139. Wood, Laurence I. "The Supreme Court and a Changing Antitrust Concept." *University of Pennsylvania Law Review* 97 (February 1949): 309-344.

5140. Zlinkoff, Sergei S., and Robert C. Barnard. "Mergers and the Antitrust Laws: The *Columbia Steel* Case, the Supreme Court and a Competitive Economy, 1947 Term." *University of Pennsylvania Law Review* 97 (December 1948): 151-179.

Banking

5141. Bleier, Michael E., and Robert A. Eisenbeis. "Commercial Banking as the 'Line of Commerce' and the Role of Thrifts." *Banking Law Journal* 98 (April 1981): 374-386.

5142. Darnell, Jerome C. "Merger Guidelines from the *Phillipsburg National Bank* Case." *Magazine of Bank Administration* 47 (June 1971): 30-33.

5143. Finnegan, Michael D. "*Perdue v. Crocker National Bank*: The Attack on Pricing." *Business Lawyer* 41 (May 1986): 997-1006.

5144. Hanson, Hugh C. "Greeley Bank: Some Speculations." *Banking Law Journal* 90 (July 1973): 578-593.

5145. Kiebanner, Benjamin J. "Potential Competition in Banking and the Supreme Court." *Banking Law Journal* 92 (June/July 1975): 545-605.

5146. Lifland, William T. "Supreme Court and the Bank Merger Act of 1966." *Bankers Magazine* 150 (Autumn 1967): 20-25.

5147. Lifland, William T. "The Supreme Court, Congress, and Bank Mergers." *Law and Contemporary Problems* 32 (Winter 1967): 15-39.

5148. McDermott, James J., Jr. "Green Light for U.S. Regional Mergers." *Banker* 135 (October 1985): 15-18.

5149. McDonald, James L., and Marcia J. Staff. "Bank Mergers after the Omnibus Banking Bill: Is *Philadelphia National Bank* Finally Dead?" *American Business Law Journal* 20 (Fall 1982): 421-434.

5150. May, Walter E. "Redefining the Product Market: Commercial Bank Mergers in the New Competitive Era." *Banking Law Journal* 103 (March/April 1986): 124-150.

5151. Murphy, C. Westbrook. "*Certiorari* Granted: What Will the Supreme Court Do to Banking Law This Term?" *Banking Law Journal* 95 (November/December 1978): 883-889.

5152. O'Brien, Stephen J. "The Legal Evolution of Potential Competition and Its Application to Banking." *Business Lawyer* 30 (July 1975): 1181-1206.

5153. Plotkin, Robert. "How the Supreme Court Viewed Bank Holding Companies." *Banking* 62 (January 1970): 47-48.

5154. Scott, Romaine S., III. "*Mennonite*: What Does It Mean to Alabama Mortgagees after *Federal Deposit Insurance Corp. v. Morrison*?" *Alabama Law Review* 36 (Summer 1985): 969-1002.

5155. Steffen, Roscoe T. "Some Recent Supreme Court Decisions Relating to Negotiable Instruments." *Indiana Law Journal* 12 (October 1936): 1-18.

5156. Wade, Alan. "Dropping the Barriers: The Supreme Court Decision on Regional Compacts Is Keying a Period of Rapid Interstate Activity." *U.S. Banker* 96 (October 1985): 48-56.

5157. Wu, Hsiu-Kwang, and Lawrence Connell, Jr. "Merger Myopia: An Economic View of Supreme Court Decisions on Bank Mergers." *Virginia Law Review* 59 (May 1973): 860-884.

5158. Zirin, James D. "Government Regulation of Bank Mergers: The Revolving Door of *Philadelphia Bank.*" *Michigan Law Review* 62 (April 1964): 990-1016.

Bankruptcy

5159. Drake, W. Homer. *Chapter 13: Practice and Procedure.* Colorado Springs, CO: Shepard's, 1983.

5160. Finletter, Thomas K. *The Law of Bankruptcy Reorganization.* Charlottesville, VA: Michie Company, 1939.

5161. Patchan, Joseph. *Bankruptcy Rules: Practice Comments.* New York: C. Boardman, 1984.

5162. Selverstone, Arthur W. *Bankruptcy and Reorganization.* Brooklyn, NY: Harmon Publications, 1940.

5163. Tabb, Charles J. "The Bankruptcy Reform Act in the Supreme Court." *University of Pittsburgh Law Review* 49 (Winter 1988): 477-589.

5164. U.S. Supreme Court. *Bankruptcy Code, Rules, and Forms: Including Federal Rules, Civil Procedure, and Federal Rules of Guidance.* St. Paul, MN: West Publishing Company, 1983.

Commerce

5165. Abel, Albert S. "The Commerce Power: An Instrument of Federalism." *Indiana Law Journal* 25 (Summer 1950): 498-531.

5166. Allen, Gary L. "Rule 10b-5 and the Burger Court: Time to Re-examine the Elements for 10b-5 Action." *Commercial Law Journal* 82 (April 1977): 118-126.

5167. Ballantine, Arthur A. "The Supreme Court and Business Planning." *Harvard Business Review* 24 (Winter 1946): 151-163.

5168. Balter, Harry G. "Supreme Court Approves Sweeping Power Commission Authority." *California State Bar Journal* 16 (March 1941): 73-78.

5169. Barnett, Vincent M., Jr. "The Supreme Court, the Commerce Clause, and State Legislation." *Michigan Law Review* 40 (November 1941): 49-77.

5170. Barnett, William M. "Ten Years of the Supreme Court, 1937-1947: The Power to Regulate Commerce." *American Political Science Review* 61 (December 1947): 1170-1181.

5171. Carmichael, Peter A. "Supreme Court and Metaphysics." *Journal of Philosophy* 34 (September 1937): 521-575.

5172. Carroll, Philip M. "The Interstate Commerce Commission, Court Decisions, and Intermodal Rate Disputes." *Quarterly Review of Economics and Business* 10 (Spring 1970): 41-56.

5173. Cummings, F. Jay, and Wayne E. Ruhter. "The *Northern Pacific* Case." *Journal of Law and Economics* 22 (October 1979): 329-350.

5174. Dos Passos, John R. "The United States Supreme Court and the Commercial Era." *Yale Law Journal* 17 (June 1908): 573-584.

5175. Evans, Alfred. "Valuation in the Supreme Court." *American Bar Association Journal* 16 (August 1930): 485-492.

5176. Fuller, Hubert B. *The Act to Regulate Commerce, Construed by the Supreme Court.* Washington, DC: Byrne, 1915.

5177. George, John J. "Motor Carrier Litigation in the Supreme Court since 1929." *Kentucky Law Journal* 22 (January 1934): 199-222.

5178. George, John J. "Supreme Court

Views Federal Authorization and Merging of Motor Carriers." *Land Economics* 26 (May 1950): 183-193; (August 1950): 274-283.

5179. Goddard, Edwin C. "The Liability of the Common Carrier as Determined by Recent Decisions of the United States Supreme Court." *Columbia Law Review* 15 (May 1915): 399-416.

5180. Harbeson, Robert W. "Recent Trends in the Regulation of Intermodal Rate Competition in Transportation." *Land Economics* 42 (August 1966): 315-326.

5181. Jarrell, Gregg A. "State Anti-Takeover Laws and the Efficient Allocation of Corporate Control: An Economic Analysis of *Edgar v. MITE Corp.*" *Supreme Court Economic Review* 2 (1983): 111-130.

5182. Johnson, Stephen J., and Lawrence N. Minch. "The Warsaw Convention before the Supreme Court: Preserving the Integrity of the System." *Journal of Air Law and Commerce* 52 (Fall 1986): 93-116.

5183. Lee, Murray G. "Supreme Court Catches Up with the Nation." *United States Law Review* 71 (April 1937): 199-210.

5184. Light, C. P., Jr. "The Supreme Court and Commerce by Motor Vehicle." *North Carolina Law Review* 7 (April 1929): 268-285.

5185. Maltz, Earl M. "Burger Court, the Regulation of Interstate Transportation, and the Concept of Local Concern: The Jurisprudence of Categories." *Tennessee Law Review* 46 (Winter 1979): 406-424.

5186. Meigher, Eugene J. "Bank Mergers and the Clayton Act: Some Chips in the Doctrine of Potential Competition?" *Boston College Industrial and Commercial Law Review* 16 (June 1975): 705-727.

5187. Michel, Jack. "*Hood v. Dumond*: A Study of the Supreme Court and the Ideology of Capitalism." *University of Pennsyl-*

vania Law Review 134 (March 1986): 657-701.

5188. Miller, George H. *Railroads and the Granger Laws.* Madison: University of Wisconsin Press, 1971.

5189. Monkkonen, Eric. "Can Nebraska or Any State Regulate Railroads? *Smyth v. Ames*, 1898." *Nebraska History* 54 (Fall 1973): 365-382.

5190. Morris, Thomas R. "The Supreme Court and Interstate Commerce." *University of Virginia News Letter* 61 (March 1985): 39-43.

5191. Murphy, Paul L. "The New Deal Agriculture Program and the Constitution." *Agricultural History* 29 (October 1955): 160-169.

5192. Phillips, Michael J. "The Declining Fortunes of *National League of Cities v. Usery.*" *American Business Law Journal* 21 (Spring 1983): 89-115.

5193. Powell, Thomas R. "Commerce, Congress, and the Supreme Court, 1922-1925." *Columbia Law Review* 26 (April/May 1926): 396-431, 521-549.

5194. Powell, Thomas R. "Supreme Court Decisions on Federal Power over Commerce, 1910-1914." *Minnesota Law Review* 6 (December 1921): 1-22; (January 1922): 123-139; (February 1922): 194-218.

5195. Powers, Fred P. "Recent Centralizing Tendencies in the Supreme Court." *Political Science Quarterly* 5 (September 1890): 389-410.

5196. Schwartz, Bernard. "Commerce, the States, and the Burger Court." *Northwestern Law Review* 74 (October 1979): 409-439.

5197. Shapiro, Martin M. "Warren Court and the Interstate Commerce Commission." *Stanford Law Review* 18 (November 1965): 110-159.

5198. Simet, Donald P., and Arthur D.

Lynn, Jr. "Interstate Commerce Must Pay Its Way: The Demise of *Spector.*" *National Tax Journal* 31 (March 1978): 53-58.

5199. Smith, Chauncey. *Cases Relating to the Law of Railways, Divided in the Supreme Court of the U.S., and in the Courts of the Several States.* Boston: Little, Brown: 1819.

5200. Tally, J. O., Jr. "The Supreme Court, the Interstate Commerce Commission, and the Freight Rate Battle." *North Carolina Law Review* 25 (February 1947): 172-191.

5201. Tucker, Eric W. "Balkanized Interstate Banking: The Supreme Court Says Yes." *American Business Law Journal* 24 (Spring 1986): 51-66.

5202. Welch, Richard E., III. "At Federalism's Crossroads: *National League of Cities v. Usery.*" *Boston University Law Review* 57 (January 1977): 178-197.

5203. Wells, David A. "How Will the United States Supreme Court Decide the *Granger Railroad* Case?" *Nation* 19 (October 29, 1874): 282-284.

Communications

5204. Francois, William E. *Mass Media Law and Regulation.* 4th ed. New York: Wiley, 1986.

5205. Guider, John W. "Courts, Radio Communication—Supreme Court of the United States: Jurisdiction, Certificates, Broadcaster's Rights, Validity of Act of Congress." *Georgetown Law Journal* 19 (March 1931): 357-360.

5206. Lee, William E. "Antitrust Enforcement, Freedom of the Press, and the Open Market: Supreme Court on the Structure and Conduct of Mass Media." *Vanderbilt Law Review* 32 (November 1979): 1249-1341.

5207. McKenna, Francis E., Jr. "An Intergovernmental Framework for the Regulation of Communications Technologies." Ph.D. diss., University of Maryland, 1983.

5208. Ramberg, Bennett. "The Supreme Court and Public Interest in Broadcasting." *Communications and the Law* 8 (December 1986): 11-29.

5209. Uldth, Dana R. *The Supreme Court: A Judicial Review of the Federal Communications Commission.* New York: Arno Press, 1979.

5210. Wilson, Gray W. "Right of Access to Broadcasting: Supreme Court Takes a Dim View." *Georgetown Law Journal* 62 (October 1973): 355-376.

Environment

5211. Brown, Omar F., and Edward M. Davis. "The Implications of the Supreme Court's California Nuclear Moratorium Decision." *Public Utilities Fortnightly* 111 (May 26, 1983): 35-38.

5212. Cleaves, Robert E. "Constitutional Protection for the Utility Investor: The Confiscation Doctrine after *Cleveland Electric Illuminating Co. v. Public Utilities Commission of Ohio.*" *Boston College Environmental Affairs Law Review* 12 (Spring 1985): 527-528.

5213. Collins, Michael. "The Dilemma of the Downstream State: The Untimely Demise of Federal Common Law Nuisance." *Boston College Environmental Affairs Law Review* 11 (January 1984): 295-412.

5214. Colton, Roger D., et al. "Seven-Cum Eleven: Rolling the Toxic Dice in the United States Supreme Court." *Boston College Environmental Affairs Law Review* 14 (Spring 1987): 345-379.

5215. Curran, William J., and Leslie I. Boden. "Occupational Health Values in the Supreme Court: Cost-Benefit Analysis." *American Journal of Public Health* 71 (November 1981): 1264-1265.

5216. DeBois, Annette N. "The United States Supreme Court Deals a Severe Blow to NEPA." *Natural Resources Journal* 22 (July 1982): 699-706.

5217. Fitzgerald, Edward A. "*Secretary of Interior v. California*: Should Continental Shelf Lease Sales Be Subject to Consistency Review?" *Boston College Environmental Affairs Law Review* 12 (Spring 1985): 425-471.

5218. Funk, William. "The Exception That Approves the Rule: FDF Variances under the Clean Water Act." *Boston College Environmental Affairs Law Review* 13 (Fall 1985): 1-60.

5219. Garcia, Timothy L. "United States Supreme Court Upholds Indiana Mineral Lapse Statute." *Natural Resources Journal* 1 (January 1984): 203-212.

5220. Glass, Stuart. *Supreme Court Decision on Impoundment of Water Pollution Control Act Funds*. Washington, DC: Congressional Research Service, 1975.

5221. Goldsmith, Richard I., and William C. Banks. "Environmental Values, Institutional Responsibility, and the Supreme Court." *Harvard Environmental Law Review* 7 (1983): 1-40.

5222. Grunbaum, Werner F. *Judicial Policy Making: The Supreme Court and Environmental Quality*. Morristown, NJ: General Learning Press, 1976.

5223. Hedal, Joseph A. "The Clean Water Act: More Section 404; The Supreme Court Gets Its Feet Wet." *Boston University Law Review* 65 (November 1985): 995-1023.

5224. Higgins, Mary R. "Supreme Court Clarifies Water Act Requirement." *Natural Resources Journal* 21 (July 1981): 607-616.

5225. Kellett, Catherine A. "The Future of the Environmental Enforcement Injunction after *Ohio vs. Kovacs*." *Boston College Environmental Affairs Law Review* 13 (Spring 1986): 397-438.

5226. Melnick, R. Shep. *Regulation and the Courts: The Case of the Clean Air Act*. Washington, DC: Brookings Institution, 1983.

5227. Peters, Lee. "Supreme Court Denies Extension of Federal Regulation of Natural Gas Producers." *Natural Resources Journal* 20 (1980): 187-198.

5228. Peters, Lee. "Supreme Court Rejects Water as Locatable Mineral for Federal Mining Claims." *Natural Resources Journal* 19 (January 1979): 183-185.

5229. Raymond, James F. "*Vermont Yankee* in King Burger's Court: Constraints on Judicial Review under NEPA." *Boston College Environmental Affairs Law Review* 7 (1979): 629-664.

5230. Reed, Phillip D. "The Supreme Court and Environmental Law: A Whole New Ballgame?" *Environmental Law Reporter* 14 (July 1984): 10262-10266.

5231. Rosenbaum, Kenneth L. "The Supreme Court Endorses a Broad Reading of Corps Wetland Jurisdiction under FWPCA 404." *Enviromental Law Reporter* 16 (January 1986): 10008-10012.

5232. Samuels, Linda B. "Surface Mining: Will Supreme Court Precedent Be Reclaimed?" *American Business Law Journal* 19 (Spring 1981): 47-62.

5233. Schwartz, Edward B. "Water as an Article of Commerce: State Embargoes Spring a Leak under *Sporhase v. Nebraska*." *Boston College Environmental Affairs Law Review* 12 (Fall 1985): 103-169.

5234. Shepard, Blake. "The Scope of Congress' Constitutional Power under the Property Clause: Regulating Non-Federal Property to Further the Purpose of National Parks and Wilderness Areas." *Bos-*

ton College Environmental Affairs Law Review 11 (April 1984): 479-538.

5235. Stenzel, Paulette L. "Toxic Substance Regulation: A Compelling Situation for Revival of the Delegation Doctrine." *American Business Law Journal* 24 (Sprng 1986): 1-24.

5236. Streubal, David A. "Reappraisal of State Interests in Outer Continental Shelf Lease Sales under the Coastal Zone Management Act: *Secretary of the Interior v. California.*" *Journal of Urban and Contemporary Law* 29 (1985): 277-295.

5237. Tobey, James A. "Public Health and the United States Supreme Court." *American Bar Association Journal* 11 (November 1925): 707-710.

5238. Vorade, Carol A. "NEPA, the Supreme Court, and the Future of Environmental Litigation." *Southwestern University Law Review* 10 (1978): 403-473.

5239. Wilbur, W. Allan. "The Supreme Court and the Environment: A New Role for the 1970s?" *Indiana Academy of the Social Sciences* 6 (1971): 88-97.

5240. Wise, Sherwood W. "*Sierra Club v. Ruckelshaus*: Symptom of a Dilemma." *Public Utilities Fortnightly* 94 (November 7, 1974): 34-38.

5241. Zinder, Norton D. "The Berg Letter: A Statement of Conscience, Not Conviction." *Hastings Center Report* 10 (October 1980): 14-15.

Labor

5242. Aaron, Benjamin. "Strikes in Breach of Collective Agreements: Some Unanswered Questions." *Columbia Law Review* 63 (June 1963): 1027-1052.

5243. Abraham, Steven E. "NLRB Jurisdiction of Secondary Boycotts: *ILA v. Allied International Inc.*, A Missed Opportu-

nity for the Supreme Court to Reevaluate *Mobile.*" *New York University Journal of International Law and Politics* 15 (Winter 1983): 395-434.

5244. Albertsworth, E. F. "Interstitial Legislation by United States Supreme Court in its Application of Federal Employers' Liability Act." *American Bar Association Journal* 19 (July 1933): 377-382, 426-428.

5245. Alchian, Armen A. "Decision Sharing and Expropriable Specific Quasi-Rents: A Theory of *First National Maintenance Corp. v. NLRB.*" *Supreme Court Economic Review* 1 (1982): 235-247.

5246. Alderman, Sidney S. "What the New Supreme Court Has Done to the Old Law of Negligence." *Law and Contemporary Problems* 18 (Spring 1953): 110-159.

5247. Atleson, James B. "Union Fines and Picket Lines: The NLRA and Union Disciplinary Power." *UCLA Law Review* 17 (March 1970): 681-757.

5248. Baird, James. "Lockout Law: The Supreme Court and the NLRB." *George Washington Law Review* 38 (March 1970): 396-430.

5249. Baird, James, and Sheila Finnegan. "Supreme Court Rulings of Interest to Public Employers and Employee Representatives." *Urban Lawyer* 18 (Fall 1986): 1017-1029.

5250. Baker, Nathan. "*Santos* Decision: A Positive Step toward Harbor Workers' Safety." *Trial* 17 (September 1981): 26-29.

5251. Ball, J. "*Barlow* Decision." *Job Safety and Health* 6 (June 1978): 15-17.

5252. Barron, Paul. "Theory of Protected Employer Rights: A Revisionist Analysis of the Supreme Court's Interpretation of the National Labor Relations Act." *Texas Law Review* 59 (March 1981): 421-475.

5253. Bartosic, Florian. "The Supreme

Court, 1974 Term: The Allocation of Power in Deciding Labor Law Policy." *Virginia Law Review* 62 (April 1976): 533-601.

5254. Bartosic, Florian, and Gary Minda. "The Labor Law Legacy of the Burger Court's Last Term: A Failure of Imagination and Vision." *Arizona Law Review* 28 (1986): 533-594.

5255. Bartosic, Florian, and Gary Minda. "Labor Law Myth in the Supreme Court, 1981 Term: A Plea for Realistic and Coherent Theory." *UCLA Law Review* 30 (December 1982): 271-326.

5256. Beck, Michael H. "The Supreme Court Decisions of the 1985-1986 Term." *Labor Lawyer* 3 (Winter 1987): 55-82.

5257. Bedolis, Robert A. "Supreme Court's *Darlington Mills* Opinion." *Conference Board Record* 2 (June 1965): 49-53.

5258. Bennett-Alexander, Dawn D. "Protection of the Individual Employee and the Bottom-Line Defense." *Labor Law Journal* 34 (November 1983): 704-713.

5259. Berger, Lawrence R., and S. Ryan Johansson. "Child Health in the Workplace: The Supreme Court in *Hammer v. Dagenhart*." *Journal of Health Politics, Policy, and Law* 5 (Spring 1980): 81-97.

5260. Berke, Jay S. "The *Stotts* Dilemma: Will *Wygant* Resolve It?" *Employee Relations Law Journal* 11 (Spring 86): 635-661.

5261. Bethel, Terry A. "Recent Labor Law Decisions of the Supreme Court." *Maryland Law Review* 45 (Winter 1986): 179-240.

5262. Blumrosen, Alfred W. "Labor Arbitration and Discrimination: The Situation after *Griggs* and *Rios*." *Arbitration Journal* 28 (September 1973): 145-158.

5263. Boudin, Louis B. "The Supreme Court and Labor: 1946 Term." *Columbia Law Review* 47 (September 1947): 979-1008.

5264. Broadwater, Margaret R. "Labor and the First Amendment: *Thornhill* to *Logan Valley Plaza*." Ph.D. diss., Rutgers University, 1976.

5265. Brotman, Billie A. "The Existence of Shared Jurisdiction between the National Labor Relations Board and Arbitrators." *Labor Law Journal* 37 (July 1986): 423-431.

5266. Browne, Harry L. "The Court, the NLRB, and Free Collective Bargaining: A Second Look." *American Bar Association Journal* 54 (June 1986): 560-565.

5267. Cady, Elwyn L. "The Impact of the Wagner Act: Supreme Court Decisions upon Reconversion." *University of Kansas City Law Review* 14 (December 1945/ January 1946): 1-25.

5268. Castle, Robert C., and Paul Lansing. "Arbitration of Labor Grievances Brought under Contractual and Statutory Provisions: The Supreme Court Grows Less Deferential to the Arbitration Process." *American Business Law Journal* 21 (Spring 1983): 49-88.

5269. Castle, Robert C., and Richard Pegnetter. "Secondary Picketing: The Supreme Court Limits the *Tree Fruits* Exception." *Labor Law Journal* 33 (January 1982): 3-16.

5270. Christensen, Thomas G., and Andrea H. Svanoe. "Motive and Intent in the Commission of Unfair Labor Practices: The Supreme Court and the Fictive Formality." *Yale Law Journal* 77 (June 1968): 1269-1332.

5271. Come, Norton J. "Federal Preemption of Labor-Management Relations: Current Problems in the Application of *Garmon*." *Virginia Law Review* 56 (December 1970): 1435-1452.

5272. Cortner, Richard C. *The Jones and Laughlin Case*. New York: Knopf, 1970.

5273. Cortner, Richard C. *The Wagner Act Cases.* Knoxville: University of Tennessee Press, 1964.

5274. Cox, Archibald. "Labor Decisions of the Supreme Court at the October Term, 1957." *Virginia Law Review* 44 (November 1958): 1057-1092.

5275. Craver, Charles B. "The 1986-1987 Supreme Court Labor and Employment Law Term: The Expanding Focus on Individual Rights and Preemption." *Labor Lawyer* 3 (Fall 1987): 755-807.

5276. Currier, Thomas S. "Defamation in Labor Disputes: Preemption and the New Federal Common Law." *Virginia Law Review* 53 (January 1967): 1-41.

5277. Cushman, Robert E. "National Police Power under the Taxing Clause of the Constitution." *Minnesota Law Review* 4 (March 1920): 247-281.

5278. Day, James F. "Supreme Court Decides Hiring and Placement Procedures Must Be Valid." *Journal of Employment Counseling* 9 (June 1972): 74-77.

5279. DeParcq, William H. "The Supreme Court and the Federal Employers' Liability Act, 1957-58 Term." *Rocky Mountain Law Review* 31 (December 1958): 22-32.

5280. Dockery, William J. "Judicial Enforcement of Labor Union Fines in State Courts." *North Carolina Law Review* 46 (February 1968): 441-451.

5281. Dodd, E. Merrick. "Supreme Court and Fair Labor Standards, 1941-1945." *Harvard Law Review* 59 (February 1946): 321-375.

5282. Dodd, E. Merrick. *The Supreme Court and Organized Labor [and] the Supreme Court and Fair Labor Standards.* New York: Practising Law Institute, 1946.

5283. Dodd, E. Merrick. "Supreme Court and Organized Labor, 1941-1945." *Har-*

vard Law Review 58 (September 1945): 1018-1071.

5284. Douglas, Joel M. "Faculty Collective Bargaining in the Aftermath of *Yeshiva.*" *Change* 13 (March 1981): 36-43.

5285. Due, Paul H. "Proof of Negligence under the LHWCA." *Trial* 20 (February 1984): 60-66.

5286. Due, Paul H., and David W. Robertson. "Remedies for Injured Offshore Oil Workers: Finding the Way through the Maze of Applicable Law." *Trial* 20 (December 1984): 48-52.

5287. Duram, James C. "Labor Union Journals and the Constitutional Issues of the New Deal: The Case for Court Restriction." *Labor History* 15 (Spring 1974): 216-238.

5288. Edwards, Harry T. "Coming of Age of the Burger Court: Labor Law Decisions of the Supreme Court during the 1976 Term." *Boston College Law Review* 19 (November 1977): 1-99.

5289. Elwell, Karen, and Peter Feuille. "Arbitration Awards and Gardner-Denver Lawsuits: One Bite or Two?" *Industrial Relations* 23 (Spring 1984): 286-297.

5290. Englestein, Stanley. "Supreme Court Sets Back Union Democracy." *Dissent* 29 (Fall 1982): 394-399.

5291. Estes, R. Wayne. "Review of Labor and Employment Law Decisions: United States Supreme Court, October 1979 Term." *Marquette Law Review* 64 (Fall 1980): 1-60.

5292. Evans, Robert, Jr. " 'Caesar' Revisited: The NLRB and the Supreme Court." *Labor Law Journal* 36 (October 1985): 789-794.

5293. Fanning, John H. "NLRB Policies under *Landrum-Griffin* and Recent Court Rulings." *Monthly Labor Review* 84 (September 1961): 960-965.

5294. Fay, Kevin J. "Strike Breakers, the

Supreme Court, and *Belknap Incorporated v. Hale*: The Continuing Erosion of Federal Labor Preemption." *Buffalo Law Review* 33 (Fall 1984): 839-871.

5295. "Flags of Convenience and NLRB Jurisdiction." *Northwestern University Law Review* 60 (May/June 1965): 195-211.

5296. Flygare, Thomas J. "Supreme Court Says Nonunion Teacher Can Address Board on Issue under Negotiation." *Phi Delta Kappan* 58 (March 1977): 573-574.

5297. Flygare, Thomas J. "Supreme Court Upholds Boards' Right to Fire Striking Teachers." *Phi Delta Kappan* 58 (October 1976): 206-207.

5298. Flygare, Thomas J. "Supreme Court Upholds Exclusive Role for Faculty Unions in 'Meet and Confer' Sessions." *Phi Delta Kappan* 65 (June 1984): 718-719.

5299. Fowler, Aubrey R., Jr. "Arbitration, the Trilogy, and Individual Rights: Developments since *Alexander v. Gardner-Denver*." *Labor Law Journal* 36 (March 1985): 173-182.

5300. Francis, Thomas S. "The New Apportionment Rule under *Bowen v. United States Postal Service*." *Labor Law Journal* 35 (February 1984): 71-91.

5301. French, Larry L. "All Things Being Equal: *General Electric v. Gilbert*: An Analysis." *Journal of Law and Education* 7 (January 1928): 21-30.

5302. Frost, Daniel S. "Labor's Antitrust Exemption." *California Law Review* 55 (April 1967): 254-272.

5303. George, B. Glenn. "Collective Bargaining in Chapter 11 and Beyond." *Yale Law Journal* 95 (December 1985): 300-346.

5304. Goetz, Raymond. "Arbitration after Termination of a Collective Bargaining Agreement." *Virginia Law Review* 63 (June 1977): 693-730.

5305. Gohmann, Stephan E., and James E. McClure. "Supreme Court Rulings on Pension Plans: The Effect on Retirement Age and Wealth of Single People." *Gerontologist* 27 (August 1987): 471-477.

5306. Goldman, Alvin L. *Supreme Court and Labor-Management Relations Law*. Lexington, MA: Lexington Books, 1976.

5307. Goodman, Carl F. "Public Employment and the Supreme Court's 1975-1976 Term." *Public Personnel Management* 5 (September 1976): 287-302.

5308. Goodman, Carl F. "Public Employment and the Supreme Court's 1976-1977 Term." *Public Personnel Management* 6 (September 1977): 283-293.

5309. Gorsky, Morley R. "Management Rights Revisited: How the Good Ship Warrior and Gulf Sailed Up the Potomac River and Wound Up in Metropolitan Toronto." *Valparaiso University Law Review* 19 (Fall 1984): 123-152.

5310. Gould, William B. "The Burger Court and Labor Law: The Beat Goes On: *Marcato*." *San Diego Law Review* 24 (January/February 1987): 51-76.

5311. Gould, William B. "Fifty Years under the National Labor Relations Act: A Retrospective View." *Labor Law Journal* 37 (April 1986): 235-243.

5312. Gould, William B. "On Labor Injunctions, Unions, and the Judges: The *Boys Market* Case." *Supreme Court Review* 1970 (1970): 215-268.

5313. Gould, William B. "Supreme Court's Clayton Decision: Its Issues and Implications." *Employment Relations Law Journal* 8 (Summer 1982): 110-119.

5314. Gould, William B. "Supreme Court's Labor and Employment Docket in the 1980 Term: Justice Brennan's

Term." *University of Colorado Law Review* 53 (Fall 1981): 1-100.

5315. Graham, James M. "Law's Labor Lost: Judicial Politics in the Progressive Era." *Wisconsin Law Review* 1972 (1972): 447-476.

5316. Gray, Elizabeth P. "The National Origin BFOQ under Title VII: Limiting the Scope of the Exception." *Employee Relations Law Journal* 11 (Autumn 1985): 311-321.

5317. Green, William. "Supreme Court's Decision in the *Lewis* Case." *American Federationist* 54 (April 1947): 16-17.

5318. Grenig, Jay E. "The Statute of Limitations in Fair Representation Cases." *Labor Law Journal* 33 (August 1982): 483-487.

5319. Handberg, Roger B., Jr. "Supreme Court and the NLRB." *Labor Law Journal* 26 (November 1975): 737-739.

5320. Hays, Paul R. "The Supreme Court and Labor Law: October Term, 1959." *Columbia Law Review* 60 (November 1960): 901-935.

5321. Heller, James W. "Unilateral Action in a Concession Bargaining Context." *Labor Law Journal* 35 (December 1984): 747-765.

5322. Henkel, Jan W., and Norman J. Wood. "Limitations on the Uses of Union Shop Funds after *Ellis*: What Activities Are 'Germane' to Collective Bargaining?" *Labor Law Journal* 35 (December 1984): 736-746.

5323. Hettinger, Kyle B. "NLRA Preemption of State and Local Plant Relocation Laws." *Columbia Law Review* 86 (March 1986): 407-426.

5324. Hill, Marvin, Jr. "Grievance Procedure and Title VII Limitations." *Labor Law Journal* 28 (June 1977): 339-343.

5325. Hirshman, Linda R. "The Second Arbitration Trilogy: The Federalization of Arbitration Law." *Virginia Law Review* 71 (November 1985): 1305-1378.

5326. Isaacson, William J. "Chapter 11: A Haven for Beleagured Employees?" *Employee Relations Law Journal* 10 (Summer 1984): 1-4.

5327. Isaacson, William J. "The Implications of the Recent U.S. Supreme Court Decisions on Labor Arbitration." *Association of the Bar of the City of New York Record* 13 (February 1958): 67-84.

5328. Jacobs, Roger B. "Employment Discrimination and Continuing Violations: An Update of *Ricks* and Recent Decisions." *Labor Law Journal* 33 (October 1982): 684-689.

5329. Jacobs, Roger B. "Time Limitations and Section 301: A New Direction from the Supreme Court" *Labor Law Journal* 34 (January 1983): 20-33.

5330. Janofsky, Leonard S., and Andrew C. Peterson. "Exercise of Unreviewed Administrative Discretion to Reverse the U.S. Supreme Court: *Ponsford Brothers*." *Labor Law Journal* 25 (December 1974): 729-735.

5331. Jenkins, Joseph A. "The Supreme Court and the NLRB." *Labor Law Journal* 9 (June 1958): 425-438.

5332. Joyce, Robert P. "Schools and the Fair Labor Standards Act." *School Law Bulletin* (University of North Carolina) 17 (Winter 1986): 1-4.

5333. Kaden, Lewis B. "Federal Labor Preemption: The Supreme Court Draws the Lines." *Urban Lawyer* 18 (Summer 1986): 607-634.

5334. Kamer, Gregory J. "Section 8(b)(4) Publicity Proviso and *NLRB v. Servette*: A Supreme Court Mandate Ignored." *Labor Law Journal* 33 (October 1982): 645-658.

5335. Karcher, Christina A. "The Supreme Court Takes One Step Forward and the NLRB Takes One Step Backward: Redefining Constructive Concerted Activities." *Vanderbilt Law Review* 38 (October 1985): 1295-1344.

5336. Kaus, Robert M. "How the Supreme Court Sabotaged Civil Service Reform." *Washington Monthly* 10 (December 1978): 38-44.

5337. Keezer, Dexter M. "Labor Problem of the United States Supreme Court." *Social Forces* 5 (December 1926): 324-329.

5338. Kovarsky, Irving. "The Supreme Court and the Secondary Boycott: Courts Are to Some Extent Unnecessarily Divorcing Labor's Constitutional Right to Picket from the Right of the Secondary Firm to Be Free of Picketing." *Labor Law Journal* 16 (April 1965): 216-233.

5339. Kutler, Stanley I. "Labor, the Clayton Act, and the Supreme Court." *Labor History* 3 (Winter 1962): 19-38.

5340. "Labor Law: The U.S. Supreme Court Alters National Labor Policy." *New Mexico Law Review* 16 (Winter 1986): 153-169.

5341. La Follette, Robert M. "Child Labor and the Federal Courts." *American Federationist* 29 (July 1922): 469-486.

5342. Lansing, Paul, and Kevin H. Smith. "Jacksonville Bulk Terminals: Should Politically Motivated Work Stoppages Be Enjoined Where a No Strike Clause Exists in the Collective Bargaining Agreement?" *American Business Law Journal* 21 (Fall 1983): 249-289.

5343. LaRock, Seymour. "Courts Leave Little in Occupational Exemption." *Employee Benefit Plan Review* 40 (September 1985): 126-128.

5344. Lewis, Robert. "*Gissel Packing*: Was the Supreme Court Right?" *American Bar Association Journal* 56 (September 1970): 877-880.

5345. Lissy, William E. "Employees Can Refuse to Perform Hazardous Jobs." *Supervision* 42 (August 1980): 19-20.

5346. McBrearty, James C. "Aesop's Fable of the Fox and the Stork Revisited: Legality of Employment Testing." *Arizona Review* 20 (June/July 1971): 11-14.

5347. McClain, Joseph A., Jr. "The Union Shop Amendment: Compulsory 'Freedom' to Join a Union." *American Bar Association Journal* 42 (August 1956): 723-726.

5348. McGill, Linda D., and Richard G. Moon. "NLRA Preemption: The Free Play Doctrine in *Metropolitan Life Insurance v. Massachusetts*." *Employee Relations Law Journal* 11 (Autumn 1985): 206-224.

5349. McKew, John J. "Supreme Court Looks at Arbitration: Three Landmark Decisions Widening the Jurisdiction of Arbitrators, and the Possible Threat They Pose to Management's Prerogatives." *Management Record* 23 (April 1961): 17-22.

5350. McKinney, T. Charles. "Fair Representation of Employees in Unionized Firms: A Newer Directive from the Supreme Court." *Labor Law Journal* 35 (November 1984): 693-700.

5351. Marion, David E. "Some Recent Public Personnel Decisions and the 'Unconstitutional Conditions' Doctrine." *Midwest Review of Public Administration* 11 (June 1977): 151-156.

5352. Matheny, Albert R., and Bruce A. Williams. "Regulation, Risk Assessment, and the Supreme Court: The Case of OSHA's Cancer Policy." *Law and Policy Quarterly* 6 (October 1984): 425-449.

5353. Meltzer, Bernard D. "The Supreme Court, Congress, and State Jurisdiction over Labor Relations." *Columbia Law Review* 59 (January/February 1959): 6-60, 269-302.

5354. Merican, Harry B. "The Supreme Court and the National Labor Relations Act." *Georgetown Law Journal* 26 (January 1938): 412-438.

5355. Miles, James M. "Survey of the United States Supreme Court Decisions Affecting Labor-Management Relations during the 1967-1968 Term." *North Carolina Law Review* 47 (June 1969): 861-880.

5356. Modjeska, Lee. "Decisions of the Supreme Court, 1979-1980: Labor Relations and Employment Discrimination Law." *Industrial Relations Law Journal* 4 (1980): 1-28.

5357. Modjeska, Lee. "Labor and the Warren Court." *Industrial Relations Law Journal* 8 (1986): 479-546.

5358. Montgomery, David K. "The Supreme Court Affirms the Board's Pattern Makers Decisions." *Employee Relations Law Journal* 11 (Winter 1985/1986): 519-525.

5359. Moore, Joseph E. "The NLRB and the Supreme Court." *Labor Law Journal* 20 (April 1969): 216-238.

5360. Moss, George W., III. "Fate of Arbitration in the Supreme Court: An Examination." *Loyola University of Chicago Law Journal* 9 (Winter 1978): 369-395.

5361. Mounts, Gregory J. "Labor and the Supreme Court: Significant Decisions of 1976-77." *Monthly Labor Review* 101 (January 1978): 12-17.

5362. Mounts, Gregory J. "Labor and the Supreme Court: Significant Decisions of 1977-78." *Monthly Labor Review* 102 (January 1979): 51-57.

5363. Mounts, Gregory J. "Labor and the Supreme Court: Significant Decisions of 1978-79." *Monthly Labor Review* 103 (January 1980): 14-21.

5364. Mounts, Gregory J. "Labor and the Supreme Court: Significant Decisions of 1979-80." *Monthly Labor Review* 104 (April 1981): 13-22.

5365. Myers, Howard N. "The Ever Changing Labor-Management Environment." *Labor Law Journal* 37 (April 1986): 250-255.

5366. Naffziger, Fred J. "Partial Business Close-Downs by an Employer and the Duty to Bargain under the National Labor Relations Act." *American Business Law Journal* 20 (Summer 1982): 223-243.

5367. National Consumers' League. *The Supreme Court and Minimum Wage Legislation: Comment by the Legal Profession on the District of Columbia Case.* New York: New Republic, 1925.

5368. O'Connor, John J. "The Supreme Court and Labor." Ph.D. diss., Catholic University of America, 1932.

5369. Padway, Joseph A. "Supreme Court Decisions on Labor: 1941-1942 Term." *American Federationist* 49 (August 1942): 14-15; (September 1942): 18-19.

5370. Parkinson, Thomas I. "Child Labor and the Constitution." *American Labor Legislation Review* 12 (June 1922): 110-113.

5371. Peterson, William B., and Michael C. Lynch. "Limiting Employer Back-Pay Liability in Employment Discrimination Cases: *Ford Motor Co. v. EEOC.*" *Employee Relations Law Journal* 9 (Autumn 1983): 276-291.

5372. Phillips, Susan M. "Supreme Court's Decision on the *Daniel* Case: Implications for Pension Regulations." *Journal of Risk and Insurance* 47 (March 1980): 157-164.

5373. Polhemus, Craig E. "Significant Labor Decisions: An Analysis." *Monthly Labor Review* 100 (January 1977): 36-41.

5374. Portwood, James D., and Stuart M. Schmidt. "Beyond *Griggs v. Duke Power*

Company: Title VII after *Washington v. Davis*." *Labor Law Journal* 28 (March 1977): 174-181.

5375. Powell, Thomas R. "The Child Labor Law, the Tenth Amendment, and the Commerce Clause." *Southern Law Quarterly* 3 (August 1918): 175-202.

5376. Powell, Thomas R. "The Oregon Minimum-Wage Cases." *Political Science Quarterly* 32 (June 1917): 196-311.

5377. Powell, Thomas R. "Supreme Court's Control over the Issue of Injunctions in Labor Disputes." *Academy of Political Science Proceedings* 13 (June 1928): 37-77.

5378. Rains, Harry H. "Should Strikers Receive Unemployment Insurance Benefits?" *Labor Law Journal* 30 (November 1979): 700-708.

5379. Rasnic, Carol D. "Labor's Return from 'Waterloo': Congressional Response to *NLRB v. Bildisco*." *American Business Law Journal* 23 (Winter 1986): 633-648.

5380. Rich, Wilbur C. "Civil Servants, Municipalities, and Courts." *Public Administration Review* 37 (September/October 1977): 517-519.

5381. Rigler, Jane. "Status of Area Standards Picketing as Protected Conduct under Section 7." *Labor Law Journal* 32 (December 1981): 770-779.

5382. Rose, George. "*Garner v. Teamsters*: The Supreme Court and Private Rights." *Virginia Law Review* 40 (February 1954): 177-192.

5383. Rosenberg, Richard S. "*Bonanno Linen Services*: A Step Backward for Industrial Harmony." *Employee Relations Law Journal* 8 (Autumn 1982): 315-319.

5384. Rosenberg, Richard S. "Supreme Court Opts for Narrow Definition of Confidential Employee." *Employee Relations Law Journal* 8 (Summer 1982): 126-130.

5385. Royce, Alexander B. "Labor, the

Federal Anti-Trust Laws, and the Supreme Court." *New York University Law Review* 5 (January 1928): 19-28.

5386. Saad, Henry W. "The *Bildisco* Decision: Balancing Political Interests." *Employee Relations Law Journal* 10 (Autumn 1984): 200-221.

5387. St. Antoine, Theodore J. "Judicial Valour and the Warren Court's Labor Decisions." *Michigan Law Review* 67 (December 1968): 317-324.

5388. Scallon, Hugh J. "Preferential Hiring Rights of Economic Strikers." *Labor Law Journal* 19 (April 1968): 195-200.

5389. Schachter, Victor, and JoAnne Dellaverson. "Partnership Selection in the Wake of *Hishon v. King and Spalding*." *Employee Relations Law Journal* 10 (Winter 1984): 400-414.

5390. Schachter, Victor, and JoAnne Dellaverson. "Title VII Extended to Partnerships." *Employee Relations Law Journal* 10 (Autumn 1984): 303-306.

5391. Schiller, Pamella M. "New Defenses for Delinquent Contributors: The Supreme Court Changes the Rules of the Pension Plan Game." *University of Pittsburgh Law Review* 44 (Spring 1983): 773-794.

5392. Schireson, Peter L. "The National Labor Relations Board's Faculty Bargaining Unit Decisions." Ph.D. diss., Harvard University, 1980.

5393. Schmedemann, Deborah A. "Of Meetings and Mailboxes: The First Amendment and Exclusive Representation in Public Sector Labor Relations." *Virginia Law Review* 72 (February 1986): 91-138.

5394. Seaver, Douglas F. "The *Stotts* Decision: Is It the Death Knell for Seniority Systems?" *Employee Relations Law Journal* 10 (Winter 1984/1985): 497-504.

5395. Selver, Tara. "Labor Law: The U.S.

Supreme Court Alters National Labor Policy." *New Mexico Law Review* 16 (Winter 1986): 153-169.

5396. Siegel, Jay S. "Deferral to Arbitration Awards in Title VII Actions." *Labor Law Journal* 25 (July 1974): 398-403.

5397. Simmons, F. Bruce, III. "Jurisdictional Disputes: Does the Board Really Snub the Supreme Court?" *Labor Law Journal* 36 (March 1985): 183-192.

5398. Smith, Arthur B., Jr. "Supreme Court, *Boys Markets* Labor Injunctions, and Sympathy Work Stoppages." *University of Chicago Law Review* 44 (Winter 1977): 321-363.

5399. Smith, Ethel M. "Supreme Court and Minimum Wage Legislation." *American Federationist* 33 (February 1926): 197-202.

5400. Smith, Russell A. "The Supreme Court and Labor, 1950-1953." *Southwestern Law Journal* 8 (Winter 1954): 1-35.

5401. Snyder, Franklin B. "What Has the Supreme Court Done to Arbitration? Uncertainties Raised by Three Recent Decisions." *Labor Law Journal* 12 (February 1961): 93-98.

5402. Spaeth, Harold J. "An Analysis of Judicial Attitudes in the Labor Relations Decisions of the Warren Court." *Journal of Politics* 25 (May 1963): 290-311.

5403. Stephens, David B., and John P. Kohl. "The Replacement Worker Phenomenon in the Southwest: Two Years after *Belknap Inc. v. Hale*." *Labor Law Journal* 37 (January 1986): 41-49.

5404. Summers, William C., and Leslie Susskind. "*Bowen v. U.S. Postal Service*: Far-Reaching Effects on Police Unions." *Police Chief* 50 (June 1983): 18-19.

5405. Sylvester, John K. "The Effect of Recent United States Supreme Court Decisions upon Labor Relations in the United States." Ph.D. diss., University of Iowa, 1953.

5406. Syme, Herbert M. "The Supreme Court and Labor Law." *Pennsylvania Bar Association Quarterly* 13 (October 1941): 40-49.

5407. Taylor, Albion G. *Labor and the Supreme Court*. 2d ed. Ann Arbor MI: Braun-Brumfield, 1961.

5408. Tiefer, Charles. "OSHA's Toxics Program Faces a Supreme Court Test." *Labor Law Journal* 30 (November 1979): 680-688.

5409. Twomey, D. P. "*NLRB v. Yeshiva University*: Faculty as Managerial Employees under the NLRA." *American Business Law Journal* 19 (Spring 1981): 63-73.

5410. Twyeffort, Frank H. "United States Supreme Court and Employer-Employee Relations under the National Industrial Recovery Act." *New York University Law Quarterly Review* 11 (December 1933): 251-261.

5411. Van Alstyne, William W. "The Constitutional Rights of Public Employers: A Comment on the Inappropriate Uses of an Old Analogy." *UCLA Law Review* 16 (1969): 751-772.

5412. Wagner, Martin. "Have the Courts Extended a Sound Doctrine Too Far?" *Labor Law Journal* 33 (August 1982): 487-493.

5413. Watt, Richard F. "The New Deal Court, Organized Labor, and the Taft-Hartley Act." *Lawyer's Guild Review* 7 (September/October 1947): 193-217; (November/December 1947): 237-251.

5414. Weinberg, Frederick E., and Max R. Simon. "The Constitutionality of Portal-to-Portal Act of 1947 in the Light of the Decisions Affecting Retroactive Legislation in the Supreme Court." *Temple Law Quarterly* 22 (April 1949): 369-396.

5415. Weingarten, Mark P. "*Bowen v.*

United States Postal Service: The Decision and Its Effect on the Union's Duty of Fair Representation." *Labor Law Journal* 35 (October 1984): 608-623.

5416. Weistart, John C. "Judicial Review of Labor Agreements: Lessons from the Sports Industry." *Law and Contemporary Problems* 44 (August 1981): 109-146.

5417. Wellington, Harry H. "Union Fines and Workers' Rights." *Yale Law Journal* 85 (July 1976): 1022-1059.

5418. White, Harold C., and William Gibney. "Arizona Farm Labor Law: A Supreme Court Test." *Labor Law Journal* 31 (February 1980): 87-99.

5419. Williams, William E. "The Interpretation of Union Motives by the United States Supreme Court." Ph.D. diss., University of Southern California, 1950.

5420. Witt, Elder. "Zoning Compensation, Other Cases Also Resolved: Court Upholds Regulation on Disability Benefit Claims." *Congressional Quarterly Weekly Report* 45 (June 13, 1987): 1260-1262.

5421. Wolfe, Nancy T. "The Fuller Court and Employer's Liability." Ph.D. diss., University of Delaware, 1974.

5422. Woll, J. Albert. "Labor in the Supreme Court." *American Federationist* 61 (July 1954): 27-29.

5423. Woll, J. Albert. "Labor and the Supreme Court." *American Federationist* 64 (September 1957): 12-14.

5424. Wood, Norman J. "Mandatory Retirement and Equal Protection." *Labor Law Journal* 28 (March 1977): 142-146.

5425. Wood, Stephen B. "Child Labor, the Supreme Court, and the Constitution." Ph.D. diss., University of Chicago, 1964.

5426. Wood, Stephen B. *Constitutional Politics in the Progressive Era, Child Labor, and the Law.* Chicago: University of Chicago Press, 1968.

5427. Wortman, Max S., Jr. and Nathaniel Jones. "Remedial Actions of the NLRB in Representation Cases: An Analysis of the *Gissel* Bargaining Order." *Labor Law Journal* 30 (May 1979): 281-288.

5428. Young, Rowland L. "Court Rules on Job Seniority and Creates a *Miranda* Exception." *American Bar Association Journal* 70 (August 1984): 124-126.

Patents and Copyrights

5429. Allyn, Robert S. "Supreme Court Patent Cases: 1875 to 1881 v. 1935 to 1941." *Journal of the Patent Office Society* 25 (January 1943): 27-51.

5430. Barnard, Robert C., and Sergei Zlinkoff. "Patents, Procedure, and the Sherman Act: The Supreme Court and a Competitive Economy, 1947 Term." *George Washington Law Review* 17 (December 1948): 1-58.

5431. Basanta, William E. "Patents and Computer Programs: The Supreme Court Makes a Decision." *Kentucky Law Journal* 62 (1973): 533-556.

5432. Blumenthal, David A. "Supreme Court Sets Guidelines for Patentability of Computer Related Inventions: *Diamond v. Diehr.*" *Journal of the Patent Office Society* 63 (February 1981): 117-122.

5433. Cox, Rowland. "Reissued Patents: The Position of the Supreme Court." *American Law Review* 15 (November 1881): 731-739.

5434. Davis, William H. "The Impact of Recent Supreme Court Cases on the Question of Patentable Invention." *Illinois Law Review* 44 (March/April 1949): 41-48.

5435. Edell, Robert T. "Supreme Court and Section 103." *American Patent Law Association Quarterly Journal* 5 (1977): 99-116.

5436. Gilbert, Ralph J. "The Constitutionality of Supreme Court Review of Patent and Trademark Decisions of the Court of Customs and Patent Appeals." *Georgetown Law Journal* 45 (Summer 1957): 645-654.

5437. Green, Harold P. *"Chakrabarty, Tempest in a Test Tube." Hastings Center Report* 10 (October 1980): 12-13.

5438. Hall, Thomas B. *The Infringement of Patents for Inventions, Not Designs: With Sole Reference to the Opinions of the Supreme Court of the United States.* Cincinnati: R. Clarke, 1893.

5439. Harris, Robert W. "Prospects for Supreme Court Review of the Federal Circuit Standards for Obviousness of Inventions Combining Old Elements." *Journal of the Patent and Trademark Office Society* 68 (February 1986): 66-82.

5440. Jeffords, Edward A. "Home Audio Recording after Betamax: Taking a Fresh Look." *Baylor Law Review* 36 (Fall 1984): 855-876.

5441. Kurland, Philip B. *The Supreme Court and Patents and Monopolies.* Chicago: University of Chicago Press, 1975.

5442. Kurland, Philip B., and Richard F. Wolfson. "Supreme Court Review of Court of Customs and Patent Appeals: Patent Office and Tariff Commission Cases." *George Washington Law Review* 18 (February 1950): 192-200.

5443. Lutz, Karl B. "The Constitution v. the Supreme Court . . . Patents for Inventions." *University of Pittsburgh Law Review* 13 (Spring 1952): 449-461.

5444. McCann, Joseph D. "The United States Supreme Court Views Copyright on Videotape: A Case Comment on Sony Corporation of America Universal City Studios." *International Review of Industrial Property and Copyright Law* 15 (August 1984): 493-501.

5445. Nieland, Robert. "The Patent Decisions of the United States Supreme Court

1980 Term." *IIC-International Review of Industrial Property and Copyright Law* 11 (1980): 624-630.

5446. Posnack, Emanuel R. "The Judicial Erosion of Our Patent System: A Threat to Inventive Initiative." *American Bar Association Journal* 37 (May 1951): 357-360.

5447. Prager, Frank D. "Trends and Developments in American Patent Law from Jefferson to Clifford." *American Journal of Legal History* 6 (January 1962): 45-62.

5448. Rice, Willis B. "Tangle of Contributor Infringement in the Supreme Court." *New York University Law Quarterly* 11 (September 1933): 48-76.

5449. Rifkin, Jeremy. "Playing God: What the Supreme Court's Genetic Ruling Means." *Sojourners* 9 (August 1980): 9-10.

5450. Schneider, Homer J. "Non-Obviousness, Supreme Court, and Prospects for Stability." *Journal of the Patent Office Society* 60 (May 1978): 304-327.

5451. Selsky, Eileen L. "Home Video Recording: The Supreme Court Decides." *Journal of Media Law and Practice* (Great Britain) 5 (1984): 251-258.

5452. "Supreme Court and the 'Standard of Invention'." *Columbia Law Review* 49 (May 1949): 685-692.

5453. Wechsler, Robert E. "The United States Supreme Court Limits the Patentability of Computer Software in *Parker v. Flook*." *IIC-International Review of Industrial Property and Copyright Law* 11 (1980): 151-165.

5454. Williams and Wilkins Company. *The* Williams and Wilkins *Case: The* Williams and Wilkins Company v. the United States. New York: Science Association International, 1974.

Securities

5455. Banks, Warren E., and Jackson A. White. "Accountants' Malpractice." *American Business Law Journal* 14 (Winter 1977): 411-415.

5456. Blaschke, Michael J. "Going Private: *Santa Fe Industries Inc. v. Green*; Supreme Court Decision in Rule 10b-5 Actions." *Oklahoma Law Review* 30 (Summer 1977): 593-602.

5457. Conard, Alfred F. "Securities Regulation in the Burger Court." *University of Colorado Law Review* 56 (Winter 1985): 193-225.

5458. DeMott, Deborah A., ed. "Shareholder Litigation." *Law and Contemporary Problems* 48 (Summer 1985): 1-261.

5459. Denburg, Howard S. "Amortization of Bond Issue Discount: The Supreme Court Decides *National Alfalfa*." *Taxes* 52 (July 1974): 409-416.

5460. Fenwick, C. G. " 'Gold Clause' Decision in Relation to Foreign Bondholders." *American Journal of International Law* 29 (April 1935): 310-313.

5461. Fox, Karla H. "SEC Rule 10b-5: Tippee Liability Revisited." *American Business Law Journal* 22 (Fall 1984): 385-405.

5462. Freeman, Paul D. "Study in Contrasts: The Warren and Burger Courts' Approach to the Securities Laws." *Dickinson Law Review* 83 (Winter 1979): 183-215.

5463. Hart, Henry M., Jr. "Gold Clause in United States Bonds." *Harvard Law Review* 48 (May 1935): 1057-1099.

5464. Hazen, Thomas L. "Symposium Introduction: The Supreme Court and the Securities Laws: Has the Pendulum Slowed?" *Emory Law Journal* 30 (Winter 1981): 5-34.

5465. Ianni, Edmond M. "Security under the Glass-Steagall Act and the Federal Securities Act of 1933 and 1934: The Direction of the Supreme Court Analysis." *Banking Law Journal* 100 (February 1983): 100-137.

5466. Kaplan, Stanley A. "*Wolf v. Weinstein*: Another Chapter on Insider Trading." *Supreme Court Review* 1963 (1963): 273-324.

5467. Letteri, John. "Are Discretionary Commodity Trading Accounts Investment Contracts? The Supreme Court Must Decide." *Catholic University Law Review* 35 (Winter 1986): 635-661.

5468. Lowenfels, Lewis D. "Recent Supreme Court Decisions under the Federal Securities Laws: The Pendulum Swings." *Georgetown Law Journal* 65 (April 1977): 891-923.

5469. Lustbader, Philip L. "Split Sale Schemes under Section 16 B: Additional Justification for Supreme Court Majorities Approach in *Reliance Electric Co. v. Emerson Electric Co.*" *Temple Law Quarterly* 45 (Spring 1972): 501-516.

5470. Meyer, Balthasar H. "History of the *Northern Securities* Case." Ph.D. diss., University of Wisconsin, 1972.

5471. Poser, Norman S. "Stock Market Manipulation and Corporate Control Transactions." *University of Miami Law Review* 40 (March 1986): 671-735.

5472. Steinberg, Marc J., and William E. Kalbach. "The Supreme Court and the Definition of 'Security': The 'Context' Clause, 'Investment Contract' Analysis, and Their Ramifications." *Vanderbilt Law Review* 40 (April 1987): 489-539.

5473. Strickler, Jeffrey P. "Inside Information and Outside Traders: Corporate Recovery of the Outsiders Unfair Gain." *California Law Review* 73 (March 1985): 483-524.

5474. Whitaker, C. Larimore, and James

E. Rotch. "Supreme Court and the Counter-Revolution in Securities Regulation." *Alabama Law Review* 30 (Winter 1979): 335-394.

5475. Wilkinson, Hugh T. "The Affirmative Duty to Disclose after *Chiarella* and *Dirks*." *Journal of Corporation Law* 10 (Spring 1985): 581-602.

Taxes

5476. Aslanides, Peter C. "Supreme Court Rules on Grantor's Retaining Certain Rights over Property Transferred to Trust." *Taxes* 51 (March 1973): 157-162.

5477. Bender, Leslie C. "Has the Supreme Court Laid Fertile Ground for Invalidating the Regulatory Interpretation of Internal Revenue Code Section 501(C)(3)?" *Notre Dame Law Review* 58 (February 1983): 564-586.

5478. Bender, Louis. "Supreme Court's *Bishop* Decision: A Useful Clarification of 'Willful' in the Fraud Area." *Journal of Taxation* 39 (September 1973): 188-190.

5479. Bolling, Rodger A., and Philip P. Storrer. "The Supreme Court's Second Look at *Crane*: What Should It Do?" *Taxes* 61 (February 1983): 138-144.

5480. Clark, John A. "Supreme Court Says Grantor May Retain Voting Control of Stock Placed in Trust." *Journal of Taxation* 37 (September 1972): 138-140.

5481. Cox, Andrew H. "Supreme Court in *Basye* Taxes Partnership on Plan Payments Made for It by Corporation." *Journal of Taxation* 38 (May 1973): 270-273.

5482. Crouter, Earl C. "*Tellier* Decision of the Supreme Court." *Taxes* 44 (September 1966): 612-616.

5483. Davidson, Sidney. "U.S. Supreme Court Decisions Affecting Public Utility Depreciation." *Journal of Accountancy* 96 (September 1953): 331-335.

5484. Dungan, Christopher W., G. Thomas Friedlob, and Robert W. Rouse. "The Supreme Court on Tax Accrual Workpapers." *CPA Journal* 55 (February 1985): 20-26.

5485. Ferguson, M. Carr. "Supreme Court Decisions in Taxation: 1981 Term." *Tax Lawyer* 36 (Winter 1983): 421-430.

5486. Grauer, Myron C. "The Supreme Court Approach to Annual and Transactional Accounting for Income Taxes: A Common Law Malfunction in a Statutory System?" *Georgia Law Review* 21 (Fall 1986): 329-398.

5487. Hamovit, Jerry M., and Joel Z. Silver. "Analysis of the Loss-Wastage Problem in View of Supreme Court's *Foster Lumber* Decision." *Journal of Taxation* 46 (February 1977): 100-103.

5488. Hass, Lawrence J. "Supreme Court in *Daniel* Leaves Open Possibility That Some Plans May Be Subject to Securities Laws." *Journal of Taxation* 50 (May 1979): 263-267.

5489. Holbert, Robert L. "The Politics of Lobbying Regulation: The Roles of the Congress, Supreme Court, and Internal Revenue Service." Ph.D. diss., University of Arizona, 1970.

5490. Horwood, Richard M., and Ronald Hindin. "Supreme Court Adopts Liberal Definition of R&D Deductibility under Section 174." *Journal of Taxation* 41 (July 1974): 2-5.

5491. Kornhauser, Marjorie E. "The Origins of Capital Gains Taxation: What's Law Got to Do with It?" *Southwestern Law Journal* 39 (November 1985): 869-928.

5492. Lenrow, Gerald I. and Ralph Milo. "Recent Court Decisions Highlight the Importance of Reserve Methods in Taxation of Life Companies." *Bests Review* 79 (July 1978): 51-54.

5493. Lewis, James B. "Note: Supreme Court Decisions in Taxation, 1979 Term." *Tax Lawyer* 34 (Winter 1981): 423-431.

5494. Lindholm, Richard W. "The Constitutionality of a Federal Net Wealth Tax: A Socioeconomic Analysis of a Strategy Aimed at Ending the Under-Taxation of Land." *American Journal of Economics and Sociology* 43 (October 1984): 451-454.

5495. Lowndes, Charles L. "Spurious Conceptions of the Constitutional Law of Taxation." *Harvard Law Review* 47 (February 1934): 628-659.

5496. McCure, Charles E., Jr. "Incidence Analysis and the Supreme Court: An Examination of Four Cases from the 1980 Term." *Supreme Court Economic Review* 1 (1982): 69-112.

5497. Miller, Joel E. "The Supreme Court Does It Again in *Tufts*: Right Answer, Wrong Reason." *Journal of Real Estate Taxation* 11 (Fall 1983): 3-33.

5498. Nad, Leon M., and Charles T. Crawford. "Supreme Court's Decision in 482 Case Is Not as Limited as First Appeared." *Journal of Taxation* 37 (October 1972): 226-230.

5499. Nolan, John S. "Note: Supreme Court Decisions in Taxation, 1982 Term." *Tax Lawyer* 37 (Winter 1984): 359-365.

5500. Power, James E., and Francis P. Carolan. "Supreme Court Strikes Down Estimated Inventory Reserves." *Journal of Corporate Taxation* 6 (Autumn 1979): 273-277.

5501. Riddle, J. H. "The Supreme Court's Theory of a Direct Tax." *Michigan Law Review* 15 (May 1917): 566-578.

5502. Sanders, Michael J. "Supreme Court, Ending *Crane* Controversy, Says Nonrecourse Debt Is Always Part of Sales Price." *Journal of Taxation* 59 (July 1983): 2-5.

5503. Seat, Donald L. "A Logical and Empirical Investigation of the Relevant Decision Variables in Supreme Court Estate and Gift Tax Cases." Ph.D. diss., University of Kentucky, 1980.

5504. Sheldon, Stuart A., and George H. Bostick. "Supreme Court Severely Limits Third Party's Right to Contest Exempt Status." *Journal of Taxation* 45 (September 1976): 140-143.

5505. Steger, Meritt H. "The Recent Supreme Court Tax Cases from a Federal Viewpoint." *Catholic University of America Law Review* 8 (January 1959): 13-22.

5506. Stoffel, Joseph C. "Bad Debt Reserves: Supreme Court's *Nash* Decision Leaves Many Questions Unanswered." *Journal of Taxation* 33 (August 1970): 92-94.

5507. "Supreme Court Decisions in Taxation, 1985 Term." *Tax Lawyer* 40 (Winter 1987): 383-429.

5508. Teschner, Paul A. "*First Security Bank of Utah*, Taxpayer Disability, and the Supreme Court." *Taxes* 50 (May 1972): 260-273.

5509. Turley, James A. "Supreme Court's *Estate of Grace* Decision: What Does It Mean?" *Journal of Taxation* 31 (September 1969): 130-134.

5510. Weisman, David E. "Brother-Sister Controlled Corporations: On and Off Road to Supreme Court with an Edsel." *Taxes* 56 (August 1978): 475-485.

5511. Wolfman, Bernard. "Supreme Court Decisions in Taxation, 1980 Term: Foreword." *Tax Lawyer* 35 (Winter 1982): 443-576.

Trade

5512. Baumann, Roland. "M. John Swanwick: Spokesman for 'Merchant-Republicanism' in Philadelphia, 1790-1798." *Pennsylvania Magazine of History and Biography* 97 (April 1973): 131-182.

5513. Beer, Henry W. *Federal Trade Law and Practice before the Federal Trade Commission, United States District Courts, United States Circuit Courts of Appeals, and United States Supreme Court in Federal Trade Commission Cases.* Chicago: Callaghan, 1942.

5514. Bucklo, Elaine E. "Supreme Court Attempts to Define Scienter under Rule 10b-5: *Ernst and Ernst v. Hochfelder.*" *Stanford Law Review* 29 (January 1977): 213-240.

5515. Carrott, M. Browning. "The Supreme Court and American Trade Associations, 1921-1925." *Business History Review* 44 (Autumn 1970): 320-338.

5516. Howe, Jonathan T. "*Noerr-Pennington* Doctrine and Inroads into It: Recent Supreme Court Decisions and Some Guidelines for Trade Association Activity." *Mercer Law Review* 26 (Spring 1975): 527-545.

5517. Klug, Harry V. "An Analysis of Supreme Court Decisions Concerning the Federal Trade Commission and the Basing Point System." Ph.D. diss., University of Iowa, 1951.

5518. Marvel, Howard P. "Hybrid Trade Restraints: The Legal Limits of a Government's Helping Hand." *Supreme Court Economic Review* 2 (1983): 165-186.

5519. Mayer, Morris L., et al. "The *Borden* Case: A Legal Basis for Private Brand Price Discrimination." *Michigan State University Business Topics* 18 (Winter 1970): 56-63.

5520. Montague, Gilbert H. "New Opportunities and Responsibilities of Trade Associations as a Result of Recent United States Supreme Court Decisions." *Academy of Political Science Proceedings* 11 (January 1926): 579-583.

5521. Peterman, John L. "The International Salt Case." *Journal of Law and Economics* 22 (October 1979): 351-364.

5522. Schutte, Thomas F., et al. "What Management Can Learn from the *Borden* Case: Implications of the Supreme Court Interpretation of 'Like Grade and Quality'." *Business Horizons* 9 (Winter 1966): 23-30.

5523. Werner, Ray O. "The Knowing Inducement of Discriminatory Prices." *Journal of Purchasing* 4 (May 1968): 5-16.

5524. Werner, Ray O. "Marketing and the Supreme Court in Transition, 1982-1984." *Journal of Marketing* 49 (Summer 1985): 97-105.

5525. Werner, Ray O. "Marketing and the United States Supreme Court." *Journal of Marketing* 31 (January 1967): 4-8.

5526. Werner, Ray O. "Marketing and the United States Supreme Court, 1965-1968." *Journal of Marketing* 33 (January 1969): 16-23.

5527. Werner, Ray O. "Marketing and the U.S. Supreme Court, 1968-1974." *Journal of Marketing* 41 (January 1977): 32-43.

5528. Werner, Ray O. "Marketing and the United States Supreme Court, 1975-1981." *Journal of Marketing* 46 (Spring 1982): 73-81.

5529. Werner, Ray O. "New Supreme Court and Marketing Environment, 1975-1977." *Journal of Marketing* 42 (April 1978): 56-62.

Utilities

5530. Bauer, John. "Reproduction Cost Has Not Been Adopted by Supreme Court: Further Decisions on Fair Value for Rate Making." *National Municipal Review* 12 (November 1923): 644-648.

5531. Bauer, John. "Supreme Court and Reproduction Value in Rate Making." *National Municipal Review* 12 (September 1923): 529-532.

5532. Bauer, John. "Supreme Court Limits Public Utility Valuations." *National Municipal Review* 24 (August 1935): 440-443.

5533. Chiappetta, Vincent F. "United States Nuclear Energy Policy after *Pacific Gas* and *Silkwood*." *Arizona State Law Journal* 1985 (1985): 79-112.

5534. Clay, Cassius M. "Control of Public Utility Rates and the Supreme Court." *U.S. Law Review* 64 (September 1930): 464-470.

5535. Drobak, John N. "From Turnpike to Nuclear Power: The Constitutional Limits on Utility Rate Regulation." *Boston University Law Review* 65 (January 1985): 65-125.

5536. Fitzpatrick, Christopher. "Public Utilities and State Action: The Supreme Court Takes a Stand." *Catholic University Law Review* 24 (Spring 1975): 622-636.

5537. Fraenkel, Osmond K. "Supreme Court and the Rate Base." *U.S. Law Review* 73 (June 1939): 315-330.

5538. Freed, Eli. "Public Service Corporations: Holding Companies and the United States Supreme Court." *California Law Review* 19 (May 1931): 431-441.

5539. Powell, Thomas R. "State Rate Regulation and the Supreme Court, 1922-1930." *Kentucky Law Journal* 20 (March 1932): 191-223.

5540. Powell, Thomas R. "State Utilities and the Supreme Court, 1922-1930." *Michigan Law Review* 29 (May 1931): 811-838; (June 1931): 1001-1030

5541. Priest, A.J.G. "Major Public Utility Decisions in Perspective." *Virginia Law Review* 46 (November 1960): 1327-1344.

5542. Priest, A.J.G. "Supreme Court Decisions on Gas Rate Cases." *Public Utilities Fortnightly* 82 (October 10, 1968): 29-34.

5543. Storey, Douglas D. "The United States Supreme Court and Rate Regulation." *University of Pennsylvania Law Review* 64 (November 1915): 1-41; (December 1915): 151-185; (January 1916): 270-300.

IX. The Court and Economic Issues

General Studies

5544. Albertsworth, E. F. "The Federal Supreme Court and Industrial Development." *American Bar Association Journal* 16 (May 1930): 317-322.

5545. Braemer, Richard J. "Recent Developments in Government Contract Law." *Business Lawyer* 22 (July 1967): 1057-1073.

5546. Caruso, Lawrence P. "An Analysis of the Evolution of the Supreme Court's Concept of the Federal Tort Claims Act." *Federal Bar Journal* 26 (Winter 1966): 35-46.

5547. Cox, James C., Mark R. Isaac, and Vernon L. Smith. "OCS Leasing and Auctions: Incentives and the Performance of Alternative Bidding Institutions." *Supreme Court Economic Review* 2 (1983): 43-88.

5548. "Economic Liberties and the Judiciary." *Cato Journal* 4 (Winter 1985): 661-980.

5549. Fluegel, Edna R. "Concepts of Economic Liberty and the United States Supreme Court: A Study in Judicial Thought." Ph.D. diss., Duke University, 1938.

5550. Jensen, Tamila C. "Supreme Court Zoning Decision." *Business Horizons* 20 (August 1977): 72-75.

5551. Prendergast, William A. "Do the Valuation Rulings of the United States Supreme Court Involve an Unworkable or Cumbersome Plan?" *American Bar Association Report* 55 (August 1930): 760-771.

5552. Shapiro, Martin M. "The Court and Economic Rights." In *Essays on the Constitution of the United States*, edited by M. Judd Harmon, 74-98. Port Washington, NY: Kennikat Press, 1978.

Internal Revenue Service

5553. Allen, Lafon. "The Income Tax Decision: An Answer to Governor Pennoyer." *American Law Review* 29 (November/December 1895): 847-856.

5554. Anspach, William N., Paul L. Marlin, and Charles J. Muller. "Deferred Compensation—A Case-Study of Purposeful Negation of Supreme Court Jurisdiction over Income Tax Laws." *Taxes* 59 (October 1981): 691-711.

5555. Babbitt, Gerald D., and William Morris. "Introduction to the Tax Court of the United States." *Tax Lawyer* 21 (Spring 1968): 615-638.

5556. Bickford, Hugh C. *Court Procedure in Federal Tax Cases.* New York: Prentice-Hall, 1928.

5557. Blum, Walter J. "The Role of the Supreme Court in Federal Income Tax Controversies: *Hillsboro National Bank and Bliss Dairy Inc.*" *Taxes* 61 (June 1983): 363-369.

5558. Bray, John M. "Supreme Court's *Shapiro* Decision Restricts Use of Jeopardy Assessments." *Journal of Taxation* 44 (May 1976): 264-266.

5559. Bray, John M., and David J. Curtin. "IRS Power to Summons Handwriting: Analyzing the Supreme Court's *Euge* Decision." *Journal of Taxation* 52 (May 1980): 290-292.

5560. Buchholz, David L., and Joseph F. Moraglio. "IRS Access to Auditors' Work Papers—the Supreme Court Decision." *Journal of Accountancy* 158 (September 1984): 1-94.

5561. Craig, Sandra J. "Federal Income Tax and the Supreme Court: The Case against a National Court of Tax Appeals." *Utah Law Review* 1983 (1983): 679-736.

5562. Creedon, John J. "On Mortgage Foreclosures and Federal Tax Liens: The Lender's Defeat in Victory." *Business Lawyer* 18 (July 1963): 1117-1151.

5563. Dauber, Milton A., George H. Jewell, and John H. Hall. "Supreme Court in *Brown* Allows Capital Gain on Bootstrap Sale to Charity." *Journal of Taxation* 23 (July 1965): 2-5.

5564. Deberry, Henry D. "Supreme Court in *Engel* Allows Percentage Depletion on Bonuses and Advance Royalties." *Journal of Taxation* 60 (May 1984): 274-278.

5565. Dougherty, J. Chrys. "Supreme Court Holds Wife Liable in *Mitchell*: A Too Harsh Adherence to Precedence." *Journal of Taxation* 35 (November 1971): 296-298.

5566. Duhl, Stuart, and Jeffery L. Kwall. "Supreme Court Holds That Net Gift Triggers Income to Donor: An Analysis of *Deidrich*." *Journal of Taxation* 57 (September 1982): 130-135.

5567. Edwards, Mark B. "Interest-Free Loans Are Held to Be Gifts in Supreme Court's Recent *Dickman* Decision." *Journal of Taxation* 60 (May 1984): 266-268.

5568. Eggert, Gerald G. "Richard Olney and the Income Tax Cases." *Mississippi Valley Historical Review* 48 (June 1961): 24-42.

5569. Eisenstein, Louis. "Estate Taxes and the Higher Learning of the Supreme Court." *Tax Law Review* 3 (April/May 1948): 395-565.

5570. Eliasberg, Kenneth C. "Bootstrap Sales Still Subject to Attack Despite Supreme Court's Holding in *Brown*." *Journal of Taxation* 23 (July 1965): 42-45.

5571. Falk, Charles E. "Nominees, Dummies, and Agents: Is It Time for the Supreme Court to Take Another Look?" *Taxes* 63 (October 1985): 725-730.

5572. Flewellen, W. C. "Concept of Depreciation Accounting Held by the United States Supreme Court." *Accounting Review* 35 (July 1960): 413-421.

5573. Fox, Michael E. "Supreme Court Limits Dividends Paid Deduction to Adjusted Basis of Distributed Property." *Journal of Taxation* 48 (May 1978): 266-268.

5574. Garbis, M. J., and L. P. Marvel. "Supreme Court's Decision in *Fisher* Requires Greater Alertness in Handling Tax Fraud Cases." *Practical Accountant* 9 (July 1976): 35-38.

5575. Goldberg, Louis S. "The Supreme Court and the Federal Income Tax since Pearl Harbor: A Study in Trends of Decision." *Iowa Law Review* 33 (November 1947): 22-47.

5576. Gregory, Francis M., Jr., and Carolyn P. Chiechi. "Supreme Court Decides Key Case on Insurance Taxation of Deferred and Uncollected Premiums." *Journal of Taxation* 47 (September 1977): 170-172.

5577. Gregory, Francis M., Jr., and Carolyn P. Chiechi. "Supreme Court Settles Conflict Involving Life Insurance Company Qualification." *Journal of Taxation* 47 (July 1977): 40-41.

5578. Handberg, Roger B., Jr. "Tax Man Cometh: The Paradox of Judicial Conservatism or Great Expectations Disappointed." *North Dakota Law Review* 55 (1979): 169-183.

5579. Holden, James P., and Matthew J. Zinn. "Note: Supreme Court Decisions in Taxation, 1983 Term." *Tax Lawyer* 38 (Winter 1985): 421-434.

5580. Huffaker, John B., and Erica L. Gut. "Supreme Court Holds Advertising Revenue Was Not Substantially Related Income." *Journal of Taxation* 65 (July 1986): 2-5.

5581. Kaplan, Philip T. "The Unitary Tax Debate, the United States Supreme Court, and Some Plain English." *British Tax Review* 1983 (1983): 203-220.

5582. Karjala, Dennis S. "Deferred Compensation and the Supreme Court." *Taxes* 160 (Summer 1982): 684-694.

5583. Kaster, Lewis R. "Another View of Implications of Supreme Court Decision in *Lyon*." *Journal of Taxation* 49 (July 1978): 44-45.

5584. Kovey, Mark H., and Peter H. Winslow. "Supreme Court in *Rowan* Holds Wages Excludable from Income Are Exempt from FICA, FUTA." *Journal of Taxation* 55 (September 1981): 130-136.

5585. Lachman, Roy E. "Liability under Section 6672 of the Internal Revenue Code: Recent Developments." *Taxes* 57 (September 1979): 593-596.

5586. Lantry, Terry. "*Thor Power Tool Co. v. CIR* Further Erodes CPA's Defense of Observing Professional Standards." *American Business Law Journal* 19 (Spring 1981): 87-96.

5587. Liebtag, Bill. "U.S. Supreme Court Decision on Tax Accrual Work Papers Draws Response by IRS, Profession."

Journal of Accountancy 157 (May 1984): 11-12.

5588. Lore, Martin M. "Review of Significant 1950 Federal Tax Decisions." *Journal of Accountancy* 91 (January 1951): 78-85.

5589. Lowndes, Charles L. "A Day in the Supreme Court with the Federal Estate Tax." *Virginia Law Review* 22 (January 1936): 261-286.

5590. Lowndes, Charles L. "Federal Taxation and the Supreme Court." *Supreme Court Review* 1960 (1960): 222-257.

5591. Lowndes, Charles L. "The Supreme Court on Taxation, 1936 Term." *University of Pennsylvania Law Review* 86 (November/December 1937): 1-24, 149-172.

5592. Lowndes, Charles L. "Tax Decisions of the Supreme Court, 1938 Term." *University of Pennsylvania Law Review* 88 (November 1939): 1-34.

5593. Lowndes, Charles L. "Tax Decisions of the Supreme Court, 1940 Term." *University of Pennsylvania Law Review* 90 (December 1941): 156-191.

5594. Lowndes, Charles L. "Taxation and the Supreme Court, 1937 Term." *University of Pennsylvania Law Review* 87 (November/December 1938): 1-33, 165-200.

5595. McAndrews, Joseph E. "Supreme Court's *Davis* Decision: Does It Do Away with the 302(b)(1) Redemption?" *Journal of Taxation* 32 (June 1970): 328-331.

5596. McLane, Larry. "Supreme Court Raises More Questions Than It Answers in *Skelly Oil* Decision." *Journal of Taxation* 31 (August 1969): 66-69.

5597. Magill, Roswell. "The Supreme Court on Federal Taxation, 1939-1940."

University of Chicago Law Review 8 (December 1940): 1-19.

5598. Myers, John H. "Supreme Court in Unenlightening Decision Holds Scholarship Taxable." *Journal of Taxation* 31 (July 1969): 20-23.

5599. Paul, Randolph E. "*Dobson v. Commissioner*: The Strange Ways of Law and Fact." *Harvard Law Review* 57 (July 1944): 753-851.

5600. Saltzman, Michael I. "Supreme Court's *Garner* Decision Puts Illegal Income Earners in a Bind." *Journal of Taxation* 44 (June 1976): 334-337.

5601. Shapiro, Harry D., and Robert K. Briskin. "Supreme Court Opens Door to Tax Court Review of Jeopardy Terminations." *Journal of Taxation* 44 (April 1976): 194-198.

5602. Shapiro, Martin M. "The Warren Court and Federal Tax Policy." *South California Law Review* 36 (1963): 208-228.

5603. Snyder, John L. "Supreme Court Holds Reinsurance Agreements Effective to Produce Life Insurance Company Status." *CLU Journal* 32 (January 1978): 58-63.

5604. Statham, Robert R., and Richard W. Buek. "Supreme Court's Holding in *National Muffler* Precludes Exemption for Franchise Associations." *Journal of Taxation* 51 (August 1979): 80-83.

5605. Thibodeau, Joseph H. "Supreme Court in *Payner* Admits Stolen Third-Party Evidence in Tax Prosecutions." *Journal of Taxation* 53 (September 1980): 152-154.

5606. Tucker, Stephen F. "The Warren Court: Its Impact on the Capital as Ordinary Concept under the Internal Revenue Code." *University of Kansas Law Review* 17 (1968): 53-78.

5607. Uretz, Lester R. "How IRS Adapts Its Practice to Adverse Supreme Court Decisions." *Journal of Taxation* 26 (May 1967): 290-293.

5608. Welz, Elzbieta, and Teryl L. Minasian. "Supreme Court in *Vogel* Voids IRS Eighty Percent Brother-Sister Group Test: Wide Impact Seen." *Journal of Taxation* 56 (April 1982): 202-205.

5609. Yin, George K. "Supreme Court's Tax Benefit Rule Decision: Unanswered Questions Invite Future Litigation." *Journal of Taxation* 59 (September 1983): 130-133.

5610. Zarrow, Stanton H., and David E. Gordon. "Supreme Court's Sale-Leaseback Decision in *Lyon* Lists Multiple Criteria." *Journal of Taxation* 49 (July 1978): 42-47.

X. The Court and Education

General Studies

5611. Allen, James E., Jr. "The Supreme Court and Public Education." *New York State Bar Journal* 38 (August 1966): 364-369; (October 1966): 435-441; (December 1966): 516-522; 39 (February 1967): 61-66.

5612. Badger, William V. "A Systematic Analysis of the United States Supreme Court Cases Dealing with Education, 1790-1951." Ed.D. diss., Florida State University, 1953.

5613. Bartlett, Lester W. "State Control of Private Incorporated Institutions of Higher Education as Defined in Decisions of the United States Supreme Court, Laws of the States Governing the Incorporation of Institutions of Higher Education, and Charters of Selected Private Colleges and Universities." Ph.D. diss., Columbia University, 1926.

5614. Bostwick, Kenneth, Jr. "The Supreme Court and Education." Ph.D. diss., Stanford University, 1956.

5615. Collier, James M., and John J. George. "Education and the Supreme Court." *Journal of Higher Education* 21 (February 1950): 77-83.

5616. Corwin, Edward S. "The Supreme Court as National School Board." *Thought* 23 (December 1948): 665-683.

5617. Drake, William E. "Educational Policy and the United States Supreme Court." *Journal of Thought* 4 (April 1969): 142-153.

5618. "Education and the Court: The Supreme Court's Educational Ideology." *Vanderbilt Law Review* 40 (May 1987): 939-981.

5619. Faber, Charles F. "The Warren Court and the Burger Court: Some Comparisons of Education-Related Decisions." *NOLPE School Law Journal* 10 (Winter 1981): 30-60.

5620. Flygare, Thomas J. "U.S. Supreme Court Reaffirms Role of Educators in Making Academic Decisions." *Phi Delta Kappan* 67 (March 1986): 537-538.

5621. Hazard, William R. "Law and Schooling: Some Observations and Questions." *Education and Urban Society* 8 (August 1976): 417-440.

5622. Hazard, William R. "Schooling and the Law: Reflections on Social Change." *Education and Urban Society* 8 (May 1976): 307-332.

5623. Heaney, Joseph P. "A Free Appropriate Public Education: Has the Supreme Court Misinterpreted Congressional Intent?" *Exceptional Children* 50 (February 1984): 456-462.

5624. Kirp, David L. "Student Classification, Public Policy, and the Courts." *Harvard Educational Review* 44 (February 1974): 7-52.

5625. Miller, Maxwell A. "Can Education Survive the 'New Equality'?" *Journal of*

Social Political and Economic Studies 9 (Spring 1984): 4-16.

5626. O'Brien, Kenneth B., Jr. "The Supreme Court and Education." Ph.D. diss., Stanford University, 1956.

5627. Schwartz, Richard A., and Ann L. Majestic. "The Supreme Court and Public Education: A Year in Review." *Urban Lawyer* 18 (Fall 1986): 991-1003.

5628. Shannon, Thomas A. "Your Stake, Mr. (or Ms.) Administrator, in Three 1974 Supreme Court Decisions." *Phi Delta Kappan* 55 (March 1974): 460-461.

5629. Spurlock, Clark P. *Education and the Supreme Court*. Urbana: University of Illinois Press, 1955.

5630. Stacey, Charles E. "The Supreme Court and the Elevation of Education to the Status of a Fundamental Right." Ph.D. diss., University of Pittsburgh, 1974.

5631. Swiger, Elinor P., Edgar H. Bittle, and Gwendolyn H. Gregory. "The Supreme Court and Public Education: A View of the Past Year." *Urban Lawyer* 17 (Fall 1985): 911-943.

5632. Turman, Ira N. "United States Supreme Court Decisions Affecting Compulsory School Attendance Laws." Ed.D. diss., East Texas State University, 1975.

5633. Van Geel, Tyll. *The Courts and American Education Law*. Buffalo, NY: Prometheus Books, 1987.

5634. Witkowiak, Stanislaus B. "The Limitations of the Rights and Powers of the State over Education According to the Decisions of the United States Supreme Court." Ph.D. diss., Catholic University of America, 1942.

5635. Zirkel, Perry A. "Checklist Based on Supreme Court Decisions Affecting Education." *NOLPE School Law Journal* 2 (1977): 199-208.

5636. Zirkel, Perry A. "A Test on Su-

preme Court Decisions Affecting Education." *Phi Delta Kappan* 59 (April 1978): 521-524.

Due Process

5637. Bangser, Henry S. "The Role of the Federal Judiciary in Directing Student-Authority Interaction." *Education and Urban Society* 8 (May 1976): 267-306.

5638. Bean, Robbie L. "Legal Rights of Elementary School Age Children." Ph.D. diss., University of Colorado, 1979.

5639. Daniels, Jack L., and C. Robert Lawson. "Procedural Due Process in Higher Education: A Protection of Students' Rights." *Southern Quarterly* 12 (April 1974): 217-223.

5640. Englander, Meryl Z. "The Court's Corporal Punishment Mandate to Parents, Local Authorities, and the Profession." *Phi Delta Kappan* 59 (April 1978): 529-532.

5641. Flygare, Thomas J. "Supreme Court Approves Corporal Punishment." *Phi Delta Kappan* 59 (January 1978): 347-348.

5642. Flygare, Thomas J. "Two Suspension Cases Supreme Court Must Decide." *Phi Delta Kappan* 56 (December 1974): 257-258.

5643. Hickman, Michael J. "The Supreme Court and the Decline of Students' Constitutional Rights: A Selective Analysis." *Nebraska Law Review* 65 (Winter 1986): 161-187.

5644. Lemley, Charles R. "Supreme Court and Corporal Punishment." *Education* 98 (Winter 1977): 228-231.

5645. Mahon, J. Patrick. "*Ingraham v. Wright*: The Continuing Debate over Corporal Punishment." *Journal of Law and Education* 6 (October 1977): 473-479.

5646. Manley-Casimer, Michael E. "Supreme Court, Students' Rights, and School Discipline." *Journal of Research and Development in Education* 11 (Summer 1978): 101-115.

5647. Mars, Michael A. "Due Process Rights of Students: Limitations on *Goss v. Lopez*: A Repeat Out of the Thicket." *Journal of Law and Education* 9 (October 1980): 449-462.

5648. Maxson, Marilyn M., and Thomas C. Hunt. "Supreme Court and Student Rights: Evolution and Emancipation?" *Contemporary Education* 52 (Summer 1981): 219-222.

5649. Piele, Phillip K. "Neither Corporal Punishment Cruel nor Due Process Due: The United States Supreme Court's Decision in *Ingraham v. Wright*." *Journal of Law and Education* 7 (January 1978): 1-19.

5650. Strope, John L. "The Impact of the United States Supreme Court on the Educational Policies of the United States with Particular Emphasis on *Goss v. Lopez* in Nebraska." Ph.D. diss., University of Nebraska, 1979.

5651. Zeffiro, William T. "The Pupil, the Constitution, and the Supreme Court." Ed.D. diss., University of Pittsburgh, 1969.

XI. Liability

Civil Rights

5652. Plotkin, Robert. "Rotten to the 'Core of *Habeas Corpus*': The Supreme Court and the Limitations on a Prisoner's Right to Sue: *Preiser v. Rodriguez.*" *Criminal Law Bulletin* 9 (July/August 1973): 518-527.

5653. Schofield, Daniel L. "Summary of Section 1983 Court Decisions Concerning Governmental Liability." *Police Chief* 53 (March 1986): 108-112.

5654. Scuro, Joseph E., Jr. "Recent Developments in Government Liability under 42 U.S.C. 1983." *Police Chief* 49 (April 1982): 20-22.

5655. Stewart, David O. "The Supreme Court Rewrites a Law: Municipal Liability under Section 1983." *Urban Lawyer* 15 (Spring 1983): 503-513.

5656. Travis, Edna H., and Bernard R. Adams. "The Supreme Court's Shell Game: The Confusion of Jurisdiction and Substantive Rights in Section 1983 Litigation." *Boston College Law Review* 24 (May 1983): 635-658.

5657. Zagrans, Eric H. "Under Color of What Law: A Reconstructed Model of Section 1983 Liability." *Virginia Law Review* 71 (May 1985): 499-598.

Other

5658. Carlson, Patricia B. "Liability of Government Appointed Attorneys in State Tort Actions." *Journal of Criminal Law and Criminology* 71 (Summer 1980): 136-146.

5659. Cooper, Phillip J. "The Supreme Court on Governmental Liability: The Nature and Origins of Sovereign and Official Immunity." *Administration and Society* 16 (November 1984): 259-288.

5660. Ellis, Dorsey D., Jr. "Economic Efficiency and Vicarious Liability for Punitive Damages: Economic Implications of *City of Newport v. Falts Concerts Inc.*" *Supreme Court Economic Review* 1 (1982): 135-162.

5661. Kales, Albert M. "The Fellow Servant Doctrine in the United States Supreme Court." *Michigan Law Review* 2 (November 1903): 79-105.

5662. McCarthy, Martha M. "Liability of School Boards and School Officials for Violations of Federal Rights." *Journal of Education Finance* 7 (Summer 1981): 128-134.

5663. McDermott, Edwin J. "The Court of Claims: The Nation's Conscience." *American Bar Association Journal* 57 (June 1971): 594-596.

5664. Malloy, Jane E. "Department of Defense Authorization Act: Leaving Atomic Veterans at Ground Zero." *Valparaiso University Law Review* 20 (Spring 1986): 413-444.

5665. Marfin, Gary C., and Jerome J. Hanus. "Supreme Court Restraints on State and Local Officials." *National Civic Review* 70 (February 1981): 83-89.

5666. Plotkin, Steven R., and Carol P. Mazorol. "Judicial Malpractice: *Pulliam* Is Not the Answer." *Trial* 20 (December 1984): 24-26.

5667. Rabin, Jack, Gerald J. Miller, and Bartley W. Hildreth. "Suing Federal Executives for Damages." *Bureaucrat* 8 (Spring 1979): 54-57.

5668. Scuro, Joseph E., Jr. "*Hensley v. Eckerhart*: The Supreme Court Strikes Back." *Police Chief* 50 (September 1983): 16.

5669. Siegel, Michael S. "High Court Rules Inmates May Seek Punitive Damages." *Trial* 19 (July 1983): 14-17.

5670. Zillman, Donald N. "Regulatory Discretion: The Supreme Court Reexamines the Discretionary Function Exception to the Federal Tort Claims Act." *Military Law Review* 110 (Fall 1985): 115-143.

XII. Public Opinion of the Court

General Studies

5671. Armstrong, Walter P. "The Supreme Court and Our Attitude towards It." *Mississippi Law Journal* 12 (May 1940): 385-392.

5672. Berkson, Larry C. *The Supreme Court and Its Publics: The Communication of Policy Decisions.* Lexington, MA: D. C. Heath, 1978.

5673. Blumenthal, Heinz. "The Supreme Court, the New Deal, and Public Opinion." Master's thesis, University of California, 1943.

5674. Caldeira, Gregory A. "Children's Images of the Supreme Court: A Preliminary Mapping." *Law and Society Review* 11 (Summer 1977): 851-871.

5675. Caldeira, Gregory A. "Neither the Purse nor the Sword: Dynamics of Public Confidence in the U.S. Supreme Court." *American Political Science Review* 80 (December 1986): 1209-1226.

5676. Caldeira, Gregory A. "Public Opinion and the U.S. Supreme Court: FDR's Court-Packing Plan." *American Political Science Review* 81 (December 1987): 1139-1154.

5677. Cantwell, Frank V. "Public Opinion and the Legislative Process." *American Political Science Review* 40 (October 1946): 924-935.

5678. Casey, Gregory. "Popular Perceptions of Supreme Court Rulings." *American Politics Quarterly* 4 (January 1976): 3-46.

5679. Casey, Gregory. "Supreme Court and Myth: An Empirical Investigation." *Law and Society Review* 8 (Spring 1974): 385-419.

5680. Casey, Gregory. "The Supreme Court: Sectors of Support among Elite and Mass." Ph.D. diss., Georgetown University, 1968.

5681. Dennis, Everette E. "Another Look at Press Coverage of the Supreme Court." *Villanova Law Review* 20 (March 1975): 765-799.

5682. Fahlund, G. Gregory. "Retroactivity and the Warren Court: The Strategy of a Revolution." *Journal of Politics* 35 (August 1973): 570-593.

5683. Gaziano, C. "Relationship between Public Opinion and Supreme Court Decisions: Was Dooley Right?" *Communication Research* 5 (April 1978): 131-149.

5684. Giles, Michael W. "Dimensions of Support for the Supreme Court." Ph.D. diss., University of Kentucky, 1971.

5685. Giles, Michael W. "Lawyers and the Supreme Court: A Comparative Look at Some Attitudinal Linkages." *Journal of Politics* 35 (May 1973): 480-486.

5686. Grey, David L. "The Supreme Court as a Communicator." *Houston Law Review* 5 (January 1968): 405-429.

5687. Handberg, Roger B., Jr. "Public

Opinion and the United States Supreme Court, 1935-1981." *International Social Science Review* 59 (Winter 1984): 3-13.

5688. Kessel, John H. "Public Perceptions of the Supreme Court." *Midwest Journal of Political Science* 10 (May 1966): 167-191.

5689. Lewis, Anthony. "The Supreme Court and Its Critics." *Minnesota Law Review* 45 (January 1961): 302-332.

5690. Morgner, Fred. "Ultra Conservative Response to Supreme Court Judicial Behavior: A Study in Political Alienation, 1935-1965." Ph.D. diss., University of Minnesota, 1970.

5691. Moynihan, Daniel P. "What Do You Do When the Supreme Court Is Wrong?" *Public Interest* 57 (Fall 1979): 3-24.

5692. Murphy, Walter F., and Joseph Tanenhaus. "Explaining Diffuse Support for the United States Supreme Court: An Assessment of Four Models." *Notre Dame Law Review* 49 (June 1974): 1037-1044.

5693. Murphy, Walter F., and Joseph Tanenhaus. "Public Opinion and Supreme Court: The Goldwater Campaign." *Public Opinion Quarterly* 32 (Spring 1968): 31-51.

5694. Murphy, Walter F., and Joseph Tanenhaus. "Public Opinion and the United States Supreme Court." *Law and Society Review* 2 (May 1968): 357-384.

5695. Murphy, Walter F., Joseph Tanenhaus, and Daniel Kastner. *Public Evaluations of Constitutional Courts: Alternative Explanations.* Beverly Hills, CA: Sage Publications, 1973.

5696. Nowak, John E. "Professor Rodell, the Burger Court, and Public Opinion." *Constitutional Commentary* 1 (Winter 1984): 107-130.

5697. Ogden, R. " 'Attacking' the Supreme Court." *Nation* 73 (August 29, 1901): 162-163.

5698. Rankin, J. Lee. "An Independent Supreme Court." *University of Pittsburgh Law Review* 20 (June 1958): 785-794.

5699. Rhyne, Charles S. "Defending Our Courts: The Duty of the Legal Profession." *American Bar Association Journal* 44 (February 1958): 121-124.

5700. Schweppe, Alfred J. "Criticism of the Supreme Court." *Massachusetts Law Quarterly* 44 (April 1959): 31-32.

5701. Sheldon, Charles H. "Public Opinion and High Courts: Communist Party Cases in Four Constitutional Systems." *Western Political Quarterly* 20 (June 1967): 341-360.

5702. Sigelman, Lee. "Black-White Differences in Attitudes toward the Supreme Court: A Replication in the 1970s." *Social Science Quarterly* 60 (June 1979): 113-119.

5703. Smith, Sylvester C., Jr. "Public Opinion Defeated the Court Bill." *American Bar Association Journal* 23 (August 1937): 575-582, 647-648.

5704. Stafford, Charles F. "The Public's View of the Judicial Role." *Judicature* 52 (August/September 1968): 73-77.

5705. Steinert, Neal S. "The Supreme Court as an Effector of Attitude Change in Mass Publics: A Quasi-Experimental Approach." Ph.D. diss., Emory University, 1973.

5706. Sutherland, Arthur E., Jr. "Supreme Court and the General Will." *American Academy of Arts and Science Proceedings* 82 (April 1954): 169-197.

5707. Tanenhaus, Joseph, and Walter F. Murphy. "Patterns of Public Support for the Supreme Court: A Panel Study." *Journal of Politics* 43 (February 1981): 24-39.

5708. Tresolini, Rocco J. "In Defense of the Supreme Court." *Social Science* 36 (January 1961): 37-44.

5709. Turner, William B. "From the Tanner Hearings to *The Brethren* and Beyond: Judicial Accountability and Judicial Independence." *California State Bar Journal* 55 (July 1980): 292-297.

Media and the Court

5710. Anderson, Douglas A., Joe W. Milner, and Mary-Lou Galician. "How Editors View Legal Issues and the Rehnquist Court." *Journalism Quarterly* 65 (Summer 1988): 294-298.

5711. Bow, James, and Ben Silver. "Attitudes of New Directors and Managing Editors." *Journalism Quarterly* 60 (Fall 1983): 533-535; 71 (October 1983): 30-33.

5712. Dahms, William R. "Press Coverage of the Supreme Court: A Troubling Question." *Intellect* 106 (February 1978): 299-301.

5713. Davis, Richard. "Lifting the Shroud: News Media Portrayal of the U.S. Supreme Court." *Communications and the Law* 9 (October 1987): 43-59.

5714. Ericson, David. "Newspaper Coverage of the Supreme Court: A Case Study." *Journalism Quarterly* 54 (Autumn 1977): 605-607.

5715. Grey, David L. *The Supreme Court and the News Media.* Evanston, IL: Northwestern University Press, 1968.

5716. Hachten, William A. *The Supreme Court and the Press.* Washington, DC: Public Affairs Press, 1965.

5717. Haltom, William T. "The Judicial and Social Construction of Constitutionality: The Supreme Court and Newspaper Editorials." Ph.D. diss., University of Washington, 1984.

5718. Katsh, Ethan. "The Supreme Court Beat: How Television Covers the United States Supreme Court." *Judicature* 67 (June/July 1983): 7-12.

5719. Kurzman, Charles. "ABC's Timothy O'Brien: The High Court in a Minute-Twenty." *American Lawyer* 6 (December 1984): 85-88.

5720. McGurn, Barret. "Public Information at the United States Supreme Court." *American Bar Association Journal* 69 (January 1983): 40-45.

5721. Morris, Jeffrey B. "Niles Register and the Supreme Court." *Supreme Court Historical Society Yearbook* 1978 (1978): 50-60.

5722. Newland, Chester A. "Press Coverage of the United States Supreme Court." *Western Political Quarterly* 17 (March 1964): 15-36.

5723. Rivers, William L. "Justice Takes the Veil." *Quill* 70 (June 1982): 33-36.

5724. Sobel, Lionel S. "News Coverage of the Supreme Court." *American Bar Association Journal* 56 (June 1970): 547-550.

5725. Solimine, Michael E. "Newsmagazine Coverage of the Supreme Court." *Journalism Quarterly* 57 (Winter 1980): 661-663.

5726. Sultan, Alan. " 'Deep Throat' Journalism and the Supreme Court: A Case of 'Burning the Barn to Roast the Pig'?" *Northern Kentucky Law Review* 7 (1980): 323-350.

5727. Tarpley, J. Douglas. "American Newsmagazine Coverage of the Supreme Court, 1978-1981." *Journalism Quarterly* (Winter 1984): 801-804, 826.

5728. Weisberger, Joseph R. "Supreme Court and the Press: Is Accommodation Possible?" *Judges Journal* 19 (Winter 1980): 14-15.

5729. Weisberger, Joseph R. "Supreme Court and the Press: Is Accommodation Possible?" *Michigan State Bar Journal* 59 (December 1980): 846, 848-849.

XIII. The Impact and Implementation of Decisions

5730. Agree, George E. "Public Financing after the Supreme Court Decision." *Annals of the American Academy of Political and Social Science* 425 (May 1976): 134-142.

5731. Allen, Edmund T., III. "Constitutional Law: Four to Three Decisions of the United States Supreme Court Are Not Binding on the State of Arizona." *Law and Social Order* 1973 (1973): 543-549.

5732. Aronson, Albert H. The Duke Power Company *Case: An Interpretative Commentary on the U.S. Supreme Decision, with Particular Reference to Its Implications for Governmental Personnel Selection Practices.* Chicago: Public Personnel Association, 1971.

5733. Atleson, James B. "The Aftermath of *Baker v. Carr*: An Adventure in Judicial Experimentation." *California Law Review* 51 (August 1963): 535-572.

5734. Ban, Michael M. "Local Compliance with *Mapp v. Ohio*: The Power of the Supreme Court." Ph.D. diss., Harvard University, 1973.

5735. Barker, Lucius J. "Black Americans and the Burger Court: Implications for the Political System." *Washington University Law Quarterly* 1973 (Fall 1973): 747-777.

5736. Barth, Thomas E. "Perception and Acceptance of Supreme Court Decisions at the State and Local Level: The Case of Obscenity Policy in Wisconsin." Ph.D. diss., University of Wisconsin, 1968.

5737. Baum, Lawrence. "Lower Court Response to Supreme Court Decisions: Reconsidering a Negative Picture." *Justice System Journal* 3 (Spring 1978): 208-219.

5738. Beatty, Jerry K. "State Court Evasion of United States Supreme Court Mandates during the Last Decade of the Warren Court." *Valparaiso University Law Review* 6 (Spring 1972): 260-285.

5739. Becker, Theodore L., and Malcolm M. Feeley, eds. *The Impact of Supreme Court Decisions: Empirical Studies.* 2d ed. New York: Oxford University Press, 1973.

5740. Behan, Thomas R. "The Post-Warren Freedom Survey: Report 1." *American Bar Association Journal* 56 (January 1970): 54-56.

5741. Bender, Louis, and Steven Bender. "Is the Supreme Court's Decision in *Baggot* Retroactive in Application?" *Journal of Taxation* 60 (March 1984): 138-144.

5742. Benjamin, Robert E., and Martin T. Farris. "The Implications of the Colorado River Suit to Arizona." *Arizona Business Bulletin* 10 (September 1963): 3-11.

5743. Binion, Gayle. "Implementation of Section 5 of the 1965 Voting Rights Act: A Retrospective on the Role of Courts." *Western Political Quarterly* 32 (June 1979): 154-173.

5744. Bond, Jon R., and Charles A. Johnson. "Implementing a Permissive Policy: Hospital Abortion Services after *Roe v.*

Wade." American Journal of Political Science 26 (February 1982): 1-24.

5745. Boyte, Sam. "Federal *Habeas Corpus* after *Stone v. Powell*: A Remedy Only for the Arguably Innocent?" *University of Richmond Law Review* 11 (Winter 1977): 291-331.

5746. Bratz, David C. "*Stare Decisis* in Lower Courts: Predicting the Demise of Supreme Court Precedent." *Washington Law Review* 60 (December 1984): 87-100.

5747. Bridges, S. Powell. "The *Schwinn* Case: A Landmark Decision." *Business Horizons* (August 1968): 77-85.

5748. Broderick, Albert. "Affirmative Action after *Stotts*: The United States Supreme Court's 1985 Term." *North Carolina Central Law Journal* 15 (1985): 145-212.

5749. Browne, Harry L. "The Impact of Supreme Court Decisions on Free Collective Bargaining." *American Bar Association Journal* 51 (February 1965): 137-142.

5750. Bryner, Gary. "Congress, Courts, and Agencies: Equal Employment and the Limits of Policy Implementation." *Political Science Quarterly* 96 (Fall 1981): 411-430.

5751. Butler, Daniel P., and Timothy C. Cook. "After *Rowley*: An Effective Education for Handicapped Children." *Trial* 18 (September 1982): 71-75.

5752. Caldeira, Gregory A. "Judges Judge the Supreme Court: State and Federal Judges Sometimes Disagree with Specific Decisions, but They Generally Support the Nation's Highest Court." *Judicature* 61 (November 1977): 208-219.

5753. Caldeira, Gregory A. "Lower Court Judges and the American Supreme Court: Legitimacy, Judicial Power, and Public Policy." Ph.D. diss., Princeton University, 1978.

5754. Canon, Bradley C. "Reactions of State Supreme Courts to a United States Supreme Court Civil Liberties Decision." *Law and Society Review* 8 (Fall 1973): 109-134.

5755. Canon, Bradley C. "Testing the Effectiveness of Civil Liberties Policies at the State and Federal Levels: The Case of the Exclusionary Rule." *American Politics Quarterly* 5 (January 1977): 57-82.

5756. Carmen, Ira H. "State and Local Motion Picture Censorship and Constitutional Liberties with Special Emphasis on the Communal Acceptance of Supreme Court Decision Making." Ph.D. diss., University of Michigan, 1964.

5757. Cayton, Charles E. "Relationship of the Probation Officer and the Defense Attorney after *Gault*." *Federal Probation* 34 (March 1970): 8-13.

5758. Chamberlain, Daniel H. "*Osborn versus the Bank of the United States*." *Harvard Law Review* 1 (December 1887): 223-225.

5759. Chapman, Samuel G. "Functional Problems Facing Law Enforcement Stemming from Supreme Court Decisions." *Police* 11 (September/October 1966): 44-48.

5760. Choper, Jesse H. "Consequences of Supreme Court Decisions Upholding Individual Constitutional Rights." *Michigan Law Review* 83 (October 1984): 1-212.

5761. Clarke, Carlene A. "*Yeshiva* Case: An Analysis and an Assessment of Its Potential Impact on Public Universities." *Journal of Higher Education* 52 (September/October 1987): 449-469.

5762. Coleburn, David R., and Richard K. Scher. "Aftermath of the *Brown* Decision: The Politics of Interposition in Florida." *Tequesta* 37 (1977): 62-81.

5763. Dalton, Thomas C. "The State Politics of Congressional and Judicial Reform: Implementing Criminal Records Policy." Ph.D. diss., University of Massachusetts, 1984.

5764. Dane, John, Jr. "Some Implications of the Recent Supreme Court Decisions on State Taxation of Income from Interstate Commerce." *Tax Policy* 26 (June/July 1959): 3-11.

5765. Dasburg, John H., and Donald E. Flannery. "Inventory Valuation after *Thor Power Tool*: Analyzing the Supreme Court Decision and Its Impact." *Journal of Taxation* 50 (April 1979): 200-205.

5766. Dometruis, Nelson C., and Lee Sigelman. "Modeling the Impact of Supreme Court Decisions: *Wygant v. Board.*" *Journal of Politics* 50 (February 1988): 131-149.

5767. Dukette, Rita, and Nicholas Stevenson. "Legal Rights of Unmarried Fathers: The Impact of Recent Court Decisions." *Social Service Review* 47 (March 1973): 1-15.

5768. "Effect of U.S. Supreme Court Decisions on Lower Federal Courts." *Texas Bar Journal* 11 (May 1948): 303.

5769. Eisenstein, James. "The Impact of Higher Courts." In *Politics and the Legal Process*, by James Eisenstein, 277-306. New York: Harper and Row, 1973.

5770. Erler, Edward J. "Sowing the Wind: Judicial Oligarchy and the Legacy of *Brown v. Board of Education.*" *Harvard Journal of Law and Public Policy* 8 (Spring 1985): 398-426.

5771. Falwell, Jerry, ed. "Judgement without Justice: Abortion on Demand Ten Years Later." *Fundamentalists Journal* 2 (January 1983): 8-35.

5772. Gassman, Benjamin. "The Effect of Recent U.S. Supreme Court Decisions on Law Enforcement." *Bar Bulletin* (New York County) 22 (1964/1965): 210-219.

5773. Gregory, Donald D. "Compliance in Three Cities: The Impact of *Freedman v. Maryland.*" Ph.D. diss., Southern Illinois University, 1977.

5774. Gruhl, John. "Anticipatory Compli-ance with Supreme Court Rulings." *Polity* 14 (Winter 1981): 294-313.

5775. Gruhl, John. "State Supreme Courts and the U.S. Supreme Court's Post-*Miranda* Rulings." *Journal of Criminal Law and Criminology* 72 (Fall 1981): 886-913.

5776. Gruhl, John. "The Supreme Court's Impact on the Law of Libel: Compliance by Lower Federal Courts." *Western Political Quarterly* 33 (December 1980): 502-519.

5777. Gruhl, John, and Cassia Spohn. "The Supreme Court's Post-*Miranda* Rulings: Impact on Local Prosecutors." *Law and Policy Quarterly* 3 (January 1981): 29-54.

5778. Gryski, Gerard S., Eleanor C. Main, and William J. Dixon. "Models of State High Court Decision Making in Sex Discrimination Cases." *Journal of Politics* 48 (February 1986): 143-155.

5779. Haas, Kenneth C. "New Federalism and Prisoners' Rights: State Supreme Courts in Comparative Perspective." *Western Political Quarterly* 34 (December 1981): 552-577.

5780. Haas, Kenneth C. "Reactions of Lower Federal and State Courts to United States Supreme Court Prisoners' Rights Decisions: A Comparative Analysis." Ph.D. diss., Rutgers University, 1978.

5781. Hansen, Susan B. "State Implementation of Supreme Court Decisions: Abortion Rates since *Roe v. Wade.*" *Journal of Politics* 42 (May 1980): 372-395.

5782. Hazard, William R., and Victor G. Rosenblum. "Education, the Law, and Social Change." *Education and Urban Society* 8 (May 1976): 259-374.

5783. Higgins, Chester A. "Boycott Decision Has Wrought Miracle Changes in Port Gibson." *Crisis* 89 (October 1982): 19-22.

5784. Hiller, Janine S. "Civil Rights Enforcement and Japanese Subsidiaries." *American Business Law Journal* 21 (Winter 1984): 463-474.

5785. Houck, Robert F. "The Impact of Federal, Judicial, and Legislative Decisions of Educational Practices during the Warren Years: 1953 to 1969." Ph.D. diss., St. Louis University, 1978.

5786. Hughes, Robert M. "Writs of Error from the United States Supreme Court to Virginia Courts." *Virginia Law Review* 1 (February 1914): 361-378.

5787. Iannone, Ronald H. "The 1975 *Wood v. Strickland* Supreme Court Decision: Its Impact on School Board Members and School Board Candidates in Los Angeles County, California." Ed.D. diss., Brigham Young University, 1978.

5788. "Issue of District Court's Compliance with Supreme Court Mandate Held Not Appealable to Circuit Court of Appeals." *Harvard Law Review* 55 (December 1941): 288-289.

5789. Jacobs, Robert. "The State of *Miranda*: The Effects of the *Quarles* Decision." *Trial* 21 (January 1985): 44-48.

5790. Johnson, Charles A. "Do Lower Courts Anticipate Changes in Supreme Court Policies? A Few Empirical Notes." *Law and Policy Quarterly* 3 (January 1981): 55-68.

5791. Johnson, Charles A. "Law, Politics, and Judicial Decisionmaking: Lower Federal Court Uses of Supreme Court Decisions." *Law and Society Review* 21 (Fall 1987): 325-340.

5792. Johnson, Charles A. "Lower Court Reactions to Supreme Court Decisions: A Quantitative Examination." *American Journal of Political Science* 23 (November 1979): 792-804.

5793. Johnson, Charles A., and Bradley C. Canon. *Judicial Policies: Implementation and Impact.* Washington, DC: Congressional Quarterly Press, 1984.

5794. Johnson, Richard M. "Compliance and Supreme Court Decision-making." *Wisconsin Law Review* 1967 (Winter 1967): 170-185.

5795. Johnson, Richard M. *The Dynamics of Compliance: Supreme Court Decision Making from a New Perspective.* Evanston, IL: Northwestern University Press, 1967.

5796. Jones, Nathaniel R. "The *Brown* Decision: 25 Years Later." *Crisis* 86 (June/July 1979): 211-214.

5797. Koob, C. Albert. "Look at the *Oregon School* Case after Fifty Years." *Religious Education* 71 (March/April 1976): 164-170.

5798. Kovey, Mark H. "Impact of Supreme Court Decision Limiting Withholding on Employee's Meal Allowances." *Journal of Taxation* 48 (May 1978): 276-279.

5799. Kozlowicz, John F. "The Impact of Recent Supreme Court Decisions on Tucson Law Enforcement." Ph.D. diss., University of Arizona, 1970.

5800. Kurland, Philip B. *The Constitutional Impact on Public Policy: From the Warren Court to the Burger Court and Beyond.* Washington, DC: Washington Institute for Values in Public Policy, 1984.

5801. Lander, Ernest M., Jr., and Richard J. Calhoun. *Two Decades of Change: The South since the Supreme Court Desegregation Decision.* Columbia: University of South Carolina Press, 1975.

5802. Lange, Glen E. "An Appraisal of the Effect of Supreme Court Decisions on Deprecation for Rate-Making Purposes in Selected Public Utilities." Ph.D. diss., University of Missouri, 1969.

5803. Leff, Donna R. "Journalists and Jurists: The Evolution of Reporter's Privilege after *Branzburg*." Ph.D. diss., University of California, Berkeley, 1982.

5804. Levine, James P. "Methodological

Concerns in Studying Supreme Court Efficacy." *Law and Society Review* 4 (May 1970): 583-611.

5805. Levine, James P., and Theodore L. Becker. "Toward and Beyond a Theory of Supreme Court Impact." *American Behavioral Scientist* 13 (March 1970): 561-573.

5806. Lewis, John B., and Bruce L. Ottley. "*New York Times v. Sullivan*: Its Continuing Impact on Libel Law." *Trial* 21 (October 1985): 59-65.

5807. Lewis, Peter W., and Harry E. Allen. "The Impact of Supreme Court Decisions of the Crime Rate in America: An Empirical Test Utilizing Regression Analysis." *Chitty's Law Journal* 25 (September 1977): 229-234.

5808. Long, Joseph R. "The Enforcement of Judgements against a State." *Vanderbilt Law Review* 4 (December 1916): 154-173.

5809. Luce, Willard R. "*Cohens v. Virginia* (1821), the Supreme Court and States Rights: A Reevaluation of Influences and Impacts." Ph.D. diss., University of Virginia, 1978.

5810. McAllister, Breck P. "*Ex Post Facto* Laws in Supreme Court of United States." *California Law Review* 15 (May 1927): 269-288.

5811. Malbin, Michael J. "Supreme Court's Ruling on Election Law Causes Confusion." *National Journal* 8 (February 7, 1976): 167-168.

5812. Malone, Patrick A. " 'You Have the Right to Remain Silent': *Miranda* after Twenty Years." *American Scholar* 55 (Summer 1986): 367-380.

5813. Manwaring, David R., Donald R. Reich, and Stephen L. Wasby. *The Supreme Court as Policy Maker: Three Studies on the Impact of Judicial Decisions*. Carbondale: Public Affairs Research Bureau, Southern Illinois University, 1968.

5814. Menacker, Julius, and Ernest

Pascarella. "How Aware Are Educators of Supreme Court Decisions That Affect Them?" *Phi Delta Kappan* 64 (February 1983): 424-426.

5815. Milner, Neal A. "Comparative Analysis of Patterns of Compliance with Supreme Court Decisions: 'Miranda' and the Police in Four Communities." *Law and Society Review* 5 (August 1970): 119-134.

5816. Milner, Neal A. *Court and Local Law Enforcement: The Political Impact of Miranda*. Beverly Hills, CA: Sage Publications, 1971.

5817. Milner, Neal A. "Supreme Court Effectiveness and the Police Organization." *Law and Contemporary Problems* 36 (Autumn 1971): 467-487.

5818. O'Leary, Vincent, and Kathleen Hanrahan. "The Impact of *Morrissey* and *Gagnon* on Parole Revocation Proceedings." *Journal of Criminal Law and Criminology* 69 (Summer 1978): 160-169.

5819. Ostrager, Barry R. "Retroactivity and Prospectivity of Supreme Court Constitutional Interpretations." *New York Law Forum* 19 (Fall 1973): 289-308.

5820. Patric, Gordon. "The Impact of a Court Decision: Aftermath of the *McCollum* Case." *Journal of Public Law* 6 (Fall 1957): 455-464.

5821. Peters, C. David "The Demise of 'One Man, One Vote': Changes in Legislative Representation in the United States since *Baker v. Carr* and *Reynolds v. Sims*." Ph.D. diss., University of Oklahoma, 1977.

5822. Petrick, Michael J. "The Supreme Court and Authority Acceptance." *Western Political Quarterly* 21 (March 1968): 5-19.

5823. Plitt, Emory A., Jr. "The Impact of *Leon* and *Sheppard* on Police Training: Remarks." *Police Chief* 52 (March 1985): 76-78.

5824. Rivell, Gerard J. "Aid to Private Schools and the 'Child Benefit' Theory: A Historical Study of the Legal Impact of Two Key Supreme Court Decisions." Ed.D. diss., Boston University, 1972.

5825. Rodgers, Harrell R., Jr. "The Supreme Court and School Desegregation: Twenty Years Later." *Political Science Quarterly* 89 (Winter 1974/1975): 751-776.

5826. Romans, Neil T. "*Escobedo* and the State Supreme Courts: A Study in Judicial Impact Analysis." Ph.D. diss., University of Massachusetts, 1969.

5827. Romans, Neil T. "The Role of State Supreme Courts in Judicial Policy Making: *Escobedo, Miranda,* and the Use of Judicial Impact Analysis." *Western Political Quarterly* 27 (March 1974): 38-59.

5828. Rosenblum, Robert. "Politics of the Judiciary: The Impact of Supreme Court and Lower Court Interdependence on Policy Outcome." Ph.D. diss., University of Colorado, Boulder, 1974.

5829. Rossum, Ralph A. "Problems in Municipal Court Administration and the Stress of Supreme Court Decisions: A Memphis Case Study." *American Journal of Criminal Law* 3 (Summer 1974): 53-84.

5830. Shiras, Oliver P. *Equity Practice in the United States Circuit Courts: A Compilation of the Provisions Governing the Same as Found in the Statutes of the United States, Rules in Equity, and Decisions of the Supreme Court.* 2d ed. Chicago: Callaghan, 1898.

5831. Sindt, Roger P., and Donald A. Nielsen. "A Conceptual Analysis of Financial Impacts of the 1982 U.S. Supreme Court Due-On-Sale Clause Decision." *Appraisal Journal* 52 (January 1984): 60-74.

5832. Smolin, David M. "State Regulation of Private Education: Ohio Law in the Shadow of the United States Supreme Court Decisions." *University of Cincinnati Law Review* 54 (1986): 1003-1033.

5833. Songer, Donald R. "The Impact of the Supreme Court on Trends in Economic Policy Making in the United States Court of Appeals." *Journal of Politics* 49 (August 1987): 830-844.

5834. Spencer, Eber A. "The Role of Federal District Courts in Securing Obedience to Supreme Court Mandates." Ph.D. diss., Columbia University, 1964.

5835. Stidham, Ronald, and Robert A. Carp. "Trial Courts' Responses to Supreme Court Policy Changes: Three Case Studies." *Law and Policy Quarterly* 4 (April 1982): 215-234.

5836. Tarr, George A. *Judicial Impact and State Supreme Courts.* Lexington, MA: Lexington Books, 1977.

5837. Temple, David G. "Facing Up to *Gideon*: Florida, Swiftly Obeying Supreme Court Decisions, Opens Prison Doors for More Than 1,000 Convicts." *National Civic Review* 54 (July 1965): 354-356, 386.

5838. Teschner, Paul A. "*Basye* Projected: Fringe Benefits and the Supreme Court." *Taxes* 51 (June 1973): 324-354.

5839. Thomas, David V. "World Court and the United States Supreme Court." *American Review* 4 (May 1926): 257-267.

5840. Thompson, Robert S. "Burger Court in the California Crystal Ball." *Southwestern University Law Review* 5 (Summer 1973): 238-261.

5841. Thompson, William N. "Transmission or Resistance: Opinions of State Attorneys General and the Impact of the Supreme Court." *Valparaiso University Law Review* 9 (Fall 1974): 55-86.

5842. Thornberry, Mary C. "Local Level Compliance with Supreme Court Decisions." Ph.D. diss., University of Michigan, 1975.

5843. Ulmer, S. Sidney. "Supreme Court Opinions: Getting the Message." *Law and Policy Quarterly* 3 (July 1981): 263-290.

5844. Wald, Michael, et al. "Interrogations in New Haven: The Impact of *Miranda*." *Yale Law Journal* 76 (July 1967): 1521-1648.

5845. Wasby, Stephen L. "Getting the Message Across: Communicating Court Decisions to the Police." *Justice System Journal* 1 (Winter 1974): 29-38.

5846. Wasby, Stephen L. *The Impact of the United States Supreme Court: Some Perspectives.* Homewood, IL: Dorsey Press, 1970.

5847. Wasby, Stephen L. "Police and the Law in Illinois: A First Look at the Communication of Supreme Court Decisions." *Public Affairs Bulletin* 5 (September/October 1972): 1-10.

5848. Wasby, Stephen L. *Small Town Police and the Supreme Court: Hearing the Word.* Lexington, MA: Lexington Books, 1976.

5849. Wasby, Stephen L. "The Study of Supreme Court Impacts: A Round-Up." *Policy Studies Journal* 2 (Winter 1973): 136-140.

5850. Wasby, Stephen L. "The Supreme Court's Impact: Some Problems of Conceptualization and Measurement." *Law and Society Review* 5 (August 1970): 41-60.

5851. Wasby, Stephen L. "United States Supreme Court's Impact: Broadening Our Focus." *Notre Dame Lawyer* 49 (June 1974): 1023-1036.

5852. Wood, David M. *The Effect of Recent Decisions of the United States Supreme Court upon State and Municipal Bonds.* New York: Municipal Forum of New York, 1957.

XIV. The Members of the Court

General Studies

5853. Ackerman, Bruce. "Transformative Appointments." *Harvard Law Review* 101 (April 1988): 1146-1229.

5854. Adams, Rodney, Jr. "No Outside Work: Supreme Court Justices." *Alabama Lawyer* 9 (October 1948): 468-469.

5855. Allman, Redmond J. "Variation in the Number of Associate Justices on the Supreme Court of the United States." *Confluence* 3 (December 1953): 22-36.

5856. Allman, Redmond J. "Variation in the Number of Associate Justices on the Supreme Court of the United States from 1801 to 1869." Ph.D. diss., University of Notre Dame, 1955.

5857. Altfeld, Michael F., and Harold J. Spaeth. "Measuring Influence on the U.S. Supreme Court." *Jurimetrics Journal* 24 (Spring 1984): 236-247.

5858. Armstrong, Walter P. "Books of Interest to the Supreme Court Members: What Do the Justices Read?" *American Bar Association Journal* 35 (April 1949): 295-298.

5859. Asch, Sidney H. *The Supreme Court and Its Great Justices.* New York: Arco, 1971.

5860. Atkinson, David N. "Minor Supreme Court Justices: Their Characteristics and Importance." *Florida State University Law Review* 3 (Summer 1975): 348-359.

5861. Baker, Leonard. "The Circuit Riding Justices." *Supreme Court Historical Society Yearbook* 1977 (1977): 63-69.

5862. Baldwin, Elbert F. "Supreme Court Justices." *Outlook* 97 (January 1911): 156-165.

5863. Ballantine, Arthur A. "The Supreme Court: Principles and Personalities." *American Bar Association* 31 (March 1945): 113-115.

5864. Bancroft, Frederic. "Some Radicals as Statesmen: Chase, Sumner, Adams, and Stevens." *Atlantic Monthly* 86 (August 1900): 276-283.

5865. Barbar, James. *Honorable Eighty-eight.* New York: Vantage, 1957.

5866. Barnes, Catherine A. *Men of the Supreme Court: Profiles of the Justices.* New York: Facts on File, 1978.

5867. Barnes, William H. *The Supreme Court of the United States: A Series of Biographies.* Washington, DC: Barnes, 1877.

5868. Barth, Alan. *Prophets with Honor: Great Dissents and Great Dissenters in the Supreme Court.* New York: Knopf, 1974.

5869. Bell, Peter A. "Extrajudicial Activity of Supreme Court Justices." *Stanford Law Review* 22 (February 1970): 587-617.

5870. Berkson, Larry C. "Supreme Court Justices: Effective Encoders of Supreme Court Decisions." *American Business Law Journal* 14 (Winter 1977): 391-404.

5871. Bickel, Alexander M. "The Making of Supreme Court Justices." *New Leader* 53 (May 25, 1970): 14-18.

5872. Blackman, Paul H. "Judicial Biography and Public Law: An Analysis with Emphasis on the New Deal Court." Ph.D. diss., University of Virginia, 1971.

5873. Blaustein, Albert P., and Roy M. Mersky. *The First One Hundred Justices: Statistical Studies on the Supreme Court of the United States*. Hamden, CT: Archon Books, 1978.

5874. Blaustein, Albert P., and Roy M. Mersky. "Rating Supreme Court Justices." *American Bar Association Journal* 58 (November 1952): 1183-1189.

5875. Brenner, Saul. "Another Look at Freshman Indecisiveness on the United States Supreme Court." *Polity* 16 (Winter 1983): 320-328.

5876. Buchanan, John G. "Justices of the United States Supreme Court from Pennsylvania." *Pennsylvania Bar Association Quarterly* 16 (January 1945): 143-151.

5877. Campbell, Tom W. *Four Score Forgotten Men: Sketches of the Justices of the U.S. Supreme Court*. Little Rock, AR: Pioneer, 1950.

5878. Chafee, Zechariah, Jr. "Liberal Trends in the Supreme Court." *Current History* 35 (December 1931): 338-344.

5879. Chase, Harold W. "Catholics on the Court." *New Republic* 143 (September 26, 1960): 13.

5880. Christensen, George A. "Here Lies the Supreme Court: Gravesites of the Justices." *Supreme Court Historical Society Yearbook* 1983 (1983): 17-30.

5881. Christman, Henry M. "Supreme Court from Taft to Warren." *Saturday Review* 41 (October 11, 1958): 40.

5882. Cibes, William J., Jr. "Extra-Judicial Activities of Justices of the United States Supreme Court, 1790-1960." Ph.D. diss., Princeton University, 1975.

5883. Coleman, Elizabeth D. "Till Death Did Them Part." *Virginia Cavalcade* 5 (Autumn 1955): 14-19.

5884. Conry, Joseph A. "Massachusetts in the Supreme Court of the United States and in the Office of the Attorney General." *Massachusetts Law Quarterly* 21 (July 1936): 29-37.

5885. Corwin, Edward S. "Statesmanship on the Supreme Court." *American Scholar* 9 (Spring 1940): 159-163.

5886. Currie, George R. "A Judicial All-Star Nine." *Wisconsin Law Review* 1964 (January 1964): 3-31.

5887. Curtis, William E. "The Seven Chief Justices of the United States." *Chautauquan* 25 (July 1897): 339-347.

5888. Danelski, David J. "A Supreme Court Justice Steps Down." *Yale Review* 54 (March 1965): 411-425.

5889. DeVergie, Adrienne, and Mary K. Kell. *Locations Guide to the Manuscripts of Supreme Court Justices*. Austin: Tarlton Law Library, University of Texas School of Law, 1981.

5890. Dorin, Dennis D. "Social Leadership, Humor, and Supreme Court Decision Making." *Judicature* 66 (May 1983): 462-468.

5891. Ducat, Craig R., and Victor Z. Flango. "The Outsider on the Court." *Journal of Politics* 47 (February 1985): 282-289.

5892. Dunham, Allison, and Philip B. Kurland, eds. *Mr. Justice: Biographical Studies of Twelve Supreme Court Justices*. Rev. ed. Chicago: University of Chicago Press, 1965.

5893. Easterbrook, Frank H. "The Most Insignificant Justice: Further Evidence." *University of Chicago Law Review* 50 (Spring 1983): 481-503.

5894. Eastland, James O. *Is the Supreme Court Pro-Communist? Here Are Facts as Disclosed by U.S. Senator James O. Eastland.* Richmond, VA: Patrick Henry Group, 1962.

5895. Ewing, Cortez A. *The Judges of the Supreme Court, 1789-1937: A Study of Their Qualifications.* Minneapolis: University of Minnesota Press, 1938.

5896. Fairman, Charles. "Retirement of Federal Judges." *Harvard Law Review* 51 (January 1938): 397-430.

5897. Felleman, Frank, and John C. Wright, Jr. "The Powers of the Supreme Court Justice Acting in an Individual Capacity." *University of Pennsylvania Law Review* 112 (April 1964): 981-1024.

5898. Fellman, David. "The Diminution of Judicial Salaries." *Iowa Law Review* 24 (November 1938): 89-126.

5899. Flanders, Henry. *The Lives and Times of the Chief Justices of the Supreme Court of the United States.* 2 vols. Philadelphia: Johnson, 1881.

5900. Flynn, James J. *Famous Justices of the Supreme Court.* New York: Dodd, Mead, 1968.

5901. Foulke, William D. *A Generation of Judges by Their Reporter.* Buffalo, NY: William S. Hein, 1973.

5902. Frank, John P. "Conflict of Interest and U.S. Supreme Court Justices." *American Journal of Comparative Law* 18 (1970): 744-761.

5903. Freund, Paul A. "Appointment of Justices: Some Historical Perspectives." *Harvard Law Review* 101 (April 1988): 1146-1229.

5904. Friedman, Leon, and Fred L. Israel, eds. *The Justices of the United States Supreme Court: 1789-1978.* 5 vols. New York: Chelsea House, 1980.

5905. Funston, Richard Y. "Great Presi-

dents, Great Justices?" *Presidential Studies Quarterly* 7 (Fall 1977): 191-199.

5906. Gardner, Woodford L., Jr. "Kentucky Justices on the U.S. Supreme Court." *Kentucky Historical Society Register* 70 (April 1972): 121-142.

5907. Garment, Suzanne. "The War against Robert H. Bork." *Commentary* 85 (January 1988): 17-26.

5908. Gibson, James L. "Judges' Role Orientations, Attitudes, and Decisions: An Interactive Model." *American Political Science Review* 72 (September 1978): 911-924.

5909. Goff, John S. "Old Age and the Supreme Court." *American Journal of Legal History* 4 (April 1960): 95-106.

5910. Goldwater, Barry. "Political Philosophy and Supreme Court Justices." *American Bar Association Journal* 58 (February 1972): 135-140.

5911. Griggs, John W. "Have the United States Judges Adequate Salaries?" *Independent* 65 (November 19, 1908): 1155-1158.

5912. Grossman, Joel B. "Dissenting Blocs on the Warren Court: A Study in Judicial Role Behavior." *Journal of Politics* 30 (November 1968): 1068-1090.

5913. Hambleton, James E. "All-Time All-Star All-Era Supreme Court." *American Bar Association Journal* 69 (April 1983): 462-464.

5914. Handberg, Roger B., Jr., and Harold F. Hill. "Predicting the Judicial Performance of Presidential Appointments to the United States Supreme Court." *Presidential Studies Quarterly* 14 (Fall 1984): 538-547.

5915. Hart, W. O. "Chief Justices of the United States." *American Bar Association Journal* 7 (July 1921): 332-333.

5916. Heck, Edward V. "Changing Voting Patterns in the Burger Court: The Impact of Personnel Change." *San Diego Law Review* 17 (August 1980): 1021-1046.

5917. Heck, Edward V. "Civil Liberties Voting Patterns in the Burger Court, 1975-1978." *Western Political Quarterly* 34 (June 1981): 193-202.

5918. Howell, Ronald F. "The Judicial Conservatives Three Decades Ago: Aristocratic Guardians of the Prerogatives of Property and the Judiciary." *Virginia Law Review* 49 (December 1963): 1447-1483.

5919. Jackson, Donald D. *Judges.* New York: Atheneum, 1974.

5920. Jacobs, Roger F. *Memorials of the Justices of the Supreme Court of the United States.* Littleton, CO: Fred B. Rothman, 1981.

5921. Jaschik, Scott. "Impact of Supreme Court Shake-up May Come Slowly, Legal Experts Say." *Chronicle of Higher Educaton* 32 (June 25, 1986): 9-10.

5922. Johnson, Charles A. "Personnel Change and Policy Change on the U.S. Supreme Court." *Social Science Quarterly* 62 (December 1981): 751-757.

5923. Johnson, Frances B. "The Justices of the Supreme Court." *American Illustrated Magazine* 61 (April 1906): 634-642.

5924. Karfunkel, Thomas. *The Jewish Seat: Anti-Semitism and the Appointment of Jews to the Supreme Court.* Hicksville, NY: Exposition Press, 1978.

5925. Kaye, David. "And Then There Were 12: Statistical Reasoning, the Supreme Court, and the Size of the Jury." *California Law Review* 68 (September 1980): 1004-1043.

5926. Kelbley, Charles A. "Bad Judgement on Judges: Why Screening Judges on Single Issues Threatens to Corrupt Our Legal System." *Human Rights* 15 (Fall 1987): 14-19.

5927. Kennedy, Walter B. "Portrait of the New Supreme Court." *Fordham Law Review* 13 (March 1944): 1-16; 14 (March 1945): 8-36.

5928. Langran, Robert W. "Why Are Some Supreme Court Justices Rated as Failures?" *Supreme Court Historical Society Yearbook* 1985 (1985): 8-14.

5929. Lawrence, David. *Nine Honest Men.* New York: Appleton and Company, 1936.

5930. Lewis, Anthony. "Portraits of Nine Men under Attack." *New York Times Magazine* 107 (May 18, 1958): 14-15.

5931. Lindstrom, Eugene E. "Attributes Affecting the Voting Behavior of Supreme Court Justices: 1889-1959." Ph.D. diss., Stanford University, 1968.

5932. McCune, Wesley. *The Nine Young Men.* New York: Harper and Brothers, 1947.

5933. McKay, Robert B. "The Judiciary and Non-Judicial Activities." *Law and Contemporary Problems* 35 (Winter 1970): 9-36.

5934. MacKenzie, John P. *The Appearance of Justice.* New York: Charles Scribner's Sons, 1974.

5935. Magrath, C. Peter. "Nine Deliberative Bodies: A Profile of the Warren Court." *Commentary* 32 (September 1961): 399.

5936. Mason, Ed. *Chief Justices of the United States.* Columbus, OH: Dispatch Printing Company, 1977.

5937. Masterson, William E. "Proposal to Enlarge the Membership of the Supreme Court." *Missouri Bar Journal* 8 (April 1937): 68-72.

5938. Maury, Nannie-Belle. "Personnel of the Supreme Court." *Cosmopolitan* 24 (February 1898): 369-374.

5939. Millen, William A. "Supreme Court Justices Are Kindly and Human in Conduct on Bench." *I.C.C. Practitioners Journal* 14 (December 1946): 225-227.

5940. Miller, Arthur S., and Jeffrey H. Bowman. "Break the Monopoly of Lawyers on the Supreme Court." *Vanderbilt Law Review* 39 (March 1986): 305-320.

5941. Miller, Arthur S., and Ronald F. Howell. "The Myth of Neutrality in Constitutional Adjudication." *University of Chicago Law Review* 27 (Summer 1960): 661-695.

5942. Mitchell, James G. "Hypocrisy of the Disability Argument for Retiring Supreme Court Justices." *Annalist* 49 (February 19, 1937): 302-303.

5943. Mitchell, Morris B. "The Judicial Salary Crisis: An Increase Is Urgently Needed." *American Bar Association Journal* 30 (March 1953): 197-200.

5944. Mitchell, Stephen R. "The Justices." *Western Political Quarterly* 15 (September 1962): 42-43.

5945. Mizell, Winton R. "The United States Senate Committee on the Judiciary and Presidential Nominations to the Supreme Court, 1965-1971: A Study of Role and Function of a Legislative Subsystem." Ph.D. diss., University of Oklahoma, 1974.

5946. Morrison, Alan B., and D. Scott Stenhouse. "The Chief Justice of the United States: More Than Just the Highest Ranking Judge." *Constitutional Commentary* 1 (Winter 1984): 57-79.

5947. Nagel, Stuart S. "Characteristics of Supreme Court Greatness." *American Bar Association Journal* 56 (October 1970): 957-959.

5948. Noonan, John T., Jr. "Catholic Justices of the United States Supreme Court." *Catholic Historical Review* 67 (July 1981): 369-385.

5949. Norton, John J. "Changes on the High Court." *Police Chief* 53 (August 1986): 8.

5950. Nowak, John E. "Resurrecting Realist Jurisprudence: The Political Bias of Burger Court Justices." *Suffolk University Law Review* 17 (Fall 1983): 549-620.

5951. Pannick, David. "Judges and Brothers." *Encounter* 55 (October 1980): 29-30.

5952. Patterson, T. Elliot. "History of Three Chief Justices of the United States Supreme Court." *Law Student's Helper* 5 (September 1897): 321-323; (October 1897): 353-355; (November 1897): 383-385.

5953. Pearson, Drew. *The Nine Old Men at the Crossroads.* Garden City, NY: Doubleday, Doran, 1937.

5954. "Pensions for Judges." *Albany Law Journal* 66 (February 1904): 33.

5955. Pollitt, Basil H. *Justice and the Justices.* Daytona Beach, FL: College Publishing Company, 1954.

5956. Pusey, Merlo J. "Disability on the Court." *Supreme Court Historical Society Yearbook* 1979 (1979): 63.

5957. Richardson, William A. "Chief Justice of the United States, or Chief Justice of the Supreme Court of the United States." *New England Historical and Geneological Register* 49 (July 1895): 275-279.

5958. Rodell, Fred. "Gallery of Justices." *Saturday Review* 41 (November 15, 1958): 9-11.

5959. Ruskowski, C. W. "Catholics on the United States Supreme Court." *University of Detroit Law Journal* 34 (April 1957): 650-658.

5960. Sandalow, Terrance. "Nonjudicial Activities of Supreme Court Justices and Other Federal Judges." *Law Quadrangle Notes* 14 (Spring 1970): 23-26.

5961. Schmidhauser, John R. *Judges and Justices: The Federal Appellate Judiciary.* Boston: Little, Brown, 1979.

5962. Schmidhauser, John R. "The Justices of the Supreme Court: A Collective Portrait." *Midwest Journal of Political Science* 3 (February 1959): 1-57.

5963. Schmidhauser, John R. "*Stare Decisis*, Dissent, and the Background of the Justices of the Supreme Court of the United States." *University of Toronto Law Journal* 14 (1962): 194-212.

5964. Schubert, Glendon A. *The Judicial Mind: Attitudes and Ideologies of Supreme Court Justices, 1946-1963.* Evanston, IL: Northwestern University Press, 1965.

5965. Schubert, Glendon A. *The Judicial Mind Revisited: Psychometric Analysis of Supreme Court Ideology.* New York: Oxford University Press, 1974.

5966. Scott, Alfred M. *The Supreme Court v. the Constitution: An Essay on How Judges Become Dictators.* New York: Exposition Press, 1963.

5967. Sedgwick, A. G. "The New United States Judges." *Nation* 9 (December 1869): 477-479.

5968. Semmes, Thomas J. "The Personal Characteristics of the Chief Justices." In *The Supreme Court of the United States,* by Hampton L. Carson, 664-692. Philadelphia: A. R. Keller, 1892.

5969. Sheldon, Charles H. *The Supreme Court: Politicians in Robes.* Beverly Hills, CA: Glencoe Press, 1970.

5970. Sherwood, Frederick, T. "New Men, Other Minds in the Supreme Court." *Lincoln Law Review* 5 (October 1931): 12-17.

5971. Steamer, Robert J. *Chief Justice: Leadership and the Supreme Court.* Columbia: University of South Carolina Press, 1986.

5972. Sterne, Simon. "The Salaries of the United States Supreme Court Justices." *Counsellor* 1 (January 1892): 93-98.

5973. Stewart, David M. "Supreme Court Appointments during the Harding and Coolidge Administrations: Influence, Critics, and Voting." Ph.D. diss., Wayne State University, 1974.

5974. Surrency, Erwin C. "The First Judges of the Federal Courts." *American Journal of Legal History* 1 (January 1957): 76-78.

5975. Swindler, William F. "The Chief Justice and Law Reform, 1921-1971." *Supreme Court Review* 1971 (1971): 241-264.

5976. Swindler, William F. "Fifty-one Chief Justices." *Kentucky Law Journal* 60 (1972): 851-871.

5977. Swindler, William F. "Justices in Academe." *Supreme Court Historical Society Yearbook* 1979 (1979): 31-37.

5978. Thornton, John E. "Balancing Various Community Interests: Should This Be Part of the Judicial Function?" *American Bar Association Journal* 35 (June 1949): 473-475.

5979. Totenberg, Nina. "The Confirmation Process and the Public: To Know or Not to Know." *Harvard Law Review* 101 (April 1988): 1213-1229.

5980. Tribe, Laurence H. "God Save This Honorable Court: How the Choice of Supreme Court Justices Shapes Our History." *Yale Law Journal* 95 (May 1986): 1283-1320.

5981. Tribe, Laurence H. "What Difference Can a Justice or Two Make?" *American Bar Association Journal* 71 (September 1985): 60-62.

5982. Tyler, Frederick S. "An All-Time Star Supreme Court." *Journal of the Bar Association of the District of Columbia* 12 (April 1945): 124-125.

5983. Ulmer, S. Sidney. "Public Office in the Social Background of Supreme Court Justices." *American Journal of Economics and Sociology* 21 (January 1962): 57-68.

5984. Ulmer, S. Sidney. "Supreme Court

Justices as Strict and Not-So-Strict Constructionists: Some Implications." *Law and Society Review* 8 (Fall 1973): 13-32.

5985. Umbreit, Kenneth B. *Our Eleven Chief Justices: A History of the Supreme Court in Terms of Their Personalities.* New York: Harper and Brothers, 1969.

5986. Vanderbilt, Arthur T., and Jacob M. Lashly. "New Members of the Supreme Court of the United States." *American Bar Association Journal* 43 (June 1957): 526-527, 545.

5987. Van Santvoord, George. *Sketches of the Lives, Times, and Judicial Services of the Chief Justices of the Supreme Court of the United States: Jay, Rutledge, Ellsworth, Marshall, Taney, Chase, and Waite.* 2d ed. Albany, NY: W. C. Little, 1882.

5988. Vorspan, Albert. *Giants of Justice.* New York: Thomas Y. Crowell, 1960.

5989. Weber, Paul J. "The Birth Order Oddity in Supreme Court Appointments." *Presidential Studies Quarterly* 14 (Fall 1984): 561-568.

5990. Westin, Alan F. "Out-of-Court Commentary by U.S. Supreme Court Justices, 1790-1962: Of Free Speech and Judicial Lockjaw." *Columbia Law Review* 62 (March 1962): 633-669.

5991. Wheeler, David H. "The Justices of the Supreme Court." *Chautauquan* 23 (August 1896): 531-539.

5992. Wheeler, Russell. "Extrajudicial Activities of Early Supreme Court." *Supreme Court Review* 1973 (1973): 123-158.

5993. Wheeler, Russell. "Extrajudicial Activities of United States Supreme Court Justices, the Constitutional Period, 1790-1809." Ph.D. diss., University of Chicago, 1971.

5994. White, G. Edward. *The American Judicial Tradition: Profiles of Leading American Judges.* Rev. ed. New York: Oxford University Press, 1988.

5995. White Burkett Miller Center. *The Office of the Chief Justice.* Lanham, MD: University Press of America, 1984.

Qualifications

5996. Bayh, Birch. "How Should We Judge Our Judges? In the Wake of the Senate Rejection of Judges Haynsworth and Carswell and the Drive to Impeach Justice Douglas." *Lithopinion* 5 (Fall 1970): 6-8.

5997. Beth, Loren P. "Judge into Justice: Should Supreme Court Appointees Have Judicial Experience?" *South Atlantic Quarterly* 58 (Autumn 1959): 521-527.

5998. Black, Charles L. "A Note on Senatorial Consideration of Supreme Court Nominees." *Yale Law Journal* 79 (March 1970): 657-664.

5999. Davenport, Ronald R. "Judicial Conservatism and the Supreme Court." *Duquesne Law Review* 10 (Winter 1971): 168-176.

6000. Gest, Ted, et al. "Justice under Reagan: With the Opening of a New Supreme Court Session on October 7, Legal Debate Is Building to Challenge an Administration Determined to Reshape the Law." *U.S. News and World Report* 99 (October 14, 1985): 58-62.

6001. Hamilton, Walton H., and George D. Braden. "The Special Competence of the Supreme Court." *Yale Law Journal* 50 (June 1941): 1319-1375.

6002. Mowry, Duane. "Some Qualifications for a Judge of the Supreme Court of the United States." *Albany Law Journal* 70 (August 1908): 275.

Selection

6003. Abraham, Henry J. "Influence of Sitting and Retired Justices on Presidential Supreme Court Nominations." *Hastings Constitutional Law Quarterly* 3 (Winter 1976): 37-63.

6004. Abraham, Henry J. *Justices and Presidents: A Political History of Appointments to the Supreme Court.* 2d. ed. New York: Oxford University Press, 1985.

6005. Abraham, Henry J., and Edward M. Goldberg. "A Note on the Appointment of Justices of the Supreme Court of the United States." *American Bar Association Journal* 46 (February 1960): 147-150, 219-222.

6006. Ashby, John B. "Supreme Court Appointments since 1937." Ph.D. diss., University of Notre Dame, 1972.

6007. "Attorney General Mitchell Terminates Association's Advance Screening of Supreme Court Nominees." *American Bar Association Journal* 57 (December 1971): 1175-1179.

6008. Beiser, Edward N. "The Haynsworth Affair Reconsidered: The Significance of Conflicting Perceptions of the Judicial Role." *Vanderbilt Law Review* 23 (March 1970): 263-292.

6009. Black, Forrest R. "The Role of the United States Senate in Passing on the Nominations to Membership in the Supreme Court of the United States." *Kentucky Law Journal* 19 (March 1931): 226-238.

6010. Black, Forrest R. "Should the Senate Pass On Social and Economic Views of Nominees to the Supreme Court of the United States?" *St. John's Law Review* 6 (May 1932): 257-271.

6011. Brownstein, Ronald. "With or without Supreme Court Changes, Reagan Will Reshape the Federal Bench." *National Journal* 16 (December 8, 1984): 2338-2341.

6012. Bryden, David P. "How to Select a Supreme Court Justice: The Case of Robert Bork." *American Scholar* 57 (Spring 1988): 210-217.

6013. Burke, Richard K. "The Path to the Court: A Study of Federal Judicial Appointments." Master's thesis, Vanderbilt University, 1958.

6014. Cadman, Wilson K. *Distribution of Nominations and Appointments to the United States Supreme Court.* Wichita, KS: n.p., 1951.

6015. Carter, Stephen. "The Confirmation Mess." *Harvard Law Review* 101 (April 1988): 1185-1201.

6016. Chase, Harold W. *Federal Judges: The Appointing Process.* Minneapolis: University of Minnesota Press, 1972.

6017. Clark, Walter. "The Election of Federal Judges by the People." *Albany Law Journal* 67 (August 1905): 235-237.

6018. Cohen, Richard E. "Conservatives Step Up Efforts to Promote Reagan-Minded Judges to U.S. Bench." *National Journal* 17 (July 6, 1985): 1560-1563.

6019. Cole, Kenneth C. "The Role of the Senate in the Confirmation of Judicial Nominations." *American Political Science Review* 28 (October 1934): 875-894.

6020. Commager, Henry S. "Choosing Supreme Court Judges." *New Republic* 162 (May 2, 1970): 13-16.

6021. Cook, Beverly B. "The First Woman Candidate for the Supreme Court: Florence E. Allen." *Supreme Court Historical Society Yearbook* 1981 (1981): 19-35.

6022. Danelski, David J. *A Supreme Court Justice Is Appointed.* New York: Random House, 1964.

6023. Daniel, Josiah M., III. " 'Chief Justice of the United States': History and Historiography of the Title." *Supreme Court Historical Society Yearbook* 1983 (1983): 109-112.

6024. Daniels, William J. "Geographic Factor in Appointments to United States Supreme Court: 1789-1976." *Western Political Quarterly* 31 (June 1978): 226-237.

6025. Dynia, Philip A. "Senate Rejection of Supreme Court Nominees: Factors Affecting Rejection, 1795-1972." Ph.D. diss., Georgetown University, 1973.

6026. Erickson, William H. "The Impact of the Judicial Confirmation Process on the U.S. Supreme Court." *Colorado Law Review* 17 (February 1988): 223-224.

6027. "The Federal Judiciary: What Role Politics?" *Judicature* 68 (April/May 1985): 330-336.

6028. Flower, Frank A. *Edwin McMasters Stanton, the Autocrat of Rebellion, Emancipation, and Reconstruction.* New York: Saalfield Publishing Company, 1905.

6029. Frank, John P. "The Appointment of Supreme Court Justices: Prestige, Principles, and Politics." *Wisconsin Law Review* 1941 (March 1941): 172-210; (May 1941): 343-379; (July 1941): 461-512.

6030. Frank, John P. "Judicial Appointments: Controversy and Accomplishment." *Supreme Court Historical Society Yearbook* 1977 (1977): 79-85.

6031. Frank, John P. "Supreme Court Justice Appointments." *Wisconsin Law Review* 1941 (March 1941): 172-210.

6032. Frank, John P. "Supreme Court Justice Appointments II." *Wisconsin Law Review* 1941 (May 1941): 343-379.

6033. Friedman, Richard D. "The Transformation in Senate Response to Supreme Court Nominations: From Reconstruction to the Taft Administration and Beyond." *Cardozo Law Review* 5 (Fall 1983): 1-95.

6034. Friedman, Richard D. "Tribal Myths: Ideology and the Confirmation of Supreme Court Nominations." *Yale Law Journal* 95 (May 1986): 1283-1320.

6035. Friendly, Fred W. "The Federal Judiciary: What Role Politics?" *Judicature* 68 (April/May 1985): 330-336.

6036. Gest, Ted. "Reagan's Court: Two Steps to the Right." *U.S. News and World Report* 100 (June 30, 1986): 16-19.

6037. Goff, John S. "Rejection of United States Supreme Court Appointments." *American Journal of Legal History* 5 (October 1961): 357-368.

6038. Gorham, George C. *Life and Public Services of Edwin M. Stanton.* 2 vols. New York: Houghton Mifflin, 1899.

6039. Grachek, Arthur F. "United States Senate Debate on Supreme Court Nominations between 1925 and 1970." Ph.D. diss., Wayne State University, 1974.

6040. Grossman, Joel B. *Lawyers and Judges: The ABA and the Politics of Judicial Selection.* New York: John Wiley, 1965.

6041. Grossman, Joel B., and Stephen L. Wasby. "Haynsworth and Parker: History Does Live Again." *South Carolina Law Review* 23 (1971): 345-359.

6042. Grossman, Joel B., and Stephen L. Wasby. "The Senate and Supreme Court Nominations: Some Reflections." *Duke Law Journal* 1972 (August 1972): 557-591.

6043. Halper, Thomas. "Demographic Factors and Supreme Court Appointments." *Drake Law Review* 21 (January 1972): 238-251.

6044. Halper, Thomas. "Senate Rejection of Supreme Court Nominees." *Drake Law Review* 22 (September 1972): 102-113.

6045. Halper, Thomas. "Supreme Court Appointments: Criteria and Consequences." *New York Law Forum* 21 (Spring 1976): 563-584.

6046. Harris, Joseph P. *The Advice and Consent of the Senate: A Study of the Confirmation and Appointments by the United States Senate.* Berkeley: University of California Press, 1953.

6047. Harris, Richard. "Annals of Politics: Judge Carswell and the Senate." Parts 1 and 2. *New Yorker* 46 (December 5, 1970): 60-160; (December 12, 1970): 53-131.

6048. Harris, Richard. *Decision.* New York: Dutton, 1971.

6049. Hulbary, William E., and Thomas G. Walker. "The Supreme Court Selection Process: Presidential Motivations and Judicial Performance." *Western Political Quarterly* 33 (June 1980): 185-196.

6050. Jager, Ronald B. "The Democracy's Demise: Grover Cleveland's Rejected Supreme Court Nominations." Ph.D. diss., University of Texas, 1972.

6051. King, Gary. "Presidential Appointments to the Supreme Court: Adding Systematic Explanation to Probabilistic Description." *American Politics Quarterly* 15 (July 1987): 373-386.

6052. Kurland, Philip B. "Appointment and Disappointment of Supreme Court Justices." *Law and the Social Order* 1972 (1972): 183-237.

6053. Lawlor, John M. "Court Packing Revisited: A Proposal for Rationalizing the Timing of Appointments to the Supreme Court." *University of Pennsylvania Law Review* 134 (April 1986): 967-1000.

6054. Lewis, Anthony. "Constitutionality of Recess Appointments of Judges to Federal Bench Doubted." *American Judicature Society Journal* 41 (December 1957): 122-123.

6055. Lively, Donald E. "The Supreme Court Appointment Process: In Search of Constitutional Roles and Responsibilities."

Southern California Law Review 59 (March 1986): 551-579.

6056. McCaffree, Floyd E. "The Nomination and Confirmation of Justices of the Supreme Court of the United States, 1789-1849." Ph.D. diss., University of Michigan, 1938.

6057. McConnell, A. Mitchell, Jr. "Haynsworth and Carswell: A New Senate Standard of Excellence." *Kentucky Law Journal* 59 (Fall 1970): 7-34.

6058. McHargue, Daniel S. "Factors Influencing the Selection and Appointment of Members of the United States Supreme Court, 1784-1932." Ph.D. diss., University of California at Los Angeles, 1949.

6059. McHargue, Daniel S. "Sectional Representation on the Supreme Court." *Marquette Law Review* 35 (Summer 1951): 13-28.

6060. McKay, Robert B. "Selection of United States Supreme Court Justices." *University of Kansas Law Review* 9 (December 1960): 109-137.

6061. McLain, J. Dudley. "Supreme Court Controversies of Presidents Roosevelt and Nixon: A Consideration of the Political Nature of the Presidential Power of Judicial Appointment." *Georgia State Bar Journal* 8 (November 1971): 145-179.

6062. Massaro, John L. "Advice and Dissent: Factors in the Senate's Refusal to Confirm Supreme Court Nominees with Special Emphasis on the Cases of Abe Fortas, Clement F. Haynsworth, and G. Harrold Carswell." Ph.D. diss., Southern Illinois University, 1973.

6063. Massaro, John L. "Fortascast: Dark Clouds over President Ford's Forthcoming Supreme Court Nominations." *Federal Bar Journal* 34 (Fall 1975): 257-278.

6064. Massaro, John. L. " 'Lame-Duck' Presidents, Great Justices?" *Presidential Studies Quarterly* 8 (Summer 1978): 296-302.

6065. Mendelsohn, Rona H. "Senate Confirmation of Supreme Court Appointments: The Nomination and Rejection of John J. Parker." *Howard Law Journal* 14 (Winter 1967): 105-148.

6066. Mersky, Roy M., and J. Myron Jacobstein. *The Supreme Court of the United States: Hearings and Reports on Successful and Unsuccessful Nominations of Supreme Court Justices by the Senate Judiciary Committee, 1916-1972.* Buffalo, NY: Hein, 1975.

6067. Monaghan, Henry P. "The Confirmation Process: Law or Politics?" *Harvard Law Review* 101 (April 1988): 1146-1229.

6068. O'Brien, David M. "Packing the Supreme Court." *Virginia Quarterly Review* 62 (Spring 1986): 189-212.

6069. O'Brien, F. William. "The Nine Rejected Men." *Baylor Law Review* 19 (Winter 1967): 1-19.

6070. Overmeyer, Philip H. "Attorney General George H. Williams and the Chief Justiceship." *Pacific Northwest Quarterly* 28 (July 1937): 251-262.

6071. Palmer, Jan. "Senate Confirmation of Appointments to the U.S. Supreme Court." *Review of Social Economy* 41 (October 1983): 152-162.

6072. Peck, Robert S. "Can Presidents Pack the Court? The Answer Is Yes, No, and Maybe." *Update* 8 (Spring 1984): 12-15.

6073. Perry, James R. "Supreme Court Appointments, 1789-1801: Criteria, Presidential Style, and the Press of Events." *Journal of the Early Republic* 6 (Winter 1986): 371-410.

6074. Piatt, Donn. "Edwin M. Stanton." *North American Review* 142 (May 1886): 466-477; (June 1886): 540-548.

6075. Pierce, Carl A. "Vacancy on the Supreme Court: The Politics of Judicial Appointment." *Tennessee Law Review* 39 (Summer 1972): 555-612.

6076. Powe, L. A., Jr. "Senate and the Court: Questioning a Nominee." *Texas Law Review* 54 (May 1976): 891-901.

6077. Pusey, Merlo J. "Court Nominations and Presidential Cronyism." *Supreme Court Historical Society Yearbook* 1981 (1981): 68-73.

6078. Ripple, Kenneth F. " 'Fitting In' at the Court: Some Reflections on the Selection of Supreme Court Justices." *Res Gestae* 25 (March 1981): 120-123.

6079. Rogers, William P. "Judicial Appointments in the Eisenhower Administration." *American Judicature Society Journal* 41 (August 1957): 38-42.

6080. Romine, Ronald H. "The Politics of Supreme Court Nominations from Theodore Roosevelt to Ronald Reagan: The Construction of a 'Politicization Index'." Ph.D. diss., University of South Carolina, 1984.

6081. Ross, William G. "The Functions, Roles, and Duties of the Senate in the Supreme Court Appointment Process." *William and Mary Law Review* 28 (Summer 1987): 633-682.

6082. Schouler, James. "Appointments to the United States Supreme Court." *Green Bag* 18 (December 1906): 657-661.

6083. Segal, Jeffrey A. "Senate Confirmation of Supreme Court Justices: Partisan and Institutional Politics." *Journal of Politics* 49 (November 1987): 998-1015.

6084. Segal, Jeffrey A., and Harold J. Spaeth. "If a Supreme Court Vacancy Occurs, Will the Senate Confirm a Reagan Nominee?" *Judicature* 69 (December 1985): 186-190.

6085. Songer, Donald R. "The Relevance of Policy Values for the Confirmation of Supreme Court Nominees." *Law and Society Review* 13 (Summer 1979): 927-948.

6086. Steele, John L. "Haynsworth v. the U.S. Senate: The Historic Confrontation over a Supreme Court Seat Was a Vivid Demonstration of the Uses of Power in Washington and of the Pressure Tactics in American Politics." *Fortune* 81 (March 1970): 90-93, 155-161.

6087. Stowe, Harriet B. "Edwin M. Stanton." In *Men of Our Times*, by Harriet B. Stowe, 363-377. Hartford, CT: Hartford Publishing Company, 1868.

6088. Sulfridge, Wayne. "Ideology as a Factor in Senate Consideration of Supreme Court Nominations." *Journal of Politics* 42 (May 1980): 560-567.

6089. Swindler, William F. "Politics of 'Advice and Consent'." *American Bar Association Journal* 56 (June 1970): 533-542.

6090. Swindler, William F. " 'Robin Hood', Congress, and the Court." *Supreme Court Historical Society Yearbook* 1977 (1977): 39-43.

6091. Teger, Stuart H. "Presidential Strategy for the Appointment of Supreme Court Justices." Ph.D. diss., University of Rochester, 1976.

6092. Teger, Stuart H. "Presidential Strategy for the Appointment of Supreme Court Justices." *Public Choice* 31 (Fall 1977): 1-22.

6093. Thorpe, James A. *The Appearance of Supreme Court Nominees before the Senate Judiciary Committee: The Evolution of a Problem in the Separation of Powers*. 2d ed. Superior, WI: Superior Publications, 1977.

6094. Tramontine, John O. "Recess Appointments to the Supreme Court." *Intramural Law Review of New York University* 17 (1962): 157-185.

6095. Ulmer, S. Sidney. "Supreme Court Appointments as a Poisson Distribution." *American Journal of Political Science* 26 (February 1982): 113-116.

6096. Vatz, Richard E., and Theodore O. Windt. "The Defeats of Judges Haynsworth and Carswell: Rejection of Supreme Court Nominees." *Quarterly Journal of Speech* 60 (December 1974): 477-488.

6097. Vigilante, Richard. "Beyond the Burger Court: Four Supreme Court Candidates Who Could Lead a Judicial Counterrevolution." *Policy Review* 28 (Spring 1984): 20-26.

6098. Voorhees, Theodore. "It's Time for Merit Selection of Supreme Court Justices." *American Bar Association Journal* 61 (June 1975): 705-708.

6099. Walker, Thomas G., and William E. Hulbary. "The Supreme Court Selection Process: Presidential Motivations and Judical Performances." *Western Political Quarterly* 33 (June 1980): 185-196.

6100. Wallis, W. Allen. "Poisson Distribution and the Supreme Court." *American Statistical Association Journal* 31 (June 1936): 376-380.

6101. Walsh, Lawrence E. "Selection of Supreme Court Justices." *American Bar Association Journal* 56 (June 1970): 555-560.

6102. Watson, George, and John Stookey. "Supreme Court Confirmation Hearings: A View from the Senate." *Judicature* 71 (December/January 1988): 186-196.

6103. Watson, Richard L., Jr. "Defeat of Judge Parker: A Study in Pressure Groups and Politics." *Mississippi Valley Historical Review* 50 (September 1963): 213-234.

6104. Weissman, Gary A. "Legal Esoterica." *Advocate* (Idaho) 29 (January 1986): 26-28.

6105. Wigmore, John H. "A New Way to Nominate Supreme Court Judges." *American Judicature Society Journal* 29 (December 1945): 106-107.

6106. Wigmore, John H. "New Way to

Nominate Supreme Court Judges." *Kentucky State Bar Journal* 10 (March 1946): 153-154.

6107. Wilson, Henry. "Jeremiah S. Black and Edwin M. Stanton." *Atlantic Monthly* 26 (October 1870): 463-475.

6108. Winters, Glenn R., ed. *Selected Readings: Judicial Selection and Tenure.* Chicago: American Judicature Society, 1967.

Tenure

6109. Atkinson, David N. "Bowing to the Inevitable: Supreme Court Deaths and Resignations, 1789-1864." *Arizona State Law Journal* 1982 (1982): 615-640.

6110. Atkinson, David N. "Retirement and Death on the United States Supreme Court: From Van Devanter to Douglas." *University of Missouri at Kansas City Law Review* 45 (Fall 1976): 1-27.

6111. Callen, Earl, and Henning Leidecker, Jr. "A Mean Life on the Supreme Court: The Use of a Mathematics Technique Called Poisson Distribution Can Provide Some Startling and Informative Insights into the Age and Length of Service of Supreme Court Justices both in the Past and the Future." *American Bar Association Journal* 57 (December 1971): 1188-1192.

6112. Carpenter, William S. *Judicial Tenure in the United States with Special Reference to the Tenure of Federal Judges.* New Haven, CT: Yale University Press, 1918.

6113. Collier, Charles S. "The Supreme Court and the Principle Rotation in Office." *George Washington Law Review* 6 (May 1938): 401-435.

6114. Kaufman, Irving R. "Chilling Judicial Independence." *Yale Law Journal* 88 (March 1979): 681-716.

6115. Nunn, Sam. "Judicial Tenure." *Chicago-Kent Law Review* 54 (1977): 29-44.

6116. O'Connor, Alice. *During Good Behavior: Judicial Independence and Accountability: A Guide for Discussion of Proposals to Establish Terms of Office for the Federal Judiciary.* Washington, DC: Jefferson Foundation, 1984.

6117. Oliver, Philip D. "Systematic Justice: A Proposed Constitutional Amendment to Establish Fixed, Staggered Terms for Members of the United States Supreme Court." *Ohio State Law Journal* 47 (1986): 799-834.

XV. The Justices

Henry Baldwin

General Studies

6118. Brown, David P. "Henry Baldwin, LL.D." In *The Forum*, vol. 2, edited by David P. Brown, 76-90. Philadelphia: R. H. Small, 1856.

6119. Taylor, Flavia M. "The Political and Civil Career of Henry Baldwin." *Western Pennsylvania Historical Magazine* 24 (March 1941): 37-50.

Writings

6120. Baldwin, Henry. *A General View of the Origin and Nature of the Constitution and Government of the United States.* Philadelphia: American Constitutional and Legal History Service, 1837.

Philip P. Barbour

General Studies

6121. Cynn, Paul P. "Philip Pendleton Barbour." *John P. Branch Historical Papers of Randolph-Macon College* 4 (1913): 67-77.

6122. Mooney, Booth. *Mr. Speaker.* Chicago: Follett, 1964.

6123. "Philip P. Barbour: Obituary Notice." *Law Reporter* 3 (April 1841): 465.

6124. Scott, William W. *A History of Orange County, Virginia.* Richmond, VA: Waddey, 1907.

Hugo L. Black

General Studies

6125. Anastaplo, George. "Mr. Justice Black, His Generous Common Sense, and the Bar Admission Cases." *Southwestern University Law Review* 9 (1977): 977-1048.

6126. Armstrong, Walter P. "Mr. Justice Black." *Tennessee Law Review* 20 (April 1949): 638-643.

6127. Ash, Michel. "The Growth of Justice Black's Philosophy on Freedom of Speech, 1962-1966." *Wisconsin Law Review* 1967 (Fall 1967): 860-862.

6128. Atkins, Burton M., and Terry Sloope. "The 'New' Hugo Black and the Warren Court." *Polity* 18 (Summer 1986): 621-637.

6129. Ball, Howard. "Hugo L. Black: A Twentieth Century Jeffersonian." *Southwestern University Law Review* 9 (1977): 1049-1068.

6130. Ball, Howard. "Justice Hugo L. Black: A Magnificent Product of the South." *Alabama Law Review* 36 (Spring 1985): 791-834.

6131. Ball, Howard. *The Vision and the*

Dream of Justice Hugo L. Black: An Examination of a Judicial Philosophy. University: University of Alabama Press, 1975.

6132. Barnett, Vincent M., Jr. "Mr. Justice Black and the Supreme Court." *University of Chicago Law Review* 8 (December 1940): 20-41.

6133. Berman, Daniel M. "Freedom and Mr. Justice Black: The Record after Twenty Years." *Missouri Law Review* 25 (1960): 155-174.

6134. Berman, Daniel M. "Hugo Black, Southerner." *American University Law Review* 10 (January 1961): 35-42.

6135. Berman, Daniel M. "Hugo L. Black at Seventy-five." *American University Law Review* 10 (January 1961): 43-52.

6136. Berman, Daniel M. "Hugo L. Black: The Early Years." *Catholic University of America Law Review* 8 (May 1959): 103-116.

6137. Berman, Daniel M. "The Political Philosophy of Hugo L. Black." Ph.D. diss., Rutgers University, 1957.

6138. Berman, Daniel M. "The Racial Issue and Mr. Justice Black." *American University Law Review* 16 (June 1967): 386-402.

6139. Beth, Loren P. "Mr. Justice Black and the First Amendment: Comments on the Dilemma of Constitutional Interpretation." *Journal of Politics* 41 (November 1979): 1105-1124.

6140. Black, Charles L. "Mr. Justice Black, the Supreme Court, and the Bill of Rights." *Harper's Magazine* 222 (February 1961): 63-73.

6141. Black, Elizabeth. "Hugo Black: A Memorial Portrait." *Supreme Court Historical Society Yearbook* 1982 (1982): 72-94.

6142. Black, Elizabeth. "Hugo Black: The Magnificent Rebel." *Southwestern University Law Review* 9 (1977): 889-898.

6143. Black, Hugo L., Jr. *My Father, A Remembrance.* New York: Random House, 1975.

6144. Bloch, Charles J. "Mr. Justice Hugo L. Black." *Georgia Bar Journal* 25 (August 1962/1963): 56-59.

6145. Burke, Andrew F. "Discussion of Senator Black's Legal Position under the Constitution of the United States." *Massachusetts Law Quarterly* 22 (July/September 1937): 1-5.

6146. Cahn, Edmond N. "Justice Black and the First Amendment 'Absolutes'." *New York University Law Review* 37 (1962): 549-563.

6147. Campbell, Jeter L. "Justices Douglas and Black and the Democratic Ethos: Rhetorical Criticism of Concurring and Dissenting Opinions on Obscenity, 1954-1975." Ph.D. diss., University of Minnesota, 1979.

6148. Cohen, William. "Justices Black and Douglas and the 'Natural-Law-Due-Process Formula'." *U.C. Davis Law Review* 20 (Winter 1987): 381-395.

6149. Cole, Kenneth C. "Mr. Justice Black and 'Senatorial Courtesy'." *American Political Science Review* 31 (December 1937): 1113-1115.

6150. Cooper, Jerome A. "Mr. Justice Hugo Black: A Free Man." *Alabama Law Review* 17 (Fall 1964): 195-200.

6151. Cooper, Jerome A. "Mr. Justice Hugo Lafayette Black of Alabama." *Alabama Law Review* 24 (Fall 1972): 1-9.

6152. Cooper, Jerome A. "Mr. Justice Hugo Lafayette Black of Alabama." *Alabama Lawyer* 33 (January 1972): 17-22.

6153. Cooper, Jerome A. *"Sincerely Your Friend:" Letters of Mr. Justice Hugo L. Black to Jerome A. Cooper.* Tuscaloosa: University of Alabama Press, 1973.

6154. Davis, Hazel B. *Uncle Hugo: An In-*

timate Portrait of Mr. Justice Black. Amarillo, TX: n.p., 1965.

6155. Decker, Raymond G. "Justice Hugo L. Black: The Balancer of Absolutes." *California Law Review* 59 (November 1971): 1335-1355.

6156. Dennis, Everette E., Donald M. Gillmor, and David L. Grey, eds. *Justice Hugo Black and the First Amendment.* Ames: Iowa State University Press, 1978.

6157. Dilliard, Irving. "Hugo Black and the Importance of Freedom." *American University Law Review* 10 (January 1961): 7-26.

6158. Dilliard, Irving. "Mr. Justice Black and *In Re Anastaplo.*" *Southwestern University Law Review* 9 (1977): 953-976.

6159. Dilliard, Irving, ed. *One Man's Stand for Freedom: Mr. Justice Black and the Bill of Rights.* New York: Knopf, 1963.

6160. Dommici, Peter J. "Protector of the Minorities: Mr. Justice Hugo L. Black." *University of Missouri at Kansas City Law Review* 32 (Summer 1964): 266-291.

6161. Dorsen, Norman. "Mr. Justice Black and Mr. Justice Harlan." *New York University Law Review* 46 (October 1971): 649-652.

6162. Douglas, William O. "Mr. Justice Black." *Yale Law Journal* 65 (February 1956): 449-450.

6163. Dunne, Gerald T. *Hugo Black and the Judicial Revolution.* New York: Simon and Schuster, 1977.

6164. Dunne, Gerald T. "Justice Hugo Black and Robert Jackson: The Great Feud." *St. Louis University Law Journal* 19 (Summer 1975): 465-487.

6165. Durr, Clifford J. "Hugo Black, Southerner, the Southern Background." *American University Law Review* 10 (January 1961): 27-42.

6166. Durr, Clifford J. "Hugo L. Black: A Personal Appraisal." *Georgia Law Review* 6 (Fall 1971): 1-13.

6167. Frank, John P. "Hugo L. Black: He Has Joined the Giants." *American Bar Association Journal* 58 (January 1972): 21-25.

6168. Frank, John P. "Justice Black and the New Deal." *Arizona Law Review* 9 (Summer 1967): 26-58.

6169. Frank, John P. "Mr. Justice Black: A Biographical Appreciation." *Yale Law Journal* 65 (February 1956): 454-463.

6170. Frank, John P. *Mr. Justice Black: The Man and His Opinion.* New York: Knopf, 1949.

6171. Freund, Paul A. "Mr. Justice Black and the Judicial Function." *UCLA Law Review* 14 (January 1967): 467-474.

6172. Freyer, Tony A. "Hugo L. Black: Alabamian and American, 1886-1937." *Alabama Law Review* 36 (Spring 1985): 789-926.

6173. Gambill, Joel T. "Hugo Black: The First Amendment and the Mass Media." Ph.D. diss., Southern Illinois University, 1973.

6174. Gordon, Murray A. "Justice Hugo Black: First Amendment Fundamentalist." *Lawyers Guild Review* 20 (Spring 1960): 1-5.

6175. Green, Leon. "Jury Trial and Mr. Justice Black." *Yale Law Journal* 65 (February 1956): 482-494.

6176. Green, Richard F. "Mr. Justice Black versus the Supreme Court." *University of Newark Law Review* 4 (Winter 1939): 113-138.

6177. Gregory, William A., and Rennard Strickland. "Hugo Black's Congressional Investigation of Lobbying and the Public Utilities Holding Company Act: A Historical View of the Power Trust, New Deal Politics, and Regulatory Propaganda." *Oklahoma Law Review* 29 (Summer 1976): 543-576.

6178. Grinnell, Frank W. "Can Senator Black Become a Member of the Supreme Court under the Constitution?" *Massachusetts Law Quarterly* 22 (July/September 1937): 20-23.

6179. Grossman, Joel B. "Justice Black and the Absolute." *Commentary* 36 (September 1963): 244-248.

6180. Hackney, Sheldon. "The Clay County Origins of Mr. Justice Black: The Populist as Insider." *Alabama Law Review* 36 (Spring 1985): 835-844.

6181. Haigh, Roger W. "Defining Due Process of Law: The Case of Mr. Justice Hugo Black." *South Dakota Law Review* 17 (Winter 1972): 1-40.

6182. Haigh, Roger W. "The Judicial Opinions of Mr. Justice Hugo L. Black." *Southwestern University Law Review* 9 (1977): 1069-1126.

6183. Haigh, Roger W. "Mr. Justice Black and the Written Constitution." *Albany Law Review* 24 (Fall 1972): 15-44.

6184. Haigh, Roger W. "Mr. Justice Hugo L. Black, Due Process of Law, and the Judicial Role." Ph.D. diss., Fordham University, 1971.

6185. Hamilton, Virginia V. "Hugo Black and the K.K.K." *American Heritage* 19 (April 1968): 60-65, 108-111.

6186. Hamilton, Virginia V. *Hugo Black: The Alabama Years.* Baton Rouge: Louisiana State University Press, 1972.

6187. Hamilton, Virginia V. "Hugo Black: The Road to the Court." *Southwestern University Law Review* 9 (1977): 859-888.

6188. Hamilton, Virginia V. "Listen Hill, Hugo Black, and the Albatross of Race." *Alabama Law Review* 36 (Spring 1985): 845-860.

6189. Hamilton, Virginia V. "The Senate Career of Hugo L. Black." Ph.D. diss., University of Alabama, 1968.

6190. Hamilton, Virginia V., ed. *Hugo Black and the Bill of Rights: Proceedings of the First Hugo Black Symposium in American History on "The Bill of Rights and American Democracy".* University: University of Alabama Press, 1978.

6191. Havighurst, Harold C. "Mr. Justice Black." *National Lawyer's Guild Quarterly* 1 (May 1938): 181-185.

6192. Hobbs, Truman M. "Justice Black: Qualities of Greatness." *Alabama Law Review* 24 (Fall 1972): 11-13.

6193. Hook, Sidney. "Justice Black's Illogic: A Case Study in Professional Ethics." *New Leader* 40 (December 2, 1957): 17-20.

6194. Howard, A. E. Dick. "Mr. Justice Black: The Negro Protest Movement and the Rule of Law." *Virginia Law Review* 53 (June 1967): 1030-1084.

6195. Hudon, Edward G. "John Lilburne, the Levellers, and Mr. Justice Black." *American Bar Association Journal* 60 (June 1974): 686-689.

6196. Johnson, Nicholas. "Senator Black and the American Merchant Marine." *UCLA Law Review* 14 (January 1967): 399-427.

6197. Kalven, Harry, Jr. "Upon Rereading Mr. Justice Black on the First Amendment." *UCLA Law Review* 14 (1967): 428-445.

6198. Kalven, Harry, Jr., and Roscoe T. Steffen. "The Bar Admission Cases: An Unfinished Debate between Justice Frankfurter and Justice Black." *Law in Transition* 21 (Fall 1961): 155-196.

6199. Keefe, Arthur J. "Justice Black Leaves His Mark." *American Bar Association Journal* 58 (January 1972): 63-65.

6200. Kirkpatrick, W. Wallace. "Justice

Black and Antitrust." *UCLA Law Review* 14 (1967): 475-500.

6201. Klein, Michael. "Hugo L. Black: A Judicial View of American Constitutional Democracy." *University of Miami Law Review* 22 (Spring 1968): 753-799.

6202. Krislov, Samuel. "Mr. Justice Black Reopens the Free Speech Debate." *UCLA Law Review* 11 (1964): 189-211.

6203. Landynski, Jacob W. "In Search of Justice Black's Fourth Amendment." *Fordham Law Review* 45 (December 1976): 453-496.

6204. Lee, Edward T. "Resolution Relative to Appointment of Hugo L. Black as a Justice of the United States." *John Marshall Law Quarterly* 4 (September 1938): 71-77.

6205. Lerner, Max. "Hugo Black: A Personal History." *Nation* 145 (October 1937): 367-369.

6206. Lerner, Max. "Mr. Justice Black." In *Ideas Are Weapons: The History and Uses of Ideas*, edited by Max Lerner, 254-266. New York: Viking Press, 1939.

6207. Leuchtenburg, William E. "A Klansman Joins the Court: The Appointment of Hugo L. Black." *University of Chicago Law Review* 41 (Fall 1973): 1-31.

6208. Lewis, Anthony. "Justice Black at 75: Still the Dissenter." *New York Times Magazine* 110 (February 26, 1961): 13, 73-75.

6209. McBride, Patrick. "Justice Black's Jurisprudence: A Study of His Interpretations of the Bill of Rights and the Due Process Clause of Amendment XIV." Ph.D. diss., University of California, Los Angeles, 1969.

6210. McBride, Patrick. "Mr. Justice Black and His Qualified Absolutes." *Loyola University of Los Angeles Law Review* 2 (April 1969): 37-70.

6211. McGovney, Dudley O. "Is Hugo L. Black a Supreme Court Justice *de Jure*?" *California Law Review* 26 (November 1937): 1-32.

6212. Madison, Charles A. "Justice Black: Defender of the Bill of Rights." *Chicago Jewish Forum* 12 (Spring 1954): 175-181.

6213. Magee, James J. *Mr. Justice Black: Absolutist on the Court.* Charlottesville: University Press of Virginia, 1980.

6214. Magee, James J. "Mr. Justice Black and the First Amendment: The Development and Dilemmas of an Absolutist." Ph.D. diss., University of Virginia, 1976.

6215. Mason, Gene L. "Hugo Black and the United States Senate." Master's thesis, University of Kansas, 1964.

6216. Mauney, Connie. "Justice Black and First Amendment Freedoms: Thirty-four Influential Years." *Emporia State Research Studies* 35 (Fall 1986): 5-51.

6217. Mauney, Connie. "Mr. Justice Black and the First Amendment Freedoms: A Study in Constitutional Interpretation." Ph.D. diss., University of Tennessee, 1975.

6218. Meador, Daniel J. "Justice Black and His Law Clerks." *Alabama Law Review* 15 (Fall 1962): 57-63.

6219. Meador, Daniel J. *Mr. Justice Black and His Books.* Charlottesville: University Press of Virginia, 1974.

6220. Meek, Roy L. "Justices Douglas and Black: Political Liberalism and Judicial Activism." Ph.D. diss., University of Oregon, 1964.

6221. Meiklejohn, Donald. "Public Speech in the Burger Court: The Influence of Mr. Justice Black." *University of Toledo Law Review* 8 (Winter 1977): 301-341.

6222. Mendelson, Wallace. "Hugo Black and Judicial Discretion." *Political Science Quarterly* 85 (March 1970): 17-39.

6223. Mendelson, Wallace. *Justices Black and Frankfurter: Conflict in the Court.* 2d ed. Chicago: University of Chicago Press, 1966.

6224. Mendelson, Wallace. "Justices Black and Frankfurter: Supreme Court Majority and Minority Trends." *Journal of Politics* 12 (February 1950): 66-92.

6225. Mendelson, Wallace. "Mr. Justice Black and the Rule of Law." *Midwest Journal of Political Science* 4 (April 1960): 250-266.

6226. Mendelson, Wallace. "Mr. Justice Black's Fourteenth Amendment." *Minnesota Law Review* 53 (March 1969): 711-727.

6227. Murphy, Paul L. "The Early Social and Political Philosophy of Hugo Black: Liquor as a Test Case." *Alabama Law Review* 36 (Spring 1985): 861-880.

6228. Mykkeltvedt, Roald Y. "Justice Black and the Intentions of the Framers of the Fourteenth Amendment's First Section." *Mercer Law Review* 20 (Spring 1969): 423-442.

6229. Nock, Albert J. "The State of the Union: The Picking of Hugo Black." *American Mercury* 42 (October 1937): 229-233.

6230. Olivarius, Ann. "Absolutely Black: A Judicial Philosophy." *Beverly Hills Bar Association Journal* 11 (November/December 1977): 11-24.

6231. Paul, Randolph E. "Mr. Justice Black and Federal Taxation." *Yale Law Journal* 65 (February 1956): 495-528.

6232. Peladeau, Marius B. "Predilections of Supreme Court Justices: A Quarter-Century Analysis of U.S. Supreme Court Rate Decisions Involving Public Utility Companies, With Special Attention to Justices Black and Douglas." *Public Utilities Fortnightly* 71 (January 17, 1963): 32-39.

6233. Pressman, Steven. "Black's Books Give Glimpse of His Life." *New Jersey Law Journal* 109 (January 14, 1982): 10.

6234. Pruden, Durward. "The Opposition of the Press to the Ascension of Hugo Black to the Supreme Court of the United States." Ph.D. diss., New York University, 1945.

6235. Ray, Ben F. "Justice Black Adorns the Bench." *Alabama Lawyer* 10 (October 1949): 455-457.

6236. Reich, Charles A. "Mr. Justice Black and the Living Constitution." *Harvard Law Review* 76 (February 1963): 673-754.

6237. Reich, Charles A. "Mr. Justice Black as One Who Saw the Future." *Southwestern Law Review* 9 (1977): 845-858.

6238. Resnik, Solomon. "Black and Douglas: Variations in Dissent." *Western Political Quarterly* 16 (June 1963): 305-322.

6239. Rice, Charles E. "Justice Black, the Demonstrators, and a Constitutional Rule of Law." *UCLA Law Review* 14 (1967): 454-466.

6240. Rodell, Fred. "A Sprig of Laurel for Hugo Black at 75." *American University Law Review* 10 (January 1961): 1-6.

6241. Rostow, Eugene V. "Mr. Justice Black: Some Introductory Observations." *Yale Law Journal* 65 (February 1956): 450-453.

6242. Rutledge, Ivan C. "Justice Black and Labor Law." *UCLA Law Review* 14 (1967): 501-523.

6243. Shannon, David A. "Hugo Lafayette Black as United States Senator." *Alabama Law Review* 36 (Spring 1985): 881-898.

6344. Shores, David F. "Justice Black and the Antitrust Laws." *Antitrust Bulletin* 27 (Summer 1982): 389-432.

6245. Silverstein, Mark. *Constitutional Faiths: Felix Frankfurter, Hugo Black, and the Process of Judicial Decision Mak-*

ing. New York: Cornell University Press, 1984.

6246. Slayman, Charles H., Jr. "Speeches and Articles by Mr. Justice Hugo L. Black." *American University Law Review* 10 (January 1961): 116-119.

6247. Snowiss, Sylvia. "Justice Black and the First Amendment." Ph.D. diss., University of Chicago, 1968.

6248. Snowiss, Sylvia. "The Legacy of Justice Black." *Supreme Court Review* 1973 (1973): 187-252.

6249. Soles, James R. "Mr. Justice Black and the Defendant's Constitutional Rights." Ph.D. diss., University of Virginia, 1968.

6250. Strickland, Stephen P. "Mr. Justice Black: A Reappraisal." *Federal Bar Journal* 25 (Fall 1965): 365-382.

6251. Strickland, Stephen P., ed. *Hugo Black and the Supreme Court: A Symposium*. Indianapolis: Bobbs-Merrill, 1967.

6252. Sutherland, Arthur E., Jr. "Justice Black on Counsel and Non-Voluntary Confessions." *UCLA Law Review* 14 (1967): 536-552.

6253. Targan, Donald G. "Justice Black, Inherent Coercion: An Analytical Study of the Standard for Determining the Voluntariness of a Confession." *American University Law Review* 10 (January 1961): 53-61.

6254. Thornton, J. Mills, III. "Hugo Black and the Golden Age." *Alabama Law Review* 36 (Spring 1985): 899-914.

6255. Tillet, Paul. "Mr. Justice Black, Chief Justice Marshall, and the Commerce Clause." *Nebraska Law Review* 43 (December 1963): 1-26.

6256. Ulmer, S. Sidney. "The Longitudinal Behavior of Hugo Lafayette Black: Parabolic Support for Civil Liberties, 1937-1971." *Florida State University Law Review* 1 (Winter 1973): 131-153.

6257. Van Alstyne, William W. "Mr. Justice Black, Constitutional Review, and the Talisman of State Action." *Duke Law Journal* 1965 (Spring 1965): 219-247.

6258. Weissman, David L., and Murray A. Gordon. "Mr. Justice Black at 70: The Man and His Influence." *Lawyers Guild Review* 16 (Fall 1956): 101-103.

6259. Williams, Charlotte. "Hugo L. Black: A Study in the Judicial Process." Ph.D. diss., Johns Hopkins University, 1949.

6260. Winters, John W. "Opinion Variation as a Measure of Attitude Change in the Supreme Court: A Study of the Opinions of Justice Hugo L. Black from 1957 to 1968." Ph.D. diss., University of Kentucky, 1974.

6261. Wright, Charles A. "Hugo L. Black: A Great Man and a Great American." *Texas Law Review* 50 (December 1971): 1-5.

6262. Wright, J. Skelly. "Justice at the Dock: The Maritime Worker and Justice Black." *UCLA Law Review* 14 (1967): 521-535.

6263. Wyatt-Brown, Bertram. "Ethical Background of Hugo Black's Career: Thoughts Prompted by the Articles of Sheldon Hackney and Paul L. Murphy." *Alabama Law Review* 36 (Spring 1985): 915-926.

6264. Yarbrough, Tinsley E. "Justice Black and Equal Protection." *Southwestern University Law Review* 9 (1977): 899-936.

6265. Yarbrough, Tinsley E. "Justice Black, the First Amendment, and the Burger Court." *Mississippi Law Journal* 46 (Spring 1975): 203-246.

6266. Yarbrough, Tinsley E. "Justice Black, the Fourteenth Amendment, and Incorporation." *University of Miami Law Review* 30 (Winter 1976): 231-276.

6267. Yarbrough, Tinsley E. "Justices

Black and Douglas: The Judicial Function and the Scope of Constitutional Liberties." *Duke Law Journal* 1973 (January 1973): 441-486.

6268. Yarbrough, Tinsley E. *Mr. Justice Black and His Critics*. Durham, NC: Duke University Press, 1988.

6269. Yarbrough, Tinsley E. "Mr. Justice Black and Legal Positivism." *Virginia Law Review* 57 (April 1971): 375-407.

Writings

6270. Black, Hugo L. "About Edmond Cahn." *New York University Law Review* 40 (April 1965): 207-208.

6271. Black, Hugo L. "Address." *Missouri Bar Journal* 13 (September 1942): 173-176.

6272. Black, Hugo L. "The Bill of Rights." *New York University Law Review* 35 (April 1960): 865-881.

6273. Black, Hugo L. *A Constitutional Faith*. New York: Knopf, 1968.

6274. Black, Hugo L. "*Erie Railroad v. Tompkins.*" *Missouri Bar Journal* 13 (October 1942): 173-176.

6275. Black, Hugo L. "Inside a Senate Investigation." *Harper's Magazine* 172 (February 1936): 275-286.

6276. Black, Hugo L. "The Lawyer and Individual Freedom." *Tennessee Law Review* 21 (December 1950): 461-471.

6277. Black, Hugo L. "Mr. Justice Black." *Indiana Law Journal* 25 (Summer 1950): 423.

6278. Black, Hugo L. "Mr. Justice Frankfurter." *Harvard Law Review* 78 (June 1965): 1521-1522.

6279. Black, Hugo L. "Mr. Justice Murphy." *Michigan Law Review* 48 (February 1950): 739.

6280. Black, Hugo L. "Mr. Justice Rutledge." *Indiana Law Journal* 25 (Summer 1950): 423.

6281. Black, Hugo L. *One Man's Stand for Freedom: Mr. Justice Black and the Bill of Rights: A Collection of His Supreme Court Opinions*. New York: Knopf, 1963.

6282. Black, Hugo L. "Reminiscences." *Alabama Law Review* 18 (Fall 1963): 3-11.

6283. Black, Hugo L. "There Is a South of Union and Freedom." *Georgia Law Review* 2 (Fall 1967): 10-15.

6284. Black, Hugo L. "William Orville Douglas." *Yale Law Journal* 73 (May 1964): 915.

6285. Black, Hugo L., and Edmond Cahn. "Justice Black and First Amendment 'Absolutes': A Public Interview." *New York University Law Review* 37 (June 1962): 549-563.

Harry A. Blackmun

General Studies

6286. Arnold, Richard S. "Mr. Justice Blackmun: An Appreciation." *Hamline Law Review* 8 (January 1985): 20-26.

6287. Foote, Joseph. "Mr. Justice Blackmun." *Harvard Law School Bulletin* 21 (June 1970): 18-21.

6288. Fuqua, David. "Justice Harry A. Blackmun: The Abortion Decisions." *Arkansas Law Review* 34 (Winter 1980): 278-286.

6289. Gostin, Larry O. "Justice Harry A. Blackmun: The Supreme Court and the Limits of Medical Privacy, Guest Editor's Introduction." *American Journal of Law and Medicine* 13 (Summer/Fall 1987): 153-162.

6290. Kobylka, Joseph F. "The Court, Justice Blackmun, and Federalism: A Subtle Movement with Potentially Great

Ramifications." *Creighton Law Review* 19 (Winter 1986): 9-49.

6291. Koh, Harold H. "Equality with a Human Face: Justice Blackmun and the Equal Protection of Aliens." *Hamline Law Review* 8 (January 1985): 51-104.

6292. Koh, Harold H. "Rebalancing the Medical Triad: Justice Blackmun's Contributions to Law and Medicine." *American Journal of Law and Medicine* 13 (Summer/Fall 1987): 153-364.

6293. Lay, Donald P. "The Cases of Blackmun, J. on the U.S. Court of Appeals for the Eighth Circuit, 1959-1970." *Hamline Law Review* 8 (January 1985): 2-19.

6294. Mahoney, Joan. "Justice Blackmun, Congress, and the States: From *National League of Cities* to *Garcia*." *University of Missouri at Kansas City Law Review* 54 (Winter 1986): 215-242.

6295. Moore, Karen N. "Justice Blackmun's Contributions on the Court: The Commercial Speech and State Taxation Examples." *Hamline Law Review* 8 (January 1985): 29-50.

6296. Stone, Alan A. "Justice Blackmun: A Survey of His Decisions in Psychiatry and Law." *American Journal of Law and Medicine* 13 (Summer/Fall 1987): 291-313.

Writings

6297. Blackmun, Harry A. "Allowances of *In Forma Pauperis* Appeals in Section 2255 and *Habeas Corpus* Cases." *Federal Rules Decisions* 43 (1968): 343-361.

6298. Blackmun, Harry A. "Dedication Remarks." *Arkansas Law Review* 30 (Spring 1976): 14-22.

6299. Blackmun, Harry A. "Marital Deduction and Its Use in Minnesota." *Minnesota Law Review* 36 (December 1951): 50-64.

6300. Blackmun, Harry A. "Section 1983 and Federal Protection of Individual Rights: Will the Statute Remain Alive or Fade Away?" *New York University Law Review* 60 (April 1985): 1-29.

6301. Blackmun, Harry A. "Some Goals for Legal Education." *Ohio Northern University Law Review* 1 (1974): 403-410.

6302. Blackmun, Harry A. "Thoughts about Ethics." *Emory Law Journal* 24 (Winter 1975): 3-20.

John Blair, Jr.

General Studies

6303. Drinard, J. Elliott. "John Blair." *Proceedings of the Virginia State Bar Association* 39 (1927): 436-449.

6304. Horner, Fredrick. *History of the Blair, Banister, and Braxton Families.* Philadelphia: Lippincott, 1898.

6305. Uhle, John B. "John Blair." *Current Comment* 3 (April 15, 1891): 193-194.

Samuel Blatchford

General Studies

6306. Blatchford, Harriet W., ed. *The Blatchford Memorial.* New York: Privately printed, 1871.

6307. Hall, A. Oakey. "Justice Samuel Blatchford." *Green Bag* 5 (November 1893): 489-492.

6308. "Honors to the Memory of Mr. Justice Blatchford." *Albany Law Journal* 48 (November 18, 1893): 415-416.

6309. Paul, Arnold M. *Conservative Crisis and the Rule of Law: Attitudes of Bar and Bench, 1887-1895.* Ithaca, NY: Cornell University Press, 1960.

Joseph P. Bradley

General Studies

6310. Champagne, Anthony, and Dennis Pope. "Joseph P. Bradley: An Aspect of a Judicial Personality." *Political Psychology* 6 (September 1985): 481-493.

6311. Fairman, Charles. "The Education of a Justice: Justice Bradley and Some of His Colleagues." *Stanford Law Review* 1 (January 1949): 217-255.

6312. Fairman, Charles. "Mr. Justice Bradley's Appointment to the Supreme Court and the *Legal Tender Cases.*" *Harvard Law Review* 54 (April 1941): 977-1034; (May 1941): 1128-1155.

6313. Fairman, Charles. "The So-Called *Granger Cases,* Lord Hale, and Justice Bradley." *Stanford Law Review* 5 (July 1953): 587-679.

6314. Fairman, Charles. "What Makes a Great Justice: Mr. Justice Bradley and the Supreme Court, 1870-1892." *Boston University Law Review* 30 (January 1950): 49-102.

6315. Hackett, Frank W. "Mr. Justice Bradley." *Green Bag* 4 (April 12, 1892): 145-152.

6316. Keasbey, A. Q. "Joseph P. Bradley—A Tribute." *New Jersey Law Journal* 15 (March 1892): 65-69.

6317. Klinkhamer, Marie C. "Joseph P. Bradley: Private Public Opinions of a 'Political' Justice." *University of Detroit Law Journal* 38 (December 1960): 150-172.

6318. Lurie, Jonathan. "Mr. Justice Bradley: A Reassessment." *Seton Hall Law Review* 16 (1986): 343-380.

6319. Parker, Cortlandt. "Justice Joseph P. Bradley." *American Review* 28 (July/August 1894): 481-509.

6320. Parker, Cortlandt. "Mr. Justice Bradley of the United States Supreme Court." *New Jersey Historical Society Proceedings* 12 (1893): 143-177.

6321. Parker, Cortlandt. *Mr. Justice Bradley of the United States Supreme Court.* Newark, NJ: Advertiser Printing House, 1893.

6322. Scott, John A. "Justice Bradley's Evolving Concept of the Fourteenth Amendment from the *Slaughterhouse Cases* to the *Civil Rights Cases.*" *Rutgers Law Review* 25 (Summer 1971): 552-569.

6323. Stern, Horace. "Joseph Bradley." In *Great American Lawyers*, vol. 6, edited by William D. Lewis, 345-404. Philadelphia: J. C. Winston Company, 1907-1909.

6324. Whiteside, Ruth A. "Justice Joseph Bradley and the Reconstruction Amendment." Ph.D. diss., Rice University, 1981.

6325. Worth, George C. "Honorable Joseph P. Bradley: The Passing of a Great Lawyer." *New Jersey Law Journal* 20 (October 1897): 299-304.

Writings

6326. Bradley, Joseph P. *Family Notes Respecting the Bradley Family of Fairfield.* Newark, NJ: A. Pierson, 1894.

6327. Bradley, Joseph P. *Miscellaneous Writings of the Late Honorable Joseph P. Bradley and a Review of His "Judicial Record".* Edited by Charles Bradley. Newark, NJ: L. J. Hardham, 1902.

6328. Bradley, Joseph P. "Saint Memin's Portrait of Marshall." *Century Magazine* 38 (September 1889): 778-781.

Louis D. Brandeis

General Studies

6329. Abrams, Richard M. "Brandeis and the New Haven-Boston and Main Merger Battle Revisited." *Business History Review* 36 (Winter 1962): 408-430.

6330. Acheson, Dean G. "Mr. Justice Brandeis." *Harvard Law Review* 55 (December 1941): 191-192.

6331. Alexander, Raymond P. "Louis Dembitz Brandeis: The End of an Era." *National Bar Journal* 1 (October 1941): 143-146.

6332. Armstrong, Walter P. "Louis D. Brandeis: Lawyer and Jurist." *American Bar Association Journal* 32 (October 1946): 649-652.

6333. Aronson, Moses J. "Democracy in Action: The Brandeis Way." *Journal of Social Philosophy* 4 (January 1939): 151-161.

6334. "As a Friend Sees Justice Brandeis." *Literary Digest* 53 (July 1, 1916): 28.

6335. Auerbach, Jerold J. "From Rags to Robes: The Legal Profession, Social Mobility, and the American Jewish Experience." *American Jewish Historical Quarterly* 66 (December 1976): 249-284.

6336. Badger, William V. "Louis D. Brandeis: Judge, Legal Scholar, and Statesman." *Social Science* 34 (April 1959): 80-88.

6337. Bagan, Earl S. "Louis Dembitz Brandeis: Of the People, by the People, for the People." *Oklahoma City University Law Review* 9 (Fall 1984): 505-539.

6338. Baker, Leonard. *Brandeis and Frankfurter.* New York: New York University Press, 1986.

6339. Balogh, Elmer. "Mr. Justice Bran-

deis." *Harvard Law Review* 45 (November 1931): 1-3.

6340. Bander, Edward J. "The Justice of Louis Dembitz Brandeis." *Commentary* 22 (November 1956): 453-455.

6341. Bartlett, Louis. "Mr. Brandeis." *Nation* 102 (March 2, 1916): 257.

6342. Bartlett, Robert M. *The Way of Liberty: Louis Dembitz Brandeis, They Did Something About It.* New York: Association Press, 1939.

6343. Berlin, George S. "The Brandeis-Weizmann Dispute." *American Jewish Historical Quarterly* 60 (September 1970): 37-68.

6344. Bernard, Burton C. "Brandeis in St. Louis." *St. Louis University Law Journal* 11 (Fall 1966): 10-11.

6345. Biddle, Francis. "Louis Dembitz Brandeis." *American Bar Association Journal* 29 (February 1943): 71-73.

6346. Bikle, Henry W. "Mr. Justice Brandeis and the Regulation of Railroads." *Harvard Law Review* 45 (November 1931): 4-32.

6347. Bloom, Solomon. "The Liberalism of Louis D. Brandeis, the Father of the New Deal." *Commentary* 6 (October 1968): 313-321.

6348. Brin, Joseph G. "Louis D. Brandeis." *Law Society Journal* 7 (November 1936): 640-642.

6349. Coburn, Frederick W. "Who Is This Man Brandeis?" *Human Life* 12 (February 9, 1911): 9.

6350. Dawson, Nelson L. "Curbing Leviathan: The Social Philosophy of Louis D. Brandeis." *Kentucky Historical Society Register* 77 (Winter 1979): 30-45.

6351. Dawson, Nelson L. *Louis D. Brandeis, Felix Frankfurter, and the New Deal.* Hamden, CT: Archon Books, 1980.

6352. DeHaas, Jacob. *Louis D. Brandeis:*

A Biographical Sketch with Special Reference to His Contribution to Jewish and Zionist History. New York: Bloch, 1929.

6353. Dilliard, Irving. "Saint Louis Recalls Brandeis." *St. Louis University Law Journal* 11 (Fall 1966): 12-14.

6354. Dilliard, Irving, ed. *Mr. Justice Brandeis, Great American: Press Opinion and Public Appraisal.* St. Louis: Modern View Press, 1941.

6355. Doro, Marion E. "The Brandeis Brief." *Vanderbilt Law Review* 11 (June 1958): 783-799.

6356. Douglas, William O. "The Lasting Influence of Mr. Justice Brandeis." *Temple Law Quarterly* 19 (April 1946): 361-370.

6357. Drushal, John G. "The Speeches of Louis Dembitz Brandeis (1908-1916)." *Speech Monographs* 19 (June 1952): 124.

6358. Dunham, Allison. "The Legacy of Brandeis, Holmes, and Stone." *Saturday Review* 39 (December 15, 1956): 13-15.

6359. Dunnington, Miles W. *Senator Thomas E. Walsh and the Vindication of Louis D. Brandeis.* Chicago: Department of History, University of Chicago, 1940.

6360. Ehrenhaft, Peter D. "Bruce Allen Murphy, The Brandeis-Frankfurter Connection: The Secret Political Activities of Two Supreme Court Justices." *American Journal of Legal History* 27 (July 1983): 302-307.

6361. Ellmann, James I. "Mr. Justice Brandeis." *Commercial Law Journal* 38 (August 1933): 363-372.

6362. Ernst, Morris L. *Justice Brandeis' Five Points.* Philadelphia: Brandeis Lawyers' Society, 1947.

6363. Evans, Elizabeth G. "Mr. Justice Brandeis: New Associate Justice of the United States Supreme Court." *Case and Comment* 23 (August 1916): 254-255.

6364. Farnum, George R. "Brandeis: Prophet of Industrial Era." *Case and Comment* 47 (November/December 1941): 16-17.

6365. Farnum, George R. "Brandeis: Prophet of Industrial Era." *Law Notes* 45 (November 1941): 26-27.

6366. Farnum, George R. "Brandeis: Prophet of Industrial Era." *New Jersey Law Journal* 64 (October 23, 1941): 483.

6367. Farnum, George R. "Justice Brandeis: Gentleman and Jurist." *Massachusetts Law Society Journal* 3 (November 1931): 306.

6368. Farnum, George R. "Louis D. Brandeis: A Chapter Closed." *Lawyer* 2 (April 1939): 8-9.

6369. Flexner, Bernard. *Mr. Justice Brandeis and the University of Louisville.* Louisville: University of Louisville, 1938.

6370. Fox, George A. *Hearings before the Subcommittee of the Committee on the Judiciary, United States Senate ... on the Nomination of Louis D. Brandeis to be an Associate Justice of the Supreme Court of the United States.* New York: Evening Post Job Printing Office, 1916.

6371. Frank, John P. "The Legal Ethics of Louis D. Brandeis." *Stanford Law Review* 17 (April 1965): 683-709.

6372. Frankel, Joseph. *Louis D. Brandeis: Patriot, Judge, Zionist.* Washington, DC: B'nai B'rith Hillel Foundation, 1959.

6373. Frankfurter, Felix. "Mr. Justice Brandeis." *Harvard Law Review* 55 (December 1941): 181-183.

6374. Frankfurter, Felix. "Mr. Justice Brandeis and the Constitution." *Harvard Law Review* 45 (November 1931): 33-105.

6375. Frankfurter, Felix, ed. *Mr. Justice Brandeis.* New Haven, CT: Yale University Press, 1932.

6376. Freund, Paul A. "An Appreciation

of Mr. Justice Brandeis." *St. Louis University Law Journal* 11 (Fall 1966): 4-5.

6377. Freund, Paul A. "The Evolution of a Brandeis Dissent." *Manuscripts* 10 (Spring 1958): 18-25.

6378. Freund, Paul A. "Holmes and Brandeis in Retrospect." *Boston Bar Journal* 28 (September/October 1984): 7-10.

6379. Freund, Paul A. "Justice Brandeis: A Law Clerk's Remembrance." *American Jewish History* 68 (September 1978): 7-18.

6380. Freund, Paul A. "The Liberalism of Justice Brandeis." *American-Jewish Archives* 10 (April 1958): 3-11.

6381. Freund, Paul A. "Mr. Justice Brandeis." *Harvard Law Review* 55 (December 1941): 195-196.

6382. Freund, Paul A. "Mr. Justice Brandeis." *Harvard Law Review* 70 (March 1957): 769-792.

6383. Freund, Paul A. *Portrait of a Liberal Judge: Mr. Justice Brandeis, on Understanding the Supreme Court.* Boston: Little, Brown, 1957.

6384. Freund, Paul A. "The Supreme Court: A Tale of Two Terms." *Ohio State Law Journal* 26 (Spring 1965): 225-238.

6385. Friendly, Henry J. "Mr. Justice Brandeis: The Quest for Reason." *University of Pennsylvania Law Review* 108 (May 1960): 985-999.

6386. Gal, Allon. *Brandeis of Boston.* Cambridge: Harvard University Press, 1980.

6387. Gersh, Harry. *These Are My People.* New York: Behrman House, 1959.

6388. Goedecke, Robert. "Holmes, Brandeis, and Frankfurter: Differences in Pragmatic Jurisprudence." *Ethics* 74 (January 1964): 83-96.

6389. Goldstein, Joseph M. "The Individualism of Mr. Justice Brandeis." *New Jersey Law Journal* 64 (November 1941): 505, 509-511.

6390. Hamilton, Walton H. "The Jurist's Art of Louis D. Brandeis." *Columbia Law Review* 31 (November 1931): 1073-1093.

6391. Hand, Learned. "Birthday Tribute on 82nd Birthday." *United States Law Review* 72 (November 1938): 632-634.

6392. Hand, Learned. "Justice Louis D. Brandeis and the Good Life." *Journal of Social Philosophy* 4 (January 1939): 144-147.

6393. Hand, Learned. "Louis Dembitz Brandeis: Memorial Session, Supreme Court of the United States." *American Bar Association Journal* 29 (February 1943): 67.

6394. Hapgood, Norman. "Americans We Like: Justice Brandeis, Apostle of Freedom." *Nation* 125 (October 5, 1927): 330-331.

6395. Hapgood, Norman. *Mr. Brandeis, the Changing Years.* New York: Farrar and Rinehart, 1930.

6396. Hard, William. "Brandeis." *Outlook* 113 (May 31, 1916): 271.

6397. Hofstadter, Samuel H. "In Memoriam: Louis Dembitz Brandeis." *American Bar Association Journal* 47 (October 1961): 978-980.

6398. Honigman, Jason L. "Louis D. Brandeis: The People's Lawyer." *University of Detroit Law Journal* 18 (January 1955): 127-133.

6399. Howell, R.B.C. "Louis Dembitz Brandeis." *Tennessee Law Review* 16 (June 1940): 441-450.

6400. Hughes, Charles E. "Mr. Justice Brandeis." *Columbia Law Review* 31 (November 1931): 1071-1072.

6401. Hughes, Charles E., ed. *Mr. Justice Brandeis.* New Haven, CT: Yale University Press, 1932.

6402. Hutcheson, Joseph C. "Louis Dembitz Brandeis." *Texas Law Review* 20 (November 1941): 1-3.

6403. Jacobs, Rose G. "Justice Brandeis and Hadassah." *New Palestine* 32 (November 14, 1941): 17.

6404. Jaffe, Louis L. "The Contributions of Mr. Justice Brandeis to Administrative Law." *Iowa Law Review* 18 (January 1932): 213-227.

6405. Jaffe, Louis L. "An Impression of Mr. Justice Brandeis." *Harvard Law School Bulletin* 8 (April 1957): 10-11.

6406. Jaffe, Louis L. "Was Brandeis an Activist? The Search for Intermediate Premises." *Harvard Law Review* 80 (March 1967): 986-1004.

6407. Kallen, Horace M. "The Faith of Louis Brandeis." *New Palestine* 32 (November 14, 1941): 23.

6408. Kallen, Horace M. *The Faith of Louis D. Brandeis, Zionist.* New York: Hadassah, Women's Zionist Organization of America, 1943.

6409. Kaplan, Jacob J. "Mr. Justice Brandeis: Prophet." *New Palestine* 32 (November 14, 1941): 27.

6410. Katz, Irving. "Henry Lee Higginson vs. Louis Dembitz Brandeis: A Collision between Tradition and Reform." *New England Quarterly* 41 (March 1968): 67-81.

6411. Kelly, Florence. "Mr. Brandeis." *Survey* 36 (May 13, 1916): 191-193.

6412. Kennedy, W.P.M. "Justice Louis D. Brandeis." *University of Toronto Law Journal* 4 (1941): 402.

6413. Kobler, Franz. *Her Children Call Her Blessed: A Portrait of the Jewish Mother.* New York: Stephen Daye Press, 1955.

6414. Konefsky, Samuel J. "A Fresh Glimpse of Brandeis." *Virginia Law Review* 44 (November 1958): 1093-1097.

6415. Konefsky, Samuel J. "Holmes and Brandeis: Companies in Dissent." *Vanderbilt Law Review* 10 (February 1957): 269-300.

6416. Konefsky, Samuel J. *The Legacy of Holmes and Brandeis: A Study in the Influence of Ideas.* New York: Macmillan, 1957.

6417. Kronstein, Heinrich, and Joachmin Volhard. "Brandeis before the FTC in 1915: Should Advisory Opinions Be Given?" *Federal Bar Journal* 24 (Fall 1964): 609-621.

6418. Landis, James M. "Mr. Justice Brandeis." *Legal Intelligencer* 106 (January 29, 1942): 1.

6419. Landis, James M. "Mr. Justice Brandeis: A Law Clerk's View." *American Jewish Historical Society Publications* 46 (June 1957): 467-473.

6420. Landis, James M. "Mr. Justice Brandeis and the Harvard Law School." *Harvard Law Review* 55 (December 1941): 184-190.

6421. Laski, Harold J. "Mr. Justice Brandeis." *Harper's Magazine* 209 (January 1934): 168-218.

6422. Lerner, Max. "Homage to Brandeis." *Nation* 148 (February 15, 1939): 222.

6423. Lerner, Max. *Homage to Louis D. Brandeis.* New York: Viking Press, 1939.

6424. Lerner, Max. "Mr. Justice Brandeis." In *Ideas Are Weapons: The History and Uses of Ideas*, edited by Max Lerner, 70-112. New York: Viking Press, 1939.

6425. Lerner, Max. "The Social Thought of Mr. Justice Brandeis." *Yale Law Journal* 41 (November 1931): 1-32.

6426. Leventhal, Louis E. "Louis Dembitz Brandeis." *American Jewish Year Book* 44 (1942/1943): 37-52.

6427. Levy, Beryl H. *Our Constitution:*

Tool or Testament? 'Democracy Militant'. Port Washington, NY: Kennikat Press, 1965.

6428. Levy, David W. "The Lawyer as Judge: Brandeis' View of the Legal Profession." *Oklahoma Law Review* 22 (November 1969): 374-395.

6429. Levy, David W., and Bruce A. Murphy. "Preserving the Progressive Spirit in Conservative Times: The Joint Reform Efforts of Justice Brandeis and Professor Frankfurter, 1916-1933." *Michigan Law Review* 78 (August 1980): 1252-1304.

6430. Lief, Alfred. *The Personal History of an American Ideal.* Harrisburg, PA: Telegraph Press, 1936.

6431. "Louis Dembitz Brandeis, 1856-1941." *American Bar Association Journal* 27 (November 1941): 689.

6432. Luban, David. "The Noblesse Oblige Tradition in the Practice of Law: Assessing Change." *Vanderbilt Law Review* 41 (May 1988): 717-740.

6433. Luney, Kenneth D. "Mr. Justice Brandeis and the Problems of Labor." Ph.D. diss., University of Illinois, 1932.

6434. McGraw, Thomas K. *Prophets of Regulation.* Cambridge: Harvard University Press, 1984.

6435. McLennen, Edward F. "Louis D. Brandeis as a Lawyer." *Massachusetts Law Quarterly* 33 (September 1948): 1-28.

6436. Madison, Charles A. "Louis D. Brandeis: Jew and Zionist." *Chicago Jewish Forum* 10 (Summer 1952): 262-267.

6437. Magruder, Calvert. "Louis Dembitz Brandeis." *American Bar Association Journal* 29 (February 1943): 69-71.

6438. Magruder, Calvert. "Mr. Justice Brandeis." *Harvard Law Review* 55 (December 1941): 193-194.

6439. Manning, George H. "Brandeis Defends Newspaper Crusading as Minnesota 'Gag' Law." *Editor and Publisher* 63 (February 7, 1931): 5-6.

6440. Mason, Alpheus T. "A Birthday Tribute: Address Delivered on the Eighty-second Birthday of Mr. Justice Brandeis." *United States Law Review* 72 (November 1938): 634-636.

6441. Mason, Alpheus T. *Brandeis: A Free Man's Life.* New York: Viking Press, 1946.

6442. Mason, Alpheus T. *Brandeis and the Modern State.* Washington, DC: National Home Library Foundation, 1936.

6443. Mason, Alpheus T. *Brandeis: Lawyer and Judge in the Modern State.* Princeton, NJ: Princeton University Press, 1933.

6444. Mason, Alpheus T. *The Brandeis Way: A Case Study in the Workings of Democracy.* Princeton, NJ: Princeton University Press, 1938.

6445. Mason, Alpheus T. "Louis Brandeis: People's Attorney." *American Mercury* 64 (April 1947): 440-447.

6446. Mason, Alpheus T. "Louis Dembitz Brandeis: Tempered Boldness in a Stand-Pat Society." *University of Pittsburgh Law Review* 28 (March 1967): 421-441.

6447. Mason, Alpheus T. "Mr. Justice Brandeis: A Student of Social and Economic Science." *University of Pennsylvania Law Review* 79 (April 1930): 665-706.

6448. Mason, Alpheus T. "Mr. Justice Brandeis and the Constitution." *University of Pennsylvania Law Review* 80 (April 1931): 799-841.

6449. Mason, Alpheus T. "Mr. Justice Brandeis: Exponent of Social Intelligence." *American Political Science Review* 25 (November 1931): 965-979.

6450. Mason, Alpheus T. "The Social Statesmanship of Mr. Justice Brandeis." *Journal of Social Philosophy* 4 (January 1939): 148-150.

6451. Mason, Alpheus T. *Variations on*

the Liberal Theme: Mr. Justice Brandeis. Philadelphia: Brandeis Lawyer's Society, 1947.

6452. Mendelson, Wallace. "The Influence of James B. Thayer upon the Work of Holmes, Brandeis, and Frankfurter." *Vanderbilt Law Review* 31 (January 1978): 71-87.

6453. Mersky, Roy M. *Louis Dembitz Brandeis, 1856-1941: A Bibliography.* New Haven, CT: Yale Law Library, 1958.

6454. Miller, Neville. "Justice Brandeis and the University of Louisville School of Law." *Filson Club Historical Quarterly* 34 (April 1960): 156-159.

6455. Mitchell, Jonathon. "Brandeis: Heavenly Visitor." *New Republic* 89 (December 2, 1936): 150.

6456. Morris, Jeffrey B. "The American Jewish Judge: An Appraisal on the Occasion of the Bicentennial." *Jewish Social Studies* 38 (Summer/Fall 1976): 195-223.

6457. Murphy, Bruce A. *The Brandeis-Frankfurter Connection: The Secret Political Activities of Two Supreme Court Justices.* Oxford, England: Oxford University Press, 1982.

6458. Murphy, Bruce A. "Supreme Court Justices as Politicians: The Extrajudicial Activities of Justices Louis D. Brandeis and Felix Frankfurter." Ph.D. diss., University of Virginia, 1978.

6459. Nathanson, Nathaniel L. "Mr. Justice Brandeis: A Law Clerk's Recollection of the October Term, 1934." *American Jewish Archives* 15 (April 1963): 6-16.

6460. Nathanson, Nathaniel L. "The Philosophy of Mr. Justice Brandeis and Civil Liberties Today." *University of Illinois Law Forum* 1979 (1979): 261-300.

6461. Newland, Chester A. "Innovation in Judicial Technique: The Brandeis Opin-

ion." *Southwestern Social Science Quarterly* 42 (June 1961): 22-31.

6462. Noble, Iris. *Firebrand for Justice, a Biography of Louis Dembitz Brandeis.* Philadelphia: Westminster Press, 1969.

6463. Oko, A. S. "Mr. Brandeis." *Nation* 102 (March 2, 1916): 251-252.

6464. Padway, Joseph A. "Brandeis and Labor." *American Federationist* 48 (December 1941): 12-13, 32.

6465. Paper, Lewis J. *Brandeis: An Intimate Biography of One of America's Truly Great Supreme Court Justices.* Englewood Cliffs, NJ: Prentice-Hall, 1983.

6466. Parzen, Herbert. *Brandeis and the Balfour Declaration.* New York: Herzl Press, 1963.

6467. Patterson, Edwin W. "Mr. Justice Brandeis: Seventy-five Years Old." *Nation* 133 (November 1931): 513-514.

6468. Pearce, Catherine O. *The Louis D. Brandeis Story.* New York: Crowell, 1970.

6469. Pollack, Ervin H., ed. *The Brandeis Reader: The Life and Contributions of Mr. Justice Louis D. Brandeis.* New York: Oceana Publications, 1956.

6470. Pollard, Joseph P. *Justice Brandeis and the Constitution.* New York: Charles Scribner's Sons, 1930.

6471. Poole, Ernest. "Brandeis: A Remarkable Record of Unselfish Work Done in the Public Interest." *American Magazine* 71 (February 1911): 481-493.

6472. Rabinowitz, Ezekiel. *Justice Louis D. Brandeis, the Zionist Chapter of His Life.* New York: Philosophical Library, 1968.

6473. Rand, I. C. "Louis D. Brandeis." *Canadian Bar Review* 25 (March 1947): 240-250.

6474. Richberg, Donald R. "The Industrial Liberalism of Justice Brandeis." *Columbia Law Review* 31 (November 1931): 1094-1103.

6475. Robbins, Alexander H. "Louis D. Brandeis, Associate Justice of the U.S. Supreme Court." *Central Law Journal* 82 (June 9, 1916): 403-404.

6476. Robbins, Alexander H. "Louis D. Brandeis, the Apostle of Efficiency in the Management of Public Service Corporations." *Central Law Journal* 80 (January 22, 1915): 78-79.

6477. Rosenfalb, Joseph. "Reflections on a Visit to Mr. Justice Brandeis." *Iowa Law Review* 27 (March 1942): 359-366.

6478. Ross, Charles G. "The Philosophy of Justice Brandeis, Credited with Fathering Woodrow Wilson's Theory of Regulated Competition." *St. Louis Post-Dispatch* (June 19, 1927): 1B.

6479. Sargent, Francis W. "Louis D. Brandeis: The Idea of Federalism and the Concept of Responsibility: A Lesson for Our Times." *Massachusetts Law Quarterly* 54 (Summer 1969): 187-203.

6480. Shapiro, Jonathan. "American Jews in Politics: The Case of Louis D. Brandeis." *American Jewish History Quarterly* 55 (December 1965): 199-211.

6481. Shishkin, Boris. "Brandeis: A Name to Remember." *American Federationist* 64 (February 1957): 24-25.

6482. Shulman, Harry. "Mr. Justice Brandeis." *Yale Law Journal* 48 (March 1939): 717-718.

6483. Siskin, Edgar E. "Mr. Justice Brandeis: A Rabbi's Recollection." *American Jewish Archives* 18 (November 1966): 129-132.

6484. Smith, Reginald H. "Mr. Justice Brandeis and Justice and the Poor." *Legal Aid Brief Case* 15 (February 1957): 103-107.

6485. Smyth, William E. "Judge Brandeis in Palestine." *Review of Reviews* 60 (December 1919): 609-615.

6486. Staples, Henry L. *The Fall of the Railroad Empire: Brandeis and the New Haven Merger Battle.* Syracuse, NY: Syracuse University Press, 1947.

6487. Stone, Harlan F. "Louis Dembitz Brandeis." *American Bar Association Journal* 29 (February 1943): 73-75, 109.

6488. Strum, Philippa. *Louis D. Brandeis: Justice for the People.* Cambridge: Harvard University Press, 1984.

6489. Tobriner, Matthew O. "Brandeis, Architect of the Law." *California State Bar Journal* 13 (August 1938): 20-23.

6490. Todd, Alden L. *Justice on Trial: The Case of Louis D. Brandeis.* New York: McGraw-Hill, 1964.

6491. Ulrich, Walter. "The Creation of a Legacy: Brandeis' Concurring Opinion in *Whitney v. California.*" *Southern Speech Communication Journal* 50 (Winter 1945): 143-155.

6492. Urofsky, Melvin I. "The Brandeis-Frankfurter Conversations." *Supreme Court Review* 1985 (1985): 299-339.

6493. Urofsky, Melvin I. "Conservatism of Mr. Justice Brandeis." *Modern Age* 23 (Winter 1979): 39-48.

6494. Urofsky, Melvin I. "The Lawyer-Qua-Citizen: The Relevance of Brandeis Today." *Filson Club Historical Quarterly* 47 (January 1973): 5-13.

6495. Urofsky, Melvin I. *Louis D. Brandeis and the Progressive Tradition.* Boston: Little, Brown, 1981.

6496. Urofsky, Melvin I. *A Mind of One Piece: Brandeis and American Reform.* New York: Charles Scribner's Sons, 1971.

6497. Urofsky, Melvin I. "The 'Outrageous' Brandeis Nomination." *Supreme Court Historical Society Yearbook* 1979 (1979): 8-19.

6498. Urofsky, Melvin I. "Wilson, Brandeis, and the Trust Issue, 1912-1914." *MidAmerica* 49 (January 1967): 3-28.

6499. Van Doren, Charles. *Letters to Mother.* Manhasset, NY: Channel Press, 1959.

6500. Vose, Clement E. "The National Consumers' League and the Brandeis Brief." *Midwest Journal of Political Science* 1 (November 1957): 267-290.

6501. Waite, John B. "Mr. Brandeis." *Nation* 102 (February 24, 1916): 220-221.

6502. Warren, Samuel D., and Louis D. Brandeis. "The Right to Privacy." *Harvard Law Review* 4 (December 15, 1890): 193-220.

6503. Weisman, Morris. "Brandeis and the *Lennox* Case." *Commercial Law Journal* 47 (February 1942): 36-41.

6504. Welliver, Judson C. "Louis D. Brandeis, Troublemaker." *The World Today* 21 (1912): 1603.

6505. Whittaker, Charles E. "Reflections on Mr. Justice Brandeis." *St. Louis University Law Journal* 11 (Fall 1966): 6-9.

6506. Winant, John G. "Mr. Justice Brandeis." *Law Society Journal* 7 (May 1936): 774-777.

6507. Winograd, Max. "Brandeis: Profile of a Commercial Lawyer." *Commercial Law Journal* 62 (February 1957): 54-57.

6508. Wise, James W. *Louis D. Brandeis: Jews Are Like That!* New York: Brenlanos, 1928.

6509. Woldman, Albert A. "Justice Louis D. Brandeis: Crusader for Human Rights." *Cleveland Bar Association Journal* 28 (March 1957): 67, 72-80.

6510. Wyzanski, Charles E., Jr. "Brandeis." *Atlantic* 198 (November 1956): 66-72.

Writings

6511. Brandeis, Louis D. *Brandeis and (Brandeis): The Reversible Mind of Louis D. Brandeis, 'the People's Lawyer', as It Stands Revealed in His Public Utterances, Briefs, and Correspondences.* Boston: United Shoe Machinery, 1912.

6512. Brandeis, Louis D. *The Brandeis Guide to the Modern World.* Edited by Alfred Lief. Boston: Little, Brown, 1941.

6513. Brandeis, Louis D. *Brandeis on Zionism: A Collection of Addresses and Statements.* Washington, DC: Zionist Organization of America, 1942.

6514. Brandeis, Louis D. *Business: A Profession.* Boston: Small, Maynard, 1914.

6515. Brandeis, Louis D. *The Curse of Bigness: Miscellaneous Papers of Louis D. Brandeis.* Edited by Osmond K. Fraenkel. New York: Viking Press, 1934.

6516. Brandeis, Louis D. *The Letters of Louis D. Brandeis.* Edited by Melvin I. Urofsky. Albany: State University of New York Press, 1971-1978.

6517. Brandeis, Louis D. "The Living Law." *Illinois Law Review* 10 (February 1916): 461-471.

6518. Brandeis, Louis D. *Mr. Justice Brandeis, Mr. Justice.* Edited by Paul A. Freund. Chicago: University of Chicago Press, 1956.

6519. Brandeis, Louis D. *Other People's Money: And How the Bankers Use It.* New York: Stokes, 1914.

6520. Brandeis, Louis D. *The Social and Economic Views of Mr. Justice Brandeis.* Edited by Alfred Lief. New York: Vanguard Press, 1930.

6521. Brandeis, Louis D. *The Unpublished Opinions of Mr. Justice Brandeis: The Supreme Court at Work.* Edited by Alexander M. Bickel. Chicago: University of Chicago Press, 1967.

6522. Brandeis, Louis D. *The Words of Justice Brandeis.* Edited by Soloman Goldman. New York: H. Schuman, 1953.

6523. Brandeis, Louis D., and Josephine

Goldmark. *Women in Industry*. New York: Arno, 1969.

6524. Brandeis, Louis D., and Samuel D. Warren. "The Right to Privacy." *Harvard Law Review* 4 (December 15, 1890): 193-220.

William J. Brennan, Jr.

General Studies

6525. Aldave, Barbara B. "Brennan: Embattled Defender of Liberalism." *National Law Journal* 2 (February 18, 1980): 22.

6526. Alexander, Jack. "Mr. Justice from Jersey." *Saturday Evening Post* 230 (September 28, 1957): 25, 128-130, 132-133.

6527. Berman, Daniel M. "Mr. Justice Brennan." *Nation* 183 (October 3, 1956): 298.

6528. Berman, Daniel M. "Mr. Justice Brennan: A Preliminary Appraisal." *Catholic University of America Law Review* 7 (January 1958): 1-15.

6529. Berman, Daniel M. "Mr. Justice Brennan after Five Years." *Catholic University of America Law Review* 11 (1962): 1-2.

6530. Cooper, Charles J., and Nelson Lund. "Landmarks of Constitutional Interpretation: Seven Lessons in the Rule of Law for Justice Brennan." *Policy Review* 40 (Spring 1987): 10-24.

6531. Defeis, Elizabeth F. "Justice William J. Brennan, Jr." *Seton Hall Law Review* 16 (1986): 429-461.

6532. Del Guidice, Richard J. "Justice Brennan and Freedom of Expression." Ph.D. diss., University of Massachusetts, 1975.

6533. Denniston, Lyle. "Justices Brennan, Stevens Say High Court Favors Prosecu-

tion." *Criminal Justice Newsletter* 17 (February 3, 1986): 2-3.

6534. Denvir, John. "Justice Brennan, Justice Rehnquist, and Free Speech." *Northwestern University Law Review* 80 (November 1985): 285-320.

6535. Dorman, Charles. "Justice Brennan: The Individual and Labor Law." *Chicago-Kent Law Review* 58 (Fall 1982): 1003-1052.

6536. Foote, Joseph. "Mr. Justice Brennan, a Profile." *Harvard Law School Bulletin* 18 (November 1966): 4-6.

6537. Friedman, Stephen J. "Mr. Justice Brennan: The First Decade." *Harvard Law Review* 80 (November 1966): 7-22.

6538. Friedman, Stephen J., ed. *An Affair with Freedom: Justice William J. Brennan, Jr.* New York: Atheneum, 1967.

6539. Gaze, James A. "Justice Brennan's Reflections on Judicial Modernization." *Rutgers Law Review* 10 (Fall 1978): 1-24.

6540. Gibbons, John J. "Tribute to Justice Brennan." *Rutgers Law Review* 36 (Summer 1984): 729-739.

6541. Gillmor, Donald M. "Justice William Brennan and the Failed 'Theory' of Actual Malice." *Journalism Quarterly* 59 (Summer 1982): 249-255.

6542. Goldberg, Arthur J. "Mr. Justice Brennan and the First Amendment." *Rutgers Law Review* 4 (Fall 1972): 8-43.

6543. Harrison, Joseph. "Mr. Justice Brennan: Eleventh from Harvard Law School." *Harvard Law School Bulletin* 8 (February 1957): 7-8.

6544. Heck, Edward V. "Justice Brennan and Freedom of Expression Doctrine in the Burger Court." *San Diego Law Review* 24 (September/October 1987): 1153-1183.

6545. Heck, Edward V. "Justice Brennan

and the Changing Supreme Court." Ph.D. diss., Johns Hopkins University, 1978.

6546. Heck, Edward V. "Socialization of a Freshman Justice: The Early Years of Justice Brennan." *Pacific Law Journal* 10 (July 1979): 707-728.

6547. "Justice Brennan Calls National Court of Appeals Proposal Unnecessary and Ill-Advised." *American Bar Association Journal* 59 (August 1973): 835-840.

6548. McKay, Robert B. "Mr. Justice Brennan, *Baker v. Carr*, and the Judicial Function." *Rutgers Camden Law Journal* 4 (Fall 1972): 44-57.

6549. McQuade, Francis P., and Alexander T. Kardos. "Mr. Justice Brennan and His Legal Philosophy." *Notre Dame Lawyer* 33 (May 1958): 321-349.

6550. Michelman, Frank I. "States' Rights and States' Roles: Permutations of 'Sovereignty' in *National League of Cities v. Usery*." *Yale Law Journal* 86 (May 1977): 1165-1195.

6551. O'Neill, Robert M. "Mr. Justice Brennan and the Conditions of Unconstitutional Conditions." *Rutgers Camden Law Journal* 4 (Fall 1972): 58-84.

6552. Phelps, Glenn A., and Timothy A. Martinez. "Brennan v. Rehnquist: The Politics of Constitutional Jurisprudence." *Gonzaga Law Review* 22 (June 1987): 307-325.

6553. Regan, John J. "Freedom of the Mind and Justice Brennan." *Catholic Lawyer* 9 (Autumn 1963): 269-296.

6554. Rezneck, Daniel A. "Justice Brennan and Discovery in Criminal Cases." *Rutgers Law Review* 4 (Fall 1972): 85-102.

6555. Robins, William. "A Bibliography of Associate Justice William J. Brennan." *Seton Hall Law Review* 12 (Spring 1982): 430-444.

6556. Rothblatt, Morris. "Mr. Justice Brennan and the First Amendment." Ph.D. diss., New School for Social Research, 1967.

6557. Shannon, William V. "The Common Sense of Mr. Justice Brennan." *Catholic University of America Law Review* 11 (January 1962): 3-14.

6558. Sheerin, John B. "Catholic Comes to Court." *Catholic World* 184 (November 1956): 81-85.

6559. Speiser, Lawrence. "Mr. Justice Brennan and the Bill of Rights." *Catholic University of America Law Review* 11 (January 1962): 15-39.

6560. Stephens, Pamela J. "The Single Contract as Minimum Contracts: Justice Brennan 'Has It His Way'." *William and Mary Law Review* 28 (Fall 1986): 89-118.

Writings

6561. Brennan, William J., Jr. "Address to the New Jersey Bar." *Guild Practitioner* 33 (Fall 1976): 152-168.

6562. Brennan, William J., Jr. "The Administrative Judge: The Key to Effective Court Management." *Journal of the American Judicature Society* 45 (April 1962): 272-278.

6563. Brennan, William J., Jr. *An Affair with Freedom*. New York: Atheneum, 1967.

6564. Brennan, William J., Jr. "The Bill of Rights and the States." *New York University Law Review* 36 (April 1961): 761-778.

6565. Brennan, William J., Jr. "The Constitution of the United States: Contemporary Ratification." *South Texas Law Review* 27 (Fall 1986): 433-445.

6566. Brennan, William J., Jr. "Constitutional Adjudication." *Notre Dame Lawyer* 40 (August 1965): 559-569.

6567. Brennan, William J., Jr. "Constitutional Adjudication and the Death Penalty: A View from the Court." *Harvard Law Review* 100 (December 1986): 313-331.

6568. Brennan, William J., Jr. "The Criminal Prosecution: Sporting Event or Quest for Truth?" *Washington University Law Quarterly* 1963 (June 1963): 279-295.

6569. Brennan, William J., Jr. "Efficient Organization and Effective Administration for Today's Courts . . . The Citizens' Responsibility." *Journal of the American Judicature Society* 48 (December 1964): 145-150.

6570. Brennan, William J., Jr. "Federal *Habeas Corpus* and State Prisoners: An Exercise in Federalism." *Utah Law Review* 7 (Fall 1961): 423-442.

6571. Brennan, William J., Jr. "How Goes the Supreme Court?" *Mercer Law Review* 36 (Spring 1985): 781-794.

6572. Brennan, William J., Jr. "How the Supreme Court Arrives at a Decision." In *American Government*, 8th ed., by Peter Woll, 550-558. Boston: Little, Brown, 1984.

6573. Brennan, William J., Jr. "Inside View of the High Court." *New York Times Magazine* 113 (October 6, 1963): 35, 100, 102, 103.

6574. Brennan, William J., Jr. "Interpreting the Constitution." *Social Policy* 18 (Summer 1987): 24-28.

6575. Brennan, William J., Jr. "The National Court of Appeals: Another Dissent." *University of Chicago Law Review* 40 (Spring 1973): 473-485.

6576. Brennan, William J., Jr. "Remarks on Discovery by Honorable William J. Brennan, Jr." *Federal Rules Decisions* 33 (1963): 56-66.

6577. Brennan, William J., Jr. "The Responsibilities of the Legal Profession." *American Bar Association* 54 (February 1968): 121-126.

6578. Brennan, William J., Jr. "Some Aspects of Federalism." *New York University Law Review* 39 (December 1964): 945-961.

6579. Brennan, William J., Jr. "Some Thoughts on the Supreme Court's Workload." *Judicature* 66 (December/January 1982-1983): 230-235.

6580. Brennan, William J., Jr. "State Constitutions and the Protection of Individual Rights." *Harvard Law Review* 90 (January 1977): 489-504.

6581. Brennan, William J., Jr. "State Court Decisions and the Supreme Court." *Pennsylvania Bar Association Quarterly* 31 (June 1960): 393-407.

6582. Brennan, William J., Jr. "The Supreme Court and the Meiklejohn Interpretation of the First Amendment." *Harvard Law Review* 79 (November 1965): 1-20.

6583. Brennan, William J., Jr. "Supreme Court Review of State Court Decisions." *Michigan State Bar Journal* 38 (November 1959): 14-22.

6584. Brennan, William J., Jr. "The United States Supreme Court: Reflections Past and Present." *Marquette Law Review* 48 (Spring 1965): 437-444.

6585. Brennan, William J., Jr. "Why Protect the Press?" *Columbia Journalism Review* 18 (January 1980): 59-60.

6586. Brennan, William J., Jr., et al. "Chief Justice Warren." *Harvard Law Review* 88 (November 1974): 1-12.

David J. Brewer

General Studies

6587. Bergan, Francis. "Mr. Justice Brewer: A Perspective of a Century." *Albany Law Review* 25 (June 1961): 191-202.

6588. Brodhead, Michael J. "Justice David J. Brewer: A Voice for Peace on the Supreme Court." *Supreme Court Historical Society Yearbook* 1985 (1985): 93-102.

6589. Butler, Charles H. "Melville Weston Fuller, David Josiah Brewer, Memorial Note." *American Journal of International Law* 4 (October 1910): 909-921.

6590. "David Josiah Brewer." *Case and Comment* 3 (June 1896): 1-2.

6591. Eitzen, D. Stanley. *David J. Brewer, 1837-1910: A Kansan on the United States Supreme Court.* Emporia: Graduate Division, Kansas State Teacher's College, 1964.

6592. Fairman, Charles. "The Education of a Justice: Justice Bradley and Some of His Colleagues." *Stanford Law Review* 1 (January 1949): 217-255.

6593. Gamer, Robert E. "Justice Brewer and Substantive Due Process: A Conservative Court Revisited." *Vanderbilt Law Review* 18 (March 1965): 615-641.

6594. Lardner, Lynford A. "The Constitutional Doctrines of Justice David Josiah Brewer." Ph.D. diss., Princeton University, 1938.

6595. "Mr. Justice Brewer." *American Law Review* (January/February 1890): 137-140.

6596. Moline, Brian. "David Josiah Brewer, Kansas Jurist." *Kansas Bar Association Journal* 55 (January/February 1986): 7-11.

6597. Watson, Warren. "David Josiah Brewer." In *Distinguished American Lawyer*, edited by Henry W. Scott, 75-88. New York: C. L. Webster, 1891.

Writings

6598. Brewer, David J. *Address: Two Periods in the History of the Supreme Court,* *Delivered by Justice David J. Brewer . . . at the Eighteenth Annual Meeting Held at Hot Springs of Virginia, August 7th, 8th, and 9th, 1906.* Richmond, VA: Richmond Press, 1906.

6599. Brewer, David J. *American Citizenship.* New Haven, CT: Yale University Press, 1911.

6600. Brewer, David J. *The Income Tax Cases and Some Comments Thereon.* Iowa City: University of Iowa, 1895.

6601. Brewer, David J. "The Nation's Anchor." *Albany Law Journal* 57 (March 12, 1898): 166-170.

6602. Brewer, David J. "The Nation's Safeguard." *Report of the New York State Bar Association* 16 (1893): 37-47.

6603. Brewer, David J. *Orators and Oratory of Texas.* Edited by William Vincent Byars. Chicago: F. P. Kaiser, 1923.

6604. Brewer, David J. "The Supreme Court of the United States." *Scribner's* 33 (March 1903): 273-284.

6605. Brewer, David J. *The United States as a Christian Nation.* Philadelphia: J. C. Winston Company, 1905.

Henry B. Brown

General Studies

6606. Butler, Charles H. "Mr. Justice Brown." *Greenbag* 18 (June 1906): 321-330.

6607. Eger, Paul G. "Justice Brown." *Michigan State Bar Journal* 24 (May 1945): 347-349.

6608. Fairman, Charles. "The Education of a Justice: Justice Bradley and Some of His Colleagues." *Stanford Law Review* 1 (January 1949): 217-255.

6609. Glennon, Robert J., Jr. "Justice

Henry Billings Brown: Values in Tension." *University of Colorado Law Review* 44 (1973): 553-604.

6610. "Henry Billings Brown." *Case and Comment* 2 (March 1896): 1-2.

6611. Kent, Charles A. *Memoir of Henry Billings Brown, Late Justice of the Supreme Court of the United States, Consisting of an Autobiographical Sketch, with Additions to His Life.* New York: Duffield and Company, 1915.

6612. "Portrait." *World's Work* 12 (May 1906): 7473.

Writings

6613. Brown, Henry B. "The Dissenting Opinions of Mr. Justice Daniel." *American Law Review* 21 (November/December 1887): 869-900.

6614. Brown, Henry B. "The Dissenting Opinions of Mr. Justice Harlan." *American Law Review* 46 (May/June 1912): 321-352.

6615. Brown, Henry B. "The Distribution of Property." *American Bar Association Reports* 16 (1893): 213-242.

6616. Brown, Henry B. "Judicial Independence." *American Bar Association Reports* 12 (1889): 265-288.

6617. Brown, Henry B. "The Judiciary." In *Celebration of the One Hundredth Anniversary of the Laying of the Corner Stone of the Capitol of the United States,* by Duncan S. Walker, 74-79, Washington: U.S. Government Printing Office, 1986.

6618. Brown, Henry B. "Proposed International Prize Court." *American Journal of International Law* 2 (July 1908): 476-489.

Warren E. Burger

General Studies

6619. Bosmajian, Haig. "Chief Justice Warren Burger and Freedom of Speech." *Midwest Quarterly* 15 (January 1974): 121-140.

6620. Buckner, Kermit G. "Analysis of Chief Burger's Influence in Supreme Court Cases Affecting Public Education." Ph.D. diss., University of North Carolina, Greensboro, 1980.

6621. "Chief Justice Burger Proposes First Step toward Certification of Trial Advocacy Specialists." *American Bar Association Journal* 60 (February 1974): 171-174.

6622. Cohen, Richard E. "Mixed Cases, Burger Activism Mark Supreme Court Record." *National Journal Reports* 6 (July 6, 1974): 1005-1013.

6623. Davenport, John. "The U.S., the Law, and Chief Justice Burger." *Fortune* 82 (September 1970): 146-150, 180-182.

6624. Dennis, Everette E. "Overcoming Occupational Heredity at the Supreme Court." *American Bar Association Journal* 66 (January 1980): 41-45.

6625. Eggert, Gerald G., and Phillip E. Stebbins. "The Chief Justice: Image of an Office." *American History Illustrated* 5 (May 1970): 32-41.

6626. Gazell, James A. "Chief Justice Burger's Quest for Judicial Administrative Efficiency." *Detroit College of Law Review* 1977 (Fall 1977): 455-497.

6627. Hengstler, Gary A. " 'Crowning Chapter': Burger's Energies Now Directed toward Constitution's Birthday." *American Bar Association Journal* 72 (August 1986): 19.

6628. Lamb, Charles M. "The Making of a Chief Justice: Warren Burger on Criminal Procedure, 1956-1969." *Cornell Law Review* 60 (June 1975): 743-788.

6629. Lamb, Charles M. "Warren Burger and the Insanity Defense: Judicial Philosophy and Voting Behavior on a U.S. Court of Appeals." *American University Law Review* 24 (Fall 1974): 91-128.

6630. Lamb, Charles M. "When Judicial Agreement Seems Impossible: Warren Burger, David Bazelon, and the D.C. Court of Appeals." *American Journal of Political Science* 11 (Spring 1984): 75-82.

6631. Miller, Arthur S. "Lord Chancellor Warren Earl Burger." *Transaction, Social Science, and Modern Society* 10 (March/April 1973): 18-27.

6632. Ostrow, Donald. "Burger and the Press." *Nieman Reports* 24 (September 1970): 3-5.

6633. "Q and A with the Chief Justice." *American Bar Association Journal* 71 (January 1985): 91-96.

6634. Swindler, William F. "The Court, the Constitution, and Chief Justice Burger." *Vanderbilt Law Review* 27 (April 1974): 443-474.

6635. Zion, Sidney. "Burger v. Bill of Rights." *Bill of Rights Journal* 16 (December 1983): 15-27.

Writings

6636. Burger, Warren E. "Address . . . before the Fifth Judicial Circuit Conference." *Journal of Public Law* 21 (1972): 271-278.

6637. Burger, Warren E. "Address to the American Law Institute, Washington, D.C., May 19, 1970." *American Law Institute Annual Proceedings* 47 (1970): 24-28.

6638. Burger, Warren E. "Agenda for Change." *Judicature* 54 (January 1971): 232-236.

6639. Burger, Warren E. "Annual Report on the State of the Judiciary." *American Bar Association Journal* 69 (April 1983): 442-450.

6640. Burger, Warren E. "Bringing the Judicial Machinery Up to the Demands Made on It." *Pennsylvania Bar Association Quarterly* 42 (March 1971): 262-267.

6641. Burger, Warren E. "Burger's Law." *Across the Board* 15 (May 1978): 80-82.

6642. Burger, Warren E. "Can We Cope? The Constitution after 200 Years." *American Bar Association Journal* 65 (February 1979): 203-207.

6643. Burger, Warren E. "Conclusion: Marking the Bicentennial of the United States Constitution." *Seton Hall Law Review* 16 (1986): 462-464.

6644. Burger, Warren E. "Conference on Supreme Court Advocacy." *Catholic University Law Review* 33 (Spring 1984): 525-527.

6645. Burger, Warren E. "Counsel for the Prosecution and the Defense: Their Role under Minimum Standards." *American Criminal Law Quarterly* 8 (Fall 1969): 2-9.

6646. Burger, Warren E. "Court Administrators: Where Would We Find Them?" *Judicature* 53 (October 1969): 108-110.

6647. Burger, Warren E. "The Courts on Trial." *Federal Rules Decisions* 22 (1959): 71-83.

6648. Burger, Warren E. "Deferred Maintenance of Judicial Machinery Remarks . . . National Conference on the Judiciary, Williamsburg, VA, March 12, 1971." *Judicature* 54 (May 1971): 410-417.

6649. Burger, Warren E. *For Whom the Bell Tolls, Remarks . . . Association of the Bar of the City of New York, February 17, 1970.* Washington, DC: Association of the Bar of the City of New York, 1970.

6650. Burger, Warren E. "Has the Time Come? Remarks ... at Opening Session, American Law Institute, May 16, 1972, Washington, DC." *American Law Institute Annual Proceedings* 1972 (1972): 23-32.

6651. Burger, Warren E. "The Image of Justice." *Judicature* 55 (December 1971): 200-202.

6652. Burger, Warren E. "The Necessity for Civility: Remarks at the Opening Session, American Law Institute, May 18, 1971, Washington, DC." *Federal Rules Decisions* 52 (1971): 211-218.

6653. Burger, Warren E. "New Chief Justice's Philosophy of Law in America." *New York State Bar Journal* 41 (October 1969): 454-479.

6654. Burger, Warren E. "The Office of the United States Attorney General." *Louisiana Bar Journal* 2 (October 1954): 124-133.

6655. Burger, Warren E. "Paradoxes in the Administration of Criminal Justice." *Journal of Criminal Law, Criminology, and Police Science* 58 (December 1967): 428-432.

6656. Burger, Warren E. "Psychiatry and the Law." *Federal Rules Decisions* 32 (1963): 557-567.

6657. Burger, Warren E. "Reflections on Law and Experimental Medicine." *UCLA Law Review* 15 (1968): 436-442.

6658. Burger, Warren E. *Remarks ... at Federal Bar Council Law Day Dinner, May 3, 1971.* New York: Federal Bar Council, 1971.

6659. Burger, Warren E. "Remarks of Chief Justice Warren E. Burger, Read by Chief Judge S. W. Robinson." *Federal Rules Decisions* 100 (March 1984): 207-212.

6660. Burger, Warren E. "Remarks of Honorable Warren E. Burger, Chief Justice Supreme Court of the United States." *Federal Rules Decisions* 100 (April 1984): 534-538.

6661. Burger, Warren E. "Report on the Federal Judicial Branch: 1973." *American Bar Association Journal* 59 (October 1973): 1125-1130.

6662. Burger, Warren E. "Rx for Justice: Modernize the Courts." *Nation's Business* 62 (September 1974): 61-63.

6663. Burger, Warren E. "School for Judges." *Federal Rules Decisions* 33 (1964): 139-150.

6664. Burger, Warren E. "A Sick Profession." *Federal Bar Journal* 27 (Summer 1967): 228-234.

6665. Burger, Warren E. "The Special Skills of Advocacy: Are Specialized Training and Certification of Advocates Essential to Our System of Justice?" *Fordham Law Review* 42 (December 1973): 227-242.

6666. Burger, Warren E. "Stanley F. Reed." *Supreme Court Historical Society Yearbook* 1981 (1981): 10-13.

6667. Burger, Warren E. "The State of the Federal Judiciary: 1979." *American Bar Association Journal* 65 (March 1979): 358-365.

6668. Burger, Warren E. "Symposium: Standards of Conduct for Prosecution and Defense Personnel." *American Criminal Law Quarterly* 5 (Winter 1966): 8-31.

6669. Burger, Warren E. "Thinking the Unthinkable." *Loyola Law Review* 31 (Spring 1985): 205-220.

6670. Burger, Warren E. "The Time Is Now for the Intercircuit Panel." *American Bar Association Journal* 71 (April 1985): 86-91.

6671. Burger, Warren E., and Earl Warren. "Retired Chief Justice Warren Attacks Chief Justice Burger: Defends Freud Study Group's Composition and Proposal." *American Bar Association Journal* 59 (July 1973): 721-730.

6672. Burger, Warren E., and W. A. Lawrence. *Conversation with the Chief Justice, July 5, 1971.* Washington, DC: American Broadcasting Company, 1971.

6673. Burger, Warren E., Benjamin Heinman, George Bush, and Laurence H. Tribe. "In Tribute of Honorable Potter Stewart." *Yale Law Journal* 95 (June 1986): 1321-1333.

Harold H. Burton

General Studies

6674. Atkinson, David N. "American Constitutionalism under Stress: Mr. Justice Burton's Response to National Security Issues." *Houston Law Review* 9 (November 1971): 271-288.

6675. Atkinson, David N. "Justice Harold H. Burton and the Work of the Supreme Court." *Cleveland State Law Review* 27 (1978): 69-83.

6676. Berry, Mary F. *Stability, Security, and Continuity: Mr. Justice Burton and Decision-Making in the Supreme Court, 1945-1958.* Westport, CT: Greenwood Press, 1978.

6677. Bricker, John J. "Justice Harold H. Burton." *American Bar Association Journal* 31 (November 1945): 558.

6678. Forrester, Ray. "Mr. Justice Burton and the Supreme Court." *Tulane Law Review* 20 (October 1945): 1-21.

6679. Hudon, Edward G., ed. *The Occasional Papers of Mr. Justice Burton.* Brunswick, ME: Bowdoin College, 1969.

6680. McHargue, Daniel S. "One of Nine: Mr. Justice Burton's Appointment to the Supreme Court." *Western Reserve Law Review* 4 (Winter 1953): 128-131.

6681. Marquardt, Ronald G. "The Judicial Justice: Mr. Justice Burton and the Supreme Court." Ph.D. diss., University of Missouri, 1973.

6682. Wilkin, Robert, and John Hadden. "Harold Hitz Burton, 1888-1964." *American Bar Association Journal* 50 (December 1964): 1148-1149.

Writings

6683. Burton, Harold H. "The Continuity of the United States Supreme Court." *Case and Comment* 55 (July/August 1950): 3-8.

6684. Burton, Harold H. "The *Dartmouth College* Case: A Dramatization." *American Bar Association Journal* 38 (December 1952): 991-994.

6685. Burton, Harold H. "An Independent Judiciary: The Keystone of Our Freedom." *American Bar Association Journal* 39 (December 1953): 1067-1070.

6686. Burton, Harold H. "John Marshall: The Man." *University of Pennsylvania Law Review* 104 (October 1955): 3-8.

6687. Burton, Harold H. "Judging Is Also Administration: An Appreciation of Constructive Leadership." *Temple Law Quarterly* 21 (October 1947): 77-90.

6688. Burton, Harold H. "Justice, the Guardian of Liberty: John Marshall at the Trial of Aaron Burr." *American Bar Association Journal* 37 (October 1951): 735-738.

6689. Burton, Harold H. "The *Legal Tender* Cases: A Celebrated Supreme Court Reversal." *American Bar Association Journal* 42 (March 1956): 231.

6690. Burton, Harold H. *The Story of the Place Where First and A Streets Formerly Met at What Is Now the Site of the Supreme Court Building.* Washington, DC: Library of Congress, 1952.

6691. Burton, Harold H. "The Supreme Court: Mr. Justice Burton Gives Interesting Comparisons." *American Bar Association Journal* 33 (July 1947): 645-648.

6692. Burton, Harold H. "Two Significant Decisions: *Ex Parte Milligan* and *Ex Parte McCardle*." *American Bar Association Journal* 41 (February 1955): 121-124.

6693. Burton, Harold H. "The United States Supreme Court." *Women Lawyers Journal* 34 (Summer 1948): 4-6, 33, 43-45.

6694. Burton, Harold H. "Unsung Services of Supreme Court of the United States." *Referees' Journal* 24 (January 1950): 4-8.

6695. Burton, Harold H. "Unsung Services of the Supreme Court of the United States." *Fordham Law Review* 24 (Summer 1955): 169-177.

6696. Burton, Harold H. "Unsung Services of the Supreme Court of the United States." *Ohio Bar* 21 (December 27, 1948): 517-521.

6697. Burton, Harold H., and Thomas E. Waggaman. "The Story of the Place." *George Washington Law Review* 21 (January 1953): 253-264.

Pierce Butler

General Studies

6698. Brown, Francis J. *The Social and Economic Philosophy of Pierce Butler.* Washington, DC: Catholic University of America Press, 1945.

6699. Howell, Ronald F. "Conservative Influence on Constitutional Development, 1923-1937: The Judicial Theory of Justices Van Devanter, McReynolds, Sutherland, and Butler." Ph.D. diss., Johns Hopkins University, 1952.

6700. Hughes, Charles E. "In Memory of Mr. Justice Butler." *United States Reports* 310 (May 1940): xv-xx.

6701. Langran, Robert W. "Why Are Some Supreme Court Justices Rated as 'Failures'?" *Supreme Court Historical Society Yearbook* 1985 (1985): 8-14.

6702. Purcell, Richard J. "Mr. Justice Pierce Butler." *Catholic Educational Review* 42 (April 1944): 193-215; (September 1944): 420-432.

6703. Sikes, Lewright B. "The Public Life of Pierce Butler." Ph.D. diss., University of Tennessee, 1973.

Writings

6704. Butler, Pierce. "Some Opportunities and Duties of Lawyers." *American Bar Association Journal* 9 (September 1923): 583-587.

James F. Byrnes

General Studies

6705. Burns, Ronald D. *James F. Byrnes.* New York: McGraw-Hill, 1961.

6706. Conover, Denise O. "James F. Byrnes, Germany, and the Cold War, 1946." Ph.D. diss., Washington State University, 1978.

6707. Curry, George. "James F. Byrnes." In *The American Secretaries of State and Their Diplomacy*, edited by Robert H. Ferrell, 87-317, 340-396, 405-414. New York: Cooper Square Publishers, 1965.

6708. Davenport, Walter. "The Non-Bureaucratic M. Byrnes." *Collier's* 111 (January 30, 1943): 11, 28-29.

6709. Figg, Robert M., Jr. "James F. Byrnes and the Supreme Court, 1941-1942." *South Carolina Law Review* 25 (1973): 543-548.

6710. Hogan, Frank J. "Associate Justice James F. Byrnes." *American Bar Association Journal* 27 (August 1941): 475-478.

6711. McGill, Ralph. "What Is Jimmy Byrnes Up to Now?" *Saturday Evening Post* 223 (October 14, 1950): 32-33, 183-188.

6712. Pettit, William. "Justice Byrnes and the U.S. Supreme Court." *South Carolina Law Quarterly* 6 (June 1954): 423-428.

Writings

6713. Byrnes, James F. *All in One Lifetime.* New York: Harper, 1958.

6714. Byrnes, James F. "Communist Influence, Home and Abroad." *Texas Bar Journal* 23 (August 22, 1960): 416-422.

6715. Byrnes, James F. "Despite These Honors." In *Twenty-seven Masters of Politics,* edited by Raymond Moley, 250-259. New York: Funk and Wagnalls, 1949.

6716. Byrnes, James F. "Segregation." *Vermont Bar Association Proceedings* 50 (1956): 86.

6717. Byrnes, James F. "The South Respects the Written Constitution: Supreme Court Has No Power to Amend the Constitution." *Vital Speeches* 23 (March 1957): 331-335.

6718. Byrnes, James F. *Speaking Frankly.* New York: Harper, 1947.

6719. Byrnes, James F. "The Supreme Court and States Rights." *Alabama Lawyer* 20 (October 1959): 396-403.

John A. Campbell

General Studies

6720. Connor, Henry G. *John Archibald Campbell, Associate Justice of the United States Supreme Court, 1853-1861.* Boston: Houghton Mifflin, 1920.

6721. Connor, Henry G. "John Archibald Campbell, 1811-1889." *American Law Review* 52 (March/April 1918): 161-214.

6722. Duncan, George W. *John Archibald Campbell.* Montgomery: Alabama Historical Society, 1905.

6723. Holt, Thad, Jr. "The Resignation of Mr. Justice Campbell." *Alabama Review* 12 (April 1954): 105-118.

6724. McAllister, Henry. "Mr. Justice Campbell's Contribution to the Law of Colorado." *Rocky Mountain Law Review* 5 (December 1932): 4-16.

6725. Mann, Justice S. "The Political Thought of John Archibald Campbell: The Formative Years, 1847-1851." *Alabama Law Review* 22 (Spring 1970): 275-302.

6726. Schmidhauser, John R. "Jeremy Bentham, the Contract Clause, and Justice John Archibald Campbell." *Vanderbilt Law Review* 11 (June 1958): 801-820.

6727. Skult, Ronald. "John Archibald Campbell, A Study in Divided Loyalties." *Alabama Lawyer* 20 (July 1959): 233-264.

6728. Williams, Samuel C. "A Remarkable Bench: Campbell, Jackson, and White." *Tennessee Law Review* 16 (June 1941): 907-914.

Benjamin N. Cardozo

General Studies

6729. Acheson, Dean G. "Mr. Justice Cardozo and Problems of Government." *Michigan Law Review* 37 (February 1939): 513-539.

6730. Aronson, Moses J. *Cardozo's Doc-*

trine of Sociological Jurisprudence. New York: n.p., 1938.

6731. Atkinson, David N. "Mr. Justice Cardozo: A Common Law Judge on a Public Law Court." *California Western Law Review* 17 (Winter 1981): 257-285.

6732. Atkinson, David N. "Mr. Justice Cardozo on the Supreme Court: State and Federal Taxation." *Houston Law Review* 5 (October 1967): 254-273.

6733. Beer, Henry W. "Late Justice Benjamin Nathan Cardozo." *New Jersey Law Journal* 62 (December 28, 1939): 1-3, 437.

6734. Brubaker, Stanley C. "Benjamin Nathan Cardozo: An Intellectual Biography." Ph.D. diss., University of Virginia, 1979.

6735. Carmen, Ira H. "One Civil Libertarian among Many: The Case of Mr. Justice Cardozo." *Michigan Law Review* 65 (December 1966): 301-336.

6736. Carmen, Ira H. "The President, Politics, and the Power of Appointment: Hoover's Nomination of Mr. Justice Cardozo (February 15, 1932)." *Virginia Law Review* 55 (May 1969): 616-659.

6737. Carswell, William B. "Benjamin Nathan Cardozo." *Brooklyn Law Review* 8 (October 1938): 1-3.

6738. Clark, Lester. "The Palsgraf Theory: What Established Doctrines It Attempted to Alter." *Hastings Law Journal* 1 (Fall 1949): 22-27.

6739. Cohen, Morris R. "Benjamin Nathan Cardozo." *National Lawyers Guild Quarterly* 1 (September 1938): 238-286.

6740. Corbin, Arthur L. "Mr. Justice Cardozo and the Law of Contracts." *Columbia Law Review* 39 (January 1939): 56-87.

6741. Corbin, Arthur L. "Mr. Justice Cardozo and the Law of Contracts." *Harvard Law Review* 52 (January 1939): 408-439.

6742. Corbin, Arthur L. "Mr. Justice Cardozo and the Law of Contracts." *Yale Law Journal* 48 (January 1939): 426-457.

6743. Cummings, Homer S. *An Address of Attorney General Cummings before the Supreme Court of the United States in Memory of Associate Justice Benjamin N. Cardozo.* Washington, DC: U.S. Government Printing Office, 1938.

6744. Cummings, Homer S., and Charles E. Hughes. "Bar Presents Resolutions in Memory of Justice Cardozo to the Supreme Court." *American Bar Association Journal* 25 (January 1939): 33-37.

6745. Douglas, William O. "Mr. Justice Cardozo." *Michigan Law Review* 58 (February 1960): 549-556.

6746. Evatt, Herbert V. "Mr. Justice Cardozo." *Columbia Law Review* 39 (January 1939): 5-8.

6747. Evatt, Herbert V. "Mr. Justice Cardozo." *Harvard Law Review* 52 (January 1939): 357-360.

6748. Evatt, Herbert V. "Mr. Justice Cardozo." *Yale Law Journal* 48 (January 1939): 375-378.

6749. Fairman, Charles. "The Late Mr. Justice Cardozo." *California State Bar Journal* 13 (December 1938): 19-23.

6750. Farnum, George R. "Benjamin N. Cardozo: Lights and Shadows." *Lawyer* 2 (September 1938): 5-6.

6751. Farnum, George R. "Justice Benjamin Cardozo, Philosopher." *Boston University Law Review* 12 (November 1932): 587-599.

6752. Finch, Edward R. "Memorial to Justice Cardozo." *American Bar Association Journal* 24 (September 1938): 728-730.

6753. Frankfurter, Felix. "Mr. Justice Cardozo." *American Bar Association Journal* 24 (August 1938): 638-639.

6754. Frankfurter, Felix. "Mr. Justice

Cardozo and Public Law." *Columbia Law Review* 39 (January 1939): 88-118.

6755. Frankfurter, Felix. "Mr. Justice Cardozo and Public Law." *Yale Law Journal* 48 (January 1939): 458-488.

6756. Friendly, Henry J. "Reactions of a Lawyer—Newly Become Judge." *Yale Law Journal* 71 (December 1961): 218-238.

6757. Goldstein, Joseph M. "Justice Benjamin Nathan Cardozo." *New Jersey Law Journal* 61 (July 14, 1938): 248.

6758. Goodhart, Arthur L. *Five Jewish Lawyers of the Common Law.* New York: Oxford University Press, 1949.

6759. Gouch, Walter T. "The Judicial Philosophy of Justice Cardozo: The Basis of a Definitive Jurisprudence." *University of Maryland Law Forum* 6 (1976): 49-63.

6760. Gouch, Walter T. "The Legal Theory of Justice Benjamin Cardozo." Ph.D. diss., Johns Hopkins University, 1954.

6761. Green, Leon. "Benjamin Nathan Cardozo." *Illinois Law Review* 33 (June 1938): 123-125.

6762. Hamilton, Walton H. "Cardozo the Craftsman." *University of Chicago Law Review* 6 (December 1938): 1-22.

6763. Hamilton, Walton H. "Justice Cardozo: The Great Tradition." *New Republic* 95 (July 27, 1938): 329.

6764. Hand, Learned. "Justice Cardozo's Work as a Judge." *United States Law Review* 72 (September 1938): 496-498.

6765. Hardman, Thomas P. "Mr. Justice Cardozo." *West Virginia Law Quarterly* 38 (April 1932): 187-194.

6766. Hellman, George S. *Benjamin N. Cardozo, American Judge.* New York: McGraw-Hill, 1940.

6767. Holland, Henry M. "Juristic Philosophy of Justice Cardozo: A Study in Mediation." Ph.D. diss., University of Washington, 1958.

6768. Howell, Charles B. "Contract and Consideration: Mansfield and Cardozo." *Intramural Law Review* 1 (May 1949): 75-90.

6769. Hughes, Charles E. "Proceeding in Memory of Mr. Justice Cardozo." *United States Reports* 305 (October 1938): xxii-xxvii.

6770. Jackson, Samuel. "Cardozo and the Supreme Court." *Indiana Law Journal* 7 (June 1932): 513-535.

6771. Knox, John. "Recollections of Justice Cardozo." *Chicago Bar Review* 21 (October 1939): 9-10, 25.

6772. Lehman, Irving. *The Influence of Judge Cardozo (1870-1938): A Memorial.* Stanford, CT: Overbook Press, 1938.

6773. Lehman, Irving. *The Influence of Judge Cardozo on the Common Law.* Garden City, NY: Doubleday, Doran, 1942.

6774. Lehman, Irving. "The Influence of Judge Cardozo on the Common Law." *Law Library Journal* 35 (January 1942): 2-9.

6775. Lehman, Irving. "Judge Cardozo in the Court of Appeals." *Columbia Law Review* 39 (January 1939): 12-19.

6776. Levy, Beryl H. *Cardozo and Frontiers of Legal Thinking, with Selected Opinions.* Cleveland: Press of Case Western Reserve University, 1969.

6777. McDougal, Myres S. "The Application of Constitutive Prescriptions: An Addendum to Justice Cardozo." *Record of the Association of the Bar of the City of New York* 33 (May/June 1978): 255-297.

6778. Mars, David. "Justice Benjamin Nathan Cardozo: His Life and Character." *American Jewish Historical Society Publications* 49 (September 1959): 5-15.

6779. Massa, Edward C. "Cardozo Succeeds Holmes." *Notre Dame Lawyer* 7 (March 1932): 387-389.

6780. Maugham, Frederic H. "Mr. Justice Cardozo." *Columbia Law Review* 39 (January 1939): 4.

6781. Maugham, Frederic H. "Mr. Justice Cardozo." *Harvard Law Review* 52 (January 1939): 356.

6782. Maugham, Frederic H. "Mr. Justice Cardozo." *Yale Law Journal* 48 (January 1939): 374.

6783. Morris, Jeffrey B. "The American Jewish Judge: An Appraisal on the Occasion of the Bicentennial." *Jewish Social Studies* 38 (Summer/Fall 1976): 195-223.

6784. Nash, Francis C. "Mr. Justice Cardozo and the Law of Torts." Ph.D. diss., Georgetown University, 1935.

6785. Noonan, John T., Jr. *Persons and Masks of the Law: Cardozo, Holmes, Jefferson, and Wythe as Makers of the Masks.* New York: Farrar, Straus, and Giroux, 1976.

6786. Oppenheim, Leonard. "The Civil Liberties Doctrines of Mr. Justice Holmes and Mr. Justice Cardozo." *Tulane Law Review* 20 (December 1945): 177-219.

6787. Otis, Merrill E. "Benjamin N. Cardozo." *Missouri Bar Journal* 3 (March 1932): 36-38.

6788. Patterson, Edwin W. "Cardozo's Philosophy of Law." *University of Pennsylvania Law Review* 88 (November 1939): 71-91; (December 1939): 156-176.

6789. Pollard, Joseph P. *Mr. Justice Cardozo: A Liberal Mind in Action.* New York: Yorktown Press, 1935.

6790. Roberts, William H. "Justice Cardozo Revisited: Phenomenological Contributions to Jurisprudence." *Catholic University of America Law Review* 12 (May 1963): 92-112.

6791. Seavey, Warren A. "Mr. Justice Cardozo and the Law of Torts." *Columbia Law Review* 39 (January 1939): 20-55.

6792. Seavey, Warren A. "Mr. Justice Cardozo and the Law of Torts." *Harvard Law Review* 52 (January 1939): 372-407.

6793. Seavey, Warren A. "Mr. Justice Cardozo and the Law of Torts." *Yale Law Journal* 48 (January 1939): 390-425.

6794. Shientag, Bernard L. *The Opinions and Writings of Judge Benjamin N. Cardozo.* New York: Columbia University Press, 1930.

6795. Snook, Janice B. "Judicial Philosophy and Judicial Behavior: The Case of Mr. Justice Cardozo." Ph.D. diss., University of Maryland, 1969.

6796. Stone, Harlan F. "Mr. Justice Cardozo." *Columbia Law Review* 39 (January 1939): 1-3.

6797. Stone, Harlan F. "Mr. Justice Cardozo." *Harvard Law Review* 52 (January 1939): 353-355.

6798. Stone, Harlan F. "Mr. Justice Cardozo." *Yale Law Journal* 48 (January 1939): 371-373.

6799. Swygert, Luther M. "Benjamin N. Cardozo." *Notre Dame Lawyer* 22 (January 1947): 142-149.

6800. Taft, Henry W. "Honorable B. N. Cardozo: He Does Not Remain Static." *Missouri Bar Journal* 3 (February 1932): 23-24.

6801. Taft, Henry W. "One Aspect of Judge Cardozo's Noteworthy Career." *American Bar Association Journal* 18 (March 1932): 172-173.

6802. Titus, James E. "Studies in American Liberalism of the 1930s: John Dewey, Benjamin Cardozo, and Thurmond Arnold." Ph.D. diss., University of Wisconsin, 1957.

6803. Tullis, Robert L. "Benjamin Nathan Cardozo: Jurist, Philosopher, Humanitarian." *Louisiana Law Review* 1 (November 1938): 147-156.

6804. Voorhis, John Van. "Cardozo and the Judicial Process Today." *Yale Law Journal* 71 (December 1961): 202-217.

Writings

6805. Cardozo, Benjamin N. *The Growth of the Law.* New Haven, CT: Yale University Press, 1924.

6806. Cardozo, Benjamin N. *The Jurisdiction of the Court of Appeals of the State of New York.* Albany, NY: Banks, 1903.

6807. Cardozo, Benjamin N. *Law and Literature and Other Essays and Addresses.* New York: Harcourt, Brace, 1931.

6808. Cardozo, Benjamin N. *Law Is Justice: Notable Opinions of Mr. Justice Cardozo.* Edited by A. Sainer. New York: Ad Press Limited, 1938.

6809. Cardozo, Benjamin N. "Mr. Justice Holmes." *Harvard Law Review* 44 (March 1931): 682-692.

6810. Cardozo, Benjamin N. *The Nature of the Judicial Process.* New Haven, CT: Yale University Press, 1921.

6811. Cardozo, Benjamin N. *The Paradoxes of Legal Science.* New York: Columbia University Press, 1928.

6812. Cardozo, Benjamin N. *Selected Writings.* Edited by Margaret E. Hill. New York: Fallon Publications, 1947.

John Catron

General Studies

6813. Chandler, Walter. *Address on the Centenary of Associate Justice John Catron of the United States Supreme Court.* Washington, DC: U.S. Government Printing Office, 1937.

6814. Chandler, Walter. "Centenary of Associate Justice John Catron of the United States Supreme Court." *Tennessee Law Review* 15 (December 1937): 32-51.

6815. Chase, Salmon P. "Memoranda: Mr. Justice Catron." *United States Reports* 70 (1865): ix-xiv.

6816. Dunlap, Boutwell. "Judge John Catron of the United States Supreme Court." *Virginia Magazine of History and Biography* 28 (April 1920): 171-174.

6817. Foote, Henry S. "Judge Catron." In *The Bench and Bar of the South and Southwest*, by Henry S. Foote, 145-153. St. Louis: Soule, Thomas, and Wentworth, 1876.

6818. Gass, Edmund C. "The Constitutional Opinions of Justice John Catron." *Eastern Tennessee Historical Society Publications* 8 (1936): 54-81.

6819. Ingersoll, John. "John Catron." In *Great American Lawyers*, vol. 4, edited by William D. Lewis, 121-186. Philadelphia: J. C. Winston Company, 1907-1909.

6820. Livingston, John. "Biographical Letter from Justice Catron." In *Portraits of Eminent Americans Now Living*, vol. 2, by John A. Livingstone, 805-812. New York: Cornish, Lamport, 1853.

Salmon P. Chase

General Studies

6821. Belden, Marva R., and Thomas G. Belden. "Kate Was Too Ambitious." *American Heritage* 7 (August 1956): 40.

6822. Belden, Thomas G. "The Salmon P. Chase Family in the Civil War and Reconstruction: A Study in Ambition and

Corruption." Ph.D. diss., University of Chicago, 1952.

6823. Belden, Thomas G., and Marva R. Belden. *So Fell the Angels.* Boston: Little, Brown, 1956.

6824. Benson, John S. *The Judicial Record of the Late Chief Justice Chase.* New York: Baker, Voorhis, and Company, 1882.

6825. Bidwell, W. H. "Salmon P. Chase." *Eclectic Magazine* 81 (September 1873): 373-374.

6826. Blue, Fredrick. "Kate's Paper Chase: The Race to Publish the First Biography of Salmon P. Chase." *Old Northwest* 8 (Winter 1982-1983): 353-363.

6827. Brockett, Linus P. "Salmon Portland Chase." In *Men of Our Day: Biographical Sketches of Patriots, Orators, Statesmen, Generals, Reformers, Financiers, and Merchants, Now on the Stage of Action . . .*, by Linus P. Brockett, 179-200. Philadelphia: Ziegler and McCurdy, 1872.

6828. Brooks, Noah. "Lincoln, Chase, and Grant." *Century Magazine* 49 (February 1895): 607-619.

6829. Brooks, Noah. "Salmon P. Chase." In *Statesman*, by Noah Brooks, 143-173. New York: Charles Scribner's Sons, 1893.

6830. Chittenden, Lucius E. "Secretary Chase and His Financial Policy." *Personal Reminiscences, 1840-1890, Including Lincoln*, by Lucius E. Chittenden, 99-100. New York: Richmond, Croscup, 1984.

6831. Cutler, H. M. Tracy. "Salmon Portland Chase." *Chicago Times* 1 (November 1886): 1-10.

6832. "Dedication of Memorial to Chief Justice Salmon Portland Chase." *American Bar Association Journal* 9 (June 1923): 347-352.

6833. Denslow, V. B. "Chief Justice Chase." *Putnam's Magazine* 12 (July 1868): 111-112.

6834. Didier, Eugene L. "Personal Recollections of Chief Justice Chase." *Green Bag* 7 (July 1895): 313-317.

6835. Dunne, Gerald T. "President Grant and Chief Justice Chase: A Footnote to the *Legal Tender Cases*." *St. Louis University Law Journal* 5 (Fall 1959): 539-553.

6836. Evarts, William M. *Eulogy on Chief Justice Chase, Delivered by William M. Evarts, before the Alumni of Dartmouth College, at Hanover, June 24, 1874.* Hanover, NH: J. B. Parker, 1874.

6837. Evarts, William M. "Evarts' Eulogy of the Late Chief Justice Chase." *Albany Law Journal* 10 (July 1, 1874): 21-25.

6838. Field, Stephen J. "The Late Chief Justice Chase." *Overland Monthly* 11 (October 1873): 305-310.

6839. Foraker, Joseph B. "Salmon P. Chase." *Ohio Archaeological and Historical Society Publications* 15 (July 1906): 311-340.

6840. Foulke, William D. "Hart: Salmon Portland Chase." *American Historical Review* 5 (April 1900): 583-588.

6841. Gerteis, Louis S. "Salmon P. Chase, Radicalism, and the Politics of Emancipation, 1861-1864." *Journal of American History* 60 (June 1973): 42-62.

6842. Graves, Harmon S. "Chief Justice Chase." *Yale Law Journal* 4 (October 1894): 27-31.

6843. Grayson, T. T. "Salmon P. Chase and Jay Cooke." In *Leaders and Periods of American Finance*, by T. T. Grayson, 234-265. New York: John Wiley, 1932.

6844. Hale, Frank W., Jr. "A Rhetorical Exegesis of the Life and Speeches of Salmon Portland Chase." Ph.D. diss., Ohio State University, 1955.

6845. Hale, Frank W., Jr. "Salmon Portland Chase: Rhetorician of Abolition." *Negro History Bulletin* 26 (February 1963): 165.

6846. Hamlin, Edward S. "Salmon Portland Chase." *International Review* 2 (September 1875): 662-691.

6847. Hart, Albert B. *Salmon Portland Chase.* Boston: Houghton, Mifflin, 1899.

6848. Hoadly, George. *Address at Music Hall, Cincinnati, Ohio, on the Occasion of the Removal of the Remains of Salmon P. Chase to Spring Grove Cemetery, Thursday, October 14, 1886.* Cincinnati: R. Clarke, 1887.

6849. Hoadly, George. "Honorable George Hoadly's Oration on Salmon P. Chase, October 14, 1886." *Weekly Law Bulletin* 16 (November 1, 1886): 321-329.

6850. Hollingsworth, Harold M. "The Confirmation of Judicial Review under Taney and Chase." Ph.D. diss., University of Tennessee, 1966.

6851. "Home Life of the Late Chief Justice Chase." *Albany Law Journal* 8 (October 25, 1873): 258-260.

6852. Hughes, David F. "Chief Justice Chase at the Impeachment Trial of Andrew Johnson." *New York State Bar Journal* 41 (April 1969): 218-233.

6853. Hughes, David F. "Salmon P. Chase, Chief Justice." Ph.D. diss., Princeton University, 1963.

6854. Hughes, David F. "Salmon P. Chase, Chief Justice." *Vanderbilt Law Review* 18 (March 1965): 569-614.

6855. Johnson, Bradley T. *Reports on Cases Decided by Chief Justice Chase in the Circuit Court of the United States for the Fourth Circuit.* New York: Da Capo Press, 1972.

6856. Jones, Francis R. "Salmon Portland Chase." *Green Bag* 14 (April 1902): 155-165.

6857. Lloyd, Henry D. "The Home Life of Salmon Portland Chase." *Atlantic Monthly* 32 (November 1873): 526-538.

6858. Luthin, Reinhard H. "Salmon P. Chase's Political Career before the Civil War." *Mississippi Valley Historical Review* 29 (March 1943): 517-540.

6859. McCulloch, Hugh. "Salmon P. Chase." In *Men and Measures of Half a Century*, by Hugh McCulloch, 181-188. New York: Charles Scribner's Sons, 1888.

6860. "Monument to the Late Chief Justice Chase." *American Bar Association Journal* 8 (April 1922): 198.

6861. Nott, C. C. "Chief Justice Chase." *Nation* 16 (May 15, 1873): 330-331.

6862. Owen, Robert D. "Letter from Honorable S. P. Chase to the Loyal National League." In *The Conditions of Reconstruction*, by Robert D. Owen, 22-24. New York: W. C. Bryant and Company, 1863.

6863. Phelps, Mary M. *Kate Chase, Dominant Daughter: The Life Story of a Brilliant Woman and Her Famous Father.* New York: Crowell, 1935.

6864. Piatt, Donn. *Memories of the Men Who Saved the Union.* New York: Belford, Clarke, 1887.

6865. Piatt, Donn. "Salmon P. Chase." *North American Review* 143 (December 1886): 599-614.

6866. Pike, James S. *Chief Justice Chase.* New York: Powers, Macgowan, and Slipper, 1873.

6867. Redfield, Isaac F. "Chief Justice Chase." *North American Review* 122 (April 1876): 337-357.

6868. Rice, Clinton. "Salmon Portland Chase, Chief Justice of the United States." In *Sketches of Representative Men, North and South*, edited by Augustus C. Rogers, 129-134. New York: Atlantic Publishing Company, 1872.

6869. Savage, John. "Salmon P. Chase, of Ohio." In *Our Living Representative Men*, by John Savage, 102-113. Philadelphia: Childs and Peterson, 1860.

6870. Schlesinger, Arthur M. *Salmon Portland Chase, Undergraduate and Pedagogue.* Columbus, OH: F. J. Heer Printing Company, 1919.

6871. Schuckers, Jacob W. *The Life and Public Services of Salmon Portland Chase.* New York: D. Appleton, 1874.

6872. Scott, Henry W. "Salmon Portland Chase." In *Distinguished American Lawyers*, by Henry W. Scott, 133-142. New York: C. L. Webster, 1891.

6873. Sefton, James E., ed. "Chief Justice Chase as an Advisor on Presidential Reconstruction." *Civil War History* 12 (September 1967): 247-264.

6874. Smith, Donald V. *Chase and Civil War Politics.* Columbus, OH: F. J. Heer Printing Company, 1931.

6875. Smith, Donald V. "Salmon P. Chase and the Nomination of 1868." In *Essays in Honor of William E. Dodd, by His Former Students at the University of Chicago*, edited by Avery Craven, 291-319. Chicago: University of Chicago Press, 1935.

6876. Stowe, Harriet B. "Salmon P. Chase." In *Men of Our Times*, by Harriet B. Stowe, 241-266. Hartford, CT: Hartford Publishing Company, 1868.

6877. Townshend, Norton S. "Salmon P. Chase." *Ohio Archaeological and Historical Quarterly* 1 (September 1887): 111-126.

6878. Trowbridge, J. T. "The First Visit to Washington: Salmon P. Chase." *Atlantic Monthly* 13 (April 1864): 448-457.

6879. Viele, Egbert L. "A Trip with Lincoln, Chase, and Stanton." *Scribner's Monthly* 16 (October 1878): 813-822.

6880. Wambaugh, Eugene. "Salmon Portland Chase." In *Great American Lawyers* vol. 5, edited by William D. Lewis, 327-371. Philadelphia: J. C. Winston, 1908.

6881. Warden, Robert B. *An Account of the Private Life and Public Services of Salmon Portland Chase.* Cincinnati: Wilstach, Baldwin, 1874.

Writings

6882. Chase, Salmon P. *Inside Lincoln's Cabinet: The Civil War Diaries of Salmon P. Chase.* Edited by David Donald. New York: Longman's Green, 1954.

6883. Chase, Salmon P. *Maintain Plighted Faith: Speech . . . in the Senate, February 3, 1854, against the Repeal of the Missouri Prohibition of Slavery North of 36°30.* Washington, DC: J. T. and L. Towers, 1854.

6884. Chase, Salmon P., and Charles D. Cleveland. *Anti-Slavery Addresses of 1844 and 1845.* Philadelphia: S. Low, Son, and Marston, 1867.

Samuel Chase

General Studies

6885. Adams, Henry. "Yazoo and Judge Chase." In *John Randolph*, edited by Henry Adams, 122-152. Boston: Houghton, Miflin, 1908.

6886. Atwood, Edward W. "Chase's Trial." *Portland University Law Review* 2 (Spring 1951): 11-23.

6887. Bair, Robert R., and Robin D. Coblentz. "The Trials of Mr. Justice Samuel Chase." *Maryland Law Review* 27 (Fall 1967): 365-386.

6888. Blackmar, Charles B. "On the Removal of Judges: The Impeachment Trial of Samuel Chase." *Judicature* 48 (February 1965): 183-187.

6889. Carrington, R. W. "The Impeachment Trial of Samuel Chase." *Virginia Law Review* 9 (May 1923): 485-500.

6890. Dwight, Nathanial. "Samuel

Chase." In *The Lives of the Signers of the Declaration of Independence*, by Nathanial Dwight, 245-252. New York: Barnes, 1876.

6891. Elsmere, Jane S. "The Impeachment Trial of Justice Samuel Chase." Ph.D. diss., Indiana University, 1962.

6892. Elsmere, Jane S. *Justice Samuel Chase.* Muncie, IN: Janevar, 1980.

6893. Evans, Charles. *Report of the Trial of the Honorable Samuel Chase. . . .* Baltimore: Printed for Samuel Butler and George Keatings, 1805.

6894. Ford, Worthington C. "The 'Publius' Letters Attacking Samuel Chase." *The Nation* 85 (November 14, 1907): 441-442.

6895. Goodrich, Charles A. "Samuel Chase." In *Lives of the Signers of the Declaration of Independence*, by Charles A. Goodrich, 338-346. New York: W. Reed and Company, 1829.

6896. Gould, Ashley M. "Luther Martin and the Trials of Chase and Burr." *Georgetown Law Journal* 1 (November 1912): 17-22; (January 1912): 13-19.

6897. Harris, Charles D. "The Impeachment Trial of Samuel Chase." *American Bar Association Journal* 57 (January 1971): 53-57.

6898. Haw, James A. "Samuel Chases's 'Objections to the Federal Government'." *Maryland Historical Magazine* 76 (Fall 1981): 272-285.

6899. Haw, James A., et al. *Stormy Patriot: The Life of Samuel Chase.* Baltimore: Maryland Historical Society, 1980.

6900. Hunt, William. "Samuel Chase." In *American Biographical Panorama*, by William Hunt, 59. Albany, NY: J. Munsell, 1849.

6901. Judson, L. Carroll. "Samuel Chase." In *A Biography of the Signers of the Declaration of Independence and of*

Washington and Patrick Henry, by L. Carroll Judson, 236-248. Philadelphia: J. Dobson and Thomas Cowperthwait, 1839.

6902. Judson, L. Carroll. "Samuel Chase." In *Sages and Heroes of the American Revolution*, by L. Carroll Judson, 68-77. Philadelphia: Mass and Brother, 1853.

6903. Lillich, Richard B. "The Chase Impeachment." *American Journal of Legal History* 4 (January 1960): 49-72.

6904. Lossing, Benson J. "Samuel Chase." In *Lives of the Signers of the Declaration of American Independence*, by Benson J. Lossing, 146-150. Philadelphia: Evans, Stoddart, and Company, 1870.

6905. O'Connell, Daniel. *Liberty or Slavery? Daniel O'Connell on American Slavery: Reply to O'Connell by Honorable S. P. Chase.* Cincinnati: Chronicle Print, 1863.

6906. Presser, Stephen B. "A Tale of Two Judges: Richard Peters, Samuel Chase, and the Broken Promise of Federalist Jurisprudence." *New York University Law Review* 73 (March/April 1978): 26-111.

6907. Presser, Stephen B., and Becky B. Hurley. "Saving God's Republic: The Jurisprudence of Samuel Chase." *University of Illinois Law Review* 1984 (Summer 1984): 771-882.

Thomas C. Clark

General Studies

6908. Baier, Paul R. "Justice Clark, the Voice of the Past, and the Exclusionary Rule." *Texas Law Review* 64 (October 1985): 415-419.

6909. Dorin, Dennis D. "Justice Tom Clark and the Right of Defendants in State Courts." Ph.D. diss., University of Virginia, 1974.

6910. Dorin, Dennis D. "Mr. Justice

Clark and State Criminal Justice, 1949-1967." Ph.D. diss., University of Virginia, 1974.

6911. Dorin, Dennis D. "Tom C. Clark: The Justice as Administrator." *Judicature* 61 (January 1978): 271-277.

6912. Dutton, C. B. "Mr. Justice Tom C. Clark." *Indiana Law Journal* 26 (Winter 1951): 169-184.

6913. Frank, John P. "Justice Tom Clark and Judicial Administration." *Texas Law Review* 46 (November 1967): 5-56.

6914. Gazell, James A. "Justice Tom C. Clark as Judicial Reformer." *Houston Law Review* 15 (January 1978): 307-330.

6915. Mengler, Thomas M. "Public Relations in the Supreme Court: Justice Tom Clark's Opinion in the School Prayer Case." *Constitutional Commentary* 6 (Summer 1989): 331-349.

6916. O'Donnell, Alice L. "Tom Clark's Unique Vision." *Judges Journal* 27 (Fall 1988): 8-10.

6917. Rostow, Eugene V. "Judge Clark." *Yale Law Journal* 73 (November 1963): 1.

6918. Srere, Mark. "Justice Tom C. Clark's Unconditional Approach to Individual Rights in the Courtroom." *Texas Law Review* 64 (October 1985): 421-442.

6919. Temple, Larry. "Mr. Justice Clark: A Tribute." *American Journal of Criminal Law* 5 (October 1977): 271-274.

6920. Warren, Earl. "Judicial Tributes: Judge Clark." *Connecticut Bar Journal* 38 (March 1964): 1-3.

6921. West, Ellis M. "Justice Tom Clark and American Church-State Law." *Journal of Presbyterian History* 54 (Winter 1976): 387-404.

Writings

6922. Clark, Thomas C. "Administrative Law." *Journal of the Bar Association of the District of Columbia* 18 (July 1951): 254-261.

6923. Clark, Thomas C. "The American Bar Association Standards for Criminal Justice: Prescription for an Ailing System." *Notre Dame Lawyer* 47 (February 1972): 429-441.

6924. Clark, Thomas C. "Bill Douglas: A Portrait." *Baylor Law Review* 28 (Spring 1976): 215-220.

6925. Clark, Thomas C. "Citizens, Courts, and the Effective Administration of Justice." *Journal of the American Judicature Society* 49 (June 1965): 6-13.

6926. Clark, Thomas C. "Colorado at the Judicial Crossroads." *Judicature* 50 (December 1966): 118-124.

6927. Clark, Thomas C. "Constitutional Adjudication and the Supreme Court." *Drake Law Review* 9 (May 1960): 59-65.

6928. Clark, Thomas C. "Constitutional Responsibility, Concomitants." *University of Colorado Law Review* 37 (Fall 1964): 1-10.

6929. Clark, Thomas C. "The Court and Its Functions." *Albany Law Review* 34 (Spring 1970): 497-502.

6930. Clark, Thomas C. "The Decisional Processes of the Supreme Court." *Cornell Law Quarterly* 50 (Spring 1965): 385-393.

6931. Clark, Thomas C. "Federal Courts in the United States: Their Work and Administration." *Australian Law Journal* 41 (November 1967): 251-260.

6932. Clark, Thomas C. "The Federal Judicial Center." *Arizona State Law Journal* 1974 (1974): 537-547.

6933. Clark, Thomas C. "The Federal Judiciary: Fifty Years of Progress." *Federal Bar Journal* 29 (Fall 1970): 245-249.

6934. Clark, Thomas C. "The First Amendment and Minority Rights." *University of Chicago Law Review* 36 (Winter 1969): 257-267.

6935. Clark, Thomas C. "*Gideon* Revisited." *Arizona Law Review* 15 (1973): 343-353.

6936. Clark, Thomas C. "Implementation Story: Where We Must Go." *Judicature* 55 (May 1972): 383-388.

6937. Clark, Thomas C. "Importance of Improving the Image of the Judge." *Trial Judges' Journal* 3 (January 1964): 1-5.

6938. Clark, Thomas C. "Internal Operation of the United States Supreme Court." *American Judicature Society Journal* 43 (August 1959): 45-51.

6939. Clark, Thomas C. "Justice: Truth in Action." *New York University Law Review* 43 (May 1968): 419-428.

6940. Clark, Thomas C. "Mr. Justice Frankfurter: 'A Heritage for All Who Love the Law'." *American Bar Association Journal* 51 (April 1965): 330-332.

6941. Clark, Thomas C. "Mr. Justice Murphy: A Review Article." *Michigan History* 53 (Fall 1969): 247-254.

6942. Clark, Thomas C. "The New Federal Judicial Center." *American Bar Association Journal* 54 (1968): 743-746.

6943. Clark, Thomas C. "Parajudges and the Administration of Justice." *Vanderbilt Law Review* 24 (November 1971): 1167-1179.

6944. Clark, Thomas C. "The Present State of Trial Advocacy." *DePaul Law Review* 12 (Spring/Summer 1963): 185-196.

6945. Clark, Thomas C. "Problems of Change." *Utah Law Review* 1968 (September 1968): 347-354.

6946. Clark, Thomas C. "Religion and the Law." *South Carolina Law Review* 15 (1963): 855-866.

6947. Clark, Thomas C. "Remarks on the Supreme Court of the United States." *Pennsylvania Bar Association Quarterly* 31 (June 1960): 430-436.

6948. Clark, Thomas C. "Reminiscences of an Attorney General Turned Associate Justice." *Houston Law Review* 6 (March 1969): 623-629.

6949. Clark, Thomas C. "Sentencing and Corrections." *University of San Francisco Law Review* 5 (October 1970): 1-9.

6950. Clark, Thomas C. "The Sixties: A Historic Decade in Judicial Improvement." *Brooklyn Law Review* 36 (Spring 1970): 331-338.

6951. Clark, Thomas C. "The Supreme Court as a Protector of Liberty under the Rule of Law." *Marquette Law Review* 43 (Summer 1959): 11-19.

6952. Clark, Thomas C. "The Supreme Court Conference." *Federal Rules Decisions* 19 (1956): 303-310.

6953. Clark, Thomas C. "The Supreme Court Conference." *Texas Law Review* 37 (February 1959): 273-278.

John H. Clarke

General Studies

6954. Levitan, David M. "The Jurisprudence of Mr. Justice Clarke." *Miami Law Review* 7 (December 1952): 44-72.

6955. Warner, Hoyt L. *The Life of Mr. Justice Clarke: A Testament to the Power of Liberal Dissent in America.* Cleveland: Western Reserve University, 1959.

6956. Wittke, Carl. "Mr. Justice Clarke: A Supreme Court Justice in Retirement." *Mississippi Valley Historical Review* 36 (June 1949): 27-50.

6957. Zilber, Harry. "Mr. Justice

Clarke." Master's thesis, University of Wisconsin, 1949.

Writings

6958. Clarke, John H. "How the United States Supreme Court Works." *American Bar Association Journal* 9 (February 1923): 80-82.

6959. Clarke, John H. "Judicial Power to Declare Legislation Unconstitutional." *American Bar Association Journal* 9 (November 1923): 689-692.

6960. Clarke, John H. "Methods of Work of the United States Supreme Court Judges." *Ohio Law Reporter* 20 (November 27, 1922): 398-408.

6961. Clarke, John H. "The Naked Question of the Constitutionality of the Court Proposal." *Vital Speeches* 3 (April 1937): 369-370.

6962. Clarke, John H. "The 'New Federalist Series': Judicial Power to Declare Legislation Unconstitutional." *American Bar Association Journal* 9 (November 1923): 689-692.

6963. Clarke, John H. "Practice before the Supreme Court." *Virginia Law Register* 8 (August 1922): 241-252.

6964. Clarke, John H. "Reminiscences of the Courts and Law." *Proceedings of the California State Bar Association* 5 (1932): 20-31.

Nathan Clifford

General Studies

6965. Bradbury, James W. "Memoir of Nathan Clifford." *Maine Historical Society Collections* 9 (1887): 235-257.

6966. Chandler, Walter. "Nathan Clifford: A Triumph of Untiring Effort."

American Bar Association Journal 11 (January 1925): 57-60.

6967. Clifford, Philip G. *Nathan Clifford, Democrat, 1803-1881.* New York: Putnam's, 1922.

6968. Hunt, William. "Nathan Clifford." In *American Biographical Sketch Book*, by William Hunt, 128-129. New York: Cornish, Lamport, and Company, 1848.

6969. "Nathan Clifford." *United States Magazine and Democratic Review* 21 (October 1847): 360-364.

Benjamin R. Curtis

General Studies

6970. "Boston Bar Forty Years Ago: Reminiscences of the Days of Webster, Choate, Loring, Curtis, and Bartlett." *American Law Review* 23 (July/August 1889): 649-652.

6971. Ellis, Charles M. *The Power of the Commander-in-Chief to Declare Emancipation: As Shown from Benjamin R. Curtis.* Boston: A. Williams, 1862.

6972. Grinnell, Frank W. "Glimpses of the Life of Benjamin Robbins Curtis." *Massachusetts Historical Society Proceedings* 64 (1932): 244-249.

6973. Leach, Richard H. "Benjamin R. Curtis: Case Study of a Supreme Court Justice." Ph.D. diss., Princeton University, 1951.

6974. Leach, Richard H. "Benjamin Robbins Curtis: A Model for a Successful Legal Career." *American Bar Association Journal* 41 (March 1955): 225-228.

6975. Leach, Richard H. "Benjamin Robbins Curtis: Judicial Misfit." *New England Quarterly* 25 (December 1952): 448-462.

6976. Leach, Richard H. "Justice Curtis

and the *Dred Scott* Case." *Essex Institute Historical Collection* 94 (January 1958): 37-56.

6977. Morse, John T., Jr. "Benjamin Robbins Curtis." *Atlantic Monthly* 45 (February 1880): 265-270.

6978. Robbins, Chandler. "Memoir of the Honorable Benjamin Robbins Curtis, LL.D." *Massachusetts Historical Society Proceedings* 16 (January 1878): 16-35.

6979. Scott, Henry W. "Benjamin Robbins Curtis." In *Distinguished American Lawyers*, by Henry W. Scott, 277-282. New York: C. L. Webster, 1891.

6980. Sedgwick, A. G. "Benjamin Robbins Curtis." *Nation* 29 (December 11, 1879): 405-407.

6981. Warner, Joseph B. "Benjamin Robbins Curtis." In *Great American Lawyers*, vol. 5, edited by William D. Lewis, 421-458. Philadelphia: J. C. Winston, 1908.

Writings

6982. Curtis, Benjamin R. "Character and Public Service of Chief Justice Taney: Remarks Made at a Meeting of the Boston Bar, October 15, 1864." In *Memoir*, vol. 2, by Benjamin R. Curtis, 336-342. Boston: Little, Brown, 1879.

6983. Curtis, Benjamin R. *Executive Power*. Cambridge, MA: H. O. Houghton, 1862.

6984. Curtis, Benjamin R. "Mr. Justice Curtis." *Albany Law Journal* 20 (October 25, 1879): 324-326.

6985. Curtis, Benjamin R. "Mr. Justice Curtis." *Albany Law Journal* 20 (November 22, 1879): 404-405.

6986. Curtis, Benjamin R. "The Supreme Court." In *Jurisdiction, Practice, and Peculiar Jurisprudence of the Courts of the United States*, edited by Henry C. Merwin, 1-63. Boston: Little, Brown, 1896.

6987. Curtis, Benjamin R., ed. *Life and Writings of Benjamin R. Curtis*. Boston: Little, Brown, 1879.

6988. Curtis, Benjamin R., ed. *A Memoir of Benjamin Robbins Curtis, LL.D., with Some of His Professional and Miscellaneous Writings*. Boston: Little, Brown, 1879.

William Cushing

General Studies

6989. Cushing, John D. "Revolutionary Conservative: The Public Life of William Cushing, 1732-1810." Ph.D. diss., Clark University, 1960.

6990. Grinnell, Frank W. "William Cushing's Judicial Career in Massachusetts from 1777-1789." *Massachusetts Law Quarterly* 43 (March 1958): 64-69.

6991. O'Brien, F. William. "Justice Cushing and State Sovereignty." *South Carolina Law Quarterly* 9 (Summer 1957): 572-590.

6992. O'Brien, F. William. "Justice Cushing's Undelivered Speech on the Federal Constitution." *William and Mary Quarterly* 15 (January 1958): 74-92.

6993. O'Brien, F. William. "Justice William Cushing and the Treaty-Making Power." *Vanderbilt Law Review* 10 (February 1957): 351-367.

6994. O'Brien, F. William. "The Pre-Marshall Court and the Role of William Cushing." *Massachusetts Law Quarterly* 43 (March 1958): 52-63.

6995. Olsson, George C. "Judge William Cushing." *Case and Comment* 46 (July 1940): 19-20.

6996. Rugg, Arthur P. "William Cushing." *Yale Law Journal* 30 (December 1920): 128-144.

Peter V. Daniel

General Studies

6997. Brown, Henry B. "The Dissenting Opinions of Mr. Justice Daniel." *American Law Review* 21 (November/December 1887): 869-900.

6998. Burnette, Lawrence. "Peter V. Daniel: Agrarian Justice." *Virginia Magazine of History and Biography* 62 (July 1954): 289-305.

6999. Frank, John P. *Justice Daniel Dissenting: A Biography of Peter V. Daniel, 1784-1860.* Cambridge: Harvard University Press, 1964.

David Davis

General Studies

7000. Brockett, Linus P. "David Davis, Associate Justice of the Supreme Court of the U.S." In *Men of Our Day: Biographical Sketches of Patriots, Orators, Statesmen, Generals, Reformers, Financiers, and Merchants, Now on the Stage of Action . . .*, by Linus P. Brockett, 346-351. Philadelphia: Ziegler and McCurdy, 1872.

7001. Dent, Thomas. "David Davis of Illinois: A Sketch." *American Law Review* 53 (July/August 1919): 535-560.

7002. Flynn, William J., and Howard N. Morse. "David Davis, Justice, U.S. Supreme Court, in Retrospect." *Alabama Lawyer* 13 (October 1952): 392-395.

7003. Flynn, William J., and Howard N. Morse. "U.S. Supreme Court Justice David Davis of Illinois." *Chicago Bar Record* 34 (October 1952): 29-30.

7004. King, Willard L. *Lincoln's Manager, David Davis.* Cambridge: Harvard University Press, 1960.

7005. Linder, Usher F. "David Davis." In *Reminiscences of the Early Bench and Bar in Illinois*, by Usher F. Linder, 181-188. Chicago: Chicago Legal News, 1879.

7006. Pratt, Harry E. "David Davis, 1815-1856." Ph.D. diss., University of Illinois, 1930.

7007. Wilson, Rufus R. "Mr. Lincoln's First Appointment to the Supreme Court." *Lincoln Herald* 50 (December 1948): 26-27; 51 (February 1949): 39.

William R. Day

General Studies

7008. "Character of Mr. Justice Day." *American Law Review* 37 (May/June 1903): 402-403.

7009. Day, William R. "Judge Luther Day." *Western Reserve Law Journal* 1 (November 1895): 153-159.

7010. Duncan, George W. "The Diplomatic Career of William Rufus Day, 1897-1898." Ph.D. diss., Case Western Reserve University, 1976.

7011. McLean, Joseph E. *William Rufus Day: Supreme Court Justice from Ohio.* Baltimore: Johns Hopkins Press, 1946.

7012. Roelofs, Vernon W. "Justice William R. Day and Federal Regulation." *Mississippi Valley Historical Review* 37 (June 1950): 39-60.

7013. Roelofs, Vernon W. "William R. Day: A Study in Constitutional History." Ph.D. diss., University of Michigan, 1942.

7014. Shippee, Lester B., and Royal B. Way. "William Rufus Day." In *American Secretaries of State and Their Diplomacy*, vol. 9, edited by Samuel F. Bemis, 22-112. New York: Pageant Book Company, 1958.

William O. Douglas

General Studies

7015. Adler, Sheldon S. "Toward a Constitutional Theory of Individuality: The Privacy Opinions of Justice Douglas." *Yale Law Journal* 87 (July 1978): 1579-1600.

7016. Allen, James, ed. *Democracy and Finance: Addresses and Public Statements of William O. Douglas.* New Haven, CT: Yale University Press, 1940.

7017. Allen, Richard B. "The Supreme Court Is a Lot of Laughs, on the Stage, at Least." *American Bar Association Journal* 64 (May 1978): 672.

7018. Amsterdam, Anthony G. "The Genius of Justice William O. Douglas." *Beverly Hills Bar Association Journal* 12 (May/June 1978): 114-117.

7019. Ares, Charles E. "Mr. Justice Douglas." *Harvard Civil Rights-Civil Liberties Law Review* 11 (Spring 1976): 229-242.

7020. Armstrong, Walter P. "Mr. Justice Douglas on *Stare Decisis*: A Condensation of the Eighth Cardozo Lecture." *American Bar Association Journal* 35 (July 1949): 541-544.

7021. Baude, Patrick. "An Appreciative Note on Mr. Justice Douglas' View of the Court's Role in Environmental Cases." *Indiana Law Journal* 51 (Fall 1975): 22-26.

7022. Bayh, Birch. "How Should We Judge Our Judges? In The Wake of the Senate Rejection of Judges Haynsworth and Carswell and the Drive to Impeach Justice Douglas." *Lithopinion* 5 (Fall 1970): 6-8.

7023. Beaney, William M. "Justice William O. Douglas: The Constitution in a Free Society." *Indiana Law Journal* 51 (Fall 1975): 18-21.

7024. Brenner, Saul, and Theodore S. Arrington. "William O. Douglas: Consistent Civil Libertarian or Parabolic Supporter?" *Journal of Politics* 45 (May 1983): 490-496.

7025. Brownfeld, Alan C. *Dossier on Douglas.* Washington, DC: New Majority Book Club, 1970.

7026. Campbell, Jeter L. "Justices Douglas and Black and the Democratic Ethos: Rhetorical Criticism of Concurring and Dissenting Opinions on Obscenity, 1954-1975." Ph.D. diss., University of Minnesota, 1979.

7027. Casper, Gerhard. "The Liberal Faith: Some Observations on the Legal Philosophy of Mr. Justice William O. Douglas." *Federal Bar Journal* 22 (Summer 1962): 179-194.

7028. Clark, Thomas C. "Bill Douglas: A Portrait." *Baylor Law Review* 28 (Spring 1976): 215-220.

7029. Cohen, William. "Freedom to Be Foolish: The Douglas Inquiry." *Center Magazine* 11 (June 1978): 2-6.

7030. Cohen, William. "Justice Douglas: A Law Clerk's View." *University of Chicago Law Review* 26 (Autumn 1958): 6-8.

7031. Cohn, Henry S. "Mr. Justice Douglas and Federal Taxation." *Connecticut Bar Journal* 45 (June 1971): 218-243.

7032. Cooper, Phillip J. "Justice Douglas and Administrative Law." Ph.D. diss., Syracuse University, 1978.

7033. Cooper, Phillip J. "William O. Douglas on Law and Administration in the Modern Government Context." *International Journal of Public Administration* 5 (1983): 1-56.

7034. Countryman, Vern. "Contribution of the Douglas Dissents." *Georgia Law Review* 10 (Winter 1976): 331-352.

7035. Countryman, Vern. *The Judicial Record of Justice William O. Douglas.*

Cambridge: Harvard University Press, 1974.

7036. Countryman, Vern. "Justice Douglas and Freedom of Expression." *University of Illinois Law Forum* 1978 (1978): 301-328.

7037. Countryman, Vern. "Justice Douglas and the Law of Business Regulation." *Banking Law Journal* 91 (April 1974): 312-319.

7038. Countryman, Vern. "Justice Douglas: Expositor of the Bankruptcy Law." *American Bankruptcy Law Journal* 51 (Spring 1971): 127-194; (Summer 1971): 247-275.

7039. Countryman, Vern. "Justice Douglas: Expositor of the Bankruptcy Law." *UCLA Law Review* 16 (1969): 773-838.

7040. Countryman, Vern. "Scholarship and Common Sense." *Harvard Law Review* 93 (May 1980): 1407-1415.

7041. Countryman, Vern, ed. *The Douglas Opinions.* New York: Random House, 1977.

7042. "Dissenter on the Bench and on World Policy, Too." *U.S. News and World Report* 38 (February 11, 1955): 78.

7043. Douglas, Cathleen H. "William O. Douglas: The Man." *Supreme Court Historical Society Yearbook* 1981 (1981): 6-9.

7044. Duke, Steven. "Mr. Justice Douglas." *Harvard Civil Rights-Civil Liberties Law Review* 11 (Spring 1976): 229-242.

7045. Dunne, Gerald T. "Justice Douglas and the Law of Banking." *Banking Law Journal* 91 (April 1974): 307-311.

7046. Duram, James C. *Justice William O. Douglas.* Boston: Twayne, 1981.

7047. Elson, Edward L., and Warren E. Burger. "William O. Douglas: 1898-1980." *American Bar Association Journal* 66 (March 1980): 320-321.

7048. Emerson, Thomas I. "Justice Doug-

las and Lawyers with a Cause." *Yale Law Journal* 89 (March 1980): 616-623.

7049. Epstein, Leon D. "Economic Predilections of Justice Douglas." *Wisconsin Law Review* 1949 (May 1949): 531-562.

7050. Epstein, Leon D. "Justice Douglas: A Case Study in Judicial Review." Ph.D. diss., University of Chicago, 1949.

7051. Epstein, Leon D. "Justice Douglas and Civil Liberties." *Wisconsin Law Review* 151 (January 1951): 125-157.

7052. Fortas, Abe. "Mr. Justice Douglas." *Yale Law Journal* 73 (May 1964): 917.

7053. Fortas, Abe. "William O. Douglas: A Eulogy." *Yale Law Journal* 89 (March 1980): 613-615.

7054. Fortas, Abe. "William O. Douglas: An Appreciation." *Indiana Law Journal* 51 (Fall 1975): 3-5.

7055. Gazell, James A. "Justice Douglas and Judicial Administration: A Libertarian Approach." *Gonzaga Law Review* 14 (Summer 1979): 785-818.

7056. Glennon, Robert J., Jr. "Do Not Go Gentle: More Than an Epitaph." *Wayne Law Review* 22 (September 1976): 1305-1334.

7057. Goldman, Eliot. "Justice William O. Douglas: The 1944 Vice Presidential Nomination and His Relationship with Roosevelt, a Historical Perspective." *Presidential Studies Quarterly* 12 (Summer 1982): 377-385.

7058. Goldman, Sheldon. "In Defense of Justice: Some Thoughts on Reading Professor Mendelson's 'Mr. Justice Douglas and Government by the Judiciary'." *Journal of Politics* 39 (February 1977): 148-165.

7059. Gressman, Eugene, William O. Douglas, and William S. Thompson. "The World of Earl Warren." *American Bar Association Journal* 60 (October 1974): 1228-1236.

7060. Hazeltine, Alice J. *We Grew Up in America.* Nashville: Abingdon, 1954.

7061. Hopkirk, John W. "William O. Douglas: His Work in Policy Bankruptcy Proceedings." *Vanderbilt Law Review* 18 (March 1965): 663-699.

7062. Hopkirk, John W. "William O. Douglas, Individualist: A Study in the Development and Application of a Judge's Attitudes." Ph.D. diss., Princeton University, 1960.

7063. Huber, Richard G. "William O. Douglas and the Environment." *Environmental Affairs* 5 (Spring 1976): 209-212.

7064. Irish, Marian D. "Mr. Justice Douglas and Judicial Restraint." *University of Florida Law Review* 6 (Winter 1953): 537-553.

7065. Isenbergh, Max. "Thoughts on William O. Douglas' *The Court Years*: A Confession and Avoidance." *American University Law Review* 30 (Winter 1981): 415-428.

7066. James, Dorothy. "Judicial Philosophy and Accession to the Court: The Cases of Justices Jackson and Douglas." Ph.D. diss., Columbia University, 1966.

7067. Jennings, Richard W. "Mr. Justice Douglas: His Influence on Corporate and Securities Regulation." *Yale Law Journal* 73 (May 1964): 920-974.

7068. Karst, Kenneth L. "Invidious Discrimination: Justice Douglas and the Return of the 'Natural-Law-Due-Process Formula'." *UCLA Law Review* 16 (1969): 716-750.

7069. Karst, Kenneth L. "Justice Douglas and the Equal Protection Clause." *Indiana Law Journal* 51 (Fall 1975): 14-17.

7070. Keller, Robert H., Jr. *In Honor of Justice Douglas: A Symposium on Individual Freedom and the Government.* Westport, CT: Greenwood Press, 1979.

7071. Keller, Robert H., Jr. "William O. Douglas, the Supreme Court, and American Indians." *American Indian Law Review* 3 (Winter 1975): 333-360.

7072. Kennedy, Harry L. "Justice William O. Douglas on Freedom of the Press." Ph.D. diss., Ohio University, 1980.

7073. Linde, Hans A. "Constitutional Rights in the Public Sector: Justice Douglas on Liberty in the Welfare State." *Washington Law Review* 40 (April 1965): 10-77.

7074. Linde, Hans A. "Justice Douglas on Freedom in the Welfare State: Constitutional Rights in the Public Sector." *Washington Law Review* 39 (Spring 1964): 4-46.

7075. Louisell, David W. "The Man and the Mountain: Douglas on Religious Freedom." *Yale Law Journal* 73 (May 1964): 975-998.

7076. McBride, Howard E., and William O. Douglas. *Impeach Justice Douglas.* Vol. 1 of *Subversion.* Hicksville, NY: Exposition, 1971.

7077. Manning, Leonard F. "The Douglas Concept of God in Government." *Washington Law Review* 39 (Spring 1964): 47-73.

7078. Maverick, Maury, Jr. "Douglas and the First Amendment: Visiting Old Battlegrounds." *Baylor Law Review* 28 (Spring 1976): 235-248.

7079. Meek, Roy L. "Justices Douglas and Black: Political Liberalism and Judicial Activism." Ph.D. diss., University of Oregon, 1964.

7080. Mendelson, Wallace. "Mr. Justice Douglas and Government by the Judiciary." *Journal of Politics* 38 (November 1976): 918-937.

7081. Mosk, Stanley. "William O. Douglas." *Ecology Law Quarterly* 5 (Spring 1976): 229-232.

7082. Neuberger, Richard L. "Much-Discussed 'Bill' Douglas." *New York Times Magazine* 91 (April 19, 1942): 10-11.

7083. Oddo, Gilbert L. "The Judicial Opinions of Mr. Justice Douglas Concerning the Question of Civil Liberty." Master's thesis, Georgetown University, 1950.

7084. Oddo, Gilbert L. "Justice Douglas and the Roosevelt Court." Ph.D. diss., Georgetown University, 1952.

7085. Parrish, Michael E. "Justice Douglas and the *Rosenberg* Case: A Rejoinder." *Cornell Law Review* 70 (August 1985): 1048-1057.

7086. Peladeau, Marius B. "Predilections of Supreme Court Justices: A Quarter-Century Analysis of U.S. Supreme Court Rate Decisions Involving Public Utility Companies; With Special Attention to Justices Black and Douglas." *Public Utilities Fortnightly* 71 (January 17, 1963): 32-39.

7087. Pollock, Paul K. "Judicial Libertarianism and Judicial Responsibilities: The Case of Justice William O. Douglas." Ph.D. diss., Cornell University, 1968.

7088. Powe, L. A., Jr. "Evolution to Absolutism: Justice Douglas and the First Amendment." *Columbia Law Review* 74 (April 1974): 371-411.

7089. Rabinove, Samuel. "Justice Douglas and the *DeFunis* Case: A Critique." *Humanist* 35 (March 1975): 25-26.

7090. Resnik, Solomon. "Black and Douglas: Variations in Dissent." *Western Political Quarterly* 16 (June 1963): 305-322.

7091. Richards, David R. "Justice Douglas and the Availability of the Federal Forum to Civil Rights Litigants." *Baylor Law Review* 28 (Spring 1976): 221-234.

7092. Rodell, Fred. "As Justice Bill Douglas Completes His First Thirty Years on the Court: Herewith a Random Anniversary Sample, Complete with Casual Commentary, of Divers Scraps, Sherds, and Shards, Gleaned from a Forty-Year

Friendship." *UCLA Law Review* 16 (1969): 704-715.

7093. Rodell, Fred. "Bill Douglas, American." *American Mercury* (December 1945): 656-665.

7094. Rodell, Fred. "I'd Prefer Bill Douglas." *Nation* 174 (April 26, 1952): 400-402.

7095. Rodell, Fred. "Justice Douglas: An Anniversary Fragment for a Friend." *University of Chicago Law Review* 26 (Autumn 1958): 2-6.

7096. Rodgers, Raymond S. "Absolutism and Natural Law Argument: William O. Douglas on Freedom of Expression." *Southern Speech Communication Journal* 48 (Fall 1982): 22-37.

7097. Rodgers, Raymond S. "Generic Tendencies in Majority and Non-Majority Supreme Court Opinions: The Case of Justice Douglas." *Communication Quarterly Journal* 30 (Summer 1982): 232-236.

7098. Rodgers, Raymond S. "Justice William O. Douglas on the First Amendment: Rhetorical Genres in Judicial Opinions." Ph.D. diss., University of Oklahoma, 1979.

7099. Romero, Patricia W. "A Look at Supreme Court Justice William O. Douglas." *Negro History Bulletin* 29 (March 1966): 129-130, 137.

7100. Sevareid, Eric. "Mr. Justice Douglas Speaks His Mind." *Bill of Rights Journal* 5 (December 1972): 17-37.

7101. Silber, Jonathan, and Marjorie A. Silver. *Dissent without Opinion: The Behavior of Justice William O. Douglas in Federal Tax Cases.* Philadelphia: University of Pennsylvania Press, 1975.

7102. Simon, James F. *Independent Journey: The Life of William O. Douglas.* New York: Harper and Row, 1980.

7103. Sprecher, Robert A. "Mr. Justice

Douglas." *Indiana Law Journal* 51 (Fall 1975): 6-13.

7104. Thomas, Helen S. "Justice William O. Douglas and the Concept of a 'Fair Trial'." *Vanderbilt Law Review* 18 (March 1965): 701-716.

7105. Ulmer, S. Sidney. "Parabolic Support of Civil Liberty Claims: The Case of William O. Douglas." *Journal of Politics* 41 (May 1979): 634-639.

7106. Urofsky, Melvin I. "Conflict among the Brethren: Felix Frankfurter, William O. Douglas, and the Clash of Personalities and Philosophies on the United States Supreme Court." *Duke Law Journal* 1988 (February 1988): 71-113.

7107. Wallfisch, Mark C. "The Conflict between Freedom and Control in the Education Opinions of Justice William O. Douglas." Ph.D. diss., Duke University, 1978.

7108. Wallfisch, Mark C. "Justice Douglas: Advocate of Free Expression in Schools." *High School Journal* 63 (April 1980): 303-307.

7109. Wallfisch, Mark C. "William O. Douglas and Religious Liberty." *Journal of Presbyterian History* 58 (Fall 1980): 193-208.

7110. Warren, Earl. "Introduction: A Tribute to Justice Douglas." *Washington Law Review* 39 (Spring 1964): 1-3.

7111. Way, H. Frank, Jr. "The Study of Judicial Attitudes: The Case of Mr. Justice Douglas." *Western Political Quarterly* 24 (March 1971): 12-27.

7112. Wechsler, Burton. "A Tribute to Justice Douglas." *Antioch Law Journal* 1 (Fall 1981): 1-6.

7113. Williams, Julian E. *The Case against William O. Douglas.* Tulsa, OK: Christian Crusade Publications, 1970.

7114. Williams, Stephen F. "Free Trade in Water Resources: *Sporhase v. Nebraska*

ex. re. Douglas." *Supreme Court Economic Review* 2 (1983): 89-110.

7115. Wolfman, Bernard, Jonathan L. F. Silver, and Marjorie A. Silver. "Behavior of Justice Douglas in Federal Tax Cases." *University of Pennsylvania Law Review* 122 (December 1973): 235-365.

7116. Wolfman, Bernard, Jonathan L. F. Silver, and Marjorie A. Silver. *Dissent without Opinion: The Behavior of Justice William O. Douglas in Federal Tax Cases.* Philadelphia: University of Pennsylvania Press, 1975.

7117. Yarbrough, Tinsley E. "Justices Black and Douglas: The Judicial Function and the Scope of Constitutional Liberties." *Duke Law Journal* 1973 (January 1973): 441-486.

Writings

7118. Douglas, William O. *An Almanac of Liberty.* Garden City, NY: Doubleday, 1954.

7119. Douglas, William O. *America Challenged.* Princeton, NJ: Princeton University Press, 1960.

7120. Douglas, William O. *The Anatomy of Liberty: The Rights of Man without Force.* New York: Trident, 1963.

7121. Douglas, William O. *Being an American.* New York: J. Day, 1948.

7122. Douglas, William O. *Beyond the High Himalayas.* Garden City, NY: Doubleday, 1952.

7123. Douglas, William O. *The Bible and the Schools.* Boston: Little, Brown, 1966.

7124. Douglas, William O. "The Bill of Rights, Due Process, and Federalism in India." *Minnesota Law Review* 40 (December 1955): 1-40.

7125. Douglas, William O. "The Bill of Rights Is Not Enough." *New York Uni-*

versity Law Review 38 (April 1963): 207-242.

7126. Douglas, William O. "The Black Silence of Fear." *New York Times Magazine* (January 13, 1952): 7, 37-38.

7127. Douglas, William O. *Cases and Materials on the Law of Corporate Reorganization.* St. Paul, MN: West Publishing Company, 1931.

7128. Douglas, William O. "Chief Justice Stone." *Columbia Law Review* 46 (September 1946): 693-695.

7129. Douglas, William O. *The Court Years, 1939-1975: The Autobiography of William O. Douglas.* New York: Random House, 1980.

7130. Douglas, William O. "A Crusade for the Bar: Due Process in a Time of World Conflict." *American Bar Association Journal* 39 (October 1953): 871-875.

7131. Douglas, William O. *Democracy and Finance.* New Haven, CT: Yale University Press, 1940.

7132. Douglas, William O. "Democracy Charts Its Course." *University of Florida Law Review* 1 (Summer 1948): 133-148.

7133. Douglas, William O. *Democracy's Manifesto.* Garden City, NY: Doubleday, 1962.

7134. Douglas, William O. "The Dissent: A Safeguard of Democracy." *Journal of the American Judicature Society* 32 (December 1948): 104-107.

7135. Douglas, William O. "The Dissenting Opinion." *Lawyers Guild Review* 8 (November/December 1948): 467-469.

7136. Douglas, William O. "The Dissenting Opinion of Mr. Justice Douglas in the Supreme Court Case of *Adler v. Board of Education*: Reprinted from April 1952." *Education Digest* 51 (November 1985): 64-66.

7137. Douglas, William O. "The Dissent-ing Opinions of William O. Douglas." *Lithopinion* 8 (Winter 1973): 31-33.

7138. Douglas, William O. *Douglas of the Supreme Court: A Selection of His Opinions.* Edited by Vern Countryman. Garden City, NY: Doubleday, 1959.

7139. Douglas, William O. *Exploring the Himalayas.* New York: Random House, 1958.

7140. Douglas, William O. *Farewell to Texas: A Vanishing Wilderness.* New York: McGraw-Hill, 1967.

7141. Douglas, William O. "Federal Courts and the Democratic System." *Alabama Law Review* 21 (Spring 1969): 179-190.

7142. Douglas, William O. "Foreword." *University of California at Los Angeles Law Review* 15 (September 1968): 1374-1376.

7143. Douglas, William O. *Freedom of the Mind.* Garden City, NY: Doubleday, 1962.

7144. Douglas, William O. "French Are Facing Danger again in Morocco." *Look* 18 (October 19, 1954): 33-37.

7145. Douglas, William O. *From Marshall to Mukherjea: Studies in American and Indian Constitutional Law.* Calcutta: Eastern Law House, 1956.

7146. Douglas, William O. *Go East, Young Man.* New York: Random House, 1974.

7147. Douglas, William O. "The Grand Design of the Constitution." *Gonzaga Law Review* 7 (Spring 1972): 239-260.

7148. Douglas, William O. "Harlan Fiske Stone Centennial Lecture: The Meaning of Due Process." *Columbia Journal of Law and Social Problems* 10 (Fall 1973): 1-14.

7149. Douglas, William O. "The Hastings Bill and Lessons Learned from the Bankruptcy Studies." *National Association of*

Referees in Bankruptcy 7 (October 1932): 25-28.

7150. Douglas, William O. *Holocaust or Hemispheric Co-op: Cross Currents in Latin America.* New York: Random House, 1971.

7151. Douglas, William O. "*In Forma Pauperis* Practice in the United States." *New Hampshire Bar Journal* 2 (October 1959): 5-10.

7152. Douglas, William O. "Indo-China: A House Divided." *Reader's Digest* 62 (March 1953): 144-148.

7153. Douglas, William O. "Insulation from Liability through Subsidiary Corporations." *Yale Law Journal* 39 (December 1929): 193-218.

7154. Douglas, William O. *International Dissent: Six Steps toward World Peace.* New York: Random House, 1971.

7155. Douglas, William O. "Interposition and the *Peters* Case, 1778-1809." *Stanford Law Review* 9 (December 1956): 3-12.

7156. Douglas, William O. "John Marshall, A Life in Law: An Essay Review." *Louisiana History* 16 (Spring 1975): 193-200.

7157. Douglas, William O. "Landlord's Claims in Reorganizations." *Yale Law Journal* 42 (May 1933): 1003-1050.

7158. Douglas, William O. "The Lasting Influence of Mr. Justice Brandeis." *Temple Law Quarterly* 19 (April 1946): 361-370.

7159. Douglas, William O. *A Living Bill of Rights.* New York: Doubleday, 1961.

7160. Douglas, William O. "Managing the Docket of the Supreme Court of the United States." *Record of the Association of the Bar of the City of New York* 25 (May 1970): 279-298.

7161. Douglas, William O. "The Meaning of Due Process." *Columbia Journal of Law and Social Problems* 10 (Fall 1973): 1-14.

7162. Douglas, William O. "The Means and the End." *Washington University Law Quarterly* 1959 (April 1959): 103-120.

7163. Douglas, William O. *Meur of the Mountains.* Boston: Houghton Mifflin, 1961.

7164. Douglas, William O. "Mr. Justice Black." *Yale Law Journal* 65 (February 1956): 449-450.

7165. Douglas, William O. "Mr. Justice Cardozo." *Michigan Law Review* 58 (February 1960): 549-556.

7166. Douglas, William O. *Mr. Lincoln and the Negroes: The Long Road to Equality.* New York: Atheneum, 1963.

7167. Douglas, William O. "My Father's Evening Star." In *This I Believe*, edited by Edward R. Murrow, 43-44. New York: Simon and Schuster, 1955.

7168. Douglas, William O. "My Favorite Vacation Land." *American Magazine* 154 (July 1952): 38-41, 94-99.

7169. Douglas, William O. *My Wilderness: East by Katahden.* Garden City, NY: Doubleday, 1961.

7170. Douglas, William O. *My Wilderness: The Pacific West.* Garden City, NY: Doubleday, 1960.

7171. Douglas, William O. "Nature's Constitutional Rights." *North American Review* 258 (Spring 1973): 11-14.

7172. Douglas, William O. *North from Malaya: Adventure on Five Fronts.* Garden City, NY: Doubleday, 1953.

7173. Douglas, William O. *Of Men and Mountains.* New York: Harper and Brothers, 1950.

7174. Douglas, William O. "On Misconception of the Judicial Function and the Responsibility of the Bar." *Columbia Law Review* 59 (February 1959): 227-233.

7175. Douglas, William O. "Peace within

Our Grasp." *Nation* 168 (April 30, 1949): 497-498.

7176. Douglas, William O. *Points of Rebellion*. New York: Random House, 1970.

7177. Douglas, William O. "The Press and First Amendment Rights." *Idaho Review* 7 (Spring 1970): 1-15.

7178. Douglas, William O. "Procedural Safeguards in the Bill of Rights." *Journal of the American Judicature Society* 31 (April 1948): 166-170.

7179. Douglas, William O. "Protecting the Investor." *Yale Review* 23 (March 1934): 521-533.

7180. Douglas, William O. "Recent Trends in Constitutional Law." *Oregon Law Review* 30 (June 1951): 279-288.

7181. Douglas, William O. "Remarks." *Rutgers Law Review* 28 (Winter 1975): 616-624.

7182. Douglas, William O. "Revolution Is Our Business." *Nation* 174 (May 31, 1952): 516-519.

7183. Douglas, William O. *The Right of the People*. Garden City, NY: Doubleday, 1958.

7184. Douglas, William O. "The Role of the Lawyer." *Oklahoma Law Review* 12 (February 1959): 1-12.

7185. Douglas, William O. *Russian Journey*. Garden City, NY: Doubleday, 1958.

7186. Douglas, William O. "Some Dicta on Discrimination." *Loyola University Los Angeles Law Review* 3 (April 1970): 207-216.

7187. Douglas, William O. "Some Functional Aspects of Bankruptcy." *Yale Law Journal* 41 (January 1932): 329-364.

7188. Douglas, William O. "*Stare Decisis*." *Columbia Law Review* 49 (June 1949): 735-758.

7189. Douglas, William O. *Strange Lands and Friendly People*. New York: Harper and Brothers, 1951.

7190. Douglas, William O. "The Supreme Court and Its Case Load." *Cornell Law Quarterly* 45 (Spring 1960): 401-414.

7191. Douglas, William O. *The Supreme Court and the Bicentennial: Two Lectures*. Rutherford, NJ: Fairleigh Dickinson University Press, 1978.

7192. Douglas, William O. *The Three Hundred Year War: A Chronicle of Ecological Disaster*. New York: Random House, 1972.

7193. Douglas, William O. "Too Many Short Cuts." *New Republic* 129 (November 23, 1953): 9-11.

7194. Douglas, William O. "Toward Greater Vitality." *Today's Health* 51 (May 1973): 54-57, 72.

7195. Douglas, William O. *Towards a Global Federalism*. New York: New York University Press, 1968.

7196. Douglas, William O. "Underhill Moore." *Yale Law Journal* 59 (January 1950): 187-188.

7197. Douglas, William O. "Vagrancy and Arrest on Suspicion." *Yale Law Journal* 70 (November 1960): 1-14.

7198. Douglas, William O. "Vicarious Liability and Administration of Risk: II." *Yale Law Journal* 38 (April 1929): 720-745.

7199. Douglas, William O. "Wage Earner Bankruptcies: State vs. Federal Control." *Yale Law Journal* 42 (February 1933): 591-642.

7200. Douglas, William O. *We the Judges: Studies in American and Indian Constitutional Law from Marshall to Mukherjea*. Garden City, NY: Doubleday, 1956.

7201. Douglas, William O. *West of the Indies*. Garden City, NY: Doubleday, 1958.

7202. Douglas, William O. *A Wilderness Bill of Rights*. Boston: Little, Brown, 1965.

7203. Douglas, William O., and Dorothy S. Thomas. "The Business Failures Project—II: An Analysis of Methods of Investigation." *Yale Law Journal* 40 (May 1931): 1034-1054.

7204. Douglas, William O., and J. Howard Marshall. "A Factual Study of Bankruptcy Administration and Some Suggestions." *Columbia Law Review* 32 (January 1932): 25-59.

7205. Douglas, William O., William Clark, and Dorothy S. Thomas. "The Business Failures Project: A Problem in Methodology." *Yale Law Journal* 39 (May 1930): 1013-1024.

Gabriel Duvall

General Studies

7206. Currie, David P. "The Most Insignificant Justice: A Preliminary Inquiry." *University of Chicago Law Review* 50 (Spring 1983): 466-480.

7207. Dilliard, Irving. "Gabriel Duvall." In *Dictionary of American Biography*, supplement 1, 272-274. New York: Charles Scribner's Sons, 1944.

7208. Singer, Elizabeth D. "Gabriel Duvall." *Daughters of the American Revolution Magazine* 83 (April 1949): 291-292.

Oliver Ellsworth

General Studies

7209. "Biographical Sketch of Chief Justice Ellsworth." *American Law Magazine* 3 (July 1844): 249-272.

7210. Brown, William G. "A Continental Congressman: Oliver Ellsworth, 1777-1783." *American Historical Review* 10 (July 1905): 751-781.

7211. Brown, William G. "The Early Life of Oliver Ellsworth." *American Historical Review* 10 (April 1905): 534-564.

7212. Brown, William G. *The Life of Oliver Ellsworth*. New York: Macmillan, 1905.

7213. Buel, Elizabeth C. "Oliver Ellsworth." *New England Magazine* 30 (July 1904): 611-626.

7214. Cook, Frank G. "Oliver Ellsworth and Federation." *Atlantic Monthly* 89 (April 1902): 524-536.

7215. Cook, Frank G. "Oliver Ellsworth, 1745-1807." In *Great American Lawyers: The Lives and Influence of Judges and Lawyers Who Have Acquired Permanent National Reputation, and Have Developed the Jurisprudence of the United States*, vol. 1, edited by William D. Lewis, 305-354. Philadelphia: J. C. Winston Company, 1907.

7216. Davis, Roger W. "An Illustrious Connecticut Statesman." *National History Magazine* 74 (April 1940): 29-31, 72.

7217. Jones, Francis R. "Oliver Ellsworth." *Green Bag* 13 (November 1901): 503-508.

7218. Lettieri, Ronald J. *Connecticut's Young Man of the Revolution, Oliver Ellsworth*. Hartford: American Revolution Bicentennial Commission of Connecticut, 1978.

7219. Lossing, Benson J. "Oliver Ellsworth." In *Eminent Americans*, by Benson J. Lossing, 102-103. New York: Hurst, 1886.

7220. Perry, Benjamin F. "Oliver Ellsworth." In *Biographical Sketches of Eminent American Statesmen*, by Benjamin F. Perry, 403-409. Philadelphia: Ferree Press, 1887.

7221. Shepard, Henry M. "Oliver Ellsworth." *Chicago Law Times* 2 (April 1888): 109-128.

7222. Uhle, John B. "Oliver Ellsworth." *Current Comment* 2 (February 15, 1890): 65-76.

7223. Verplanck, Julian C. "Biographical Memoir of Oliver Ellsworth." *Analectic Magazine* 3 (May 1814): 382-403.

Writings

7224. Ellsworth, Oliver. *Essays on the Constitution of the United States, Published during Its Discussion by the People, 1787-1788.* Brooklyn, NY: Historical Printing Club, 1892.

Stephen J. Field

General Studies

7225. Black, Chauncey F., and Samuel B. Smith, eds. *Some Account of the Work of Stephen J. Field, as Legislator, State Judge, and Justice of the Supreme Court of the United States.* New York: S. B. Smith, 1895.

7226. Durfee, Calvin. "Stephen Johnson Field." In *Williams Biographical Annals,* by Calvin Durfee, 503-504. Boston: Lee and Shepard, 1871.

7227. Fairman, Charles. "The Education of a Justice: Justice Bradley and Some of His Colleagues." *Stanford Law Review* 1 (January 1949): 217-255.

7228. Field, Henry M. *Life of David Dudley Field.* New York: Charles Scribner's Sons, 1898.

7229. Goedecke, Robert. "Justice Field and Inherent Rights." *Review of Politics* 27 (April 1965): 198-207.

7230. Goedecke, Robert. "Rights, Interests, and the Constitution: The Jurisprudence of Mr. Justice Stephen Johnson Field." Ph.D. diss., University of Chicago, 1958.

7231. Graham, Howard J. "Four Letters of Mr. Justice Field." *Yale Law Journal* 47 (May 1938): 1100-1108.

7232. Graham, Howard J. "Justice Field and the Fourteenth Amendment." *Yale Law Journal* 52 (September 1943): 851-889.

7233. Hogan, John C., ed. "The Last Will and Testament of Stephen J. Field." *California History Quarterly* 36 (March 1957): 41-55.

7234. House, A. F. "Mr. Justice Field and Attorney General Garland." *Arkansas Law Review* 3 (Summer 1949): 266-277.

7235. Hunt, Rockwell D. *California's Stately Hall of Fame.* Stockton, CA: College of the Pacific, 1950.

7236. Johnson, J. Edward. "Stephen J. Field." *State Bar of California Journal* 23 (March/April 1948): 82-90.

7237. Jones, William C. "Justice Field's Opinions on Constitutional Law." *California Law Review* 5 (January 1917): 108-128.

7238. "Justice Field's Resignation Accepted." *Albany Law Journal* 56 (October 23, 1897): 295-298.

7239. Kroninger, Robert. "The Justice (Stephen J. Field) and the Lady (Sarah Althea Hill)." *Supreme Court Historical Society Yearbook* 1977 (1977): 11-19.

7240. Lenihan, Joseph L. "Supreme Court Justice Encounters Violence." *Kentucky State Bar Journal* 16 (September 1952): 193-196.

7241. McCloskey, Robert G. *American Conservatism in the Age of Enterprise: A Study of Summer, Field, and Carnegie.* Cambridge: Harvard University Press, 1951.

7242. MacCraken, Brooks W. "Althea and the Judges." *American Heritage* 18 (June 1967): 60-63, 75-79.

7243. McCurdy, Charles W. "Economic Growth and Judicial Conservatism in the Age of Enterprise: Studies in the Jurisprudence of Stephen J. Field, 1850-1900." Ph.D. diss., University of California, San Diego, 1976.

7244. McCurdy, Charles W. "Justice Field and the Jurisprudence of Government-Business Relations: Some Parameters of Laissez-Faire Constitutionalism, 1863-1897." *Journal of American History* 61 (March 1975): 970-1005.

7245. McCurdy, Charles W. "Stephen J. Field and Public Land Law Development in California, 1850-1866: A Case Study of Judicial Resource Allocation in Nineteenth-Century America." *Law and Society Review* 10 (Winter 1976): 235-266.

7246. McMurray, Orrin K. "Field's Work as a Lawyer and Judge in California." *California Law Review* 5 (January 1917): 87-107.

7247. Mendelson, Wallace. "Mr. Justice Field and Laissez-Faire." *Virginia Law Review* 36 (February 1950): 45-58.

7248. Morice, Joseph R. "Justice Stephen J. Field and the Fourteenth Amendment: A Re-evaluation." Ph.D. diss., University of Pittsburgh, 1962.

7249. New York State Bar Association. Judiciary Centennial Committee. *Centennial Celebration of the Organization of the Federal Judiciary, Held in the City of New York February 4, 1890: Addresses of Chief Justice Fuller and Associate Justice Field, Delivered at the Metropolitan Opera House, Together with the Speech of Associate Justice Harlan, Made at the Banquet in the Evening.* Washington, DC: New York State Bar Association, 1890.

7250. Pomeroy, John N., Jr. "Stephen Johnson Field." In *Great American Lawyers*, vol. 7, edited by William D. Lewis, 1-51. Philadelphia: J. C. Winston Company, 1907-1909.

7251. Schweppe, Alfred J. "The Justice and the Lady: A Postscript." *Supreme Court Historical Society Yearbook* 1981 (1981): 114-116.

7252. Scott, Henry W. "Stephen Johnson Field." In *Distinguished American Lawyers*, by Henry W. Scott, 373-378. New York: C. L. Webster, 1891.

7253. Shipman, George A. The Constitutional Doctrines of Stephen J. Field." Ph.D. diss., Cornell University, 1931.

7254. Stern, Horace. "An Examination of Justice Field's Work in Constitutional Law." In *Great American Lawyers*, vol. 7, edited by William D. Lewis, 52-86. Philadelphia: J. C. Winston Company, 1907-1909.

7255. Swisher, Carl B. *Stephen J. Field: Craftsman of the Law.* Washington, DC: Brookings Institution, 1930.

7256. Taylor, John M. "Justice Stephen M. Field." *American History Illustrated* 9 (October 1974): 34-38.

7257. Turner, William. *Documents in Relation to the Charges Preferred by Stephen J. Field.* New York: Harper, 1853.

7258. Weidner, Paul A. "Justices Field and Miller: A Comparative Study in Judicial Attitudes and Values." Ph.D. diss., University of Michigan, 1959.

7259. Westin, Alan F. "Stephen J. Field and the Headnote to *O'Neil v. Vermont*: A Snapshot of the Fuller Court." *Yale Law Journal* 67 (January 1958): 363-383.

Writings

7260. Field, Stephen J. "Address, The Supreme Court of the United States, Centennial Celebration of the Organization of the

Federal Judiciary." *United States Reporter* 134 (February 4, 1890): 729-746.

7261. Field, Stephen J. "The Centenary of the Supreme Court of the United States." *American Law Review* 24 (May/June 1890): 351-368.

7262. Field, Stephen J. "The Late Chief Justice Chase." *Overland Monthly* 11 (October 1873): 305-310.

7263. Field, Stephen J. *Personal Reminiscences of Early Days in California with Other Sketches.* Washington, DC: n.p., 1893.

Abe Fortas

General Studies

7264. Baldwin, Gordon B. "Justice Fortas on Dissent and Civil Disobedience: Heretic or Hero?—A Little of Both." *Wisconsin Law Review* 1969 (November 1969): 218-230.

7265. Cory, John. "Fortas Controversy, Strom's Dirty Movies: Washington Report." *Harpers* 237 (December 1968): 30-40.

7266. Graham, Deborah. "Fortas Fiasco Revisited." *American Bar Association Journal* 72 (August 1986): 19.

7267. Graham, Fred P. "The Many Sided Justice Fortas." *New York Times Magazine* 96 (June 4, 1967): 26, 86-96.

7268. Griffin, Robert P., and Philip A. Hart. "The Fortas Controversy: The Senate's Role of Advice and Consent to Judicial Nominations: The Broad Role by Griffin, the Discriminating Role by Hart." *Prospectus* 2 (April 1969): 283-310.

7269. Handberg, Roger B., Jr. "After the Fall: Justice Fortas' Judicial Values and Behavior after the Failure of His Nomina-

tion as Chief Justice." *Capital University Law Review* 15 (Winter 1986): 205-222.

7270. Heckart, Ronald J. "Justice Fortas and the First Amendment." Ph.D. diss., State University of New York at Albany, 1973.

7271. Jones, Hugh E. "The Defeat of the Nomination of Abe Fortas as Chief Justice of the United States: A Case Study in Judicial Politics." Ph.D. diss., Johns Hopkins University, 1976.

7272. Kalin, Berkley. "Young Abe Fortas." *West Tennessee Historical Society Papers* 34 (October 1980): 96-100.

7273. Lambert, William. "Fortas of the Supreme Court: A Question of Ethics; The Justice and the Stock Manipulator." *Life* 66 (May 9, 1969): 32-37.

7274. Lewis, Anthony. "A Tough Lawyer Goes to the Supreme Court." *New York Times Magazine* 114 (August 8, 1965): 11, 65-67.

7275. Mason, Alpheus T. "Pyrrhic Victory: The Defeat of Abe Fortas." *Virginia Quarterly Review* 45 (Winter 1969): 19-28.

7276. Massaro, John L. "LBJ and the Fortas Nomination for Chief Justice." *Political Science Quarterly* 97 (Winter 1982/1983): 589-621.

7277. Murphy, Bruce A. *Fortas: The Rise and Ruin of a Supreme Court Justice.* New York: Morrow, 1987.

7278. Rioch, Margaret J. "In Memoriam: Abe Fortas." *Psychiatry* 46 (February 1983): 83-86.

7279. Roth, Larry M. "Remembering 1965: Abe Fortas and the Supreme Court." *Mercer Law Review* 28 (Spring 1977): 961-976.

7280. Seib, Charles B., and A. L. Otten. "Abe, Help!: LBJ." *Esquire* 63 (June 1965): 86-110.

7281. Shogan, Robert. *A Question of Judgment: The Fortas Case and the Struggle for the Supreme Court.* Indianapolis: Bobbs-Merrill, 1972.

7282. Wukasch, Barry C. "The Abe Fortas Controversy: A Research Note on the Senate's Role in Judicial Selection." *Western Political Quarterly* 24 (March 1971): 24-27.

Writings

7283. Fortas, Abe. "Chief Justice Warren: The Enigma of Leadership." *Yale Law Journal* 84 (January 1975): 405-412.

7284. Fortas, Abe. *Concerning Dissent and Civil Disobedience.* New York: New American Library, 1968.

7285. Fortas, Abe. "Criminal Justice 'without Pity'." *Trial Lawyers Quarterly* 9 (Summer 1973): 9-14.

7286. Fortas, Abe. "Mr. Justice Douglas." *Yale Law Journal* 73 (May 1964): 917.

7287. Fortas, Abe. "William O. Douglas: A Eulogy." *Yale Law Journal* 89 (March 1980): 613-615.

7288. Fortas, Abe. "William O. Douglas: An Appreciation." *Indiana Law Journal* 51 (Fall 1975): 3-5.

Felix Frankfurter

General Studies

7289. Abrams, Richard. "The Reputation of Felix Frankfurter." *American Bar Foundation Research Journal* 1985 (Summer 1985): 639-652.

7290. Acheson, Dean G. "Felix Frankfurter." *Harvard Law Review* 76 (November 1962): 14-16.

7291. Baker, Liva. *Felix Frankfurter.* New York: Coward-McCann, 1969.

7292. Baskerville, Stephen W. "Frankfurter, Keynes, and the Fight for Public Works, 1932-1935." *Maryland Historian* 9 (Spring 1978): 1-16.

7293. Belknap, Michael R. "Frankfurter and the Nazi Saboteurs." *Supreme Court Historical Society Yearbook* 1982 (1982): 66-71.

7294. Berman, Daniel M. "The Case of Justice Frankfurter." *New Jersey State Bar Journal* 2 (Fall 1958): 149, 168-169.

7295. Bickel, Alexander M. "Frankfurter and Friend." *New Republic* 158 (February 3, 1968): 27-28, 32-33.

7296. Black, Hugo L. "Mr. Justice Frankfurter." *Harvard Law Review* 78 (June 1965): 1521-1522.

7297. Brown, Ernest J. "The Open Economy: Justice Frankfurter and the Position of the Judiciary." *Yale Law Journal* 67 (December 1957): 219-239.

7298. Brown, John M. "Frankfurter and the Uniform of Justice." In *Through These Men*, by John M. Brown, 167-197. New York: Harper, 1956.

7299. Clark, Thomas C. "Mr. Justice Frankfurter: 'A Heritage for All Who Love the Law'." *American Bar Association Journal* 51 (April 1965): 330-332.

7300. Cohen, Jerome A. "Mr. Justice Frankfurter." *California Law Review* 50 (October 1962): 591-597.

7301. Coleman, William T., Jr. "Mr. Justice Felix Frankfurter: Civil Libertarian as Lawyer and as Justice: Extent to Which Judicial Responsibilities Affected His Pre-Court Convictions." *University of Illinois Law Forum* 1978 (1978): 279-300.

7302. Crockett, Sam. *Frankfurter's Red Record.* Union, NJ: Christian Educational Association, 1961.

7303. Danzig, Richard. "How Questions

Begot Answers in Felix Frankfurter's First Flag Salute Opinion." *Supreme Court Review* 1977 (1977): 257-274.

7304. Davison, J. Forrester. "Mr. Justice Frankfurter: An Appreciation." *George Washington Law Review* 31 (December 1962): 327-334.

7305. Dawson, Nelson L. *Louis D. Brandeis, Felix Frankfurter, and the New Deal.* Hamden, CT: Archon Books, 1980.

7306. Dixon, Owen. "Mr. Justice Frankfurter: A Tribute from Australia." *Yale Law Journal* 67 (December 1957): 179-186.

7307. Ehrenhaft, Peter D. "Bruce Allen Murphy, The Brandeis-Frankfurter Connection: The Secret Political Activities of Two Supreme Court Justices." *American Journal of Legal History* 27 (July 1983): 302-307.

7308. Evershed, Lord. "Mr. Justice Frankfurter." *Harvard Law Review* 76 (November 1962): 3-6.

7309. Farnum, George R. "Felix Frankfurter: An Unfinished Portrait." *New Jersey Law Journal* 65 (March 12, 1942): 125.

7310. Farnum, George R. "Justice Frankfurter: An Intriguing Figure." *Law Notes* 45 (September 1941): 21-22.

7311. Forkosch, Morris D., ed. *Essays in Legal History in Honor of Felix Frankfurter.* Indianapolis: Bobbs-Merrill, 1966.

7312. Freund, Paul A. "Mr. Justice Frankfurter." *Harvard Law Review* 76 (November 1962): 17-19.

7313. Freund, Paul A., and Albert M. Sacks. "Mr. Justice Frankfurter." *University of Chicago Law Review* 26 (Winter 1959): 205-221.

7314. Gerber, Larry G. "The Limits of Liberalism: A Study of the Careers and Ideological Development of Josephus Daniels, Henry Stimson, Bernard Baruch,

Donald Richberg, and Felix Frankfurter." Ph.D. diss., University of California, Berkeley, 1979.

7315. Gilkey, Royal C. "Felix Frankfurter and the *Oregon Maximum Hour* Case." *University of Missouri at Kansas City Law Review* 35 (Winter 1967): 149-156.

7316. Gilkey, Royal C. "Felix Frankfurter's Years of Preparation: From Immigrant Status to Service with Stimson." *University of Missouri at Kansas City Law Review* 32 (Summer 1964): 322-328.

7317. Gilkey, Royal C. "Frankfurter's Career as a Law Officer under Henry L. Stimson." *University of Missouri at Kansas City Law Review* 33 (Winter 1965): 61-67.

7318. Gilkey, Royal C. "Justice Frankfurter and Labor's Constitutional Rights." *Labor Law Journal* 1 (September 1950): 955-960.

7319. Gilkey, Royal C. "Mr. Justice Frankfurter and Civil Liberties as Manifested in and Suggested by the Compulsory Flag Salute Controversy: A Study of Fifteen Years of Supreme Court Opinions, 1939-1953." Ph.D. diss., University of Minnesota, 1957.

7320. Gilkey, Royal C. "Mr. Justice Frankfurter and Freedom of Religion in Terms of Separation of Church and State." *University of Missouri at Kansas City Law Review* 27 (Fall 1958): 3-59.

7321. Gilkey, Royal C. "Mr. Justice Frankfurter's Interpretation of the Constitutional Rights of Labor in a Statutory Context with Special Attention to Picketing and Associated Union Activity." *University of Missouri at Kansas City Law Review* 18 (December/February 1950): 1-33; (April/June 1950): 133-168.

7322. Goedecke, Robert. "Holmes, Brandeis, and Frankfurter: Differences in Pragmatic Jurisprudence." *Ethics* 74 (January 1964): 83-96.

7323. Grant, J.A.C. "Felix Frankfurter: A

Dissenting Opinion." *UCLA Law Review* 12 (1965): 1013-1042.

7324. Griswold, Erwin N. "Felix Frankfurter: Teacher of the Law." *Harvard Law Review* 76 (November 1962): 7-13.

7325. Grossman, James. "A Note on Felix Frankfurter." *Commentary* 41 (March 1966): 59-64.

7326. Haimbaugh, George D., Jr. "Free Press versus Fair Trial: The Contribution of Mr. Justice Frankfurter." *University of Pittsburgh Law Review* 26 (March 1965): 491-520.

7327. Hand, Augustus N. "Mr. Justice Frankfurter." *Harvard Law Review* 62 (January 1949): 353-356.

7328. Handler, Emmerich. "The Fourth Amendment, Federalism, and Mr. Justice Frankfurter." *Syracuse Law Review* 8 (Spring 1957): 166-190.

7329. Heffron, Paul T. "Felix Frankfurter: Manuscript Historians." *Manuscripts* 23 (Summer 1971): 178-184.

7330. Henson, Ray D. "Study in Style: Mr. Justice Frankfurter." *Villanova Law Review* 6 (Spring 1961): 377-387.

7331. Hirsch, Harry N. *The Enigma of Felix Frankfurter*. New York: Basic Books, 1981.

7332. Hirsch, Harry N. "The Uses of Psychology in Judicial Biography: Felix Frankfurter and the Ambiguities of Self-Image." Ph.D. diss., Princeton University, 1948.

7333. Hofstadter, Samuel H., and Theodore B. Richter. "Mr. Justice Frankfurter, Legal Craftsman." *Association of the Bar of the City of New York* 20 (May 1965): 273-287.

7334. Hutchinson, Dennis J. "Felix Frankfurter and the Business of the Supreme Court." *Supreme Court Review* 1980 (1980): 143-209.

7335. Jacobs, Clyde E. *Justice Frankfurter and Civil Liberties*. Berkeley: University of California Press, 1961.

7336. Jacobsohn, Gary J. "Felix Frankfurter and the Ambiguities of Judicial Statesmanship." *New York University Law Review* 49 (April 1974): 1-44.

7337. Jaffe, Louis L. "Judicial Universe of Mr. Justice Frankfurter." *Harvard Law Review* 62 (January 1949): 357-412.

7338. Jaffe, Louis L. "Professors and Judges as Advisors to Government: Reflections on the Roosevelt-Frankfurter Relationship." *Harvard Law Review* 83 (December 1969): 366-376.

7339. Kalven, Harry, Jr., and Roscoe T. Steffen. "The Bar Admission Cases: An Unfinished Debate between Justice Frankfurter and Justice Black." *Law in Transition* 21 (Fall 1961): 155-196.

7340. King, Willard L. "Mr. Justice Frankfurter Retires." *American Bar Association Journal* 48 (December 1962): 1143-1145.

7341. Konefsky, Samuel J. "Justice Frankfurter and the Conscience of a Constitutional Judge." *Brooklyn Law Review* 31 (April 1965): 213-219.

7342. Kurland, Philip B. *Mr. Justice Frankfurter and the Constitution*. Chicago: University of Chicago Press, 1971.

7343. Kurland, Philip B. "Mr. Justice Frankfurter, the Supreme Court, and the Erie Doctrine in Diversity Cases." *Yale Law Journal* 67 (December 1957): 187-218.

7344. Kurland, Philip B., ed. *James Bradley Thayer, Oliver Wendell Holmes, and Felix Frankfurter on John Marshall*. Chicago: University of Chicago Press, 1967.

7345. Kurland, Philip B., Paul A. Freund, and Albert M. Sacks. "Mr. Justice Frankfurter." *University of Chicago Law Review* 26 (Autumn/Winter 1959): 1-2, 205-216, 217-221.

7346. Lash, Joseph P., and Jonathan Lash. *From the Diaries of Felix Frankfurter.* New York: W. W. Norton, 1975.

7347. Lavery, Emmet. "Felix Frankfurter and the Theater." *American Bar Association Journal* 51 (December 1965): 1162-1164.

7348. Levy, David W., and Bruce A. Murphy. "Preserving the Progressive Spirit in Conservative Times: The Joint Reform Efforts of Justice Brandeis and Professor Frankfurter, 1916-1933." *Michigan Law Review* 78 (August 1980): 1252-1304.

7349. MacLeish, Archibald. "Felix Frankfurter: A Lesson of Faith." *Supreme Court Review* 1966 (1966): 1-6.

7350. MacLeish, Archibald. "Felix Frankfurter: Frame for a Portrait." *Harvard Law Review* 76 (November 1962): 22-24.

7351. May, Geoffrey. "Dear Felix." *Harvard Law School Bulletin* 14 (April 1963): 3-5.

7352. Mendelson, Wallace. "The Influence of James B. Thayer upon the Work of Holmes, Brandeis, and Frankfurter." *Vanderbilt Law Review* 31 (January 1978): 71-87.

7353. Mendelson, Wallace. *Justices Black and Frankfurter: Conflict in the Court.* 2d ed. Chicago: University of Chicago Press, 1966.

7354. Mendelson, Wallace. "Justices Black and Frankfurter: Supreme Court Majority and Minority Trends." *Journal of Politics* 12 (February 1950): 66-92.

7355. Mendelson, Wallace. "Mr. Justice Frankfurter and the Process of Judicial Review." *University of Pennsylvania Law Review* 103 (December 1954): 295-320.

7356. Mendelson, Wallace. "Mr. Justice Frankfurter: Law and Choice." *Vanderbilt Law Review* 10 (February 1961): 333-350.

7357. Mendelson, Wallace. "Mr. Justice Frankfurter on Administrative Law." *Journal of Politics* 19 (August 1957): 441-460.

7358. Mendelson, Wallace. "Mr. Justice Frankfurter on the Construction of Statutes." *California Law Review* 43 (October 1955): 652-673.

7359. Mendelson, Wallace. "Mr. Justice Frankfurter on the Distribution of Judicial Power in the United States." *Midwest Journal of Political Science* 2 (February 1958): 40-61.

7360. Mendelson, Wallace, ed. *Felix Frankfurter: A Tribute.* New York: William Morrow, 1964.

7361. Mendelson, Wallace, ed. *Felix Frankfurter: The Judge.* New York: Reynal, 1964.

7362. Morris, Jeffrey B. "The American Jewish Judge: An Appraisal on the Occasion of the Bicentennial." *Jewish Social Studies* 38 (Summer/Fall 1976): 195-223.

7363. Murphy, Bruce A. *The Brandeis-Frankfurter Connection: The Secret Political Activities of Two Supreme Court Justices.* Oxford: Oxford University Press, 1982.

7364. Murphy, Bruce A. "A Supreme Court Justice as Politician: Felix Frankfurter and Federal Court Appointments." *American Journal of Legal History* 21 (October 1977): 316-334.

7365. Murphy, Bruce A. "Supreme Court Justices as Politicians: The Extrajudicial Activities of Justices Louis D. Brandeis and Felix Frankfurter." Ph.D. diss., University of Virginia, 1978.

7366. Nathanson, Nathaniel L. "Mr. Justice Frankfurter and Administrative Law." *Yale Law Journal* 67 (December 1957): 240-265.

7367. Nathanson, Nathaniel L. "Mr. Justice Frankfurter and the Holmes Chair: A Study in Liberalism and Judicial Self-Restraint." *Northwestern University Law Review* 71 (May/June 1976): 135-160.

7368. Newman, Jon O. "Mr. Justice Frankfurter." *Connecticut Bar Journal* 36 (December 1962): 527-532.

7369. Niebuhr, Reinhold. "Tribute to Felix Frankfurter." *Harvard Law Review* 76 (November 1962): 20-21.

7370. O'Connell, Jeffrey, and Nancy Dart. "The House of Truth: Home of the Young Frankfurter and Lippmann." *Catholic University Law Review* 35 (Fall 1985): 79-95.

7371. Parrish, Michael E. *Felix Frankfurter and His Times.* New York: Free Press, 1982.

7372. Peebles, Thomas H. "Mr. Justice Frankfurter and the Nixon Court: Some Reflections on Contemporary Judicial Conservatism." *American University Law Review* 24 (Fall 1974): 1-90.

7373. Pollak, Louis H. "Mr. Justice Frankfurter: Judgement and the Fourteenth Amendment." *Yale Law Journal* 67 (December 1957): 304-323.

7374. Pollock, Frederick, John H. Wigmore, Morris R. Cohen, Felix Frankfurter, Eugene Ehrlich, Learned Hand, and Roscoe Pound. "A Symposium in Honor of Holmes, Dedicated to Him on His Seventy-fifth Birthday." *Harvard Law Review* 29 (April 1916): 565-704.

7375. Rauh, Joseph L., Jr. "Felix Frankfurter: Civil Libertarian." *Harvard Civil Rights-Civil Liberties Law Review* 11 (Summer 1976): 496-500.

7376. "Retired Justice Felix Frankfurter Receives American Bar Association Medal." *American Bar Association Journal* 49 (September 1963): 876-877.

7377. Rice, Daniel. "Felix Frankfurter and Reinhold Niebuhr: 1940-1964." *Journal of Law and Religion* 1 (1983): 325-426.

7378. Sacks, Albert M. "Mr. Justice Frankfurter." *University of Chicago Law Review* 26 (Winter 1958): 217-221.

7379. Schwartz, Bernard. "The Administrative World of Mr. Justice Frankfurter." *Yale Law Journal* 59 (June 1950): 1228-1265.

7380. Silverstein, Mark. *Constitutional Faiths: Felix Frankfurter, Hugo Black, and the Process of Judicial Decision Making.* New York: Cornell University Press, 1984.

7381. Spaeth, Harold J. "The Judicial Restraint of Mr. Justice Frankfurter: Myth or Reality?" *Midwest Journal of Political Science* 8 (February 1964): 22-38.

7382. Stevens, Richard G. "Reason and History in Judicial Judgement: Mr. Justice Frankfurter's Treatment of Due Process." Ph.D. diss., University of Chicago, 1963.

7383. Summers, Clyde W. "Frankfurter, Labor Law, and the Judge's Function." *Yale Law Journal* 67 (December 1957): 266-303.

7384. Thomas, Helen S. *Felix Frankfurter: Scholar on the Bench.* Baltimore: Johns Hopkins University Press, 1960.

7385. Thomas, Helen S. "Scholar on the Bench: The Judicial Performance of Justice Felix Frankfurter." Ph.D. diss., Johns Hopkins University, 1959.

7386. Tugwell, Rexford G. "Roosevelt and Frankfurter: An Essay Review." *Political Science Quarterly* 85 (March 1970): 99-114.

7387. Umbreit, Kenneth B. "Review of the Commerce Clause under Marshall, Taney, and White by Felix Frankfurter." *American Bar Association Journal* 23 (September 1937): 706.

7388. Urofsky, Melvin I. "The Brandeis-Frankfurter Conversations." *Supreme Court Review* 1985 (1985): 299-339.

7389. Urofsky, Melvin I. "Conflict among the Brethren: Felix Frankfurter, William O. Douglas, and the Clash of Personalities and Philosophies on the United States Supreme Court." *Duke Law Journal* 1988 (February 1988): 71-113.

7390. Urofsky, Melvin I. "The Incomparable Felix." *Reviews in American History* 11 (March 1983): 118-123.

7391. Varney, Harold L. "Frankfurter: The Man Behind the Scenes." *American Mercury* 84 (May 1957): 113-118.

7392. Vom Baur, F. Trowbridge. "Introduction of Mr. Justice Frankfurter." *Federal Bar Journal* 18 (January/March 1958): 21-23.

7393. Walsh, James A. "The Political Ideas of Felix Frankfurter, 1911-1939." Ph.D. diss., American University, 1976.

7394. White, G. Edward. "Felix Frankfurter, the Old Boy Network, and the New Deal: The Placement of Elite Lawyers in Public Service in the 1930s." *Arkansas Law Review* 39 (Spring 1986): 631-667.

Writings

7395. Frankfurter, Felix. *The Case of Sacco and Vanzetti: A Critical Analysis for Lawyers and Laymen.* Boston: Little, Brown, 1927.

7396. Frankfurter, Felix. "Chief Justices I Have Known." *Supreme Court Historical Society Yearbook* 1980 (1980): 3-9.

7397. Frankfurter, Felix. "Chief Justices I Have Known." *Virginia Law Review* 39 (November 1953): 883.

7398. Frankfurter, Felix. *The Commerce Clause under Marshall, Taney, and White.* Chapel Hill: University of North Carolina Press, 1937.

7399. Frankfurter, Felix. "The Constitutional Opinions of Justice Holmes." *Harvard Law Review* 29 (April 1916): 683-702.

7400. Frankfurter, Felix. *The Constitutional World of Mr. Justice Frankfurter: Some Representative Opinions.* Edited by Samuel J. Konefsky. New York: Hafner, 1971.

7401. Frankfurter, Felix. "Distribution of Judicial Power between United States and State Courts." *Cornell Law Quarterly* 13 (June 1928): 499-530.

7402. Frankfurter, Felix. "Felix Frankfurter." *Harvard Law School Bulletin* 21 (June 5, 1970): 15-17.

7403. Frankfurter, Felix. *Felix Frankfurter: A Register of His Papers in the Library of Congress.* Washington, DC: Library of Congress, Manuscript Division, 1971.

7404. Frankfurter, Felix. *Felix Frankfurter on the Supreme Court: Extrajudicial Essays on the Court and the Constitution.* Edited by Philip B. Kurland. Cambridge: Harvard University Press, 1970.

7405. Frankfurter, Felix. *Felix Frankfurter Reminisces.* Edited by Harlan B. Phillips. Garden City, NY: Doubleday, 1962.

7406. Frankfurter, Felix. "Harlan Fiske Stone." *American Philosophical Society Year Book* 1946 (1946): 334-339.

7407. Frankfurter, Felix. "Hours of Labor and Realism in Constitutional Law." *Harvard Law Review* 29 (February 1916): 353-373.

7408. Frankfurter, Felix. "The Job of a Supreme Court Justice." *New York Times Magazine* 104 (November 1954): 14.

7409. Frankfurter, Felix. "John Marshall and the Judicial Function." *Harvard Law Review* 69 (December 1955): 217-238.

7410. Frankfurter, Felix. "Justice Holmes Defines the Constitution." *Atlantic Monthly* 162 (October 1938): 484-495.

7411. Frankfurter, Felix. *Law and Politics: Occasional Papers of Felix Frankfurter.* Edited by Archibald MacLeish. New York: Harcourt, Brace, 1939.

7412. Frankfurter, Felix. "Memorandum on 'Incorporation of the Bill of Rights into the Fourteenth Amendment'." *Harvard Law Review* 78 (February 1965): 746-783.

7413. Frankfurter, Felix. "Mr. Justice Brandeis." *Harvard Law Review* 55 (December 1941): 181-183.

7414. Frankfurter, Felix. "Mr. Justice Brandeis and the Constitution." *Harvard Law Review* 45 (November 1931): 33-105.

7415. Frankfurter, Felix. "Mr. Justice Cardozo." *American Bar Association Journal* 24 (August 1938): 638-639.

7416. Frankfurter, Felix. "Mr. Justice Cardozo and Public Law." *Columbia Law Review* 39 (January 1939): 88-118.

7417. Frankfurter, Felix. "Mr. Justice Cardozo and Public Law." *Yale Law Journal* 48 (January 1939): 458-488.

7418. Frankfurter, Felix. *Mr. Justice Holmes.* New York: Coward-McCann, 1931.

7419. Frankfurter, Felix. *Mr. Justice Holmes and the Constitution.* Cambridge: Harvard University Press, 1938.

7420. Frankfurter, Felix. "Mr. Justice Holmes and the Constitution: A Review of His Twenty-five Years on the Supreme Court." *Harvard Law Review* 41 (December 1927): 121-173.

7421. Frankfurter, Felix. *Mr. Justice Holmes and the Supreme Court.* 2d ed. Cambridge: Harvard University Press, 1961.

7422. Frankfurter, Felix. "Mr. Justice Holmes, March 8, 1841 to March 6, 1935." *Harvard Law Review* 48 (June 1935): 1279-1280.

7423. Frankfurter, Felix. "Mr. Justice Jackson." *Columbia Law Review* 55 (April 1955): 435-437.

7424. Frankfurter, Felix. "Mr. Justice Jackson." *Harvard Law Review* 68 (April 1955): 937-939.

7425. Frankfurter, Felix. *Of Law and Life and Other Things That Matter: Papers and Addresses of Felix Frankfurter, 1956-1963.* Edited by Philip B. Kurland. Cambridge: Harvard University Press, 1965.

7426. Frankfurter, Felix. *Of Law and Men: Papers and Addresses, 1939-1956.* Edited by Philip Elman. New York: Harcourt, 1956.

7427. Frankfurter, Felix. "Oliver Holmes, Jr." In *Dictionary of American Biography,* vol. 21, supplement 1, 417-427. New York: Charles Scibner's Sons, 1981.

7428. Frankfurter, Felix. *Oliver W. Holmes.* Boston: Starr King Press, 1956.

7429. Frankfurter, Felix. "Personal Ambition of Judges: Should a Judge Think beyond the Judicial?" *American Bar Association Journal* 34 (August 1948): 656-659, 747-749.

7430. Frankfurter, Felix. *The Public and Its Government.* Boston: Beacon Press, 1964.

7431. Frankfurter, Felix. *Roosevelt and Frankfurter: Their Correspondence, 1928-1945.* Edited by Max Freedman. Boston: Little, Brown, 1968.

7432. Frankfurter, Felix. *Sketch of the Life of Oliver Wendell Holmes.* New York: American Council of Learned Societies, 1944.

7433. Frankfurter, Felix. "Some Observations on the Nature of the Judicial Process of Supreme Court Litigation." *American Philosophical Society Proceedings* 98 (April 1954): 233-239.

7434. Frankfurter, Felix. *Some Observations on Supreme Court Litigation and Legal Education.* Chicago: Chicago Law

School, University of Chicago, 1954.

7435. Frankfurter, Felix. "Some Reflections on the Reading of Statutes." *Columbia Law Review* 47 (May 1947): 527.

7436. Frankfurter, Felix. "The Supreme Court." *Parliamentary Affairs* 3 (Winter 1949): 55-71.

7437. Frankfurter, Felix. "The Supreme Court in the Mirror of Justices." *American Bar Association Journal* 44 (August 1958): 723-726.

7438. Frankfurter, Felix. "The Supreme Court in the Mirror of Justices." *University of Pennsylvania Law Review* 105 (April 1957): 781-796.

7439. Frankfurter, Felix. "A Symposium on Statutory Construction: Foreword." *Vanderbilt Law Review* 3 (April 1950): 365-368.

7440. Frankfurter, Felix. "Taney and the Commerce Clause." *Harvard Law Review* 49 (June 1936): 1286-1302.

7441. Frankfurter, Felix. "Twenty Years of Mr. Justice Holmes' Constitutional Opinions." *Harvard Law Review* 36 (June 1923): 909-939.

7442. Frankfurter, Felix. "Zeitgeist and the Judiciary." *Survey* 29 (January 25, 1913): 542-544.

7443. Frankfurter, Felix, ed. "The Early Writings of O. W. Holmes." *Harvard Law Review* 64 (March 1931): 717-827.

7444. Frankfurter, Felix, ed. *Mr. Justice Brandeis.* New Haven, CT: Yale University Press, 1932.

7445. Frankfurter, Felix, and Adrian S. Fisher. "Business of the Supreme Court at the October Terms, 1935 and 1936." *Harvard Law Review* 51 (February 1938): 577-637.

7446. Frankfurter, Felix, and Edwin McElwain. "The Administrative Side of Chief Justice Hughes: The Business of the Supreme Court as Conducted by Chief Justice Hughes." *Harvard Law Review* 63 (November 1949): 1-26.

7447. Frankfurter, Felix, and James M. Landis. *The Business of the Supreme Court: A Study in the Federal Judicial System.* New York: Macmillan, 1928.

7448. Frankfurter, Felix, and James M. Landis. "The Business of the Supreme Court at October Term, 1928." *Harvard Law Review* 43 (November 1929): 33-62.

7449. Frankfurter, Felix, and James M. Landis. "The Business of the Supreme Court of the United States: A Study in the Federal Judicial System." *Harvard Law Review* 38 (June 1925): 1005-1059; 39 (November 1925): 35-81; 39 (January 1926): 325-367; 39 (March 1926): 587-627; 39 (June 1926): 1046-1075; 40 (January 1927): 431-468; 40 (April 1927): 831-877; 40 (June 1927): 1110-1149.

7450. Frankfurter, Felix, and James M. Landis. *The Compact Clause of the Constitution.* New Haven, CT: Yale Law Journal Company, 1925.

7451. Frankfurter, Felix, and James M. Landis. "The Supreme Court under the Judiciary Act of 1925." *Harvard Law Review* 42 (November 1928): 1-29.

7452. Frankfurter, Felix, and Nathan Green. *The Labor Injunction.* New York: Macmillan, 1930.

7453. Frankfurter, Felix, and Nathaniel L. Nathanson. "Forbidden Dialogue: Standards of Judicial Review of Administrative Action." *Supreme Court Review* 1963 (1963): 206-210.

Melville W. Fuller

General Studies

7454. Butler, Charles H. "Melville Weston Fuller, David Josiah Brewer, Memorial Note." *American Journal of International Law* 4 (October 1910): 909-921.

7455. Choate, Joseph H. "Melville Weston Fuller." *Harvard Graduates' Magazine* 19 (September 1910): 11-14.

7456. Hill, Don G. *Chief Justice Fuller: A Descendant of One of the Early Settlers of Dedham*. Dedham, MA: Dedham Historical Society, 1888.

7457. King, Willard L. "Melville Weston Fuller: Chief Justice of the United States, 1888-1910." *American Bar Association Journal* 36 (March 1950): 183-186, 255-258.

7458. King, Willard L. *Melville Weston Fuller: Chief Justice of the United States, 1888-1910*. New York: Macmillan, 1950.

7459. King, Willard L. "Melville Weston Fuller: 'The Chief and the Giants on the Court'." *American Bar Association Journal* 36 (April 1950): 293-296, 349-351.

7460. New York State Bar Association. Judiciary Centennial Committee. *Centennial Celebration of the Organization of the Federal Judiciary, Held in the City of New York February 4, 1890: Addresses of Chief Justice Fuller and Associate Justice Field, Delivered at the Metropolitan Opera House, Together with the Speech of Associate Justice Harlan, Made at the Banquet in the Evening*. Washington, DC: New York State Bar Association, 1890.

7461. Reeder, Robert F. "Chief Justice Fuller." *University of Pennsylvania Law Review* 59 (October 1910): 1-14.

7462. Robson, Charles, ed. "Melville W. Fuller." In *A Biographical Encyclopedia of Illinois of the Nineteenth Century*, edited by Charles Robson, 34-35. Philadelphia: Galaxy, 1875.

7463. Scott, Henry W. "Melville Weston Fuller." In *Distinguished American Lawyers*, by Henry W. Scott, 387-392. New York: C. L. Webster, 1891.

7464. Stephenson, D. Grier, Jr. "Charles Henry Butler on the Death of Chief Justice Fuller." *New York State Bar Journal* 47 (October 1975): 47.

7465. Walz, William E. "Chief Justice Fuller, The Individualist on the Bench." *Maine Law Review* 10 (January 1917): 77-84.

7466. White, Edward D. "Proceedings on the Death of Mr. Chief Justice Fuller." *United States Reports* 219 (1911): 15.

7467. White, Matthew, Jr. "Chief Justice Fuller." *Munsey's Magazine* 11 (April 1894): 80-82.

Arthur J. Goldberg

General Studies

7468. Bickel, Alexander M. "A Reply to Arthur J. Goldberg: The Overworked Court." *New Republic* 168 (February 1973): 17-18.

7469. Donelski, David. "A Supreme Court Justice Steps Down." *Yale Review* 54 (Spring 1965): 411-425.

7470. Goldberg, Dorothy. *A Private View of a Public Life*. New York: Charterhouse, 1975.

7471. Lewin, Nathan. "Helping the Court with Its Work: A Response to Goldberg and Bickel." *New Republic* 168 (March 1973): 15-19.

7472. Marsel, Robert S. "Mr. Justice Arthur J. Goldberg and the Death Penalty." *South Texas Law Review* 27 (Fall 1986): 467-492.

7473. Marvin, John F. "A Constitutional Prejudice for Liberty and Equality: Mr. Justice Arthur Goldberg." *University of Missouri at Kansas City Law Review* 34 (Summer 1966): 289-324.

7474. "Mr. Justice Arthur J. Goldberg."

American Bar Association Journal 48 (December 1962): 1146.

7475. Morris, Jeffrey B. "The American Jewish Judge: An Appraisal on the Occasion of the Bicentennial." *Jewish Social Studies* 38 (Summer/Fall 1976): 195-223.

7476. Moynihan, Daniel P., ed. *The Defenses of Freedom: The Public Papers of Arthur J. Goldberg.* New York: Harper and Row, 1966.

7477. Watts, Tim J. "A Bibliography of Arthur J. Goldberg." *Law Library Journal* 77 (Spring 1984): 307-388.

Writings

7478. Goldberg, Arthur J. *AFL-CIO: Labor United.* New York: McGraw-Hill, 1956.

7479. Goldberg, Arthur J. "Death and the Supreme Court." *Hastings Constitutional Law Quarterly* 15 (Fall 1987): 1-6.

7480. Goldberg, Arthur J. "The Death Penalty and the Supreme Court." *Arizona Law Review* 15 (1973): 355-368.

7481. Goldberg, Arthur J. *Equal Justice: The Warren Era of the Supreme Court.* Evanston, IL: Northwestern University Press, 1971.

7482. Goldberg, Arthur J. "Equality and Government Action." *New York University Law Review* 39 (April 1964): 205-227.

7483. Goldberg, Arthur J. "Law and the United Nations." *American Bar Association Journal* 52 (September 1966): 813-816.

7484. Goldberg, Arthur J. "Managing the Supreme Court's Workload." *Hastings Constitutional Law Quarterly* 11 (Spring 1984): 353-357.

7485. Goldberg, Arthur J. "Memorandum to the Conference Re: Capital Punishment." *South Texas Law Review* 27 (Fall 1986): 493-506.

7486. Goldberg, Arthur J. "Mr. Justice Brennan and the First Amendment." *Rutgers Law Review* 4 (Fall 1972): 8-43.

7487. Goldberg, Arthur J. "One Supreme Court: It Doesn't Need Its Cases 'Screened'." *New Republic* 168 (February 1973): 14-16.

7488. Goldberg, Arthur J. "Reflections about the United States Supreme Court." *Nova Law Journal* 5 (Winter 1981): 159-166.

7489. Goldberg, Arthur J. "Reflections on the Role of the Supreme Court." *Chicago Bar Record* 58 (January/February 1977): 182-189.

7490. Goldberg, Arthur J. "Stanley Mosk: A Federalist for the 1980s." *Hastings Constitutional Law Quarterly* 12 (Spring 1985): 395-419.

7491. Goldberg, Arthur J. "The Supreme Court, Congress, and Rules of Evidence." *Seton Hall Law Review* 5 (Spring 1974): 667-687.

7492. Goldberg, Arthur J. "Supreme Court Review 1972." *Journal of Criminal Law, Criminology, and Police Science* 63 (December 1972): 463-529.

7493. Goldberg, Arthur J. "There Shall Be One Supreme Court." *Hastings Constitutional Law Quarterly* 3 (Spring 1976): 339-344.

7494. Goldberg, Arthur J., and Alan Dershowitz. "Declaring the Death Penalty Unconstitutional." *Harvard Law Review* 83 (June 1970): 1773-1819.

Horace Gray

General Studies

7495. Adams, Charles F., and Solomon Lincoln. "Tribute to Horace Gray."

Massachusetts Historical Society Proceedings 16 (1902): 251-268.

7496. Davis, Elbridge B., and Harold A. Davis. "Mr. Justice Horace Gray: Some Aspects of His Judicial Career." *American Bar Association Journal* 41 (May 1955): 421-424, 468-471.

7497. Hoar, George F. "Memoir of Horace Gray." *Massachussetts Historical Society Proceedings* 18 (January 1904): 155-187.

7498. Jones, Francis R. "Horace Gray, An Encomium." *Green Bag* 14 (September 1902): 403-407.

7499. Lowell, Francis C. "Horace Gray." *American Academy of Arts and Science* 39 (1904): 627-637.

7500. Mitchell, Stephen R. "Mr. Justice Horace Gray." Ph.D. diss., University of Wisconsin, 1961.

7501. Smith, John M. "Mr. Justice Horace Gray of the United States Supreme Court." *South Dakota Law Review* 6 (Fall 1961): 221-247.

7502. Spector, Robert M. "Legal Historian on the United States Supreme Court: Justice Horace Gray, Jr., and the Historical Method." *American Journal of Legal History* 12 (July 1968): 181-210.

7503. Storey, Moorfield. "Horace Gray." In *Later Years of the Saturday Club, 1870-1920*, edited by M. A. DeWolfe Howe, 49-53. Boston: Houghton Mifflin, 1927.

7504. Thayer, Ezra R. "Horace Gray." *Harvard Graduates' Magazine* 11 (March 1903): 345-350.

7505. Williston, Samuel. "Horace Gray." In *Great American Lawyers*, vol. 8, edited by William D. Lewis, 137-188. Philadelphia: J. C. Winston Company, 1907-1909.

Writings

7506. Gray, Horace. *An Address on the Life, Character, and Influence of Chief Justice Marshall, Delivered at Richmond on the Fourth Day of February 1901 at the Request of the State Bar Association of Virginia and the Bar Association of the City of Richmond.* Washington, DC: Pearson, 1901.

7507. Gray, Horace. *Catalogue of the Valuable Law Library of the Late Honorable Horace Gray.* Boston: Libbie, 1903.

7508. Gray, Horace. *A Legal Review of the Case of* Dred Scott. Boston: Crosby, Nichols, 1857.

Robert C. Grier

General Studies

7509. Brown, David P. "Robert Cooper Grier, LL.D." In *The Forum*, vol. 2, edited by David P. Brown, 91-101. Philadelphia: R. H. Small, 1856.

7510. Chase, Salmon P. "Resignation of Mr. Justice Grier." *United States Reports* 75 (1870): vii-xix.

7511. Jones, Francis R. "Robert Cooper Grier." *Green Bag* 16 (April 1904): 221-224.

7512. "The Late Robert Cooper Grier." *Albany Law Journal* 2 (October 15, 1870): 294-295.

7513. Livingston, John. "Honorable Robert C. Grier." In *Portraits of Eminent Americans Now Living*, vol 2., by John A. Livingstone, 813-817. New York: Cornish, Lamport, 1853.

John M. Harlan, 1899-1971

General Studies

7514. Adams, Arlin M. "Justice John Marshall Harlan and the Antitrust Laws." *Record of the Association of the Bar of the City of New York* 32 (May/June 1977): 269-338.

7515. Ballantine, Arthur A. "John M. Harlan for the Supreme Court." *Iowa Law Review* 40 (Spring 1955): 391-399.

7516. Bartosic, Florian. "The Constitution, Civil Liberties, and John Marshall Harlan." *Kentucky Law Journal* 46 (Spring 1958): 807-847.

7517. Bean, Michael J. "The Legitimacy of Civil Law Reasoning in the Common Law: Justice Harlan's Contribution." *Yale Law Review Journal* 82 (December 1972): 258-285.

7518. Beth, Loren P. "Justice Harlan and the Uses of Dissent." *American Political Science Review* 49 (December 1955): 1085-1104.

7519. Bourguignon, Henry J. "The Second Mr. Justice Harlan: His Principles of Judicial Decision Making." *Supreme Court Review* 1979 (1979): 251-328.

7520. Canfield, Monte, Jr. "Our Constitution Is Colorblind: Mr. Justice Harlan and Modern Problems of Civil Rights." *University of Missouri at Kansas City Law Review* 32 (Summer 1964): 292-332.

7521. Dane, Stephen M. " 'Ordered Liberty' and Self-Restraint: The Judicial Philosophy of the Second Justice Harlan." *University of Cincinnati Law Review* 51 (1982): 545-573.

7522. Dorsen, Norman. "Mr. Justice Black and Mr. Justice Harlan." *New York University Law Review* 46 (October 1971): 649-652.

7523. Dorsen, Norman. "The Second Mr. Justice Harlan." *New York University Law Review* 44 (April 1969): 249-271.

7524. Friedman, Edward L., Jr. "Mr. Justice Harlan." *Notre Dame Lawyer* 30 (May 1955): 349-359.

7525. Friendly, Henry J. "Mr. Justice Harlan, as Seen by a Friend and Judge of an Inferior Court." *Harvard Law Review* 85 (December 1971): 382-389.

7526. Gressman, Eugene. "New Justice Harlan." *New Republic* 132 (April 4, 1955): 8-9.

7527. Howard, Lowell B. "Mr. Justice John Marshall Harlan and the Supreme Court, 1955-1971: A Study in Federalism and Judicial Self-Restraint." Ph.D. diss., Ohio State University, 1975.

7528. Hughes, John C. "John Marshall Harlan, the Warren Court, and the Freedoms of Speech and Press." Ph.D. diss., New School for Social Research, 1978.

7529. Landynski, Jacob W. "John Marshall Harlan and the Bill of Rights: A Centennial View." *Social Research* 49 (Winter 1982): 899-926.

7530. Laporte, Cloyd. "John M. Harlan Saves the Ella Wendel Estate." *American Bar Association Journal* 59 (August 1973): 668-872.

7531. Ledbetter, William H., Jr. "Mr. Justice Harlan: Due Process and Civil Liberties." *South Carolina Law Review* 20 (1968): 389-407.

7532. Lewin, Nathan. "Justice Harlan: 'The Full Measure of the Man'." *American Bar Association Journal* 58 (June 1972): 579-583.

7533. Lewis, Ellwood W. "The Appointment of Mr. Justice Harlan." *Indiana Law Journal* 29 (Fall 1953): 46-74.

7534. Lumbard, J. Edward. "John Harlan: In Public Service, 1955-1971." *Harvard Law Review* 85 (December 1971): 372-376.

7535. Lumbard, J. Edward. "Of Mr. Justice Harlan." *New York County Bar Bulletin* 16 (November/December 1958): 93.

7536. Maddocks, Lewis I. "Two Justices Harlan on Civil Rights and Liberties: A Study in Judicial Contrasts." *Kentucky Law Journal* 68 (1979/1980): 301-343.

7537. Seymour, Whitney N. "John Marshall Harlan." *American Bar Association Journal* 41 (May 1955): 434.

7538. Shapiro, David L., ed. *The Evolution of a Judicial Philosophy: Selected Opinions and Papers of Justice John Harlan*. Cambridge: Harvard University Press, 1969.

7539. Vasicko, Sally J. "John Marshall Harlan: Neglected Advocate of Federalism." *Modern Age* 24 (Fall 1980): 387-395.

7540. Warren, Earl. "Mr. Justice Harlan, as Seen by a Colleague." *Harvard Law Review* 85 (December 1971): 369-371.

7541. Werner, Ray O. "The Economics of the Joint Antitrust Dissents of Justices Harlan and Stewart." *Washington Law Review* 48 (May 1973): 555-591.

7542. Wilkinson, J. Harvie. "Justice John Marshall Harlan and the Values of Federalism." *Virginia Law Review* 57 (October 1971): 1185-1221.

7543. Wood, John E. F. "John M. Harlan, as Seen by a Colleague in the Practice of Law." *Harvard Law Review* 85 (December 1971): 377-381.

Writings

7544. Harlan, John M. "Address to the Fifty-eighth Annual Meeting of the American Association of Law Libraries." *Law Library Journal* 58 (November 1965): 370-379.

7545. Harlan, John M. "The Bill of Rights and the Constitution." *American Bar Association Journal* 50 (October 1964): 918-920.

7546. Harlan, John M. "The Frankfurter Imprint as Seen by a Colleague." *Harvard Law Review* 76 (November 1962): 1-2.

7547. Harlan, John M. "Glimpse of the Supreme Court at Work." *Oklahoma Bar Association Journal* 34 (September 28, 1963): 1649-1655.

7548. Harlan, John M. "John M. Harlan's One Day Diary, August 21, 1877: An Interpretation of the Harlan-Bristow Controversy." *Filson Club History Quarterly* 24 (April 1958): 158-168.

7549. Harlan, John M. "Keeping the Judicial Function in Balance." *American Bar Association Journal* 49 (October 1963): 943-945.

7550. Harlan, John M. *Manning the Dikes: Some Comments on the Statutory Certiorari Jurisdiction and Jurisdictional Statement Practice of the Supreme Court of the United States*. New York: Association of the Bar of the City of New York, 1958.

7551. Harlan, John M. "Mr. Justice Black: Remarks of a Colleague." *Harvard Law Review* 81 (November 1967): 1-3.

7552. Harlan, John M. "Some Aspects of the Judicial Process in the Supreme Court of the United States." *Australian Law Journal* 33 (August 1959): 108-125.

7553. Harlan, John M. "The Supreme Court Years." *Texas Law Review* 40 (June 1962): 748.

John M. Harlan, 1833-1911

General Studies

7554. Abraham, Henry J. "John Marshall Harlan: A Justice Neglected." *Valparaiso Law Review* 41 (November 1955): 871-891.

7555. Abraham, Henry J. "John Marshall Harlan: The Justice and the Man." *Kentucky Law Journal* 46 (Spring 1958): 448-475.

7556. Beth, Loren P. "Justice Harlan and the Chief Justiceship." *Supreme Court Historical Society Yearbook* 1983 (1983): 73-79.

7557. Billman, Obed C. "John Marshall Harlan (1833-1911)." *Case and Comment* 23 (July 1916): 120-125.

7558. Brown, Henry B. "The Dissenting Opinions of Mr. Justice Harlan." *American Law Review* 46 (May/June 1912): 321-352.

7559. Clark, Floyd B. *Constitutional Doctrines of Justice Harlan.* Baltimore: Johns Hopkins Press, 1915.

7560. "Dinner to Mr. Justice Harlan in Celebration of His Completion of Twenty-five Years of Judicial Service." *American Law Review* (January/February 1903): 92-96.

7561. Duke, R. T., Jr. "John Marshall Harlan." *Virginia Law Register* 17 (November 1911): 497-504.

7562. Farnum, George R. "John Marshall Harlan: Portrait of a Great Dissenter." *American Bar Association Journal* 30 (October 1944): 576-578.

7563. Farrelly, David G. "John M. Harlan's Formative Period: The Years before the War." *Kentucky Law Journal* 46 (Spring 1958): 367-406.

7564. Farrelly, David G. "Justice Harlan's Dissent in the *Pollock* Case." *Southern California Law Review* 24 (February 1951): 175-182.

7565. Farrelly, David G. "Sketch of John Marshall Harlan's Pre-Court Career." *Vanderbilt Law Review* 10 (February 1957): 209-225.

7566. Goff, John S. "Justice John Marshall Harlan of Kentucky." *Kentucky Historical Society Register* 55 (April 1957): 109-133.

7567. Hartz, Louis. "John M. Harlan in Kentucky, 1855-1877: The Story of His Pre-Court Political Career." *Filson Club History Quarterly* 14 (January 1940): 17-40.

7568. Knight, Thomas J. "The Dissenting Opinions of Justice Harlan." *American Law Review* 51 (July/August 1917): 481-506.

7569. Latham, Frank B. *The Great Dissenter: Supreme Court Justice John Marshall Harlan, 1833-1911.* New York: Cowles Book Company, 1970.

7570. McCracken, Robert T. "Justice Harlan." *University of Pennsylvania Law Review* 60 (February 1912): 297-310.

7571. Maddocks, Lewis I. "Justice John Marshall Harlan: Defender of Individual Rights." Ph.D. diss., Ohio State University, 1959.

7572. Maddocks, Lewis I. "Two Justices Harlan on Civil Rights and Liberties: A Study in Judicial Contrasts." *Kentucky Law Journal* 68 (1979/1980): 301-343.

7573. New York State Bar Association. Judiciary Centennial Committee. *Centennial Celebration of the Organization of the Federal Judiciary, Held in the City of New York February 4, 1890: Addresses of Chief Justice Fuller and Associate Justice Field, Delivered at the Metropolitan Opera House, Together with the Speech of Associate Justice Harlan, Made at the Banquet in the Evening.* Washington, DC: New York State Bar Association, 1890.

7574. Pillsbury, Albert E. "John Marshall Harlan." *Twentieth Century Magazine* 5 (November 1911): 69-71.

7575. Porter, Mary C. A. "John Marshall Harlan and the Laissez-Faire Court." Ph.D. diss., University of Chicago, 1970.

7576. Porter, Mary C. A. "John Marshall

Harlan, the Elder, and Federal Common Law: A Lesson from History." *Supreme Court Review* 1972 (1972): 103-134.

7577. Read, William E., and William C. Berman. "Papers of the First Justice Harlan at the University of Louisville." *American Journal of Legal History* 11 (January 1967): 57-68.

7578. Stein, Simon B. "John Marshall Harlan, the Great Dissenter." *Bar Bulletin of Boston* 26 (October 1955): 257-259.

7579. U.S. Supreme Court Bar. *Dinner Given by the Bar of the Supreme Court of the United States to Mr. Justice John Marshall Harlan, in Recognition of the Completion of Twenty-five years of Distinguished Service on the Bench, December 9, 1902.* New York: Press of Cameron and Bulkeley, 1902.

7580. Watt, Richard F., and Richard M. Orlikoff. "The Coming Vindication of Mr. Justice Harlan." *Illinois Law Review* 44 (March/April 1949): 13-40.

7581. Westin, Alan F. "The First Justice Harlan: A Self-Portrait from His Private Papers." *Kentucky Law Journal* 46 (Spring 1958): 321-366.

7582. Westin, Alan F. "John Marshall Harlan and the Constitutional Rights of Negroes: The Transformation of a Southerner." *Yale Law Journal* 66 (April 1957): 637-710.

7583. White, Edward D. "Proceedings on the Death of Mr. Justice Harlan." *United States Reports* 222 (1911): 25.

7584. White, G. Edward. "John Marshall Harlan I: The Precursor." *American Journal of Legal History* 19 (January 1975): 1-21.

7585. Willson, Augustus E. "John Marshall Harlan." In *The Lawyers and the Lawmakers of Kentucky*, edited by H. Levin, 151-155. Chicago: Lewis Publishing Company, 1897.

Writings

7586. Harlan, John M. "Government under the Constitution." *Law Notes* 11 (February 1908): 206-208.

7587. Harlan, John M. "James Wilson and the Formation of the Constitution." *American Law Review* 34 (July/August 1900): 481-504.

7588. Harlan, John M. "Mr. Justice Harlan's Address, at the Banquet Given on December Ninth in Honor of the Twenty-fifth Anniversary of His Appointment to the Supreme Court." *Albany Law Journal* 65 (January 1903): 16-18.

7589. Harlan, John M. "The Supreme Court of the United States." In *The Supreme Court of the United States*, edited by Hampton L. Carson, 725-732. Philadelphia: A. R. Keller, 1882.

7590. Harlan, John M. "The Supreme Court of the United States and Its Work." *American Law Review* 30 (November/December 1896): 900-902.

Oliver W. Holmes, Jr.

General Studies

7591. Adams, Edward B. "Oliver Wendell Holmes." *Green Bag* 15 (January 1903): 1-9.

7592. Aitchison, Clyde B. "Justice Holmes and the Development of Administrative Law." *George Washington Law Review* 1 (January 1933): 165-171.

7593. Allen, Francis A. "Mr. Justice Holmes and 'The Life of the Mind'." *Boston University Law Review* 52 (Winter 1972): 229-235.

7594. Allen, Francis A. "Mr. Justice Holmes: Criminal Law." *University of Chicago Law Review* 31 (Winter 1964): 257-262.

7595. Anderson, D. I. *Public Speeches of Justice Oliver Wendell Holmes.* Columbia: University of Missouri Press, 1961.

7596. Auchincloss, Louis. "The Long Life and Broad Mind of Mr. Justice Holmes." *American Heritage* 29 (June 1978): 68-77.

7597. Bander, Edward J. "Holmespun Humor." *Villanova Law Review* 10 (Fall 1964): 92-99.

7598. Bander, Edward J., ed. *Justice Holmes: Wisdom and Humor of and about Justice Oliver Wendell Holmes.* Charlottesville, VA: Michie, 1966.

7599. Beard, Charles A. "Justice Oliver Wendell Holmes." *Current History* 33 (March 1931): 801-806.

7600. Beck, James M. "Justice Holmes and the Supreme Court." *Federal Bar Journal* 1 (March 1932): 36-39, 61.

7601. Bent, Silas. *Justice Oliver Wendell Holmes, A Biography.* New York: Vanguard Press, 1932.

7602. Bernstein, Irving. "The Conservative Mr. Justice Holmes." *New England Quarterly* 23 (December 1950): 435-452.

7603. Biddle, Francis. *Justice Holmes, Natural Law, and the Supreme Court.* New York: Macmillan, 1961.

7604. Biddle, Francis. *Mr. Justice Holmes.* New York: Charles Scribner's Sons, 1942.

7605. Biddle, Francis. "Mr. Justice Holmes." *Temple Law Quarterly* 6 (February 1932): 139-140.

7606. Biddle, Francis. "Reminiscences of Mr. Justice Holmes." *Case and Comment* 49 (Fall 1943): 5-9.

7607. Biddle, Francis. "Reminiscences of Mr. Justice Holmes." *Chicago Bar Review* 24 (May 1943): 313-314, 352-358.

7608. Bishop, James. *The Holmes-Einstein Letters.* London: Macmillan, 1964.

7609. Bodger, William V. "Some Ideas of

Mr. Justice Holmes Regarding Education." *Peabody Journal of Education* 28 (July 1950): 2-8.

7610. Bogen, David S. "The Free Speech Metamorphosis of Mr. Justice Holmes." *Hofstra Law Review* 11 (Fall 1982): 97-189.

7611. Boorstin, Daniel J. "The Elusiveness of Mr. Justice Holmes." *New England Quarterly* 14 (September 1941): 478-487.

7612. Boudin, Louis B. "Justice Holmes and His World." *Law Guild Review* 3 (July/August 1943): 24-41.

7613. Bowen, Catherine D. *Yankee from Olympus: Justice Holmes and His Family.* Boston: Little, Brown, 1944.

7614. Briggs, Charles W. "Justice Holmes Was Not a Ladder to Hitler." *American Bar Association Journal* 32 (October 1946): 631-634.

7615. Brody, Burton F. "The Pragmatic Naturalism of Mr. Justice Holmes." *Chicago-Kent Law Review* 46 (Spring/Summer 1969): 9-33.

7616. Brown, Elliot A. "Case Histories, Interest Group Litigation, and Mr. Justice Holmes: Some Unexplored Questions on Psycho-Political Behavior." *Emory Law Journal* 24 (Fall 1975): 1037-1074.

7617. Burton, David H. "Curious Correspondence of Justice Oliver Wendell Holmes and Franklin Ford." *New England Quarterly* 53 (June 1980): 196-211.

7618. Burton, David H. "The Friendship of Justice Holmes and Canon Sheehan." *Harvard Library Bulletin* 25 (April 1977): 155-169.

7619. Burton, David H. "The Intellectual Kinship of Oliver Wendell Holmes, Jr., Frederick E. Pollock, and Harold J. Laski." *American Philosophical Society Proceedings* 119 (April 1975): 133-142.

7620. Burton, David H. "Mr. Justice

Holmes in England, 1866." *History Today* 29 (May 1979): 304-309.

7621. Burton, David H. *Oliver Wendell Holmes, Jr.* Boston: Twayne, 1980.

7622. Burton, David H. *Oliver Wendell Holmes: What Manner of Liberal?* Huntington, NY: R. E. Krieger, 1979.

7623. Burton, David H., ed. *Progressive Masks: Letters of Oliver Wendell Holmes, Jr. and Franklin Ford.* Newark: University of Delaware Press, 1982.

7624. Cardozo, Benjamin N. "Mr. Justice Holmes." *Harvard Law Review* 44 (March 1931): 682-692.

7625. Clark, Samuel I. "The Political Philosophy of Justice Oliver Wendell Holmes." Ph.D. diss., University of Chicago, 1950.

7626. Cohen, Felix S. "The Holmes-Cohen Correspondence." *Journal of the History of Ideas* 9 (January 1948): 3-52.

7627. Cohen, Jeremy. *Congress Shall Make No Law: Oliver Wendell Holmes, the First Amendment, and Judicial Decision Making.* Ames: Iowa State University Press, 1989.

7628. Cohen, Morris R. "Justice Holmes and the Nature of Law." *Columbia Law Review* 31 (March 1931): 352-367.

7629. Cohen, Saul. "Justice Holmes and the Copyright Law." *Southern California Law Review* 32 (Spring 1959): 263-279.

7630. Commager, Henry S. "Oliver Wendell Holmes, Jr." *Cambridge Journal* 1 (July 1948): 604-612.

7631. Conklin, William E. "The Political Theory of Mr. Justice Holmes." *Chitty's Law Journal* 26 (June 1978): 200-211.

7632. Coogan, John E. "The Religious Ultimates of Justice Holmes." *American Ecclesiastical Review* 132 (February 1955): 73-83.

7633. Cook, Walter W. "Oliver Wendell Holmes: Scientist." *American Bar Association Journal* 21 (April 1935): 211-213.

7634. Cushing, Carolyn K. "The Gallant Captain and the Little Girl." *Atlantic Monthly* 155 (May 1935): 545-550.

7635. Davis, Horace B. "The End of the Holmes Tradition." *University of Kansas City Law Review* 19 (December/February 1950-1951): 53-65.

7636. Dennon, Lester E. *The Wit and the Wisdom of Oliver W. Holmes, Father and Son.* Boston: Beacon Press, 1953.

7637. Derby, Augustin. "Recollection of Mr. Justice Holmes." *New York University Law Quarterly Review* 12 (March 1935): 345-353.

7638. Dobyns, Fletcher. "Justice Holmes and the Fourteenth Amendment." *Illinois Law Review* 13 (June 1918): 71-96.

7639. Dudziak, Mary L. "Oliver Wendell Holmes as a Eugenic Reformer: Rhetoric in the Writing of Constitutional Law." *Iowa Law Review* 71 (March 1986): 833-867.

7640. Dumbauld, Edward. "Valedictory Opinions of Mr. Justice Holmes." *ICC Practitioner's Journal* 12 (December 1944): 224-234.

7641. Dumbauld, Edward. "Valedictory Opinions of Mr. Justice Holmes." *Michigan Law Review* 42 (April 1944): 1037-1048.

7642. Dunham, Allison. "The Legacy of Brandeis, Holmes, and Stone." *Saturday Review* 39 (December 15, 1956): 13-15.

7643. "Eighty-eight Years Old and Still Active." *American Bar Association Journal* 15 (April 1929): 211.

7644. Eldridge, F. Howard. "Justice Holmes: Another Aspect of His Life and Philosophy." *University of Chicago Law Record* 10 (July 1943): 417-436.

7645. Elliot, E. Donald. "Holmes and Evolution: Legal Process as Artificial

Intelligence." *Journal of Legal Study* 13 (January 1984): 113-146.

7646. Ellmann, James I. "Justice Holmes Today." *Commercial Law Journal* 39 (January 1934): 5-12.

7647. Emmy, Walter B. "Legal and Political Philosophy of Mr. Justice Holmes." *Oklahoma State Bar Journal* 3 (September 1932): 150-157.

7648. Enselman, Isidor. "Mr. Justice Holmes." *Case and Comment* 54 (July/August 1949): 48-55.

7649. Espinosa, Jose F. "Observations on Justice Holmes' and Cardozo's Philosophy of Law." *Philadelphia Law Journal* 22 (April 1947): 87-92.

7650. Fallon, Perlie P. "The Judicial World of Mr. Justice Holmes." *Notre Dame Lawyer* 14 (November 1938): 52-97.

7651. Fallon, Perlie P. "Mystery of Justice Holmes." *Nebraska Law Review* 37 (1958): 442-448.

7652. Fallon, Perlie P. "Some Influences of Justice Holmes' Thought on Current Law." *Dickinson Law Review* 56 (1951-1952): 387-401.

7653. Fallon, Perlie P. "Some Influences of Justice Holmes' Thought on Current Law: Assessments, Bankruptcy, Citizenship, and Commerce." *Temple Law Quarterly* 19 (March 1945): 15-25.

7654. Fallon, Perlie P. "Some Influences of Justice Holmes' Thought on Current Law: Conflict of Laws, Contempt, Contracts, Copyright, and Corporations." *Tennessee Law Review* 19 (February 1946): 118-128.

7655. Fallon, Perlie P. "Some Influences of Justice Holmes' Thought on Current Law: Contracts with the United States, Suits against the United States." *Minnesota Law Review* 30 (February 1946): 185-203.

7656. Fallon, Perlie P. "Some Influences of Justice Holmes' Thought on Current Law: Federal Taxation of Instrumentalities of the United States." *Tulane Law Review* 20 (October 1945): 56-82.

7657. Fallon, Perlie P. "Some Influences of Justice Holmes' Thought on Current Law: Interstate Commerce; Fourteenth Amendment." *Minnesota Law Review* 29 (April 1945): 318-338.

7658. Fallon, Perlie P. "Some Influences of Justice Holmes' Thought on Current Law: The Full Faith and Credit Clause." *Nebraska Law Review* 26 (March 1947): 367-381.

7659. Fallon, Perlie P. "Some Influences of Justice Holmes' Thought on Current Law: The Police Power; Theories of Local Law." *Nebraska Law Review* 24 (June 1945): 182-194.

7660. Farnum, George R. *Holmes: The Soldier Philosopher.* Brooklyn, NY: American Law Book Company, 1939.

7661. Farnum, George R. "Holmes: The Solitary Scholar, A Study in Spiritual Values." *Lawyer* 1 (June 1938): 13-14.

7662. Farnum, George R. "Justice Holmes: Philosopher and Humanitarian." *Law Society Journal* 3 (November 1930/February 1931): 3-6.

7663. Farnum, George R. "Justice Holmes: Philosopher and Humanitarian." *Lawyer* 5 (November 1941): 25-27.

7664. Farnum, George R. "Oliver Wendell Holmes: Jurist, Soldier, and Philosopher." *American Bar Association Journal* 29 (January 1943): 17-21.

7665. Fiechter, Frederick C., Jr. "The Preparation of an American Aristocrat." *New England Quarterly* 6 (March 1933): 3-28.

7666. Fisch, Max H. "Justice Holmes: The Predictive Theory of Law and Pragmatism." *Journal of Philosophy* 39 (February 1962): 85-97.

7667. Ford, John C. "The Fundamentals of Holmes' Juristic Philosophy." *Fordham Law Review* 9 (November 1942): 255-278.

7668. Frank, Jerome. "Mr. Justice Holmes and Non-Euclidian Legal Thinking." *Cornell Law Quarterly Review* 17 (June 1932): 568-603.

7669. Frankfurter, Felix. "The Constitutional Opinions of Justice Holmes." *Harvard Law Review* 29 (April 1916): 683-702.

7670. Frankfurter, Felix. "Holmes and the Sorcerer's Apprentice." In *Twenty-seven Masters of Politics*, edited by Raymond Moley, 151-164. New York: Funk and Wagnalls, 1949.

7671. Frankfurter, Felix. "Justice Holmes Defines the Constitution." *Atlantic Monthly* 162 (October 1938): 484-495.

7672. Frankfurter, Felix. *Mr. Justice Holmes*. New York: Coward-McCann, 1931.

7673. Frankfurter, Felix. *Mr. Justice Holmes and the Constitution*. Cambridge: Harvard University Press, 1938.

7674. Frankfurter, Felix. "Mr. Justice Holmes and the Constitution: A Review of His Twenty-five Years on the Supreme Court." *Harvard Law Review* 41 (December 1927): 121-173.

7675. Frankfurter, Felix. *Mr. Justice Holmes and the Supreme Court*. 2d ed. Cambridge: Harvard University Press, 1961.

7676. Frankfurter, Felix. "Mr. Justice Holmes, March 8, 1841 to March 6, 1935." *Harvard Law Review* 48 (June 1935): 1279-1280.

7677. Frankfurter, Felix. "Oliver Holmes, Jr." In *Dictionary of American Biography*, vol. 21, supplement 7, 417-427. New York: Charles Scribner's Sons, 1981.

7678. Frankfurter, Felix. *Oliver W. Holmes*. Boston: Starr King Press, 1956.

7679. Frankfurter, Felix. *Sketch of the Life of Oliver Wendell Holmes*. New York: American Council of Learned Societies, 1944.

7680. Frankfurter, Felix. "Twenty Years of Mr. Justice Holmes' Constitutional Opinions." *Harvard Law Review* 36 (June 1923): 909-939.

7681. Frankfurter, Felix, ed. "The Early Writings of O. W. Holmes, Jr." *Harvard Law Review* 44 (March 1931): 717-827.

7682. Freund, Paul A. "Holmes and Brandeis in Retrospect." *Boston Bar Journal* 28 (September/October 1984): 7-10.

7683. Gall, Morris. *Judicial Decision and Practical Judgment*. New York: King's Crown Press, 1946.

7684. Gallagher, Eugene R. "Two Interpretations of the State and Government: The Pragmatic Skepticism of Mr. Justice Oliver Wendell Holmes Contrasted with the Natural Law Philosophy of Mr. Justice James Wilson." Ph.D. diss., Fordham University, 1940.

7685. Garraty, John A. "Holmes' Appointment to the United States Supreme Court." *New England Quarterly* 22 (September 1949): 291-303.

7686. Gerhart, Eugene C. *American Liberty and "Natural Law"*. Boston: Beacon Press, 1953.

7687. Goedecke, Robert. "Holmes, Brandeis, and Frankfurter: Differences in Pragmatic Jurisprudence." *Ethics* 74 (January 1964): 83-96.

7688. Goldsmith, Arnold L. "Oliver Wendell Holmes, Father and Son." *Journal of Criminal Law, Criminology, and Political Science* 48 (November/December 1957): 394-398.

7689. Goldstein, Joseph M. "The Philosophy of Mr. Justice Holmes." *New Jersey*

Law Journal 69 (December 12, 1946): 401-403.

7690. Greene, Nathan. "Mr. Justice Holmes and the Age of Man." *Wayne Law Review* 6 (Summer 1960): 394-412.

7691. Gregg, Paul S. "The Pragmatism of Mr. Justice Holmes." *Georgetown Law Journal* 31 (March 1943): 262-295.

7692. Hamilton, Doris J. "Oliver Wendell Holmes." *Hobbies* 64 (August 1959): 110-111.

7693. Hamilton, Walton H. "On Dating Mr. Justice Holmes." *University of Chicago Law Review* 9 (December 1941): 1-29.

7694. Hand, Learned. "Mr. Justice Holmes." *Harvard Law Review* 43 (April 1930): 857-862.

7695. Hart, Henry M., Jr. "Holmes' Positivism: An Addendum." *Harvard Law Review* 64 (February 1951): 929-937.

7696. Hickman, Martin B. "Mr. Justice Holmes: A Reappraisal." *Western Political Quarterly* 5 (March 1952): 66-83.

7697. Hill, Arthur D. "Oliver Wendell Holmes, Justice of the Supreme Court of the United States." *Harvard Graduates' Magazine* 39 (March 1931): 265-288.

7698. Hofstadter, Samuel H. "Mr. Justice Holmes: Exponent of Judicial Relativity." *American Bar Association Journal* 42 (January 1956): 19-23.

7699. Holt, George C. "The New Justice of the Supreme Court." *Independent* 54 (October 2, 1902): 2361-2364.

7700. Howe, Mark D. "Holmes' Positivism: A Brief Rejoinder Comment." *Har-*

vard Law Review 64 (April 1951): 937-939.

7701. Howe, Mark D. *Justice Oliver Wendell Holmes.* Vol. 1. *The Shaping Years, 1841-1870.* Vol. 2. *The Proving Years, 1870-1882.* Cambridge: Harvard University Press, 1957-1963.

7702. Howe, Mark D. "Mr. Justice Holmes and His Secretaries." *New York Times Magazine* 100 (April 8, 1951): 15, 42-46.

7703. Howe, Mark D. "Mr. Justice Holmes Seeks His Friends." *Atlantic Monthly* 199 (April 1957): 71-73.

7704. Howe, Mark D. "Oliver Wendell Holmes at Harvard Law School." *Harvard Law Review* 70 (January 1957): 401-421.

7705. Howe, Mark D. "The Positivism of Mr. Justice Holmes." *Harvard Law Review* 64 (February 1951): 529-546.

7706. Howe, Mark D. "The Positivism of Mr. Justice Holmes." *Measure* 1 (Spring 1950): 118-132.

7707. Hughes, Charles E. "Mr. Justice Holmes." *Harvard Law Review* 44 (March 1931): 677-679.

7708. Hughes, Charles E. *Mr. Justice Holmes and the Supreme Court.* Cambridge: Harvard University Press, 1961.

7709. Hurst, James W. *Justice Holmes on Legal History.* New York: Macmillan, 1964.

7710. Jones, Leonard A. "Oliver Wendell Holmes, the Jurist." *American Law Review* 36 (September/October 1902): 710-722.

7711. Judson, Clara. *Mr. Justice Holmes.* Chicago: Follett, 1956.

7712. "Justice Holmes at Ninety." *American Bar Association Journal* 17 (April 1931): 251-253.

7713. Kalven, Harry, Jr. "Mr. Justice

Holmes: Torts." *University of Chicago Law Review* 31 (Winter 1964): 263-267.

7714. Kaplan, Benjamin. "Encounters with O. W. Holmes." *Harvard Law Review* 96 (June 1983): 1828-1852.

7715. Kellogg, Frederic R. *The Formative Essays of Justice Holmes: The Making of an American Legal Philosophy*. Westport, CT: Greenwood Press, 1984.

7716. Kellogg, Frederic R. "Law, Morals, and Justice Holmes." *Judicature* 69 (December 1985): 214-217.

7717. Knox, John. "Some Correspondence with Holmes and Pollock." *Chicago Bar Review* 21 (March 1940): 219-224.

7718. Konefsky, Samuel J. "Holmes and Brandeis: Companies in Dissent." *Vanderbilt Law Review* 10 (February 1957): 269-300.

7719. Konefsky, Samuel J. *The Legacy of Holmes and Brandeis: A Study in the Influence of Ideas*. New York: Macmillan, 1957.

7720. Kraines, Oscar. "The Holmes Tradition." *American Jewish History Society Publications* 42 (June 1953): 341-359.

7721. Kremm, Walter P. "Justice Holmes on Constitutionality and Evidence of His Influence upon the Vinson Court, 1946-1949." Ph.D. diss., University of North Carolina, 1961.

7722. Krislov, Samuel. "Oliver Wendell Holmes: The Ebb and Flow of Judicial Legendry." *Northwestern University Law Review* 52 (September/October 1957): 514-525.

7723. Kulp, Victor H. "A Great Jurist, Oliver Wendell Holmes." *Oklahoma State Bar Journal* 4 (May 1933): 34-37.

7724. Kurland, Philip B., ed. *James Bradley Thayer, Oliver Wendell Holmes, and Felix Frankfurter on John Marshall*. Chicago: University of Chicago Press, 1967.

7725. Laski, Harold J. "Mr. Justice Holmes: For His Eighty-ninth Birthday." *Harper's* 160 (March 1930): 415-423.

7726. Laski, Harold J. "The Political Philosophy of Mr. Justice Holmes." *Yale Law Journal* 40 (March 1931): 683-695.

7727. Lavery, Emmet. "Justice Holmes and Canon Sheehan." *Catholic World* 172 (October 1950): 13-19.

7728. Lerner, Max. "Mr. Justice Holmes." In *Ideas Are Weapons: The History and Uses of Ideas*, edited by Max Lerner, 54-67. New York: Viking Press, 1939.

7729. Levy, Beryl H. *Our Constitution: Tool or Testament? 'Holmes: Above the Battle'*. New York: Knopf, 1941.

7730. Llewellyn, Karl N. "Holmes." *Columbia Law Review* 35 (April 1935): 485-492.

7731. Llewellyn, Karl N. "Review of Mr. Justice Holmes." *Columbia Law Review* 31 (May 1931): 902.

7732. Lowry, Walker. "Mr. Justice Holmes: The Community vs. the Individual." *California Law Review* 36 (September 1948): 390-404.

7733. Lucey, Francis E. "Holmes: Liberal, Humanitarian, Believer in Democracy?" *Georgetown Law Journal* 39 (May 1951): 523-562.

7734. Lundquist, William A. "Oliver Wendell Holmes and External Standards of Criminal and Tort Liability: Application on the Massachusetts Bench." *Buffalo Law Review* 28 (Summer 1979): 607-625.

7735. McKinnon, Harold R. "The Secret of Mr. Justice Holmes: An Analysis." *American Bar Association Journal* 36 (April 1950): 261-264, 342-346.

7736. Marke, Julius J. "A Law Student's Guide to Mr. Justice Holmes." *University of Florida Law Review* 28 (Winter 1976): 376-391.

7737. Mellen, Francis J., Jr. "Ralph

Waldo Emerson, Mr. Justice Holmes, and the Idea of Organic Form in American Law." *New England Law Review* 14 (Fall 1978): 147-168.

7738. Mendelson, Wallace. "The Influence of James B. Thayer upon the Work of Holmes, Brandeis, and Frankfurter." *Vanderbilt Law Review* 31 (January 1978): 71-87.

7739. Mendelson, Wallace. "Mr. Justice Holmes: Humility, Skepticism, and Democracy." *Minnesota Law Review* 36 (March 1952): 343-363.

7740. Meyer, Edith P. *That Remarkable Man, Justice Oliver Wendell Holmes.* Boston: Little, Brown, 1967.

7741. Miller, James D. "Holmes, Pierce, and Legal Pragmatism." *Yale Law Journal* 84 (April 1975): 1123-1140.

7742. Miller, Loren, and Harold J. Sinclair. "Justice Holmes and the Civil War Amendments." *National Bar Journal* 6 (June 1948): 95-132.

7743. Morris, George P. "Oliver Wendell Holmes, Jurist." *American Monthly Review of Reviews* 26 (September 1902): 307-309.

7744. Morse, John T., Jr. *Life and Letters of Oliver Wendell Holmes.* Boston: Houghton Mifflin, 1896.

7745. Muller, Henry. "A Reappraisal of Oliver Wendell Holmes, Jr." *California State Bar Journal* 26 (March/April 1951): 94-101.

7746. Mullock, Philip. "Holmes on Contractual Duty." *University of Pittsburgh Law Review* 33 (Spring 1972): 471-482.

7747. Nelles, Walter, and Samuel Mermin. "Holmes and Labor Law." *New York University Law Quarterly Review* 13 (May 1936): 517-555.

7748. Nettleton, Tully. "The Philosophy of Mr. Justice Holmes on Freedom of Speech." *Southwestern Social Science Quarterly* 3 (March 1923): 287-305.

7749. Odom, Luther W. "Justice Holmes, the Fourteenth Amendment, and the Reasonable Man Standard." Ph.D. diss., University of Texas, 1966.

7750. Oppenheim, Leonard. "The Civil Liberties Doctrines of Mr. Justice Holmes and Mr. Justice Cardozo." *Tulane Law Review* 20 (December 1945): 177-219.

7751. O'Shaughnessy, James B. "Justice Holmes and Chancellor More." *Catholic University of America Law Review* 3 (May 1953): 145-148.

7752. Palmer, Ben W. "Hobbes, Holmes, Hitler." *American Bar Association Journal* 31 (November 1945): 569-573.

7753. Palmer, Ben W. "The Totalitarianism of Mr. Justice Holmes: Another Chapter in the Controversy." *American Bar Association Journal* 37 (November 1951): 809-811.

7754. Patterson, C. Perry. "Jurisprudence of Oliver Wendell Holmes." *Minnesota Law Review* 31 (March 1947): 355-370.

7755. Perry, Ralph B. "The Common Enemy: Early Letters of Oliver Wendell Holmes, Jr., and William James." *Atlantic* 156 (September 1935): 293-303.

7756. Pettengill, Samuel B. "Tribute to Justice Holmes." *Indiana Law Journal* 10 (April 1935): 411-413.

7757. Plucknett, Theodore F. T. "Holmes, the Historian." *Harvard Law Review* 44 (March 1931): 820-827.

7758. Pohlman, H. L. *Justice Oliver Wendell Holmes and Utilitarian Jurisprudence.* Cambridge: Harvard University Press, 1984.

7759. Pollard, Joseph P. "Justice Holmes Dissents." *Scribner's Magazine* 85 (January 1929): 22-29.

7760. Pollock, Frederick. "Mr. Justice

Holmes." *Harvard Law Review* 44 (March 1931): 693-696.

7761. Pollock, Frederick. "Mr. Justice Holmes." *Harvard Law Review* 48 (June 1935): 1277-1278.

7762. Pollock, Frederick. "Mr. Justice Oliver Wendell Holmes: In Memoriam." *Law Quarterly Review* 51 (April 1955): 263-264.

7763. Pollock, Frederick, John H. Wigmore, Morris R. Cohen, Felix Frankfurter, Eugene Ehrlich, Learned Hand, and Roscoe Pound. "A Symposium in Honor of Holmes, Dedicated to Him on His Seventy-fifth Birthday." *Harvard Law Review* 29 (April 1916): 565-704.

7764. Pollock, Seton. "Mr. Justice Holmes: Philosopher and Lawyer." *Law and Society Gazette* 52 (August 1955): 349.

7765. Post, A. C. "Judge Oliver Wendell Holmes." *McClure's Magazine* 19 (October 1902): 523-524.

7766. Pound, Roscoe. "Dedicated to Holmes on His Eightieth Birthday." *Harvard Law Review* 34 (March 1921): 449-453.

7767. Pound, Roscoe. "Judge Holmes' Contributions to the Science of Law." *Harvard Law Review* 34 (March 1921): 449-453.

7768. Powell, Thomas R. "Holmes and Pollock." *Nation* 152 (May 17, 1941): 589-590.

7769. Pritchett, C. Herman. "Justice Holmes and a Liberal Court." *Virginia Quarterly Review* 24 (Winter 1948): 43-58.

7770. Rader, Benjamin G., and Barbara K. Rader. "The Ely-Holmes Friendship, 1901-1912." *American Journal of Legal History* 10 (April 1966): 128-147.

7771. Ragan, Fred D. "Justice Oliver Wendell Holmes, Jr., Zechariah Chafee, Jr., and the Clear and Present Danger Test for Free Speech: The First Year, 1919." *Journal of American History* 58 (June 1971): 24-45.

7772. Reiblich, G. Kenneth. "Conflict of Laws, Philosophy of Mr. Justice Holmes." *Georgetown Law Journal* 28 (October 1939): 1-23.

7773. Reid, John P. "Brandy in His Water: Correspondence between Doe, Holmes, and Wigmore." *Northwestern University Law Review* 57 (September/October 1962): 522-535.

7774. Reid, John P. "Experience or Reason: The Tort Theories of Holmes and Doe." *Vanderbilt Law Review* 18 (March 1965): 405-436.

7775. Reid, Sydney, and George P. Morris. "Oliver Wendell Holmes, a Biographical Sketch: Jurist and Stylist." *Independent* 54 (August 28, 1902): 2057-2059.

7776. Reuschlein, Harold G. "An Outline of Taught Law Notes on American Legal Philosophy: The Beginnings to Holmes and Pound." *Minnesota Law Review* 28 (December 1943): 1-42.

7777. Rice, Mary C. "Holmes and Laski on Natural Law." Ph.D. diss., Boston University, 1962.

7778. Richardson, Dorsey. *Constitutional Doctrines of Justice Oliver Wendell Holmes.* Baltimore: Johns Hopkins Press, 1924.

7779. Roberts, E. F. "Mining with Mr. Justice Holmes." *Vanderbilt Law Review* 39 (March 1986): 287-304.

7780. Rodell, Fred. "Holmes and His Hecklers." *Progressive* 15 (April 1951): 9-11.

7781. Rodell, Fred. "Justice Holmes and His Hecklers." *Yale Law Journal* 60 (April 1951): 620-624.

7782. Rogat, Yosal. "Mr. Justice Holmes: A Dissenting Opinion." *Stanford Law Review* 15 (December 1962): 3-44.

7783. Rogat, Yosal. "Mr. Justice Holmes: Some Modern Views; A Symposium: The Judge as Spectator." *University of Chicago Law Review* 31 (Winter 1964): 213-256.

7784. Roth, Larry M. "Touched with Fire, Forged in Flame: Holmes and a Different Perspective." *University of Florida Law Review* 28 (Winter 1976): 365-375.

7785. Rumble, Wilfrid E., Jr. "Legal Realism: Sociological Jurisprudence and Mr. Justice Holmes." *Journal of the History of Ideas* 26 (October/December 1965): 547-566.

7786. Sankey, C. "Mr. Justice Holmes: On Behalf of the English Judiciary." *Harvard Law Review* 44 (March 1931): 680.

7787. Sayre, Paul. "Mr. Justice Holmes: Philosopher." *Iowa Law Review* 27 (January 1942): 187-212.

7788. Schwartz, Joan I. "Oliver Wendell Holmes' 'The Path of the Law': Conflicting Views of the Legal World." *American Journal of Legal History* 29 (July 1985): 235-250.

7789. Seagle, William. "The Significance of Justice Holmes." *South Atlantic Quarterly* 45 (April 1946): 155-164.

7790. Sharp, Malcolm P. "Mr. Justice Holmes: Contracts." *University of Chicago Law Review* 31 (Winter 1964): 268-278.

7791. Shriver, Harry C. "Great Dissenter: Whose Dissents Now Prevail." *Case and Comment* 47 (September/October 1941): 6-9.

7792. Shriver, Harry C. "Oliver Wendell Holmes: Lawyer." *American Bar Association Journal* 24 (February 1938): 157-162.

7793. Shriver, Harry C. *What Gusto: Stories and Anecdotes about Justice Oliver Wendell Holmes.* Potomac, MD: Fox Hills Press, 1970.

7794. Shriver, Harry C. *What Justice Holmes Wrote and What Has Been Written about Him: A Bibliography, 1866-1976.* Potomac, MD: Fox Hills Press, 1978.

7795. Shuman, Howard E. "The Style of Mr. Justice Oliver Wendell Holmes's Ceremonial Speeches." *Speech Monographs* 16 (September 1949): 307.

7796. Simms, E. W. "A Dissent from Greatness." *Virginia Law Review* 28 (February 1942): 467-487.

7797. Stanlis, Peter J. "Dr. Wu and Justice Holmes: A Reappraisal on Natural Law." *University of Detroit Law Journal* 18 (March 1955): 149-179.

7798. Stechow, Wolfgang. "Justice Holmes' Notes on Albert Durer." *Journal of Aesthetics and Art Criticism* 8 (December 1949): 119-124.

7799. Thompson, Milton W. "The Social Thought of Justice Oliver Wendell Holmes." Ph.D. diss., Marquette University, 1931.

7800. "To Justice Oliver Wendell Holmes: An Anniversary Oblation." *Illinois Law Review* 10 (April 1916): 617-632.

7801. Touster, Saul. "Holmes: The Years of the Common Law." *Columbia Law Review* 64 (February 1964): 230-247.

7802. Touster, Saul. "In Search of Holmes from Within." *Vanderbilt Law Review* 18 (March 1965): 437-472.

7803. Townsend, Henry H. "Justice Holmes, the Dissenter." *Connecticut Bar Journal* 11 (1937): 167-183.

7804. Tufts, James H. "The Legal and Social Philosophy of Mr. Justice Holmes." *American Bar Association Journal* 7 (July 1921): 359-363.

7805. Turner, Helen. "Mr. Justice Holmes." *Tennessee Law Review* 10 (February 1932): 127-128.

7806. Tushnet, Mark V. "The Logic of Experience: Oliver Wendell Holmes on the Supreme Judicial Court." *Virginia Law Review* 63 (October 1977): 975-1052.

7807. University of Virginia. Barrett Library. *Oliver Wendell Holmes: A Checklist of Printed and Manuscript Works of Oliver W. Holmes in the Library of the University of Virginia.* Charlottesville: University of Virginia Press, 1960.

7808. Walker, Alexander J. "The Growth and Expression of the Constitutional Philosophy of Mr. Justice Holmes." Ph.D. diss., University of Iowa, 1941.

7809. White, G. Edward. "The Rise and Fall of Justice Holmes." *Chicago Law Review* 39 (Fall 1971): 55-77.

7810. Wigmore, John H. "Justice Holmes and the Law of Torts." *Harvard Law Review* 29 (April 1916): 601.

7811. Wu, John C. H. "The Juristic Philosophy of Justice Holmes." *Michigan Law Review* 21 (March 1923): 523-531.

7812. Wu, John C. H. "Justice Holmes and the Common-Law Tradition." *Vanderbilt Law Review* 14 (December 1960): 221-238.

7813. Wyzanski, Charles E., Jr. "The Democracy of Justice Oliver Wendell Holmes." *Vanderbilt Law Review* 7 (April 1954): 311-324.

7814. Yntema, Hessel E. "Mr. Justice Holmes' View of Legal Science." *Yale Law Journal* 40 (March 1931): 696-703.

Writings

7815. Holmes, Oliver W., Jr. *Collected Legal Papers.* Selected by Harold Laski. New York: Harcourt, Brace, 1920.

7816. Holmes, Oliver W., Jr. *The Common Law.* Boston: Little, Brown, 1881.

7817. Holmes, Oliver W., Jr. *The Dissenting Opinions of Mr. Justice Holmes.*

Edited by Alfred Lief. New York: Vanguard Press, 1929.

7818. Holmes, Oliver W., Jr. "The Early Reading of Justice Oliver Wendell Holmes." *Harvard Library Bulletin* 8 (Spring 1954): 163-203.

7819. Holmes, Oliver W., Jr. *The Holmes Reader: The Life, Writings, Speeches, Constitutional Decisions, etc., of the Late Oliver Wendell Holmes, Associate Justice of the Supreme Court of the United States, as Well as an Evaluation of His Work and Achievements by Eminent Authorities.* Edited by Julius J. Marke. New York: Oceana Publications, 1955.

7820. Holmes, Oliver W., Jr. *The Holmes-Einstein Letters: Correspondence of Mr. Justice Holmes and Lewis Einstein, 1903-1935.* Edited by James B. Peabody. New York: St. Martin's Press, 1964.

7821. Holmes, Oliver W., Jr. *Holmes-Laski Letters: The Correspondence of Mr. Justice Holmes and Harold J. Laski.* 2 vols. Edited by Mark D. Howe. Cambridge: Harvard University Press, 1953.

7822. Holmes, Oliver W., Jr. *Holmes-Pollock Letters: The Correspondence of Mr. Justice Holmes and Sir Frederick Pollock, 1874-1932.* Edited by Mark D. Howe. Cambridge: Harvard University Press, 1941.

7823. Holmes, Oliver W., Jr. *The Judicial Opinions of Oliver Wendell Holmes: Constitutional Opinions, Selected Excerpts, and Epigrams as Given in the Supreme Judicial Court of Massachusetts, 1885-1902.* Edited by Harry C. Shriver. Buffalo, NY: Dennis, 1940.

7824. Holmes, Oliver W., Jr. *Justice Holmes to Doctor Wu: An Intimate Correspondence, 1921-1932.* New York: Central Book Company, n.d.

7825. Holmes, Oliver W., Jr. *Justice Oliver Wendell Holmes: His Book Notices and Uncollected Letters and Papers.*

Edited by Harry C. Shriver. New York: Central Book Company, 1936.

7826. Holmes, Oliver W., Jr. *The Mind and Faith of Justice Holmes: His Speeches, Essays, Letters, and Judicial Opinions.* Edited by Max Lerner. Boston: Little, Brown, 1943.

7827. Holmes, Oliver W., Jr. *The Occasional Speeches of Justice Oliver Wendell Holmes.* Edited by Mark D. Howe. Cambridge: Harvard University Press, 1962.

7828. Holmes, Oliver W., Jr. *Representative Opinions of Mr. Justice Holmes.* Edited by Alfred Lief. New York: Vanguard Press, 1931.

7829. Holmes, Oliver W., Jr. *Speeches.* Boston: Little, Brown, 1934.

7830. Holmes, Oliver W., Jr. *Touched with Fire: Civil War Letters and Diary of Oliver Wendell Holmes, Jr., 1861-1864.* Edited by Mark D. Howe. Cambridge: Harvard University Press, 1946.

7831. Holmes, Oliver W., Jr., and Patrick Sheehan. *Holmes-Sheehan Correspondence: The Letters of Justice Oliver Wendell Holmes and Canon Patrick Augustine Sheehan.* Edited by David H. Burton. Port Washington, NY: Kennikat Press, 1976.

Charles E. Hughes

General Studies

7832. Allen, Arthur M. "The Opinions of Mr. Justice Hughes." *Columbia Law Review* 16 (October 1916): 565-584.

7833. Bates, Earnest S. "McReynolds, Roberts, and Hughes." *New Republic* 87 (July 1, 1936): 232.

7834. Chafee, Zechariah, Jr. "Charles Evans Hughes." *American Philosophical Society Proceedings* 93 (June 1959): 267-281.

7835. "Charles Evans Hughes, 1862-1948: America's Great Diplomat-Jurist Dies." *American Bar Association Journal* 34 (October 1948): 902-903.

7836. Cummings, Homer S., and Charles E. Hughes. "Bar Presents Resolutions in Memory of Justice Cardozo to the Supreme Court." *American Bar Association Journal* 25 (January 1939): 33-37.

7837. Danelski, David J., and Joseph S. Tulchin, eds. "Charles Evans Hughes at Cornell: Excerpts from Hughes' Autobiographical Notes." *Cornell Law Review* 50 (November 1972): 9-22.

7838. Ellis, L. Ethan. "Charles Evans Hughes: A Profile." *American History Illustrated* 3 (October 1968): 28-37.

7839. Fish, Peter G. "William Howard Taft and Charles Evans Hughes: Conservative Politicians as Chief Judicial Reformers." *Supreme Court Review* 1975 (1975): 123-145.

7840. Foley, William E. "Chief Justice Hughes and the Due Process of Law." Ph.D. diss., Harvard University, 1940.

7841. Fosdick, Raymond B. *Secretary Hughes and the League of Nations.* New York: New York Times, 1924.

7842. Freund, Paul A. "Charles Evans Hughes as Chief Justice." *Harvard Law Review* 81 (November 1967): 4-43.

7843. Friedman, Richard D. "Charles Evans Hughes as Chief Justice, 1930-1941." D.Ph. diss., University of Oxford, 1978.

7844. Galloway, Gail. "Charles Evans Hughes: The Eleventh Chief Justice." *Supreme Court Historical Society Yearbook* 1981 (1981): 94-112.

7845. Glad, Betty. *Charles Evans Hughes and the Illusions of Innocence: A Study in American Diplomacy.* Urbana: University of Illinois Press, 1966.

7846. Gossett, Elizabeth H. "My Father

the Chief Justice." *Supreme Court Historical Society Yearbook* 1976 (1976): 7-15.

7847. Gossett, William T. "Chief Justice Hughes: A Recollection." *Supreme Court Historical Society Yearbook* 1981 (1981): 74-77.

7848. Gossett, William T. "The Human Side of Chief Justice Hughes." *American Bar Association Journal* 59 (December 1973): 1413-1419.

7849. Greer, Virginia L. "Charles Evans Hughes and Nicaragua, 1921-1925." Ph.D. diss., University of New Mexico, 1954.

7850. Guffey, Joseph F. *How Liberal Is Justice Hughes?* Washington, DC: U.S. Government Printing Office, 1937.

7851. Guthrie, William D. "Charles Evans Hughes." *American Bar Association Journal* 15 (March 1929): 266-267.

7852. Hendel, Samuel. *Charles Evans Hughes and the Supreme Court.* New York: King's Crown Press, 1951.

7853. Hendel, Samuel. "The 'Liberalism' of Chief Justice Hughes." *Vanderbilt Law Review* 10 (February 1959): 259-268.

7854. Hendrick, Burton J. "Governor Hughes." *McClure's* 30 (March 1908): 521-536; (April 1908): 670-681.

7855. Hill, Leslie B. "Charles Evans Hughes and United States Adherence to an International Court: A Rhetorical Analysis." Ph.D. diss., University of Illinois, 1968.

7856. Horwill, Herbert S. "Charles Evans Hughes." *Contemporary Review* 120 (November 1921): 593-599.

7857. Howland, Harold J. "Hughes, Governor." *Outlook* 88 (February 8, 1908): 303-309.

7858. Hoyt, Edwin P. *Lost Statesman.* Philadelphia: Peter Reilly, 1961.

7859. Huthmacher, J. Joseph. "Charles Evans Hughes and Charles Francis Murphy: The Metamorphosis of Progressivism." *New York History* 46 (January 1965): 25-40.

7860. Hyde, Charles C. "Charles Evans Hughes." In *The American Secretaries of State and Their Diplomacy*, edited by Samuel F. Bemis, 221-402. New York: Pageant Book Company, 1958.

7861. Hyde, Charles C. "Charles Evans Hughes: An Appreciation." *American Journal of International Law* 43 (April 1949): 335-338.

7862. Jackson, Robert H. "Judicial Career of Chief Justice Hughes." *American Bar Association Journal* 27 (July 1941): 408.

7863. Kane, N. Stephen. "Charles Evans Hughes and Mexican-American Relations, 1921-1924." Ph.D. diss., University of Colorado, 1970.

7864. Kennedy, John F. *Profiles in Courage.* New York: Harper, 1956.

7865. Knox, John. "Some Comments on Chief Justice Hughes." *Supreme Court Historical Society Yearbook* 1984 (1984): 34-44.

7866. Kornberg, Harvey R. "Charles Evans Hughes and the Supreme Court: A Study in Judicial Philosophy and Voting Behavior." Ph.D. diss., Brown University, 1972.

7867. McElwain, Edwin. "Business of the Supreme Court as Conducted by Chief Justice Hughes." *Harvard Law Review* 63 (November 1949): 5-26.

7868. Mason, Alpheus T. "Charles Evans Hughes: An Appeal to the Bar of History." *Vanderbilt Law Review* 6 (December 1952): 1-19.

7869. Meloney, William B. "Hughes." *Everybody's* 35 (October 1916): 385-397.

7870. Moore, Allen. "Our Eleventh Chief Justice." *Dicta* 7 (April 1930): 11-27.

7871. Navarrete, George. "The Latin American Policy of Charles Evans Hughes, 1921-1925." Ph.D. diss., University of California, Berkeley, 1964.

7872. Northrup, Clark S. "Mr. Hughes' Career." *Phi Beta Kappa Key* 5 (March 1925): 683-690.

7873. O'Brian, John L. "Charles Evans Hughes as Governor." *American Bar Association Journal* 27 (July 1941): 412-413.

7874. Pepper, George W. "Charles Evans Hughes: Publication of New Biography Is Major Event." *American Bar Association Journal* 38 (March 1952): 200-204, 262.

7875. Perkins, Dexter. *Charles E. Hughes: . . . A Statesman of the First Order.* Manhasset, NY: Channel Press, 1960.

7876. Perkins, Dexter. *Charles Evans Hughes and American Democratic Statesmanship.* Boston: Little, Brown, 1956.

7877. Powell, Thomas R. "Charles Evans Hughes." *Political Science Quarterly* 67 (June 1952): 161-172.

7878. Pusey, Merlo J. *Charles Evans Hughes.* 2 vols. New York: Macmillan, 1951.

7879. Pusey, Merlo J. "The Hughes Biography: Some Personal Reflections." *Supreme Court Historical Society Yearbook* 1984 (1984): 45-52.

7880. Pusey, Merlo J. *Mr. Chief Justice Hughes.* Chicago: University of Chicago Press, 1956.

7881. Pusey, Merlo J. "The Nomination of Charles Evans Hughes as Chief Justice." *Supreme Court Historical Society Yearbook* 1982 (1982): 95-99.

7882. Raff, Lawrence B. "Charles Evans Hughes: Public Servant." *Case and Comment* 54 (May/June 1949): 17-23.

7883. Ransom, William L. *Charles E. Hughes, the Statesman, as Shown in the Opinions of the Jurist.* New York: E. P. Dutton, 1916.

7884. Ribble, F.D.G. "The Constitutional Doctrines of Chief Justice Hughes." *Columbia Law Review* 41 (November 1941): 1190-1215.

7885. Rogers, James G. "Hughes as Secretary of State." *American Bar Association Journal* 27 (July 1941): 411-412.

7886. Schurman, George W. "Charles Evans Hughes." *Independent* 61 (October 4, 1906): 779-783.

7887. Sentell, R. Perry, Jr. "The Opinions of Hughes and Sutherland and the Rights of the Individual." *Vanderbilt Law Review* 15 (March 1962): 559-615.

7888. Simmons, David A. "Charles Evans Hughes." *Journal of the American Judicature Society* 25 (August 1941): 35-36.

7889. Simonds, Frank H. "Governor Hughes." *Putnam's Monthly* 3 (October 1907): 30-36.

7890. Stone, Harlan F. "The Chief Justice." *American Bar Association Journal* 27 (July 1941): 407-408.

7891. Thompson, Guy A., John W. Davis, and Chief Justice Hughes. "Laying of the Corner-Stone of the Supreme Court Building." *Federal Bar Association Journal* 1 (October 1932): 11-19.

7892. Vinson, John C. *Charles Evans Hughes.* New York: McGraw-Hill, 1961.

7893. Warren, Earl. *Hughes and the Court.* Hamilton, NY: Colgate University, 1962.

7894. Wesser, Robert F. "Charles Evans Hughes and the Urban Sources of Political Progressivism." *New York Historical Society Quarterly* 50 (October 1966): 365-400.

7895. Wesser, Robert F. *Charles Evans Hughes: Politics and Reform in New York, 1905-1910.* Ithaca, NY: Cornell University Press, 1967.

7896. Wickersham, George W. "Hughes: Man and Statesman." *Independent* 86 (June 19, 1916): 481.

7897. Wiener, Frederick B. "Justice Hughes' Appointment: The Cotton Story Re-examined." *Supreme Court Historical Society Yearbook* 1981 (Annual 1981): 78-91.

7898. Woodard, Nelson E. "Postwar Reconstruction and International Order: A Study of the Diplomacy of Charles Evans Hughes, 1921-1925." Ph.D. diss., University of Wisconsin, 1970.

Writings

7899. Hughes, Charles E. "Address at Judicial Conference." *American Bar Association Journal* 18 (July 1932): 445-448.

7900. Hughes, Charles E. "Address: Making Democracy Workable; 150th Anniversary of the First Meeting of Congress, Washington, DC, March 4, 1939." *Vital Speeches* 5 (March 1939): 327-328.

7901. Hughes, Charles E. *Addresses of Charles Evans Hughes, 1906-1916.* 2d ed. New York: Putnam's, 1916.

7902. Hughes, Charles E. "Associate Justice Van Devanter: An Appraisal by the Chief Justice." *American Bar Association Journal* 28 (July 1942): 458-459.

7903. Hughes, Charles E. *The Autobiographical Notes of Charles Evans Hughes.* Edited by David J. Danelski and Joseph F. Tulchin. Cambridge: Harvard University Press, 1973.

7904. Hughes, Charles E. "Chief Justice Hughes Addresses Judicial Conference of Fourth Circuit." *American Bar Association Journal* 18 (July 1932): 445-448.

7905. Hughes, Charles E. *Conditions of Progress in Democratic Government.* New Haven, CT: Yale University Press, 1910.

7906. Hughes, Charles E. *Foreign Relations.* Chicago: Republican National Committee, 1924.

7907. Hughes, Charles E. "An Imperishable Ideal of Liberty under Law." *Journal of the American Judicature Society* 25 (December 1941): 99.

7908. Hughes, Charles E. "In Memory of Mr. Justice Butler." *United States Reports* 310 (May 1940): xv-xx.

7909. Hughes, Charles E. " 'Justice Our Anchor': 150th Anniversary of the First Sitting of the Supreme Court, Washington, DC, February 1, 1940." *Vital Speeches* 6 (February 1940): 259-260.

7910. Hughes, Charles E. "Liberty and Law." *American Bar Association Proceedings* 1925 (1925): 183-199.

7911. Hughes, Charles E. "Mr. Justice Brandeis." *Columbia Law Review* 31 (November 1931): 1071-1072.

7912. Hughes, Charles E. "Mr. Justice Holmes." *Harvard Law Review* 44 (March 1931): 677-679.

7913. Hughes, Charles E. *Mr. Justice Holmes and the Supreme Court.* Cambridge: Harvard University Press, 1961.

7914. Hughes, Charles E. "The Obligations of the Bar." *California State Bar Journal* 3 (May 1929): 223-225, 240-241.

7915. Hughes, Charles E. "Observations on the Monroe Doctrine." *American Journal of International Law* 17 (1923): 611-628.

7916. Hughes, Charles E. *Our Relations to the Nations of the Western Hemisphere.* Princeton, NJ: Princeton University Press, 1928.

7917. Hughes, Charles E. *Pan American Peace Plans.* New Haven, CT: Yale University Press, 1929.

7918. Hughes, Charles E. *The Pathway of Peace.* New York: Harper and Brothers, 1925.

7919. Hughes, Charles E. "Proceeding in Memory of Mr. Justice Cardozo." *United States Reports* 305 (October 1938): xxii-xxvii.

7920. Hughes, Charles E. "Roger Brooke Taney." *American Bar Association Journal* 17 (December 1931): 785-790.

7921. Hughes, Charles E. "Some Aspects in the Development of American Law." *Chicago Legal News* 48 (January 20, 1916): 198-200.

7922. Hughes, Charles E. *The Supreme Court of the United States: Its Foundation, Methods, and Achievements, an Interpretation.* New York: Columbia University, 1928.

7923. Hughes, Charles E. "War Powers under the Constitution." *Massachusetts Law Quarterly* 2 (August 1917): 575-590.

7924. Hughes, Charles E., ed. *Mr. Justice Brandeis.* New Haven, CT: Yale University Press, 1932.

7925. Hughes, Charles E., Robert H. Jackson, and Charles A. Beardsley. "Sesquicentennial of the Supreme Court of the United States." *New York Law Review* 74 (March 1940): 142-150.

Ward Hunt

General Studies

7926. "Old Judge and the New." *Albany Law Journal* 6 (December 14, 1872): 400-401.

7927. Wyman, Thomas B. *Genealogy of the Name and Family of Hunt.* Boston: Wilson, 1862-1863.

James Iredell

General Studies

7928. Boyd, Julian P. "Letter to the Editor." *William and Mary Quarterly* 8 (April 1951): 317-319.

7929. Carson, Hampton L. "James Wilson and James Iredell: A Parallel and a Contrast." *American Bar Association Journal* 7 (March 1921): 123-136.

7930. Connor, Henry G. "James Iredell: Lawyer, Statesman, Judge, 1751-1799." *University of Pennsylvania Law Review* 60 (January 1912): 225-253.

7931. Davis, Junius. *Alfred Moore and James Iredell: Revolutionary Patriots and Associate Justices of the Supreme Court of the United States.* Raleigh: North Carolina Society of the Sons of the Revolution, 1899.

7932. Davis, Junius. "James Iredell." *Green Bag* 12 (April 1900): 165-172.

7933. Fordham, Jefferson B. "Iredell's Dissent in *Chisholm v. Georgia.*" *North Carolina Historical Review* 8 (April 1931): 155-167.

7934. Hubbell, Jay B. *South in American Literature: 1607-1900.* Durham, NC: Duke University Press, 1954.

7935. McRee, Griffith J. *Life and Correspondence of James Iredell, One of the Associate Justices of the Supreme Court of the United States.* New York: D. Appleton, 1857.

7936. Shulhafer, Lucia. "James Iredell, Patriot." *Daughters of the American Revolution Magazine* 113 (September 1979): 994-999.

7937. Smith, Fitz H., Jr. "Mr. Justice Iredell's Opinion in 1798 on the Duty of the Federal Courts in Regard to Legislation." *Massachusetts Law Quarterly* 22 (July/September 1937): 51-52.

Writings

7938. Iredell, James. "Letter of James Iredell to Johnson." *Massachussetts Historical Society Proceedings* 53 (1920): 27-28.

7939. Iredell, James. *The Papers of James Iredell.* Edited by Don Higgenbotham. Raleigh: North Carolina Department of Archives and History, 1976.

Howell E. Jackson

General Studies

7940. Calvani, Terry. "The Early Legal Career of Howell Jackson." *Vanderbilt Law Review* 30 (January 1977): 39-72.

7941. Doak, Henry M. "Howell Edmunds Jackson." *Green Bag* 5 (May 1893): 209-215.

7942. Green, John W. "Two United States Circuit Judges." *Tennessee Law Review* 18 (June 1944): 311-322.

7943. Hardaway, Roger D. "Howell Edmunds Jackson: Tennessee Legislator and Jurist." *West Tennessee Historical Society Papers* 30 (1976): 104-119.

Robert H. Jackson

General Studies

7944. "American Lawyers Mourn the Passing of Mr. Justice Jackson." *American Bar Association Journal* 40 (November 1954): 970-972.

7945. Barnett, Vincent M., Jr. "Mr. Justice Jackson and the Supreme Court." *Western Political Quarterly* 1 (September 1948): 223-242.

7946. Bishop, William W., Jr. "Robert H. Jackson, Editorial." *American Journal of International Law* 49 (January 1955): 44-50.

7947. Cancian, John. "Justice Jackson: Civil Liberties and State Action under the Due Process Clause of the Fourteenth Amendment." *Northeastern Law Review* 1951 (May 1951): 3-48.

7948. Cox, Susan J. "Justice Robert Jackson and the Evolution of Administrative Law." Ph.D. diss., Virginia Polytechnic Institute and State University, 1983.

7949. Dean, Gordon. "Mr. Justice Jackson: His Contribution at Nuremberg." *American Bar Association Journal* 41 (October 1955): 912-915.

7950. Desmond, Charles S., et al. *Mr. Justice Jackson: Four Lectures in His Honor.* New York: Columbia University Press, 1969.

7951. Dunne, Gerald T. "Justices Hugo Black and Robert Jackson: The Great Feud." *St. Louis University Law Journal* 19 (Summer 1975): 465-487.

7952. Fairman, Charles. "Robert H. Jackson: 1892-1954, Associate Justice of the Supreme Court." *Columbia Law Review* 55 (April 1955): 445-487.

7953. Frankfurter, Felix. "Mr. Justice Jackson." *Columbia Law Review* 55 (April 1955): 435-437.

7954. Frankfurter, Felix. "Mr. Justice Jackson." *Harvard Law Review* 68 (April 1955): 937-939.

7955. Freund, Paul A. "Individual and Commonwealth in the Thought of Mr. Justice Jackson." *Stanford Law Review* 8 (December 1955): 9-25.

7956. Gardner, Warner W. "Robert H. Jackson, 1892-1954, Government Attorney." *Columbia Law Review* 55 (April 1955): 438-444.

7957. Gerhart, Eugene C. *America's Advocate: Robert H. Jackson.* Indianapolis: Bobbs-Merrill, 1958.

7958. Gerhart, Eugene C. "Decade of Mr. Justice Jackson." *New York University Law Review* 28 (May 1953): 927-974.

7959. Gerhart, Eugene C. *Supreme Court Justice Jackson: Lawyer's Judge.* New York: Q Corporation, 1961.

7960. Halpern, Phillip. "Robert H. Jackson, 1892-1954." *Stanford Law Review* 8 (December 1955): 3-8.

7961. Harpaz, Leora. "Justice Jackson's Flag Salute Legacy: The Supreme Court Struggles to Protect Intellectual Individualism." *Texas Law Review* 64 (March 1986): 817-914.

7962. Harris, Whitney R. "Justice Jackson at Nuremberg." *International Lawyer* 20 (Summer 1986): 867-896.

7963. Hubbard, Robert C. "Mr. Justice Robert H. Jackson." Senior thesis, Princeton University, 1950.

7964. Hughes, Charles E., Robert H. Jackson, and Charles A. Beardsley. "One Hundred and Fiftieth Anniversary of First Session of Supreme Court: Addresses." *American Bar Association Journal* 26 (March 1940): 203-208.

7965. Jaffe, Louis L. "Mr. Justice." *Harvard Law Review* 68 (April 1955): 940-998.

7966. James, Dorothy. "Judicial Philosophy and Accession to the Court: The Cases of Justices Jackson and Douglas." Ph.D. diss., Columbia University, 1966.

7967. Klimuir, D. P. "Justice Jackson and Nuremberg: A British Tribute." *Stanford Law Review* 8 (December 1955): 54-59.

7968. Kurland, Philip B. "Justice Robert H. Jackson: Impact on Civil Rights and Civil Liberties." *University of Illinois Law Forum* 1977 (1977): 551-576.

7969. Lawless, William B. "Mr. Justice Jackson: The Struggle for Federal Supremacy." *Notre Dame Law Review* 37 (May 1962): 489-498.

7970. McDonough, John R., Jr. "Mr. Justice Jackson and Full Faith and Credit to Divorce Decrees: A Critique." *Columbia Law Review* 56 (June 1956): 860-886.

7971. Marsh, James M. "The Genial Justice: Robert H. Jackson." *American Bar Association Journal* 60 (March 1974): 306-309.

7972. Murphy, Walter F. "Mr. Justice Jackson: Free Speech and the Judicial Function." *Vanderbilt Law Review* 12 (October 1959): 1019-1046.

7973. Nielson, James A. "Robert H. Jackson: The Middle Ground." *Louisiana Law Review* 6 (May 1945): 381-405.

7974. Penfold, John B. "The Verdict Is 'Guilty'." *U.S. Naval Institute Proceedings* 72 (May 1946): 675-679.

7975. Pew, Mary J. "An Analysis of Justice Robert H. Jackson's Interpretation of the Religious Clauses of the First Amendment." Ph.D. diss., Fordham University, 1961.

7976. Pound, Roscoe. "Supreme Court in Our System: A Review of Mr. Justice Jackson's Last Book." *American Bar Association Journal* 42 (May 1956): 427-432.

7977. Ransom, William L. "Associate Justice Robert H. Jackson." *American Bar Association Journal* 27 (August 1941): 478-482.

7978. Reese, William E. "Mr. Justice Jackson." *Federal Bar Association Journal* 4 (November 1941): 226-229, 259.

7979. "Robert Houghwout Jackson, 1892-1954." *Albany Law Review* 19 (January 1955): 1.

7980. Schubert, Glendon A. "Jackson's Judicial Philosophy: An Exploration in Value Analysis." *American Political Science Review* 59 (December 1965): 940-963.

7981. Seymour, Whitney N., Potter Stewart, and Paul A. Freund. *Mr. Justice Jack-*

son: *Four Lectures in His Honor.* New York: Columbia University Press, 1969.

7982. Shawcross, Lord. "Robert H. Jackson's Contribution during the Nuremberg Trial." *Record of the Association of the Bar of the City of New York* 23 (June 1968): 393-428.

7983. Shellow, James M. "An Analysis of Judicial Methodology: Selected Opinions of Justice Robert H. Jackson." *Marquette Law Review* 45 (Summer 1961): 103-116.

7984. Simpson, Dwight J. "Robert H. Jackson and the Doctrine of Judicial Restraint." *UCLA Law Review* 3 (April 1956): 325-359.

7985. Steamer, Robert J. "The Constitutional Doctrines of Mr. Justice Robert H. Jackson." Ph.D. diss., Cornell University, 1954.

7986. Steamer, Robert J. "Mr. Justice Jackson and the First Amendment." *University of Pittsburgh Law Review* 15 (Winter 1954): 193-221.

7987. Stewart, Potter. "Robert H. Jackson's Influence on Federal State Relationships." *Record of the Association of the Bar of the City of New York* 23 (January 1968): 7-32.

7988. Taylor, Telford. "Robert H. Jackson, 1892-1954: The Nuremberg Trials." *Columbia Law Review* 55 (1955): 488-525.

7989. Weidner, Paul A. "Justice Jackson and the Judicial Function." *Michigan Law Review* 53 (February 1955): 567-594.

7990. Williams, Samuel C. "A Remarkable Bench: Campbell, Jackson, and White." *Tennessee Law Review* 16 (June 1941): 907-914.

Writings

7991. Jackson, Robert H. "Address, Our American Legal Philosophy." *Vital Speeches of the Day* 8 (June 24, 1942): 356-358.

7992. Jackson, Robert H. "Advocacy before the Supreme Court: Suggestions for Effective Case Presentations." *American Bar Association Journal* 37 (November 1951): 801-804.

7993. Jackson, Robert H. *Advocacy before the United States Supreme Court.* San Francisco: Morrison Foundation Lecture, 1951.

7994. Jackson, Robert H. "The Advocate: Guardian of Our Traditional Liberties." *American Bar Association Journal* 36 (August 1950): 607-610.

7995. Jackson, Robert H. "American Courts." *New York State Bar Association Proceedings* 67 (1944): 424-429.

7996. Jackson, Robert H. *The Case Against the Nazi War Criminals.* New York: Knopf, 1946.

7997. Jackson, Robert H. "Decisional Law and *Stare Decisis.*" *American Bar Association Journal* 30 (June 1944): 334-335.

7998. Jackson, Robert H. "Decline of *Stare Decisis* Is Due to Volume of Opinions." *Journal of American Judicature Society* 28 (June 1944): 6-8.

7999. Jackson, Robert H. *Dispassionate Justice: A Synthesis of the Judicial Opinions of Robert H. Jackson.* Edited by Glendon Schubert. Indianapolis: Bobbs-Merrill, 1969.

8000. Jackson, Robert H. *Full Faith and Credit: The Lawyer's Clause of the Constitution.* New York: Columbia University Press, 1945.

8001. Jackson, Robert H. "Judicial Career of Chief Justice Hughes." *American Bar Association Journal* 27 (July 1941): 408.

8002. Jackson, Robert H. "The Law Is a

Rule for Men to Live By." *Vital Speeches of the Day* 9 (June 24, 1943): 664-667.

8003. Jackson, Robert H. "Lawyers Today: The Legal Profession in a World of Paradox." *American Bar Association Journal* 33 (January 1947): 24-27, 85-89.

8004. Jackson, Robert H. "Maryland at the Supreme Court Bar." In *Report of the Forty-fourth Annual Meeting of the Maryland State Bar Association*, 11-124. Baltimore: Maryland State Bar Association, 1939.

8005. Jackson, Robert H. "The Meaning of Statutes: What Congress Says or What the Court Says." *American Bar Association Journal* 34 (July 1948): 535-538.

8006. Jackson, Robert H. "The Rise and Fall of *Swift* and *Tyson*." *American Bar Association Journal* 24 (1938): 609-614, 644.

8007. Jackson, Robert H. *The Struggle for Judicial Supremacy: A Study of a Crisis in American Power Politics*. New York: Knopf, 1941.

8008. Jackson, Robert H. *The Supreme Court in the American System of Government*. Cambridge: Harvard University Press, 1955.

8009. Jackson, Robert H. "The Task of Maintaining Our Liberties: The Role of the Judiciary." *American Bar Association Journal* 37 (November 1951): 801-804, 861-864.

John Jay

General Studies

8010. Barre, W. L. "John Jay." In *Lives of Illustrious Men of America: Distinguished in the Annals of the Republic as Legislators, Warriors, and Philosophers*, by W. L. Barre, 334-348. Cincinnati: W. A. Clarke, 1859.

8011. Baxter, Katharine S. "John Jay: Statesman and First Chief Justice of the United States." In *Godchild of Washington: A Picture of the Past*, by Katharine S. Baxter, 87-94. New York: F. T. Neely, 1897.

8012. Becker, Carl. "John Jay and Peter Van Schaak." *New York State Historical Association Journal* 50 (October 1969): 1-12.

8013. Bemis, Samuel F. *Jay's Treaty*. New York: Macmillan, 1924.

8014. Brooks, Elbridge S. "The Story of John Jay, of Bedford, First Chief Justice of the United States." In *Historic Americans: Sketches of the Lives and Characters of Certain Famous Americans Held Most in Reverence by the Boys and Girls of America*, by Elbridge S. Brooks, 146-160. New York: Crowell, 1899.

8015. Dietze, Gottfried. "Jay's *Federalist*: Treatise for Free Government." *Maryland Law Review* 17 (Summer 1957): 217-230.

8016. Dorfman, Joseph H., and Rexford G. Tugwell. "John Jay: Revolutionary Conservative." In *Early American Policy: Six Columbia Contributions*, by Joseph H. Dorfman and Rexford G. Tugwell, 43-98. New York: Columbia University Press, 1960.

8017. Durham, G. Homer. "John Jay and the Judicial Powers." *Brigham Young University Studies* 16 (Spring 1976): 349-361.

8018. Hackett, William H. "Sketch of the Life and Character of John Jay." *American Review* 2 (July 1845): 59-68.

8019. Halsey, John J. "A Modern Roman." *Dial* 11 (September 1890): 111-112.

8020. Herring, James. "John Jay." In *The National Portrait Gallery*, vol. 2, by James Herring and James B. Longacre, 47-62. Philadelphia: Henry Perkins, 1835.

8021. Hubbard, Elbert. "John Jay." In

Little Journeys to the Homes of American Statesmen, by Elbert Hubbard, 327-361. New York: Putnam's, 1898.

8022. Hubbard, Elbert. "John Jay." *Magazine of American History* 1 (December 1901): 1-6; 1 (January/March 1902): 24-30; 2 (April/May 1902): 46-57.

8023. Hubbard, Elbert. *John Jay, the First Chief Justice of the United States.* New York: Hartford Lunch Company, 1918.

8024. Ide, John J. *The Portraits of John Jay.* New York: New York Historical Society, 1938.

8025. Jay, William. *The Life of John Jay: With Selections from His Correspondence and Miscellaneous Papers.* 2 vols. New York: J. and J. Harper, 1833.

8026. Jenkins, John S. "John Jay." In *Lives of the Governors of the State of New York*, edited by John S. Jenkins, 74-131. Auburn, NY: Derby and Miller, 1851.

8027. Johnson, Herbert A. "Civil Procedure in John Jay's New York." *American Journal of Legal History* 11 (January 1967): 69-80.

8028. Johnson, Herbert A. "John Jay: Colonial Lawyer." Ph.D. diss., Columbia University, 1965.

8029. Johnson, Herbert A. "John Jay: Lawyer in a Time of Transition, 1764-1775." *University of Pennsylvania Law Review* 124 (May 1976): 1260-1292.

8030. Jones, Francis R. "John Jay." *Green Bag* 13 (January 1901): 1-4.

8031. Kelland, Clarence B. "John Jay: A Brief Study of the Life of a Great Master of International Law." *Law Students' Helper* 17 (April 1909): 106-108.

8032. Lossing, Benson J. "John Jay." In *Eminent Americans*, by Benson J. Lossing, 171-172. New York: Hurst, 1886.

8033. Monaghan, Frank. "Anti-Slavery Papers of John Jay." *Journal of Negro History* 17 (October 1932): 481-497.

8034. Monaghan, Frank. *The Diary of John Jay during the Peace Negotiations of 1782.* New Haven, CT: Bibliographical Press, Yale University, 1934.

8035. Monaghan, Frank. *John Jay, Defender of Liberty against Kings and Peoples, Author of the Constitution and Governor of New York, President of the Continental Congress, Co-author of the Federalist, Negotiator of the Peace of 1783 and the Jay Treaty of 1794, First Chief Justice of the United States.* New York: Bobbs-Merrill, 1935.

8036. Morris, Richard B. "John Jay and the Adoption of the Federal Constitution in New York: A New Reading of Persons and Events." *New York History* 63 (April 1982): 133-164.

8037. Morris, Richard B. "John Jay and the New England Connection." *Massachusetts Historical Society Proceedings* 80 (February 1968): 16-37.

8038. Morris, Richard B. "The John Jay Court: An Intimate Profile." *Journal of Contemporary Law* 5 (Spring 1979): 163-179.

8039. Morris, Richard B. *John Jay, the Nation, and the Court.* Boston: Boston University Press, 1968.

8040. Morris, Richard B., ed. "The Jay Papers I: Mission to Spain." *American Heritage* 19 (February 1968): 8-21.

8041. Morris, Richard B., ed. "The Jay Papers II: The Forging of the Nation." *American Heritage* 20 (December 1968): 24-29.

8042. Morris, Richard B., ed. "The Jay Papers III: The Trials of Chief Justice Jay." *American Heritage* 20 (June 1969): 80-90.

8043. Morris, Richard B., ed. *John Jay: The Making of a Revolutionary; Unpub-*

lished Papers, 1745-1780. New York: Harper and Row, 1975.

8044. Pellew, George. *John Jay.* Boston: Houghton Mifflin, 1890.

8045. Perry, Benjamin F. "John Jay." In *Biographical Sketches of Eminent American Statesmen,* by Benjamin F. Perry, 393-402. Philadelphia: Ferree Press, 1887.

8046. Proctor, L. B. "John Jay and Other Chief Justices of the Supreme Court of the United States." *Michigan Law Journal* 5 (May 1896): 153-164.

8047. Renwick, Henry B., and James Renwick. *Lives of John Jay and Alexander Hamilton.* New York: Harper and Brothers, 1840.

8048. Scott, James B. "John Jay." *Columbia Law Review* 6 (May 1906): 289-325.

8049. Smith, Donald L. *John Jay: Founder of a State and Nation.* New York: Teacher's College Press, Columbia University, 1968.

8050. Tuckerman, Henry T. "Violations of Literary Property: *The Federalist*: Life and Character of John Jay." *Continental Monthly* 6 (September 1864): 336-355.

8051. Uhle, John B. "John Jay." *Current Comment* 1 (November 15, 1889): 411-415.

8052. Van Burkelo, Sandra F. "Honour, Justice, and Interest: John Jay's Republican Politics and Statesmanship of the Federal Bench." *Journal of the Early Republic* 4 (Fall 1984): 239-274.

8053. Waite, Charles B. "John Jay." *Chicago Law Times* 1 (July 1887): 215-223.

8054. Wheeler, Charles B. "John Jay, 1926." *New York Historical Association Proceedings* 7 (July 1926): 180-194.

8055. Whitelock, William. *The Life and Times of John Jay, Secretary of Foreign Affairs under the Confederation and First Chief Justice of the United States, with a Sketch of Public Events from the Opening of the Revolution to the Election of Jefferson.* New York: Dodd, Mead, 1887.

8056. Zuver, John H. *The Earthly Pilgrimage of John Jay.* Battle Creek, MI: Associated Lawyer's Publishing Company, 1904.

Writings

8057. Jay, John. *An Address to the People of the State of New York on the Subject of the Constitution, Agreed upon at Philadelphia, September 17, 1787.* New York: S. and J. Loudon, 1788.

8058. Jay, John. *The Correspondence and Public Papers of John Jay.* 4 vols. Edited by Henry P. Johnston. New York: Putnam's, 1890-1893.

8059. Jay, John. *Letters, Being the Whole of the Correspondence between the Hon. John Jay, Esq. and Mr. Lewis Littlepage: A Young Man Whom Mr. Jay, When in Spain, Patronized, and Took into His Family.* New York: F. Childs, 1786.

8060. Jay, John. *Unpublished Correspondence of William Livingston and John Jay.* Newark: New Jersey Historical Society, 1934.

Thomas Johnson

General Studies

8061. Delaplaine, Edward S. "The Life of Thomas Johnson." *Maryland Historical Magazine* 20 (March/December 1925): 33-42; (March/June 1926): 39-54, 181-201.

8062. Delaplaine, Edward S. *The Life of Thomas Johnson: Member of the Continental Congress, First Governor of the State of Maryland, and Associate Justice of* the United States Supreme Court. New York: F. H. Hitchcock, 1927.

8063. Offult, T. Scott. "Thomas Johnson and Constitutional Government." *Constitutional Review* 13 (October 1929): 204-211.

William Johnson

General Studies

8064. Greenberg, Irwin F. "Justice William Johnson: South Carolina Unionist, 1823-1830." *Pennsylvania History* 36 (July 1969): 307-334.

8065. Levin, A. J. "Mr. Justice William Johnson and the Common Incidents of Life." *Michigan Law Review* 44 (August 1945): 59-112; (October 1945): 243-293.

8066. Levin, A. J. "Mr. Justice William Johnson and the Unenviable Dilemma." *Michigan Law Review* 42 (April 1944): 803-830.

8067. Levin, A. J. "Mr. Justice William Johnson, Creative Dissenter." *Michigan Law Review* 43 (December 1944): 497-548.

8068. Levin, A. J. "Mr. Justice William Johnson, Jurist *in Limine:* Dissent and the Judging Faculty." *Michigan Law Review* 47 (February 1949): 477-536.

8069. Levin, A. J. "Mr. Justice William Johnson, Jurist *in Limine:* The Judge as Historian and Maker of History." *Michigan Law Review* 46 (December 1947): 131-186.

8070. Levin, A. J. "Mr. Justice William Johnson, Jurist *in Limine:* Views on Judicial Precedent." *Michigan Law Review* 46 (February 1948): 481-520.

8071. McCaughey, Elizabeth P. "William Samuel Johnson, Loyalist and Founding Father." Ph.D. diss., Columbia University, 1976.

8072. Morgan, Donald G. "The Constitutional Philosophy of Associate Justice William Johnson, 1771-1834." Ph.D. diss., Harvard University, 1943.

8073. Morgan, Donald G. "Justice William Johnson on the Treaty-Making Power." *George Washington Law Review* 22 (December 1953): 187-215.

8074. Morgan, Donald G. *Justice William Johnson, the First Dissenter: The Career and Constitutional Philosophy of a Jeffersonian Judge.* Columbia: University of South Carolina Press, 1971.

8075. Morgan, Donald G. "Mr. Justice William Johnson and the Constitution." *Harvard Law Review* 57 (January 1944): 328-361.

8076. O'Neall, John B. "William Johnson." In *Biographical Sketches of the Bench and Bar of South Carolina*, vol. 1, by John B. O'Neall, 72-79. Charleston, SC: S. G. Courtenay, 1859.

8077. Schroeder, Oliver, Jr. "Life and Judicial Work of Justice William Johnson, Jr." *University of Pennsylvania Law Review* 95 (December 1946): 164-201.

Writings

8078. Johnson, William. *Sketches of the Life and Correspondence of Nathanael Greene.* 2 vols. Charleston, SC: A. E. Miller, 1822.

Anthony Kennedy

General Studies

8079. Bell, Robin O. "Justice Anthony M. Kennedy: Will His Appointment to the United States Supreme Court Have an Impact on Employment Discrimination?" *University of Cincinnati Law Review* 57 (1989): 1037-1071.

8080. Biskupic, Joan. "Justice Kennedy: The Fifth Vote." *Congressional Quarterly Weekly Report* 47 (February 6, 1989): 1695.

8081. Cohodas, Nadine. "Cautious Senate Wants to Like Judge Kennedy." *Congressional Quarterly Weekly Report* 45 (November 14, 1987): 2786-2788.

8082. Cohodas, Nadine. "Kennedy Hearings Indicate Easy Confirmation." *Congressional Quarterly Weekly Report* 45 (December 19, 1987): 3129-3133.

8083. Hale, Vicky C. "Abortion Waiting Period Statutes: *Hartigan v. Zbaraz*: 108 S. Ct. 479: And Justice Anthony Kennedy's Impact on Future Decisions." *Tulsa Law Journal* 24 (Winter 1988): 189-213.

8084. "A Survey of Justice Anthony Kennedy's Ninth Circuit International Law Opinions." *Connecticut Journal of International Law* 3 (Spring 1988): 501-512.

8085. Williams, Charles F. "The Opinions of Anthony Kennedy: No Time for Ideology." *American Bar Association Journal* 74 (March 1988): 56-61.

Joseph R. Lamar

General Studies

8086. Gilbert, S. Price. "The Lamars of Georgia: L.Q.C., Mirabeau B., and Joseph R. Lamar." *American Bar Association Journal* 34 (December 1948): 1100-1102, 1156-1158.

8087. Lamar, Clarinda P. *The Life of Joseph Rucker Lamar, 1857-1916*. New York: Putnam, 1926.

8088. Sibley, Samuel H. *Georgia's Contribution to Law: The Lamars*. New York: Newcomen Society of England, American Branch, 1948.

Writings

8089. Lamar, Joseph R. *A Century's Progress in Law*. Augusta, GA: Richards and Shaver, 1900.

8090. Lamar, Joseph R. "History of the Establishment of the Supreme Court of Georgia." *Report of the Georgia Bar Association* 24 (1907): 85-103.

Lucius Q. Lamar

General Studies

8091. Cate, Wirt A. *Lamar and the Frontier Hypothesis*. Baton Rouge: Franklin Press, 1935.

8092. Cate, Wirt A. *Lucius Q. C. Lamar: Secession and Reunion*. Chapel Hill: University of North Carolina Press, 1935.

8093. Gilbert, S. Price. "The Lamars of Georgia: L.Q.C., Mirabeau B., and Joseph R. Lamar." *American Bar Association Journal* 34 (December 1948): 1100-1102, 1156-1158.

8094. Halsell, Willie D. "Appointment of L.Q.C. Lamar to the Supreme Court: A Political Battle of Cleveland's Administration." *Mississippi Valley Historical Review* 28 (December 1941): 399-412.

8095. Halsell, Willie D. "The Friendship of L.Q.C. Lamar and Jefferson Davis." *Journal of Mississippi History* 6 (July 1944): 131-144.

8096. Halsell, Willie D. "L.Q.C. Lamar, Associate Justice of the Supreme Court." *Journal of Mississippi History* 5 (April 1943): 59-78.

8097. Halsell, Willie D. "L.Q.C. Lamar's Taylor Farm: An Experiment in Diversified Farming." *Journal of Mississippi History* 5 (January 1943): 185-196.

8098. Halsell, Willie D. "A Mississippi *Habeas Corpus* Case and Justice L.Q.C. Lamar." *Journal of Mississippi History* 4 (January 1942): 31-33.

8099. Hamilton, J. G. de Roulhac. "Lamar of Mississippi." *Virginia Quarterly Review* 8 (January 1932): 77-89.

8100. Hill, Walter B. "L.Q.C. Lamar." *Green Bag* 5 (April 1893): 153-165.

8101. Hill, Walter B. "Sketch of Mr. Justice L. Q. C. Lamar." *Georgia Bar Association Report* 11 (1894): 149-169.

8102. Kennedy, John F. *Profiles in Courage.* New York: Harper, 1956.

8103. Knight, Lucian L. "L.Q.C. Lamar, of Mississippi." In *Reminiscences of Famous Georgians*, by Lucian L. Knight, 176-193. Atlanta: Franklin-Turner, 1907.

8104. Mayes, Edward. *Lucius Q. C. Lamar: His Life, Times, and Speeches; 1825-1893.* Nashville, TN: Publishing House of the Methodist Episcopal Church, South, 1896.

8105. Meador, Daniel J. "Lamar and the Law at the University of Mississippi." *Mississippi Law Journal* 34 (May 1963): 227-256.

8106. Morris, Clara. "Some Reminiscences of L.Q.C. Lamar." *Cosmopolitan* 36 (March 1904): 566-573.

8107. Murphy, James B. *L.Q.C. Lamar: Pragmatic Patriot.* Baton Rouge: Louisiana State University Press, 1973.

8108. Sibley, Samuel H. *Georgia's Contribution to Law: The Lamars.* New York: Newcomen Society of England, American Branch, 1948.

Henry B. Livingston

General Studies

8109. Bigelow, John. "A Chapter in Chancery of New Jersey: Livingston, Paterson, and Howell." *New Jersey Historical Society Proceedings* 54 (October 1936): 268-279.

8110. Davis, Curtis C. *The King's Chevalier.* New York: Bobbs-Merrill, 1961.

8111. Dunne, Gerald T. "The Story-Livingston Correspondence, 1812-1822." *American Journal of Legal History* 10 (July 1966): 224-236.

8112. Livingston, Edwin B. *The Livingstons of Livingston Manor.* New York: Knickerbocker Press, 1910.

8113. Troup, Robert. *A Letter to the Honorable Brockholst Livingston ... on the Lake Canal Policy of the State of New York, with a Supplement, and Additional Documents.* Albany, NY: Packard and Van Benthuysen, 1822.

Horace H. Lurton

General Studies

8114. Tucker, David M. "Justice Horace Harmon Lurton: The Shaping of a Natural Progressive." *American Journal of Legal History* 13 (July 1969): 223-232.

8115. Williams, Samuel C. "Judge Horace H. Lurton." *Tennessee Law Review* 18 (April 1944): 242-250.

John Marshall

General Studies

8116. Abbott, Lawrence F. "John Marshall and Constitution Day." *Outlook* 135 (September 26, 1923): 131-132.

8117. Abbott, Lawrence F. "John Marshall, the Democrat." In *Twelve Great Modernists*, edited by Lawrence F. Abbott, 125-147. New York: Doubleday, Page, 1927.

8118. Adams, James T. "John Marshall." *American Scholar* 1 (May 1932): 261-264.

8119. Adams, William H. "John Marshall." *Vermont Bar Association Proceedings* 49 (1955): 16.

8120. Anderson, Dice R. "The Teacher of Jefferson and Marshall." *South Atlantic Quarterly* 15 (October 1916): 327-342.

8121. Baker, Leonard. *John Marshall: A Life in Law*. New York: Macmillan, 1974.

8122. Barkley, Alben W. "The Lessons of John Marshall." *Federal Bar Association Journal* 3 (April 1937): 3-11.

8123. Barlin, Barbara. "John Marshall: Usurper or Grantee?" *Social Education* 22 (March 1958): 116-118, 121.

8124. Barre, W. L. "John Marshall." In *Lives of Illustrious Men of America: Distinguished in the Annals of the Republic as Legislators, Warriors, and Philosophers*, by W. L. Barre, 426-452. Cincinnati: W. A. Clarke, 1859.

8125. Bartosic, Florian. "With John Marshall from William and Mary to Dartmouth College." *William and Mary Law Review* 7 (May 1966): 259-266.

8126. Beck, James M. "The Memory of Marshall." *American Bar Association Journal* 21 (June 1935): 345-351.

8127. Belgrad, Eric A. "John Marshall's Contribution to American Neutrality Doctrines." *William and Mary Law Review* 9 (Winter 1967): 430-457.

8128. Bell, Landon C. "John Marshall: Albert J. Beveridge as a Biographer." *Virginia Law Register* 12 (February 1927): 640-655.

8129. Berger, Raoul. "Jefferson v. Marshall in the *Burr* Case." *American Bar Association Journal* 60 (June 1974): 702-706.

8130. Berger, Raoul. "Jefferson v. Marshall in the *Burr* Case." *American Business Law Journal* 14 (Winter 1977): 391-404.

8131. Beveridge, Albert J. "Commentaries on the Life of John Marshall." *Journal of Missouri Bar* 3 (June 1947): 115-117, 126-127.

8132. Beveridge, Albert J. "The Development of the American Constitution under John Marshall." *American Law Review* 61 (May/June 1927): 449-477.

8133. Beveridge, Albert J. "The Development of the American Constitution under John Marshall." *Michigan Bar Journal* 1 (March 1922): 121-133; (April 1922): 141-182.

8134. Beveridge, Albert J. "The Development of the American Constitution under John Marshall." *Minnesota Law Review* 7 (November 1922): 102-121.

8135. Beveridge, Albert J. "The Development of the Constitution under John Marshall." *American Law Review* 56 (November/December 1922): 921-948.

8136. Beveridge, Albert J. "The Development of the United States Constitution under John Marshall." In *Proceedings of the Bar Association of the State of New Hampshire, 1923*, 7-49. Concord, NH: Rumford Press, 1924.

8137. Beveridge, Albert J. "John Marshall: His Personality and Development." *Ohio Law Report* 14 (February 21, 1916): 24-32.

8138. Beveridge, Albert J. "John Marshall, the Man and the Lawyer." *Case and Comment* 23 (March 1917): 809-812.

8139. Beveridge, Albert J. *The Life of John Marshall.* 4 vols. Boston: Houghton Mifflin, 1916-1919.

8140. Binney, Horace. "Binney's Eulogy on Chief Justice Marshall." *American Jurist* 14 (October 1835): 462-465.

8141. Binney, Horace. *Eulogy on John Marshall Delivered at Philadelphia, September 24, 1835.* Chicago: Callaghan, 1900.

8142. Binney, Horace. *An Eulogy on the Life and Character of John Marshall, Chief Justice of the Supreme Court of the United States.* Philadelphia: J. Crissy and G. Goodman, 1835.

8143. Bischoff, Ralph F. "The Supreme Court Then and Now." *Albany Law Review* 20 (January 1956): 16-22.

8144. Bishop, H. O. "Chief Justice John Marshall, Transportation Expert." *American Bar Association Journal* 21 (March 1935): 184-185.

8145. Black, John C. "John Marshall." *Albany Law Journal* 54 (July 25, 1896): 55-62.

8146. Black, John C. "John Marshall." *Illinois State Bar Association Proceedings* 20, part 2 (July 14-15, 1896): 25-45.

8147. Bloch, Susan L., and Maeva Marcus. "John Marshall's Selective Use of History in *Marbury v. Madison.*" *Wisconsin Law Review* 1986 (1986): 301-337.

8148. Bonaparte, Charles J. *John Marshall as Lawyer and Judge.* Baltimore: Williams, 1901.

8149. Boudin, Louis B. "John Marshall and Roger B. Taney." *Georgetown Law Journal* 24 (May 1936): 864-909.

8150. Boyd, Julian P. "The Chasm That Separated Thomas Jefferson and John Marshall." In *Essays on the American Constitution: A Commemorative Volume in Honor of Alpheus T. Mason,* edited by Gottfried Dietze, 3-20. Englewood Cliffs, NJ: Prentice-Hall, 1964.

8151. Boynton, W. W. "John Marshall and the Western Reserve." *Western Reserve Law Journal* 7 (April 1901): 61-64.

8152. Bradley, Joseph P. "Saint Memin's Portrait of Marshall." *Century Magazine* 38 (September 1889): 778-781.

8153. Brant, Irving. "John Marshall and the Lawyers and Politicians." In *Chief Justice John Marshall: A Reappraisal,* edited by William M. Jones, 38-60. Ithaca, NY: Cornell University Press, 1956.

8154. Bronner, Frederick L. "John Marshall: A Layman's Approach." *Albany Law Journal* 20 (January 1956): 1-5.

8155. Brooks, Elbridge S. "The Story of John Marshall of Richmond, Called 'The Great Chief Justice'." In *Historic Americans: Sketches of the Lives and Characters of Certain Famous Americans Held Most in Reverence by the Boys and Girls of America,* by Elbridge S. Brooks, 161-174. New York: Crowell, 1899.

8156. Brown, Hugh H. "John Marshall." *Case and Comment* 23 (July 1916): 127-130.

8157. Brown, Neal. *Critical Confessions and John Marshall and His Times.* 2d ed. Wausau, WI: Philosopher Press, 1902.

8158. Browne, Irving. "John Marshall." In *Short Studies of Great Lawyers,* by Irving Browne, 201-217. Albany, NY: Albany Law Journal, 1878.

8159. Brownell, Herbert, Jr. "John Marshall, the Chief Justice." *Cornell Law Quarterly* 41 (Fall 1955): 93-104.

8160. Bryant, James R. *Eulogium on Chief Justice Marshall Delivered in the Unitarian Church, Washington City, on the 24th of September, 1835, at the Request of the Union Literary Society.* Washington, DC: Jacob Gideon, Jr., 1835.

8161. Burton, Harold H. "John Marshall: The Man." *University of Pennsylvania Law Review* 104 (October 1955): 3-8.

8162. Burton, Harold H. "Justice, the Guardian of Liberty: John Marshall at the Trial of Aaron Burr." *American Bar Association Journal* 37 (October 1951): 735-738.

8163. "Bust of John Marshall Placed in Hall of Fame." *American Bar Association Journal* 11 (June 1925): 381-382.

8164. Byran, George. *The Imperialism of John Marshall: A Study in Expediency.* Boston: Stratford, 1924.

8165. Caldwell, Russell L. "The Influence of the Federal Bar upon the Interpretation of the Constitution by the Supreme Court under John Marshall." Ph.D. diss., University of Southern California, 1948.

8166. Campbell, Bruce A. "John Marshall, the Virginia Political Economy, and the *Dartmouth College* Decision." *American Journal of Legal History* 19 (January 1975): 40-65.

8167. Campbell, Thomas P., Jr. "Chancellor Kent, Chief Justice Marshall, and the Steamboat Cases." *Syracuse Law Review* 25 (Spring 1974): 497-534.

8168. Carlton, Mabel M. *John Marshall, the Great Chief Justice.* Boston: John Hancock Mutual Life Insurance Company, 1925.

8169. Carney, J. C. "John Marshall." *Iowa State Bar Association Proceedings* 17 (1911): 59-73.

8170. Carson, Hampton L. "John Marshall." *Western Reserve Law Journal* 7 (March 1901): 31-47.

8171. Cassoday, John B. "John Scott and John Marshall." *American Law Review* 33 (January/February 1899): 1-27.

8172. Chesley, J. Harry. "The Ancestry of Chief Justice Marshall." *American Law Review* 35 (January/February 1901): 112-115.

8173. Conant, Harrison J. "John Marshall and the Recall." *Central Law Journal* 81 (August 1927): 147-154.

8174. Cook, Fred J. *Fighting for Justice: John Marshall.* Chicago: Kingston House, 1961.

8175. Cooke, John E. "Early Days of John Marshall." *Historical Magazine* 3 (June 1859): 165-169.

8176. Corwin, Edward S. *John Marshall and the Constitution: A Chronicle of the Supreme Court.* New Haven, CT: Yale University Press, 1919.

8177. Corwin, Edward S. "John Marshall, Revisionist *Malgre Lui*." *University of Pennsylvania Law Review* 104 (October 1955): 9-22.

8178. Coxe, Alfred C. "In Marshall's Day and Ours." *Columbia Law Review* 3 (February 1903): 88-107.

8179. Cozart, A. W. "Marshall and Taney: A Parallel." *Georgia Law Review* 1 (December 1927): 33-37.

8180. Craighill, Robert T. "John Marshall." In *The Virginia "Peerage": Sketches of Virginians*, by Robert T. Craighill, 231-284. Richmond, VA: Jones, 1880.

8181. Craigmyle, Thomas S. *John Marshall in Diplomacy and in Law.* New York: Charles Scribner's Sons, 1933.

8182. Crosskey, William W. "John Marshall and the Constitution." *University of Chicago Law Review* 23 (Spring 1956): 377-397.

8183. Crosskey, William W. *Mr. Chief Justice Marshall.* Chicago: University of Chicago Press, 1956.

8184. Cullen, Charles T. "New Light on John Marshall's Legal Education and His Admission to the Bar." *American Journal of Legal History* 16 (October 1972): 345-351.

8185. Cullen, Charles T. "St. George Tucker, John Marshall, and Constitutionalism in the Post-Revolutionary South." *Vanderbilt Law Review* 32 (January 1979): 341-345.

8186. Cuneo, John R. *John Marshall: Judicial Statesman.* New York: McGraw-Hill, 1975.

8187. Cunningham, Joe. *Remember John Marshall: A Biography of the Great Chief Justice.* Dallas: Biographic Press, 1956.

8188. Cushman, Robert E. "Marshall and the Constitution." *Minnesota Law Review* 5 (December 1920): 1-31.

8189. Custer, Lawrence B. "Bushrod Washington and John Marshall: A Preliminary Inquiry." *American Journal of Legal History* 4 (January 1960): 34-78.

8190. Dabney, Virginius. "He Made the Court Supreme." *Saturday Evening Post* 228 (September 24, 1955): 36, 121-122, 124.

8191. Day, Edward M. "John Marshall." *Connecticut Bar Journal* 9 (April 1935): 95-113.

8192. Deniston, Elinore. *John Marshall: Famous Makers of America.* New York: Dodd, Mead, 1963.

8193. Dewey, Donald O. *Marshall versus Jefferson: The Political Background of Marbury v. Madison.* New York: Knopf, 1970.

8194. Dickinson, Marquis Fayette, Jr. *John Marshall: The Tribute of Massachusetts: Being the Addresses Delivered at Boston and Cambridge February 4, 1901, in Commemoration of the One Hundredth Anniversary of His Elevation to the Bench as Chief Justice of the United States.* Boston: Little, Brown, 1901.

8195. Dillon, John F. "A Commemorative Address on Chief Justice Marshall." *American Law Review* 35 (March/April 1901): 161-189.

8196. Dillon, John F. *John Marshall: Life, Character, and Judicial Services as Portrayed in the Centenary and Memorial Addresses and Proceedings throughout the United States on Marshall Day, 1901, and in the Classic Orations of Binney, Story, Phelps, Waite, and Rawle.* 3 vols. Chicago: Callaghan, 1903.

8197. Dixon, Owen. "Marshall and the Australian Constitution." *Australian Law Journal* 29 (December 1955): 420-427.

8198. Dodd, William E. "Chief Justice Marshall and Virginia, 1813-1821." *American Historical Review* 12 (July 1907): 776-787.

8199. Dodd, William E. *Chief Justice Marshall and Virginia, 1813-1821.* New York: Macmillan, 1907.

8200. Donnan, Elizabeth, and Leo Stock, eds. "Senator Beveridge, J. Franklin Jameson, and John Marshall." *Mississippi Valley Historical Review* 35 (December 1948): 463-492; (March 1949): 639-673.

8201. Dorfman, Joseph. "John Marshall: Political Economist." In *Chief Justice John Marshall: A Reappraisal*, edited by William M. Jones, 124-144. Ithaca, NY: Cornell University Press, 1956.

8202. Douglas, William O. "John Marshall, A Life in Law: An Essay Review." *Louisiana History* 16 (Spring 1975): 193-200.

8203. Dumbauld, Edward. "John Marshall and the Law of Nations." *University of Pennsylvania Law Review* 104 (October 1955): 38-56.

8204. Dumbauld, Edward. "John Marshall and Treaty Law." *American Journal of International Law* 50 (January 1956): 69-80.

8205. Farr, Chester N., Jr. "John Marshall." *University of Pennsylvania Law Review* 42 (June 1894): 426-434.

8206. Faulkner, Robert K. "John Marshall and the Burr Trial." *Journal of*

American History 53 (September 1966): 247-258.

8207. Faulkner, Robert K. *The Jurisprudence of John Marshall.* Princeton, NJ: Princeton University Press, 1968.

8208. Finch, Francis M. *Chief Justice John Marshall.* Philadelphia: T. and J. W. Johnson, 1905.

8209. Finch, Francis M. "John Marshall." *Yale Law Journal* 10 (March 1901): 171-183.

8210. Flanders, Henry. "The Life of John Marshall." *The Dial* 6 (May 1885): 10-12.

8211. Flanders, Henry. *The Life of John Marshall.* Philadelphia: T. and J. W. Johnson, 1905.

8212. Foran, William A. "John Marshall as a Historian." *American Historical Review* 43 (October 1937): 51-64.

8213. Fordham, Jefferson B., and Theodore Husted, Jr. "John Marshall and the Rule of Law." *University of Pennsylvania Law Review* 104 (October 1955): 57-68.

8214. Frankfurter, Felix. *The Commerce Clause under Marshall, Taney, and White.* Chapel Hill: University of North Carolina Press, 1937.

8215. Frankfurter, Felix. "John Marshall and the Judicial Function." *Harvard Law Review* 69 (December 1955): 217-238.

8216. Frierson, William L. "Chief Justice John Marshall." *Tennessee Law Review* 12 (April 1934): 167-173.

8217. Frisch, Morton J. "John Marshall's Philosophy of Constitutional Republicanism." *Review of Politics* 20 (January 1958): 34-45.

8218. Gaines, Clarence H. "John Marshall and the Spirit of America." *North American Review* 205 (February 1917): 287-292.

8219. Gaines, William H., Jr. "Bench, Bar, and Barbecue Club." *Virginia Cavalcade* 5 (Autumn 1955): 8-13.

8220. Garvey, Gerald. "The Constitutional Revolution of 1837 and the Myth of Marshall's Monolith." *Western Political Quarterly* 18 (March 1965): 27-34.

8221. Goebel, Julius, Jr. "The Common Law and the Constitution." In *Chief Justice John Marshall: A Reappraisal*, edited by William M. Jones, 101-123. Ithaca, NY: Cornell University Press, 1956.

8222. Gordon, Douglas H. "John Marshall: The Fourth Chief Justice." *American Bar Association Journal* 41 (August 1955): 698-702, 766-771.

8223. Green, John W. "How Some Famous Men Came to Be Lawyers." *Tennessee Law Review* 20 (April 1948): 223-230.

8224. Griswold, Rufus W. "John Marshall." In *Homes of American Statesmen: With Anecdotical, Personal, and Descriptive Sketches, by Various Writers*, edited by Rufus W. Griswold, 263-274. New York: A. W. Upham, 1858.

8225. Griswold, Rufus W. "John Marshall." In *The Prose Writers of America*, edited by Rufus W. Griswold, 85-88. Philadelphia: Carey and Hart, 1847.

8226. Gunther, Gerald, ed. *John Marshall's Defense of McCulloch v. Maryland.* Stanford, CA: Stanford University Press, 1969.

8227. Hardy, Sallie E. "Chief Justice John Marshall." *Magazine of American History* 12 (July 1884): 62-71.

8228. Hardy, Sallie E. "John Marshall, Third Chief Justice of the United States, as Son, Brother, Husband, and Friend." *Green Bag* 8 (December 1896): 479-492.

8229. Hardy, Sallie E. "The Will of a Great Lawyer: How Chief Justice Marshall Devised His Estates." *Green Bag* 8 (January 1896): 4-6.

8230. Haskins, George L. "John Marshall

and the Commerce Clause of the Constitution." *University of Pennsylvania Law Review* 104 (October 1955): 23-68.

8231. Haskins, George L., and Herbert A. Johnson. *Foundations of Power: John Marshall, 1801-1815. The History of the Supreme Court of the United States*, edited by Paul A. Freund and Stanley N. Katz, vol. 5. New York: Macmillan, 1981.

8232. Hatcher, William H. "John Marshall and States' Rights." *Solicitor Quarterly* 3 (April 1965): 207-216.

8233. Haymond, Frank C. "John Marshall: His Influence on the Constitution and the Courts." *West Virginia Law Quarterly* 42 (December 1935): 14-30.

8234. Hedrick, Charles E. "John Marshall and the West." *Marshall Review* 1 (1937): 42-47.

8235. Hildreth, Melvin A. "John Marshall." *Bar Briefs* 12 (January 1936): 175-177.

8236. Holcombe, Arthur N. "John Marshall as Politician and Political Theorist, 1788-1835." In *Chief Justice John Marshall: A Reappraisal*, edited by William M. Jones, 24-37. Ithaca, NY: Cornell University Press, 1956.

8237. Hooker, Richard J., ed. "John Marshall on the Judiciary, the Republicans, and Jefferson, March 4, 1801." *American Historical Review* 53 (April 1948): 518-520.

8238. Houghton, Walter R. "John Marshall." In *Kings of Fortune*, by Walter R. Houghton, 437-456. Chicago: A. E. Davis, 1885.

8239. Hughes, Robert M. "Chief Justice John Marshall and His Work." In *Genesis and Birth of the Federal Constitution: Addresses and Papers in the Marshall-Wythe School of Government and Citizenship of the College of William and Mary*, edited by J.A.C. Chandler, 351-374. New York: Macmillan, 1924.

8240. Isaacs, Nathan. "John Marshall on Contracts: Study in Early American Juristic Theory." *Virginia Law Review* 7 (March 1921): 413-428.

8241. Jaeger, Walter. "John Marshall: The Man, the Judge, and the Law of Nations." *American University Law Review* 8 (January 1959): 28-33.

8242. "John Marshall." *Albany Law Journal* 13 (June 24, 1876): 442-445.

8243. "John Marshall: Judge and Jurist." *Green Bag* 13 (May 1901): 213-267.

8244. "John Marshall: Soldier, Lawyer, Statesman, and Man." *Green Bag* 13 (April 1901): 157-195.

8245. Johnson, Herbert A. "The Tribulations of Conway Robinson, Jr.: John Marshall's 'Washington Lotts'." *Virginia Magazine of History and Biography* 79 (October 1971): 427-435.

8246. Jones, Francis R. "John Marshall." *Green Bag* 13 (February 1901): 53-64.

8247. Jones, William M., ed. *Chief Justice John Marshall: A Reappraisal*. Ithaca, NY: Cornell University Press, 1956.

8248. Karst, Kenneth L. "Justice Marshall and the First Amendment." *Black Law Journal* 6 (Fall 1979): 26-42.

8249. Kaufman, Irving R. "John Marshall: A Dedication." *Fordham Law Review* 24 (Autumn 1955): xi-xvii.

8250. Keeble, John B. "Influence of John Marshall on American Jurisprudence." *Tennessee Bar Association Proceedings* 32 (1913): 169-196.

8251. Keefe, Arthur J. "John Marshall, Magnificent Mugwump." *Catholic University of America Law Review* 6 (December 1956): 103-115.

8252. Kerr, Charles. "If Spencer Roane Had Been Appointed Chief Justice Instead of John Marshall." *American Bar Association Journal* 20 (March 1934): 167-172.

8253. Klinkhamer, Marie C. "John Marshall's Use of History." *Catholic University of America Law Review* 6 (December 1956): 78-96.

8254. Konefsky, Samuel J. *John Marshall and Alexander Hamilton: Architects of the American Constitution.* New York: Macmillan, 1967.

8255. Kurland, Philip B., ed. *James Bradley Thayer, Oliver Wendell Holmes, and Felix Frankfurter on John Marshall.* Chicago: University of Chicago Press, 1967.

8256. Kutler, Stanley I., ed. *John Marshall.* Englewood Cliffs, NJ: Prentice-Hall, 1972.

8257. Lerner, Max. "John Marshall and the Campaign of History." *Columbia Law Review* 39 (March 1939): 396-431.

8258. Lerner, Max. "John Marshall's Long Shadow." In *Ideas Are Weapons: The History and Uses of Ideas*, edited by Max Lerner, 27-37. New York: Viking Press, 1939.

8259. Levy, Martin L. "Supreme Court in Retreat: Wealth Discrimination and Mr. Justice Marshall." *Texas Southern University Law Review* 4 (Spring 1977): 209-242.

8260. Lewis, William D. "John Marshall." In *Great American Lawyers*, vol. 2, edited by William D. Lewis, 311-408. Philadelphia: J. C. Winston Company, 1907-1909.

8261. Libby, Charles F. *John Marshall: An Address Delivered at . . . [Bowdoin] College on February 4, 1901, the Centenary of the Installation of John Marshall as Chief Justice of the United States.* Brunswick, ME: Bowdoin College, 1901.

8262. Lodge, Henry C. *An Address upon Chief Justice Marshall, Delivered at the Auditorium in Chicago on the Fourth Day of February 1901, at the Request of the Bar Associations of the State of Illinois and the City of Chicago.* Washington, DC: Pearson Printing Office, 1901.

8263. Lossing, Benson J. "John Marshall." In *Eminent Americans*, by Benson J. Lossing, 216-218. New York: Hurst, 1886.

8264. Loth, David G. *Chief Justice: John Marshall and the Growth of the Republic.* New York: W. W. Norton, 1949.

8265. McCabe, James D. "John Marshall." In *Great Fortunes*, edited by James D. McCabe, 417-434. Cincinnati: Hannaford, 1871.

8266. McClain, Emlin. "Chief Justice Marshall as a Constructive Statesman." *Iowa Journal of History* 1 (October 1903): 427-466.

8267. MacDonald, William. "The Indebtedness of John Marshall to Alexander Hamilton." *Massachusetts Historical Society Proceedings* 46 (May 1913): 412-426.

8268. McGinty, Brian. "The Great Chief Justice." *American History Illustrated* 21 (September 1986): 8-14, 46-47.

8269. McKenna, Daniel J. "John Marshall, the Man." *University of Detroit Law Journal* 34 (October 1956): 70-74.

8270. McLaughlin, Andrew C. "The Life of John Marshall." *American Bar Association Journal* 7 (May 1921): 231-233.

8271. MacVeagh, Wayne. *John Marshall: An Address, Delivered upon the Invitation of the American Bar Association and a Joint Committee of the Congress in the Hall of the House of Representatives, February 4, 1901.* Washington, DC: Judd and Detweiler, 1901.

8272. Magruder, Allan B. *John Marshall.* Boston: Houghton Mifflin, 1985.

8273. Maltbie, William M. "John Marshall: A Tribute." *Connecticut Bar Journal* 29 (December 1955): 335-349.

8274. Marshall, Maria N. "The Marshall

Memorial Tablet." *Green Bag* 14 (August 1902): 372-373.

8275. Martini, Teri. *John Marshall.* Philadelphia: Westminster Press, 1974.

8276. Mason, Francis N. *My Dearest Polly: Letters of Chief Justice Marshall to His Wife, with Their Background, Political and Domestic, 1779-1831.* Richmond, VA: Garrett and Massie, 1961.

8277. Means, D. M. "Chief Justice John Marshall." *The Nation* 72 (February 7, 1901): 104-105.

8278. Mendelson, Wallace. "Chief Justice John Marshall and the Mercantile Tradition." *Southwestern Social Science Quarterly* 29 (June 1948): 27-37.

8279. Mendelson, Wallace. "John Marshall's Short Way with Statutes: A Study in the Judicial Use of Legislation to Expound the Constitution." *Kentucky Law Journal* 36 (March 1948): 284-289.

8280. Moore, Frank. "John Marshall." In *American Eloquence*, vol. 2, edited by Frank Moore, 1-32. New York: D. Appleton, 1862.

8281. Moore, John B. *John Marshall.* Boston: Ginn and Company, 1901.

8282. Morgan, Donald G. "Marshall, the Marshall Court, and the Constitution." In *Chief Justice John Marshall: A Reappraisal*, edited by William M. Jones, 168-185. Ithaca, NY: Cornell University Press, 1956.

8283. Morison, S. E. "The Education of John Marshall." *Atlantic* 126 (July 1920): 45-54.

8284. Moses, Adolph. "The Friendship between Marshall and Story." *American Law Review* 35 (May/June 1901): 321-342.

8285. Moses, Adolph. *How to Celebrate "John Marshall Day".* Chicago: Illinois Bar Association, 1900.

8286. Moses, Belle. *John Marshall, Our Greatest Chief Justice.* New York: Appleton-Century, 1938.

8287. Munro, William B. "John Marshall and the Achievement of Nationalism." In *The Makers of the Unwritten Constitution*, edited by William B. Munro, 53-84. New York: Macmillan, 1930.

8288. Nelson, William E. "The Eighteenth Century Background of John Marshall's Constitutional Jurisprudence." *Michigan Law Review* 76 (May 1978): 893-960.

8289. Nurick, Gilbert. "Impeach John Marshall." *North Carolina Central Law Journal* 2 (Spring 1970): 100-109.

8290. Nutting, Charles B. "John Marshall and the Federal Union." *Carnegie Magazine* 29 (September 1955): 232-235.

8291. Oliver, Andrew. *The Portraits of John Marshall.* Charlottesville: University Press of Virginia, 1976.

8292. Olney, Richard. "Chief Justice Marshall." *Outlook* 67 (March 9, 1901): 573-576.

8293. Olney, Warren. "Chief Justice Marshall." *American Law Review* 34 (July/August 1900): 550-561.

8294. Padover, Saul K. "Political Ideas of John Marshall." *Social Research* 26 (Spring 1959): 47-70.

8295. Palmer, Ben W. *Marshall and Taney: Statesmen of the Law.* New York: Russell and Russell, 1966.

8296. Paulding, William I. "A Contribution to History." *Lippincott's Magazine* 2 (December 1868): 623-626.

8297. Perkins, Charles E. "Celebration of John Marshall Day in Connecticut." *Yale Law Journal* 10 (March 1901): 187-203.

8298. Perry, Benjamin F. "John Marshall." In *Biographical Sketches of Eminent American Statesmen*, by Benjamin F.

Perry, 467-477. Philadelphia: Ferree Press, 1887.

8299. Phelps, Edward J. *Chief Justice Marshall and the Constitutional Law of His Time: An Address before the American Bar Association at Saratoga, August 21, 1879.* Philadelphia: E. C. Malkley and Son, 1879.

8300. "Portrait." *Scholastic* 30 (March 6, 1937): 17.

8301. Powell, Lewis F., Jr. "Three Giants of the Law." *American Bar Association Journal* 50 (February 1964): 158-161.

8302. Powell, Thomas R. "The Great Chief Justice: His Leadership in Judicial Review." *William and Mary Law Review* 2 (July 1955): 72-93.

8303. Prentice, E. Parmalee. "Chief Justice Marshall on Federal Regulations of Interstate Carriers." *Cleveland Bar Association Journal* 5 (February 1905): 77-106.

8304. Proctor, L. B. "Jefferson's Contempt of Chief Justice Marshall's Opinions." *Albany Law Journal* 44 (October 24, 1891): 342-343.

8305. Purcell, Richard J. "Marshall v. Taney." *Catholic Education Review* (1940): 160-170.

8306. Ramage, C. J. "John Marshall." *Central Law Journal* 92 (May 13, 1921): 336-339.

8307. Rawle, William. *Unveiling of the Statue of Chief Justice Marshall, at Washington, May 10, 1884 Oration.* Philadelphia: Allen, Lane, and Scott's Printing House, 1884.

8308. Rhode Island Bar Association. *John Marshall Day: Celebration by the Rhode Island Bar Association and Brown University, February 4, 1901: Address by Le Baron Bradford Colt.* Providence: Rhode Island Printing Company, 1901.

8309. Rhodes, Irwin S., ed. *The Papers of John Marshall, a Descriptive Calendar.* Norman: University of Oklahoma Press.

8310. Richards, Gale L. "Alexander Hamilton's Influence on John Marshall's Judiciary Speech in the 1788 Virginia Federal Ratifying Convention." *Quarterly Journal of Speech* 44 (February 1958): 31-39.

8311. Richards, Gale L. "A Criticism of the Public Speaking of John Marshall Prior to 1801." Ph.D. diss., State University of Iowa, 1954.

8312. Richards, Gale L. "Invention in John Marshall's Legal Speaking." *Southern Speech Journal* 19 (December 1953): 108-115.

8313. Roberts, William A. "John Marshall and the New Deal." *Federal Bar Association Journal* 2 (April 1934): 33-36.

8314. Roche, John P. *John Marshall: Major Opinions and Other Writings.* Indianapolis: Bobbs-Merrill, 1966.

8315. Rodell, Fred. "The Great Chief Justice." *American Heritage* 7 (December 1955): 10-13, 106-111.

8316. Roosevelt, Theodore. "Beveridge's *Life of Marshall*: A Review." *Outlook* 116 (July 18, 1917): 448-449.

8317. Russell, Alfred. "John Marshall." *American Law Review* 35 (January/February 1901): 1-7.

8318. Seddig, Robert G. "John Marshall and the Origins of Supreme Court Leadership." *University of Pittsburgh Law Review* 36 (Summer 1975): 785-835.

8319. Servies, James A., comp. *A Bibliography of John Marshall.* Washington, DC: U.S. Commission for the Celebration of the Two Hundreth Anniversary of the Birth of John Marshall, 1956.

8320. Severn, William. *John Marshall, the Man Who Made the Court Supreme.* New York: David McKay, 1969.

8321. Shinn, Preston A. "Chief Justice

Marshall and the American Indian." *Case and Comment* 23 (March 1917): 842-843.

8322. Small, Joseph. "Bicentennial of Chief Justice Marshall." *America* 93 (September 17, 1955): 588-589.

8323. Smyth, Clifford. *John Marshall, Father of the Supreme Court.* New York: Funk and Wagnalls Company, 1931.

8324. Speer, Emory. *Exercises on the Evening of February 4, 1901, in the U.S. District Courtroom at Savannah in Honor of the Memory of Chief Justice John Marshall.* Macon, GA: Burke, 1901.

8325. Stanard, Mary N. *John Marshall: An Address.* Richmond, VA: William Ellis Jones's Sons Printers, 1913.

8326. Stebbins, Calvin. *John Marshall: A Discourse.* Framingham, MA: Printed by request, 1901.

8327. Steinberg, Alfred. *John Marshall.* New York: Putnam, 1962.

8328. Stinson, Joseph W. "Marshall and the Supremacy of the Unwritten Law." *American Law Review* 58 (November/December 1924): 856-871.

8329. Stinson, Joseph W. "Marshall on the Jurisdiction of the Littoral Sovereign over Territorial Waters." *American Law Review* 57 (July/August 1923): 567-578.

8330. Stites, Francis. *John Marshall: Defender of the Constitution.* Boston: Little, Brown, 1981.

8331. Story, Joseph. *Discourse upon the Life, Character, and Services of the Honorable John Marshall.* Boston: J. Munroe, 1835.

8332. Strong, Frank R. "John Marshall: Hero or Villain?" *Ohio State Law Journal* 6 (December 1939): 42-62; (March 1940): 158-189.

8333. Suddath, R. L. "Life and Services of John Marshall." *Oklahoma State Bar Journal* 7 (June 1936): 56-60.

8334. Surrency, Erwin C., ed. *The Marshall Reader: The Life and Contributions of Chief Justice John Marshall.* New York: Oceana Publications, 1955.

8335. Sutherland, Arthur E., Jr., ed. *Government under Law: A Conference Held at Harvard Law School on the Occasion of the Bicentennial of Justice Marshall.* Cambridge: Harvard University Press, 1956.

8336. Swindler, William F. *The Constitution and Chief Justice Marshall.* New York: Dodd, Mead, 1979.

8337. Swindler, William F. "John Marshall's Preparation for the Bar: Some Observations on His Law Notes." *American Journal of Legal History* 11 (April 1967): 207-273.

8338. Swindler, William F. "See Marshall Exhibit at Supreme Court Building." *American Bar Association Journal* 59 (July 1973): 746-748.

8339. Swisher, Carl B. "The Achievement of John Marshall." *Thought* 31 (Spring 1956): 5-26.

8340. Thayer, James B. *John Marshall.* Boston: Houghton Mifflin, 1901.

8341. Thompson, William D. "John Marshall: His Constitutional Decisions." *Marquette Law Review* 7 (April 1923): 111-130.

8342. Thorpe, Francis N. "Hamilton's Ideas in Marshall's Decisions." *Boston University Law Review* 1 (April 1921): 60-98.

8343. Tillet, Paul. "Mr. Justice Black, Chief Justice Marshall, and the Commerce Clause." *Nebraska Law Review* 43 (December 1963): 1-26.

8344. Tucker, Caroline. *John Marshall, the Chief Justice.* New York: Ariel Books, 1962.

8345. Tunstall, Robert B. "John Marshall: One Hundred Years After." *Ameri-*

can Bar Association Journal 21 (September 1935): 561-567.

8346. Turner, Kathryn. "The Appointment of Chief Justice Marshall." *William and Mary Quarterly* 17 (April 1960): 143-163.

8347. Umbanhowar, Charles E. "Marshall on Judging." *American Journal of Legal History* 7 (July 1963): 210-227.

8348. Umbreit, Kenneth B. "Review of the Commerce Clause under Marshall, Taney, and White by Felix Frankfurter." *American Bar Association Journal* 23 (September 1937): 706.

8349. Waite, Catharine V. "John Marshall." *Chicago Law Times* 1 (April 1887): 109-121.

8350. Warren, Aldice G. "A Comparison of the Tendencies in Constitutional Construction Shown by the Supreme Court under Chief Justices Marshall and Taney Respectively." Ph.D. diss., New York University, 1913.

8351. Warren, Charles. *The Story-Marshall Correspondence.* New York: New York University School of Law, 1942.

8352. Warren, Earl. "Chief Justice John Marshall: A Heritage of Freedom and Stability." *American Bar Association Journal* 41 (November 1955): 1008-1010.

8353. Warren, Earl. "Chief Justice Marshall: The Expounder of the Constitution." *American Bar Association Journal* 41 (August 1955): 687.

8354. White, Edward J. "The Life of John Marshall." *American Law Review* 55 (July 1921): 503-511.

8355. White, G. Edward. *The Marshall Court and Cultural Change: 1815-35. The History of the Supreme Court of the United States,* edited by Paul A. Freund and Stanley N. Katz, vols. 3-4. New York: Macmillan, 1988.

8356. Williams, George H. *Address on John Marshall, Delivered by Honorable George H. Williams before the Legislative Assembly of the State of Oregon, February 4, 1901.* Salem, OR: W. H. Leeds, 1901.

8357. Wilson, Andrew. "The Influence of John Marshall on the Political History of the U.S." Ph.D. diss., George Washington University, 1904.

8358. Wilson, Henry H. "The Influence of Chief Justice Marshall on American Institutions." *Nebraska Law Bulletin* 6 (February 1928): 327-354.

8359. Wilson, John R. "John Marshall." *American Law Review* 22 (September/October 1988): 706-730.

8360. Wolfe, Christopher. "John Marshall and Constitutional Law." *Polity* 15 (Spring 1982): 5-25.

8361. Woodbridge, Dudley W. "John Marshall in Perspective." *Pennsylvania Bar Association Quarterly* 27 (January 1956): 192-204.

8362. Ziegler, Benjamin M. *The International Law of John Marshall: A Study in First Principles.* Chapel Hill: University of North Carolina Press, 1939.

Writings

8363. Marshall, John. *An Autobiographical Sketch by John Marshall: Written at the Request of Joseph Story.* Edited by John S. Adams. Ann Arbor: University of Michigan Press, 1937.

8364. Marshall, John. *Complete Constitutional Decisions.* Edited by John M. Dillon. Chicago: Callaghan, 1903.

8365. Marshall, John. *The Constitutional Decisions of John Marshall.* 2 vols. Edited by Joseph P. Cotton, Jr. New York: Putnam's, 1905.

8366. Marshall, John. *Day: Centennial Proceedings of the Chicago Bar, February 4, 1901; Including Proceedings before the*

Supreme Court of Illinois. Chicago: Press of Hollister Brothers, 1901.

8367. Marshall, John. *A History of the Colonies Planted by the English on the Continent of North America, from Their Settlement, to the Commencement of That War Which Terminated in Their Independence.* Philadelphia: A. Small, 1824.

8368. Marshall, John. "John Marshall on the French Revolution and on American Politics." Edited by Jack L. Cross. *Wisconsin Law Review* 12 (October 1955): 631-649.

8369. Marshall, John. "A Letter of Marshall to Jefferson, 1783 by R. G. Thwaites." *American Historical Review* 10 (July 1905): 815-817.

8370. Marshall, John. "Letters from John Marshall to His Wife." *William and Mary Quarterly* 3 (April 1923): 73-90.

8371. Marshall, John. *Letters of Joseph Story.* New York: Macmillan, 1958.

8372. Marshall, John. *The Life of George Washington.* Compiled by Bushrod Washington. 5 vols. Philadelphia: C. P. Wayne, 1804-1807.

8373. Marshall, John. "Marshall-Story Correspondence." *Massachusetts Historical Society Proceedings* 14 (1901): 324-360.

8374. Marshall, John. *Papers of John Marshall.* 2 vols. Norman: University of Oklahoma Press, 1969.

8375. Marshall, John. *The Papers of John Marshall.* 4 vols. Edited by Herbert A. Johnson and Charles T. Cullen. Chapel Hill: University of North Carolina Press, 1974-1984.

8376. Marshall, John. *The Political and Economic Doctrines of John Marshall, Who for Thirty-four Years Was Chief Justice of the United States, and Also His Letters, Speeches, and Hitherto Unpublished and Uncollected Writings.* Edited by John E. Oster. New York: Neale Publishing Company, 1914.

8377. Marshall, John. *The Writing of John Marshall upon the Federal Constitution.* Boston: J. Munroe, 1839.

Thurgood Marshall

General Studies

8378. Bazelon, David L. "Humanizing the Criminal Process: Some Decisions of Mr. Justice Marshall." *Black Law Journal* 6 (Fall 1979): 3-11.

8379. Bergan, Francis. "Marshall, the Constitution, and the Common Law." *Alabama Lawyer* 25 (June 1974): 702-706.

8380. Bland, Randall W. "Examination of the Legal Career of Thurgood Marshall Prior to His Elevation to the Supreme Court of the United States, 1934-1967." Ph.D. diss., Notre Dame University, 1971.

8381. Bland, Randall W. "Justice Thurgood Marshall: An Analysis of His First Years on the Court, 1967-1971." *North Carolina Central Law Journal* 4 (Spring 1973): 183-202.

8382. Bland, Randall W. *Private Pressure on Public Law: Legal Career of Justice Thurgood Marshall.* Port Washington, NY: Kennikat Press, 1973.

8383. Carter, Robert L. "Mr. Justice Marshall: Some Private Reflections." *Bombay Law Journal* 6 (1979): 12-22.

8384. Contee, Clarence G. "Teacher, Healer, Lawyer: The Supreme Court Bar's First Black Member." *Supreme Court Historical Society Yearbook* 1976 (1976): 82-85.

8385. Daniels, William J. "Thurgood Marshall and the Administration of Criminal Justice: An Analysis of Dissenting

Opinions." *Black Law Journal* 6 (Fall 1979): 43-66.

8386. Davenport, Ronald R. "The Second Justice Marshall." *Duquesne Law Review* 7 (Fall 1968): 44-60.

8387. Galie, Peter J., and Lawrence P. Galie. "State Constitutional Guarantees and Supreme Court Review: Justice Marshall's Proposal in *Oregon v. Hass.*" *Dickinson Law Review* 82 (Winter 1978): 273-293.

8388. Kaufman, Irving R. "Thurgood Marshall: A Tribute from a Former Colleague." *Black Law Journal* 6 (Fall 1979): 23-25.

8389. Laurence, Robert. "Thurgood Marshall's Indian Law Opinions." *Howard Law Journal* 27 (Winter 1984): 3-89.

8390. Ripple, Kenneth F. "Thurgood Marshall and the Forgotten Legacy of *Brown v. Board of Education.*" *Notre Dame Law Review* 55 (April 1980): 471-484.

8391. Roy, Jessie H. "Pin Point Portrait of Attorney Thurgood Marshall." *Negro History Bulletin* 25 (1961): 20.

8392. Stone, Geoffrey R. "Marshall: He's the Frustrated Conscience of the High Court." *National Law Journal* 2 (February 18, 1980): 24.

8393. Watson, Denton L. "Civil Rights Law: Concept to Reality." *Crisis* 86 (June/July 1979): 233-239.

8394. "Where Are They Now?" *Newsweek* 63 (May 11, 1964): 16.

8395. Williams, Jamye C. "Rhetorical Analysis of Thurgood Marshall's Arguments before the Supreme Court in the Public School Segregation Controversy." Ph.D. diss., Ohio State University, 1959.

8396. Wilson, Margaret B., and Diane Ridley. "A New Birth of Liberty: The Role of Thurgood Marshall's Civil Con-

tribution." *Bombay Law Journal* 6 (1979): 67-87.

8397. Young, Margaret B. *The Picture Life of Thurgood Marshall.* New York: Watts, 1971.

Writings

8398. Marshall, Thurgood. "The Continuing Challenge of the Fourteenth Amendment." *Georgia Law Review* 3 (Fall 1968): 1-10.

8399. Marshall, Thurgood. "The Continuing Challenge of the Fourteenth Amendment." *Wisconsin Law Review* 1968 (1968): 979-987.

8400. Marshall, Thurgood. "Dissent in the *Bakke* Case." *Freedomways* 18 (1978): 127-135.

8401. Marshall, Thurgood. "Financing Public Interest Law Practice: The Role of the Organized Bar." *American Bar Association Journal* 61 (December 1975): 1487-1491.

8402. Marshall, Thurgood. "Group Action in the Pursuit of Justice." *New York University Law Review* 44 (October 1969): 661-672.

8403. Marshall, Thurgood. "Justice Thurgood Marshall's Opinion in the *Bakke* Case." *Crisis* 86 (February 1979): 45-50.

8404. Marshall, Thurgood. "Mr. Justice Murphy and Civil Rights." *Michigan Law Review* 48 (February 1950): 745-766.

8405. Marshall, Thurgood. "Mr. Justice Murphy and Civil Rights." *National Bar Journal* 9 (March 1951): 1-25.

8406. Marshall, Thurgood. "Remarks on the Death Penalty Made at the Judicial Conference of the Second Circuit." *Columbia Law Review* 86 (January 1986): 1-8.

8407. Marshall, Thurgood. "Search and

Seizure: A New Horizon: Dissent by Mr. Justice Marshall in *United States v. Robinson*." *Contemporary Drug Problems* 3 (Spring 1974): 21-44.

8408. Marshall, Thurgood. "The Supreme Court as Protector of Civil Rights: Equal Protection of the Laws." *Annals of the American Academy of Political and Social Sciences* 275 (May 1951): 101-110.

8409. Marshall, Thurgood, and Roy Wilkins. "Interpretation of Supreme Court Decision and the NAACP Program." *Crisis* 86 (June/July 1979): 205-209.

Stanley Matthews

General Studies

8410. Helfman, Harold M. "The Contested Confirmation of Stanley Matthews to the United States Supreme Court." *Historical and Philosophical Society of Ohio* 8 (July 1958): 154-170.

8411. Jager, Ronald B. "Stanley Matthews for the Supreme Court: 'Lord Roscoe's' Downfall." *Cincinnati Historical Society Bulletin* 38 (Fall 1980): 191-208.

8412. "Stanley Matthews." *American Bar Association Report* 12 (1889): 360-367.

Writings

8413. Matthews, Stanley. *The Function of the Legal Profession in the Progress of Civilization.* Cincinnati: R. Clarke, 1881.

Joseph McKenna

General Studies

8414. "Joseph McKenna." *Case and Comment* 4 (March 1898): 109.

8415. McDevitt, Matthew. *Joseph McKenna, Associate Justice of the United States.* Washington, DC: Catholic University of America Press, 1946.

John McKinley

General Studies

8416. Hicks, Jimmie. "Associate Justice John McKinley: A Sketch." *Alabama Review* 18 (July 1965): 227-233.

8417. Levin, H. "John McKinley." In *The Lawyers and Law Makers of Kentucky*, by H. Levin, 150. Chicago: Lewis Publishing Company, 1897.

8418. Martin, John M. "John McKinley: Jacksonian Phase." *Alabama Historical Quarterly* 28 (Spring/Summer 1966): 7-31.

8419. Whatley, George C. "Justice John McKinley." *North Alabama History Association, Bulletin* 4 (1959): 15-18.

John McLean

General Studies

8420. Livingston, John. "Honorable John McLean." In *Portraits of Eminent Americans Now Living*, vol. 2, by John A. Livingstone, 789-796. New York: Cornish, Lamport, 1853.

8421. Longacre, James B., and James Herring. "John McLean." In *The National Portrait Gallery*, vol. 4, by James B. Longacre and James Herring, 257-262. Philadelphia: Robert E. Peterson and Company, 1839.

8422. Maury, Sarah M. "The Honourable John McLean, Associate-Justice in the Supreme Court of the United States." In *The Statesmen of America in 1846*, by Sarah M. Maury, 164-182. London: Brown, Green, and Longmans, 1847.

8423. Savage, John. "John McLean of Ohio." In *Our Living Representative Men*, by John Savage, 373-381. Philadelphia: Childs and Peterson, 1860.

8424. Weisenberger, Francis P. "John McLean, Postmaster-General." *Mississippi Valley Historical Review* 18 (June 1931): 23-33.

8425. Weisenberger, Francis P. *The Life of John McLean: A Politician on the United States Supreme Court.* Columbus: Ohio State University Press, 1937.

Writings

8426. McLean, John. *Letters of John McLean to John Teesdale.* Edited by William Salter. Oberlin, OH: Bibliotheca Sacra, 1899.

James C. McReynolds

General Studies

8427. Bates, Earnest S. "McReynolds, Roberts, and Hughes." *New Republic* 87 (July 1, 1936): 232.

8428. Birkby, Robert H. "Teaching Congress How to Do Its Work: Mr. Justice McReynolds and Maritime Torts." *Congressional Studies* 8 (1981): 11-20.

8429. Blaisdell, Donald P. "Mr. Justice James Clark McReynolds." Ph.D. diss., University of Wisconsin, 1948.

8430. Blaisdell, Doris A. "The Constitutional Law of Mr. Justice McReynolds." Ph.D. diss., University of Wisconsin, 1954.

8431. Collyer, Rita. *In Defense of the Constitution: Excerpts from Addresses and Opinions of the Chief Justices of the United States and an Excerpt from the Recent Mi-* nority *Opinion in the So-Called "Gold Clause" Case by Associate Justice McReynolds of the Supreme Court.* Washington, DC: n.p., 1935.

8432. Early, Stephen T. "James Clark McReynolds and the Judicial Process." Ph.D. diss., University of Virginia, 1952.

8433. Fletcher, R. V. "Mr. Justice McReynolds: An Appreciation." *Vanderbilt Law Review* 2 (December 1948): 35-46.

8434. Ganoe, John T. "The Passing of the Old Dissent." *Oregon Law Review* 21 (April 1942): 285-297.

8435. Howell, Ronald F. "Conservative Influence on Constitutional Development, 1923-1937: The Judicial Theory of Justices Van Devanter, McReynolds, Sutherland, and Butler." Ph.D. diss., Johns Hopkins University, 1952.

8436. Jones, Calvin P. "Kentucky's Irascible Conservative: Supreme Court Justice James Clark McReynolds." *Filson Club History Quarterly* 57 (January 1983): 20-30.

8437. McCraw, John B. "James Clark McReynolds and the Supreme Court, 1914-1941." Ph.D. diss., University of Texas, 1951.

8438. Ribble, F.D.G. "James Clark McReynolds." *Virginia Law Review* 32 (August 1946): 909.

8439. Schimmel, Barbara B. "The Judicial Policy of Mr. Justice McReynolds." Ph.D. diss., Yale Universiy, 1964.

Writings

8440. McReynolds, James C. "Address." *Tennessee Bar Association Proceedings* 54 (1935): 65.

8441. McReynolds, James C. "Remarks." *Tennessee Bar Association Proceedings* 42 (1923): 121.

8442. McReynolds, James C. "Speech." *Tennessee Bar Association Proceedings* 45 (1926): 132.

Samuel F. Miller

General Studies

8443. Clute, O. "Justice Samuel F. Miller." *Iowa Historical Record* 7 (April 1891): 90-95.

8444. "Death of Mr. Justice Miller." *American Law Review* 24 (November/December 1890): 997-1003.

8445. Fairman, Charles. "The Education of a Justice: Justice Bradley and Some of His Colleagues." *Stanford Law Review* 1 (January 1949): 217-255.

8446. Fairman, Charles. "Justice Miller and the Mortgaged Generation." *Iowa Law Review* 23 (March 1938): 351-378.

8447. Fairman, Charles. "Justice Samuel Miller: A Study of a Judicial Statesman." *Political Science Quarterly* 50 (March 1935): 15-44.

8448. Fairman, Charles. "Justice Samuel F. Miller and the Barbourville Debating Society." *Mississippi Valley Historical Review* 17 (March 1931): 595-601.

8449. Fairman, Charles. *Mr. Justice Miller and the Supreme Court, 1862-1890.* Cambridge: Harvard University Press, 1939.

8450. Fairman, Charles. "Samuel F. Miller: Justice of the Supreme Court, 1862-1890." *Vanderbilt Law Review* 10 (February 1957): 193-208.

8451. Gregory, Charles N. *Samuel Freeman Miller.* Iowa City: State Historical Society of Iowa, 1907.

8452. Gregory, Charles N. "Samuel Freeman Miller: Associate Justice of the Supreme Court of the United States." *Yale Law Journal* 17 (April 1908): 422-442.

8453. Herriott, Frank I. "Justice Samuel F. Miller and His First Circuit Court." *Annals of Iowa* 9 (July/October 1910): 539-545.

8454. Lathrop, Henry W. "Judge Miller's Appointment to the Supreme Court." *Iowa Historical Record* 7 (January 1891): 16-17.

8455. Levin, H. "Samuel F. Miller." In *The Lawyers and Law Makers of Kentucky*, by H. Levin, 151. Chicago: Lewis Publishing Company, 1897.

8456. Stern, Horace. "Samuel Freeman Miller." In *Great American Lawyers*, vol. 6, edited by William D. Lewis, 539-585. Philadelphia: J. C. Winston Company, 1907-1909.

8457. Strong, Henry. "Justice Samuel Freeman Miller." *Annals of Iowa* 3 (January 1894): 241-257.

8458. Swinford, Mac. "Mr. Justice Samuel Freeman Miller (1816-1873)." *Filson Club History Quarterly* 34 (January 1960): 35-44.

8459. Weidner, Paul A. "Justices Field and Miller: A Comparative Study in Judicial Attitudes and Values." Ph.D. diss., University of Michigan, 1959.

Writings

8460. Miller, Samuel F. *The Constitution and the Supreme Court of the United States of America: Addresses.* New York: D. Appleton, 1889.

8461. Miller, Samuel F. *Lectures on the Constitution of the United States.* New York: Banks and Brothers, 1891.

8462. Miller, Samuel F. "Oration." In *History of the Celebration of the One Hundredth Anniversary of the Promulgation of the Constitution of the United States*, edited by Hampton L. Carson, 262-290. Philadelphia: J. B. Lippincott Company, 1889.

8463. Miller, Samuel F. "The Removal of Judges and the Jury System." *Central Law Journal* 8 (January 10, 1879): 35-36.

8464. Miller, Samuel F. "The Study and Practice of the Law in the United States." *Law Times* 48 (January 1, 1870): 171.

8465. Miller, Samuel F. *The Supreme Court of the United States.* Washington, DC: W. H. Barnes, 1877.

Sherman Minton

General Studies

8466. Atkinson, David N. "From New Deal Liberal to Supreme Court Conservative: The Metamorphosis of Justice Sherman Minton." *Washington University Law Quarterly* 1975 (1975): 361-394.

8467. Atkinson, David N. "Justice Sherman Minton and Behavior Patterns Inside the Supreme Court." *Northwestern University Law Review* 69 (November/December 1975): 716-739.

8468. Atkinson, David N. "Justice Sherman Minton and the Balance of Liberty." *Indiana Law Journal* 50 (Fall 1974): 34-59.

8469. Atkinson, David N. "Justice Sherman Minton and the Protection of Minority Rights." *Washington and Lee Law Review* 34 (Winter 1977): 97-117.

8470. Atkinson, David N. "Mr. Justice Minton and the Supreme Court, 1949-1956." Ph.D. diss., University of Iowa, 1969.

8471. Atkinson, David N. "Opinion Writing on the Supreme Court, 1949-1956: The Views of Justice Sherman Minton." *Temple Law Quarterly* 49 (Fall 1975): 105-118.

8472. Braden, George D. "Mr. Justice Minton and the Truman Bloc." *Indiana Law Journal* 26 (Winter 1951): 153-168.

8473. Hull, Elizabeth A. "Sherman Minton and the Cold War Court." Ph.D. diss., New School for Social Research, 1977.

8474. Lerner, Max. "Supreme Court." *Holiday* 7 (February 1950): 73-82, 119-122.

8475. Wallace, Henry L. "Mr. Justice Minton: Hoosier Justice on the Supreme Court." *Indiana Law Journal* 34 (Winter 1959): 145-205.

8476. Wallace, Henry L. "Mr. Justice Minton: Hoosier Justice on the Supreme Court." *Indiana Law Journal* 34 (Spring 1959): 377-424.

William H. Moody

General Studies

8477. Heffron, Paul T. "Profile of a Public Man." *Supreme Court Historical Society Yearbook* 1980 (1980): 30-31, 48.

8478. Heffron, Paul T. "Theodore Roosevelt and the Appointment of Mr. Justice Moody." *Vanderbilt Law Review* 18 (March 1965): 545-568.

8479. McDonough, Judith R. "William Henry Moody." Ph.D. diss., Auburn University, 1983.

8480. Morrow, James B. "The Honorable William H. Moody: The New Justice of the United States Supreme Court." *Law Students' Helper* 15 (February 1907): 42-46.

8481. Paradise, Scott H. *Men of the Old School.* Andover, MA: Phillips Academy, 1956.

8482. Whitelock, George. "Mr. Justice Moody, Lately Attorney General." *Green Bag* 21 (June 1909): 263-266.

8483. Wiener, Frederick B. "The Life and Judicial Career of William Henry Moody." Master's thesis, Harvard University Law School, 1937.

Alfred Moore

General Studies

8484. Davis, Junius. *Alfred Moore and James Iredell: Revolutionary Patriots and Associate Justices of the Supreme Court of the United States.* Raleigh: North Carolina Society of the Sons of the Revolution, 1899.

Francis W. Murphy

General Studies

8485. Arnold, Thurman W. "Mr. Justice Murphy." *Harvard Law Review* 63 (December 1949): 289-293.

8486. Barnett, Vincent M., Jr. "Mr. Justice Murphy, Civil Liberties, and the Holmes Tradition." *Cornell Law Quarterly* 32 (November 1946): 177-221.

8487. Bates, Henry M. "New Supreme Court Judge: An Appraisal." *American Bar Association Journal* 26 (January 1940): 107.

8488. Black, Hugo L. "Mr. Justice Murphy." *Michigan Law Review* 48 (February 1950): 739.

8489. Clark, Tom C. "Mr. Justice Murphy: A Review Article." *Michigan History* 53 (Fall 1969): 247-254.

8490. Clarke, Mary M. "Justice Murphy and the Problem of Civil Liberties." Ph.D. diss., Johns Hopkins University, 1952.

8491. Cox, Archibald. "The Influence of Mr. Justice Murphy on Labor Law." *Michigan Law Review* 48 (April 1950): 767-810.

8492. "Death of an Apostle." *Time* 54 (August 1, 1949): 12.

8493. Fahy, Charles. "Judicial Philosophy of Mr. Justice Murphy." *Yale Law Journal* 60 (May 1951): 812-820.

8494. Fine, Sidney. *Frank Murphy: The Detroit Years.* Ann Arbor: University of Michigan Press, 1975.

8495. Fine, Sidney. *Frank Murphy: The New Deal Years.* Chicago: University of Chicago Press, 1979.

8496. Fine, Sidney. "Frank Murphy, the *Thornhill* Decision, and Picketing as Free Speech." *Labor History* 6 (Spring 1965): 99-120.

8497. Fine, Sidney. *Frank Murphy: The Washington Years.* Ann Arbor: University of Michigan Press, 1984.

8498. Fine, Sidney. "Mr. Justice Murphy and the *Hirabayashi* Case." *Pacific Historical Review* 33 (May 1964): 195-209.

8499. Fine, Sidney. "Mr. Justice Murphy in World War II." *Journal of American History* 53 (June 1966): 90-106.

8500. Frank, John P. "Justice Murphy: The Goals Attempted." *Yale Law Journal* 58 (December 1949): 1-26.

8501. Gressman, Eugene. "The Catholic Issue and the Supreme Court." *U.S. News and World Report* 49 (October 24, 1960): 66-67.

8502. Gressman, Eugene. "The Controversial Image of Mr. Justice Murphy." *Georgetown Law Journal* 47 (Summer 1959): 631-654.

8503. Gressman, Eugene. "Mr. Justice Murphy: A Preliminary Appraisal." *Columbia Law Review* 50 (January 1950): 29-47.

8504. Gressman, Eugene, John H. Pickering, and T. L. Tolan, Jr. "Mr. Justice

Murphy, 1890-1949." *Michigan Law Review* 48 (February 1950): 742-744.

8505. Howard, J. Woodford, Jr. "Frank Murphy and the Philippine Commonwealth." *Pacific Historical Review* 33 (February 1964): 45-68.

8506. Howard, J. Woodford, Jr. "Frank Murphy and the Sit Down Strikes of 1937." *Labor History* 1 (Spring 1960): 103-140.

8507. Howard, J. Woodford, Jr. "Frank Murphy: A Liberal's Creed." Ph.D. diss., Princeton University, 1959.

8508. Howard, J. Woodford, Jr. "Justice Murphy: The Freshman Years." *Vanderbilt Law Review* 18 (March 1965): 473-505.

8509. Howard, J. Woodford, Jr. *Mr. Justice Murphy: A Political Biography.* Princeton, NJ: Princeton University Press, 1968.

8510. Huthmacher, J. Joseph. "Charles Evans Hughes and Francis Murphy: The Metamorphosis of Progressivism." *New York History* 46 (January 1965): 25-40.

8511. Irons, Peter. "Politics and Principle: An Assessment of the Roosevelt Record on Civil Rights and Liberties." *Washington Law Review* 59 (September 1984): 693-772.

8512. Jolly, James A. "The Social Philosophy of Frank Murphy." *University of Detroit Law Journal* 42 (June 1965): 585-604.

8513. Lunt, Richard D. *The High Ministry of Government: The Political Career of Frank Murphy.* Detroit: Wayne State University Press, 1965.

8514. Man, Albon P., Jr. "Mr. Justice Murphy and the Supreme Court." *Virginia Law Review* 36 (November 1950): 889-943.

8515. Marshall, Thurgood. "Mr. Justice Murphy and Civil Rights." *Michigan Law Review* 48 (February 1950): 745-766.

8516. Marshall, Thurgood. "Mr. Justice Murphy and Civil Rights." *National Bar Journal* 9 (March 1951): 1-25.

8517. Norris, Harold. "Mr. Justice Frank Murphy: A Michigan Contribution to Law and Politics." *Michigan Bar Journal* 64 (August 1985): 55-56.

8518. Norris, Harold. *Mr. Justice Murphy and the Bill of Rights.* Dobbs Ferry, NY: Oceana Publications, 1965.

8519. O'Rourke, Basil. "An Historical Interpretation of Some of Justice Frank Murphy's Decisions." Ph.D. diss., St. John's University, 1959.

8520. Potts, Margaret H. "Justice Murphy: A Reexamination." *Supreme Court Historical Society Yearbook* 1982 (1982): 57-67.

8521. Pressman, Steven, and Frank Murphy. "ABA Votes New Youth Standards: Delegates Also Reject New Federal Courts, Delay Law School Action." *New Jersey Law Journal* 105 (February 21, 1980): 17.

8522. Roche, John P. "The Utopian Pilgrimage of Mr. Justice Murphy." *Vanderbilt Law Review* 10 (February 1957): 369-394.

8523. Scanlan, Alfred L. "The Passing of Justice Murphy: The Conscience of a Court." *Notre Dame Lawyer* 25 (Fall 1949): 7-39.

8524. Stason, E. Blythe. "Mr. Justice Murphy: Alumnus of the University of Michigan." *Michigan Law Review* 48 (April 1950): 737.

8525. Vinson, Fred M. "Mr. Justice Murphy." *Michigan Law Review* 48 (April 1950): 738.

8526. Warner, Robert M. "Detroit's First Supreme Court Justice." *Detroit Historical Society Bulletin* 13 (May 1957): 8-13.

8527. Weiss, Leo. "Justice Murphy and

the Welfare Questions." *Michigan Law Review* 53 (February 1955): 541-566.

8528. Woll, J. Albert. "Two Great Men Gone: A Tribute to Wiley Rutledge and Frank Murphy." *American Federationist* 56 (October 1949): 36.

Samuel Nelson

General Studies

8529. Countryman, Edwin. "Samuel Nelson." *Green Bag* 19 (June 1907): 329-334.

8530. Leach, Richard H. "Rediscovery of Samuel Nelson." *New York History* 34 (January 1953): 64-71.

8531. "Old Judge and the New." *Albany Law Journal* 6 (December 14, 1872): 400-401.

Sandra D. O'Connor

General Studies

8532. Ailshie, Lee W., and John M. Scheb, II. "Justice Sandra Day O'Connor and the 'Freshman Effect'." *Judicature* 69 (June/July 1985): 9-12.

8533. Bentley, Judith. *Justice Sandra Day O'Connor.* Englewood Cliffs, NJ: Messner, 1983.

8534. Beschle, Donald L. "The Conservative as Liberal: The Religion Clauses, Liberal Neutrality, and the Approach of Justice O'Connor." *Notre Dame Law Review* 62 (1987): 151-191.

8535. Brill, Steven. "What Ron Didn't Know about Sandra." *American Lawyer* 3 (November 1981): 5-7.

8536. Bruckmann, Barbara O. "Justice Sandra Day O'Connor: Trends toward

Judicial Restraint." *Washington and Lee Law Review* 42 (Fall 1985): 1185-1231.

8537. Cordray, Richard, and James Vrodelis. "The Emerging Jurisprudence of Justice O'Connor." *University of Chicago Law Review* 52 (Spring 1985): 389-459.

8538. Feder, Benjamin D. "And a Child Shall Lead Them: Justice O'Connor, the Principle of Religious Liberty, and Its Practical Application." *Pace Law Review* 8 (Spring 1988): 249-302.

8539. Fox, Mary V., ed. *Justice Sandra Day O'Connor.* Hillside, NJ: Enslow Publishers, 1983.

8540. Greenhouse, Linda. "Justice Sandra Day O'Connor on the Supreme Court." In *American Government*, 8th ed., edited by Peter Woll, 547-550. Boston: Little, Brown, 1984.

8541. Heck, Edward V., and Melinda G. Hall. "Bloc Voting and the Freshman Justice Revisited." *Journal of Politics* 43 (August 1981): 852-860.

8542. Heck, Edward V., and Paula C. Arledge. "Justice O'Connor and the First Amendment, 1981-1984." *Pepperdine Law Review* 13 (May 1986): 993-1019.

8543. Kelso, Charles D. "Justice O'Connor Replaces Justice Stewart: What Effect on Constitutional Cases?" *Pacific Law Journal* 13 (January 1982): 259-272.

8544. Loewy, Arnold H. "Rethinking Government Neutrality towards Religion under the Establishment Clause: The Untapped Potential of Justice O'Connor's Insight." *North Carolina Law Review* 60 (December 1985): 1049-1070.

8545. Miller, Margaret A. "Justice Sandra Day O'Connor: Token or Triumph from a Feminist Perspective." *Golden Gate University Law Review* 15 (Fall 1985): 493-525.

8546. Riggs, Robert E. "Justice O'Connor: A First Term Appraisal." *Brigham*

Young University Law Review 1983 (Winter 1983): 1-46.

8547. Scheb, John M., II, and Lee W. Ailshie. "Justice Sandra Day O'Connor and the 'Freshman Effect': Contrary to Expectations, the Newest Justice Quickly Adapted to Her Environment and Almost Immediately Began Participating Fully in the Work of the Court." *Judicature* 69 (June/July 1985): 9-12.

8548. Schenker, Carl. " 'Reading' Justice Sandra Day O'Connor." *Catholic University Law Review* 32 (Spring 1983): 487-503.

8549. Shea, Barbara C. S. "Sandra Day O'Connor: Woman, Lawyer, Justice; Her First Four Terms on the Supreme Court." *University of Missouri at Kansas City Law Review* 55 (Fall 1986): 1-32.

8550. Sheridan, Kathleen. "Women in Law: With a Woman on the Supreme Court, Has Anything Changed?" *Barrister* 8 (Summer 1981): 44-48.

8551. Spring, Beth. " 'Abhorrent and Offensive': From the Witness Chair, Sandra O'Connor Said That about Abortion." *Christianity Today* 25 (October 23, 1981): 52-53.

8552. Sylvester, Kathleen. "Justice O'Connor Makes Her Mark on the High Court." *National Law Journal* 4 (July 19, 1982): 3.

8553. Witt, Elder. *A Different Justice: Reagan and the Supreme Court.* Washington, DC: Congressional Quarterly, 1985.

8554. Woods, Harold, and Geraldine Woods. *Equal Justice: A Biography of Sandra Day O'Connor.* Minneapolis: Dillon Press, 1985.

Writings

8555. O'Connor, Sandra D. "The Changing of the Circuit Justice." *University of*

Toledo Law Review 17 (Spring 1986): 521-526.

8556. O'Connor, Sandra D. "Swinford Lecture." *Kentucky Bench and Bar* 49 (Summer 1985): 20-22, 51-53.

William Paterson

General Studies

8557. Boyd, Julian P. "William Paterson, Forerunner of John Marshall." In *Lives of Eighteen from Princeton*, edited by Williard Thorp, 194-196. Princeton, NJ: Princeton University Press, 1946.

8558. Clark, Joseph. *A Sermon on the Death of the Honorable William Paterson.* New Brunswick, NJ: A. Blauvelt, 1806.

8559. Degnan, Daniel A. "Justice William Paterson: Founder." *Seton Hall Law Review* 16 (1986): 313-342.

8560. Haskett, Richard C. "Prosecuting the Revolution." *American Historical Review* 59 (April 1954): 578-587.

8561. Haskett, Richard C. "Village Clerk and Country Lawyer: William Paterson's Legal Experience, 1763-1772." *New Jersey Historical Society Proceedings* 66 (October 1948): 155-171.

8562. Haskett, Richard C. "William Paterson, Attorney General of New Jersey: Public Office and Private Profit in the American Revolution." *William and Mary Quarterly* 7 (January 1950): 26-38.

8563. Haskett, Richard C. "William Paterson, Counsellor at Law." Ph.D. diss., Princeton University, 1952.

8564. Honeyman, A. Van Doren. "Early Career of Governor William Paterson, 1745-1806." *Somerset County Historical Quarterly* 1 (July/October 1912): 161-179, 241-256.

8565. McCormick, Richard P. *Experi-*

ment in *Independence: New Jersey in the Critical Period, 1781-1789.* New Brunswick, NJ: Rutgers University Press, 1950.

8566. O'Connor, John E. "William Paterson and the American Revolution, 1763-1787." Ph.D. diss., City University of New York, 1974.

8567. O'Connor, John E. *William Paterson: Lawyer and Statesman, 1745-1806.* New Brunswick, NJ: Rutgers University Press, 1979.

8568. Parker, Cortlandt. "Address on Governor William Paterson." *New Jersey Historical Society Proceedings* 5 (October 1920): 230-236.

8569. Parker, Cortlandt. "Alexander Hamilton and William Paterson." *American Bar Association Reports* 3 (August 18, 19, 20, 1880): 149-166.

8570. Parker, Cortlandt. "William Paterson." In *Great American Lawyers,* vol. 1, edited by William D. Lewis, 223-245. Philadelphia: J. C. Winston Company, 1907.

8571. Rosenberg, Leonard B. "The Political Thought of William Paterson." Ph.D. diss., New School for Social Research, 1967.

8572. Rosenberg, Leonard B. "William Paterson: New Jersey's Nation-Maker." *New Jersey History* 85 (Spring 1967): 7-40.

8573. Shriner, Charles A. *William Paterson.* Paterson, NJ: Paterson Industrial Commission, 1940.

8574. Wood, Gertrude S. "William Paterson of New Jersey, 1745-1806." Ph.D. diss., Columbia University, 1933.

Writings

8575. Paterson, William. "Extracts from Unpublished Letters of Governor Pater-

son." *Somerset County Historical Quarterly* 3 (January/April 1913): 1-6, 83-88.

Rufus W. Peckham

General Studies

8576. Hall, A. Oakey. "The New Supreme Court Justice." *Green Bag* 8 (January 1896): 1-4.

8577. Proctor, L. B. "Rufus W. Peckham." *Albany Law Journal* 55 (May 1, 1897): 286-288.

Mahlon Pitney

General Studies

8578. Belknap, Michael R. "Mr. Justice Pitney and Progressivism." *Seton Hall Law Review* 16 (1986): 381-428.

8579. Breed, Alan R. "Mahlon Pitney." Senior thesis, Princeton University, 1932.

8580. Levitan, David M. "Mahlon Pitney: Labor Judge." *Virginia Law Review* 40 (October 1954): 733-770.

Lewis F. Powell, Jr.

General Studies

8581. DuVall, Randolph C., John E. Ely, Mark S. Gardner, William C. Goodwin, and H. P. Williams. "Balanced Justice: Mr. Justice Powell and the Constitution." *University of Richmond Law Review* 11 (Winter 1977): 335-430.

8582. Fingarette, Herbert. "The Perils of Powell: In Search of a Factual Foundation of the Disease Concept of Alcoholism."

Harvard Law Review 83 (February 1970): 793-812.

8583. Gunther, Gerald. "In Search of Judicial Quality on a Changing Court: The Case of Justice Powell." *Stanford Law Review* 24 (June 1972): 1001-1035.

8584. Howard, A. E. Dick. "Mr. Justice Powell and the Emerging Nixon Majority." *Michigan Law Review* 70 (January 1972): 445-468.

8585. Kahn, Paul W. "The Court, the Community, and the Judicial Balance: The Jurisprudence of Justice Powell." *Yale Law Journal* 97 (November 1987): 1-60.

8586. Leedes, Gary C. "Mr. Justice Powell's Standing." *University of Richmond Law Review* 11 (Winter 1977): 269-290.

8587. Lessard, Suzannah. "Rehnquist, Powell, and the Cult of the Pro." *Washington Monthly* 3 (December 1972): 48-56.

8588. Maltz, Earl M. "Portrait of a Man in the Middle: Mr. Justice Powell, Equal Protection, and the Pure Classification Problem." *Ohio State Law Journal* 40 (1979): 941-966.

8589. Urofsky, Melvin I. "Mr. Justice Powell and Education: The Balancing of Competing Values." *Journal of Law and Education* 13 (October 1984): 581-627.

8590. Watkins, John J. "Newsgathering and the First Amendment: Supreme Court Has Dealt Directly with Question of a Right of Newsgathering." *Journalism Quarterly* 53 (Autumn 1976): 406-416.

8591. Watkins, Michael C. "United States Supreme Court Justice Lewis F. Powell: A Study of His Philosophy and Application of the Law in Education Cases." Ph.D. diss., University of Missouri, Columbia, 1984.

8592. Wilkinson, J. Harvie. "Honorable Lewis F. Powell, Jr.: Five Years on the Supreme Court." *University of Richmond Law Review* 11 (Winter 1977): 259-267.

8593. Wilkinson, J. Harvie. *Serving Justice: A Supreme Court Clerk's View.* New York: Charterhouse, 1974.

8594. Wilkinson, J. Harvie, Sandra D. O'Connor, Richard H. Fallon, Jr., George C. Freeman, Jr., Gerald Gunther, and Oliver W. Hill. "A Tribute to Justice Lewis F. Powell, Jr." *Harvard Law Review* 101 (December 1987): 395-420.

8595. Wilson, James Q. "The Flamboyant Mr. Powell." *Commentary* 41 (January 1966): 31-35.

8596. Yackle, Larry W. "Thoughts on *Rodriguez:* Mr. Justice Powell and the Demise of Equal Protection Analysis in the Supreme Court." *University of Richmond Law Review* 9 (Winter 1975): 181-247.

Writings

8597. Powell, Lewis F., Jr. "The Burger Court." *Washington and Lee Law Review* 44 (Winter 1987): 1-10.

8598. Powell, Lewis F., Jr. "Myths and Misconceptions about the Supreme Court." *American Bar Association Journal* 61 (November 1975): 1344-1347.

8599. Powell, Lewis F., Jr. "Of Politics and the Court." *Supreme Court Historical Society Yearbook* 1982 (1982): 23-26.

8600. Powell, Lewis F., Jr. "Supreme Court Justices from Virginia." *Virginia Magazine of History and Biography* 84 (April 1976): 131-141.

8601. Powell, Lewis F., Jr. "Three Giants of the Law." *American Bar Association Journal* 50 (February 1964): 158-161.

8602. Powell, Lewis F., Jr. "What Really Goes on at the Supreme Court." *American Bar Association Journal* 66 (June 1980): 721-723.

8603. Powell, Lewis F., Jr., and William

H. Rehnquist. "What the Justices Are Saying." *American Bar Association Journal* 62 (November 1976): 1454-1456.

Stanley F. Reed

General Studies

8604. Bickel, Alexander M. "On the Retirement of Justice Reed." *New Republic* 136 (March 1957): 6.

8605. Burger, Warren E. "Stanley F. Reed." *Supreme Court Historical Society Yearbook* 1981 (1981): 10-13.

8606. Fitzgerald, Mark J. "Justice Reed: A Study of a Center Judge." Ph.D. diss., University of Chicago, 1950.

8607. O'Brien, F. William. *Justice Reed and the First Amendment: The Religion Clauses.* Washington, DC: Georgetown University Press, 1958.

8608. O'Brien, F. William. "Mr. Justice Reed and Democratic Pluralism." *Georgetown Law Journal* 45 (Spring 1957): 364-387.

8609. O'Brien, F. William. "Mr. Justice Reed and the Liberties of the First Amendment." Ph.D. diss., Georgetown University, 1956.

8610. O'Brien, F. William. "Unshaken Reed." *America* 96 (February 23, 1957): 571.

8611. Prickett, Morgan D. "Stanley Forman Reed: Perspectives on a Judicial Epitaph." *Hastings Constitutional Law Quarterly* 8 (Winter 1981): 343-369.

Writings

8612. Reed, Stanley F. "Our Constitutional Philosophy: Concerning the Significance of Judicial Review in the Evolution of American Democracy." *Kentucky State Bar Journal* 2 (June 1961): 136-146.

William H. Rehnquist

General Studies

8613. Berger, Raoul. "*Benno Schmidt vs. Rehnquist and Scalia.*" *Ohio State Law Journal* 47 (November 1986): 709-712.

8614. Boles, Donald E. *Mr. Justice Rehnquist, Judicial Activist: The Early Years.* Ames: Iowa State University Press, 1987.

8615. Castle, Linda L. "Rehnquist, the Partisan, Meets the Press." *American Bar Association Journal* 71 (May 1985): 132.

8616. Davis, Sue. *Justice Rehnquist and the Constitution.* Princeton, NJ: Princeton University Press, 1989.

8617. Davis, Sue. "Justice Rehnquist's Equal Protection Clause: An Interim Analysis." *Nebraska Law Review* 63 (Spring 1984): 288-313.

8618. Davis, Sue. "Justice Rehnquist's Judicial Philosophy: Democracy v. Equality." *Polity* 17 (Fall 1984): 88-117.

8619. Denniston, Lyle. "Rehnquist, Scalia Not Expected to Shift High Court's Balance." *Criminal Justice Newsletter* 17 (July 1986): 1-3.

8620. Denvir, John. "Justice Brennan, Justice Rehnquist, and Free Speech." *Northwestern University Law Review* 80 (November 1985): 285-320.

8621. Denvir, John. "Justice Rehnquist and Constitutional Interpretation." *Hastings Law Journal* 34 (May 1983): 1011-1053.

8622. Dwyer, Paula. "Rehnquist and Scalia: A One-Two Punch for the Right." *Business Week* (June 30, 1986): 36-37.

8623. French, Bruce C. "The Views of

Justice Rehnquist Concerning the Proper Role of the State in National Labor Relations Policy." *Tulsa Law Journal* 17 (Fall 1981): 76-96.

8624. "The Gavel Passes." *National Law Journal* 7 (June 30, 1986): 1-20.

8625. Graham, Deborah. "The Rehnquistision: Part II." *American Bar Association Journal* 72 (August 1986): 17-18.

8626. Heilman, Arthur D. "Preserving the Essential Role of the Supreme Court: A Comment on Justice Rehnquist's Proposal." *Florida State University Law Review* 14 (Spring 1986): 15-34.

8627. Kleven, Thomas. "The Constitutional Philosophy of Justice William H. Rehnquist." *Vermont Law Review* 8 (Spring 1983): 1-53.

8628. Lauter, David. "The Justices Again Repudiate Rehnquist: Is His Dominance of the Court a Myth?" *National Law Journal* 7 (April 1, 1985): 5.

8629. Lessard, Suzannah. "Rehnquist, Powell, and the Cult of the Pro." *Washington Monthly* 3 (December 1972): 48-56.

8630. Lind, Robert C. "Justice Rehnquist: First Amendment Speech in the Labor Context." *Hastings Constitutional Law Quarterly* 8 (Fall 1980): 93-123.

8631. Luneburg, William V. "Justice Rehnquist, Statutory Interpretation, the Policies of Clear Statement, and Federal Jurisdiction." *Indiana Law Journal* 58 (Winter 1982/1983): 211-285.

8632. McClurg, Andrew J. "Logical Fallacies and the Supreme Court: A Critical Examination of Justice Rehnquist's Decisions on Criminal Procedure Cases." *University of Colorado Law Review* 59 (Autumn 1988): 741-844.

8633. MacKenzie, John P. "Rehnquist Recuse: Judging Your Own Case." *Washington Monthly* 6 (May 1974): 54-61.

8634. Massey, Stephen. "Justice Rehnquist's Theory of Property." *Yale Law Journal* 93 (January 1984): 541-560.

8635. Nelson, Dale. "Dateline—Washington: Rehnquist, Scalia, and the First Amendment." *Wilson Library Bulletin* 61 (October 1986): 30-31.

8636. Nelson-Horchler, Joani. "Supreme Court: How Far Will Rehnquist Tilt It to the Right?" *Industry Week* 230 (July 7, 1986): 24-25.

8637. Phelps, Glenn A., and Timothy A. Martinez. "Brennan v. Rehnquist: The Politics of Constitutional Jurisprudence." *Gonzaga Law Review* 22 (June 1987): 307-325.

8638. Powell, Jeff. "The Compleat Jeffersonian: Justice Rehnquist and Federalism." *Yale Law Journal* 91 (June 1982): 1317-1370.

8639. Powell, Lewis F., Jr., and William H. Rehnquist. "What the Justices Are Saying." *American Bar Association Journal* 62 (November 1976): 1454-1456.

8640. Riemenschneider, John. "The Judicial Philosophy of William H. Rehnquist." *Mississippi Law Journal* 45 (January 1974): 224-245.

8641. Riggs, Robert E., and Thomas D. Proffitt. "The Judicial Philosophy of Justice Rehnquist." *Akron Law Review* 16 (Spring 1983): 555-604.

8642. Rydell, John R., II. "Mr. Justice Rehnquist and Judicial Self-Restraint." *Hastings Law Journal* 26 (February 1975): 875-915.

8643. Shapiro, David L. "Mr. Justice Rehnquist: A Preliminary View." *Harvard Law Review* 90 (December 1976): 293-357.

8644. Stempel, Jeffrey W. "Rehnquist, Recusal, and Reform." *Brooklyn Law Review* 53 (Fall 1987): 589-667.

8645. Stewart, David O. "What's Ahead

with Rehnquist and Scalia." *American Bar Association Journal* 72 (August 1986): 36-40.

8646. Tushnet, Mark V. "The Constitutional Right to One's Good Name: An Examination of the Scholarship of Mr. Justice Rehnquist." *Kentucky Law Journal* 64 (1976): 753-766.

8647. Washington, Harold H. "Essays in Repression: First Term Opinion of Mr. Justice Rehnquist." *North Carolina Central Law Journal* 4 (Fall 1972): 53-67.

8648. Weaver, Warren, Jr. "Mr. Justice Rehnquist, Dissenting." *New York Times Magazine* 124 (October 13, 1974): 36, 94-99.

8649. White, Charles. "A View from the Gallery: Rehnquist Shows No Mercy to an Opening Day Lawyer, and Curletti Gives a Polished Performance on Short Notice." *American Lawyer* 2 (December 1980): 39-40.

8650. Williams, Mark E. "The Pendulum Swings: Rehnquist and the De-emphasis of Individual Liberty in Criminal Procedure Analysis." *University of Detroit Law Review* 65 (Winter 1988): 291-314.

Writings

8651. Rehnquist, William H. "Act Well Your Part: Therein All Honor Lies." *Human Rights* 9 (Spring 1980): 42-47.

8652. Rehnquist, William H. "Act Well Your Part: Therein All Honor Lies." *Pepperdine Law Review* 7 (Winter 1980): 227-239.

8653. Rehnquist, William H. " 'All Discord Harmony Not Understood': The Performance of the Supreme Court of the United States." *Arizona Law Review* 22 (1980): 973-986.

8654. Rehnquist, William H. "The Bar Admission Cases: A Strange Judicial Aberration." *American Bar Association Journal* 44 (March 1958): 229-232.

8655. Rehnquist, William H. "The Changing Role of the Supreme Court." *Florida State University Law Review* 14 (Spring 1986): 1-14.

8656. Rehnquist, William H. "Civility and Freedom of Speech." *Indiana Law Journal* 49 (Fall 1973): 1-7.

8657. Rehnquist, William H. "A Comment on the Instruction of Constitutional Law." *Pepperdine Law Review* 14 (March 1987): 563-566.

8658. Rehnquist, William H. "Constitutional Law and Public Opinion." *Suffolk University Law Review* 20 (Winter 1986): 751-769.

8659. Rehnquist, William H. "The First Amendment: Freedom, Philosophy, and the Law." *Gonzaga Law Review* 12 (Fall 1976): 1-18.

8660. Rehnquist, William H. "Is an Expanded Right of Privacy Consistent with Fair and Effective Law Enforcement?" *Kansas Law Review* 23 (Fall 1974): 1-22.

8661. Rehnquist, William H. "The Making of a Supreme Court Justice." *Harvard Law Record* 29 (October 8, 1959): 7-10.

8662. Rehnquist, William H. "The Notion of a Living Constitution." *Texas Law Review* 54 (May 1976): 693-706.

8663. Rehnquist, William H. "The Old Order Changeth: The Department of Justice under John Mitchell." *Arizona Law Review* 12 (Summer 1970): 251-259.

8664. Rehnquist, William H. "A Plea for Help: Solutions to Serious Problems Currently Experienced by the Federal Judicial System." *St. Louis University Law Journal* 28 (February 1984): 1-10.

8665. Rehnquist, William H. "Political Battles for Judicial Independence." *Wash-*

ington Law Review 50 (August 1975): 835-851.

8666. Rehnquist, William H. "Presidential Appointments to the Supreme Court." *Constitutional Commentary* 2 (Summer 1985): 319-330.

8667. Rehnquist, William H. "Sense and Nonsense about Judicial Ethics." *Record of the Association of the Bar of the City of New York* 28 (November 1973): 694-713.

8668. Rehnquist, William H. "Sunshine in the Third Branch." *Washburn Law Journal* 16 (Spring 1977): 559-570.

8669. Rehnquist, William H. *The Supreme Court, 1988*. New York: Morrow, 1988.

8670. Rehnquist, William H. "Supreme Court of the United States: The Ohio Connection." *University of Dayton Law Review* 4 (Summer 1979): 271-281.

8671. Rehnquist, William H. "Supreme Court: Past and Present." *American Bar Association Journal* 59 (April 1973): 361-364.

8672. Rehnquist, William H. *The Supreme Court: The Way It Was—the Way It Is*. New York: Morrow, 1987.

8673. Rehnquist, William H. "Whither the Courts." *American Bar Association Journal* 60 (July 1974): 787-790.

8674. Rehnquist, William H. "Who Writes Decisions of the Supreme Court?" *U.S. News and World Report* 43 (December 13, 1957): 74-75.

8675. Rehnquist, William H., Anthony L. Mondello, and Marvin D. Hugan. "Rights in Conflict: Reconciling Privacy with the Public's Right to Know: A Panel at the 63rd Annual Meeting of the American Association of Law Libraries." *Law Library Journal* 63 (November 1970): 551-563.

Owen J. Roberts

General Studies

8676. Adrian, Leonard E. "Mr. Justice Roberts and the Constitutional Revolution of 1937." Ph.D. diss., University of Notre Dame, 1967.

8677. Bates, Earnest S. "McReynolds, Roberts, and Hughes." *New Republic* 87 (July 1, 1936): 232.

8678. Chambers, John. "The Big Switch: Justice Roberts and the Minimum-Wage Cases." *Labor History* 10 (Winter 1969): 44-73.

8679. Clark, Frederic L. "Mr. Justice Roberts: A Sketch." *Pennsylvania Bar Association Quarterly* 17 (January 1946): 158-163.

8680. Grinnell, Frank W. "Proposed Amendments to the Constitution: A Reply to Former Justice Roberts." *American Bar Association Journal* 35 (August 1949): 648-651.

8681. Griswold, Erwin N. "Owen J. Roberts as a Judge." *University of Pennsylvania Law Review* 104 (December 1955): 332-349.

8682. Keedy, Edwin R. "Owen J. Roberts and the Law School." *University of Pennsylvania Law Review* 104 (December 1955): 318-321.

8683. Leonard, Charles. "A Revolution Runs Wild." *Supreme Court Historical Society Yearbook* 1980 (1980):55-61.

8684. Leonard, Charles. *A Search for a Judicial Philosophy: Mr. Justice Roberts and the Constitutional Revolution of 1937*. Port Washington, NY: Kennikat Press, 1971.

8685. Lingelbach, William E. "Owen J. Roberts and the American Philosophical Society." *University of Pennsylvania Law Review* 104 (December 1955): 368-371.

8686. McCloy, John J. "Owen J. Roberts'

Extra Curia Activities." *University of Pennsylvania Law Review* 104 (December 1955): 332-349.

8687. McCracken, Robert T. "Justice Roberts Leaves the Court." *American Bar Association Journal* 31 (August 1945): 407-435.

8688. McCracken, Robert T. "Owen J. Roberts, 1875-1955." *American Bar Association Journal* 41 (July 1955): 616.

8689. McCracken, Robert T. "Owen J. Roberts: Master Advocate." *University of Pennsylvania Law Review* 104 (December 1955): 322-331.

8690. Mason, Alpheus T. "Owen Josephus Roberts." In *Dictionary of American Biography: Supplement Five, 1951-1955*, edited by John A. Garraty, 571-577. New York: Charles Scribner's Sons, 1977.

8691. Nelson, Paul E. "Constitutional Theory of Mr. Justice Roberts." Master's thesis, University of Chicago, 1960.

8692. "Owen J. Roberts, 1875-1955." *American Bar Association Journal* 41 (July 1955): 616.

8693. "Owen J. Roberts: In Memoriam." *University of Pennsylvania Law Review* 104 (December 1955): 311-317.

8694. Pepper, George W. "Owen J. Roberts: The Man." *University of Pennsylvania Law Review* 104 (December 1955): 372-379.

8695. Pepper, George W. "Owen Josephus Roberts." *American Philosophical Society Yearbook* 1955 (December/January 1955): 494-502.

8696. Pusey, Merlo J. "Justice Roberts' 1937 Turnaround." *Supreme Court Historical Society Yearbook* 1983 (1983): 102-107.

8697. Streit, Clarence K. "Owen J. Roberts and Atlantic Union." *University of Pennsylvania Law Review* 104 (December 1955): 354-367.

8698. Trapp, William O. "Constitutional Doctrines of Owen J. Roberts." Ph.D. diss., Cornell University, 1943.

Writings

8699. Roberts, Owen J. "American Constitutional Government: The Blueprint and Structure." In *Gaspar G. Bacon Lectures on the Constitution of the United States, 1940-1950*, by Arthur N. Holcombe, et al., 379-422. Boston: Boston University Press, 1953.

8700. Roberts, Owen J. *The Court and the Constitution*. Cambridge: Harvard University Press, 1951.

8701. Roberts, Owen J. "Now Is the Time: Fortifying the Supreme Court's Independence." *American Bar Association Journal* 35 (January 1949): 1-4.

John Rutledge

General Studies

8702. Barnwell, Robert W. "Rutledge, 'The Dictator'." *Journal of Southern History* 7 (May 1941): 215-224.

8703. Barre, W. L. "John Rutledge." In *Lives of Illustrious Men of America: Distinguished in the Annals of the Republic as Legislators, Warriors, and Philosophers*, by W. L. Barre, 408-425. Cincinnati: W. A. Clarke, 1859.

8704. Barry, Richard. *Mr. Rutledge of South Carolina*. New York: Duell, Sloan, and Pearce, 1942.

8705. Cook, Frank G. "John Rutledge." *Atlantic Monthly* 67 (February 1891): 225-236.

8706. Flanders, Henry. "Chief Justice Rutledge." *University of Pennsylvania Law Review* 54 (April 1906): 203-213.

8707. Hartley, Cecil B. "Life of Governor John Rutledge." In *Heroes and Patriots of the South*, by Cecil B. Hartley, 291-301. Philadelphia: G. G. Evans, 1860.

8708. Lossing, Benson J. "John Rutledge." In *Eminent Americans*, by Benson J. Lossing, 153-154. New York: Hurst, 1886.

8709. McCowan, George S., Jr. "Chief Justice John Rutledge and the Jay Treaty." *South Carolina Historical Magazine* 62 (January 1961): 10-23.

8710. Mendelson, Wallace. "Mr. Justice Rutledge's Mark upon the Bill of Rights." *Columbia Law Review* 50 (January 1950): 48-51.

8711. Middleton, Kent R. "The Partisan Press and the Rejection of a Chief Justice: John Rutledge." *Journalism Quarterly* 53 (Spring 1976): 106-110.

8712. O'Neall, John B. "John Rutledge." In *Biographical Sketches of the Bench and Bar of South Carolina*, vol. 1, by John B. O'Neall, 17-27. Charleston, SC: S. G. Courtenay, 1859.

8713. Perry, Benjamin F. "John Rutledge." In *Biographical Sketches of Eminent American Statesmen*, by Benjamin F. Perry, 254-258. Philadelphia: Ferree Press, 1887.

8714. Uhle, John B. "John Rutledge." *Current Comment* 1 (December 15, 1889): 443-446.

8715. Waite, Charles B. "John Rutledge." *Chicago Law Times* 1 (October 1887): 305-311.

8716. Webber, Mabel L. "Dr. John Rutledge and His Descendants." *South Carolina Historical and Genealogical Magazine* 31 (January 1930): 7-25.

Writings

8717. Rutledge, John. *Cyclopedia of Eminent and Representative Men of the Caro-* linas of the Nineteenth Century. Vol. 1. Madison: Brant and Fuller, 1892.

Wiley B. Rutledge

General Studies

8718. Bar of the Supreme Court of the United States. "In Memory of Honorable Wiley Rutledge: Proceedings before United States Supreme Court." *Iowa Law Review* 36 (Summer 1951): 591-606.

8719. "Biographical Notes." *U.S. News and World Report* 27 (August 5, 1949): 20.

8720. Black, Hugo L. "Mr. Justice Rutledge." *Indiana Law Journal* 25 (Summer 1950): 423.

8721. Brant, Irving. "Mr. Justice Rutledge: The Man." *Indiana Law Journal* 25 (Summer 1950): 424-443.

8722. Brudney, Victor, and Richard F. Wolfson. "Mr. Justice Rutledge: Law Clerks' Reflections." *Indiana Law Journal* 25 (Summer 1950): 455-461.

8723. Canon, Alfred O. "Mr. Justice Rutledge and the Roosevelt Court." *Vanderbilt Law Review* 10 (February 1957): 167-192.

8724. Davies, A. Powell. "Memorial for Justice Wiley Blount Rutledge." *American Bar Association Journal* 35 (December 1949): 1008-1009.

8725. Edgerton, Henry W. "Mr. Justice Rutledge." *Harvard Law Review* 63 (December 1949): 293-298.

8726. Forrester, Ray. "Mr. Justice Rutledge: A New Factor." *Tulane Law Review* 17 (April 1943): 511-536.

8727. Fuchs, Ralph F. "In Memory of Mr. Justice Wiley B. Rutledge." *Rocky Mountain Law Review* 24 (December 1951): 1-8.

8728. Fuchs, Ralph F. "The Judicial Art of Wiley B. Rutledge." *Washington University Law Quarterly* 28 (April 1943): 115-146.

8729. Fuchs, Ralph F. "Wiley B. Rutledge, 1894-1949." *National Bar Journal* 7 (December 1949): 393-397.

8730. Harper, Fowler V. *Justice Rutledge and the Bright Constellation*. Indianapolis: Bobbs-Merrill, 1965.

8731. Harper, Fowler V. "Mr. Justice Rutledge and Full Faith and Credit." *Indiana Law Journal* 25 (Summer 1950): 480-497.

8732. Levitan, David M. "Mr. Justice Rutledge." *Virginia Law Review* 34 (May/June 1948): 393-416; (July 1948): 526-552.

8733. Mann, W. Howard. "Mr. Justice Rutledge and Civil Liberties." *Iowa Law Review* 35 (Summer 1950): 663-692.

8734. Mann, W. Howard. "Rutledge and Civil Liberties." *Indiana Law Journal* 25 (Summer 1950): 532-559.

8735. Mosher, Lester E. "The Constitutional Philosophy of Mr. Justice Rutledge: A Study of His Approach to Problems of Civil Rights and the Commerce Clause." Ph.D. diss., New York University, 1951.

8736. Mosher, Lester E. "Mr. Justice Rutledge's Philosophy of Civil Rights." *New York University Law Quarterly Review* 24 (October 1949): 661-706.

8737. Mosher, Lester E. "Mr. Justice Rutledge's Philosophy of the Commerce Clause." *New York University Law Review* 27 (April 1952): 218-247.

8738. Nathanson, Nathaniel L. "Statutory Interpretation and Mr. Justice Rutledge." *Indiana Law Review* 25 (Summer 1950): 462-479.

8739. Pollak, Louis H. "Wiley Blount Rutledge: Profile of a Judge." *University of Illinois Law Forum* 1979 (1979): 310-336.

8740. Rockwell, Landon G. "Justice Rutledge on Civil Liberties." *Yale Law Journal* 59 (December 1949): 27-59.

8741. Rockwell, Landon G. "Justice Rutledge on State Taxation of Commerce." *Cornell Law Quarterly* 35 (Spring 1950): 493-513.

8742. Stevens, John P. *Mr. Justice Rutledge*. Chicago: University of Chicago Press, 1956.

8743. Treiman, Israel. "Mr. Justice Rutledge." *Dicta* 20 (April 1943): 85-94.

8744. Treiman, Israel. "Mr. Justice Rutledge: An Appraisal Based upon His Opinions While on the U.S. Court of Appeals." *Missouri Bar Journal* 14 (January 1943): 4-6.

8745. Wiley, Eugene V. "Justice Rutledge and State Taxation of Interstate Commerce." *Washington Law Quarterly* 1950 (June 1950): 399-422.

8746. "Wiley B. Rutledge, Humanitarian." *American Bar Association Journal* 35 (October 1949): 842.

8747. Wirtz, W. Willard. "Mr. Justice Rutledge: Teacher of Men." *Indiana Law Journal* 25 (Summer 1950): 444-454.

8748. Woll, J. Albert. "Two Great Men Gone: A Tribute to Wiley Rutledge and Frank Murphy." *American Federationist* 56 (October 1949): 36.

Writings

8749. Rutledge, Wiley B. *A Declaration of Legal Faith*. Lawrence: University of Kansas Press, 1947.

8750. Rutledge, Wiley B. "Foreword to a Symposium on Constitutional Rights in Wartime." *Iowa Law Review* 29 (March 1944): 379-382.

8751. Rutledge, Wiley B. "Harlan Fiske Stone: A Great American Judge." *Temple Law Quarterly* 19 (April 1946): 9-10.

Edward T. Sanford

General Studies

8752. Cook, Stanley A. "Path to the High Bench: The Pre-Supreme Court Career of Justice Edward Terry Sanford." Ph.D. diss., University of Tennessee, 1977.

8753. Fowler, James A. "Mr. Justice Edward Terry Sanford." *American Bar Association Journal* 17 (April 1931): 229-233.

8754. Green, John W. "Tennessee, Some Judges of the United States District Court of 1878-1939." *Tennessee Law Review* 18 (April 1944): 227-241.

8755. Laska, Lewis L. "Mr. Justice Sanford and the Fourteenth Amendment." *Tennessee Historical Quarterly* 33 (Summer 1974): 210-227.

8756. Ragan, Allen E. "Mr. Justice Sanford." *Eastern Tennessee Historical Society Publications* 15 (1943): 74-88.

Writings

8757. Sanford, Edward T. *Blount College and the University of Tennessee.* Knoxville: University of Tennessee, 1894.

Antonin Scalia

General Studies

8758. Adler, Stephen. "Live Wire on the D.C. Circuit." *American Lawyer* 7 (March 1985): 86.

8759. "Appellate Jurisprudence of Justice Antonin Scalia." *University of Chi-* *cago Law Review* 54 (Spring 1987): 705-739.

8760. Baker, Stewart A., and Katherine H. Wheatley. "Justice Scalia and Federalism: A Sketch." *Urban Lawyer* 20 (Spring 1988): 353-366.

8761. Denniston, Lyle. "Rehnquist, Scalia Not Expected to Shift High Court's Balance." *Criminal Justice Newsletter* 17 (July 1986): 1-3.

8762. Dwyer, Paula. "Rehnquist and Scalia: A One-Two Punch for the Right." *Business Week* (June 30, 1986): 36-37.

8763. King, Michael P. "Justice Antonin Scalia: The First Term on the Supreme Court, 1986-1987." *Rutgers Law Journal* 20 (Fall 1988): 1-77.

8764. Lawrence, Barnett M. "The Supreme Court: The 1985-86 Term in Review and a Look Ahead." *Environmental Law Reporter* 16 (November 1986): 10325-10329.

8765. Nelson, Dale. "Dateline—Washington: Rehnquist, Scalia, and the First Amendment." *Wilson Library Bulletin* 61 (October 1986): 30-31.

8766. Perino, Michael A. "Justice Scalia: Standing, Environmental Law, and the Supreme Court." *Boston Affairs Law Review* 15 (Fall 1987): 135-179.

8767. Ross, Steve. "A Question of Judgement: Rehnquist and Scalia Advance toward Supreme Court Posts Despite Their Dismal Church-State Opinions." *Church and State* 39 (September 1986): 4-6.

8768. Rubin, Thea E., and Albert P. Melone. "Justice Antonin Scalia: A First Year Freshman Effect?" *Judicature* 72 (August/September 1988): 98-102.

8769. Stewart, David O. "What's Ahead with Rehnquist and Scalia." *American Bar Association Journal* 72 (August 1986): 36-40.

8770. Viscusi, W. Kip. "Regulatory Economics in the Courts: An Analysis of Judge Scalia's NHTSA Bumper Decision." *Law and Contemporary Problems* 50 (Autumn 1987): 17-31.

8771. Wilson, James G. "Constraints of Power: The Constitutional Opinions of Judges Scalia, Bork, Posner, Easterbrook, and Winter." *University of Miami Law Review* 40 (September 1986): 1171-1266.

8772. Wogeler, William. "Scalia Says Justices Wield Little Influence over Each Other." *Los Angeles Daily Journal* 102 (March 13, 1989): 2.

Writings

8773. Scalia, Antonin. "An Address by Justice Antonin Scalia, United States Supreme Court." *Federal Bar News and Journal* 34 (July/August 1987): 252-254.

8774. Scalia, Antonin. "Historical Anomalies in Administrative Law." *Supreme Court Historical Society Yearbook* 1985 (1985): 101-111.

8775. Scalia, Antonin. "Vermont Yankee: The APA, the D.C. Circuit, and the Supreme Court." *Supreme Court Review* 1978 (1978): 345-409.

George Shiras, Jr.

General Studies

8776. "George Shiras, Jr." *Case and Comment* 2 (February 1896): 1-2.

8777. Shiras, George, III. *Justice George Shiras, Jr., of Pittsburgh . . . A Chronicle of His Family, Life, and Times.* Edited by Winfield Shiras. Pittsburgh: University of Pittsburgh Press, 1953.

John P. Stevens

General Studies

8778. Becker, Brandon, and Michael F. Walsh. "The Interpretation of Narrow Construction and Policy: Mr. Justice Stevens' Circuit Opinions." *San Diego Law Review* 13 (July 1976): 899-930.

8779. Beytagh, Francis X., Jr. "Mr. Justice Stevens and the Burger Court's Uncertain Trumpet." *Notre Dame Lawyer* 51 (July 1976): 946-955.

8780. Cummings, Walter J. "Tribute to Justice John Paul Stevens." *Chicago-Kent Law Review* 56 (Winter 1980): 11-12.

8781. Denniston, Lyle. "Justices Brennan, Stevens Say High Court Favors Prosecution." *Criminal Justice Newsletter* 17 (February 3, 1986): 2-3.

8782. Fairchild, Thomas E., F. Ryan Duffy, Win G. Knoch, Latham Castle, Luther M. Swygert, Walter J. Cummings, Wilbur F. Pell, Jr., Robert A. Sprecher, Philip W. Tone, William J. Bauer, and Harlington Wood, Jr. "Tribute to Justice John Paul Stevens." *Chicago-Kent Law Review* 56 (Winter 1980): 1-10.

8783. Harmon, Kenneth, et al. "The One Hundred and First Justice: An Analysis of the Opinions of Justice John Paul Stevens, Sitting as a Judge on the Seventh Court of Appeals." *Vanderbilt Law Review* 29 (January 1976); 125-209.

8784. Jones, Jeffrey J. "Justice Steven's Proposal to Establish a Sub-Supreme Court." *Harvard Journal on Legislation* 20 (Winter 1983): 201-218.

8785. Lamb, George C., III, et al. "Justice Stevens: The First Three Terms." *Vanderbilt Law Review* 32 (April 1979): 671-754.

8786. Melusky, Joseph A. "Justice John

Paul Stevens' Equal Protection Analysis." Ph.D. diss., University of Delaware, 1983.

8787. Perry, R. Christopher, and John L. Carmichael, Jr. "Have Four-Vote *Certiorari* Cases Been Unimportant? Qualitative and Quantitative Tests of Justice Stevens' Argument." *Cumberland Law Review* 16 (1985/1986): 419-446.

8788. Shenfield, Arthur. "Mr. Justice Stevens and the Zeitgeist." *Modern Age* 23 (Spring 1979): 130-139.

8789. Sickels, Robert J. *John Paul Stevens and the Constitution: The Search for Balance.* University Park: Pennsylvania State University Press, 1988.

Writings

8790. Stevens, John P. "Legal Questions in Perspective." *Florida State University Law Review* 13 (Spring 1985): 1-7.

8791. Stevens, John P. *Mr. Justice Rutledge.* Chicago: University of Chicago Press, 1956.

8792. Stevens, John P. "Remarks on the U.S. Supreme Court: Its Work, Its Workload, and the Appropriate Scope of Its Work." *Federal Bar News and Journal* 33 (March 1986): 109-111.

8793. Stevens, John P. "Some Thoughts on Judicial Restraint." *Judicature* 66 (November 1983): 177-183.

8794. Stevens, John P. "The Supreme Court of the United States: Reflections after a Summer Recess." *South Texas Law Review* 27 (Fall 1986): 447-453.

8795. Stevens, John P. "The Third Branch of Liberty." *University of Miami Law Review* 41 (December 1986): 277-293.

Potter Stewart

General Studies

8796. Barnett, Helaine M., and Kenneth Levine. "Mr. Justice Potter Stewart." *New York University Law Review* 40 (May 1965): 526-562.

8797. Bendiner, Robert. "The Law and Potter Stewart: An Interview with Justice Potter Stewart." *American Heritage* 35 (December 1983): 98-104.

8798. Berman, Daniel M. "Mr. Justice Stewart: A Preliminary Appraisal." *University of Cincinnati Law Review* 28 (Fall 1959): 401-421.

8799. Binion, Gayle. "An Assessment of Potter Stewart." *Center Magazine* 14 (September 1981): 2-5.

8800. Binion, Gayle. "The Evolution of Constitutional Doctrine: The Role of Justice Stewart on a Changing Supreme Court." Ph.D. diss., University of California, Los Angeles, 1977.

8801. Borgersen, Ellen. "On the Power of Balance: A Remembrance of Justice Potter Stewart." *Hastings Constitutional Law Quarterly* 13 (Winter 1986): 173-183.

8802. Galloway, Russell W., Jr. "Potter Stewart: Just a Lawyer." *Santa Clara Law Review* 25 (Autumn 1985): 523-528.

8803. Gupta, Shawn L. "Potter Stewart, Lawyer." *Barrister* 11 (Spring 1984): 22-23, 58-63.

8804. Johnson, George C. "Special Privilege for an Autonomous Press: Justice Stewart's Structural Approach." Ph.D. diss., Southern Illinois University, 1984.

8805. Lewis, Peter W. "Justice Stewart and Fourth Amendment Probable Cause: 'Swing Voter' or Participant in a 'New Majority'?" *Loyola Law Review* 22 (Summer 1976): 713-742.

8806. Morris, Earl F. "Mr. Justice Stewart." *American Bar Association Journal* 44 (December 1950): 1174-1175.

8807. Padgett, George E. "Voting Record of Justice Stewart on First Amendment Cases." *Journalism Quarterly* 59 (Winter 1982): 554-559.

8808. Palmer, Larry I. "Two Perspectives on Structuring Discretion: Justices Stewart and White on the Death Penalty." *Journal of Criminal Law and Criminology* 70 (Summer 1979): 194-213.

8809. Paschal, Joel F. "Mr. Justice Stewart on the Court of Appeals." *Duke Law Journal* 1959 (Summer 1959): 325-340.

8810. Stewart, David O. "Remember Potter Stewart." *American Bar Association Journal* 72 (March 1, 1986): 98-103.

8811. Terrell, Timothy P. " 'Property', 'Due Process', and the Distinction between Definition and Theory in Legal Analysis." *Georgetown Law Journal* 70 (February 1982): 881-941.

8812. Thompson, John R. "Mr. Justice Stewart Serves on Approval." *Reporter* 20 (February 5, 1959): 31-32.

8813. Werner, Ray O. "The Economics of the Joint Antitrust Dissents of Justices Harlan and Stewart." *Washington Law Review* 48 (May 1973): 555-591.

Writings

8814. Stewart, Potter. "The Nine of Us: 'Guardians of the Constitution'." *Florida Bar Journal* 41 (October 1967): 1090-1097.

8815. Stewart, Potter. "Or of the Press." *Hastings Law Journal* 26 (January 1975): 631-637.

8816. Stewart, Potter. "Reflections on the Supreme Court." *Litigation* 8 (Spring 1982): 8-13.

8817. Stewart, Potter. "Robert H. Jackson's Influence on Federal-State Relationships." *Record of the Association of the Bar of the City of New York* 23 (January 1968): 7-32.

8818. Stewart, Potter. "A View from Inside the Court." *Cleveland Bar Association Journal* 39 (January 1968): 69-92.

Harlan F. Stone

General Studies

8819. Aronson, Moses J. "Mr. Justice Stone and the Spirit of the Common Law." *Cornell Law Quarterly* 25 (June 1940): 489-509.

8820. Bates, Henry M. "Chief Justice Harlan F. Stone." *American Bar Association Journal* 27 (August 1941): 469-475.

8821. Biddle, Francis. "Dedicatory Issue of the *Columbia Law Review* to Harlan Fiske Stone, Columbia Law, 1898, Chief Justice of the United States; and Charles Evans Hughes, Columbia Law, 1884, Retired Chief Justice of the United States." *Columbia Law Review* 41 (November 1941): 1157.

8822. Blaesi, George M. "Chief Justice Stone." *Law Notes* 50 (May 1946): 5-6.

8823. Boskey, Bennett. "Mr. Chief Justice Stone." *Harvard Law Review* 59 (October 1966): 1200-1202.

8824. Burlingham, Charles C. "Harlan Fiske Stone." *American Bar Association Journal* 32 (June 1946): 322-324.

8825. Cheatham, Elliott E. "Stone on Conflicts of Laws." *Columbia Law Review* 46 (September 1946): 719-734.

8826. Danelski, David J. "The Chief Justice and the Supreme Court." Ph.D. diss., University of Chicago, 1961.

8827. Douglas, William O. "Chief Justice Stone." *Columbia Law Review* 46 (September 1946): 693-695.

8828. Dowling, Noel T. "The Methods of Mr. Justice Stone in Constitutional Cases." *Columbia Law Review* 41 (November 1941): 1160-1189.

8829. Dunham, Allison. "The Legacy of Brandeis, Holmes, and Stone." *Saturday Review* 39 (December 15, 1956): 13-15.

8830. Dunham, Allison. "Mr. Chief Justice Stone." In *Mr. Justice*, by Allison Dunham, 229-249. Chicago: University of Chicago Press, 1956.

8831. Fahy, Charles. "Mr. Chief Justice Stone." *Harvard Law Review* 59 (October 1966): 1196-1199.

8832. Farnum, George R. "Chief Justice Stone Is Militant Leader." *New Jersey Law Journal* 64 (November 13, 1941): 521.

8833. Frank, John P. "Harlan Fiske Stone: An Estimate." *Stanford Law Review* 9 (May 1957): 621-632.

8834. Frankfurter, Felix. "Harlan Fiske Stone." *American Philosophical Society Year Book* 1946 (1946): 334-339.

8835. Freund, Paul A. "Chief Justice Stone and the Conflict of Laws." *Harvard Law Review* 59 (October 1946): 1210-1236.

8836. Gardner, Warner W. "Mr. Chief Justice Stone." *Harvard Law Review* 59 (1946): 1203-1209.

8837. Gellhorn, Walter. "Stone on Administrative Law." *Columbia Law Review* 46 (September 1946): 734-746.

8838. Givens, Richard A. "Chief Justice Stone and the Developing Functions of Judicial Review." *Virginia Law Review* 47 (December 1961): 1321-1365.

8839. Gold, George. "Loose Tongues: How Stone Cautioned Clerks." *American Bar Association Journal* 71 (October 1985): 28.

8840. Hand, Learned. "Stone's Conception of the Judicial Function." *Columbia Law Review* 46 (July 1946): 696-699.

8841. "Harlan Fiske Stone, Attorney General of the United States." *American Law Review* 58 (July/August 1924): 574-580.

8842. Hollander, Samuel M. "Chief Justice Harlan Fiske Stone." *Commercial Law Journal* 52 (October 1947): 193-195.

8843. Hollander, Samuel M. "Chief Justice Stone." *New Jersey Law Journal* 70 (September 1947): 307.

8844. Holtzoff, Alexander. "Chief Justice Harlan F. Stone." *Federal Bar Association Journal* 4 (November 1941): 207-209, 214.

8845. Hughes, Charles E., Jr. "Mr. Chief Justice Stone." *Harvard Law Review* 59 (October 1946): 1193-1236.

8846. Konefsky, Samuel J. *Chief Justice Stone and the Supreme Court.* New York: Macmillan, 1945.

8847. Laufer, David D. "*Hague v. C.I.O.*: Mr. Justice Stone's Test of Federal Jurisdiction: A Reappraisal." *Buffalo Law Review* 19 (Spring 1970): 547-564.

8848. Levy, Beryl H. "A Solid Chief Justice: Harlan Fiske Stone." *Indiana Law Journal* 17 (October 1941): 23-29.

8849. Lusky, Louis. "Fragmentation of the Supreme Court: An Inquiry into Causes." *Hofstra Law Review* 10 (Summer 1982): 1137-1148.

8850. Magill, Roswell. "Stone on Taxation." *Columbia Law Review* 66 (September 1946): 747-763.

8851. Mason, Alpheus T. "The Core of Free Government, 1938-1940: Mr. Justice Stone and 'Preferred Freedoms'." *Yale Law Journal* 65 (April 1956): 597-628.

8852. Mason, Alpheus T. "Extra-Judicial Work for Judges: The Views of Chief Justice Stone." *Harvard Law Review* 67 (December 1953): 193-216.

8853. Mason, Alpheus T. "Harlan Fiske

Stone and FDR's Court Plan." *Yale Law Journal* 61 (June/July 1952): 791-817.

8854. Mason, Alpheus T. "Harlan Fiske Stone Assays Social Justice, 1912-1923." *University of Pennsylvania Law Review* 99 (May 1951): 887-918.

8855. Mason, Alpheus T. "Harlan Fiske Stone: In Defense of Individual Freedom, 1918-1920." *Columbia Law Review* 51 (February 1951): 147-169.

8856. Mason, Alpheus T. *Harlan Fiske Stone: Pillar of the Law.* New York: Viking Press, 1956.

8857. Mason, Alpheus T. "Inter Arma Silent Leges: Chief Justice Stone's Views." *Harvard Law Review* 69 (March 1956): 806-838.

8858. Mount, Annice P. "Chief Justice Harlan Fiske Stone." *Women Lawyers Journal* 32 (June/July 1966): 102.

8859. Parker, John J. "Harlan F. Stone: A Liberal in the American Pattern." *Syracuse Law Review* 1 (Spring 1949): 2-8.

8860. Powell, Richard R. "Harlan F. Stone." *University of Pennsylvania Law Review* 94 (July 1957): 355-364.

8861. Rutledge, Wiley B. "Harlan Fiske Stone: A Great American Judge." *Temple Law Quarterly* 19 (April 1946): 9-10.

8862. Smith, Young B. "Harlan Fiske Stone: Teacher, Scholar, Dean." *Columbia Law Review* 46 (September 1946): 700-709.

8863. Stone, Lauson H. "Harlan F. Stone: My Father the Chief Justice." *Supreme Court Historical Society Yearbook* 1978 (1978): 7-17.

8864. Vinson, Fred M. "An Observation about Judge Stone's Judicial Life." *University of Kansas City Law Review* 16 (1947-1948): 1.

8865. Wechsler, Herbert. "Mr. Chief Justice Stone." *Case and Comment* 54 (September/October 1949): 14-20.

8866. Wechsler, Herbert. "Mr. Chief Justice Stone." *Indiana Law Journal* 24 (Winter 1949): 195-202.

8867. Wechsler, Herbert. "Stone and the Constitution." *Columbia Law Review* 46 (September 1946): 764-800.

Writings

8868. Stone, Harlan F. "The Chief Justice." *American Bar Association Journal* 27 (July 1941): 407-408.

8869. Stone, Harlan F. "The Common Law in the United States." *Harvard Law Review* 50 (November 1936): 4-26.

8870. Stone, Harlan F. "Dissenting Opinions Are Not without Value." *Journal of the American Judicature Society* 26 (October 1942): 78.

8871. Stone, Harlan F. "Fifty Years' Work of the United States Supreme Court." *American Bar Association Journal* 14 (August/September 1928): 428-436.

8872. Stone, Harlan F. "Fifty Years' Work of the United States Supreme Court." *American Bar Association Report* 53 (1928): 259-281.

8873. Stone, Harlan F. "Fifty Years' Work of the United States Supreme Court." *Oregon Law Review* 8 (April 1929): 248-268.

8874. Stone, Harlan F. *Law and Its Administration.* New York: Columbia University Press, 1915.

8875. Stone, Harlan F. "Louis Dembitz Brandeis." *American Bar Association Journal* 29 (February 1943): 73-75, 109.

8876. Stone, Harlan F. "Mr. Justice Cardozo." *Columbia Law Review* 39 (January 1939): 1-3.

8877. Stone, Harlan F. "Mr. Justice Cardozo." *Harvard Law Review* 52 (January 1939): 353-355.

8878. Stone, Harlan F. "Mr. Justice Cardozo." *Yale Law Journal* 48 (January 1939): 371-373.

8879. Stone, Harlan F. *Public Control of Business, Selected Opinions by Harlan Fiske Stone.* Edited by Alfred Lief. New York: Howell, Soskin, 1940.

8880. Stone, Harlan F. "The Public Influence of the Bar." *Harvard Law Review* 48 (November 1934): 1-14.

8881. Stone, Harlan F. "Some Aspects of the Problem of Law Simplification." *Columbia Law Review* 23 (March 1923): 319-337.

Joseph Story

General Studies

8882. Bacon, Ezekiel. *A Lecture Delivered before the Young Men's Association of the City of Utica, December 15, 1843.* Utica, NY: R. W. Roberts, 1844.

8883. Banks, N. Huston. "Abby Folsom and Judge Story: A Curious Incident." *Magazine of American History* 10 (November 1883): 427-429.

8884. Bishirjian, Richard. "Justice Story's Influence on American Law." *Intercollegiate Review* 8 (Winter 1972-1973): 127-130.

8885. Bork, Robert H. "Styles in Constitutional Theory." *Supreme Court Historical Society Yearbook* 1984 (1984): 53-60.

8886. Brown, George S. "A Dissenting Opinion of Mr. Justice Story Enacted as Law within Thirty-six Days." *Virginia Law Review* 26 (April 1940): 759-767.

8887. Browne, Irving. "Joseph Story." In *Short Studies of Great Lawyers*, by Irving Browne, 28. Albany, NY: Albany Law Journal, 1878.

8888. Buttre, Lillian C. "Joseph Story." In *American Portrait Gallery*, vol. 2, by Lillian C. Buttre, 45-46. New York: J. C. Buttre, 1877.

8889. Cassoday, John B. "James Kent and Joseph Story." *Yale Law Journal* 12 (January 1903): 146-153.

8890. Commager, Henry S. "Joseph Story." In *Gaspar G. Bacon Lectures on the Constitution of the United States, 1940-1950*, by Arthur N. Holcombe, et al., 31-94. Boston: Boston University Press, 1953.

8891. Culver, Michael. "An Examination of the July 8, 1838 Letter from Harriet Martineau to United States Supreme Court Justice Joseph Story as It Pertains to United States Copyright Law." *Journal of the Copyright Society* 32 (October 1984): 38-45.

8892. Dowd, Morgan D. "Justice Joseph Story: A Study of the Contributions of a Jeffersonian Judge to the Development of American Constitutional Law." Ph.D. diss., University of Massachusetts, 1964.

8893. Dowd, Morgan D. "Justice Joseph Story: A Study of the Legal Philosophy of a Jeffersonian Judge." *Vanderbilt Law Review* 18 (March 1965): 643-662.

8894. Dowd, Morgan D. "Justice Joseph Story and the Politics of Appointment." *American Journal of Legal History* 9 (October 1965): 265-285.

8895. Dowd, Morgan D. "Justice Story and the Slavery Conflict." *Massachusetts Law Quarterly* 52 (September 1967): 239-253.

8896. Dowd, Morgan D. "Justice Story, the Supreme Court, and the Obligation of Contract." *Case Western Reserve Law Review* 19 (April 1968): 493-527.

8897. Dunne, Gerald T. "American Blackstone." *Washington University Law Quarterly* 1963 (June 1963): 321-337.

8898. Dunne, Gerald T. "Joseph Story: 1812 Overture." *Harvard Law Review* 77 (December 1963): 240-278.

8899. Dunne, Gerald T. "Joseph Story: The Age of Jackson." *Missouri Law Review* 34 (Summer 1969): 307-355.

8900. Dunne, Gerald T. "Joseph Story: The Germinal Years." *Harvard Law Review* 75 (February 1962): 707-754.

8901. Dunne, Gerald T. "Joseph Story: The Great Term, 1837." *Harvard Law Review* 79 (March 1966): 877-913.

8902. Dunne, Gerald T. "Joseph Story: The Lowering Storm." *American Journal of Legal History* 13 (January 1969): 1-41.

8903. Dunne, Gerald T. "Joseph Story: The Middle Years." *Harvard Law Review* 80 (June 1967): 1679-1709.

8904. Dunne, Gerald T. "Joseph Story: The Salem Years." *Essex Institute Historical Collections* 101 (October 1965): 307-332.

8905. Dunne, Gerald T. *Justice Joseph Story and the Rise of the Supreme Court.* New York: Simon and Schuster, 1970.

8906. Dunne, Gerald T. "Justice Story and the Modern Corporation: A Closing Circle?" *American Journal of Legal History* 17 (July 1973): 262-270.

8907. Dunne, Gerald T. "Mr. Joseph Story and the American Law of Banking." *American Journal of Legal History* 5 (July 1961): 205-229.

8908. Dunne, Gerald T. "The Story-Livingston Correspondence, 1812-1822." *American Journal of Legal History* 10 (July 1966): 224-236.

8909. Eddy, Ruth S. "The Ancestry of Judge Joseph Story: Justice of the Supreme Court of the United States." *Essex Institute Historical Collections* 83 (January 1947): 59-66.

8910. Gould, Elizabeth P. "Joseph Story: An Additional Word." *Chicago Law Times* 3 (July 1889): 231-236.

8911. Greenleaf, Simon. "Biographical Sketch of Joseph Story, LL.D." *American Law Magazine* 6 (January 1846): 241-268.

8912. Greenleaf, Simon. *A Discourse Commemorative of the Life and Character of the Honorable Joseph Story.* Boston: Little, Brown, 1845.

8913. Griswold, Rufus W. "Joseph Story." In *The Prose Writers of America*, edited by Rufus W. Griswold, 138-139. Philadelphia: Carey and Hart, 1847.

8914. Guernsey, Rocellus S. *A Key to Story's Equity Jurisprudence.* New York: Diossy, 1876.

8915. Heaney, Howell J. "The Letters of Joseph Story, 1779-1845, in the Hampton L. Carson Collection of the Free Library of Philadelphia." *American Journal of Legal History* 2 (April 1958): 75-85.

8916. Hillard, George S. "Memoir of Joseph Story, LL.D." *Massachusetts Historical Society Proceedings* 10 (April 1868): 176-205.

8917. Hogan, John C. "Blackstone and Joseph Story: Their Influence on the Development of Criminal Law in America." *Minnesota Law Review* 40 (January 1956): 107-124.

8918. Hogan, John C. "Joseph Story on Juries." *Oregon Law Review* 37 (April 1958): 234-255.

8919. Hogan, John C. "Joseph Story's Anonymous Law Articles." *Michigan Law Review* 52 (April 1954): 869-884.

8920. Hogan, John C. "Joseph Story's Essay on 'Domicil'." *Buffalo Law Review* 35 (April 1955): 215-224.

8921. Hogan, John C. "Joseph Story's Essay on 'Natural Law'." *Oregon Law Review* 34 (February 1955): 88-105.

8922. Hogan, John C. "Joseph Story's

Unsigned Article on *Common Law Lines.*" *Case and Comment* 62 (November/December 1957): 34-36.

8923. Hogan, John C. "Justice Story on Capital Punishment." *California Law Review* 43 (March 1955): 76-84.

8924. Hogan, John C. "Justice Story on the Common Law of Evidence." *Vanderbilt Law Review* 9 (December 1955): 51-67.

8925. Hogan, John C., ed. "Three Essays on the Law by Joseph Story." *Southern California Law Review* 28 (December 1954): 19-32.

8926. Howland, Francis. "Story." In *Homes of American Statesmen: With Anecdotical, Personal, and Descriptive Sketches by Various Authors,* 427-445. New York: A. W. Upham, 1858.

8927. Hunt, William. "Joseph Story." In *The American Biographical Sketch Book,* by William Hunt, 302. New York: Cornish, Lamport, 1848.

8928. Joyce, Craig. "Supreme Court Justice Joseph Story: Statesman of the Old Republic." *Michigan Law Review* 84 (February/April 1986): 846-860.

8929. Leslie, William R. "The Influence of Joseph Story's Theory of the Conflict of Laws on Constitutional Nationalism." *Mississippi Valley Historical Review* 35 (September 1948): 203-220.

8930. Leslie, William R. "Similarities in Lord Mansfield's and Joseph Story's View of Fundamental Law." *American Journal of Legal History* 1 (October 1957): 278-307.

8931. Loerenzen, Ernest G. "Story's Commentaries on the Conflict of Laws: One Hundred Years After." *Harvard Law Review* 48 (November 1934): 15-38.

8932. McClellan, James. "Comments on Kent Newmyer's Paper, 'Justice Joseph Story, the *Charles River Bridge* Case, and

the Crisis of Republicanism'." *American Journal of Legal History* 17 (June 1973): 271-273.

8933. McClellan, James. *Joseph Story and the American Constitution: A Study in Political and Legal Thought.* Norman: University of Oklahoma Press, 1971.

8934. McDowell, Gary L. "Joseph Story's 'Science' of Equity." *Supreme Court Review* 1979 (1979): 153-172.

8935. Marshall, John. *Letters of Joseph Story.* New York: Macmillan, 1958.

8936. Marshall, John. "Marshall-Story Correspondence." *Massachusetts Historical Society Proceedings* 14 (1901): 324-360.

8937. Mathews, William. "Recollections of Judge Story." In *Hours with Men and Books,* 13th ed., edited by William Mathews, 97-116. Chicago: Scott, Foresman, 1879.

8938. Moore, Frank. "Joseph Story." In *American Eloquence,* vol. 2, edited by Frank Moore, 422-437. New York: D. Appleton, 1862.

8939. Moses, Adolph. "The Friendship between Marshall and Story." *American Law Review* 35 (May/June 1901): 321-342.

8940. Nadelmann, Kurt H. "Joseph Story's Sketch of American Law." *American Journal of Comparative Law* 3 (Winter 1954): 3-8.

8941. Newell, William. *A Discourse Occasioned by the Death of the Honorable Joseph Story, LL.D.* Cambridge, MA: Metcalf, 1845.

8942. Newmyer, R. Kent. "Joseph Story and the War of 1812: A Judicial Nationalist." *Historian* 26 (August 1964): 486-501.

8943. Newmyer, R. Kent. "Justice Joseph Story: A Political and Constitutional Study." Ph.D. diss., University of Nebraska, 1959.

8944. Newmyer, R. Kent. "Justice Joseph Story, the *Charles River Bridge* Case, and the Crisis of Republicanism." *American Journal of Legal History* 17 (July 1973): 232-245.

8945. Newmyer, R. Kent. "Note on the Whig Politics of Justice Joseph Story." *Mississippi Valley Historical Review* 48 (December 1961): 480-491.

8946. Newmyer, R. Kent. *Supreme Court Justice Joseph Story: Statesman of the Old Republic*. Chapel Hill: University of North Carolina Press, 1985.

8947. Peabody, Andrew P. "Joseph Story." In *Harvard Reminiscences*, by Andrew P. Peabody, 56-60. Boston: Ticknor and Company, 1888.

8948. Prager, Frank D. "The Changing Views of Justice Story on the Constitution of Patents." *American Journal of Legal History* 4 (January 1960): 1-21.

8949. Prager, Frank D. "The Influence of Mr. Justice Story on American Patent Law." *American Journal of Legal History* 5 (July 1961): 254-264.

8950. Robbins, Donald C. "Joseph Story: The Early Years, 1779-1811." Ph.D. diss., University of Kentucky, 1965.

8951. Schofield, William. "Joseph Story." In *Great American Lawyers*, vol. 3, edited by William D. Lewis, 121-186. Philadelphia: J. C. Winston Company, 1907-1909.

8952. Schotten, Peter M. "A Government of Laws: The Constitutional Understanding of Mr. Justice Story." Ph.D. diss., Claremont Graduate School, 1974.

8953. Schwartz, Mortimer D., and John C. Hogan. "A National Library: Mr. Justice Story Speaks." *Journal of Legal Education* 8 (1955): 328-330.

8954. Scott, Henry W. "Joseph Story." In *Distinguished American Lawyers*, by Henry W. Scott, 627-636. New York: C. L. Webster, 1891.

8955. "Story." *Albany Law Journal* 13 (February 5, 1876): 90-94.

8956. Story, William W. *Life and Letters of Joseph Story*. 2 vols. Boston: Little, Brown, 1851.

8957. Sumner, Charles. *The Scholar, the Jurist, the Artist, the Philanthropist: An Address before the Phi Beta Kappa Society of Harvard University, at Their Anniversary, August 27, 1846*. Boston: W. D. Ticknor and Company, 1846.

8958. Sumner, Charles. "Some Account of Judge Story of the United States." *Bentleys Miscellaney* 29 (1851): 376-384.

8959. Taney, Roger B. "Proceedings of Court Had upon the Death of Judge Story." *United States Reports* 45 (1846): v-viii.

8960. Tucker, Henry S. "Judge Story's Position on the So-Called General Welfare Clause." *Constitutional Review* 13 (January 1929): 13-35.

8961. Upshur, Abel P. *A Brief Enquiry into the True Nature and Charter of Our Federal Government: Being a Review of Judge Story's Commentaries on the Constitution of the United States*. New York: Da Capo Press, 1971.

8962. Valladao, Haroldo. "The Influence of Joseph Story on Latin-American Rules of Conflict of Law." *American Journal of Comparative Law* 3 (Winter 1954): 27-41.

8963. Waite, Charles B. "Joseph Story." *Chicago Law Times* 3 (January 1889): 1-13.

8964. Ware, William. "Joseph Story." In *American Unitarian Biography*, vol. 2, by William Ware, 175-186. Boston: J. Munroe, 1851.

8965. Warren, Charles. *The Story-Marshall Correspondence*. New York: New York University School of Law, 1942.

8966. Waterson, Robert C. "The Character of Joseph Story, LL.D.: A Discourse."

Monthly Religious Magazine 2 (November 1845): 361-370.

8967. Waterson, Robert C. *A Discourse on the Life and Character of Hon. Joseph Story. . . .* Boston: W. Crosby and H. P. Nichols, 1845.

8968. Webster, Daniel. "Mr. Justice Story." In *Writings and Speeches*, vol. 3, by Daniel Webster, 295-302. Boston: Little, Brown, 1903.

Writings

8969. Story, Joseph. *Commentaries on the Constitution of the United States.* 5th ed. Boston: Little, Brown, 1891.

8970. Story, Joseph. *Discourse upon the Life, Character, and Services of the Honorable John Marshall.* Boston: J. Munroe, 1835.

8971. Story, Joseph. *Joseph Story: A Collection of Writings by and about an Eminent American Jurist.* Edited by Mortimer D. Schwartz and John C. Hogan. New York: Oceana Publications, 1959.

8972. Story, Joseph. *Miscellaneous Writings of Joseph Story.* Edited by William W. Story. Boston: Little, Brown, 1852.

William Strong

General Studies

8973. Dwight, Benjamin W. *The History of the Descendants of Older John Strong.* Albany, NY: J. Munsell, 1871.

8974. "Political Portrait of William Strong." *United States Democratic Review* 27 (September 1850): 269-275.

8975. Teaford, Jon C. "Toward a Christian Nation: Religion, Law, and Justice Strong." *Journal of Presbyterian History* 54 (Winter 1976): 422-437.

8976. Teiser, Sidney. "William Strong, Associate Justice of the Territorial Courts." *Oregon Historical Quarterly* 64 (December 1963): 293-308.

Writings

8977. Strong, William. "The Needs of the Supreme Court." *North American Review* 132 (May 1881): 437-450.

8978. Strong, William. "Relief for the Supreme Court." *North American Review* 151 (November 1890): 567-575.

8979. Strong, William. *Two Lectures upon the Relations of Civil Law to Church Polity, Discipline, and Property.* New York: Dodd and Mead, 1875.

George Sutherland

General Studies

8980. Banner, James. "Mr. Justice Sutherland and the Social Welfare." Master's thesis, Columbia University, 1961.

8981. Howell, Ronald F. "Conservative Influence on Constitutional Development, 1923-1937: The Judicial Theory of Justices Van Devanter, McReynolds, Sutherland, and Butler." Ph.D. diss., Johns Hopkins University, 1952.

8982. Knox, John. "Justice George Sutherland." *Chicago Bar Review* 24 (October 1942): 16-18.

8983. Levitan, David M. "The Foreign Relations Power: An Analysis of Mr. Justice Sutherland's Theory." *Yale Law Journal* 55 (April 1946): 467-497.

8984. Maidment, Richard A. "A Study in Judicial Motivation: Mr. Justice Sutherland and Economic Regulation." *Utah Law Review* 1973 (Summer 1973): 156-163.

8985. Mason, Alpheus T. "Conservative

World of Mr. Justice Sutherland, 1883-1910." *American Political Science Review* 32 (June 1938): 443-477.

8986. Mason, Alpheus T. "The Dilemma of Liberalism." *Journal of Social Philosophy* 3 (April 1938): 223-234.

8987. Paschal, Joel F. "Man against the State: The Ordeal of George Sutherland." Ph.D. diss., Princeton University, 1948.

8988. Paschal, Joel F. *Mr. Justice Sutherland.* Chicago: University of Chicago Press, 1956.

8989. Paschal, Joel F. *Mr. Justice Sutherland, a Man against the State.* Princeton, NJ: Princeton University Press, 1951.

8990. Saks, J. Benson. "Mr. Justice Sutherland." Ph.D. diss., Johns Hopkins University, 1940.

8991. Sentell, R. Perry, Jr. "The Opinions of Hughes and Sutherland and the Rights of the Individual." *Vanderbilt Law Review* 15 (March 1962): 559-615.

8992. Stephens, Harold M. "Mr. Justice Sutherland." *American Bar Association Journal* 31 (September 1945): 446-453.

Writings

8993. Sutherland, George. *Constitutional Power and World Affairs.* New York: Columbia University Press, 1919.

8994. Sutherland, George. *Private Rights and Government Control.* Washington, DC: U.S. Government Printing Office, 1917.

Noah H. Swayne

General Studies

8995. "Honorable Noah H. Swayne: Memorial Proceedings of the Ohio State Bar Association." *Ohio State Bar Association Reports* 5 (December 30-31, 1884): 41-48.

8996. Swayne, Norman W. *The Descendants of Francis Swayne.* Philadelphia: Lippincott, 1921.

William H. Taft

General Studies

8997. Anderson, Donald F. *William Howard Taft: A Conservative's Conception of the Presidency.* Ithaca, NY: Cornell University Press, 1973.

8998. Anderson, Judith I. "A Mountain of Misery: An Intimate History of William Howard Taft." Ph.D. diss., University of California, Los Angeles, 1973.

8999. Anderson, Judith I. *William Howard Taft: An Intimate History.* New York: W. W. Norton, 1981.

9000. Ballard, Rene N. "The Administrative Theory of William Howard Taft." *Western Political Quarterly* 7 (March 1954): 65-74.

9001. Barker, Charles E. *With President Taft in the White House: Memories of William Howard Taft.* Chicago: Knoch, 1947.

9002. Bickel, Alexander M. "Mr. Taft Rehabilitates the Court." *Yale Law Journal* 79 (November 1969): 1-45.

9003. Currie, David P. "The Constitution in the Supreme Court: 1921-1930." *Duke Law Journal* 1986 (February 1986): 65-144.

9004. Danelski, David J. "The Chief Justice and the Supreme Court." Ph.D. diss., University of Chicago, 1961.

9005. Duffy, Herbert S. *William Howard Taft.* New York: Minton, Balch, 1930.

9006. Fish, Peter G. "William Howard Taft and Charles Evans Hughes: Conservative Politicians as Chief Judicial Reformers." *Supreme Court Review* 1975 (1975): 123-145.

9007. Greve, Charles T. "Personal Reminiscences of Chief Justice William Howard Taft." *Commercial Law Review* 35 (June 1930): 282-285.

9008. Hahn, Harlan. "President Taft and the Discipline of Patronage." *Journal of Politics* 28 (May 1966): 368-390.

9009. Hess, Stephen. "Big Bill Taft." *American Heritage* 17 (October 1966): 33-37, 82-86.

9010. Hicks, Frederick C. *William Howard Taft, Yale Professor of Law and New Haven Citizen.* New Haven, CT: Yale University Press, 1945.

9011. Hollister, Howard C. "William H. Taft at the Bar and on the Bench." *Green Bag* 20 (July 1908): 337-345.

9012. Kutler, Stanley I. "Chief Justice Taft and the Delusion of Judicial Exactness: A Study in Jurisprudence." *Virginia Law Review* 48 (December 1962): 1407-1426.

9013. Kutler, Stanley I. "Chief Justice Taft, Judicial Unanimity, and Labor: The *Coronado* Case." *Historian* 24 (November 1961): 68-83.

9014. Kutler, Stanley I. "Chief Justice Taft, National Regulation, and the Commerce Clause." *Journal of American History* 51 (March 1965): 651-668.

9015. Kutler, Stanley I. "The Judicial Philosophy of Chief Justice Taft and Organized Labor, 1921-1930." Ph.D. diss., Ohio State University, 1960.

9016. Larson, Robert W. "Taft, Roosevelt, and New Mexico Statehood." *Mid-America* 45 (April 1963): 99-114.

9017. Low, A. Maurice. "William Howard Taft." *Yale Review* 1 (April 1912): 349-363.

9018. McGowan, Carl. "Perspectives of

Taft's Tenure as Chief Justice and Their Special Relevance Today." *University of Cincinnati Law Review* 55 (Spring 1987): 1143-1157.

9019. McHale, Francis. *President and Chief Justice: The Life and Public Services of William Howard Taft.* Philadelphia: Dorrance and Company, 1931.

9020. McHargue, Daniel S. "President Taft's Appointments to the Supreme Court." *Journal of Politics* 12 (August 1950): 478-510.

9021. Mason, Alpheus T. "Chief Justice Taft at the Helm." *Vanderbilt Law Review* 18 (March 1965): 367-404.

9022. Mason, Alpheus T. "The Labor Decisions of Chief Justice Taft." *University of Pennsylvania Law Review* 78 (March 1930): 585-625.

9023. Mason, Alpheus T. "President by Chance, Chief Justice by Choice." *American Bar Association Journal* 55 (January 1969): 35-39.

9024. Mason, Alpheus T. *William Howard Taft, Chief Justice.* New York: Simon and Schuster, 1965.

9025. Minger, Ralph E. "Taft's Missions to Japan: A Study in Personal Diplomacy." *Pacific Historical Review* 30 (August 1961): 279-294.

9026. Minger, Ralph E. *William Howard Taft and United States Foreign Policy: The Apprenticeship Years, 1900-1908.* Urbana: University of Illinois Press, 1975.

9027. Minger, Ralph E. "William Howard Taft's Forgotten Visit to Russia." *Russian Review* 22 (April 1963): 149-156.

9028. Morris, Jeffrey B. "What Heaven Must Be Like: William Howard Taft as Chief Justice, 1921-1930." *Supreme Court Historical Society Yearbook* 1983 (1983): 80-101.

9029. Murphy, Walter F. "Chief Justice Taft and the Lower Court Bureaucracy: A

Study in Judicial Administration." *Journal of Politics* 24 (August 1962): 453-476.

9030. Murphy, Walter F. "In His Own Image: Mr. Chief Justice Taft and Supreme Court Appointments." *Supreme Court Review* 1961 (1961): 159-193.

9031. Pringle, Henry F. *Life and Times of William Howard Taft: Chief Justice.* New York: Farrar and Rhinehart, 1939.

9032. Ragan, Allen E. *Chief Justice Taft.* Columbus: Ohio State Archaeological and Historical Society, 1938.

9033. Ragan, Allen E. "Free Chief Justice Taft." Ph.D. diss., Ohio State University, 1932.

9034. Reuter, Frank R. "William Howard Taft and the Separation of Church and State in the Philippines." *Journal of Church and State* 24 (Winter 1982): 105-117.

9035. Roebuck, James R. "The United States and East Asia, 1909-1913: A Study of the Far Eastern Diplomacy of William Howard Taft." Ph.D. diss., University of Virginia, 1977.

9036. Ross, Ishbel. *An American Family: The Tafts, 1678-1964.* Cleveland: World Publishing Company, 1964.

9037. Schultz, L. Peter. "William Howard Taft: A Constitutionalist's View of the Presidency." Ph.D. diss., Northern Illinois University, 1979.

9038. Schultz, L. Peter. "William Howard Taft: A Constitutionalist's View of the Presidency." *Presidential Studies Quarterly* 9 (Fall 1979): 402-414.

9039. Smith, Dean. "Three Hundred Pounds of Solid Charity: William Howard Taft." *American History Illustrated* 11 (April 1976): 10-17.

9040. Solvick, Stanley D. "The Pre-Presidential Political and Economic Thought of William Howard Taft." *Northwest Ohio Quarterly* 43 (Fall 1971): 87-97.

9041. Spring, Samuel. "Two Chief Jus-

tices: Edward Douglas White and William Howard Taft." *Review of Reviews* 64 (August 1921): 161-170.

9042. Taft, Charles P. "My Father the Chief Justice." *Supreme Court Historical Society Yearbook* 1977 (1977): 5-10.

9043. Taft, Helen H. *Recollections of Full Years.* New York: Dodd, Mead, 1914.

9044. U.S. War Department. *Special Report of William H. Taft, Secretary of War, to the President, on the Philippines.* Washington, DC: U.S. Government Printing Office, 1908.

9045. Warren, Earl. "Chief Justice William Howard Taft." *Yale Law Journal* 67 (January 1958): 353-362.

9046. Wessel, Thomas R. "Republican Justice: The Department of Justice under Roosevelt and Taft, 1901-1903." Ph.D. diss., University of Maryland, 1922.

9047. Withers, John L. "The Administrative Theories and Practices of William Howard Taft." Ph.D. diss., University of Chicago, 1957.

Writings

9048. Taft, William H. *Address at Dedication of Alphonso Taft Hall.* Cincinnati: University of Cincinnati, 1925.

9049. Taft, William H. *The Anti-Trust Act and the Supreme Court.* New York: Harper and Row, 1914.

9050. Taft, William H. "The Boundaries between the Executive, the Legislative, and the Judicial Branches of the Government." *Yale Law Journal* 25 (June 1916): 599-616.

9051. Taft, William H. "Criticism of the Federal Judiciary." *American Law Review* 29 (September/October 1895): 641-674.

9052. Taft, William H. "Delays and Defects in the Enforcement of Law in This Country." *Albany Law Journal* 70 (October 1908): 300-304.

9053. Taft, William H. *Ethics in Service: Addresses Delivered in the Page Lecture Series, 1914, before the Senior Class of Sheffield Scientific School, Yale University.* New Haven, CT: Yale University Press, 1915.

9054. Taft, William H. *Four Aspects of Civic Duty.* New York: Charles Scribner's Sons, 1906.

9055. Taft, William H. "The Jurisdiction of the Supreme Court under the Act of February 13, 1925." *Yale Law Journal* 35 (November 1925): 1-12.

9056. Taft, William H. *Liberty under Law, An Interpretation of the Principles of Our Constitutional Government.* New Haven, CT: Yale University Press, 1922.

9057. Taft, William H. "My Conception of the Presidency." *Collier's Weekly* 41 (June 27, 1908): 7.

9058. Taft, William H. *Our Chief Magistrate and His Powers.* New York: Columbia University Press, 1916.

9059. Taft, William H. "Our New Secretary of War." *New England Magazine* 35 (November 1903): 371-373.

9060. Taft, William H. *Political Issues and Outlooks: Speeches Delivered between August, 1908, and February, 1909.* New York: Doubleday, 1909.

9061. Taft, William H. *Popular Government: Its Essence, Its Permanence, and Its Perils.* New Haven, CT: Yale University Press, 1913.

9062. Taft, William H. "Possible and Needed Reforms in the Administration of Civil Justice in the Federal Courts." *American Law Review* 57 (January 1923): 1-23.

9063. Taft, William H. "Power of the President." *Yale Review* 4 (October 1914): 25-42.

9064. Taft, William H. *Present Day Problems: A Collection of Addresses Delivered on Various Occasions.* New York: Dodd, Mead, 1908.

9065. Taft, William H. "Presidency." *Independent* 73 (November 21, 1912): 1196-1200.

9066. Taft, William H. *The Presidency: Its Duties, Its Powers, Its Opportunities, and Its Limitations: Three Lectures.* New York: Charles Scribner's Sons, 1916.

9067. Taft, William H. *The President and His Powers.* New York: Columbia University Press, 1916.

9068. Taft, William H. *Presidential Addresses and State Papers of William Howard Taft.* 2 vols. Garden City, NY: Doubleday, 1910.

9069. Taft, William H. "Proceedings on the Death of Chief Justice White." *United States Reports* 257 (1921): v-xxix.

9070. Taft, William H. *Representative Government in the United States: Being the Opening Lecture of the James Stokes Lectureship on Politics, at New York University.* New York: New York University Press, 1921.

9071. Taft, William H. "The Right of Private Property." *Michigan Law Journal* 3 (August 1894): 215-233.

9072. Taft, William H. "Salmon P. Chase Memorial." *American Bar Association Journal* 9 (June 1923): 348-352.

9073. Taft, William H. "The Supreme Court of the United States and Popular Self-Government." *Harvard Graduates' Magazine* 23 (September 1914): 1-14.

9074. Taft, William H. *Taft Papers on League of Nations.* Edited by Theodore Marburg and Horace E. Flack. New York: Macmillan, 1920.

9075. Taft, William H. *The United States and Peace.* New York: Charles Scribner's Sons, 1914.

9076. Taft, William H. *The United States Supreme Court: The Prototype of a World Court.* Baltimore: American Society for Judicial Settlement of International Disputes, 1915.

9077. Taft, William H., and George B. Edwards. "Letters of Roommates: William H. Taft and George B. Edwards." Edited by Walter P. Armstrong. *American Bar Association Journal* 34 (May 1948): 383-385.

9078. Taft, William H., and William J. Bryan. *World Peace: A Written Debate between William Howard Taft and William Jennings Bryan.* New York: Doran, 1917.

9079. Taft, William H., et al. "Appreciation of Edward Douglas White." *Loyola Law Journal* 7 (April 1926): 61-94.

Roger B. Taney

General Studies

9080. Acheson, Dean G. "Roger Brooke Taney: Notes upon Judicial Self-Restraint." *Illinois Law Review* 31 (February 1937): 705-717.

9081. Adams, Samuel B. "Roger Brooke Taney." *Georgia Bar Association Reports* 48 (1931): 262-274.

9082. Armstrong, Walter P. "The Rehabilitation of Roger Brooke Taney." *Kansas Bar Association Journal* 5 (August 1936): 13-22.

9083. Beitzinger, Alfons J. "Chief Justice Taney and the Publication of Court Opinions." *Catholic University of America Law Review* 7 (January 1958): 32-36.

9084. Borchard, Edwin. "Taney's Influence on Constitutional Law." *Georgetown Law Journal* 24 (May 1936): 843-863.

9085. Boudin, Louis B. "John Marshall and Roger B. Taney." *Georgetown Law Journal* 24 (May 1936): 864-909.

9086. Braley, Henry K. "Roger Brooke Taney, Chief Justice of the United States." *Green Bag* 22 (March 1910): 149-167.

9087. Buttre, Lillian C. "Roger Brooke Taney." In *The American Portrait Gallery,* by Lillian C. Buttre, vol. 2, 981-982. New York: J. C. Buttre, 1877.

9088. Christian, George L. "Roger Brooke Taney." *American Law Review* 46 (January 1912): 1-23.

9089. Conron, Michael A. "Law, Politics, and Chief Justice Taney: A Reconsideration of the *Luther v. Borden* Decision." *American Journal of Legal History* 11 (October 1967): 377-388.

9090. Cozart, A. W. "Marshall and Taney: A Parallel." *Georgia Law Review* 1 (December 1927): 33-37.

9091. Curtis, Benjamin R. "Character and Public Service of Chief Justice Taney: Remarks Made at a Meeting of the Boston Bar, October 15, 1864." In *Memoir,* vol. 2, by Benjamin R. Curtis, 336-342. Boston: Little, Brown, 1879.

9092. Delaplaine, Edward S. "Chief Justice Roger B. Taney: His Career as a Lawyer." *American Law Review* 52 (July/August 1918): 535-570.

9093. Delaplaine, Edward S. "Chief Justice Roger Brooke Taney: His Career at the Frederick Bar." *Maryland Historical Magazine* 13 (1918): 109-142.

9094. Delaplaine, Edward S. "The Fame of Chief Justice Taney." *Case and Comment* 37 (Winter 1931): 6-9.

9095. Delaplaine, Edward S. "Lincoln after Taney's Death." *Lincoln Herald* 79 (Winter 1977): 151-157.

9096. Edwards, Isaac. "Chief Justice Taney: A Sketch and a Criticism." *Albany Law Journal* 8 (July 19, 1873): 33-38.

9097. Ellis, Charles M. "Roger Brooke

Taney." *Atlantic Monthly* 15 (February 1865): 151-161.

9098. Estes, W. Lee. "Roger B. Taney." *American Law Review* 59 (September/October 1925): 783-798.

9099. Fehrenbacher, Don E. "Roger B. Taney and the Sectional Crisis." *Journal of Southern History* 43 (November 1977): 555-566.

9100. Flavius, Brother. *The Pride of Our Nation: A Story of Chief Justice Roger Brooke Taney.* Notre Dame, IN: Dujarie Press, 1961.

9101. Frankfurter, Felix. *The Commerce Clause under Marshall, Taney, and White.* Chapel Hill: University of North Carolina Press, 1937.

9102. Frankfurter, Felix. "Taney and the Commerce Clause." *Harvard Law Review* 49 (June 1936): 1286-1302.

9103. Gatell, Frank O., ed. "Roger B. Taney, the Bank of Maryland Rioters, and a Whiff of Grapeshot." *Maryland Historical Magazine* 59 (September 1964): 262-267.

9104. Gregory, Charles N. *A Great Judicial Character, Roger Brooke Taney.* New Haven, CT: S. Z. Field, 1908.

9105. Harris, Robert J. "Chief Justice Taney: Prophet of Reform and Reaction." *Vanderbilt Law Review* 10 (February 1957): 227-257.

9106. Holland, Kenneth M. "Statesmanship and the Law: The Jurisprudence and Political Thought of Chief Justice Roger B. Taney." Ph.D. diss., University of Chicago, 1978.

9107. Hollingsworth, Harold M. "The Confirmation of Judicial Review under Taney and Chase." Ph.D. diss., University of Tennessee, 1966.

9108. Hughes, Charles E. "Roger Brooke Taney." *American Bar Association Journal* 17 (December 1931): 785-790.

9109. Janousek, Joseph O. "Roger Brooke

Taney: Man of Conscience." *Journal of the Bar Association of the District of Columbia* 12 (May 1945): 159-169.

9110. Johnson, Monroe. "Roger Brooke Taney: A Reappraisal." *United States Law Review* 66 (September 1932): 487-496.

9111. Johnson, Monroe. "Taney and Lincoln." *American Bar Association Journal* 16 (August 1930): 499-502.

9112. Jones, Francis R. "Roger Brooke Taney." *Green Bag* 14 (January 1902): 1-7.

9113. Lerner, Max. "Taney Redivivus." In *Ideas Are Weapons: The History and Uses of Ideas,* edited by Max Lerner, 38-41. New York: Viking Press, 1939.

9114. Lewis, Walker. "At Home with Chief Justice Taney." *American Bar Association Journal* 51 (September 1965): 829-834.

9115. Lewis, Walker. "Unjust Judge: Who Wrote It?" *American Bar Association Journal* 50 (October 1964): 932-937.

9116. Lewis, Walker. *Without Fear or Favor: A Biography of Chief Justice Roger Brooke Taney.* Boston: Houghton Mifflin, 1965.

9117. Livingstone, John A. "Roger Brooke Taney, 1777-1864." *Commonwealth Law Review* 40 (May 1935): 232-236.

9118. Long, Joseph C. "*Ex Parte Merryman:* The Showdown between Two Great Antagonists: Lincoln and Taney." *South Dakota Law Review* 14 (Spring 1969): 207-249.

9119. McKinley, Andrew. "The Taney Bench." *Green Bag* 16 (June 1904): 369-372.

9120. McLaughlin, James F. "Chief Justice Taney and the Maryland Catholics." In *Catholic World* 67 (June 1898): 396-404.

9121. Mallison, Albert G. "The Political

Theories of Roger B. Taney." *Southwestern Political Science Quarterly* 1 (December 1920): 219-240.

9122. Maury, Sarah M. "The Honourable Roger B. Taney, Chief Justice of the United States." In *The Statesmen of America in 1846*, by Sarah M. Maury, 160-163. London: Brown, Green, and Longmans, 1847.

9123. Mendelson, Wallace. "Chief Justice Taney: Jacksonian Judge." *University of Pittsburgh Law Review* 12 (Spring 1951): 381-393.

9124. Merrick, Edwin. "Roger B. Taney." *The Bar* 10 (May 1903): 33-40.

9125. Mikell, William E. "Chief Justice Roger Brooke Taney." *West Virginia Law Quarterly* 30 (January 1924): 87-103.

9126. Mikell, William E. "Chief Justice Roger Brooke Taney: 1777-1864." In *South Carolina Bar Association Transactions of the 13th Annual Meeting, February 15-16, 1923*, 81-102. Columbia, SC: McCaw of Columbia, 1923.

9127. Mikell, William E. "Roger Brooke Taney: 1777-1864." In *Great American Lawyers*, vol. 4, edited by William D. Lewis, 77-194. Philadelphia: J. C. Winston Company, 1908.

9128. Murray, Nicholas. *Romanism at Home: Letters to the Honorable Roger B. Taney*. 6th ed. New York: Harper and Brothers, 1852.

9129. Palmer, Ben W. *Marshall and Taney: Statesmen of the Law*. New York: Russell and Russell, 1966.

9130. Paterson, Isabel. "The Riddle of Chief Justice Taney in the *Dred Scott* Decision." *Georgia Review* 3 (Summer 1949): 192-203.

9131. Potter, Clarkson N. *Roger Brooke Taney: The Annual Address Delivered before the American Bar Association at Its Fourth Annual Meeting*. Philadelphia: E. E. Markley and Son, 1881.

9132. Purcell, Richard J. "Marshall v. Taney." *Catholic Education Review* (1940): 160-170.

9133. Ransom, William L. "Roger Brooke Taney: Chief Justice of the United States." *Georgetown Law Journal* 24 (May 1936): 809-847.

9134. Schauck, John A. "Chief Justice Taney." *Green Bag* 14 (December 1902): 559-569.

9135. Schouler, James. "Chief Justice Taney." *United States Jurist* 3 (January 1873): 127-137.

9136. Schumacher, Alvin J. *Thunder on Capitol Hill: The Life of Chief Justice Roger B. Taney*. Milwaukee, WI: Bruce Publishing Company, 1964.

9137. Smith, Charles W., Jr. "Roger B. Taney and Mr. Biddle's Bank." *Maryland Historical Magazine* 31 (March 1936): 1-6.

9138. Smith, Charles W., Jr. *Roger B. Taney: Jacksonian Jurist*. Chapel Hill: University of North Carolina Press, 1936.

9139. Smith, F. Dumont. "Roger Brooke Taney." *Texas Law Review* 1 (April 1923): 261-280.

9140. Smith, Walter G. "Roger Brooke Taney." *University of Pennsylvania Law Review* 47 (April 1899): 201-234.

9141. Spector, Robert M. "Lincoln and Taney: A Study in Constitutional Polarization." *American Journal of Legal History* 15 (July 1971): 199-214.

9142. Steiner, Bernard C. *Life of Roger Brooke Taney, Chief Justice of the United States Supreme Court*. Baltimore: Williams and Wilkins Company, 1922.

9143. Steiner, Bernard C. "Roger B. Taney." In *Report of the Twenty-fourth Annual Meeting of the Maryland State Bar*

Association Held at Hotel Chatham, Atlantic City, N.J., June 26, 27, and 28, 1919. Baltimore: Maryland State Bar Association, 1919.

9144. Storey, Moorfield. "Tyler's Memoir of Roger Brooke Taney." *North American Review* 116 (January 1873): 194-203.

9145. Swisher, Carl B. *Mr. Chief Justice Taney.* Chicago: University of Chicago Press, 1956.

9146. Swisher, Carl B. *Roger B. Taney.* New York: Macmillan, 1935.

9147. Swisher, Carl B. "Roger B. Taney and the Tenets of Democracy." *Maryland Historical Magazine* 34 (September 1939): 207-222.

9148. Taggart, Joseph. *Biographical Sketches of the Eminent American Patriots, Charles Carroll, of Carrollton; Roger Brooke Taney; William Starke Rosecrans; John Barry; Philip Henry Sheridan; and a Sketch of the Early History of Maryland.* Kansas City, MO: Burton Company, 1907.

9149. Taney, Edward S. "Roger B. Taney." *Green Bag* 7 (August 1895): 361-364.

9150. Taney, Mary F. "Roger Brooke Taney." *American Catholic Historical Society Records* 11 (March 1900): 33-42.

9151. Tyler, Samuel. *Memoir of Roger Brooke Taney, Chief Justice of the Supreme Court of the United States.* 2d ed. Baltimore: John Murphy and Company, 1876.

9152. Uhle, John B. "Roger Brooke Taney." *Current Comment* 2 (September 15, 1890): 513-517.

9153. Umbreit, Kenneth B. "Review of Roger B. Taney by Carl Brent Swisher." *American Bar Association Journal* 22 (March 1936): 206-207.

9154. Umbreit, Kenneth B. "Review of the Commerce Clause under Marshall, Taney,

and White by Felix Frankfurter." *American Bar Association Journal* 23 (September 1937): 706.

9155. Wallis, Severn T. *Address, with the Reply of His Excellency, Governor Whyte, Delivered in the Senate Chamber, at Annapolis at the Unveiling of the Statue of Chief Justice Taney, December 10, 1872.* Baltimore: John Murphy and Company, 1872.

9156. Warren, Aldice G. "A Comparison of the Tendencies in Constitutional Construction Shown by the Supreme Court under Chief Justices Marshall and Taney Respectively." Ph.D. diss., New York University, 1913.

9157. Warren, Earl. "Roger Brook Taney: Fifth Chief Justice of the United States." *American Bar Association Journal* 41 (June 1955): 504-506.

9158. Welch, James. "Roger B. Taney: Historical Allusions in His Supreme Court Decisions." Master's thesis, Catholic University of America, 1950.

9159. Winitsky, Marvin L. "The Jurisprudence of Roger B. Taney." Ph.D. diss., University of California, Los Angeles, 1973.

9160. Winitsky, Marvin L. "Roger B. Taney: A Historiographical Inquiry." *Maryland Historical Magazine* 69 (Spring 1974): 1-26.

Writings

9161. Taney, Roger B. "Chief Justice Taney." *Albany Law Journal* 7 (January 4, 1873): 2-5.

9162. Taney, Roger B. *Decision in the* Merryman *Case, upon the Writ of* Habeas Corpus. Philadelphia: John Campbell, 1862.

9163. Taney, Roger B. "Letter of Chief Justice Taney." *Massachusetts His-*

torical Society Proceedings 12 (1873): 445-447.

9164. Taney, Roger B. "An Unpublished Letter by Roger B. Taney." *Maryland Historical Magazine* 32 (1937): 225-227.

Smith Thompson

General Studies

9165. Lobingier, Charles S. "The Judicial Opinions of Mr. Justice Thompson." *Nebraska Bar Bulletin* 12 (May 1924): 421-426.

9166. Poucher, J. Wilson. "Smith Thompson, Justice of the Supreme Court of the United States." *Dutchess County Historical Society Yearbook* 25 (1940): 26-29.

9167. Roper, Donald M. "Justice Smith Thompson: Politics and the New York Supreme Court in the Early Nineteenth Century." *New York Historical Society Quarterly* 51 (April 1967): 119-140.

9168. Roper, Donald M. "Mr. Justice Thompson and the Constitution." Ph.D. diss., Indiana University, 1963.

Thomas Todd

General Studies

9169. Levin, H. "Thomas Todd." In *The Lawyers and Law Makers of Kentucky*, by H. Levin, 149. Chicago: Lewis Publishing Company, 1897.

9170. O'Rear, Edward C. "Justice Thomas Todd." *Kentucky State Historical Society Register* 38 (February 1940): 112-119.

Robert Trimble

General Studies

9171. Goff, John S. "Mr. Justice Trimble of the United States Supreme Court." *Kentucky Historical Society Register* 58 (January 1960): 6-28.

9172. Levin, H. "Robert Trimble." In *The Lawyers and Law Makers of Kentucky*, by H. Levin, 149-150. Chicago: Lewis Publishing Company, 1897.

9173. Scheider, Alan N. "Robert Trimble: A Kentucky Justice on the Supreme Court." *Kentucky State Bar Journal* 12 (December 1947): 21-30.

Willis Van Devanter

General Studies

9174. Gould, Lewis L. "Willis Van Devanter in Wyoming Politics, 1884-1897." Ph.D. diss., Yale University, 1966.

9175. Grinnell, Frank W. "Mr. Justice Van Devanter and the Common Law 'Writ of Ease'." *Massachusetts Law Quarterly* 22 (July/September 1937): 24-27.

9176. Holsinger, M. Paul. "The Appointment of Supreme Court Justice Van Devanter." *American Journal of Legal History* 12 (October 1968): 324-335.

9177. Holsinger, M. Paul. "Mr. Justice Van Devanter and the New Deal: A Note." *Historian* 31 (November 1968): 57-63.

9178. Holsinger, M. Paul. "Willis Van Devanter: Wyoming, 1884-1897." *Annals of Wyoming* 37 (October 1965): 171-206.

9179. Howard, James O. "Constitutional Doctrines of Mr. Justice Van Devanter." Ph.D. diss., State University of Iowa, 1937.

9180. Howell, Ronald F. "Conservative Influence on Constitutional Development, 1923-1937: The Judicial Theory of Justices Van Devanter, McReynolds, Sutherland, and Butler." Ph.D. diss., Johns Hopkins University, 1952.

9181. Hughes, Charles E. "Associate Justice Van Devanter: An Appraisal by the Chief Justice." *American Bar Association Journal* 28 (July 1942): 458-459.

9182. Nelson, Daniel A. "The Supreme Court Appointment of Willis Van Devanter." *Annals of Wyoming* 53 (Fall 1981): 2-11.

Writings

9183. Van Devanter, Willis. "The Supreme Court of the United States." *Indiana Law Journal* 5 (May 1930): 553-562.

Frederick M. Vinson

General Studies

9184. Allen, Francis A. "Chief Justice Vinson and the Theory of Constitutional Government: A Tentative Appraisal." *Northwestern University Law Review* 49 (March/April 1954): 3-25.

9185. Belair, Felix. "Mr. Truman's Friend—and His Nominee?" *New York Times Magazine* 101 (December 16, 1951): 13, 43.

9186. Bolner, James. "Fred M. Vinson, 1890-1938: The Years of Relative Obscurity." *Kentucky Historical Society Register* 63 (January 1965): 3-16.

9187. Bolner, James. "Mr. Chief Justice Fred M. Vinson and Racial Discrimination." *Kentucky Historical Society Register* 64 (January 1966): 29-43.

9188. Bolner, James. "Mr. Chief Justice Vinson and the Communist Controversy: A Reassessment." *Kentucky Historical Society Register* 66 (October 1968): 378-391.

9189. Bolner, James. "Mr. Chief Justice Vinson: His Politics and His Constitutional Law." Ph.D. diss., University of Virginia, 1963.

9190. Frank, John P. "Fred Vinson and the Chief Justiceship." *University of Chicago Law Review* 21 (Winter 1954): 212-246.

9191. "Fred M. Vinson." *Northwestern University Law Review* 49 (March/April 1954): 1-75.

9192. Grant, Philip A., Jr. "Press Reaction to the Appointment of Fred M. Vinson as Chief Justice of the United States." *Kentucky Historical Society Register* 75 (October 1977): 304-313.

9193. Hatcher, John H. "The Education of the Thirteenth United States Chief Justice: Frederick Moore Vinson, Part I." *West Virginia History* 39 (July 1978): 285-323.

9194. Hatcher, John H. "Fred Vinson: Boyhood and Education in the Big Sandy Valley." *Kentucky Historical Society Register* 72 (July 1974): 243-261.

9195. Hatcher, John H. "Fred Vinson, Congressman from Kentucky: A Political Biography, 1890-1938." Ph.D. diss., University of Cincinnati, 1967.

9196. Havighurst, Harold C. "In Memoriam: Fred M. Vinson." *Northwestern University Law Review* 49 (March/April 1954): 1-2.

9197. Law Clerks of Justice Vinson. "Chief Justice Vinson and His Law Clerks." *Northwestern University Law Review* 49 (March/April 1954): 26-35.

9198. Laws, Bolitha J. "Chief Justice Fred M. Vinson." *American Bar Association Journal* 39 (October 1953): 901-921.

9199. Lefberg, Irving F. "Chief Justice

Vinson and the Politics of Desegregation." *Emory Law Journal* 24 (Spring 1975): 243-312.

9200. Lester, Wilbur R. "Fred M. Vinson in the Executive Branch." *Northwestern University Law Review* 49 (March/April 1954): 36-53.

9201. Oliver, William W. "Vinson in Congress." *Northwestern University Law Review* 49 (March/April 1954): 62-75.

9202. Parker, John J. "Chief Justice Fred M. Vinson: Meeting the Challenge to Law and Order: Evaluates the Work of the Late Chief Justice." *American Bar Association Journal* 41 (April 1955): 324-326, 363.

9203. Schwartz, Marvin, and Edwin M. Zimmerman. "Place of Chief Justice Vinson in the History of the Supreme Court." *Oklahoma Bar Association Journal* 24 (November 28, 1953): 1925-1930.

9204. Stephens, Harold M. "The Chief Justice." *American Bar Association Journal* 32 (July 1946): 387-389.

9205. Stephens, Harold M. "The Chief Justice." *Case and Comment* 51 (November/December 1946): 3-7.

9206. Stephens, Harold M. "The Chief Justice." *Kentucky State Bar Journal* 10 (September 1946): 212-214.

Writings

9207. Vinson, Frederick M. "Mr. Justice Murphy." *Michigan Law Review* 48 (April 1950): 738.

9208. Vinson, Frederick M. "Mr. Justice Rutledge." *Indiana Law Journal* 25 (Summer 1950): 421-422.

9209. Vinson, Frederick M. "An Observation about Judge Stone's Judicial Life." *University of Kansas City Law Review* 16 (1947-1948): 1.

9210. Vinson, Frederick M. "Our Endur-

ing Constitution." *Washington and Lee Law Review* 6 (1949): 1-11.

9211. Vinson, Frederick M. "Supreme Court Work: Opinion on Dissents." *Oklahoma Bar Association Journal* 20 (September 1949): 1269-1275.

9212. Vinson, Frederick M. "The Work of the United States Supreme Court." *Texas Bar Journal* 12 (December 1949): 551-553.

Morrison R. Waite

General Studies

9213. Association of the Bar of the City of New York. *Chief Justice Waite*. New York: Association of the Bar of the City of New York, 1890.

9214. Baker, William. "Memorial of Hon. Morrison Remick Waite." *Ohio State Bar Association Reports* 9 (July 11-12, 1988): 173-188.

9215. Bidwell, W. H. "Chief Justice Waite." *Eclectic Magazine* 82 (May 1874): 631.

9216. Coudert, Frederic R. "In Memoriam: Hon. Morrison R. Waite." In *Addresses: Historical, Political, Sociological*, by Frederic R. Coudert, 226-229. New York: Putnam's, 1905.

9217. Cowen, Benjamin R. "Morrison Remick Waite." In *Great American Lawyers*, vol. 7, edited by William D. Lewis, 87-126. Philadelphia: J. C. Winston Company, 1907-1909.

9218. "Death of Chief Justice Waite." *American Law Review* 22 (March/April 1888): 301-303.

9219. Jones, Francis R. "Morrison Remick Waite." *Green Bag* 14 (June 1902): 257-262.

9220. Lamb, Martha J. "Chief Justice

Morrison Remick Waite, His Home in Washington." *Magazine of American History* 20 (July 1888): 1-16.

9221. Logan, Richard D. "The Chief Justice from Northwestern Ohio." *Northwest Ohio Quarterly* 18 (January 1946): 14-24.

9222. Lovell, Arthur T. "Morrison R. Waite." *New England Magazine* 4 (January 1886): 50-52.

9223. Lovell, Arthur T. "Richard and Gamaliel Waite and Some of Their Descendants." *New England Magazine* 4 (January 1886): 48-59.

9224. Magrath, C. Peter. "Chief Justice Waite and the 'Twin Relic': *Reynolds v. United States.*" *Vanderbilt Law Review* 18 (March 1965): 507-543.

9225. Magrath, C. Peter. *Morrison R. Waite: The Triumph of Character.* New York: Macmillan, 1963.

9226. Morgan, Mathew S., ed. "How Morrison R. Waite Came to Be Nominated Chief Justice of the United States." *Northwest Ohio Quarterly* 23 (Summer 1951): 140-144.

9227. Morris, Jeffrey B. "Morrison Waite's Court." *Supreme Court Historical Society Yearbook* 1980 (1980): 38-48.

9228. Stephenson, D. Grier, Jr. "The Chief Justice as Leader: The Case of Morrison Remick Waite." *William and Mary Law Review* 14 (Summer 1973): 899-927.

9229. Trimble, Bruce R. "Chief Justice Waite and the Limitations of the *Dartmouth College* Decision." *University of Cincinnati Law Review* 9 (January 1935): 41-66.

9230. Trimble, Bruce R. *Chief Justice Waite: Defender of the Public Interest.* Princeton, NJ: Princeton University Press, 1938.

9231. Trimble, Bruce R. "The Life and Constitutional Doctrines of Chief Justice

Waite." Ph.D. diss., Cornell University, 1934.

9232. Uhle, John B. "The Opinions of Chief Justice Waite." *Current Comment* 2 (May 15, 1890): 257-261.

9233. Waite, Charles B. "Morrison R. Waite." *Chicago Law Times* 2 (July 1888): 205-212.

Writings

9234. Waite, Morrison R. *The Orations of Chief Justice Waite and of William Henry Rawle on the Occasion of the Unveiling of the Bronze Statue of Chief Justice Marshall at Washington, May 10, 1884.* Chicago: T. H. Flood, 1900.

9235. Waite, Morrison R. "Remarks of Chief Justice Waite on 'The Supreme Court of the United States'." *Albany Law Journal* 36 (October 15, 1887): 315-318.

9236. Waite, Morrison R. "The Supreme Court of the United States." *Albany Law Journal* 36 (October 15, 1887): 318.

Earl Warren

General Studies

9237. Bassett, James. "Unpartisan Chief Justice of the United States." *New York Times Magazine* 103 (October 11, 1953): 10, 19-20.

9238. Becker, Robert M. "Chief Justice Warren and Civil Liberties." Ph.D. diss., New School for Social Research, 1974.

9239. Bickel, Alexander M. "Chief Justice Warren and the Presidency." *New Republic* 134 (January 23, 1956): 8.

9240. Bickel, Alexander M. "Close of the Warren Era." *New Republic* 161 (July 12, 1969): 13-16.

9241. Blaustein, Albert P. "Some Notes on

the Chief Justice." *American Bar Association Journal* 40 (July 1954): 600-601.

9242. Bowe, Jess J. "Comparative Analysis of the Earl Warren and Warren Burger Supreme Courts." *International Journal of Comparative and Applied Criminal Justice* 11 (Spring/Winter 1987): 193-212.

9243. Bozell, L. Brent. "Should We Impeach Earl Warren?" *National Review* 11 (September 9, 1961): 153.

9244. Christman, Henry M. *The Public Papers of Chief Justice Earl Warren.* New York: Simon and Schuster, 1966.

9245. Cox, Archibald. "Chief Justice Earl Warren." *Harvard Law Review* 83 (November 1969): 1-5.

9246. Cullinan, Eustace. "New Chief Justice of the United States." *American Bar Association Journal* 39 (November 1953): 988-989.

9247. Dilliard, Irving. "Warren and the New Supreme Court." *Harper's Magazine* 211 (December 1955): 59-64.

9248. Fordham, Jefferson B. "Earl Warren, A Man for All Men." *Human Rights* 1 (July 1971): 1-12.

9249. Fortas, Abe. "Chief Justice Warren: The Enigma of Leadership." *Yale Law Journal* 84 (January 1975): 405-412.

9250. Frank, John P. "Affirmative Opinions on Justice Warren." *New York Times Magazine* 104 (October 3, 1954): 17-42.

9251. Fry, Amelia R. "The Warren Tapes: Oral History and the Supreme Court." *Supreme Court Historical Society Yearbook* 1982 (1982): 10-22.

9252. Gazell, James A. "Chief Justice Warren's Neglected Accomplishments in Federal Judicial Administration." *Pepperdine Law Review* 5 (Spring 1978): 437-464.

9253. Gerber, Albert. "Obscenity and Chief Justice Warren: Is the Chief Justice Changing His Mind on What Constitutes Obscenity?" *Censorship Today* 2 (February/March 1969): 5-11.

9254. Gressman, Eugene, William O. Douglas, and William S. Thompson. "The World of Earl Warren." *American Bar Association Journal* 60 (October 1974): 1228-1236.

9255. Griswold, Erwin N. "Earl Warren and the Supreme Court." *Christian Science Monitor* 51 (December 23, 1958): 9.

9256. Hanna, John. "Our Highest Court ... and the Man from California. . . ." *Freeman* 4 (November 2, 1953): 87-88.

9257. Harvey, Richard B. *Earl Warren: Governor of California.* Jericho, NY: Exposition Press, 1969.

9258. Harvey, Richard B. "Governor Earl Warren of California: A Study in 'Non-Partisan' Republican Politics." *California Historical Quarterly* 46 (March 1967): 33-51.

9259. Havemann, E. "Storm Center of Justice." *Life* 56 (May 22, 1964): 108-110.

9260. Henderson, Lloyd W. "Earl Warren and California Politics." Ph.D. diss., University of California, Berkeley, 1965.

9261. Heyman, Ira M. "The Chief Justice, Racial Segregation, and the Friendly Critics." *California Law Review* 49 (March 1961): 104-125.

9262. Huston, Luther. *Pathway to Judgement: A Study of Earl Warren.* Philadelphia: Chilton Books, 1966.

9263. Kagel, Sam, and Virginia B. Smith. "Chief Justice Warren and Labor Laws." *California Law Review* 49 (March 1961): 126-143.

9264. Katcher, Leo. *Earl Warren: A Political Biography.* New York: McGraw-Hill, 1967.

9265. Kilpatrick, J. J. "Warren Legacy." *National Review* 21 (August 12, 1969): 794-800.

9266. Kurland, Philip B. "Earl Warren, the 'Warren Court', and the 'Warren

Myths'." *Michigan Law Review* 67 (December 1968): 353-358.

9267. Levy, Leonard W., ed. *The Supreme Court under Earl Warren.* New York: Quadrangle Books, 1972.

9268. Lewis, Anthony. "New Look at the Chief Justice." *New York Times Magazine* 113 (January 19, 1964): 9, 63-65.

9269. Mehling, Harold. "Living Legends." *Today's Health* 37 (July 1959): 4, 57.

9270. Pollack, Jack H. *Earl Warren, the Judge Who Changed America.* Englewood Cliffs, NJ: Prentice-Hall, 1979.

9271. Rawls, James J. "The Earl Warren Oral History Project: An Appraisal." *Pacific Historical Review* 56 (February 1987): 87-97.

9272. Schreiber, Flora R. "American Dream." *Cosmopolitan* 139 (October 1955): 122-127.

9273. Schwartz, Bernard. "Chief Justice Warren and 1984." *Hastings Law Journal* 35 (July 1984): 975-989.

9274. Schwartz, Bernard. "Judicial Lives of Earl Warren." *Suffolk University Law Review* 15 (March 1981): 1-22.

9275. Schwartz, Bernard. *Super Chief.* New York: New York University Press, 1983.

9276. Severn, William M. *Mr. Chief Justice: Earl Warren.* New York: David McKay, 1968.

9277. Simmons, Stephen J. "Earl Warren, the Warren Court, and Civil Liberties." *Pepperdine Law Review* 2 (1974): 1-7.

9278. Smith, Beverly. "Earl Warren's Greatest Moment." *Saturday Evening Post* 227 (July 24, 1954): 17-19, 48, 53.

9279. Smith, Bradford. "Education of Earl Warren." *Nation* 187 (October 1958): 206-208.

9280. Stephenson, D. Grier, Jr. "The

Memoirs of Earl Warren." *Houston Law Review* 15 (October 1977): 224-244.

9281. Stone, Irving. *Earl Warren, A Great American Story.* New York: Prentice-Hall, 1948.

9282. Ulmer, S. Sidney. "Earl Warren and the *Brown* Decision." *Journal of Politics* 33 (August 1971): 689-702.

9283. Ulmer, S. Sidney. "Support for Negro Claimants in the Warren Court: The Case of the Chief Justice." *Jurimetrics Journal* 11 (June 1971): 179-188.

9284. Warren, Earl, Jr. "My Father the Chief Justice." *Supreme Court Historical Society Yearbook* 1982 (1982): 6-9.

9285. Weaver, John D. *Warren: The Man, the Court, the Era.* Boston: Little, Brown, 1967.

9286. White, G. Edward. *Earl Warren: A Public Life.* New York: Oxford University Press, 1982.

9287. White, G. Edward. "Earl Warren as Jurist." *Virginia Law Review* 67 (April 1981): 461-551.

9288. White, G. Edward. "Researching Oral History Materials: The Case of Earl Warren." *Law Library Journal* 75 (Summer 1982): 355-361.

9289. White, G. Edward. "The Unacknowledged Lesson: Earl Warren and the Japanese Relocation Controversy." *Virginia Quarterly Review* 55 (Autumn 1979): 613-629.

Writings

9290. Warren, Earl. "Address: At the Commencement Exercise of the University of San Diego School of Law." *San Diego Law Review* 11 (February 1974): 291-295.

9291. Warren, Earl. "All Men Are Created Equal." *Record of the Association of* *the Bar of the City of New York* 25 (June 1970): 351-364.

9292. Warren, Earl. "The Bill of Rights and the Military." *New York University Law Review* 37 (April 1962): 181-203.

9293. Warren, Earl. "The Blessings of Liberty." *Washington University Law Quarterly* 1955 (April 1955): 105-111.

9294. Warren, Earl. "Chief Justice John Marshall: A Heritage of Freedom and Stability." *American Bar Association Journal* 41 (November 1955): 1008-1010.

9295. Warren, Earl. "Chief Justice Marshall: The Expounder of the Constitution." *American Bar Association Journal* 41 (August 1955): 687.

9296. Warren, Earl. "Chief Justice William Howard Taft." *Yale Law Journal* 67 (January 1958): 353-362.

9297. Warren, Earl. *Hughes and the Court.* Hamilton, NY: Colgate University, 1962.

9298. Warren, Earl. "Introduction: A Tribute to Justice Douglas." *Washington Law Review* 39 (Spring 1964): 1-3.

9299. Warren, Earl. "Judicial Tributes: Judge Clark." *Connecticut Bar Journal* 38 (March 1964): 1-3.

9300. Warren, Earl. "Knight of Non-Partisanship." In *Twenty-seven Masters of Politics*, edited by Raymond Moley, 87-96. New York: Funk and Wagnalls, 1949.

9301. Warren, Earl. "Let's Not Weaken the Supreme Court." *American Bar Association Journal* 60 (June 1974): 677-680.

9302. Warren, Earl. *The Memoirs of Chief Justice Earl Warren.* New York: Doubleday, 1977.

9303. Warren, Earl. "Mr. Justice Harlan, as Seen by a Colleague." *Harvard Law Review* 85 (December 1971): 369-371.

9304. Warren, Earl. "The Notre Dame Law School Civil Rights Lectures." *Notre Dame Lawyer* 48 (October 1972): 14-48.

9305. Warren, Earl. *The Public Papers of Chief Justice Earl Warren.* Edited by Henry M. Christman. New York: Simon and Schuster, 1959.

9306. Warren, Earl. *A Republic, if You Can Keep It.* New York: Quadrangle Books, 1972.

9307. Warren, Earl. "Response to Recent Proposals to Dilute the Jurisdiction of the Supreme Court." *Loyola Law Review* 20 (1974): 221-230.

9308. Warren, Earl. "Roger Brooke Taney: Fifth Chief Justice of the United States." *American Bar Association Journal* 41 (June 1955): 504-506.

9309. Warren, Earl. "The Supreme Court Years." *Texas Law Review* 40 (June 1962): 744-745.

Bushrod Washington

General Studies

9310. Annis, David L. "Mr. Bushrod Washington: Supreme Court Justice on the Marshall Court." Ph.D. diss., University of Notre Dame, 1974.

9311. Binney, Horace. *Bushrod Washington.* Philadelphia: C. Sherman and Son, 1858.

9312. Brown, David P. "Bushrod Washington." In *The Forum; or Forty Years Full Practice at the Philadelphia Bar*, edited by David P. Brown, 350-378. Philadelphia: R. H. Small, 1856.

9313. Custer, Lawrence B. "Bushrod Washington and John Marshall: A Preliminary Inquiry." *American Journal of Legal History* 4 (January 1960): 34-78.

9314. Dunne, Gerald T. "Bushrod Washington and the Mount Vernon Slaves." *Su-*

preme Court Historical Society Yearbook 1980 (1980): 25-29.

9315. Hopkinson, Joseph. "Biographical Sketch of Bushrod Washington." *American Law Magazine* 5 (July 1845): 249-267.

9316. Hopkinson, Joseph. *Eulogium in Commemoration of the Honorable Bushrod Washington.* Philadelphia: S. Manning, 1830.

9317. Hunt, William. "Bushrod Washington." In *American Biographical Panorama*, by William Hunt, 40-41. Albany, NY: J. Munsell, 1849.

9318. Morrison, A. J. "Judge Bushrod Washington." *Tyler's Quarterly Historical and Genealology Magazine* 4 (July 1922): 32-35.

9319. Uhle, John B. "Bushrod Washington." *Current Comment* 2 (June 15, 1890): 321-325.

9320. Washington, Lawrence. *Address of Lawrence Washington in Presenting on May 3, 1910 at Montrose, Virginia, the Portrait of Judge Bushrod Washington.* Columbus, OH: F. B. Toothaker, 1912.

Writings

9321. Washington, Bushrod. "The Late Mr. Justice Bushrod Washington." *Green Bag* 9 (August 1897): 329-335.

James M. Wayne

General Studies

9322. Alexander, Lawrence A. *James Moore Wayne, Southern Unionist.* Chapel Hill: University of North Carolina Press, 1943.

9323. Battle, George G. "James Moore

Wayne: Southern Unionist." *Fordham Urban Law Journal* 14 (March 1964): 42-59.

9324. Candler, Allen D., and Clement A. Evans. "James Moore Wayne." In *Georgia: Comprising Sketches of Counties, Towns, Events, Institutions, and Persons Arranged in Cyclopedic Form*, vol. 3, edited by Allen D. Candler and Clement A. Evans, 536-537. Atlanta: Atlanta State Historical Association, 1906.

9325. Chase, Salmon P. "Memoranda: Mr. Justice Wayne." *United States Reports* 73 (1867): vii-x.

9326. Grice, Warren. "James M. Wayne." *Georgia Bar Association Proceedings* (1938): 179-200.

9327. Lawrence, Alexander A. "Justice Wayne and the *Dred Scott* Case." In *Report of Proceedings of the Fifty-seventh Annual Session of the Georgia Bar Association*, edited by John B. Harris, 196-218. Macon, GA: W. Burke Company, 1940.

9328. Livingston, John. "Hon. James M. Wayne." In *Biographical Sketches of Distinguished American Lawyers*, by John Livingston, 158-175. New York: The author, 1854.

Byron R. White

General Studies

9329. Armstrong, Michael J. "A Barometer of Freedom of the Press: The Opinions of Mr. Justice White." *Pepperdine Law Review* 8 (December 1980): 157-187.

9330. Broyde, Michael J. "The Intercircuit Tribunal and Perceived Conflicts: An Analysis of Justice White's Dissents from Denial of *Certiorari* during the 1985 Term." *New York University Law Review* 62 (June 1987): 610-650.

9331. Friendly, Fred W. "Beyond 'Caldwell': Justice White and Reporter Cald-well, Finding a Common Ground." *Columbia Journalism Review* 11 (September/October 1972): 31-37.

9332. Highsaw, Robert B. "Mr. Justice White: A Judicial Biography." Ph.D. diss., Harvard University, 1945.

9333. Hoagland, Donald W. "Byron White as a Practicing Lawyer in Colorado." *University of Colorado Law Review* 58 (Summer 1987): 365-370.

9334. Liebman, Lance. "Swing Man on the Supreme Court." *New York Times Magazine* 122 (October 8, 1972): 16-17, 94-95, 98, 100.

9335. McLean, Deckle. "Justice White and the First Amendment." *Journalism Quarterly* 56 (Summer 1979): 305-310.

9336. Mauro, Tony. "White's Quiet Trek toward a Record." *Legal Times* 9 (April 20, 1987): 87.

9337. Mirabella, Peter F. "Justice Byron R. White and Fundamental Freedoms." Ph.D. diss., New School for Social Research, 1980.

9338. Palmer, Larry I. "Two Perspectives on Structuring Discretion: Justices Stewart and White on the Death Penalty." *Journal of Criminal Law and Criminology* 70 (Summer 1979): 194-213.

9339. Price, Monroe. "White: A Justice of Studied Unpredictability." *National Law Journal.* 2 (February 18, 1980): 24.

9340. Seymour, Whitney N. "Mr. Justice White." *American Bar Association Journal* 48 (May 1962): 450-457.

9341. Weyland, Alexander M. *Football Immortals.* New York: Macmillan, 1962.

9342. Zelnick, Robert. "Whizzer White and the Fearsome Foursome." *Washington Monthly* 4 (December 1972): 46-54.

Writings

9343. White, Byron R. "Challenges for the U.S. Supreme Court and the Bar: Contemporary Reflections." *Antitrust Law Journal* 51 (August 1982): 275-282.

9344. White, Byron R. "Supreme Court Review of Agency Decisions." *Administrative Law Review* 26 (Winter 1974): 107-112.

9345. White, Byron R. "Work of the Supreme Court: A Nuts and Bolts Description." *New York State Bar Journal* 54 (October 1982): 346-349.

Edward D. White

General Studies

9346. Carolyn, Marie. "The Legal Philosophy of Edward Douglass White." *University of Detroit Law Journal* 35 (December 1957): 174-199.

9347. Carson, Hampton L. "Memorial Tribute to Edward Douglass White." *Reports of the American Bar Association* 46 (1921): 25-30.

9348. Carter, Newman. "Edward D. White in Personal Retrospect." *Supreme Court Historical Society Yearbook* 1979 (1979): 5-7.

9349. Cassidy, Lewis C. *The Catholic Ancestry of Chief Justice White.* Philadelphia: Patterson and White, 1927.

9350. Cassidy, Lewis C. "An Evaluation of Chief Justice White." *Mississippi Law Journal* 10 (February 1958): 136-153.

9351. Cassidy, Lewis C. "The Life of Edward Douglass White: Soldier, Statesman, Jurist, 1845-1921." Ph.D. diss., Georgetown University, 1923.

9352. Dart, Henry P. "Chief Justice

White." *Louisiana Historical Quarterly* 5 (April 1922): 141-151.

9353. Dart, Henry P. "Edward Douglass White." *Loyola Law Journal* 3 (November 1921): 1-13.

9354. Davis, John W. "Edward Douglass White." *American Bar Association Journal* 7 (August 1921): 377-382.

9355. Dishman, Robert B. "Mr. Justice White and the Rule of Reason." *Review of Politics* 13 (April 1951): 229-243.

9356. Fegan, Hugh E. "Edward Douglass White, Jurist and Statesman." *Georgetown Law Journal* 14 (November 1925): 1-21; 15 (January 1926): 148-168.

9357. Forman, William H. "Chief Justice Edward Douglass White." *American Bar Association Journal* 56 (May 1970): 260-262.

9358. Frankfurter, Felix. *The Commerce Clause under Marshall, Taney, and White.* Chapel Hill: University of North Carolina Press, 1937.

9359. Gannon, Frank S. "Edward D. White, Chief Justice, 1845-1921." *American Irish Historical Society Journal* 20 (June 1921): 235-257.

9360. Hagemann, Gerard. *The Man on the Bench: A Story of Chief Justice Edward Douglass White.* Notre Dame, IN: Dujarie Press, 1962.

9361. Hart, W. O. "Edward Douglass White: A Tribute." *Loyola Law Journal* 7 (July 1926): 150-158.

9362. Hartman, Harold F. "Constitutional Doctrines of Edward D. White." Ph.D. diss., Cornell University, 1936.

9363. Highsaw, Robert B. *Edward Douglass White: Defender of the Conservative Faith.* Baton Rouge: Louisiana State University Press, 1981.

9364. Jesse, Richard H. "Chief Justice White." *American Law Review* 45 (May/June 1911): 321-326.

9365. Joyce, Walter E. "Edward Douglass White: The Louisiana Years, Early Life, and on the Bench." *Tulane Law Review* 41 (June 1967): 752-768.

9366. Klinkhamer, Marie C. "Chief Justice White and Administrative Law." *Fordham Law Review* 14 (November 1944): 194-231.

9367. Klinkhamer, Marie C. "Edward Douglass White, Chief Justice of the United States." Ph.D. diss., Catholic University of America, 1943.

9368. Klinkhamer, Marie C. "Legal Philosophy of Edward Douglass White." *University of Detroit Law Journal* 35 (December 1957): 174-199.

9369. Mann, S. H. "Chief Justice White." *American Law Review* 60 (1926): 620-637.

9370. Morris, Jeffrey B. "Chief Justice Edward Douglass White and President Taft's Court." *Supreme Court Historical Society Yearbook* 1982 (1982): 27-45.

9371. Ramke, Diedrich. "Edward Douglass White, Statesman and Jurist." Ph.D. diss., Louisiana State University, 1940.

9372. Ransdell, Joseph E. "Reminiscences of Edward Douglass White." *Loyola Law Journal* 7 (April 1926): 69-73.

9373. Spring, Samuel. "Two Chief Justices: Edward Douglass White and William Howard Taft." *Review of Reviews* 64 (August 1921): 161-170.

9374. Umbreit, Kenneth B. "Review of the Commerce Clause under Marshall, Taney, and White by Felix Frankfurter." *American Bar Association Journal* 23 (September 1937): 706.

9375. Walker, Albert H. *The "Unreasonable" Obiter Dicta of Chief Justice White in the* Standard Oil *Case: A Critical Review.* New York: n.p., 1911.

9376. Williams, Samuel C. "A Remarkable Bench: Campbell, Jackson, and White." *Tennessee Law Review* 16 (June 1941): 907-914.

Writings

9377. White, Edward D. "Proceedings on the Death of Mr. Chief Justice Fuller." *United States Reports* 219 (1911): vii.

9378. White, Edward D. "Proceedings on the Death of Mr. Justice Harlan." *United States Reports* 222 (1911): v.

9379. White, Edward D. "Supreme Court of the United States." *American Bar Association Journal* 7 (July 1921): 341-343.

Charles E. Whittaker

General Studies

9380. Berman, Daniel M. "Mr. Justice Whittaker: A Preliminary Appraisal." *Missouri Law Review* 24 (January 1959): 1-15.

9381. Christensen, Barbara B. "Mister Justice Whittaker: The Man on the Right." *Santa Clara Law Review* 19 (1979): 1039-1062.

9382. Lashly, Jacob M. "Mr. Justice Whittaker." *American Bar Association Journal* 43 (June 1957): 526-527.

9383. Ridge, Albert A. "Charles Evans Whittaker: A Personal Tribute." *Texas Law Review* 40 (June 1962): 749-750.

9384. Volz, Marlin M. "Mr. Justice Whittaker." *Notre Dame Lawyer* 33 (March 1958): 159-179.

Writings

9385. Whittaker, Charles E. "Role of the Supreme Court." *Arizona Law Review* 17 (Fall 1963): 292-301.

James Wilson

General Studies

9386. Adams, Randolph. "The Legal Theories of James Wilson." *University of Pennsylvania Law Review* 68 (June 1920): 337-355.

9387. Alexander, Lucien H. *James Wilson, Patriot, and the Wilson Doctrine.* New York: n.p., 1906.

9388. Andrews, James D. "James Wilson and His Relation to Jurisprudence and Constitutional Law." *University of Pennsylvania Law Review* 49 (December 1901): 708-728.

9389. Carson, Hampton L. "James Wilson and James Iredell: A Parallel and a Contrast." *American Bar Association Journal* 7 (March 1921): 123-136.

9390. Carson, Hampton L. "Oration." *University of Pennsylvania Law Review* 55 (January 1907): 35-46.

9391. Cook, Frank G. "James Wilson." *Atlantic Monthly* 64 (September 1889): 316-330.

9392. Dennison, George M. "Revolutionary Principle: Ideology and the Constitution in the Thought of James Wilson." *Review of Politics* 39 (April 1977): 157-191.

9393. Dwight, Nathanial. "James Wilson." In *The Lives of the Signers of the Declaration of Independence*, by Nathanial Dwight, 214-218. New York: Barnes, 1876.

9394. Gallagher, Eugene R. "Two Interpretations of the State and Government: The Pragmatic Skepticism of Mr. Justice Oliver Wendell Holmes Contrasted with the Natural Law Philosophy of Mr. Justice James Wilson." Ph.D. diss., Fordham University, 1940.

9395. Goodrich, Charles A. "James Wilson." In *Lives of the Signers of the Declaration of Independence*, by Charles A. Goodrich, 300-309. New York: W. Reed and Company, 1829.

9396. Hunt, William. "James Wilson." In *American Biographical Panorama*, by William Hunt, 160. Albany, NY: J. Munsell, 1849.

9397. Jezierski, John V. "Parliament or People: James Wilson and Blackstone on the Nature and Location of Sovereignty." *Journal of the History of Ideas* 32 (January/March 1971): 95-106.

9398. Judson, L. Carroll. "James Wilson." In *A Biography of the Signers of the Declaration of Independence*, by L. Carroll Judson, 394-399. Philadelphia: Cowperthwait and Company, 1839.

9399. Kelland, Clarence B. "James Wilson, Expounder and Defender of the Constitution." *Law Student's Helper* 17 (July 1909): 209-213.

9400. Klingelsmith, Margaret C. "James Wilson." In *Great American Lawyers*, vol. 1, edited by William D. Lewis, 149-222. Philadelphia: J. C. Winston Company, 1907-1909.

9401. Klingelsmith, Margaret C. "James Wilson and the So-Called Yazoo Frauds." *University of Pennsylvania Law Review* 56 (January 1908): 1-27.

9402. Konkle, Burton A. *James Wilson and the Constitution: The Opening Address in the Official Series of Events Known as the James Wilson Memorial: Delivered before the Law Academy of Philadelphia on November 14, 1906.*

Philadelphia: Law Academy of Philadelphia, 1907.

9403. Leavelle, Arnaud B. "James Wilson and the Relation of Scottish Metaphysics to American Political Thought." *Political Science Quarterly* 57 (September 1942): 394-410.

9404. Lossing, Benson J. "James Wilson." In *Lives of the Signers of the Declaration of American Independence*, by Benson J. Lossing, 126-129. Philadelphia: Evans, Stoddart, and Company, 1870.

9405. McLaughlin, Andrew C. "James Wilson in the Philadelphia Convention." *Political Science Quarterly* 12 (March 1897): 1-20.

9406. Mell, Wayne A. "James Wilson, Alexander Hamilton, William Blackstone: Organic Principles of Constitutional Liberty." Ph.D. diss., University of Oregon, 1976.

9407. Nevin, David R. "James Wilson, of Pennsylvania." In *Continental Sketches of Distinguished Pennsylvanians*, edited by David R. Nevin, 76-84. Philadelphia: Porter and Coates, 1875.

9408. Obering, William F. *The Philosophy of Law of James Wilson, Associate Justice of the United States Supreme Court, 1789-1798: A Study in Comparative Jurisprudence.* Washington, DC: American Catholic Philosophical Association, Catholic University of America, 1938.

9409. O'Donnell, May G. *James Wilson and the Natural Law Basis of Positive Law.* New York: Fordham University Press, 1937.

9410. Pierce, James O. "James Wilson as a Jurist." *American Law Review* 38 (January/February 1904): 44-60.

9411. Quattrocchi, Anna M. "James Wilson and the Establishment of the Federal Government." *Historian* 2 (Spring 1940): 105-117.

9412. Rosenberger, Homer T. "James

Wilson's Theories of Punishment." *Pennsylvania Magazine of History and Biography* 73 (January 1949): 45-63.

9413. Schacht, James A. "Architect of the Constitution: James Wilson." *Wisconsin Bar Bulletin* 60 (May 1987): 32-36.

9414. Seed, Geoffrey. *James Wilson.* Millwood, NY: KTO Press, 1978.

9415. Smith, Charles P. *James Wilson: Founding Father, 1742-1798.* Chapel Hill: University of North Carolina Press, 1956.

9416. Smith, William C. "James Wilson and the Philosophy of Freedom in the American Revolution." *American Catholic Historical Society Record* 50 (March 1939): 65-71.

9417. Young, George L. "The Services of James Wilson in the Continental Congress." Ph.D. diss., Lehigh University, 1954.

Writings

9418. Wilson, James. *Selected Political Essays of James Wilson.* Edited by Randolph Adams. New York: Knopf, 1930.

9419. Wilson, James. *Works.* Philadelphia: Lorenzo Press, 1804.

9420. Wilson, James. *Works of James Wilson.* Edited by Robert G. McCloskey. Cambridge: Harvard University Press, 1967.

9421. Wilson, James, and Thomas Mikean. *Commentaries on the Constitution of the United States.* Philadelphia: T. Loyd, 1792.

Levi Woodbury

General Studies

9422. Capowski, Vincent J. "The Era of Good Feelings in New Hampshire: The Gubernatorial Campaigns of Levi Woodbury, 1823-1824." *Historical New Hampshire* 21 (Winter 1966): 3-30.

9423. Capowski, Vincent J. "Making of a Jacksonian Democrat: Levi Woodbury." Master's thesis, Fordham University, 1966.

9424. "Political Portrait of Levi Woodbury." *United States Magazine and Democratic Review* 2 (July 1838): 385-408.

9425. Rantoul, Robert. *Eulogy on the Honorable Levi Woodbury Pronounced at Portsmouth, New Hampshire.* Portsmouth, NH: Published by Vote of the City Council, 1852.

9426. Rantoul, Robert. "Mr. Justice Woodbury." *Law Reporter* 14 (November 1851): 349-361.

9427. Watterson, George. "Levi Woodbury." In *Gallery of American Portraits*, 3d ed., by George Watterson, 149-153. Washington, DC: F. Taylor, 1836.

9428. Wheaton, Philip D. "Levi Woodbury: Jacksonian Financier." Ph.D. diss., University of Maryland, 1955.

9429. Woodbury, Charles L. "Memoir of Honorable Levi Woodbury, LL.D." *New England Historical and Genealogical Register* 48 (January 1894): 9-17.

Writings

9430. Woodbury, Levi. *Writings of Levi Woodbury, LL.D., Political, Judicial, and Literary.* Boston: Little, Brown, 1852.

William B. Woods

General Studies

9431. Baynes, Thomas E. "Yankee from Georgia: A Search for Justice Woods." *Supreme Court Historical Society Yearbook* 1978 (1978): 31-42.

9432. Brister, E. M. P. *Centennial History of the City of Newark and Licking County, Ohio.* New York: S. J. Clarke Publishing Company, 1909.

9433. Reid, Whitelaw. *Ohio in the War. . . .* New York: Moore, Wilstach, and Baldwin, 1868.

9434. Smith, Joseph P., ed. *History of the Republican Party in Ohio.* Chicago: Lewis Publishing Company, 1898.

Author Index

Price, Monroe, 9339
Prickett, Morgan D., 8611
Priest, A.J.G., 5541, 5542
Priest, George L., 2393
Prigmore, Charles S., 4812
Prince, Toussaint L., 2613
Pringle, Henry F., 9031
Pritchett, C. Herman, 255, 288, 594, 735-740, 1073, 1074, 1177, 1647, 2509-2514, 2953, 3059-3061, 3202, 3858, 7769
Proctor, L. B., 8046, 8304, 8577
Proctor, William G., Jr., 3646
Proffitt, Thomas D., 8641
Provine, Doris M., 2394, 2395
Proviser, Norman W., 3256
Pruden, Durward, 6234
Prygoski, Philip J., 1517
Pugh, Darrell L., 1200
Pugh, James T., 2081
Pullen, Ricky D., 3331
Puner, Nicholas W., 3203
Purcell, Richard J., 6702, 8305, 9132
Puro, Steven, 2311
Pusey, Merlo J., 1648, 2082, 2083, 3647, 5956, 6077, 7878-7881, 8696
Putka, John S., 3420
Putney, Albert H., 2661
Putney, Bryant, 1649
Putzel, Henry, 2007
Pye, A. Kenneth, 4632

Quade, Quentin L., 2897
Quattrocchi, Anna M., 9411
Quick, Albert T., 3204
Quillian, Sally C., 4781
Quinlan, Patrick J., 4418

Raab, Jennifer J., 4442
Rabb, Charles, 4279
Rabban, David M., 3119
Rabin, Jack, 5667
Rabin, Robert L., 3648
Rabinove, Samuel, 7089
Rabinowitz, Ezekiel, 6472
Rabkin, Jeremy, 289, 1075, 1951
Rabkin, Peggy A., 3904
Radelet, Michael L., 4722
Rader, Barbara K., 7770
Rader, Benjamin G., 7770
Raedy, Raymond, 1952
Raff, Lawrence B., 7882
Raffel, Burton, 1650
Ragan, Allen E., 8756, 9032, 9033
Ragan, Fred D., 7771
Raggi, Reena, 3152
Ragsdale, J. Donald, 3257
Ragsdale, John W., Jr., 4825, 4826
Rains, Harry H., 5378

Ralston, Jackson H., 1518
Ralston, Robert, 2288
Ramage, C. J., 8306
Ramaswamy, M., 2853
Ramberg, Bennett, 5208
Ramke, Diedrich, 9371
Ramsay, David, 2148
Ramsey, Mary L., 957, 4955
Rand, I. C., 6473
Randall, James G., 459
Randall, Richard S., 3258
Rankin, J. Lee, 595, 5698
Rankin, Robert S., 596
Ransdell, Joseph E., 9372
Ransmeier, Joseph S., 4153
Ransom, William L., 1306, 7883, 7977, 9133
Ransopher, Tad D., 4002
Rantoul, Robert, 9425, 9426
Raps, Eric A., 3589
Rashid, Baddia J., 1307, 1864
Rasnic, Carol D., 3905, 5379
Ratcliffe, Robert H., 290
Rathjen, Gregory J., 2515, 2624-2627, 2854
Ratnaswamy, John P., 2421
Ratner, Leonard G., 1308
Ratner, Sidney, 1651
Rau, Donald, 481
Rauch, Jonathan, 1557
Rauh, Joseph L., Jr., 1309, 7375
Rava, Paul B., 2615
Rawle, William, 1076, 8307
Rawls, James J., 9271
Ray, Ben F., 1217, 6235
Raymar, Robert S., 1519
Raymond, James F., 5229
Raymond, John M., 2713
Read, Conyers, 1077
Read, Frank T., 4280
Read, William E., 7577
Reams, Bernard D., 4281
Reardan, Nancy B., 3906
Rearick, Francis G., 2211
Reddick, L. D., 4282
Redding, Louis L., 4283
Redenius, Charles M., 4419
Redfield, Isaac F., 6867
Redish, Martin H., 1865, 3096, 3120, 4633
Redlich, Norman, 427, 1310, 3649
Reed, Phillip D., 5230
Reed, Stanley F., 8612
Reed, Thomas J., 5115
Reeder, Robert F., 7461
Reeder, Robert H., 4782, 4956
Reeder, Robert P., 1983
Reedy, Cheryl D., 4023
Reese, William E., 7978
Reese, Willis L. M., 1866, 2212
Regan, Donald H., 1352

Subject Index

regulation of, 5168, 5233
resources, 7114
rights, 1870
Water Pollution Control Act, 5220
Watergate, 337, 1589, 1613, 2960
Watkins v. United States, 1311, 1371, 1373
Watson v. Jones, 3692
Wayne, James M., 9322-9328
Wealth
  discrimination, 4437
  equal protection, 3823
  John Marshall, 8259
Webster, Daniel, 113, 406
Wechsler, Herbert, 894
Welfare, 289, 507, 1950, 4063, 4994, 4997, 4998
  Burger Court, 4061, 4062
  home-visit, 4991
  Francis W. Murphy, 8527
  policy, 4993, 4999, 5000
  prior hearing cases, 4996
  residence requirements, 4443, 4444, 4995
  right to travel, 4443, 4444
  social, 2858
  state programs, 4992
Wendel, Ella, 7530
Wesberry v. Sanders, 4389
West Virginia, 518
West Virginia State Board of Education v. Barnetti, 1771
Western and Southern Life Insurance Co. v. State Board of Equalization, 5496
Wetzel v. Liberty Mutual Insurance Co., 4018
Wheaton, Henry, 1992
Wheaton v. Peters, 2001
Whipple, William, 115
White v. Johnson and Hayes, 5205
White, Byron R., 9329-9345
  biography, 9332
  certiorari, writ of, 9330
  death penalty, 9338
  First Amendment, 9335
  freedom, 9337
  as lawyer, 9333
  press, 9329
  writings, 9343-9345
White, Edward D., 9346-9379
  administrative law, 9366
  Catholic ancestry of, 9349
  commerce clause, 9358, 9373
  Constitution, 9362
  as defender of the conservative faith, 9363
  early life of, 9365
  legal philosophy of, 9346, 9368
  memorial to, 9347
  Standard Oil case, 9375
  writings, 9377-9379
White, W. F., 2689
Whitney v. California, 6491

Whittaker, Charles E., 9380-9385
  writings, 9385
Wiener v. United States, 1675
Wigmore, John H., 7773
Wigodav v. Cousins, 2846
Williams, George H., 6070
Williams and Wilkins Co. v. United States, 5454
Williams v. Florida, 2470, 4681
Williams v. Rhodes, 4367
Wilson, Henry, 489
Wilson, James, 361, 7684, 9386-9421
  William Blackstone, 9406
  Constitution, 9388, 9392, 9399, 9402
  Continental Congress, 9417
  federal government, 9411
  Alexander Hamilton, 9406
  legal theories of, 9386
  liberty, 9406
  memorial for, 9402
  natural law, 9409
  parallel with Iredell, 9389
  Philadelphia Convention, 9405
  philosophy of freedom, 9416
  philosophy of law, 9394, 9408
  political thought, 9403
  sovereignty, 9397
  punishment theories of, 9412
  writings, 9418-9421
Wilson, Woodrow, 6498
Wiretapping, 4910, 4914, 4953, 4987
Wisconsin, obscenity in, 5736
Wisconsin Railroad Commission, 1905-1917, 5012
Wisconsin v. Yoder, 3653
Wolf v. Weinstein, 5466
Wolston v. Reader's Digest Association Inc., 3768
Women, 3981
  Burger Court, 3997, 3998
  clergy, 3978
  employees, 4003
  in industry, 6523
  legal history of, 3980
  organizations, 4020
  rights groups, 2705
  working, 4029
Wood v. Strickland, 5637, 5787
Woodbury, Levi, 9422-9430
  gubernatorial campaigns of, 9422
  writings, 9430
Woods, William B., 9431
Woodson v. North Carolina, 4728
Worcester v. Georgia, 1845
World Court, 352, 1291, 5839
World War I, 3115, 3179, 3786
World War II, 657
Wright, B. F., 420
Wygant v. Board of Education of Jackson, 3921, 5260, 5766
Wyoming, 9174